THE OXFORD HANDBOOK OF
WILLIAM JAMES

THE OXFORD HANDBOOK OF
WILLIAM JAMES

Edited by
ALEXANDER MUGAR KLEIN

Oxford University Press is a department of the University of Oxford. It furthers the University's objective of excellence in research, scholarship, and education by publishing worldwide. Oxford is a registered trade mark of Oxford University Press in the UK and certain other countries.

Published in the United States of America by Oxford University Press
198 Madison Avenue, New York, NY 10016, United States of America.

© Oxford University Press 2024

All rights reserved. No part of this publication may be reproduced, stored in a retrieval system, or transmitted, in any form or by any means, without the prior permission in writing of Oxford University Press, or as expressly permitted by law, by license, or under terms agreed with the appropriate reproduction rights organization. Inquiries concerning reproduction outside the scope of the above should be sent to the Rights Department, Oxford University Press, at the address above.

You must not circulate this work in any other form
and you must impose this same condition on any acquirer.

Library of Congress Cataloging-in-Publication Data
Names: Klein, Alexander Mugar, editor.
Title: The Oxford handbook of William James / [edited by] Alexander Mugar Klein.
Description: New York, NY : Oxford University Press, [2024] |
Series: Oxford handbooks | Includes index. |
Identifiers: LCCN 2023035501 (print) | LCCN 2023035502 (ebook) |
ISBN 9780199395699 (hardback) | ISBN 9780197746271 (epub) |
ISBN 9780199395712
Subjects: LCSH: James, William, 1842–1910.
Classification: LCC B945.J24 O94 2023 (print) | LCC B945.J24 (ebook) |
DDC 191—dc23/eng/20231129
LC record available at https://lccn.loc.gov/2023035501
LC ebook record available at https://lccn.loc.gov/2023035502

DOI: 10.1093/oxfordhb/9780199395699.001.0001

Printed by Sheridan Books, Inc., United States of America

Contents

List of Contributors   ix
Primary Sources   xi

Editor's Introduction   1
   Alexander Mugar Klein

PART I: MIND

1. James and Attention: Reactive Spontaneity   19
   Jesse Prinz

2. James's Revolutionary Theory of Emotions   41
   Heleen J. Pott

3. James on the Perception of Space   61
   Gary Hatfield

4. James and Consciousness   84
   Alexander Mugar Klein

PART II: SCIENCE

5. James and Evolution   109
   Trevor Pearce

6. James and Medicine: Reckoning with Experience   134
   Paul J. Croce

7. James and Psychical Research in Context   155
   Andreas Sommer

8. Psychology and Philosophy in the Work of William James: Two Good Things   177
   David E. Leary

PART III: VALUE

9. Hortatory Ethics — Sarin Marchetti — 199

10. James and Religion — Stephen S. Bush — 216

11. Pluralism and Toleration in James's Social Philosophy — Robert B. Talisse — 232

12. James and Politics: The Radical Democracy of a Radical Empiricist — Trygve Throntveit and James T. Kloppenberg — 245

PART IV: MEANING, TRUTH, AND PRAGMATISM

13. James on Percepts, Concepts, and the Function of Cognition — James R. O'Shea — 269

14. James, Intentionality, and Analysis — Henry Jackman — 289

15. What Was James's Theory of Truth? — Tom Donaldson — 309

16. James and Pragmatism: The Road Not Taken — Philip Kitcher — 328

17. James and Epistemic Pluralism — Ignas Kęstutis Skrupskelis — 346

PART V: LATER METAPHYSICS

18. James's Radical Empiricism: Sensation and Pure Experience — Wesley Cooper — 359

19. James and the Metaphysics of Intentionality: Royce, Bergson, and the Miller-Bode Objections — Jeremy Dunham — 370

20. James and Math: On Infinite Totalities — Francesca Bordogna — 390

PART VI: CONVERSATIONS, PAST

21. James and Hume: Radical Empiricism and the Reality of Relations   411
    YUMIKO INUKAI

22. James and Hegel: Looking for a Home   430
    ROBERT STERN AND NEIL W. WILLIAMS

23. James and Emerson: On the Pragmatic Use of Terms   450
    RUSSELL B. GOODMAN

PART VII: CONVERSATIONS, PRESENT

24. William James and Renouvier's Neo-Kantianism:
    Belief, Experience and Consciousness   467
    MATHIAS GIREL

25. James and Peirce   490
    CLAUDINE TIERCELIN

26. James's and Dewey's Radical Rationalism   511
    F. THOMAS BURKE

PART VIII: CONVERSATIONS, FUTURE

27. James and British Philosophy   531
    CHERYL MISAK

28. James and Wittgenstein   549
    ANNA BONCOMPAGNI

29. James and Phenomenology   570
    STEVEN LEVINE

Index   591

Contributors

Anna Boncompagni, Associate Professor, Department of Philosophy, University of California, Irvine

Francesca Bordogna, Associate Professor, Program of Liberal Studies, University of Notre Dame

F. Thomas Burke, Professor, Philosophy Department, University of South Carolina

Stephen S. Bush, Professor of Religious Studies, Brown University

Wesley Cooper, Professor Emeritus, University of Alberta

Paul J. Croce, Professor of History and Director of American Studies, Stetson University

Tom Donaldson, Assistant Professor, Philosophy Department, Simon Fraser University

Jeremy Dunham, Associate Professor in Philosophy, Department of Philosophy, University of Durham

Mathias Girel, Associate Professor, Department of Philosophy, École normale supérieure-PSL

Russell B. Goodman, Regents Professor, Department of Philosophy, University of New Mexico

Gary Hatfield, Professor of Philosophy, Department of Philosophy, University of Pennsylvania

Yumiko Inukai, Associate Professor of Philosophy, University of Massachusetts, Boston

Henry Jackman, Associate Professor, Philosophy, York University

Philip Kitcher, John Dewey Professor of Philosophy, Emeritus, Columbia University

Alexander Mugar Klein, Canada Research Chair, Associate Professor of Philosophy, McMaster University

James T. Kloppenberg, Charles Warren Research Professor of American History, Harvard University

David E. Leary, University Professor Emeritus and Dean of Arts and Sciences Emeritus, University of Richmond

Steven Levine, Professor of Philosophy, Philosophy Department, University of Massachusetts, Boston

Sarin Marchetti, Associate Professor of Philosophy, Sapienza Università di Roma

Cheryl Misak, University Professor and Professor of Philosophy, University of Toronto

James R. O'Shea, Professor, School of Philosophy, University College Dublin

Trevor Pearce, Chair & Associate Professor of Philosophy, University of North Carolina at Charlotte

Heleen J. Pott, Emerita Professor, Erasmus University Rotterdam

Jesse Prinz, Distinguished Professor, Philosophy, City University of New York, Graduate Center

Ignas Kęstutis Skrupskelis, Professor Emeritus of Philosophy, University of South Carolina

Andreas Sommer, Research Associate, Department of History and Philosophy of Science, University of Cambridge

Robert Stern, Emeritus Professor, Department of Philosophy, University of Sheffield

Robert B. Talisse, W. Alton Jones Professor, Department of Philosophy, Vanderbilt University

Trygve Throntveit, Director of Strategic Partnership, Minnesota Humanities Center

Claudine Tiercelin, Professor, Chair Métaphysique et philosophie de la connaissance, Collège de France

Neil W. Williams, Senior Lecturer in Ethics and Environmental Philosophy, Faculty of Business and Law, University of Roehampton

Primary Sources

REFERENCES to *The Works of William James* follow these conventions:

Title	Abbreviation	
Pragmatism	P	1907
The Meaning of Truth	MT	1909
Essays in Radical Empiricism	ERE	yyyy
A Pluralistic Universe	PU	1909
Essays in Philosophy	EPh	yyyy
The Will to Believe	WB	1897
Some Problems of Philosophy	SPP	1911
The Principles of Psychology	PP	1890
Essays in Religion and Morality	ERM	yyyy
Talks to Teachers on Psychology	TTP	1899
Essays in Psychology	EPs	yyyy
Psychology: Briefer Course	PBC	1892
The Varieties of Religious Experience	VRE	1902
Essays in Psychical Research	EPR	yyyy
Essays, Comments, and Reviews	ECR	yyyy
Manuscript Essays and Notes	MEN	yyyy
Manuscript Lectures	ML	yyyy

For books originally published during James's lifetime, plus SPP, references include the year the work originally appeared (as above). For all other posthumous collections, references include the year that the cited item in the collection was originally published or composed (in lieu of "*yyyy*," above).

References to *The Correspondence of William James* follow this convention, where "*yyyy*" is the year the cited letter was composed, "*v*" is the volume number in which the letter appears, and "*p*" is a page range in the cited volume: CWJ yyyy, v.p.

Publication details for James's *Works* and *Correspondence* are as follows:

James, William. 1890/1981. *The Principles of Psychology*. Edited by Frederick H. Burkhardt, Fredson Bowers and Ignas K. Skrupskelis. Cambridge: Harvard University Press.
James, William. 1892/1984. *Psychology: Briefer Course*. Edited by Frederick H. Burkhardt, Fredson Bowers and Ignas K. Skrupskelis. Cambridge: Harvard University Press.
James, William. 1897/1979. *The Will to Believe, and Other Essays in Popular Philosophy*. Edited by Frederick H. Burkhardt, Fredson Bowers and Ignas K. Skrupskelis. Cambridge: Harvard University Press.
James, William. 1902/1985. *The Varieties of Religious Experience*. Edited by Frederick Burkhardt, Fredson Bowers and Ignas K. Skrupskelis. Cambridge: Harvard University Press.
James, William. 1907/1975. *Pragmatism*. Edited by Fredson Bowers and Ignas K. Skrupskelis. Cambridge: Harvard University Press.
James, William. 1909/1977. *A Pluralistic Universe*. Edited by Fredson Bowers and Ignas K. Skrupskelis. Cambridge: Harvard University Press.
James, William. 1909/1978. *The Meaning of Truth*. Edited by Frederick H. Burkhardt, Fredson Bowers and Ignas K. Skrupskelis. Cambridge, MA: Harvard University Press.
James, William. 1911/1979. *Some Problems of Philosophy*. Edited by Frederick H. Burkhardt, Fredson Bowers and Ignas K. Skrupskelis. Cambridge: Harvard University Press.
James, William. 1912/1976. *Essays in Radical Empiricism*. Edited by Fredson Bowers and Ignas K. Skrupskelis. Cambridge: Harvard University Press.
James, William. 1978. *Essays in Philosophy*. Edited by Frederick H. Burkhardt, Fredson Bowers and Ignas K. Skrupskelis. Cambridge: Harvard University Press.
James, William. 1982. *Essays in Religion and Morality*. Edited by Frederick Burkhardt, Fredson Bowers and Ignas K. Skrupskelis. Cambridge: Harvard University Press.
James, William. 1983a. *Essays in Psychology*. Edited by Frederick H. Burkhardt, Fredson Bowers and Ignas K. Skrupskelis. Cambridge: Harvard University Press.
James, William. 1983b. *Talks to Teachers on Psychology and to Students on Some of Life's Ideals*. Edited by Frederick Burkhardt, Fredson Bowers and Ignas K. Skrupskelis. Cambridge: Harvard University Press.
James, William. 1987. *Essays, Comments, and Reviews*. Edited by Frederick H. Burkhardt, Fredson Bowers and Ignas K. Skrupskelis. Cambridge: Harvard University Press.
James, William. 1988a. *Manuscript Essays and Notes*. Edited by Frederick H. Burkhardt, Fredson Bowers and Ignas K. Skrupskelis. Cambridge: Harvard University Press.
James, William. 1988b. *Manuscript Lectures*. Edited by Frederick H. Burkhardt, Fredson Bowers and Ignas K. Skrupskelis. Cambridge: Harvard University Press.
James, William. 1992-2004. *The Correspondence of William James*. Edited by Ignas K. Skrupskelis and Elizabeth M. Berkeley. 12 vols. Charlottesville: University Press of Virginia.

EDITOR'S INTRODUCTION

ALEXANDER MUGAR KLEIN

Overview of James's Intellectual Biography

In August of 1872, three neurasthenic years out of medical school, William James (1842–1910) accepted his first teaching appointment. Harvard offered him $300 to co-teach Comparative Anatomy and Physiology (Natural History 3). He held exercises three times a week, taking responsibility for the physiology portion of the course (Skrupskelis 1988, xxii). For the fifty-odd undergraduates enrolled, the moment James assumed the podium that fall would have been inconspicuous; but it marked the arrival at Harvard of a giant.

James would become one of his country's most influential and visible academics in any field.[1] Over the span of his career, he was elected president of both the American Psychological Association and the American Philosophical Association. He received honors from Princeton and Yale, as well as from universities in Berlin, Copenhagen, Durham, Edinburgh, Geneva, Milan, Moscow, Oxford, Padua, Paris, and Rome. He was elected an honorary member of the National Academy of Science, the American Association for the Advancement of Science, and the British Academy (Myers 1986, 1–2), and was the first foreign philosopher to become a corresponding member of the Berlin Academy of Sciences (CWJ, 9.212, 585). He also gained an international reputation for connecting with audiences of non-academics (see Cotkin 1994, 12). In short, James would become a towering figure in western intellectual life.

What was the basis for his reputation? For one thing, James was instrumental in founding the nascent field of physiological psychology. In 1875–1876, he created and taught the first graduate course in the United States in that field (at Harvard). That fall, he also opened one of the two original psychology laboratories in the world.[2] And his 1890 *Principles of Psychology* (PP) became a modern classic at a time when the distinction between textbook and research contribution in this young science remained porous. It has often been considered his masterpiece (e.g., Santayana 1955, 41; Barzun 1983/1984, 34; Myers 1986, 2; Richardson 2006, 302).

The book was in fact commissioned as a textbook on the "new psychology" for Henry Holt's American Science Series. It took James almost twelve years to produce the work, which ran to 28 chapters over two volumes. The *Principles* synthesized a kaleidoscope of experimental results and clinical observations being produced in laboratories and medical facilities especially in Europe and North America, and peppered these with homespun demonstrations readers could perform on themselves. It offered ingenious theories of spatial and temporal perception, attention, emotion, habit, will, and many other phenomena. But it also interspersed striking introspective description and conceptual reflection of a sort that today would be more at home in philosophy. The book's phenomenological analysis so struck his readers that characteristically Jamesean turns of phrase seeped into the wider English lexicon, including the "stream of consciousness," the baby's experience as a "blooming, buzzing confusion," and temporal experience as involving a "specious present" (PP 1890, 341, 462, 573). The work has apparently never gone out of print and remains a classic in both philosophy and psychology (Leary 2018, viii). The contributions to this volume most centrally concerned with James's *Principles of Psychology* are the chapters by Prinz, Pott, Hatfield, Klein, Leary, and Levine.

During the 1890s, the balance of James's intellectual energies tilted more toward philosophy and what might be called the psychology of religion. He had already established considerable scientific credibility through the *Principles* and through his provocative albeit more scholarly publications in France, Britain, and the United States. But that decade he would publish the first of three philosophical books on which his tremendous popular reputation would be built—*The Will to Believe and other Essays in Popular Philosophy* (WB 1897). The title essay took issue with William Clifford's famous dictum that "it is wrong always, everywhere, and for any one, to believe anything upon insufficient evidence" (Clifford 1877, 295). The dialectic between James and Clifford gave rise to a long-running philosophical debate over the ethics of belief—that is, over whether it is ever morally permissible to have faith in a belief for which one lacks evidence. The two essays continue to be routinely paired on philosophy syllabi today.

The year after *The Will to Believe* appeared, James visited the University of California at Berkeley in August. He spoke to the school's Philosophical Union about "Philosophical Conceptions and Practical Results," with his remarks published in Berkeley's *University Chronicle* that fall (James 1898, later reproduced in an appendix to P). This publication marks the first usage of the word "pragmatism" in connection with the philosophical movement with which James would come to be most closely associated.

Here is how he introduced the concept of pragmatism, drawing the basics from an 1878 paper by his old friend, the philosopher and logician Charles Sanders Peirce.[3] The passage is worth quoting at length because it encapsulates the spirit of this new philosophical outlook:

> The soul and meaning of thought, he [Peirce] says, can never be made to direct itself towards anything but the production of belief, belief being the demi-cadence which

closes a musical phrase in the symphony of our intellectual life. Thought in movement has thus for its only possible motive the attainment of thought at rest. But when our thought about an object has found its rest in belief, then our action on the subject can firmly and safely begin. Beliefs, in short, are really rules for action; and the whole function of thinking is but one step in the production of habits of action. If there were any part of a thought that made no difference in the thought's practical consequences, then that part would be no proper element of the thought's significance. Thus the same thought may be clad in different words; but if the different words suggest no different conduct, they are mere outer accretions, and have no part in the thought's meaning. If, however, they determine conduct differently, they are essential elements of the significance. "Please open the door," and "*Veuillez ouvrir la porte*," in French, mean just the same thing; but "D—n you, open the door," although in English, *means* something very different. Thus to develop a thought's meaning we need only determine what conduct it is fitted to produce: that conduct is for us its sole significance. And the tangible fact at the root of all our thought-distinctions, however subtle, is that there is no one of them so fine as to consist in anything but a possible difference of practice. To attain perfect clearness in our thoughts of an object, then, we need only consider what effects of a conceivably practical kind the object may involve—what sensations we are to expect from it, and what reactions we must prepare. Our conception of these effects, then, is for us the whole of our conception of the object, so far as that conception has positive significance at all. (P 1898, 259)

James gave more than a name to this movement. He also gave it a distinctive slant. Peirce's pragmatism grew out of an engagement with the exact sciences (especially logic and mathematics). But James's way of developing these philosophical ideas was informed by his own research and training in psychology, physiology, medicine, and evolutionary biology, and by his enduring interest in religion. Relationships between James's philosophy and his reflections on biology, psychology, medicine (alternative and traditional), and even parapsychology, are treated in this volume in the contributions by Pearce, Croce, Sommer, and Leary. The contributions to this volume most centrally concerned with James's pragmatism include the chapters by O'Shea, Jackman, Donaldson, Kitcher, and Skrupskelis.[4]

By the time James gave his Gifford Lectures in Edinburgh (1901–1902), a lively debate about this new pragmatist movement was beginning to heat up.[5] The Gifford Lectures would be published in 1902 as *The Varieties of Religious Experience* (VRE 1902). The contributions to this volume most centrally concerned with James's *Will to Believe* and *Varieties* are the chapters by Marchetti, Bush, Talisse, Throntveit and Kloppenberg, and Stern and Williams. This would constitute the second of three major books to cement his philosophical reputation well beyond the walls of academia. The book offered psychological and philosophical analyses of lengthy first-person accounts of (often intense) religious experience. It gave philosophical pragmatism a central place in the analysis of religion (e.g., at VRE, 351 *ff.*). And it captured the imagination of legions of readers.[6]

The third book to burnish James's status as a formidable public intellectual was his 1907 *Pragmatism*. It expanded on basic themes from his 1898 Berkeley lecture and would become the central lightning rod in the controversy over the movement, which by then had exploded across the Atlantic. What generated the most heat were his provocative accounts of meaning and truth.

A long tradition in English-language philosophy tracing back at least to Hume construes the meaning of a thought in terms of that thought's causal history—in terms of the experience from which the thought was originally copied. On such a view, when I think of the apple in my refrigerator, the thought counts as *meaning* the apple in virtue of the thought's having been copied from a past experience of the apple. In contrast, James offered a future-tensed account according to which a thought's "meaning" must be understood in terms of the future "conduct it is fitted to produce" (per the block quotation above). On this approach, my thought *means* the apple in virtue of the thought affording a capacity to produce apple-appropriate conduct, such as helping me find and eat the fruit when I'm hungry.

If one regards meaning as a matter of the future conduct a thought supports, then it is natural to regard truth as a matter of *successful* conduct. As James liked to put it, we have "human purposes" in this world (PP 1907, 122), and the true thoughts are just those that help us achieve those purposes (finding and eating the apple, to stick with the pedestrian example). In the mature years of his life, James developed a suite of more complex views about meaning, truth, and ultimately metaphysics, and at the heart of all these is the notion that better and worse when it comes to cognition is a matter of better and worse support for our practical goals.

When James died in 1910, he was still developing a metaphysical system, especially in a book he left "fragmentary and unrevised" (MT, xiv) called *Some Problems of Philosophy*, which would be published posthumously. He had also attempted to flesh out his metaphysical system in his eight-part Hibbert Lectures at Oxford's Manchester College (1908), which were subsequently published as *A Pluralistic Universe*. And a series of more academic papers would be published posthumously as *Essays in Radical Empiricism*. These latter papers developed his conception of the universe as composed of "pure experience," a stuff that is by itself neither mental nor physical, but out of which all mental and physical phenomena are built. Although James never finished working out his metaphysical system to his own satisfaction, these three books represent the most mature metaphysical reflections in his literary remains. The contributions to this volume most centrally concerned with James's late metaphysics include the chapters by Cooper, Dunham, and Bordogna.

In this section I have offered an overview of James's intellectual career. In the next section, I outline a rationale for how I have editorially organized this book.

James and Dialogic Density

Along with his pragmatist conspirators Peirce and John Dewey, James was among the earliest Americans to make a sustained and distinctive contribution to European philosophy. Perhaps unsurprisingly, pragmatism has often been thought to be *characteristically* American, although both James and Dewey resisted being pigeon-holed in this way (Klein 2021).

One basis for this estimation has been that pragmatists have often seemed happy to throw out old-world orthodoxies in philosophy. Indeed, Dewey once wrote that we do not solve philosophical problems, "we get over them" (Dewey 1910, 19). His attitude earned pragmatists a reputation as revolutionaries who are less interested in engaging with reigning philosophical problems than with changing the subject.

If being a revolutionary simply means being willing to dispense with philosophical dogmas, the label seems as apropos for James as it does for Dewey. We have seen examples of James's radicalism in this sense, above. But if being a revolutionary means having a preference for changing the subject on reigning philosophical problems rather than grappling with them, the revolutionary label seems less apt for James.

Some philosophers write in a monological voice, giving little sense that they arrived at their positions by engaging with anyone else's work. This kind of voice suits the philosopher who wishes to change the subject on old problems. But to read James is to be confronted with a battery of references to others. In his writing, his own views characteristically develop in dialogue, both with the living and the deceased. By the standards of any age, he was extraordinarily erudite, engaging with everything from laboratory research from the most famous European experimentalists (like Wilhelm Wundt) to reports on mind-expanding drug experimentation from obscure pamphleteers (like Benjamin Paul Blood), from natural-philosophical reflection by ancients (like Aristotle) to metaphysical speculation from his contemporaries (like Josiah Royce and F. H. Bradley). What is more, he was fluent in French and German and engaged extensively with literatures in those languages.

James often situated his ideas inside a complex web of others' views, in short. Readers get the impression of an author working out positions in dialogue with peers and with the mighty dead. He advocated startling views that departed from his predecessors in many interesting ways, to be sure; but these departures were often taken in the guise of new solutions to perennial problems (hence the subtitle of *Pragmatism: A New Name for Some Old Ways of Thinking*), not in the guise of turning one's back on the past.

This feeling one gets from reading James—that his writing is unusually dialogical, especially compared to Dewey's more monological prose—suggests a hypothesis that can be tested using computational techniques. One would expect to find a relatively high density of names of persons in James's writing. I have conducted just such a computational study, and the findings (of which I provide a brief report, here) are consistent with this hypothesis.

I began by constructing a digital corpus out of the ten major monographs James published. The size of this corpus is about 1.34 million words in total. I then used a machine learning algorithm (the Stanford Named Entity Recognizer, or NER; Finkel, Grenager, and Manning 2005) to tag names of persons in this corpus. Using this algorithm (and hand-correcting obvious errors), my results show 5.48 names of persons in every thousand words in James's books, on average.

Table I.1 Dialogic density in William James's 10 major monographs

Year	Work	Total Words	Total PERSON Tags	Dialogic Density (number of PERSON tags per 1000 words)
1890	*Principles of Psychology*	564,071	3,283	5.82
1892	*Psychology: The Briefer Course*	157,539	508	3.22
1897	*The Will to Believe*	100,213	536	5.35
1899	*Talks to Teachers*	62,902	177	2.81
1902	*Varieties of Religious Experience*	187,468	1,166	6.22
1904	*Essays in Radical Empiricism*	49,433	201	4.07
1907	*Pragmatism*	51,469	235	4.57
1909	*Meaning of Truth*	58,067	272	4.68
1909	*Pluralistic Universe*	61,746	534	8.65
1911	*Some Problems of Philosophy*	44,359	420	9.47
	SUM	1,337,267	7,332	
Corpus Dialogic Density: (PERSON tags sum / words sum)				5.48

For a comparison, I ran a similar analysis on 21 major monographs and book collections that Dewey published in his lifetime, which yielded a corpus of roughly 1.56 million words.[7] References to persons appear at a strikingly lower rate. Using the NER (and again hand-correcting obvious errors), my results show only 2.24 person names per every thousand words in this sample of Dewey's writing.[8]

Let us call the average density of named persons in every thousand words a corpus's "dialogic density." The dialogic density of the James corpus is well over twice what it is in the Dewey corpus (5.48 versus 2.24 person names in every thousand words). The results are summarized in Tables I.1 and I.2. These results are consistent with the hypothesis that James's writing is significantly more densely populated with references to other persons than is Dewey's writing. And it fits more generally with the idea that James tended to write in an unusually dialogically-engaged manner.

Think of an author as sitting at the center of a web of persons whom he or she explicitly discusses, cites, mentions, references, and so on. Think of the web as stretched over a surface that is determined by the size of the corpus of works under consideration—more words amounts to a larger web. And think of each node in the web as a mentioned person, so that higher rates of persons mentioned in the corpus amounts to a denser web. "Dialogic density" refers to the density of this web.

The phrase is meant to suggest that authors' rhetorical strategies can differ—often substantially—when it comes to the degree to which they develop their own ideas in

Table I.2 Dialogic density in John Dewey's 18 major monographs

Year	Work	Total Words	Total PERSON Tags	Dialogic Density (number of PERSON tags per 1000 words)
1887	Psychology	123,522	641	5.19
1891	Outlines of a Critical Theory of Ethics	57,220	276	4.82
1894	Study of Ethics	50,483	273	5.41
1899	The School and Society	38,301	38	0.99
1910	How We Think	62,861	44	0.70
1910	The Influence of Darwin on Philosophy and Other Essays in Contemporary Thought	66,835	262	3.92
1916	Democracy and Education	139,803	117	0.84
1916	Essays in Experimental Logic	104,980	244	2.32
1920	Reconstruction in Philosophy	49,644	127	2.56
1922	Human Nature and Conduct	85,692	83	0.97
1925	Experience and Nature	125,517	136	1.08
1927	The Public and its Problems	53,400	75	1.40
1929	The Quest for Certainty	97,169	165	1.70
1930	Individualism, Old and New	30,110	26	0.86
1934	A Common Faith	21,996	27	1.23
1934	Art as Experience	135,947	460	3.38
1935	Liberalism and Social Action	23,040	100	4.34
1938	Experience and Education	21,802	5	0.23
1938	Logic	193,698	254	1.31
1939	Freedom and Culture	49,028	124	2.53
1939	Theory of Valuation	24,342	1	0.04
	SUM	1,555,390	3,478	
Corpus Dialogic Density: (PERSON tags sum / words sum)				2.24

explicit dialogue with others. That James's corpus (his web) is over twice as dialogically dense as Dewey's does not mean that James was influenced by twice as many people as Dewey, or that James was somehow twice as erudite as Dewey (who was extremely learned, himself). But it does suggest that James made a consistent rhetorical habit of setting out his own positions in the context of a constellation of interlocutors. Given 1000-word samples from these corpora, a James sample is likely to contain almost two-and-a-half times the references to others as a Dewey sample.

This striking feature of James's writing presents challenges to newcomers as well as experts. It is difficult to get very far in James's corpus unless one can make sense of his attitudes toward figures like Charles Darwin and Herbert Spencer, Alexander Bain and Charles Renouvier, David Hume and G. W. F. Hegel, or indeed Peirce and Dewey.[9] So I have curated contributions to this book that elucidate James not only through theoretical analysis, but also through a kind of situational analysis—that is, through attempts to unwind important strands in his dense dialogical web.

Thus some chapters of this book are directly devoted to James's intellectual relationships with others. But treatments of James's relationships can be found throughout many of the thematic chapters as well. In addition to the interlocutors mentioned in the last paragraph, we have chapters that consider James's relationships with Royce, Henri Bergson, and Ralph Waldo Emerson. We also have chapters looking at how James was dialectically engaged *by* later figures in the British analytic tradition, including Wittgenstein, and in the phenomenological tradition.[10]

No single volume can possibly canvass the entire network of James's interlocuters, of course. But one goal of this volume is to elucidate a selection of his more important intellectual relationships, both for the benefit of the newcomer and to help advance our scholarly understanding. I suggest that what finally emerges from this treatment is a more evolutionary, less revolutionary James.

Chapter Previews

This book is divided into eight parts. The first part addresses James's work on the mind, especially in psychology. Jesse Prinz's chapter examines James's work on attention. James's theory was central to much of his other work in psychology, particularly to his theorizing about perception, the self, and will. Prinz excavates from James a compelling theory of attention that offers insight and interest even for theorizing about this topic today.

Heleen Pott's chapter is an examination of James's influential and provocative work on emotion. Pott canvasses three popular interpretations, today, of James's theory: that he offered a view much in line with Friedrich Lange; that he offered a forerunner of Basic Emotions Theory; and that he aimed to develop a phenomenology of the body. She argues that a full grasp of his approach requires integrating insights from all three readings.

Next, Gary Hatfield examines the topic to which James devoted the longest chapter in his voluminous *Principles of Psychology*: spatial perception. Hatfield situates James's approach to this complex topic in the broader history of psychological and physiological reflections, with particular reference to Wilhelm Wundt, Hermann von Helmholtz, and Alexander Bain. Hatfield examines James's case for nativism and his treatment of spatial sensation, perception, and conception.

Alexander Klein's chapter assesses James's evolutionary account of consciousness. James contended that consciousness involves actively evaluating what is in one's environment. The evolutionary function of this evaluating agency was behavior regulation, for James, and Klein reviews some empirical evidence he offered for this view.

The second part of the book turns to James's involvement with other sciences, both mainstream and alternative. Trevor Pearce's chapter examines James's engagement with evolutionary biology, especially as developed by Darwin and Spencer. James came to accept Darwin's theory, but was critical of Spencer's evolutionary philosophy, which he thought made the mind overly passive. But James also adopted Spencer's organism-environment framework, building a novel evolutionary philosophy of his own.

Paul J. Croce's chapter examines James's medical training and his lifelong engagement with alternative medical practices. Croce argues that traditional medicine taught James a rigorous adherence to fact, while his encounters with alternative medicine opened James to a wider range of spiritual experience in his work on religion. Croce suggests that alternative medicine also helped James develop his non-dualistic metaphysical account of the relationship between mind and body.

Andreas Sommer's chapter canvases James's long-standing interest in parapsychology, including his interactions with allies like Frederick Myers and critics like James McKeen Cattell. James's uncompromisingly empirical attitude toward phenomena such as telepathy and mediumship subjected him to widespread criticism in the scientific community. Sommer shows that surprisingly, many of these criticisms were based on religious or political considerations rather than on purely scientific ones.

David E. Leary's chapter considers the relationship between philosophy and psychology more broadly in James's writing. Although he once advocated a sharp separation between the two, Leary shows that James came to find their admixture to be both inevitable and productive. Leary argues that a fundamental fealty to experience ties together James's approach to both philosophy and psychology.

In part three, the book turns to examining James's reflections on value. Sarin Marchetti's chapter offers an overview of the many different interpretations to which James's work on ethics has been subject. Marchetti defends a more radical reading according to which James sees the primary aim of ethics as hortatory. This means that for James the goal of ethics is not so much to describe moral facts but to exhort certain kinds of fruitful action.

Stephen S. Bush's chapter surveys James's work on religion. He discusses James's famous argument from *The Will to Believe* that it is permissible in special cases to accept beliefs for which one does not yet have compelling evidence. James argues that such beliefs are essential not only in religion but in other areas of our moral and social lives more generally.

Robert B. Talisse, Trygve Throntveit, and James T. Kloppenberg offer complementary accounts of social and political matters in James. Talisse's chapter examines James's social philosophy in terms of his fundamental commitment to value pluralism. Talisse critically analyzes the link James saw between value pluralism and social toleration. Throntveit and Kloppenberg examine James's civic engagement and political ideals. The chapter culminates with an idea James developed toward the end of his life: what he called "radical democracy," the insistence on popular participation not only at the ballot box but at every level of social life.

In part four we turn to James's pragmatism about meaning and truth. James O'Shea opens this part of the book with an examination of a distinction that James developed throughout his career and that became central to his pragmatism—a distinction between percepts and concepts. O'Shea traces and critically assesses James's attempts to refine this distinction throughout his lifetime.

Henry Jackman's chapter examines James's pragmatic account of intentionality (aboutness) and of philosophical analysis. Unlike contemporary philosophers who seek to analyze phenomena by identifying necessary and sufficient conditions, James sought to analyze phenomena like intentionality in terms of resemblance to core cases. Jackman then argues that James's controversial account of truth can meet some important objections if one keeps his novel approaches to intentionality and analysis in view.

Tom Donaldson's chapter then evaluates James's account of truth more directly. Donaldson identifies some of James's core commitments on truth that some readers have thought to be inconsistent. Donaldson argues that they do in fact form a compelling and coherent whole, particularly when James's account of truth is tied to his pure experience metaphysics.

Philip Kitcher portrays James as a philosophical reformer, one who wanted to pull philosophy back from increasingly narrow, technical analyses to a focus on the human condition. James continually conveyed a sense that humanity was lost, as if in a dense forest, and he thought pragmatist philosophy could help us find our way again.

Ignas Kęstutis Skrupskelis's chapter examines James's pluralism about truth. James claimed that there are many different truth relations that apply in different contexts. Skrupskelis examines James's epistemic pluralism as it relates to science, religion, and philosophy in particular.

Part five addresses James's later metaphysics. It begins with Wes Cooper exploring James's radical empiricism, and in particular James's view that mind and matter are both composed of "pure experience." Cooper shows how the idea of pure experience—a stuff that is itself neither mental nor physical—grows naturally from James's earlier conception of sensation in his psychology.

Jeremy Dunham's chapter is an examination of James's long-running attempts to respond to Josiah Royce's argument from error. Royce had claimed to derive the existence of an absolute mind from the plain fact that it is possible for intentional mental states to be mistaken. Dunham argues that James repeatedly sought to overcome this argument, and only found a satisfactory answer after adopting, late in his life, some metaphysical views championed by Bergson.

Francesca Bordogna examines James's little-known reflections on the mathematics of infinite totalities. James is often thought (in part due to self-deprecation) to have been mathematically ignorant. But Bordogna shows that James in fact grappled extensively with the so called "new infinite," a formal definition of infinity developed by Richard Dedekind and Georg Cantor. Royce had put the new infinite to philosophical work in offering a mathematized conception of the Absolute. By excavating James's assessment of the new infinite, Bordogna places in a startling new light his philosophical relationship to Royce (and to Renouvier, with whom James also had important disagreements concerning the philosophy of mathematics).

Part six features chapters that focus directly on James's engagements with past figures. Yumiko Inukai examines James's relationship to David Hume. James called his worldview "radical empiricism," a moniker he used to suggest both an affinity with Hume and some important differences. Inukai argues that Hume's conception of perception is much closer to James's notion of pure experience than James (and many of his readers) have thought.

The chapter co-authored by Robert Stern and Neil W. Williams takes up James's criticisms of G. W. F. Hegel, which Hegel scholars have often regarded as shallow. Stern and Williams show that James in fact developed an interesting, internal critique of Hegel's system that deserves more attention than it has received. James shared an important commitment with Hegel—that philosophy should help us "feel at home" in the world. James's central objection is that Hegel has an overly narrow and intellectualistic conception of what it takes for creatures like us to feel at home in the world.

Russell B. Goodman turns to an important American inspiration for James—Ralph Waldo Emerson. Goodman focuses on James's Emersonian use of language, paying particular attention to schematic distinctions James draws between temperaments, for example between the "tough-" and "tender-minded," and the "once-" and "twice-born." The former distinction plays a prominent role in *Pragmatism*, and Goodman shows that Emerson made use of a similar distinction between temperaments in earlier essays.

Part seven considers James's relationships with a few key contemporaries. The French neo-Kantian Charles Renouvier is the focus of Mathias Girel's chapter. Girel argues that although Renouvier and his journal *Critique Philosophique* were instrumental in bringing James's early work to an international readership, by the 1880s philosophical fissures had already opened up between the two. Renouvier's philosophy was animated by a Kantian spirit, and Girel's investigation thus sheds light on James's attitudes toward Kantian philosophy more generally.

We usually think of classic pragmatism as having three main founders—Peirce, James, and Dewey. The next two chapters take up James's relationships with Peirce and Dewey, respectively. Claudine Tiercelin's chapter offers both comparison and contrast between James and Peirce. Scholars have often seen the pragmatist tradition as developing along two distinct paths. A more realistic path owes to Peirce, and a more nominalistic path owes to James. But Tiercelin compares their views on psychology, truth, ethics, and even realism, showing that the differences are not as extreme as many have come to imagine. F. Thomas Burke's chapter offers a new reading of the relationship between James and Dewey. While most comparisons of the two figures focus on their shared pragmatism, Burke examines their shared commitment to radical empiricism. He also argues that there is an implicit position one might call "radical rationalism" that can be found in the work of both James and Dewey. Radical rationalism constitutes a neglected respect in which Dewey developed to maturity some seeds of ideas planted but not fully cultivated by James.

Finally in part eight we consider a few respects in which later figures and traditions developed James's ideas. Cheryl Misak argues that James's pragmatism had an important and hitherto neglected influence on the development of British analytic philosophy. Although Bertrand Russell and G. E. Moore's early opposition to pragmatism is well known, Misak argues that Russell actually took a turn toward pragmatism after James's death, and passed this influence on both to Frank Ramsey and Ludwig Wittgenstein.

Anna Boncompagni's chapter puts the spotlight more tightly on Wittgenstein. He is also often thought to have been broadly critical of James, but Boncompagni shows that this is simplistic. Wittgenstein first became interested in James through the *Varieties of Religious Experience*, and one correspondent reports that the book had had such an influence that Wittgenstein considered becoming a monk. By the 1930s he was engaging James's psychological work, both critically and productively, and eventually (like Ramsey and Russell) came around to some views that resemble pragmatism.

Steven Levine's chapter examines the impact of James's *Principles of Psychology* on the phenomenological tradition. Starting with Edmund Husserl, a phenomenological reading of the *Principles* portrays that work as developing a sophisticated account of intentionality. Later figures like Richard Cobb-Stevens and Bruce Wilshire suggest that in coming to grips with intentionality in the *Principles*, James was ultimately pushed to reject the idea that psychology can be a natural science separate from philosophy. This implication has been controversial since it seems to contradict James's own professions to be building a science of psychology. Levine critically examines this reading.

I am very grateful to the talented scholars whose work constitutes this volume. I would particularly like to thank several friends and colleagues on whom I have relied for advice throughout the long process of assembling this book, including Henry Jackman, Steven Levine, Cheryl Misak, and Trevor Pearce. I also thank Pearce along with Christopher Green and Charles Pence for helpful feedback on the digital analysis in this chapter. And I would especially like to thank my editor at Oxford for his generous guidance (and patience), Peter Ohlin.

Notes

1. Upon James's death, this was the judgment of colleagues like John Dewey and Bertrand Russell, as well as of newspapers around the world. For example, his obituary in the Paris *Temps* declared James to have been "the most famous American philosopher since Emerson"; and the *Boston Evening Transcript* called his death "the removal of the greatest of contemporary Americans" (quoted at Myers 1986, 1, which also contains quotes from Dewey and Russell). His tremendous influence on the subsequent development of psychology is also apparent. Almost a hundred years later he was ranked as the fourteenth most eminent psychologist of the twentieth century in a study that combines three quantitative measures (like journal citations and textbook mentions) with three qualitative measures (like results in reputation surveys). The study reports that when American Psychological Association members were asked, "[W]ho are the greatest psychologists of the 20th century

in the *overall field of psychology*?" James was the sixth most frequently mentioned name (Haggbloom et al. 2002).
2. The first psychology laboratory is often credited to Wundt in 1879, but in fact both Wundt and James independently established psychology laboratories for the sake of teaching in 1875–1876 (Harper 1949, 1950). For more on James's early class in physiological psychology, see Skrupskelis (1988, xxii–xxvii).
3. Despite his clear intellectual gifts, Peirce floundered personally and professionally, spending periods of his life in poverty. James continually sought to help his friend find income through teaching and lecturing, and to try to bring Peirce's publications to wider attention (Misak 2013, 26–27). For instance, in an 1897 letter to James, Peirce wrote that he had not eaten in three days (CWJ, 8.243–244). James swiftly invited Peirce to give a series of lectures in Cambridge and secured donors for a much-needed stipend. Delivered in the winter of 1898 in a private house, the lectures impressed a few colleagues, but did not substantially improve Peirce's fortunes or professional reputation. Interestingly, it was in August of that same year when James unveiled pragmatism in his lecture at Berkeley, famously crediting Peirce as the movement's founder. Peirce would have been all but unknown to his audience (Menand 2001, 348–351). Although Peirce could be prickly, he apparently felt indebted to his more famous friend, even sometimes using his middle initial as "Santiago"—St. James (Misak 2013, 27). For more on Peirce and James, see Tiercelin's contribution to this volume.
4. For more on connections between James's own scientific work and his pragmatism, see Klein (forthcoming, esp. the postscript).
5. One can get a sense of how quickly the controversy heated up by consulting Shook's annotated bibliography (Shook 1998), an essential scholarly resource.
6. Richardson reports that the book sold 11,500 copies in the first year. Selling for a whopping $3.20 each—more than three times what *Pragmatism* would command five years later—*Varieties* "made James a rich man" (Richardson 2006, 421). Smith notes that the book received six printings during that first year, and in the next half century would appear in no less than fifty-six impressions, which does not begin to count the many translations (VRE xii).
7. I used the Past Masters database to access the full text of the *Works of William James* and the *Collected Works of John Dewey* (Dewey 2003, James 2008). Here is my basic rule for including or excluding volumes from my corpora. If a volume is a monograph or mono-authored essay collection published within a year of the author's death and is cited in the main *Stanford Encyclopedia Entry* for either William James or John Dewey (Goodman 2022, Hildebrand 2021), then I included the volume in the relevant corpus. No other volumes were included. Dewey lived much longer than James, and his publications were far more voluminous. The books cited in Dewey's *Stanford Encyclopedia* entry are therefore understandably selective (the volumes in James's *Stanford Encyclopedia* bibliography are more complete). But my study aims to elucidate James and Dewey's reputation specifically in philosophy, and given the *Stanford Encyclopedia*'s preeminence in the field, works cited in these entries should provide a representative sample of each author's most philosophically prominent writing. I excluded any words written by the editors of either James's *Works* or Dewey's *Collected Works*. I included prefaces or introductions written by either James or Dewey. I excluded indexes and tables of contents, whether produced by James, Dewey, or their editors. My corpus thus includes only words written by James or Dewey. I did not trim, lowercase, remove stop-words, remove page numbers, or do any other pre-processing.

8. I manually read through all the results attempting to find and fix any words or phrases that were either erroneously tagged with PERSON or erroneously not tagged with PERSON. For example, in Dewey's *Democracy and Education*, the word "Hegel" is erroneously tagged as a LOCATION. I hand-corrected that entry (and numerous similar entries) to the PERSON tag. And in James's *Pragmatism*, the German word "Wie" was erroneously tagged as referring to a PERSON; I removed that tag (James frequently used German and French phrases in his English prose, and NER sometimes mistakenly tags such words). Finally, I deleted all remaining LOCATION and ORGANIZATION tags, leaving only the PERSON tags. Note that the NER does miss some name references, occasionally. For example, it identifies 24 instances of the name "Lange" in James's *Principles*, whereas one can use a case-sensitive word search to see that *Principles* in fact contains 28 instances of this name. The results tabulated here only include names tagged by the NER. I did not supply any missing instances, such as the four overlooked "Lange" instances in the *Principles*, except in cases where I could easily notice that a name had been mis-tagged with LOCATION or ORGANIZATION (as was common with the name Bain, for example), in which case I corrected the tag to PERSON. Missed names do not undermine my comparative study on the assumption that names are likely to be undercounted at a similar rate in both the James and Dewey corpora. My complete data are freely available online, along with a more detailed discussion of methodology; see Klein (2022).
9. For more on James's attitudes toward Darwin and Spencer see the chapter by Pearce, toward Bain and Renouvier see the chapters by Hatfield, Bordogna, and Girel, toward Hume and Hegel see the chapters by Inukai and Stern and Williams, and toward Peirce and Dewey see the chapters by Tiercelin and Burke.
10. For Royce and Bergson, see the chapters by Dunham and Bordogna, and on Emerson see Goodman's chapter. For the British analytic tradition see Misak's chapter, for Wittgenstein see Boncompagni's chapter, and for the phenomenological tradition see Levine's chapter.

Works Cited

Barzun, Jacques. 1983/1984. *A Stroll with William James*. Chicago: University of Chicago Press.

Clifford, William Kingdon. 1877. "The Ethics of Belief." *The Contemporary Review*, January, 289–309.

Cotkin, George. 1994. *William James, Public Philosopher*. Champaign, IL: University of Illinois Press.

Dewey, John. 1910. *The Influence of Darwin on Philosophy, and Other Essays in Contemporary Thought*. New York: Henry Holt.

Dewey, John. 2003. *The Collected Works of John Dewey, 1882–1953 (2nd Release). Electronic Edition*. Edited by Boydston, Jo Ann and Larry Hickman. Charlottesville, VA: InteLex Corp.

Finkel, Jenny Rose, Trond Grenager, and Christopher Manning. 2005. "Incorporating Non-Local Information into Information Extraction Systems by Gibbs Sampling." *Proceedings of the 43nd Annual Meeting of the Association for Computational Linguistics* ACL 2005: 363–370.

Goodman, Russell. 2022. "William James." *The Stanford Encyclopedia of Philosophy*. Edited by Edward N. Zalta. Spring ed. https://plato.stanford.edu/archives/spr2022/entries/james/.

Haggbloom, Steven J., Renee Warnick, Jason E. Warnick, Vinessa K. Jones, Gary L. Yarbrough, Tenea M. Russell, Chris M. Borecky, Reagan McGahhey, John L. Powell, Jamie Beavers, and Emmanuelle Monte. 2002. "The 100 Most Eminent Psychologists of the 20th Century." *Review of General Psychology* 6 (2): 139–152.

Harper, Robert S. 1949. "The Laboratory of William James." *The Harvard Alumni Bulletin* 52: 169–173.
Harper, Robert S. 1950. "The First Psychological Laboratory." *Isis* 41 (2): 158–161.
Hildebrand, David. 2021. "John Dewey." *The Stanford Encyclopedia of Philosophy*. Edited by Edward N. Zalta. Winter ed. https://plato.stanford.edu/archives/win2021/entries/dewey/.
James, William. 1898. "Philosophical Conceptions and Practical Results." *The University Chronicle (University of California)* 1: 287–310.
James, William. 2008. *The Works of William James. Electronic Edition*. Edited by Burkhardt, Frederick H., Fredson Bowers, and Ignas K. Skrupskelis. Charlottesville, VA: InteLex Corp.
Klein, Alexander. 2021. "How American Is Pragmatism?" *Philosophy of Science* 88 (5): 849–859.
Klein, Alexander. 2022. "Dialogic Density in the Books of William James and John Dewey." Zenodo. https://doi.org/10.5281/zenodo.6336256.
Klein, Alexander. Forthcoming. *Consciousness Is Motor: William James on Mind and Action*. New York: Oxford University Press.
Leary, David E. 2018. *The Routledge Guidebook to James's Principles of Psychology*. London: Routledge, Taylor & Francis Group.
Menand, Louis. 2001. *The Metaphysical Club: A Story of Ideas in America*. New York: Farrar, Straus, and Giroux.
Misak, Cheryl J. 2013. *The American Pragmatists*. Oxford: Oxford University Press.
Myers, Gerald E. 1986. *William James: His Life and Thought*. New Haven: Yale University Press.
Richardson, Robert D. 2006. *William James: In the Maelstrom of American Modernism*. Boston: Houghton Mifflin.
Santayana, George. 1955. *Character and Opinion in the United States*. New York: George Braziller.
Shook, John R. 1998. *Pragmatism: An Annotated Bibliography, 1898–1940*. Atlanta: Rodopi.
Skrupskelis, Ignas K. 1988. "Introduction." In *Manuscript Lectures*, edited by Frederick H. Burkhardt, Fredson Bowers and Ignas K. Skrupskelis, xvii–lxiii. Cambridge, MA: Harvard University Press.

PART I
MIND

CHAPTER 1

JAMES AND ATTENTION
Reactive Spontaneity

JESSE PRINZ

INTRODUCTION

IN his chapter on attention in the *Principles of Psychology*, William James remarks that the topic has been neglected within Anglophone philosophy. He then offers a detailed analysis drawing on German psychology. Though presented as an empirical review, it is really much more, since James offers original theoretical perspectives on attention, and attention becomes an important player in his theory of the mind, more broadly. It factors, for example, into his theories of perception, belief, and the will. James's complaint that attention has been neglected in Anglophone philosophy remains as true today as it did 125 years ago, though that is beginning to change. Attention has been a major topic of ongoing empirical enquiry, and, in very recent years, philosophers have begun to take notice. It is therefore a perfect moment to reflect on James's views. Though prescient and influential, James's work on attention has received little commentary. The purpose of this chapter is to summarize his treatment, and to extrapolate a theory of what attention is and what attention does. The perspective that emerges from the exercise has much to contribute to contemporary discussions. In particular, I will suggest that James postulates a kind of spontaneity in mental processes that are often regarded as merely receptive, and that this has implications for philosophical psychology, the philosophy of mind, epistemology, and even ontology. Attention can no longer afford to be neglected within philosophy, and James's work helps us see why.

What Is Attention?

Does James Have One Theory or Many?

James's chapter on attention in the *Principles* offers a challenge to readers, since he does not provide a simple formula telling us what attention is. Or rather, he offers what seem to be several different analyses, raising questions about whether his views on the matter were consistent. The chapter is also arranged in a way that makes it difficult to evaluate. Rather than beginning with a detailed analysis of attention itself, he begins with much more specific questions about how many things we can attend to at once. These and other interesting questions populate the chapter, with periodic comments about the nature of attention interspersed. To make things even more difficult, he burdens his prose with lengthy quotations from psychologists describing empirical work. The initial appearance is of a rather random assortment of questions and findings, with little by way of theoretical synthesis. James occasionally turns to lofty philosophical issues (free will and the mind-body relation), but he leaves these unresolved, and there is little reason given in the chapter to think that their resolution hangs on the nature of attention in particular. Philosophical readers may be left wondering what attention really is and why they should care about it.

This first impression can be corrected with a little toil. The first task is to identify a theory of attention, and then one can trace out what attention does. Only then can one really see why it matters. Identifying a theory is not a trivial task, since there are several formulations and characterizations that appear to be in competition with each other. I will bring these out more explicitly and then suggest that there is indeed an official theory, and that theory can make sense of the characterizations that may otherwise appear inconsistent.

The claim that James characterizes attention in different ways might come as a surprise to those who have only casual acquaintance with his discussion. Near the opening, James seems to give an explicit definition of attention, and this, indeed, is the most frequently quoted remark in the chapter:

> Everyone knows what attention is. It is the taking possession by the mind, in clear and vivid form, of one out of what seem several simultaneously possible objects or trains of thought. (PP 1890, 381)

One might call this a selective enhancement theory. It states that attention selects a sub-component of a complex input and renders it salient. James even seems to tell us how this increased salience is achieved: the selected input is rendered clearer and more vivid. Difficulties immediately arise, however, when we notice that this formulation itself already encompasses several ideas, which could be separated. Perhaps there can be selection without these two forms of enhancement. And perhaps these two forms of enhancement are dissociable: clarity and vivacity, after all, are distinct. Such questions are compounded by the rest of the passage, which continues:

> Focalization, concentration, of consciousness are of its essence. It implies withdrawal from some things in order to deal effectively with others, and is a condition which has a real opposite in the confused, dazed, scatterbrained state which in French is called *distraction*, and *Zerstreutheit* in German. (PP 1890, 381–382)

Here we seem to get some new ideas. Is focalization the same as clarity? Is concentration the same as vivacity? If so, it isn't obvious. If not, these are further analyses of how attention operates. Then we get this notion of withdrawal, which is not the same as enhancement (one can make part of a stimulus salient without suppressing anything else). Finally, James contrasts attention with other states of mind, such as confusion. This raises further questions; the term "confusion" can contrast with clear-headedness or with a clearly represented stimulus. The former reading is suggested by the accompanying words, "dazed" and "scatterbrained," but the latter meaning is more consistent with the earlier remark that attention makes things "clear and vivid."

The difficulty in pinning down James's view is compounded by the fact that his opening definition of attention is later supplemented by various further observations that might also be taken as advancing a theory. He says that attention improves perception, conception, discrimination, remembering, and reaction time (PP 1890, 401). This implies that attention is a general-purpose mental facilitator. Here he mentions clarity again and also intensity, which seems, perhaps, subtly different from vivacity, and he is at pains to say that clarity and intensity differ. Thus, the improvements he is adverting to are not only general in scope, they are also varied in form. James proposes a link between attention and memory as well: he says that attention allows memory encoding (PP 1890, 403–404). This is a very different idea than perceptual enhancement, since the point about memory is neutral about whether a stimulus representation is improved in any way. He implies, too, that attention determines what gets noticed (PP 1890, 430–431). This differs from memory encoding, since noticing is something that happens here and now.

The story does not end there. James tells us that attention relates to expectations (406), implying that to attend involves what we would now call predictive coding; when we encounter a stimulus, we apply background knowledge based on prior experience and that influences what we attentively perceive. He suggests, further, that attention involves application of previously stored ideas (PP 1890, 387) and is thus a kind of interpretive activity. Thus, we have two further stories about what goes on when we attend.

To add one final dimension to the mix, we also find James frequently drawing connections between attention and action. In discussing experiments on reaction times, James indicates that attention occasions a preparation of motor response (PP 1890, 405–406). This might be taken as suggesting yet another theory, according to which attention fundamentally involves the control of behavior. That impression is amplified by James's claim that attention is a central component of conscious will (more on this in the section on Belief and the Will).

In summary, James's discussion is an embarrassment of riches. He provides so many observations about the definition of and impact of attention that one is left with the impression that there are multiple constructs at work. This could lead one to think that James is a pluralist about attention, or perhaps even an eliminativist, suggesting that the term should be abandoned because it has no fixed meaning. Less charitably, one might charge James with inconsistency and dismiss his chapter as a litany of disparate effects, with no possible unifying cause.

One can underscore the apparent disunity of James's treatment by comparing his remarks to more recent views of attention. Many of the aspects that he mentions have analogues in recent theories. Seeing these points of comparison reveals how prescient James was, while also deepening the impression that he failed to draw distinctions that animate contemporary debates. Let's begin with the notion of selective enhancement. In current discussions, there are some theories that emphasize selection (see Treisman 1960, on attenuation, and Walley and Weiden 1973, on inhibition), while others emphasize enhancement. Among enhancement theories, some emphasize changes in clarity (see Carrasco et al. 2004, on effective contrast), while others emphasize intensity (see Hillyard et al. 1998, on gain control). There are also theories that highlight the contrast between attention and distraction. For example, there has been recent work relating attention to what has been called the default mode network in the brain; according to the "sentinel hypothesis," this network corresponds to conditions under which a person is vigilantly monitoring the world for pertinent information, in contrast to conditions in which the mind wanders (see Buckner et al. 2008). In addition, there are theories that link attention to memory. In my own work on these themes, I have suggested that attention is the process that allows encoding in working memory—a short-term memory store used for decision-making (Prinz 2012). Others have emphasized the link between attention and action (see Wu 2011, who suggests that attention provides action alternatives). Another recent theorist (Mole 2011) calls on James in noting the diversity of attention's effects and concludes that attention is not a single process but rather refers to those conditions under which multiple cognitive resources are brought into "unison." With the exception of this last example, leading theories mostly correspond to a single dimension in James's rich overview. The cognitive unison account attempts to bring these together, but in actual fact only captures some of the phenomena that James identifies; it relates most to the idea that attention concentrates consciousness, and less, for example, to certain forms of enhancement.

A Unified Theory of Attention

Despite the apparent disunity, I think James does, in fact, have a unified theory of attention. The aforementioned aspects of attention are best understood as effects or symptoms of attention, and the theory provides a potential explanation of those effects. James is not entirely clear on this point, but he does explicitly label one of the sub-sections of his chapter, "Effects of Attention." There he discusses the fact that attention clarifies representations and shortens reaction time. The next section he calls, "The Intimate Nature of the Attentive Process." It is here that, I believe, he advances his unified theory. James does not walk the reader through all the explanatory details; he does not systematically summarize attention's effects and then explain how the "attentive process" accounts for them. But he says enough to give the reader an idea of how those explanations might go. I will offer an interpretation of James's theory and then meditate on its explanatory prowess.

James says that the attentive process has two components, which he calls "organic adjustment" or sometimes "accommodation," and "ideational preparation" or sometimes "anticipatory preparation" or "preperception" (PP 1890, 411). Organic adjustment is a motor response. It occurs when our sensory organs or muscles that "favor their exercise" adjust in some way so as to better respond to the object of attention. One might think of this as an orienting response (elsewhere I define orienting as a change in bodily position with regard to an object of attention or motor preparation for such a change; Prinz 2012). There are two obvious counterexamples to the claim that we always orient toward an object of attention, which James addresses. First, we sometimes talk about attention that is cognitive, rather than sensory (see later), in which case there is no need to orient our senses. Here James suggests that organic adjustment involves the withdrawal of outward senses, including the rolling of our eyes into our heads when we reflect (PP 1890, 412). This is consistent with more recent research linking eye gaze to thinking (Glenberg et al. 1998), and there is also research suggesting that gaze shifts as we form imagery corresponding to the contents of thought (Altmann 2004). Second, there are laboratory cases in which people are trained to stare at one location while attending to another. James replies that this requires great effort and can thus be regarded as an organic adjustment, and he notes that without this effort, gaze spontaneously shifts to the attended object (PP 1890, 414). One might express this by saying that there is a motor plan to shift gaze that gets actively suppressed.

James's insistence on organic adjustment makes him qualify as having an embodied theory of attention: one that says a bodily response, or preparation thereof, is an essential aspect of attention. This anticipates behaviorism, as well as more recent theories, such as ecological psychology, which emphasizes affordances (Heft 2001), and enactivism, which defines perception as a sensorimotor skill (Heras-Escribano, forthcoming). But James cannot be placed into any of these categories. His theory of perception contains a mental component as well: ideational preparation. This mental component is incompatible with behaviorism, and, since it is defined independently of the motor component, it violates the strictures of enactivism. It also departs from the view that perception is direct, which has been associated with ecological theories.

Ideational preparation is the more surprising component of James's theory, and it takes some work to see what he is proposing and why. James seems to believe that, when we attend, we endogenously generate a representation of the thing to which we are attending. Thus, in the case of sensory attention, an external stimulus will cause one representation, as it impinges on our senses, and we will then endogenously generate a representation of the stimulus as well. Attention involves an interaction between these two.

Sometimes this occurs before an object has impinged on our senses, as in what we now call visual search. The easiest cases to understand involve expectations. If, for example, I look for a bottle of wine in just the location where my bottles are usually kept, it seems plausible that I generate a representation of a wine bottle prior to actually seeing one. That representation then allows me to fix attention on a bottle, once found. James says that such anticipatory representations are generated from the "ideational centres of the brain," and this is just an archaic term for what he also calls imagination. Imagination, in turn, is the faculty that allows us to use stored records of prior experiences—it is a kind of active memory system. In the case of expectation, then, we imagine a wine bottle and use of that image facilitates our search. It is a "preperception" (a term borrowed from George Herbert Lewes 1879; PP 1890, 106f.), in that we enter something like a perceptual state prior to actually perceiving a real wine bottle. Contemporary authors agree that cases like this, in which we are looking for something in the visual field, involve an endogenously generated representation, sometimes called a template or a filter.

But what about cases in which attention is more of a passive response to what we happen to encounter? Here too, James wants to posit "ideational preparation." That may seem odd, since it is unclear how we could prepare for something we encounter unexpectedly, but I think this is essential to James's theory, so I want to offer an interpretation.

In cases in which we notice something that we weren't looking for, one might think James would offer a different account. But he does not. James makes the sweeping claim that "ideational preparation or preperception are concerned in all attentive acts" (PP 1890, 420). He defends this surprising conjecture by observing that we typically fail to notice things that we have not previously perceived; to use his example, a kindergarten child might stare at a stuffed bird for hours without noticing that it has nostrils. Noticing the nostrils—and, hence, attending to them—requires that a representation of birds' nostrils be stored in our ideational centers and engaged when looking.

This account raises three puzzles that are not addressed in the chapter on attention, making it difficult to digest James's account. First, what are we to make of James's invocation of the term *pre*-perception in the case of unexpected encounters? How can we represent something we didn't expect before seeing it? A possible answer can be extrapolated from elsewhere in the *Principles*, in particular from his chapter on the Perception of Time. There, James famously posits a specious present, saying that our experience of the present moment is always actually a memory of the recent past. If so, perceptual experience arises after a slight delay. Just prior to experience, there may be stimulation of the senses and response within the central nervous system without any awareness by the knowing subject of experience. It is possible that in this brief instant, we get a kind of feedback loop: first the stimulus engages our ideational centers, and they generate a representation that then serves as a template for us to re-sample the stimulus from the environment. This raises a complication for James since he is loath to admit unconscious mental states (see the section on Intellectual Attention), but we might think of the representation in question as a fleeting physiologically grounded trace, like an afterimage. On this view, experience arises upon this re-sampling, and the prior chain of events goes on behind the scenes, as it were. What we experience as seeing here and now is a kind of revisioning of something first registered by the brain a moment prior. On this interpretation it could work out that conscious perception is always anticipatory.

The second puzzle about James's account concerns how we first come to perceive anything attentively. If attention always involves prior representations, then how does an infant come to attend? James's answer comes in his chapter on Sensations:

> In a new-born brain this gives rise to an absolutely pure sensation. But the experience leaves its 'unimaginable touch' on the matter of the convolutions, and the next impression which a sense-organ transmits produces a cerebral reaction in which the awakened vestige of the last impression plays its part. (PP 1890, 657)

By "pure sensation," James means a sensation with absolutely no records or associations in memory. The phrase "unimaginable touch" appears nowhere else in the *Principles*. It may be an allusion to William Wordsworth, who uses this expression in his poem "Mutability" to refer to the impact of time: time itself is unfelt but it has considerable impact. Likewise, for James, the first sensations of life may be unfelt, but they leave a trace or vestige in memory. These traces can then be engaged the very next time the infant samples similar aspects of the world. Thus, by the second time an infant looks, there are already stored records that can give rise to attentive seeing.

These observations help with a third puzzle. James's talk of ideational preparation gives the impression that attentive seeing requires the deployment of ideas, and, from that, it might be inferred that he adopts a conceptual theory of perception. This would be an interesting commitment, but also a troubling one, since it would seem to imply that we cannot attend to something that we cannot conceptualize. That seems implausible, since we often see things that are difficult to interpret, and stare at them attentively in the hope that they will become decipherable. To find a way out of the puzzle, we need only recall that James borrows the term "idea" from John Locke. Ideas need not be restricted to concepts, in any intellectually demanding sense of the term (cf. PP 1890, 185–186). Ideas can include anything that we can store in memory. Moreover, James finds relevant shortcomings in Locke's terminology. He criticizes the term "idea" for blurring the distinction between thoughts and feelings, and he complains that it invites the view that each idea corresponds to a word, along with the implicit atomism this entails (PP 1890, 194–195). Ideas, then, in James's vocabulary, need not be concepts.

Helpful remarks can also be excavated from his chapters on Sensations and on The Perception of "Things." There James distinguishes sensations from perceptions in a way that is more quantitative than qualitative, allowing that both can be stored. After the first days of life, both sensations and perceptions involve stored records, but in the case of sensations these records are comparatively superficial or simple in content. Over time, we build up associations that allow us to assign meaning to the deliverances of the senses, and we thereby come to perceive "things." In cases where no such associations have been formed, we may nevertheless attend, because we can attend to superficial form. Here we use sensations, rather than ideas of specific kinds of objects for which we may have labels and elaborate beliefs. For these reasons, I don't think we should read James as a conceptualist about attentive seeing. His "ideational" theory allows for seeing with the aid of rudimentary stored sensations that we cannot verbalize; it would be misleading to call these concepts.

This interpretation inoculates James's theory against charges of intellectualism. It also sheds light on a phrase that James introduces in the first paragraph of his Attention chapter. He says that attention introduces a kind of "reactive spontaneity" into perception (PP 1890, 380). The terms "reactive" and "spontaneity" derive from the Kantian tradition, and they normally function as contrastives. In modern language, they relate to "bottom-up" and "top-down" processes. Reactive states are reactions to stimulation, and spontaneous states come from within. A reflex would be reactive, and an act of pure will (if such acts are possible) would be spontaneous. Or, sometimes, percepts are regarded as reactive and concepts are regarded as spontaneous, since the former are caused by the world, and the latter can be willfully manipulated. "Reactive spontaneity" sounds like an oxymoron, but it refers to James's proposal that, in response to external stimuli, we engage stored representations. Attention arises when the latter are applied to the former, and the resulting state is, in that sense, both reactive and spontaneous. I will therefore refer to this as the Reactive Spontaneity Theory.

The Advantages of James's View

I have been trying to make James's Reactive Spontaneity intelligible, and also addressing some immediate concerns. Still, one might wonder what motivates such a view. Why does James analyze attention in terms of ideational preparation instead of adopting any of the more familiar approaches to attention, catalogued in the first section? The answer, I think, is that James's theory has the promise of explaining those disparate aspects of attention within a unified framework.

First, consider selection. When we attend, we often select some aspects of the stuff that impinges on our senses, while ignoring the rest. The Reactive Spontaneity view explains this by supposing that we apply stored ideas to some of the things coming in and not others. The theory also offers an explanation of enhancement: the ideas we deploy may serve to make incoming impressions both sharper and more intense. Enhancement may also be facilitated by the motor component of attention; by shifting our sense organs, we can improve the quality of the input.

The Reactive Spontaneity view may also explain why attended stimuli are brought into memory. Ideas, recall, are stored records, called up from the faculty of imagination. By placing an input under an idea, we bring it into contact with memory systems. One might worry that James is on the brink of a contradiction here. When he discusses newborn babies in his chapter on Sensation, he implies that they automatically store what they see, even before they have the capacity to attend. In the chapter on Attention, he suggests that attention is necessary for memory.

We might help James here, by supplementing his account with a more modern distinction between different kinds of memory. Long-term perceptual memory is used to store sensory records. This contrasts with other kinds of memory, such as working memory (a system for holding items in mind temporarily to perform some computation) or episodic memory (a system for storing autobiographical experiences in a way that allows subsequent imaginative re-living of previous life events). Perhaps attention is a precondition for working memory and episodic memory but not mere perceptual memory. Consistent with this, in his chapter on Memory, James follows other authors who relate attention to keeping things in mind (PP 1890, 645) and vivid recollection (PP 1890, 631).

James's theory also sheds light on the relationship between attention and action. A connection is secured by the fact that stored ideas are often associated with behavioral responses. In discussing the impact of attention on reaction times, James suggests that we can reduce behavioral responses to a minimum by bringing to mind stored ideas that are linked to action plans; then, when a stimulus matches the potentiated idea, the response immediately follows (PP 1890, 406).

The contrast between attentiveness, as a state of mind, and distraction, can also find an explanation here. In a case of distraction we may be reduced to something like infancy, where inputs strike us without evoking stored records and associations. This can happen, for example, in cases of divided attention. If we are lost in thought, the sensory world may recede into oblivion. James would say that this is a situation of ideational absorption, which prevents ideas from being applied in perception. In contrast, we might enter a sentinel mode of watchfulness, by tuning ideational centers to external inputs, so that we are ready to conceptualize any incoming perturbation.

On the face of it, then, James's theory of attention seems to have a major advantage over rival theories. Others distinguish different phenomena that occur when we attend and choose between these. Each theory seems to emphasize one aspect at the expense of others. James's theory treats these aspects as effects and posits a common cause. The apparent disunity of James's treatment is illusory. He identifies many features of attention ("focalization, concentration," etc.), and then provides a way of bringing these into a single explanatory framework. Subsequent theories have missed out on this, and many have invested in a single feature at the expense of others. Meanwhile, the Reactive Spontaneity Theory has been neglected, despite its great promise.

In what follows, I will turn to some applications of James's view in an effort to show that its explanatory fruits are even more abundant than they may initially appear. His Reactive Spontaneity Theory enables James to argue that attention plays some fundamental roles in the mind, despite the fact that generations of philosophers have neglected it and generations of psychologists have seen it as nothing more than a mechanism for sharpening perception.

Applications of Attention in James

Intellectual Attention

It has become a platitude about James that his *Principles of Psychology* was so prescient that we are still catching up with its many insights. Though ostensibly a review, James constantly takes us in new directions, and many of the paths he paved remain relatively unexplored. I will explore several of these now, to show that James's theory of attention has much to teach contemporary readers.

First, I will take up an issue mentioned in passing earlier. In addition to "sensorial attention," James posits "intellectual attention"—a capacity to attend to our thoughts. Contemporary psychology has neglected this idea almost entirely (though see de Brigard 2012 on attention to memories). In fact, prevailing models of attention often involve processes that would be difficult to apply outside of the sensory domain. For example, the finding that attention boosts contrast (Carrasco et al. 2004) could have, at best, a metaphorical application in the domain of thought. What, then, are we to make of James's suggestion? Is his theory of intellectual attention also just a metaphor?

I think James took the notion of intellectual attention quite literally, and he offers an implicit argument for its existence. That argument works by pointing out functional parallels and interactions between sensorial and intellectual attention. Among the attributes he observes in the sensorial case are two key distinctions (PP 1890, 393). James notes that, when attending to sensory inputs, attention can be active or passive and immediate or derived. Active cases arise when attention is deployed voluntarily (as with visual search), and passive cases are driven by features of the stimulus (as when we gaze at a captivating artwork). In thought, there are analogues of this distinction. We can decide to think about a given topic (say, James on attention), or we might be led from thought to thought, as we notice an obvious implication. Sensorial attention is immediate when it is driven by instinctive response (as when we attend to a bright flash of light), and it is derived when salience is learned, as when the grammar maven notices an error in speech. In thought, there can be chains of ideas that are inherently exciting to us and others that are interesting only as a means to some end. A quotidian example of the latter might be thinking about what public transit to take to reach a desired destination.

Another functional parallel concerns time-course. Attention, James tells us, lasts only a few seconds without renewed effort (PP 1890, 397). He implies that this is true for both sensorial and intellectual attention. If so, that indicates similar underlying mechanisms. James also points out that sensorial and intellectual attention can interact, which speaks even more directly in favor of mechanistic convergence. In particular, he suggests that sensorial and intellectual attention can compete (PP 1890, 396). While deep in thought, a person might experience attenuation of sensorial attention. Even pains can disappear when cognitively absorbed, according to James. This suggests that attention is a finite resource shared by both perception and cognition.

These considerations support the conjecture that we can attend to our thoughts. If so, then James's account of how attention works, the Reactive Spontaneity Theory, should be applicable to intellectual attention. Recall, that the theory posits two components: organic accommodation and ideational preparation. As already noted, James does make an explicit case for the claim that intellectual attention satisfies the organic accommodation condition: when we attend to our thoughts we adjust sensory systems by withdrawing them from the eternal world. On ideational preparation, James says less than one might want, but we can try to fill in the missing pieces on his behalf. Recall that, in the sensory case, attention involves the endogenous generation of ideas; we form representations corresponding to the attended features in a perceptual stimulus. To apply this account to the intellectual case, it would follow that we attend to thoughts by forming ideational representations of what we are thinking. At first sight, this may sound completely implausible on grounds of redundancy. If thoughts are made up of ideas, then why do we need to re-represent them, using ideas, in order to bring them in to attentional focus? The apparent weirdness is dispelled, however, when we note that, for James, thoughts flow in an unbroken stream (PP 1890, 233), and they are in constant flux (PP 1890, 224). Thus, we have an over-abundance of thoughts, just as we have a massively complex flow of sensory inputs. In both cases, there is a selection problem. We often manage to bring one of the many concurrent thoughts that we are having into attentional focus. We manage to think about one thing, in a more or less linear way, despite the fact that the mind contains an ocean of ideas any of which might be vying for current attention. One solution is to re-represent the selected line of thought. Using a modern metaphor, we might think about this as a transcription from a capacious storage device, such as a hard drive, into a temporary storage system, read-only memory (RAM). By writing to RAM, computers are able to access and manipulate data, and this process involves something like ideational preparation.

These suggestions are not meant to be a full statement of how James's theory applies in the intellectual case. My more modest goal is to give some hint of how the story might go, and to indicate why it might not be implausible. If James is right to think that we can literally attend to our thoughts, that is an observation deserving serious investigation. Attention is a major research area in psychology, but it is almost exclusively dedicated to the sensory modalities. Even the observation that intense thought can attenuate perception has been largely ignored.

One can easily imagine extending James's functional comparisons as well. Is there such a thing as "pop-out" in thought? Is there "inhibition of return"? Can cognitive attention be divided? These are all terms borrowed from current research on attention in perception, and their extension to cognition would be illuminating. If intellectual attention exists, the importance of attention as a faculty may be underestimated by current theories. Its investigation might also lead to discoveries about the nature of thought—for example, it might shed light on the ways in which thinking and perceiving are intertwined.

Attention and Consciousness

Intellectual attention has not received much discussion in contemporary literature, but another application of James's theory has recently come into vogue. In various passages, he suggests that attention may be the basis of conscious experience. The study of consciousness has been a major preoccupation in recent philosophy, and James's contributions are underappreciated. Some authors who speculate about the role of attention in consciousness fail to mention James (e.g., Prinz 2012; though see Mole 2011). This is a serious oversight, since James can be read as a pioneer of the view. I say "can be read," because, as we will see, there are some exegetical thickets in this vicinity.

James makes a number of remarks relating consciousness to attention. He says, "the mind is at every stage a theatre of simultaneous possibilities. Consciousness consists in the comparison of these with each other, the selection of some, and the suppression of the rest by the reinforcing and inhibiting agency of attention" (PP 1890, 277). At another point he refers to, "Coerciveness over attention, or the mere power to possess consciousness" (PP 1890, 928). In his Stream of Consciousness chapter in the *Briefer Course*, James also says, "what is called our 'experience' is almost entirely determined by our habits of attention" (PBC 1892, 156). Such remarks suggest that attention and consciousness arise together.

James also seems to believe that attention and consciousness disappear together. The Attention chapter in the *Principles* concludes with a section on Inattention, in which he suggests that consciousness disappears when attention is withdrawn. I already mentioned cases in which we lose awareness of sensations while absorbed in thought. The chapter also discusses bodily phenomena such as "the pressure of our clothes and shoes, the beating of our hearts and arteries, our breathing, certain steadfast bodily pains, habitual odors, tastes in the mouth," which shift out of consciousness because they are too constant to maintain our attention (PP 1890, 430). Likewise for many external stimuli: "the ticking of the clock, the noise of the city streets, or the roaring of the brook near the house; and even the din of a foundry or factory." James also mentions laboratory studies of divided attention, binocular viewing, and ambiguous figures, where attention seems to fluctuate from one stimulus or interpretation to another, and to take consciousness with it.

These passages strongly suggest that James regards attention as the sine qua non for consciousness. Consciousness arises and disappears with the onset and offset of attention. There are obstacles, however, to this interpretation. First, James sometimes seems to refer to consciousness of unattended items. In a discussion of Wundt, for example, he mentions "inattentive awareness" (PP 1890, 95). Some such passages can be dismissed either as minor inconsistencies, or by positing terminological distinctions; "awareness" might not entail consciousness for James. A second obstacle is harder to circumvent. Early in the *Principles*, James has a chapter called "The Mind Stuff Theory," in which he seems to deny that mental states are *ever* unconscious. The chapter includes a series of ten arguments that James has culled from the literature purporting to establish the existence of unconscious mental states. After each, James offers a refutation. This leads many commentators to read James as a skeptic about unconscious mentation. If so, it seems implausible to credit him with the view that stimuli become unconscious when they are unattended. The chaotic stream of stimulations from which attention selects must be conscious prior to the allocation of attention, since, on this reading, all mental states are conscious.

There are several ways out of the conundrum. One recent commentator rejects the widespread view that James denies the existence of unconscious mental states (Weinberger 2000). He argues that the term "unconscious" does not have its contemporary meaning in James's chapter on the Mind Stuff Theory. Rather, it refers there to an antiquated view that makes a more specific commitment. On the view in question, conscious states are built up from unconscious mental atoms. When these atoms combine differently, or with some missing elements, there can be states that are just like conscious mental states except lacking in consciousness. Weinberger argues that James's ten refutations are intended to refute this view and not unconscious mentality in general. Unfortunately, this interpretation does not completely solve the problem. Many of the ten arguments seem to offer general considerations in favor of unconscious states. Alleged examples include habitual and automatic processes, dreams, unconscious steps in reasoning, somnambulism, trance states, the causes of emotions that we cannot justify or explain, instincts, unconscious inferences in low-level vision, and cases in which we mischaracterize our mental states because we haven't fully attended to them. James seems to take himself as showing that none of these phenomena require the postulation of unconscious states. It's not just that they don't require mental atoms; he seems to imply that the states in question are actually conscious. This would suggest he doesn't believe that unconscious mental states exist, regardless of what theory one happens to hold of them. James boldly states, "There is only one 'phase' in which an idea can be, and that is a fully conscious condition. If it is not in that condition, then it is not at all" (PP 1890, 174).

The challenge of finding a consistent interpretation of James is compounded by the fact that this discussion of unconscious mental states also includes some remarks on attention that seem to contradict what he says about attention and consciousness later on. In discussing examples of states that we mischaracterize, he credits his opponent with the argument that unattended mental states are unconscious:

> Consider, too, the difference between a sensation which we simply *have* and one which we *attend to*. Attention gives results that seem like fresh creations; and yet the feelings and elements of feeling which it reveals must have been already there—in an unconscious state. (PP 1890, 172)

James goes on to reject this suggestion, implying that he thinks unattended mental states are conscious. He says that apparent cases of unconscious, unattended mental states may, in fact, be conscious mental states that are faint, fleeting, or less richly elaborated than their attended counterparts. Granted, we might read James here as simply taking issue with specific examples, suggesting that the states in question are actually weakly attended rather than unattended. But one is left wondering why he doesn't say that explicitly. And why does he seem to explicitly deny that unconscious mental states exist?

Another interpretation is offered by Myers (1986, 167). His reading begins with the premise that, for James, consciousness is always consciousness to a self, and there can be multiple selves within the same organism. Thus, when James denied the existence of unconscious mental states, "he denied only that mental states can occur unnoticed by any self whatsoever." On this interpretation, mental states are all conscious, but it can nevertheless be true for a given self that it lacks consciousness of a mental state that is occurring for another self within the same organism. Though carefully supported (Myers cites James's enthusiasm for Edmund Gurney's theory of multiple selves), I find this hard to swallow. James does not appeal to multiple selves when trying to refute arguments for unconscious mental states.

I want to suggest a third possibility. Perhaps James denies the existence of unconscious mental states because he finds it incoherent to imagine that an inner state with psychological properties (e.g., a sensation of blue, or a state of terror) could occur unconsciously. For James, "mental" might entail "felt." This would be a kind of phenomenal essentialism of the mental. Such a position would rule out unconscious mental states on conceptual grounds, but it would leave open the possibility that there are unconscious analogues of our mental states—namely, brain states that, when conscious, are correlates of mentality. That is, we might read James as posting a distinction between unconscious brain stimulation and conscious mental states. If so, unattended sensory inputs can occur unconsciously, but it would be a mistake to call them unconscious sensations (for a similar reading, see Klein 2020).

It's unlikely that James adhered to this manner of speaking consistently, but there is some textual evidence that it is his official view. In the passage where he expressly denied unconscious mental states (quoted earlier), he continues:

> If [an idea is not conscious], then it is not at all. Something else is, in its place. The something else may be a merely physical brain-process . . . [which] may perform much the same *function* as the first idea . . . (PP 1890, 174)

Earlier, in the same section, he makes a similar move to address the case of hidden premises in reasoning: "Either [the premise] was consciously there, but the next instant forgotten, or its *brain-tract* alone was adequate to do the whole work" (PP 1890, 168). In response to the case of instincts, James says that they "are explicable as actions of the nervous system" (PP 1890, 170). To address cases of an unexplained emotion, he argues that it "is no 'unconscious idea;' it is only a particular collocation of the molecules in certain tracts of the brain" (PP 1890, 170). In response to alleged unconscious visual inferences, he notes that "[c]ertain sense-impressions directly stimulate brain-tracts, of whose activity readymade conscious percepts are [normally] the immediate psychic counterparts" (PP 1890, 170–171). Again and again, we find James explaining putative unconscious mental states by positing neural analogues.

On the interpretation I am offering here, James has a relatively consistent view about the relationship between consciousness and attention, though it is not always expressed clearly. He thinks that consciousness comes and goes with attention, and that, when attention is withdrawn, the state that remains is best described with reference to brain stimulation. Use of mental vocabulary for unconscious states is, on his view, unintelligible (see PP 1890, 174–176). In modern usage, we have become accustomed to referring to unconscious neural states as mental, and little, I think, hangs on the choice of terms.

If this reading is right, James himself is not always consistent in his language. As Alex Klein points out (personal communication), when James refers to the "mind" as a theater of possibilities, we might need to read him as referring to the brain, and it is also a bit puzzling how attention, which is, after all, a mental process, can operate on this physiological stage. One might address the worry by exploiting a familiar spotlight metaphor (James himself refers to "footlights of consciousness"; PP 1890, 426). The theater of possibilities is a stage crowded with candidates for mentality and the attention spotlight secures their mental status.

Attention and Interest

Another topic about which James has much to teach is the relationship between attention and interest. Earlier I presented a reading of James's theory of attention (see A Unified Theory of Attention). I said what attention is, according to his view. But I left aside another question, which gets passing treatment throughout his chapter: what drives attention? We saw a glimpse of James's answer, when I mentioned the distinction between immediate and derived attention in the last section. A stimulus (or thought) can grab our attention because its features engage our instincts, or because of its relationship to some independent goal. So stated, this sounds like a disjunctive answer to the question; different kinds of factors drive attention in different cases. There is, on closer analysis, also an overarching construct here. Again and again, James tells us that attention is driven by *interest*.

In keeping with the immediate/derived distinction, James makes it clear that interests can be innate or learned. In his chapter on Consciousness of the Self (and discussed again in the chapter on Instinct), James tells us that,

> [E]very species is particularly interested in its own prey or food, its own enemies, its own sexual mates, and its own young. These things fascinate by their intrinsic power to do so; they are cared for for their own sakes. (PP 1890, 304)

He adds other items to this list of things subjects are innately interested in, including one's own body, one's friends, and also "spiritual dispositions," which refers, in part, to intellectual, moral, and religious aspirations (PP 1890, 307). These latter, one might suppose, can shade off into interests that are acquired, rather than innate. James mentions practical interests (PP 1890, 487), instrumental interests (PP 1890, 550), aesthetic interests (PP 1890, 818), emotional interests (PP 1890, 929), and even interests that we acquire by habit (PP 1890, 1164).

Unfortunately, James offers little by way of a positive analysis of what interests are. He mostly offers inventories, emphasizing their variety, and their importance. At some points, he courts a kind of circularity, by suggesting that we attend to what interests us, and then defining interest as that which guides attention. At one point, he even says, "what-we-attend-to and what-interests-us are synonymous terms" (PP 1890, 1164). I think it is most charitable to read this as loose talk. James is here expressing his principle that interest determines the targets of attention, not that they are one and the same. James offers a concrete theory of what attention is (the Reactive Spontaneity Theory), and this does not look like a promising account of interest. I think it more plausible to assume that, for James, interests are functionally specifiable mental operations that *include* the disposition to bring something into attention as well as some other effects.

What might the other effects of interest include? One answer is suggested by a remark in which James describes interest as "stirring" (PP 1890, 927). Following this line of thought, it is plausible to suppose that interest has an emotional impact. Indeed, it is customary to classify interest as an emotion. For James, such a classification may seem awkward, since he has an unusual theory of emotions, according to which each emotion is the perception of a change in the body (EPs 1884, 168–187; PP 1890, ch. 25). At one point, he implies that interest might be among the exceptions to this, lacking a bodily concomitant, but he leaves the matter unsettled (EPs 1884, 169).

We can help James out here, however, by recalling that attention, for him, has a bodily aspect: we orient our senses when attending. In arousing attention, interest presumably arouses orienting responses ("organic adjustments") and these, in turn, might be felt. For James, attention is also potentiated action, so there is further room for bodily changes here; attention, which is prompted by interest, may excite action-conducive arousal. Given such bodily effects, it follows that there are likely to be emotional feelings associated with interest.

Technically, we cannot equate such feelings with interest for James, since interest is the cause of these bodily changes, not the perception thereof. But, his account does lend itself to the view that interest causes what might be called feelings of interest, in addition to causing attention. Such feelings might vary in intensity from mild curiosity to fascination or even rapture. I don't mean to suggest that this is James's official theory of interest. I aim only to point out that he has resources to develop a positive account on which interest is not synonymous with attention, but rather a cause of attention that can also be independently characterized in terms of its embodied emotional effects.

Returning to the text, I think there are two important implications of James's proposal that interest guides attention. The first is that interest helps explain the spontaneous aspect of attention. This issue is dealt with most explicitly in his discussion of whether attention is "a resultant or a force" (PP 1890, 423–430). Here, James is ostensibly addressing the question of fee will. He is asking whether attention is ever caused by us, independent of anything external to us. In this discussion, he arrives at what one might regard as a frustrating verdict that the matter cannot be empirically settled. More pertinent, for our purposes, is the way that James uses the issue to underscore his conviction that attention is both receptive and spontaneous. To make this point, he works through different cases.

Consider, first, receptivity. James notes that immediate attention is clearly receptive, in that it is driven by features of the stimulus. He then suggests that derived attention may be receptive too, at least in cases in whiche there is no voluntary effort. In particular, a standing goal or desire might make some stimulus salient to us, even when we are not actively seeking that goal. The voluntary case is the one that raises the possibility of free will, and here James entertains the determinist possibility that our voluntary efforts are, themselves, results of prior causes, in which case even voluntary attention would be a "resultant" rather than a "force." Thus, all cases of attention may be receptive. At the same time, however, they can also all be characterized as spontaneous, even if not free. The reason for this brings us back to interest. Interest, whether innate or learned, comes from within. It is not given in the external world, but rather originates in the organism. Since attention is always guided by interest, it follows that attention is always, in part, spontaneous. Thus, interest provides another perspective on this core aspect of James's account of attention. One might say, interest puts the spontaneity into his Reactive Spontaneity Theory.

The second implication that follows from James's appeal to interest is a bit less explicit in the text, but it is even more important. One can think of interests as a class of values. What we value interests us, and interest itself is a kind of evaluative imposition on the world. Put differently, the spontaneity in James's theory can be re-described as an evaluative spontaneity. It is not just that we impose our ideas onto the world. Our interests get imposed as well. This is important because perception is often presented as value-neutral. We see what's there, not what we want to see. For James, this is untenable. Because interests are values that come from us and determine the locus of attention, it follows that what we attentively see is value-laden. James says, "without selective interest, experience is an utter chaos. Interest alone gives accent and emphasis, light and shade, background and foreground—intelligible perspective, in a word" (PP 1890, 381). So, interest introduces an ordering on the world. This is a fascinating thesis, which has not always been adequately addressed in contemporary theories of perception. If we take seriously the idea that attention is required for consciousness, then James also implicitly endorses an evaluative theory of how we become conscious. This, too, is a neglected idea, worthy of exploration.

Belief and the Will

James's evaluative theory of attentive perception challenges prevailing theories, but it is not the most radical application of his views about intention. It sets the stage for some conjectures that are even more provocative. For James, attention has implications that can be characterized as ontological. The ontological implications forecast some themes in his later work, but it is rewarding to see how they get worked out in the *Principles*. I think this early formulation is easier to defend. In the *Principles*, James lays down an inroad to a pragmatist ontology without recourse to speculative metaphysics. Attention is the paving stone.

We can approach this grand conclusion by triangulating from two of the most cryptic and striking statements that James makes about attention in the *Principles*. Both appear in his chapter on the Perception of Reality and have other formulations elsewhere. In the first statement, James asserts that, "will consists in nothing but a manner of attending to certain objects" (PP 1890, 947). Then, in a footnote, he says, "belief and attention are the same fact" (949, n.31). Thus, James seems to be equating attention with both the will and belief. What could he possibly mean?

In his discussions of the will, James sometimes engages in metaphysical debates about freedom, but more often he is interested in phenomenology: what does it feel like to engage in acts of will? Or, a bit more accurately, one might say that James approaches will using a combination of phenomenology and functional analysis. He is also interested in what the will is for, when experiences of will come about, and the processes that underlie them. This method might be called functional phenomenology and it characterizes much of his approach in the *Principles* (and all the more so in the *Briefer Course*, since he truncates his review of experimental work there).

As a phenomenologist, James's analysis begins with the experience of "volitional effort" (the term "volitional" is meant to mark a contrast with muscular effort; PP 1890, 1167, n.63). His account reveals that, for him, will is something that is experienced at moments of difficulty or conflict. We strain to exercise the will. James tells us that

> the immediate point of application of the volitional effort lies exclusively in the mental world. The whole drama is a mental drama. The whole difficulty is a mental difficulty, a difficulty with an object of our thought. (PP 1890, 1168)

Will can eventuate in actions, of course, but only indirectly. Will is first and foremost a faculty that determines the objects of consciousness, and only then, by means of conscious states, do actions follow ("consciousness is *in its very nature impulsive*"; PP 1890, 1134). What, then, determines the content of consciousness? The answer has been the central theme of this chapter: attention. And here we see how will and attention coalesce. The experience of will is a felt effort to keep something in consciousness, and that is achieved by attention.

More accurately, will gets analyzed in terms of *voluntary* attention—they may even be one and the same. When attention is passively driven by a stimulus, we experience it as effortless. Will is needed when we are strongly inclined to attend to one thing, but we realize that another course of action is required. Examples include the soldier who faces bullets in battle, the exhausted sailor on a wreck who forces himself to work (PP 1890, 1167, n.63). These heroic actions begin with a mental battle. Fear and fatigue tend to dominate attention, but, through mental strain, we focus on the task at hand. There is, once again, a threat of circularity here. James seems to analyze will in terms of voluntary attention, and that makes one wonder how to cash out the term "voluntary" if not in terms of will. But James is not offering a reductive definition, here. Rather, he is making the substantive and surprising claim that will essentially involves attention. If James is right, as seems plausible, this is a genuine insight. It suggests that attention plays a role in agency that has not been fully appreciated.

Let's turn now to James's remark that belief and the will are "the same fact." James is not always clear or consistent on this point. He sometimes suggests that belief is an emotion (PP 1890, 913–914), or a sui generis state of consciousness (PP 1890, 917). Believing involves taking something to be real, and taking-to-be-real is an indiscernible feeling. But James also says that attention determines what, at any given moment, gets associated with this feeling. In the footnote where he declares that belief and attention are the same fact, he elaborates by saying, "[f]or the moment, what we attend to is reality" (PP 1890, 949, n.31). Thus, when attention brings something into consciousness, it also succeeds in making the individual believe it to be real. That is, attention causes us to believe in the reality of an object and may be necessary for that sense of reality.

One consequence of this picture is that there may be many different realities, corresponding to the shifting contents of attention:

> Each world *whilst it is attended* to is real after its own fashion; only the reality lapses with the attention.... Each thinker, however, has dominant habits of attention; and these *practically elect from among the various worlds some one to be for him the world of ultimate realities.* (PP 1890, 923)

James says there are "many worlds," including

> ... the world of absolute reality (i.e., reality believed by the complete philosopher) ... the world of collective error, ... the worlds of abstract reality, of relative or practical reality, of ideal relations, and ... the supernatural world. (PP 1890, 921)

All of these worlds are real, in some sense, and they come into being when we attend to them. In ordinary life, we shift from one to another depending on context, and while we are attentively entertaining a given world it is real for us.

On the face of it, "real" is a purely epistemic notion here. It is shorthand for "taken to be real" or "regarded as real." But I think James has something stronger than this in mind. James does not draw a sharp boundary between how we take things to be and how they really are. He allows, at most, that there are shared views about how the world is, or views that might emerge at the end of inquiry. He says that a reality is absolute if it is uncontradicted (PP 1890, 918). This is still an epistemic notion, but James's ontology is epistemic.

James's ontology is also pluralist, given that people have different realities, and, much of the time there will be no single vantage point that can be described as absolute. The pluralism is, to some degree, ineliminable, for reasons connected to the earlier observation that attention is interest-relative. Given the inevitability of divergent interests, there is always likely to be some ontological divide between people. What is real for one person might differ from what is real for another, since people have different values, and these guide attention.

In this pluralist ontology we can see roots of James's ontological pragmatism. It relates also to his pragmatic theory of truth, and his radical empiricism. James's discussion in the *Principles* also anticipates his later work on the *Will to Believe*. This brings us back to his remarks on attention and the will. For James, the will is a site of effort. It arises when there is a mental conflict between what captures our attention and what, we think, deserves our attention. To will something is to effortfully maintain it in attention. This account of will can be brought into contact with James's theory of belief. If believing is a state that is induced by attention, then there may also be cases where we believe things voluntarily. That is, we may, under certain circumstances, arrive at a belief through attentional effort. Given James's views about ontology, it would follow that realities can be created by acts of will. This, of course, is a central thread in his work on the will to believe, and by tracing out its origin in the *Principles*, we can see that attention is a crucial part of the story. Put succinctly, we can attend things into existence.

Conclusions: Attending to James

In this chapter, I have reviewed James's conjectures about attention in the *Principles of Psychology*. Some details have been left out, such as his opening discussion of divided attention, which has been heavily studied and superseded by contemporary experimentalists. I have focused on broader theoretical questions, including the nature of attention, and some surprising applications.

James's account of attention, which I called the Reactive Spontaneity Theory, differs from contemporary theories, with its emphasis on both a motor component and an anticipatory mental representation. It has advantages over some current theories, and it also bears on philosophical theories of perception, by suggesting that perceiving is more active (and value-laden) than often appreciated. James's views about attention and interest suggest that what we perceive depends on values and goals—an idea worthy of pursuing.

James also takes attention in some surprising and exciting directions. He suggests that attention can be applied to thought, and he seems to think that attention is crucial for consciousness. The former idea has been neglected and the latter has only recently entered debates. If James is right, a theory of attention will contribute to understanding the mind's fundamental capacities: thinking and feeling.

More surprisingly, perhaps, James hypothesizes links among attention, belief, and the will. Attending gives rise to beliefs, because the objects of attention become real for us while we are attending to them. Attention is also a crucial contributor to the will: we overcome conflicts through effortful attention. Together these conjectures allow that we can arrive at beliefs though acts of will. For James, such beliefs have ontological import. We can, through attention, create realities. Thus, for James attention is not just a tool for sharpening perception. It is a tool for thinking, doing, and worldmaking. In the final analysis, Reactive Spontaneity is not just a theory of how we attend; it suggests that worlds we inhabit are not simply discovered, by passive reactivity, but constructed through our ideas and interests.

Acknowledgments

It would be difficult to overstate my debt to Alex Klein. In addition to encouraging me to work on this topic, he provided copious feedback, which greatly improved the chapter and helped me avoid interpretive missteps. He also provided extensive editorial feedback and exhibited extraordinary patience throughout the process. I am also grateful to Rick Delaney for careful copy editing.

References

Altmann, G. 2004. "Language-mediated Eye Movements in the Absence of a Visual World: The 'Blank Screen Paradigm.'" *Cognition* 93: B79–B87.

Buckner, R. L., J. R. Andrews-Hanna, and D. L. Schacter. 2008. "The Brain's Default Network: Anatomy, Function, and Relevance to Disease." *Annals of the New York Academy of Science* 1124: 1–38.

Carrasco, M., S. Ling, and S. Read. 2004b. "Attention Alters Appearance." *Nature Neuroscience* 7: 308–313.

de Brigard, F. 2012. "The Role of Attention in Conscious Recollection." *Frontiers in Psychology* 3: 29.

Glenberg, A. M., J.L. Schroeder, and D. A. Robertson. 1998. "Averting the Gaze Disengages the Environment and Facilitates Remembering." *Memory & Cognition* 26: 651–658.

Heft, H. 2001. *Ecological Psychology in Context: James Gibson, Roger Barker, and the Legacy of William James's Radical Empiricism*. Mahwah, NJ: Lawrence Erlbaum Associates Publishers.

Heras-Escribano, M. (forthcoming). "Pragmatism, Enactivism, and Ecological Psychology: Towards a Unified Approach to Post-Cognitivism." *Synthese*.

Hillyard, S. A., E. K. Vogel, and S. J. Luck. 1998. "Sensory Gain Control (Amplification) as a Mechanism of Selective Attention: Electrophysiological and Neuroimaging Evidence." *Philosophical Transactions of the Royal Society: Biological Sciences* 353: 1257–1267.

Klein, A. 2020. "The Death of Consciousness? William James's Case Against Scientific Unobservables." *Journal of the History of Philosophy* 58: 293–323.

Lewes, G. H. 1879. *Problems of Life and Mind, Third Series, Problem the Second*. Cambridge, MA: The Riverside Press.

Mole, C. 2011. *Attention Is Cognitive Unison: An Essay in Philosophical Psychology*. New York, NY: Oxford University Press.

Myers, G. 1986. *William James: His Life and Thought*. New Haven, CT: Yale University Press.

Prinz, J. J. 2012. *The Conscious Brain: How Attention Engenders Experience*. New York, NY: Oxford University Press.

Treisman, A. 1960. "Contextual Cues in Selective Listening." *Quarterly Journal of Experimental Psychology* 12: 242–248.

Walley, R. E., and T. D. Weiden. 1973. "Lateral Inhibition and Cognitive Masking: A Neuropsychological Theory of Attention." *Psychological Review* 80: 284–302.

Weinberger, J. 2000. "William James and the Unconscious: Redressing a Century-Old Misunderstanding." *Psychological Science* 11: 439–445.

Wu, W. 2011. "Attention as Selection for Action." In *Attention: Philosophical and Psychological Essays*, edited by C. Mole, D. Smithies, and W. Wu, 97–116. New York, NY: Oxford University Press.

CHAPTER 2

JAMES'S REVOLUTIONARY THEORY OF EMOTIONS

HELEEN J. POTT

Introduction: James and His Critics

The first account of James's ideas about emotions appeared in 1884 in the philosophical journal *Mind*. In an essay titled "What is an Emotion?" James challenged the common sense view that emotions are mental states caused by perception, with bodily changes as their consequence: we see a bear, feel frightened, and then we run away. James famously argued that the real sequence is the reverse: the bodily changes come first, and the feeling of these changes is what we call the emotion.

> My theory, on the contrary, is that *the bodily changes follow directly the perception of the exciting fact, and that our feeling of the same changes as they occur IS the emotion.* Common sense says we lose our fortune, are sorry and weep; we meet a bear, are frightened and run; we are insulted by a rival, are angry and strike. The hypothesis here to be defended says that this order of sequence is incorrect, that the one mental state is not immediately induced by the other, that the bodily manifestations must be interposed between, and that the more rational statement is that we feel sorry because we cry, are angry because we strike, afraid because we tremble.... Without the bodily states following on the perception, the latter would be purely cognitive in form, pale, colorless, destitute of emotional warmth. We might then see the bear and judge it best to run, receive the insult and deem it right to strike, but we should not actually *feel* afraid or angry. (EPs 1884, 170; emphasis in original)

The paragraph was repeated verbatim in *The Principles of Psychology* (1890) and in *Psychology: The Briefer Course* (1892); according to Myers (1986, 215), the content would provoke more response than any other psychology topic James addressed.

Almost immediately the idea that we are angry because we hit someone, frightened because we run away, became a source of amusement among James's psychological colleagues, who pointed out that we often feel fear without running away or are angry but do not strike, and that running is certainly not the only option in fear. One of James's reviewers came up with the example that if we see a rain shower looming we may run for shelter out of fear of getting wet; but suppose that instead of running we step into a shop and buy an umbrella—is the fear in that case caused by buying an umbrella (Worcester 1893, 291)?[1]

The general impression was that James's criticism of common sense had resulted in a simplistic alternative that could not be taken too seriously—actually, it was more like "a good joke than a scientific hypothesis" (Gardiner 1896, 102). The mockery never really stopped and a decade after his *Mind* paper, James felt compelled to respond to his critics and explicitly confront what he saw as the most common misunderstandings. In "The Physical Basis of Emotion" (1894), he argues that his idea of emotion is more complicated than his critics assume and blames his sloppy language for many of the critical objections:

> I think that all the force of such objections lies in the slapdash brevity of the language used, of which I admit that my own text set a bad example when it said "we are frightened because we run." Yet let the word "run" but stand for what it was meant to stand for, namely, for many other movements in us, of which invisible visceral ones seem to be by far the most essential; discriminate also between the various grades of emotion which we designate by one name, and our theory holds up its head again. (EPs 1894, 302)

He did not mean to say that running away causes fear or that striking out at someone causes anger. As he had explained earlier in the *Principles* (PP 1890, 1061–1064), the "expression" that causes the feeling of fear can include a wide variety of bodily changes, such as expressive behaviors (crying, trembling), facial expressions (frowning), invisible visceral reactions (increased heart rate, blood pressure, muscular tension), and sometimes, depending on the intensity of the triggering event, reflex-like actions such as running away from a bear. The bodily changes are so numerous that the entire organism may be called a sounding-board, he says (PP 1890, 1066). Also, he was well aware that "[t]he same bear may truly enough excite us to either fight or flight, according as he suggests an overpowering 'idea' of his killing us, or one of our killing him" (EPs 1894, 302; c.f. Ellsworth 1994, 224). He further repeats his claim that the basis of emotion is physiological and that without the body, there is nothing to be felt.

But it was too little and too late—James's reply was hardly read or cited. The mistaken view that his theory reduces fear to nothing but the effect of physiological reflexes in the presence of a stimulus started a life of its own. It would form the backbone of the so-called James-Lange theory that dominated during most of the twentieth century. This theory was also named after the Danish physiologist Carl Lange who defined emotions more specifically as patterns of changes in the viscera—a view James explicitly refers to in his 1894 article, where he says that of the many movements in the body during emotion, "invisible visceral ones seem to be by far the most essential." Seventeen years after James's death, experimental psychologist Walter Cannon (1927) presented a devastating blow to the theory, demonstrating that visceral responses are too slow, too undifferentiated, and too insensitive to be the source of emotional feeling, and that artificial induction of visceral changes does not produce emotion. The same visceral reactions occur in very different emotions, such as fear and anger, and also in non-emotional states, according to Cannon. In his laboratory he worked with cats and dogs, and showed that in animals where feedback from the viscera had been surgically eliminated, the animals continued hissing and barking when teased. Cannon concluded that emotional experience did not seem reducible to bodily changes, and that bodily changes are insufficient to differentiate among the many different emotions we experience. In their famous 1962 study "Cognitive, Social and Physiological Determinants of Emotional State," Stanley Schachter and Jerome Singer would defend a similar conclusion and suggest that cognitive labeling on the basis of one's undifferentiated physiological arousal explains the variety of emotions.

Cannon's experimental results effectively undermined the credibility of James's view of emotion for decades to come. During behaviorism, his theory sunk into oblivion, and it would perhaps have been completely forgotten were it not that in the second half of the twentieth century, cognitivism started to dominate psychology. Cognitive emotion theorists (Arnold 1960; Solomon [1976] 1993; Nussbaum 2001) defined emotion as a complex cognitive state, individuated by "appraisals" or evaluative judgments. The striking contrast with James's body-based "feeling theory" became one of the defining characteristics of the cognitive approach. Feelings were seen as non-cognitive and inessential to emotion, and bodily changes were declared to be mere by-products of cognitive emotion processing. As Bob Solomon, the philosophical spokesman of the cognitive revolution, put it: "However predictable the association of feelings and emotion, feelings no more constitute or define emotion than an army of fleas constitutes a homeless dog. [...] Feeling is the ornamentation of emotion, not its essence" (Solomon [1976] 1993, 158).

The cognitivists' criticisms of James's theory would continue to resonate for years to come. According to cognitivist theorists, James ignores the role of judgment and trivializes emotion as an epiphenomenon, an inconsequential by-product of physiological disturbance. By identifying emotions with bodily feelings and sensations, he fails to explain the cognitive richness and individuality of emotional experience. Nor can he account for the intentionality, for the cultural variety, or for the normative dimension of emotions. What is more, if emotions were merely bodily feelings, it would be difficult to understand aesthetic and moral emotions and to justify emotions in the light of reasons. For the cognitivists, emotions are differentiated by cognitive judgments; by definition, they are "something far more sophisticated than mere feelings" (Solomon [1976] 1993, 102).

During the heyday of cognitivism, James's theory was referred to as the textbook example of a hopelessly flawed and outdated approach. But paradigms in psychology come and go, and with the dawn of the twenty-first century, things started to look a lot better for James. Cognitivism itself came under fire for overintellectualizing emotion and neglecting its biological roots. Critics pointed out that cognitive theories easily ascribe emotions to computers and intelligent robots but have a lot more trouble explaining the presence of anger and fear in non-linguistic creatures like animals and babies (Deigh 1994). Paul Griffiths, in *What Emotions Really Are: The Problem of Psychological Categories* (1997), polemically suggested that emotion researchers should radically revise their unscientific framework in order to account for such non-cognitive reactions (Griffiths 1997).

In the late 1990s, evolution-based theories started to promote the idea that there are "basic emotions": hard-wired instinctive emotions that are universal across the human species and selected by evolution because they enabled our ancestors to deal with "fundamental life tasks" such as facing danger, experiencing a loss, fighting rivals, falling in love, escaping predators, and confronting sexual infidelity. With the evolutionary turn, the (neuro)physiological dimension dismissed as inessential by cognitivism returned in the discussion, and in its slipstream James's theory was making a spectacular comeback.

Antonio Damasio played an important role in James's revival by showing that new evidence from neuroscience supports the theory that innate primary emotions are (neuro) physiologically differentiated, and that Cannon's objections were misplaced. Newly discovered pathways like the vagus nerve and hormones in the blood are responsible for the transmission of physiological changes to the brain and the nervous system; many emotions are activated by what Damasio calls "as-if body loops"—bodily changes that are not actual but are simulated by neural activity. That Cannon's animals responded angrily cannot be seen as a denial of James's theory, because the blocking of body signals to the brain in Cannon's experiments was incomplete and left the entire range of body inputs from the head free to travel to the central nervous system (Damasio 1994, 2000). In philosophy, Jesse Prinz (2004) and Jenefer Robinson (2005) came up with a "neo-Jamesian" conception of emotions as "gut reactions": they are perceptions of bodily changes representing matters of concern, like danger or loss, that prepare us for a quick response. A recent issue of *Emotion Review* (January 2014), dedicated to James's legacy, observes a growing consensus among emotion researchers that James's views are overall in line with the "autonomic specificity" hypothesis, which says that at least the basic emotions can be seen as differentiated by specific patterns of autonomic nervous system activity (Reisenzein and Stephan 2014; Laird and Lacasse 2014).

But not everyone agrees. In the same issue, Phoebe Ellsworth (2014) argues that James would have rejected the idea of basic emotions because he strongly believed in an infinite variety of emotions across individuals and cultures, whereas John Deigh (2014) maintains that all attempts to rehabilitate James are beside the point because his theory identified emotions with causally produced bodily *disturbances*, lacking all potential to motivate adaptive action. From a completely different perspective, philosophers and (neuro)scientists working in the field of psychiatry recently suggested that we should not just focus on James's early psychological writings, but also on his later work. In *The Will to Believe* (1897) and in *The Varieties of Religious Experience* (1902), James explores how emotions relate to personal beliefs and world views; he examines emotional feelings and dispositions such as hope, confidence, and religious enthusiasm, and also their counterparts insecurity, unreality, estrangement, anxiety, melancholy, depression, and nihilistic despair. Here he is not primarily interested in physiological underpinnings but investigates how these feelings are foundational to personal well-being and happiness, and how they feature in autobiographical accounts of depression and mental illness.

According to Matthew Ratcliffe (2005, 2008), a phenomenological concern with emotional feelings that provide a sense of belonging, of a self, and of reality can be found throughout James's oeuvre. In much of his writing, he is examining emotion as a fundamental structure of personal experience and action, a way of finding oneself in the world. Ratcliffe thinks these first-person explorations show remarkable affinities with twentieth-century phenomenological approaches to affectivity such as Heidegger's analysis of moods (Heidegger [1927] 1962) and Merleau-Ponty's phenomenology of the "lived body" (Merleau-Ponty 1962).

In sum, it is clear that James's theory of emotion continues to inspire discussion and debate but that the controversy over his ideas has not been resolved yet. Which of the opposing interpretations presents the true Jamesian view? In the rest of this chapter, I will go deeper into the three versions of James that are most popular today: James as a defender of the James-Lange theory, James as a forerunner of some version of basic emotion theory, and James as an embodied phenomenologist. I will argue that in a sense, all are right in focusing on a significant aspect of his theory, and all are wrong, or at least incomplete, because they are silent on how James's account of emotion relates to what was his central project: developing a new natural science of consciousness based on the principles of pragmatism. Reconstructing his view inspires a fresh outlook on emotion, one that addresses many of the unanswered questions of current emotion science.

Did James Really Defend the James-Lange Theory?

The James-Lange version of James's theory can be summarized as the view that emotion is a non-cognitive feeling, or "nothing but a bodily sensation." During most of the twentieth century, James and Lange were supposed to defend an identical position, that emotions are feelings caused and constituted by the body and differentiated by patterns of bodily changes. James gives illustrations of this physiological constitution throughout his work, pointing out, for example, that emotions can be objectless and unmotivated, or induced by chemical substances (drugs, alcohol), and can arise without the intervention of any cognitive appraisal or belief: "the emotion here is nothing but the feeling of a bodily state, and it has a purely bodily cause," he writes (PP 1890, 1074). In the eyes of his critics, this view was the ultimate example of reductionism and eliminativism.

Labelling James's theory as reductionist, however, ignores that there are significant differences between the broader framework of the two theories that make them incompatible. First, James and Lange differ about the nature of the "bodily changes" involved in emotion. Lange was an experimental physiologist working within a mechanistic paradigm; his theory focused exclusively on changes in the viscera—the kind of bodily changes that could best be measured and tested in an experimental setting. Lange's main goal was to find a one-to-one match between certain standard emotions and specific patterns of physiological changes. James, as previously noted, had a different focus. He was quite clear that the "bodily changes" include not just visceral responses but also a variety of other bodily movements: expressive behaviors, facial expressions, and impulsive actions. For James, the changes in the body are "almost infinitely numerous and subtle" and they reverberate throughout the organism; the body as a whole is a "*sounding-board*" (EPs 1884, 172; PP 1890, 1066; emphasis added) resonating with the environmental stimuli it is presented with. Many emotional feelings are so subtle that we cannot even be aware of all their behavioral and body expressions, and "*there is no limit to the number of possible different emotions which may exist*" (PP 1890, 1069, italics original).

Second, as a Darwinian psychologist, James was not interested in the bodily underpinnings of emotion as such but in how the bodily mechanism contributes to personal survival and well-being, to practical knowledge and action. Psychology is "the science of mental life, both of its phenomena and their conditions," as he writes in his introduction to the *Principles* (PP 1890, 15). A little further on, he adds that the defining criterion of mental phenomena—"such things as we call feelings, desires, cognitions, reasonings, decisions, and the like"—is that they are purposive and future-oriented.[2] Unlike Lange, James wants to find out how feelings of bodily changes play a functional, biological role in human experience. As he puts it in *Psychology*, "our various ways of feeling and thinking have grown to be what they are because of their utility in shaping our *reactions* on the outer world" (PBC 1892, xiii). Emotions, for James, are not merely sensations of changes inside the body, like feeling a lump settling in one's throat or a pounding heart. Emotions are bodily feelings that are at the same time responses to events and situations outside the body. Through emotional feeling, we are engaging with the world.

That James was well aware of this more nuanced view is already clear in the *Principles*, where he criticizes the specifics of Lange's account, arguing that "it simplifies and universalizes the phenomena a little too much" (PP 1890, 1062). The similarities however are more important here, and he opens chapter 25 on the emotions with a long quotation from Lange on grief, followed by an introduction to Lange's theory that is almost verbatim the description he gave of his own view in the *Mind* article. The trouble with traditional psychologies of emotion—"mind stuff-theories," writes James—is that they examine emotions "as absolutely individual things" (PP 1890, 1065) and endlessly describe, analyze, and classify the distinct mental qualities. This makes the psychological literature about emotions "one of the most tedious parts of psychology" (PP 1890, 1064).

> I should as lief read verbal descriptions of the shapes of the rocks on a New Hampshire farm as toil through them again. . . . They give one nowhere a central

point of view, or a deductive or generative principle. They distinguish and refine and specify at infinitum without ever getting on to another logical level. Whereas the beauty of all truly scientific work is to get to ever deeper levels. (PP 1890, 1064)

Rather than treating the emotions as purely mental feelings, a truly scientific psychology must ask for the cause of the phenomena, and in the case of emotional feelings "the general causes are indubitably physiological" (PP 1890, 1065). This is why introspective observation of emotion experience is not enough. A psychological theory needs third-person causal explanations to clarify how emotions come about and how they work, how emotional feelings *relate* to bodily changes.

As is evident from the context, James is not dismissing first-person introspection here, nor suggesting replacing it by Lange's experimental observation in the third person. On the contrary, psychology aims to explain mental life; introspection gives us primary access to emotion as a mental phenomenon, and therefore "[i]ntrospective observation is what we have to rely on first and foremost and always" (PP 1890, 185). Examples of this approach can be found throughout the *Principles*, where his evidence for the claim that emotions are "feelings of bodily changes" is based on introspective experience of what he called the "coarser" emotions: emotions accompanied by "a wave of bodily disturbance of some kind" (EPs 1884, 169), in which "everyone recognizes a strong organic reverberation" (PP 1890, 1065). They are the most direct proof that emotion should not be conceived as a purely mental phenomenon, that the bodily changes follow the perception of the exciting fact directly and automatically, and that "a disembodied emotion is a nonentity" (PP 1890, 1068). He encourages his readers to introspect on their own emotional experience:

> If we fancy some strong emotion and then try to abstract from our consciousness of it all the feelings of its characteristic body symptoms, we find we have nothing left behind, no "mind-stuff" out of which the emotion can be constituted.... What kind of an emotion of fear would be left, if the feeling neither of quickened heart beats nor of shallow breathing, neither of trembling lips nor of weakened limbs, neither of gooseflesh nor of visceral stirrings, were present, it is quite impossible to think. (PP 1890, 1067)

Given his enthusiasm for Lange's physiological theory, James's introspective methodology may surprise the contemporary reader, but it fits into the broader framework of James's psychology as developed in *Principles*. Introspective observation is the primary method of getting acquainted with emotions; as a "natural science" (PP 1890, 1230), however, psychology requires more than just introspective data—it requires empirical observation, experiments, and testing. And here is where Lange enters the story. James immediately recognized that Lange's focus on patterns of visceral changes could help to make his own claim empirically testable. He was so happy with Lange that ten years after his *Mind* article, he wrote: "Professor Lange of Copenhagen and the present writer published, independently of each other, the same theory of emotional consciousness. They affirmed it to be the effect of the organic changes, muscular and visceral, of which the so called 'expression' of the emotion consists" (EPs 1894, 299).

The outcome of James's enthusiasm was that the two approaches became mixed up and that James's theory was summarized from then on as the view that emotion is feedback from the viscera, a causally inefficacious byproduct of physiological reactions. As a result of his emphasis on the body, James was considered unable to account for how emotions can generate actions, how they can be object-directed, and how the differences between emotions are to be explained. When in the 1920s Cannon (and in the 1960s Schachter and Singer) empirically refuted the hypothesis that emotions are differentiated by visceral response patterns, it was generally assumed that they had conclusively refuted James's original claim.

What the experiments refuted, however, was not the actual claim defended by James, as a series of reviews have rightly pointed out (De Sousa 1987; Barbalet 1994; Ellsworth 1994; Ratcliffe 2005; Laird and Lacasse 2014; Southworth 2014; Deonna and Teroni 2017); as we have seen, the range of bodily changes that are taken into account in both experiments is far too narrow to count seriously against James's view. But more importantly, James never meant to reduce emotional experience to a bodily sensation. In a letter to Charles Renouvier, he writes: "I don't mean that the Emotion is the perception of bodily changes *as such*, but only that the bodily changes give us a feeling, which is the Emotion" (CWJ 1884, 5.524). Emotion is a personal feeling—and James was fascinated with how this specific emotional feeling, given in a continuous "stream of consciousness," plays a crucial role in our adjustment to the world—a fascination that is strangely overlooked by most of James's cognitive critics during the twentieth century and by many in the twenty-first.

James himself has always been clear about the importance of first-person experience in his work. In the first sentence of his 1894 article, he explicitly characterizes his theory as a "theory of emotional consciousness" (EPs 1894, 299). He was not only interested in the "coarser" emotions that illustrate the physiological mechanism of emotional responses most effectively. In "The Sentiment of Rationality" (1879), in the *Principles* (1890), and even more so in his later work, he also studies the "subtle" emotions extensively. Subtle emotions are "those emotions whose organic reverberation is less obvious and strong." The class includes the moral, aesthetic, and intellectual feelings as well as feelings of pleasure and displeasure, interest and excitement. But even these longer-lasting, cognitively complex subjective experiences

> form no exception to our account but rather an additional illustration thereof. In all cases of intellectual and moral rapture we find that, unless there be coupled a bodily reverberation of some kind with the mere thought of the object and cognition of its quality; unless we actually laugh at the neatness of a demonstration or witticism; unless we thrill at the case of justice, or tingle at the act of magnanimity, our state of mind can hardly be called emotional at all. (PP 1890, 1084)

In sum, we may conclude that James and Lange shared the view that bodily changes cause and constitute emotion, that there is no emotional feeling without underlying bodily processes, and that different bodily changes distinguish different types of emotion. But for James, the bodily changes that differentiate emotion are not limited to the viscera and resonate in the organism as a whole; moreover, he aimed to explore how these bodily changes are connected to first-person emotional experience and how feeling these bodily changes contributes to individual well-being. The ultimate goal of James's theory was not to explain away the subjective experience of emotion by reducing it to a pattern of physiological events, as was the goal of Lange's theory, but to come up with a new understanding of the adaptive role of emotional feeling in the life of individual human beings. Therefore, James was not a defender of James-Lange theory.

James and Basic Emotions Theory

Basic emotions theory (BET) claims that there is empirical evidence for the existence of a limited set of "basic emotions" that are innate, universal, adaptive, and associated with emotion-specific changes at the level of expressions, behavior, and autonomic response. BET first appeared in the work of McDougall (1923) and returned in the 1960s in Silvan Tomkins's *Affect, Imagery, Consciousness* ([1962] 2008). Tomkins analyzed emotions as affects: hardwired mechanisms, associated with distinctive facial behavior. The link between face and emotion was further explored by Paul Ekman and his associates Wallace Friesen and Phoebe Ellsworth in *Emotion in the Human Face* (1972). In the 1990s, BET became fashionable, with the popularity of Ekman's account of six universal facial expressions and their interpretation in terms of six discrete "basic emotions": anger, fear, disgust, sadness, happiness, and surprise (Ekman 1999; Ekman, Friesen, and Ellsworth 1972). Among psychologists, proof for the occurrence of such a limited set of biologically evolved emotions is still controversial; as Lisa Barrett pointed out in "Are Emotions Natural Kinds," the empirical evidence does not support it (Barrett 2006; cf. Russell 1994). Nevertheless, BET became the dominant paradigm in emotion research.

BET is widely seen as a revival of the James-Lange view that each emotion type is attached to distinct bodily changes—but with two major innovations: first, it adds some additional bodily changes—facial expressions, hormonal changes, neural changes—to the visceral ones that were central in the standard version; and second, the automatic physiological response is now explicitly considered to have adaptive value; in the standard version, James's theory was seen—incorrectly, as I pointed out in the previous section—as promoting the view that emotion is a physiological disturbance without any direct use or function. Inspired by this return to the body and encouraged by Damasio's neuroscientific rehabilitation of James (in Damasio 1994, 2000), philosophers Jesse Prinz (2004) and Jenefer Robinson (2005) presented "neo-Jamesian" theories of emotion as a "gut reaction"—a perception of changes in our bodily condition, like a heart-sinking feeling or a turning of the stomach, that give us a direct sense of the relationship between the organism's body and its environment. Gut reactions are primitive appraisals, based on rough information like Good! Bad! Danger! or Yuck! sometimes working below the level of consciousness. They are to be understood as perceptions of physiological changes that signal situations of danger, good fortune, loss, and so forth. Tracing such situations is the main function of emotion, according to the neo-Jamesians.

This update of James's theory in the twenty-first century has two direct consequences that lead to a significant change in the conception of emotion. First, from an evolutionary perspective, emotions are not inconsequential epiphenomena anymore but functional devices, solutions to environmental problems. Second, the mental and the physical sides of emotion, appraisal and arousal, are not disconnected in this new approach—as they were in the standard version—but intrinsically linked, preparing the organism as a whole for coordinated adaptive response. The result is a coherent biological understanding of emotion, and James has been highly praised for anticipating this view.

He is also criticized, however, because his approach is assumed to account only for instinctive "coarse" emotions such as fear of loud noises, dark shadows, large animals, or falling off a cliff. The neo-Jamesian update of his theory will not work for the "subtle" moral and aesthetic emotions or for other higher cognitive emotions that are informed by learning and socialization. Basic emotions, according to critics of BET, are little more than reflex-like, "quick and dirty" responses. BET-type theories have difficulty explaining how emotions can be connected to beauty, justice, hope for a better future, and other human aspirations.[3] It is James himself who is to blame for this blind spot, according to his critics. His scientific approach reduced emotion to a purely causal event, the result of a blind, instinctive reflex. By doing so, he disconnected emotional experience from evaluation, will, and intelligent action, and completely removed the traditional idea of emotion as a "passion" from human psychology (Deigh 2014; c.f. Reisenzein and Stephan 2014; Dixon 2003).

It is very unlikely, however, that James would have recognized himself in any of these criticisms. That he often speaks about the emotions as if they were instinctive dispositions is evident. But this instinctive background is compatible with emotions being subtly responsive to cultural cues. We get an illustration of the former point in a passage in the *Mind* article where he writes:

> The neural machinery is but a hyphen between determinate arrangements of matter outside the body and determinate impulses to inhibition or discharge within its organs. When the hen sees an oval egg on the ground, she cannot leave it, she must keep upon it and return to it, until at last its transformation into a little mass of moving chirping down elicits from her machinery an entirely new set of performances. The love of man for woman, or of the human mother for her baby, our wrath at snakes and our fear of precipices, may all be described similarly. (EPs 1884, 170–171)

James's approach to emotion was deeply influenced by Darwin and evolutionary theory. In the *Principles*, where the chapter on emotion follows the chapter on instincts and precedes the chapter on the will, he says that "instinctive reactions and emotional expressions . . . shade imperceptibly into each other. Every object that excites an instinct excites an emotion as well" (PP 1890, 1058). Humans have a huge variety of instincts—far more than other animals, according to James. He mentions tendencies to flee from threats, attack enemies, comfort family and friends. But unlike many of today's emotion theorists, he rejects the idea that there are two sets of emotional response, instinctive and cognitive, basic and non-basic, primary and secondary. For James, all emotions, both coarse and subtle ones, higher and lower, are based on an instinctive bodily reaction and caused by a physiological mechanism.[4]

That this instinctive background goes hand in hand with a responsiveness to culture is illustrated by "shame, pride, and their varieties" (PBC 1892, 325), which James counts under the "coarse" emotions, together with five out of Ekman's six: anger, fear, love, hate, joy, and grief. He says that most occasions of shame and pride are purely conventional and vary with the social environment. Already in his *Mind* article he points out that the most relevant emotional environment for man is social life and that we experience the most intense emotions in the world of socio-cultural beliefs and norms. Illustrating his point with the example of the social emotion "stage fright," he says:

> The most important part of the environment is my fellow-man. The consciousness of his attitude towards me is the perception that normally unlocks most of my shames and indignations and fears. The extraordinary sensitiveness of this consciousness is shown by the bodily modifications wrought in us by the awareness that our fellow-man is noticing us *at all*. No one can walk across the platform at a public meeting with just the same muscular innervation he uses to walk across his room at home. . . . It is not surprising that the . . . persuasion that my fellow-man's attitude means either well or ill for me, should awaken . . . [strong] emotions. In primitive societies, "Well" may mean handing me a piece of beef and "Ill" may mean aiming a blow at my skull. In our "cultured age," "Ill" may mean cutting me in the street and "Well," giving me an honorary degree. What the action itself may be is quite insignificant, so long as I can perceive in it intent or *animus*. *That* is the emotion-arousing perception. (EPs 1884, 176)

The passage makes it clear that James does not distinguish between non-cognitive basic emotions and cognitively constituted non-basic emotions. In his view, all emotions are based on inherited evolutionary stimulus-response connections and initiated by an "emotion-arousing perception" of the environment as "good" or "bad," "well" or "ill." Culture and social convention determine the kinds of situation that trigger the emotion, but not the physiological mechanism that underlies the emotion and produces the emotional feeling. Complex human emotions, although triggered by appraisals of complex social situations, are still caused by an automatic instinctive reaction, according to James; yet, they differ from what are commonly called "instincts" in important respects.

Instincts in the strict sense of the word are blind. They lead to mechanical, reflex-like action "without foresight of the ends, and without previous education in the performance" (PP 1890, 1004). Emotions, on the contrary, are not blind. They are receptive to social learning and do not automatically generate action. They "fall short of instincts, in that the emotional reaction usually terminates in the body" (PP 1890, 1058). Emotions may just remain "inside," as subjective feeling states. This is, says James, because

> emotional reactions are often excited by objects with which we have no practical dealing. A ludicrous object, for example, or a beautiful object are not necessarily objects to which we *do* anything; we simply laugh, or stand in admiration. The class of emotional, is thus larger than the class of instinctive, impulses, commonly so called. Its stimuli are more numerous, and its expressions are more internal and delicate, and often less practical. The physiological plan and essence of the two classes of impulse, however, is the same. (PP 1890, 1058–1059)

What James is saying here is that all emotions are caused by impulsive bodily changes, but not all emotions lead to immediate action. While there is a tight connection between emotions and specific bodily impulses, there is only a very loose connection between emotions and concrete actions. For most emotions, immediate automatic acting out is not necessary; emotion's primary effect is on individual consciousness. An individual may feel angry and undergo the instinctive bodily reactions related to anger, but resist the impulse to hit someone and instead start to consider other, more sophisticated options for revenge. "When the outward deeds are inhibited, these latter emotional expressions still remain, and we read the anger in the face, though the blow may not be struck" (PP 1890, 1058).

Here we have the fundamental difference with instinct: emotion allows for a flexible response because emotions are action-oriented feelings—forward-looking and goal-oriented experiences of the self (Barbalet 1994). They have not just evolved to prepare a rapid automatic response; emotions may also result in a person's fantasizing about future possibilities for action. Because of "memory, power of reflection, and power of inference," an emotional "tendency to obey impulses" is always experienced "accompanied with foresight of its 'end,'" says James (PP 1890, 1010; PBC 1892, 342). Remaining "inside" most of the time, emotions allow the higher centers of action-control to work out specific personal answers to the situation. By so doing, they provide us with crucial information about ourselves, about how we are doing now and what we would like to do next (Laird 2007; Slaby 2012; Laird and Lacasse 2014; Reisenzein and Stephan 2014). Emotions are forms of pre-reflective, practical self-knowledge, closely linked to notions like "self-complacency and self-dissatisfaction" (PP 1890, 292; PBC 1892, 165). They provide orientation and direction to future action, and make self-organization, self-control, and self-regulation possible.

In the same line, the Dutch psychologist Nico Frijda has argued that emotion is a state of "action readiness": a felt readiness for approach, avoidance, rejecting, engaging, dominating, submitting, and so on that does not dictate any fixed action. Emotions are merely "tendencies to establish, maintain, or disrupt a relationship with the environment." Different emotions are distinguished by different modes of "action readiness" that have distinct, self-motivational force (Frijda 1986; 2010). In "Emotion as Process," Jenefer Robinson elaborates on the idea of action tendencies in her Jamesian account of emotion as a causal process, instinctively generated by the perception of a significant situation, and having as its main function to get the person or animal to cope with the situation in an appropriate way (Robinson 2017).

In conclusion, James's theory of emotions differs from basic emotions theory because he defines emotions not in terms of a fixed set of coordinated responses that are universal and cross-culturally identical, but in terms of functional action-tendencies that allow for a flexible individual response to the situation. For James, emotion is primarily a personal "tendency to obey impulses"; his focus is on the individual, not on the species. Even though a certain stimulus situation may trigger the same kind of action tendencies in different individuals, their overall reactions will be highly individualized and related to personality and personal history, culture, and social convention. In James's scientific psychology, "there is no limit to the number of possible different emotions which may exist, and why the emotions of different individuals may vary indefinitely" (PP 1890, 1069; c.f. Ellsworth 2014; Barrett 2006).

And so, James was not a basic emotion theorist, but he was not a social or psychological constructionist either.[5] That he emphasized individual variation in the experience of emotions does not imply that he believed emotions to be differentiated by social or psychological labeling instead of by biology. All emotions have a personal, social, and cultural dimension in so far as culture and personality have impact on the appraisal that triggers the emotion and on the subjective experience and expression of the emotional response. But the response as such is instinctive, grounded in evolved, biologically functional "action tendencies" in the first place; varieties of common emotions like anger, fear, or shame share a functional resemblance. Theories that radically dissociate emotional experience from its biological roots are the kind of mind-stuff theories that James dismissed in the *Principles*.

JAMES AND PHENOMENOLOGY

Looking back at the discussion so far, what stands out is that for more than a century, James's critics and supporters have been occupied with his work on the physiology of the so-called coarse emotions, analyzed in his 1884 article and in the *Principles*. Less widely known is that in later years, James continued his studies of the affective domain from a somewhat different perspective. In *The Will to Believe* (1897) and *The Varieties of Religious Experience* (1902), he explores how emotions relate to philosophical, moral, and religious beliefs. His focus is on a rather diffuse set of phenomena that are not reactions to a sudden event but are experienced as objectless, longer-term emotional feelings and attitudes: emotions such as confidence, trust, familiarity, and being at home in the world, but also anxiety, insecurity, loneliness, vulnerability, and confusion.

Confronted with this shift in attention, psychologists often assume that James, at the end of his career, made a radical turn in his thinking and gave up his naturalistic somatic theory in favor of a more humanistic approach (Averill 1992). Evidence to support this assumption is lacking, however. James never denounced his early writings on the physiology of emotions, because he simply had no reason to do so. As I noted in the section "Did James Really Defend the James-Lange Theory" his project was to transform psychology into a genuine natural science, but he was not a physiological reductionist. He intends to study emotional experience from a pluralistic perspective that gives plenty of room to the richness of first-person experiences but at the same time seeks to integrate third-person methods and physiological causality. In the *Varieties*, subtitled "a study in human nature," James is continuing this scientific effort, now concentrating even more explicitly on the experiential side of emotion. Meanwhile, he sticks to the premise that all emotion types—coarse and subtle, foreground and background, object directed and objectless—are constituted by bodily changes. Even in his study of religious and mystical emotions, the body is never far away. His point of departure in the *Varieties* is that our deepest, most personal beliefs are rooted in feeling and that it is through the feeling body that we believe in the reality of God or some higher truth. More than a decade earlier, he had defended a similar claim in the *Principles*, stating that our reasons for believing are closely related to the "bodily commotion" that an exciting religious or metaphysical idea evokes. All our religious or supernatural beliefs are based on a sense that "nothing which I can feel like *that* [about] can be false," he writes (PP 1890, 936).

Starting from the assumption that there is a great deal of continuity in James's views on emotion, Matthew Ratcliffe (2005, 2008) has recently argued that emotion theorists should take the later work more seriously than they did so far. What James's later studies shed light on is that his actual concern was not with the "coarser" emotions but with a category of primordial emotions that are referred to by Ratcliffe as "existential feelings." Existential feelings are mood-like emotions in the background of consciousness that provide us with a sense of reality, a sense of relatedness between self and world. According to Ratcliffe, James is interested in how these pre-intentional emotional feelings constitute a background to one's experience as a whole and provide us with an a priori orientation to the world.

Unlike the short-term object-directed emotions that lie in the foreground of consciousness, existential background feelings are "more deep and more general" (VRE, 55). Examples are intense joy or deep anxiety that are not directed at a particular object or event but are more like all-encompassing orientations. Just like the standard emotions, existential feelings are feelings of bodily changes, but at the same time they are feelings of how we are doing in the world and how the world appeals to us. "World experience is not distinct from how one's body feels; the two are utterly inextricable," says Ratcliffe (2008, 1).

Ratcliffe suggests that we understand James's writings on emotion in the context of his pragmatist project to naturalize intentionality in such a way that bodily feeling is included into its structure (Ratcliffe 2005, 180; 188–189). What emotion theorists focusing on James's physiological descriptions overlook is that James was a pioneer of philosophical pragmatism, committed to investigating consciousness as world-directed, active, and selective. His theory of mind was inspired by the evolutionary view that the nervous system of organisms and persons is biologically pre-tuned to specific ecological niches and responsive only to features that are significant in relation to possible behaviors and actions. The idea of emotional background feelings, understood as a priori conditions that play a leading role in pre-structuring our world- and self-experience, nicely fits this Darwinian approach. Background emotions are inarticulate feelings that give us "premonitions, awareness of direction" (PP 1890, 452), a sense of how situations can be practically significant to us. They constitute "possibility spaces" (Ratcliffe 2010), basic layers of individual experience that first make possible our grasp of objects in the world. Ratcliffe also points out that this philosophical line of arguing shows interesting similarities with the discussion of moods in *Being and Time* (Heidegger [1927] 1962), where Heidegger referred to this fundamental layer of experience with the German word *Befindlichkeit*, to be translated as "attunement," a way of "finding oneself in the world." Philosophically speaking, moods, or better, objectless background emotions, are ways in which we are open to the world, according to Heidegger.

So was James actually doing philosophy? There are plenty of reasons to agree that his approach is in line with the project of existential phenomenology, as Ratcliffe is not the first to notice (c.f. Linschoten 1968, Edie 1987). What is striking is the shared interest in the practical structures of embodied subjectivity through which the world of experience is disclosed. Merleau-Ponty's observation that "prior to stimuli and sensory contents, we must recognize a kind of inner diaphragm which determines, infinitely more than they do, what our reflexes and perceptions will be able to aim at in the world" (1962, 79; c.f. Ratcliffe 2005, 196), might have been written by James. Moreover, in his later work, we find interesting illustrations of this "world-disclosing" quality of emotion. It is a central theme in the *Varieties*, where James is particularly interested in first-person narratives of religious conversion, mystical experience, and psychiatric illness—emotional conditions that can be so overwhelming and encompassing that they may result in a radical change of personality and world view, grounded in a completely new experience of reality.

But on the other hand, what James is trying to demonstrate throughout his career is precisely that there is no need to make room outside psychology to accommodate his interest in this kind of issue, because his goal has always been to integrate first-person analysis into his scientific project. He aims to take the study of consciousness away from abstract armchair philosophy; instead of analyzing the abstract structures of world experience, he investigates how concrete background emotions constitute an individual's temperament and personality, and how they play a role in mood disorders. He understands the dispositional background emotions along the same lines as he understood the coarser emotions in his early writings—as functional, adaptive phenomena.

Examples of this approach can be found in his chapter on the "sick soul" in *Varieties*. James gives a lot of attention to Tolstoy's autobiographical *My Confession*, where the author describes his depression in terms of an existential disposition that blocks all possibilities for meaningful action. On the brink of suicide, Tolstoy experiences his life as a failure and the world as evil, a place where we can never be safe or feel at home. The therapy for Tolstoy is a religious conversion rising from the depths of the unconscious and accompanied by a wave of positive energy, as a magical cure by which the soul is healed and Tolstoy himself becomes a new man— James speaks of a redemption, "a second birth, a deeper kind of conscious being" (VRE 1902, 131).

His description of the whole transformational experience shows a striking similarity with Sartre's famous account in *Sketch for a Theory of the Emotions* (1939), where Sartre analyzes emotion as a "magic transformation of the world," when paths are blocked but the action must move forward (Sartre [1939] 2002). In Tolstoy's case, the emotional re-orientation completely changes his self-image and his relationship with the world in a way that is experienced as positive. Sartre, from a typically moralistic point of view, would disqualify such magical transformations of self and reality as degradations of consciousness that are self-deceptive; whereas James characteristically sees the conversion as a successful coping process and concludes that religious emotions are among mankind's most important functions. "If the fruits of the state of conversion are good, we ought to venerate it" (VRE 1902, 193).

Was James a phenomenologist? The answer is positive in so far as he was fascinated by consciousness and personal experience and championed a first-person methodology. He devoted much time to wonderfully detailed descriptions of the phenomenology of feeling, clarifying how emotional feelings pre-structure possibilities for action and shape one's sense of ability. But this descriptive first-person point of view must be complemented by a physiological third-person perspective in order to find out what the potential benefits of emotional experience are from an evolutionary, biological point of view.

To wrap things up, I think James is best understood as a scientist who is on his way to a "phenomenological psychology" (Linschoten 1968): a Darwinian psychology of consciousness as "embodied subjectivity" that seeks to close the gap between phenomenological analysis and naturalistic models of the mind. In the early days of psychology as an academic discipline, science and philosophy did not differ so much in their methods and conceptual tools, and James freely alternates between empirical and phenomenological methods. He has no worries about how psychology should bridge the explanatory gap between third-person observation of (neuro)physiological processes and first-person introspection of feelings, because in his view, the two approaches do not refer to different ontological domains; they are two different ways of exploring the same emotional experience—from the inside and from the outside.

The actual goal of James's psychology was to integrate the two epistemological perspectives, intentionality and causality, first-person and third-person experience, and to clarify their mysterious co-existence in the human condition in general. Already in 1869, in a letter, he described this commitment as follows:

> I feel that we are nature through and through, that we are *wholly* conditioned, that not a wiggle of our will happens save as the result of physical laws, and yet notwithstanding we are en rapport with reason – how to conceive it? . . . It is not that we are all nature *but* some point that is reason, but that all is Nature *and* all is reason too. (CWJ 1869, 4.370)

Conclusion: Emotion as a Pragmatist Views It

Three conclusions can be drawn from this overview. First, during more than a century of heated debates, comments on James have systematically ignored the fact that his views of emotion are part of a broader psychological framework that was already in place at the time of the *Principles*.[6] James's ambition was to establish psychology as a Darwinian science of mental life, based on the idea of consciousness as adaptive and purposive. Emotion, for James, is primarily given as a mental phenomenon, more precisely as a feeling. The task of psychology as a natural science is, first, to carefully describe and analyze emotional feeling from an introspective point of view; second, to investigate the (neuro)physiology of emotion with the help of empirical and experimental methods, and third, to look for psychophysical correlations that explain the biological function of emotion. Combining data from first-person phenomenology and third-person experiment, James came up with the theory that emotion is a bodily feeling, an experience of the resonance that an event or situation arouses in our bodies. Through the emotional sounding-board, we learn how things are important to us and find our way in the world.

Second, most discussions about James's work on emotion have interpreted his theory through the lens of dualistic conceptual frameworks that James himself rejected. As a pragmatist thinker, James disliked metaphysics; he did not propose any solution to the problem of how mind and body are related. Instead, he pointed out that emotion is a response of the whole living organism and that our emotional experience is influenced by both culture and biology. Examined from within, emotions are subjective feelings that shape one's sense of action possibilities and are intimately related to a person's beliefs and perceptions, values and goals. Examined from the outside, emotions are bodily mechanisms connected to the self-regulatory skills of the biological organism. What appear to be two different accounts, related to two different ontologies, are for James two distinct perspectives on the same emotional experience. Consequently, a re-evaluation of James's claim that emotion is a "feeling of bodily changes" should start with a criticism of the traditional dualism between mind and body, culture and biology, that prevents us to see the coherence in his work.

Third, James's revolutionary conception of the bodily "sounding board" that is at work in emotion allows him to close the gap between naturalism and phenomenology and to cross boundaries between categories that psychologists of emotion traditionally seek to separate, like feeling and cognition, appraisal and arousal, episode and disposition. His theoretical framework anticipates newer research programs in affective science such as enactivism, presented in Giovanna Colombetti's *The Feeling Body: Affective Science Meets the Enactive Mind* (2014), and neurophenomenology (Varela 1996), which also emphasize the embodied, action-oriented nature of emotions and prefer a combination of third-person and first-person methodology.

With his radical anti-dualism and his pluralistic approach, James managed to elegantly integrate feelings, cognitions, action tendencies, and physiology into a functional whole. For today's emotion scientists, working in a field where the number of opposing theories has only increased over the years and has no common basis for productive exchange in sight, it might be a good idea to start rereading James's work.

Notes

1. For a comprehensive overview of early critiques, see Dixon (2003).
2. "The pursuance of future ends and the choice of means for their attainment are thus the mark and criterion of the presence of mentality in a phenomenon" (PP 1890, 21).
3. Even Damasio shares this intuition. James "gave no weight to the process of evaluating mentally the situation that causes the emotion [. . . .] James's view] works well for the first emotions one experiences in life" (Damasio 1994, 130)—but not for the complex emotions.
4. C.f. *Principles* (PP 1890, 1084): the subtle emotions "form no exception to our account but rather an additional illustration thereof."
5. See Barrett (2017) and Scarantino (2016) for an alternative account of James as a forerunner of psychological constructivism.
6. For notable exceptions, see Barbalet (1994), Ellsworth (1994), and Southworth (2014).

References

Arnold, M. B. 1960. *Emotion and Personality*. New York: Columbia University Press.
Averill, J. 1992. "William James Other Theory of Emotion." In *Reinterpreting the Legacy of William James*, edited by M. Donnelly, 221–230. Washington: American Psychological Association.
Barbalet, J. M. 1994. "William James's Theory of Emotions: Filling in the Picture." *Journal for the Theory of Social Behavior* 29 (3): 251–266.
Barrett, L. F. 2006. "Are Emotions Natural Kinds." *Perspectives on Psychological Science* 1:28–58.
Barrett, L. F. 2017. *How Emotions Are Made*. New York: Houghton-Mifflin-Harcourt.
Cannon, W. B. 1927. "The James-Lange Theory of Emotion: A Critical Examination and an Alternative Theory." *American Journal of Psychology* 39:106–124.

Colombetti, G. 2014. *The Feeling Body: Affective Science Meets the Enactive Mind*. Cambridge, MA: MIT Press.

Damasio, A. 1994. *Descartes' Error: Emotion, Reason, and the Human Brain*. New York: Putnam & Grossett.

Damasio, A. 2000. *The Feeling of What Happens: Body, Emotion and the Making of Consciousness*. London: Vintage.

Deigh, J. 1994. "Cognitivism in the Theory of Emotions." *Ethics* 104 (4): 824–854

Deigh, J. 2014. "William James and the Rise of the Scientific Study of Emotion." *Emotion Review* 6:4–12.

Deonna, J. and F. Teroni. 2017. "Getting Bodily Feelings into Emotional Experience in the Right Way." *Emotion Review* 9 (1): 55–63.

De Sousa, R. 1987. *The Rationality of Emotion*. Cambridge, MA: MIT Press.

Dixon, T. 2003. *From Passions to Emotions: The Creation of A Secular Psychological Category*. Cambridge, MA: Cambridge University Press.

Edie, J. 1987. *William James and Phenomenology*. Bloomington, IN: Indiana University Press.

Ekman, P., V. Friesen, and P. Ellsworth. 1972. *Emotion in the Human Face*. New York: Pergamon Press.

Ekman, P. 1999. "Basic Emotions." In *Handbook of Cognition and Emotion*, edited by T. Dalgleish and M. Power, 38–60. New York: John Wiley and Sons.

Ellsworth, P. 1994. "William James and Emotion: Is a Century of Fame Worth a Century of Misunderstanding?" *Psychological Review* 101:222–229.

Ellsworth, P. 2014. "Basic Emotions and the Rocks of New Hampshire." *Emotion Review* 6:21–26.

Frijda, N. H. 1986. *The Emotions*. Cambridge, MA: Cambridge University Press.

Frijda, N.H. 2010. "Impulsive Action and Motivation." *Biological Psychology* 84 (3): 570–579

Gardiner, H. N. 1896. "Recent Discussion of Emotion." *Philosophical Review* 5:102–112.

Griffiths, P. E. 1997. *What Emotions Really Are: The Problem of Psychological Categories*. Chicago: University of Chicago Press.

Heidegger, M. (1927) 1962. *Being and Time*. Translated by J. Macquarrie and E. Robinson. Oxford, UK: Blackwell.

Laird, J. D. and L. Lacasse. 2014. "Bodily Influences on Emotional Feelings: Accumulating Evidence and Extensions of William James's Theory of Emotion." *Emotion Review* 6:27–34.

Laird, J. D. 2007. *Feelings: The Perception of Self*. New York: Oxford University Press.

Linschoten, H. 1968. *On the Way toward a Phenomenological Psychology. The Psychology of William James*. Pittsburgh: Duquesne University Press.

McDougall, W. 1923. *An Outline of Psychology*. London: Methuen.

Merleau-Ponty, M. 1962. *Phenomenology of Perception*. London: Routledge.

Myers, G. 1986. *William James: His Life and Thought*. New Haven, CT: Yale University Press.

Nussbaum, M. 2001. *Upheavals of Thought. The Intelligence of Emotions*. Cambridge, MA: Cambridge University Press.

Prinz, J. 2004. *Gut Reactions: A Perceptual Theory of Emotion*. New York: Oxford University Press.

Ratcliffe, M. 2005. "William James on Emotions and Intentionality." *International Journal of Philosophical Studies* 13:179–202.

Ratcliffe, M. 2008. *Feelings of Being. Phenomenology, Psychiatry, and the Sense of Reality*. New York: Oxford University Press.

Ratcliffe, M. 2010. *Experiences of Depression. A Study in Phenomenology*. Oxford, UK: Oxford University Press.

Reisenzein, R., and A. Stephan. 2014. "More on James and the Physical Basis of Emotion." *Emotion Review* 6:35–46.

Robinson, J. (2005). *Deeper Than Reason: Emotion and its Role in Literature, Music, and Art*. Oxford: Oxford University Press.

Robinson, J. 2017. "Emotion as Process." In *The Ontology of Emotions*, edited by H. Naar and F. Teroni, 51–70. Cambridge, MA: Cambridge University Press.

Russell, James. 1994. "Is There Universal Recognition of Emotion from Facial Expressions?" *Psychological Bulletin* 115 (1): 102–141.

Sartre, J. P. (1939) 2002. *Sketch for a Theory of the Emotions*. London: Routledge Classics.

Scarantino, A. 2016. "The Philosophy of Emotions and Its Impact on Affective Science." In *Handbook of Emotions: Fourth Edition*, edited by L. Feldman Barrett, M. Lewis, and J. M. Haviland-Jones, 3–48. New York and London: The Guilford Press.

Schachter, S. and J. Singer. 1962. "Cognitive, Social, and Physiological Determinants of Emotional State." *Psychological Review* 69:379–399.

Solomon, R. (1976) 1993. *The Passions: Emotions and the Meaning of Life*. Cambridge, MA: Hackett.

Southworth, J. 2014. *William James' Theory of Emotion*. Western Electronic Thesis and Dissertation Repository. Paper 2315. https://ir.lib.uwo.ca/etd//.

Slaby, J. 2012. "Affective Self-Construal and the Sense of Ability." *Emotion Review* 4:151–156.

Tomkins, S. S. (1962) 2008. *Affect, Imagery, Consciousness: The Complete Edition*. New York: Springer Publishing Company.

Varela, F. J. 1996. "Neurophenomenology: A Methodological Remedy for the Hard Problem." *Journal of Consciousness Studies* 3 (4): 330–350.

Worcester, W. L. 1893. "Observations on Some Points in James's Psychology. II. Emotion." *The Monist* 3:285–298.

CHAPTER 3

JAMES ON THE PERCEPTION OF SPACE

GARY HATFIELD

Introduction

THE perception of space was a central topic in the philosophy, psychology, and sensory physiology of the nineteenth century. William James engaged all three of these approaches to spatial perception. On the prominent issue of nativism versus empirism, he supported nativism, holding that space is innately given in sensory perception. He thus opposed the dominant view, that sensory perception originally involves only aspatial sensations that must be organized into spatial structures (two dimensional and then three dimensional) on the basis of experience.

James became a philosopher and a psychologist early in his career. His first teaching position was in physiology at Harvard College (from 1872). He soon used this opportunity to teach psychological topics (Perry 1935, 2.10), and in support of his teaching in physiological psychology he secured some laboratory demonstration rooms (from 1875). He was also drawn to philosophical topics, especially about human agency and free will. His teaching moved to the Philosophy Department (in 1877–1878), where he offered courses in both philosophy and psychology. In 1880, his title changed from Assistant Professor of Physiology to Assistant Professor of Philosophy; he became Professor in 1886. His title changed again, in 1889, to Professor of Psychology, perhaps in anticipation of the monumental *Principles of Psychology* (PP 1890), soon to appear after twelve years of work. Ironically, he subsequently moved more fully into philosophy; in 1897, he was once again Professor of Philosophy.

From the late 1860s, James held that psychology should become a natural science, allied with biology and physiology (Perry 1935, 2.3–4; letter to President Eliot of Harvard, CWJ 1875, 4.527–528). His earliest psychological writings addressed spatial perception, determinism, introspection, and emotion (among other topics), which shows that, in James's conception, psychology as a natural science would also develop in conversation with philosophy. In his description of the history of thought on spatial perception, which began with Locke and Berkeley and included Kant as well as sensory physiologists such as Helmholtz, he alluded to various physiologists and psychologists as "space philosophers" (PP 1890, 910).

In the *Principles*, "The Perception of Space" is by far the longest chapter. Near the end of it, to start his General Summary, he wrote: "With this we may end our long and, I fear to many readers, tediously minute survey. The facts of vision form a jungle of intricacy; and those who penetrate deeply into physiological optics will be more struck by our omissions than by our abundance of detail" (PP 1890, 898). This "survey" focused on the psychology and related physiology of spatial sensation, perception, and conception. The chapter is rich and nuanced, worthy of detailed examination on its own terms.

Herein, I first examine the historical context for James's work on the physiology and psychology of spatial perception, guided by (and commenting on) his own account of that history (PP 1890, 900–912). Included here are his arguments for nativism about spatial experience. I then examine central aspects of his theory of spatial sensation, perception, and conception, focusing on the *Principles*. Finally, I touch upon the reception of his nativism, his phenomenological holism, his characterization of perception as involving active processes of discernment and construction, and his conception of perceiving organisms as environmentally embedded.

Space in Context

At the end of his chapter on space perception, James offered a critical and opinionated "historical survey" of previous theories, focusing on British and German-language contributions. His history examined the differing accounts of the reality and origin of spatial experience. James found only "three possible kinds of theory concerning space." These are:

> Either (1) there is no spatial *quality* of sensation at all, and space is a mere symbol of succession; or (2) there is an *extensive quality given* immediately in certain particular sensations; or, finally, (3) there is a *quality produced* out of the inward resources of the mind, to envelop sensations which, as given originally, are not spatial, but which, on being cast into the spatial form, become united and orderly. (PP 1890, 902; see also EPs 1879, 80)

Let us take up these three and then add a fourth.

James attributed the first position to Thomas Brown, "the Mills" (James Mill and his son John Stuart), and Alexander Bain, albeit against their will. That is, he has them replacing genuine spatial experience with a temporal series of (aspatial) sensations that are reversible, as when one runs a finger back and forth on a surface. As James notes, a mere temporal succession of sensations does not in itself manifest a spatial quality (think of a series of ascending and descending tones, ignoring any spatial localization). Taking Bain as a test case,[1] further examination reveals his position actually to have been that, through association, genuine spatial experience, or a felt spatial quality, can arise from such sequences (Bain 1868, 371–375). Sensations of movement and of tactile qualities (e.g., roughness or smoothness), as associated, produce the feeling of extension.[2] Further association combines touch and muscle movement with vision:

> The conclusion, therefore, is that Extension, Size, or Magnitude, owes, not only its origin, but its essential import, or meaning, to a combination of different effects associated together under the cohesive principle we are now considering. Extension, or space, as a quality, has *no other* origin and no other meaning than the association of these different sensitive and motor effects. The coalition of sensations of sight and of touch with felt motive energies, explains everything that belongs to our notion of extended magnitude or SPACE. (Bain 1868, 372)[3]

Association yields the new quality of extension or space. But James denied this as a "possible" position by arguing that one should regard association "as *producing* nothing" (PP 1890, 901). Accordingly, if a sequence of aspatial sensations (that is, sensations lacking any spatial quality or position in space) are associated in a series, the most one might get is a transition among aspatial qualities, but no fusion into a phenomenally new product: felt spatial extension. Hence, James ruled out such accounts of the origin of the spatial quality as being inconsistent with, at least, his own understanding of association. But Bain and others allow such an associative product (further discussion to follow).

The second position is James's own. It contends that all *sensations*—which are, we shall see, the immediate products of physiological activity, prior to any psychological modification—have what James called a primitive "voluminousness" or "extensity" (PP 1890, 685–689, 776–786; PBC 1892, 292–294). This applies to sound, tastes, and odors, as well as to sensations of movement (felt through the joints), feelings in the skin, and feelings of retinal extent in vision. Only the last three give rise to what he described as a space-*perception* (PP 1890, 898). Spatial sensations per se are a bare and unexplained product of physiological activity: "In calling the quality in question a *sensational* quality, our own account equally disclaimed ability to analyze it, but said its antecedents were cerebral, not psychical—in other words, that it was a *first* psychical thing" (PP 1890, 908). His position is strictly nativist in that spatial extent is present in sensations originally, as a bare product of neural activity. James allied his position with those of Ewald Hering, A. W. Volkmann, and Carl Stumpf, among others.

The third position is that of Kant, which accepts the aspatial sensations of the first position but maintains that "inward resources" of the mind are aroused to order and unify these sensations into the "forms" of space and time (as co-existent simultaneous sensations arranged imagistically, or as sequential sensations ordered in time). James accepted from Stumpf the descriptor "psychic stimulus" for this theory, because the aspatial sensations are viewed as "goads to the mind to put forth its slumbering power" for imposing spatial order on sensations (PP 1890, 902). Kant indeed held that sensations are ordered into space and time, via a priori "forms of intuition." And James was right that Kant regarded such forms as *supra-sensational*, that is, beyond sensations themselves. However, he was incorrect in further maintaining (PP 1890, 904–905) that, according to Kant, the forms are *intellectual*: they belong, in Kant's scheme, to "sensibility" as opposed to "understanding" or intellect.[4]

James ended up relegating most theorists, including the authors he initially placed in the first category (Brown, the Mills, Bain, and also Spencer), to the camp of "psychical stimulists" (PP 1890, 903). First, he noted that each of them attributed the origin of spatial feeling or the spatial quale to processes that arise through association or synthesis. He then contended, as we have seen, that the associative explanation fails, since he (James) maintains that association can create nothing new. In his view, association is always reproductive, never productive (PP 1890, 163–164, 899–902). In order for our group of theorists to have a workable account of the genesis of the spatial quale (in James's estimation), they must turn to the third position, in which spatiality is latent in the mind as a form of intuition and spatial experience is an actively created synthetic product. James in effect re-classified the positions not only of the British, but also of Herbart, Lotze, Wundt, and Helmholtz, as "psychical stimulists," despite themselves (PP 1890, 906, 909).

The question of whether association can yield the new result of a spatial quality is, in one way of looking at things, precisely what was at stake between James and associationists such as Herbart, Bain, Wundt, and Helmholtz.[5] James believed he had established that there can be no sui generis product of associated elements (PP 1890, 163–164). We cannot know exactly how Herbart, Helmholtz, or Bain would have responded, but these authors all accepted that association can yield a new resultant: spatial extension. Wundt (1902–1903, 2.655, 661, 684), writing after James, divided earlier theories into empirist (includes Helmholtz, the Mills, and Bain) and nativist (in a Kantian version, and in a version denying that spatiality can be derived from aspatial elements, James being a primary exemplar). Wundt described himself as holding a reformed version of empirism, which he dubbed a "genetic" (developmental) "association or fusion" theory (fusion being a type of association).

We should, therefore, augment James's threefold division of theories with a fourth type, an associationist theory which claims that a genuinely spatial quality or experience can arise from the associative combination of sensations of movement, tactile qualities, and visual qualities.[6] Herbart held that, as a result of reversible series of sensations, more than one representation seeks to enter consciousness at once; the representations then co-exist in a spatial representation. James denigrated this claim, remarking that "Heaven knows how" such a product should arise from the fusion of sensations (PP 1890, 906).[7] Wundt and Helmholtz offered their own synthetic and associative accounts of the genesis of sensory space, as did Bain. James described such accounts as invoking a kind of "mental chemistry" (a term he attributes to "the Mills"), which combines elements without spatial quality so as to yield a new product with spatial quality.[8] James rejected such chemistry, but he shouldn't be allowed simply to decree productive association out of theoretical consideration.

As James noted (PP 1890, 909), Helmholtz seems to equivocate on whether he was attempting to explain the capacity for generating spatial experience, or merely how spatial localization takes place in sensory perception; James might also have cited Wundt (1862, 28) in this regard. James saw this as a concession, as Helmholtz recanting on explaining the genesis of spatial experience. Helmholtz and Wundt might rather have regarded such discussion as reflections on the very notion of a "capacity" for spatial perception (e.g., Wundt 1880–1883, 1.455–456). If one *can* develop spatial perception, does that mean one has a capacity to do so? Perhaps the question is whether there is a specific capacity for space, or merely a general capacity for association or psychical synthesis that, when stimulated by reversible series, generates a spatial experience. Wundt and Helmholtz are not as clear on these matters as James would like. But in this taxonomy of positions, we should acknowledge their self-descriptions as offering "empirist" or "genetic" (that is, developmental) accounts of the origin of sensory spatial representation, as opposed to nativist accounts, including of the Kantian variety.[9]

Having relegated everyone besides himself and his allies to the Kantian position (as we have seen), James then quickly offered a widely cited refutation. He described the position as "thoroughly mythological" (PP 1890, 903) and then quoted Schopenhauer on the Kantian point that spatial qualitative experience is "supra-sensational,"[10] after which he offered his famous refutation:

> I call this view mythological, because I am conscious of no such Kantian machine-shop in my mind, and feel no call to disparage the powers of poor sensation in this merciless way. I have no introspective experience of mentally producing or creating space. My space-intuitions occur not in two times but in one. There is not one moment of passive inextensive sensation, succeeded by another of active extensive perception, but the form I see is as immediately felt as the color which fills it out. (PP 1890, 905; see also EPs 1879, 81)

Two key elements in his argument are that the spatial quality is phenomenally primitive and that he (James) is not introspectively aware of any supra-sensational process by which he constructs spatial qualitative experience from aspatial sensations.

In fact, at least some of the holders of the associationist position would have granted these points. They would accept that spatial experience seems primitive and that we are not aware of the synthetic processes that bring aspatial sensations into a spatial qualitative experience. Indeed, since the time of Berkeley, a standard move by empirists has been to argue that the psychological processes that underlie spatial perception become rapid and habitual and so go unnoticed by the perceiver, who then experiences the product of such processes as an immediate, underived phenomenal content (Hatfield and Epstein 1979). Helmholtz accepted this account of why the perception of depth can seem to be psychologically immediate: "whatever is imposed on the sensations at the moment, as the result of these associations of ideas based on all our experiences collectively, seems to us to be communicated directly without any effort of will or conscious activity on our part, just like the sensations themselves; that is, seems to be immediate perception" (Helmholtz 1924–1925, 3.293). Wundt, too, held that the fusional activities that yield spatial representations are typically overlooked, so that we simply experience an array of visual qualities without awareness of the mechanisms of spatial localization (1902, 143). In other words, we are aware of colors in a spatial pattern, not of the local signs and synthetic processes that underlie this perception.

Accordingly, Helmholtz and Wundt would not find James's introspective failure to discover a "Kantian machine-shop" to be a telling objection. It has the appearance of begging the question. However, James did not simply refuse to consider the possibility of unnoticed psychological operations that yield phenomenally immediate qualitative spatial experience. Rather, he had, much earlier in the *Principles*, rejected unconscious psychological operations of this sort (PP 1890, 166–177). For him, association-based synthetic fusion must either be posited on the basis of poor phenomenology or must actually be the product of physiological processes, not psychological ones. But if the underlying processes are purely physiological, then, as we have seen James opine, they enter consciousness as psychologically primitive effects (and so do not exist anywhere as felt sensations that evoke mental operations). In this earlier section, James described Helmholtz and Wundt as, in later years, becoming less attached to unconscious or unnoticed reasoning processes (PP 1890, 171). Granting this point to James anent the term "unconscious inference," we have seen that Helmholtz and Wundt nonetheless retained a commitment to unnoticed associative processes. James might then be forced to summon his claim that association cannot yield new resultants. Which means that his argument cannot merely invoke the lack of an introspected machine shop: it also depends on his claim that association cannot be productive. That premise is, presumably, more open to debate than his introspective report. His contentions that reversible temporal series must fail to produce a spatial product and that in any case we can tell directly that the mind does not organize our sensations into a spatial order have become less secure. His arguments depend on his conclusions regarding both associative productivity and unconscious states and processes.

THE PERCEPTION OF SPACE

As James began teaching physiology and psychology during the 1870s, the prior two decades had seen the proliferation of research works and synthetic treatments of psychology, with an emphasis on sensory psychology. Bain had published his *The Senses and the Intellect* (1855), Mill his *Examination of Sir William Hamilton's Philosophy* (1865), followed by his edition of his father's *Analysis of the Phenomena of the Human Mind* (1869). Spencer had published the second edition, much expanded, of his *Principles of Psychology* (1870–1872). James knew these works, as well as German authors including

Wundt (1862, 1874) and Helmholtz, who had published his monumental *Handbuch der physiologischen Optik* in 1867.[11]

The British authors and Helmholtz shared a commitment to psychological atomism. That is, they regarded the elements of the mind to be atomic sensations or feelings, varying only in quality and intensity, and so (originally) without spatial order. These elements are the product of the stimulation of a single neural fiber, and occur independently of what is happening in adjacent fibers.[12] They are combined to construct complex psychological states, such as perceptions. The original sensations and the constructive processes were typically held to be unconscious.[13] The authors differed over the details of the constructive and synthetic processes by which elemental sensations are put together. But they agreed that mental content starts from atomic elements and proceeds by various processes: associative, synthetic, and, in some cases, logical or inferential. This meant that their books typically were organized so that, after one or more chapters on the brain and nervous system, they began with sensations and then moved on to perception, imagination, memory, conception, and understanding.

Already in the 1870s, James set himself against this mainstream in his paper "The Spatial Quale" (EPs 1879). This paper not only contained many of the arguments reviewed earlier concerning the various "schools" of empirists and their failings.[14] It also foretold James's methodological tendency toward phenomenal description and holism.

These tendencies are evident in the very organization of the *Principles*. After a brief chapter on the "Scope of Psychology," it has two chapters on the functions and activities of the brain.[15] It then treats the fundamental psychological phenomenon of habit formation, which it relates to neural processes. There follow chapters on "Automaton Theory," which opposes a purely mechanistic approach and favors the causal efficacy of the mental, and the "Mind-Stuff Theory," which attacks psychological atomism and seeks to rule out unconscious mental states. James then offers a methodological chapter, favoring psychology as a natural science, endorsing introspection and experiment (along with comparative psychology), and warning against the snares of ordinary language and the tendency, called the "psychologist's fallacy," to confuse the psychologist's description of a mental state with the subject's relation to that state. The preparatory chapters end with a general characterization of the relation of the mind to the world, including the time course of consciousness, the mind–brain relation, the division between subject and object, and the structure of knowledge, as comprising "knowledge of acquaintance" and "knowledge-about." James separates *feeling* (including sensation and emotion) from *thought*, but only in a "practical" and "relative" way (PP 1890, 217–218).

These preparatory chapters pave the way for the substance of psychology. James begins with what he calls "concrete experience": "The Stream of Thought." He begins holistically. The long chapter on the stream of thought includes sensation and perception, conception, attention, reasoning, self-awareness, and indeed anything that is present to the conscious mind, dimly or strongly. He characterizes this starting point as the "study of the mind from within" and contrasts it with that of "most books" on psychology, which "start with sensation, as the simplest mental facts," and "synthetically" construct higher stages of thought. He accuses this usual beginning with "abandoning the empirical method," since: "No one ever had a simple sensation by itself. Consciousness, from our natal day, is of a teeming multiplicity of objects and relations, and what we call simple sensations are results of discriminative attention" (PP 1890, 219). In the preface to his subsequent abridgement of the *Principles*, the *Psychology: Briefer Course* (PBC 1892), he described what led him, in the big book, to initiate his psychology proper with the stream of consciousness. He was following the *analytic order*, which starts from a complex given and seeks its elements (as opposed to the synthetic order, which starts from elements and builds up the objects of study). In this case, he began with the concretely given stream and, through discrimination and discernment, discovered its various aspects (PBC 1892, 2).

In accordance with this strategy, James (PP 1890) then takes seven chapters to consider phenomenal givens and active capacities as found in "inner" life. In previous psychologies, these topics had come later. They are: first "The Consciousness of Self" (the second-longest chapter in the work), and then chapters on attention, conception, discrimination and comparison, association, perception of time, and memory. James makes abundantly clear throughout that he is working from what is phenomenally given, now expanded to include aspects of the stream of thought that had, in his view, been overlooked in previous introspective reports. In particular, he finds stable objects in the stream, "perchings," as well as "flights," "transitions," or "fringes" (see also EPs 1884). Throughout, he regularly contrasts his phenomenal holism with the associationist view that thoughts and perceptions are composed of atomic sensations.

Then come five chapters on "outer perception" (PP 1890, 651): sensation, imagination,[16] and perception. In these chapters, we learn that perceptions are not built up from sensations as constituent parts, but are developed by directing various processes toward sensations, including discrimination, association, and attentional selection. Sensation and perception are followed by reasoning, motor production, instinct, emotions, will, hypnotism, and the evolutionary basis of instincts together with the genesis of scientific thought. The chapters on instinct, emotions, and will are grouped at the end as producers of bodily motion (behavior), and also, in the case of will, as returning to metaphysics, which had been heavily present in the preparatory chapters. Reasoning is well placed at the end of the whole discussion from the stream of consciousness to perception, the grand scheme of which it draws upon.

James's *Principles* follows the analytic order in working back from the stream, and it eventually comes to sensory perception and spatial perception as aspects. But there is a further framework that must be kept in mind. In the Preface, James revealed an assumption he made in the book, on behalf of scientific psychology:

> Psychology, the science of finite individual minds, assumes as its data (1) *thoughts and feelings*, and (2) *a physical world* in time and space with which they coexist and which (3) *they know*. Of course these data themselves are discussable; but the discussion of them (as of other elements) is called metaphysics and falls outside the province of this book. (PP 1890, 6)

As the remark on metaphysics indicates, the book assumes but does not justify belief in a physical world. The import of the passage does not primarily concern the reality of that world. Rather, James here serves notice that psychology, as "The Science of Mental Life" (PP 1890, 15), will study not only thoughts and feelings, but also the environment toward which they typically are directed and the manner in which they present that environment. Mind, he says later, is a "fighter for ends" (PP 1890, 144; also, 20-23). These ends facilitate, in the Spencerian phrase (here endorsed), "the adjustment of inner to outer relations" (PP 1890, 19). While allowing that this formulation suffers from vagueness, James nevertheless praises it "because it takes into account the fact that minds inhabit environments which act on them and on which they in turn react" (PP 1890, 19).

In pursuing the portion of the stream of consciousness that manifests spatial perception—or, with finer grain, spatial sensation, perception, and conception—we must keep in mind that spatial perception is as of the world, that it facilitates the mind's adjustment to its environment. Hence, spatial perception is to be studied not only as an occurrent mental phenomenon, but as a mental phenomenon that makes present things and their properties.

Spatial Sensation and Perception

James divided sensation, as the original and immediate product of sensory stimulation, from perception, which manifests the effects of past experience (memory, association, habit) and also typically involves the activity of the mind in discriminating and attending. This division has a phenomenal or introspective aspect and a neural aspect. Taken phenomenally, "Sensation . . . differs from Perception only in the extreme simplicity of its object or content" (PP 1890, 651-652). Sensations are not bare subjective effects; like perceptions, they are of "facts" and are directed toward "an immediately present outward reality" (PP 1890, 652). But they display relatively simple properties and objects, such as can be known "by acquaintance," that is, by being "present to our minds" (PP 1890, 218). We can be acquainted with the visual quality of blue, or the flavor of a pear, without knowing "about the inner nature of these facts or what makes them what they are" (PP 1890, 217). In contrast, perception and knowledge-about involve conception and judgment (PP 1890, 218), including classifying things into individuals and kinds (pears are fruit), attending to sensational structure not previously noticed (seeing the finer parts of an object), and experience-based "knowledge about" perceived things (such as that pears are sweeter than apples).

We have already seen that James, in characterizing something as a sensation, meant to imply that "its antecedents were cerebral, not psychical—in other words, that it was a *first* psychical thing" (PP 1890, 908). However, since he believed that perception also has neural or cerebral conditions, the notion of being "first" must here be understood in relation to the correlated neural process. James used neural conditions to distinguish sensation and perception, which both arise from sensory stimulation, from those thoughts that do not. And he also used neural conditions to distinguish sensation *from* perception. In the chapter on sensation, he wrote:

> From the physiological point of view both sensations and perceptions differ from "thoughts" (in the narrower sense of the word) in the fact that nerve-currents coming in from the periphery are involved in their production. In perception these nerve-currents arouse voluminous associative or reproductive processes in the cortex; but when sensation occurs alone, or with a minimum of perception, the accompanying reproductive processes are at a minimum too. (PP 1890, 652–653)

Perceptions, as we shall see, all involve acquired elements; they are influenced by past sensory experience, which alters the cerebral cortex. Sensations, if completely pure, would arise solely from afferent nerve currents. Of course, even in that case the conditions of other parts of the brain and nervous system would affect the sensation, as when the sensation of an area of color is affected by the surrounding colors (PP 1890, 663). James held that the physiological processes that are correlated even with sensation are complex; he rejected the standard view that the same atomic sensation is produced by the same physical stimulation of an individual sensory neural fiber. Indeed, he held that present experience is a product of the entire brain state: a physiological holism to match his phenomenal holism (PP 1890, 177–179).[17]

As mentioned, James attributed voluminousness or extensity to all sensations. This extensity is the basic sensation of space. It is more than simply a grouping of ordered relations. Tones and colors can be ordered in relation to one another, without exhibiting that order spatially (even if they have internal voluminousness). Sensations all have a volumetric aspect, but these volumes are not immediately comparable nor do they all eventually give rise to spatial perception: tones and pains have volume but do not yield spatial perception because they do not exhibit spatial structure. Even sensations that do yield spatial perception are not manifestly ordered. In these sensations, variation of the extensive element "has seemed to be the immediate psychic effect of a peculiar sort of nerve-process excited; and all the nerve-processes in question agree in yielding what space they do yield, to the mind, in the shape of a simple total vastness, in which, *primitively* at least, no *order of parts* or of *subdivisions* reigns" (PP 1890, 787). The sensations that support spatial perception, which originate in the skin, retina, and joints of the limbs, are sensations of volume without (initially apprehended or delineated) order.

This intuited but unordered "vastness" is the original experience of space. The mind actively finds relations of order within spatial sensations, or by conjoining and relating the objects of such sensations:

> Let no one be surprised at this notion of a space without order. There may be a space without order just as there may be an order without space. And the primitive perceptions of space are certainly of an unordered kind. The order which the spaces first perceived potentially include must, before being distinctly apprehended by the mind, be woven into those spaces by a rather complicated set of intellectual acts. The

primordial largenesses which the sensations yield must be *measured and subdivided* by consciousness, and *added* together, before they can form by their synthesis what we know as the real Space of the objective world. (PP 1890, 787)

The perceiver must undergo learning and development in order to go from undifferentiated spatiality to the "real Space of the objective world." Someone might object: I find no unordered volumes in my experience, just as James found no Kantian machine shop. To which James might reply: volumetric sounds, internally unordered, offer a model for unordered volumes.

Although James held that an ordered space must be created through intellectual acts that "weave" the individual sensational volumes together to create a unified perceived space, at the same time he insisted that these intellectual processes do not add spatial content to the original sensations that was not there already (albeit unapprehended). At the beginning of the long chapter on space, James made his point about volumetric sensations. He then offered his "first thesis" about spatial perception proper:

Now my first thesis is that this element [voluminousness], *discernible in each and every sensation, though more developed in some than in others, is the original sensation of space,* out of which all the exact knowledge about space that we afterwards come to have is woven by processes of discrimination, association, and selection. (PP 1890, 777)

Although discrimination, association, and selection don't add structure that is not present in sensations or derivable by extrapolation, these activities are needed to make complex spatial structures manifest.

Consider, in this regard, James's rejection of the Kantian claim that intuited space is one, infinite extent (PP 1890, 905). James simply denied that we intuit the one space directly. According to him, the one space must be achieved through two stages of cognitive activity. These are, first, spatial perception, which introduces subdivisions, ordered parts, and experienced relations, including potential spaces that extend out from locally intuited space. This is a matter of bringing out or extrapolating from relations present in sensations. There results a finite system of perceived spaces that are locally unified and potentially all inter-connected. The second stage in attaining a unified spatial world is to construct an infinite space, which is a conceptual achievement.

Spatial Perception and the Construction of Real Space

Sensations and perceptions are both as of an external reality. Sensations are "simpler." The object of an early visual sensation is the entire ill-apprehended but concrete volumetric visual space with intrinsic but as yet unappreciated spatial structure (PP 1890, 657–658, 777; PBC 1892, 20–21). Such sensations cannot be had in their pure form by a visually experienced adult (reminiscent of Helmholtz's assertion about atomic sensations). But an adult can approach pure sensations through acts of abstraction and special attention (examples to come).

Perceptions arise because, as a result of sensory experience, physiological processes become associated with a given pattern of stimulation. After a period of development, "[a]ny quality of a thing which affects our sense-organs does also more than that: it arouses processes in the hemispheres which are due to the organization of that organ by past experiences, and the results of which in consciousness are commonly described as ideas which the sensation suggests" (PP 1890, 722). This past experience includes associations, habits, and memories. These lead the mature perceiver to see concrete individual things, such as tables and chairs within a room, at a distance and with their "proper" sizes and shapes (PP 1890, 723, 816–817). Because visual sensations simply give us colors arrayed in a volumetric space, perception of particular things arises from the effects of past experience on the brain, effects which are implicated in the current sensory mental state. Accordingly: "Every perception is an acquired perception" (PP 1890, 724).

The current perceptual state is, however, not determined solely by sensory stimulation and previous experience; we also actively engage present sensations and perceptions. This activity includes the marking of subdivisions, the positing of further space beyond the present one, the noting of relations, and the awareness of the sizes, shapes, and relative distances of things.

Both previous experience and active discrimination are present in a summary list, from the *Briefer Course*, of what is needed for the construction of "real" perceptual space:

> First, the total object of vision or of feeling at any time *must have smaller objects definitely discriminated within it*;
> Secondly, *objects seen or tasted must be identified with objects felt, heard*, etc., and *vice versa*, so that *the same "thing"* may come to be recognized, although apprehended in such widely differing ways;
> Third, the total extent felt at any time must be conceived as *definitely located in the midst of the surrounding extents of which the world consists*;
> Fourth, these objects *must appear arranged in definite order* in the so-called three dimensions; and
> Fifth, their relative sizes must be perceived—in other words, *they must be measured*.
> (PBC 1892, 294–295)

Let us consider each point.

The discrimination of spatial parts is done actively, heavily involving attention (see PP 1890, chs. 11, 13; PBR 1892, ch. 15). In apprehending the orientation of a line segment, we become aware of the relation between the two ends, as manifest in sensation to discriminating attention. Two line segments, each joined with the extremity of a horizontal line segment, when intersecting in a point, "give us the peculiar sensation of triangularity" (PP 1890, 791). The process of discrimination and division is fundamental to finding structure in our volumetric sensations and engendering spatial perceptions: "The bringing of subdivisions to consciousness constitutes, then, the entire process by which we pass from our first vague feeling of a total vastness to a cognition of the vastness in detail" (PP 1890, 793), that is, to perceived spatial extents replete with order and relation.

Second, properties are grouped together spatially and ascribed to one thing located in a common space. As James explained, some of these properties are considered "essential," or as stable properties that belong to this individual or this kind of thing, some as "accidental": in the perception of a library table, its rectilinear shape, its color, and its heaviness are considered essential, but its trapezoidal appearance from a certain vantage point is taken as accidental and ephemeral (PP 1890, 724, 821; also PBC 1892, 295–296).[18] Already with heaviness we have the conjoining of a tactile property with a visual property (the brown rectangle), in a unified space.

The third point is quite important. Throughout the *Principles*, James railed against the notion that spatial perceptions are composed of elemental aspatial sensations. But he did not deny that the spatial world of experience can be and is composed out of smaller spaces. In learning to apprehend a current scene, a child learns to link one region with another, as alongside each other.[19] These adjoining regions are apprehended as permitting movement through them. From these linked adjoining spatial regions, we abstract away from other properties of things to apprehend "mere extents," thereby obtaining the notion of "empty space" as that through which we can move freely (PBC 1892, 296–297; PP 1890, 822–825). This leads to the fourth point, that through eye movements, hand movements, and other limb movements, we map out a set of locations in relation to our bodies and sense organs and consequently in relation to the things that we touch or see.[20] This order includes the third dimension.

Finally, James took up the relative sizes (and the shapes) of things. Measurement involves bringing extents into relation with one another, while accepting one extent as a standard unit (PP 1890, 815–818). We do not measure something merely by running our hand down its length; we need to compare it to a standard (which could be our hand, used as a unit measure for comparison).[21] These extents do not originally occupy a unified metric space. Rather, the same object or spatial gap may produce a larger or smaller felt volume, depending on circumstances and sense modality. If the perceived extents of the same thing differ in some way, one is chosen as the "true standard." A favorite Jamesian example is the gap formed by an extracted tooth, which feels larger to the tongue than to the fingertip (or the eye). Here, the fingertip takes precedence. A similar process occurs with size and shape. When the same object is nearer or farther, the size of its retinal image varies inversely with distance. But we don't perceive the size of the object as varying with the retinal image or the sensation it would produce: "As I look along the dining-table I overlook the fact that the farther plates and glasses *feel* so much smaller than my own, for I *know* that they are all equal in size; and the feeling of them, which is a present sensation, is eclipsed in the glare of the knowledge, which is a merely imagined one" (PBC 1892, 299–300; repeated from PP 1890, 817–818). We *perceive* the distant plate as of the same size as one close by, and we perceive it to be circular rather than elliptical (the shape projected on the retina by a plate not seen from directly above), because knowledge of its true size and shape has informed our perception, eliding the smaller, elliptical sensation. James explains what is now called "perceptual constancy" not through unconscious inferences, as others (such as Helmholtz and the early Wundt) did, but as a product of discernment and choice. We accept that the appearance of the plate in an optimal viewing position reveals its true size and shape. That size and shape then constitutes our perception on other occasions. We take this perceptual experience to present the object as it is, as opposed to how it merely looks (PBC 1892, 300–301; PP 1890, 816–818, 869–871).

For James, perception typically involves conception. Perception focuses on aspects of a scene that have been conceptualized and, in the human case, for which we have names.[22] In the earlier chapter on attention, James explained how we more easily "see" the things for which we have names, as well as properties that have been drawn to our attention. James is talking about the phenomenology of sensory-perceptual tasks. I read him as saying that what we perceive is heavily influenced by attentional acts, so that perception is a product of the interaction among sensory stimulation, past experience, and current modes of attention and discrimination. He offered this charming example:

> In kindergarten-instruction one of the exercises is to make the children see how many features they can point out in such an object as a flower or a stuffed bird. They readily name the features they know already, such as leaves, tail, bill, feet. But they may look for hours without distinguishing nostrils, claws, scales, etc., until their attention is called to these details; thereafter, however, they see them every time. In short, *the only things which we commonly see are those which we preperceive*, and the only things which we preperceive are those which have been labelled for us, and the labels stamped into our mind. (PP 1890, 420)

Here, the effect of attention, guided by conceptualization (classifications such as leaves, tail, bill), is that we become better perceivers. But the effects are not merely postperceptual. By calling the attentional factors "preperceptual," James is allowing that they condition perception itself (on preperception and on attention more generally, see Prinz, this volume).

In James's view, the normal perceptual effects of experience, conception, and attentional training enrich, but ultimately elide, bare sensations. We have learned that "pure sensations" are impossible for an adult. But, as it turns out, in relation to constancy phenomena, James allows that we can recover relatively bare (not totally pure) sensations. A case in point: artists may be enjoined to draw what they see, not what they know is there, and so to approach bare sensations.

> Even where the sensation is not merely subjective, . . . we are also liable, as Reid says, to overlook its intrinsic quality and attend exclusively to the image of the "thing" it suggests. But here everyone *can* easily notice the sensation itself if he will. Usually we see a sheet of paper as uniformly white, although a part of it may be in shadow. But we can in an instant, if we please, notice the shadow as local color. A man walking towards us does not usually seem to alter his size; but we can, by setting our attention in a peculiar way, make him appear to do so. The

whole education of the artist consists in his learning to see the presented signs as well as the represented things. No matter what the field of view *means*, he sees it also as it *feels*—that is, as a collection of patches of color bounded by lines—the whole forming an optical diagram of whose intrinsic proportions one who is not an artist has hardly a conscious inkling. The ordinary man's attention passes *over* them to their import; the artist's turns back and dwells *upon* them for their own sake. (PP 1890, 874–875; see also EPs 1879, 79)

Prior to training, the artist sees the approaching person to be of constant size.[23] She sees the paper as white. In another example (PP 1890, 225–226; PBC 1892, 142), looking out the window, one sees the grass as uniformly green, whether in shade or sun. But the artist, and indeed we with appropriate effort, can see the paper as darker in shadow, the man as in some sense smaller in the distance, and the grass as being matched, in accessible sensory appearance ("sensation"), by paint that is brownish for the portion in shade and yellowish in full sun.

Presumably, James thinks that this sort of access to sensation can help sustain his claims (as an adult psychologist) about sensations, such as the voluminousness of all sensations. Interestingly, as we have seen, he does not regard the phenomenal "switch" to felt sensations as revealing how things "really look" or what we "really" perceive; rather, he classifies such sensation-based perceptions as "illusory" (PBC 1892, 298; PP 1890, 816), or as mere signs that point toward a more stable (perceptually constant) reality (PP 1890, 869–872). Relatively bare sensations are only sometimes manifest as components of perceptions (for instance, as underlying spatiality itself); often, sensations act as signs or prompts that call forth a different and dominant perceptual image (see PP 1890, 654). It seems that, in most cases of adult perception, the physiological aspects of the sensations are present (the sensory stimulation), without directly entering consciousness; these processes, together with neural products of previous learning, produce the normal perceptual image in consciousness.[24] These perceptual images are environmentally directed, as befits his conception of psychology as describing not only sensory perceptual experience, but perceptual experience as of an environment to which we adapt.

Spatial Conception

James asked how a perceiver who starts from a "blooming, buzzing" spatial confusion, a spatial "chaos" (PBC 1892, 21; PP 1890, 821), could come to perceive an orderly space. We have seen one answer in the construction of a connected visual space, which opens a connected spatial environment for us.

James gave a large role to conception in perceptual development. Suppose one is looking at objects A B C, and swings the focus of vision rightward just beyond C. Now the field includes C D E. To see A and B again, we must move the gaze to the left, losing D and E. James's idea, foreshadowed earlier, is that we come to conceive A B C D E as spatially ordered "in a space larger than that which any one sensation brings" (PP 1890, 822).

> This larger space, however, is an object of conception rather than of direct intuition, and bears all the marks of being constructed piecemeal by the mind. The blind man forms it out of tactile, locomotor, and auditory experiences, the seeing man out of visual ones almost exclusively. (PP 1890, 822)

Even though this locally ordered space cannot be intuited all at once, it is part of perception.[25] We experience a perceptual "fringe" of surrounding space. Suppose we focus on B C D. Then A might be present in a fringe on the left, E on the right. In this training, we use the persisting identity of the same "things" or objects (A, etc.) as landmarks. But we then are able to expand on this concrete situation so as to experience the local environment as embracing a spatial terrain in which we can move about.[26] In our current perception of a spatial arena, this potential space-to-be-entered exists, in the proximate neighborhood, as the fringe of our perceptual state. Accordingly, the notion, introduced in the subsection Spatial Sensation and Perception, that perception differs from thought in being supported by sensory nerve currents, must be liberally interpreted to allow that past experience and conception-based attention also contribute to present perceptual content. But there are limits. When our current mental state is extended to foresee a trip out of the house and into the park, perhaps it becomes a matter of mere conception and imagination, rather than sense perception.

The recognition, locally, that perceived space extends beyond our literal optical field of view, together with our learning the larger layout of environments (as held in memory and imagination), might be adequate for many purposes. But James allowed that we have the conception of a "consolidated, unitary continuum" (PP 1890, 819). Indeed, some thinkers conceive of a single space that encompasses the entire universe. We've seen that Kant spoke of such a unitary space. James described Kant as holding that "there are not *spaces*, but *Space*—one infinite continuous *Unit*—and that our knowledge of *this* cannot be a piecemeal sensational affair, produced by summation and abstraction" (PP 1890, 905). He responded:

> the obvious reply is that, if any known thing bears on its front the *appearance* of piecemeal construction and abstraction, it is this very notion of the infinite unitary space of the world. It is a *notion*, if ever there was one; and no intuition. Most of us apprehend it in the barest symbolic abridgment: and if perchance we ever do try to make it more adequate, we just add one image of sensible extension to another until we are tired. (PP 1890, 905)

The one unitary space transcends perception. Even an imaginary construction will not display the infinite space. We are left with the possibility of always adding another image to our picture of cosmic space.[27]

James, Space, and Psychology

In examining James on space (in the *Principles*), we have considered his arguments against atomistic accounts and sampled aspects of his own holistic, nativistic account. James himself predicted that his efforts to undermine the atomistic approach and its unconscious acts of synthesis would not fully succeed (PP 1890, 176–177). And indeed, the atomistic approach might seem even now to be alive and well, in some invocations of tuned receptor cells, such as edge detectors or motion detectors, and their compounding (Barlow 1995; but see Yuste 2015). His nativism also has not become ubiquitous, but it is no longer clearly in second place. The tide is rising in favor of innate spatial perception in three dimensions (Palmer 1999, 249–253).

James's phenomenological holism also has had a mixed reception. The Gestalt psychologist Wolfgang Köhler (1947, 249) appreciated James's anti-atomism and approved his notion of the fringe (without using the term). But he found James to be "unaware" of the concept of organization (Köhler 1947, 339). Curiously, there has been little response to James's insightful discussion of a "figured" dimension of experience, which includes elements comparable to Gestalt organization and a Gestalt switch (PP 1890, 728–729, also 885–888; PBC 1892, 276–277). James's perceptive phenomenology, as exemplified especially in his descriptions of the stream of consciousness, remains legendary.

Finally, James advanced psychology by focusing on the adjustment of the organism to the environment (see also Pearce, this volume). He intended psychology to be environmentally embedded. In spatial perception, his careful phenomenal descriptions promoted this cause. In particular, his notion of a spatial "fringe," which extends beyond what "any one sensation brings" (PP 1890, 822), that is, beyond the momentary retinal image, is of interest. It played into the Phenomenological tradition in philosophy (see Moran 2017). It has kinship with James Gibson's (1950) "visual world," which extends perceived space beyond the current field of vision. This aspect of James's theory especially reveals his conception of perception as cognitively active through focused attention and also as guiding action and incorporating the effects of motion. Like the later Gibson (1966, 1979), James linked spatial vision with the potential for motion, and he emphasized the importance of organism–environment relations (on James and Gibson, see Heft 2001). Again like Gibson, he displaced sensations as the primary object of perception in favor of the world itself; for James, this was the world as revealed through sensory input and active processes of discernment and construction—a conception too mentalistic for Gibson, but perhaps needed. Accordingly, the aim of spatial perception, as with much of cognition more generally, is to connect us with the surrounding environment and its potentialities. Recent philosophy and psychology have been catching up to James's insight.

Notes

1. James knew Bain's work well. In 1878–1879, he used Bain's *The Senses and the Intellect* and *The Emotions and the Will* (the third editions, 1868, 1875) as textbooks in his undergraduate class on Psychology, listed under Philosophy (Sever 1878, 9). He again used Bain (1868) in a course on logic in 1887–1888 (Harvard 1886, 16; PP 1890, 1301). In focusing on Bain, I don't assume that he speaks precisely for the others.
2. Bain (1868, 365): "when we add the Active or Muscular sensibility of the eye, we obtain new products. The sweep of the eye over the coloured field gives a feeling of a definite amount of *action*, an exercise of internal power, which is something totally different from the passive feeling of light." The feeling of action is not itself spatial, but becomes so when associated with movements of the whole body and with sensations of touch, these being the root source for the "feeling of linear extension" in every direction (95–96). See also (183): actively moving the hand over a surface yields the experience of "co-existence in *space*"; and (234–235).
3. Bain repeated this conclusion in the fourth edition, where he noted James's preference for nativism, conceded that the facts at present could not decide between the positions, and allowed for an (undeveloped) partial nativism, while continuing to reject the Kantian view (1894, 332, 394–398).
4. James allowed a quotation from Arthur Schopenhauer to represent Kant's position: "Our Intellect, antecedently to all experience, must bear in itself the intuitions of Space and Time" (PP 1890, 904), a description that attributes the forms to the intellect as opposed to the faculty of sensibility. On Kant's distinction between sensibility and understanding and his view that space is a form of intuition, see Höffe (1994, 54–59).
5. Herbart's associationism is discussed anon. The early Wundt held that the psychical synthesis that forms a spatial representation was a logical act (1862, 441–445); he subsequently rejected this position in favor of an associative account (1880–1883, 1.458; 1894, 142; 1902, 248–249). Helmholtz may be grouped with the associationists despite his use of the term "inference," because he gave an associative account of the inferential processes themselves (Hatfield 1990, ch. 5.3.2).
6. In "The Psychological Theory of Extension" (EPs 1889, 239), James acknowledged that Brown, Bain, Spencer, and Mill had intended their accounts to provide a positive explanation of the genesis of spatial appearances from association operating on aspatial sensations; in "The Original Datum of Space-Consciousness" (EPs 1893, 294), he repeated his claim that their accounts fail (in this instance, leaving them with mere temporal sequence, as in the first type of theory).
7. James (PP 1890, 906) summarized Herbart's position, before editorializing: "Herbart, whose influence has been widest, says 'the resting eye sees no space,' and ascribes visual extension to the influence of movements combining with the non-spatial retinal feelings so as to form gradated series of the latter. A given sensation of such a series reproduces the idea of its associates in regular order, and its idea is similarly reproduced by any one of them with the order reversed. Out of the fusion of these two contrasted reproductions comes the form of space—Heaven knows how." On Herbart and spatial genesis, see Hatfield (1990, 123–127).
8. James used "mental chemistry" also in relation to Wundt: "With the 'mental chemistry' of which the Mills speak—precisely the same thing as the 'psychical synthesis' of Wundt, which, as we shall soon see, is a principle expressly intended to do what Association can never perform—they hold the third view, but again in other places imply the first"

(PP 1890, 902). James cited Wundt (1880–1883, 1.459) using the chemical analogy; see also Wundt (1874, 484–485, 639–640; 1902, 33). I separate these associationist accounts from Kant's form of intuition, since they rely on productive association; the associationists would accept this distinction (with Helmholtz equivocating in 1878/1974, 124).

9. Helmholtz organized the third part of his *Handbuch* (on perception) around the nativist–empirist divide (1924–1925, §§26, 33); the conflict was oft-discussed (e.g., Ladd 1887, 389–392; Wundt 1880–1883, 1.452–460).

10. As previously noted, the quoted passage does not respect Kant's distinction between sensibility and intellect. But James's refutation does not require the posited supra-sensational processes of the Kantians to be intellectual; the refutation would be as effective (or ineffective) if the processes were associational or belonged to the faculty of productive imagination (the ability to form images).

11. In 1867–1868, while in Germany, James hoped to study scientific psychology in Heidelberg with Helmholtz and Wundt (letter to Thomas W. Ward, CWJ 1867, 4.226); but he left the city soon after arriving, most likely without seeing either man (Gundlach 2017). Perry (1935, 2.55) indicates that, in the *Principles*, James made the "largest use," among the "psychologists" of his day, of writings by Spencer, Helmholtz, Wundt, and Bain. On James's life and works, see Leary (2018, ch. 1).

12. This doctrine of one fiber yielding one sensation (perhaps with multiple dimensions of variation: as when retinal fibers yield both a qualitive "local sign" and a color sensation) was widely accepted in the nineteenth century, including by Helmholtz (Hatfield 1990, 157, 172). James characterized this physiological assumption as initially plausible but ultimately unsustainable (PP 1890, 88–89, 176–179; PBC 1892, 396–397). The mature Wundt (1874 and later) did not accept the one-fiber doctrine or psychical atoms as object-like (1874, 231; 1902, 15; 1902–1903, 1.327–328); he accepted elemental sensations, conceived as processes.

13. James gives as an example the contention that "what seems like one feeling, of blueness for example, or of hatred, may really and 'unconsciously' be ten thousand elementary feelings," a view he considered "unintelligible," since it makes one mental state into two things: an unnoticed synthesis of ten thousand elements and the awareness of a single, unified patch of blue (PP 1890, 176). For additional anti-atomistic arguments in James, empirically based, see Klein (2009, 433–438); on James's denial of unconscious mental states, Klein (2020, secs. 4–5).

14. James listed the same three possible kinds of theories, including two atomistic positions (associative and Kantian), variously occupied by Wundt, Helmholtz, Lotze, Mill, Bain, and Spencer (EPs 1879, 80–81). Klein (2009) shows that James's encounter with T. H. Green's criticism of Humean mental atomism was also in the background.

15. Leary (2018, 14) contrasts James's starting from brain functions with (initially unnamed) "psychologies written in the old manner." Subsequently (294), he notes that James's *Psychology: Briefer Course* (PBC 1892) ousted textbooks by Bowne (1886), Dewey (1886), McCosh (1886), and the "more scientific" Ladd (1887). These displaced textbooks do not sustain Leary's claim. First, the *Briefer Course* moved the chapter on brain function to eighth place, in order to compete with other "introductory" texts (PBC 1892, 2). Second, other works that James knew well and that were of the same kind as the *Principles*—that is, major synthetic treatments of psychology—regularly began with the brain: Bain's (1855, 1868) first substantive chapter was on the nervous system; Spencer (1870–1872) started with the nervous system; also, Wundt (1874). Ladd (1887) began with nine chapters on the nervous system. James (PP 1890) was following standard practice.

16. James (PP 1890, 690) treats imagination as closely tied to sense perception.
17. James held that because the entire brain state is (most likely) never exactly the same, we never enter the same total mental state twice, nor repeat the same sensation (PP 1890, 224–230; PBC 1892, 141–142). If this seems implausible, assume that James did not require differences in the total mental state to be noticed. Also, we can have the same object twice, since the presentation of an object need not be mentally identical to another presentation of the same object, as in seeing Memorial Hall from different vantage points.
18. The trapezoidal appearance is gained by an act of abstraction or special attention (more anon).
19. Myers ("Introduction," PP 1890, xxv), notes that James, later in life, changed his position to allow that some mental states are essentially "compounded of smaller psychic units." He cites James saying some fields of consciousness are "made of simpler 'parts'" (PU 1909, 83, n. 3); close by, James himself cites an 1895 article, "The Knowing of Things Together" (EPh), as allowing psychical compounding. But James (PU 1909) did not say that all fields of consciousness are made of parts, and in the cited article he described spatial extents as not originally composable from parts but as requiring an "original extensity" (EPh 1895, 77, n. 6). As we are seeing, in the *Principles* and *Briefer Course* James already allowed compounding or joining of spatial extents. Myers's discussion concerns the effect of James's later neutral monism on his acceptance of compounding, a topic beyond our present scope.
20. Nineteenth-century physiology examined in detail the role of eye movements in the development of spatial vision, some emphasizing the motor commands to the eye, others the feelings of muscle contraction (Hatfield 1990, chs. 4–5). James was not convinced that either is directly sensed with sufficient accuracy to underlie space perception; instead, he attributed the feeling of limb-location to sensors in the joints (PP 1890, 826–838). At the same time, James did attribute the ability to move sense organs and limbs a large role in the development of spatial perception, as when our movements lead to new patterns of tactile or retinal sensations (833).
21. Jubin (1977) argues that James's "Spatial Quale" (EPs 1879) and *Principles* differ, with the earlier work granting a larger role to the intellect in apprehending quantitative spatial relations, whereas I find similar positions in the two. Both allow that relations of measurement involving quantity are not intrinsically spatial. "More" applies to intensities and other things that admit of degree, such as ambition (EPs 1879, 63). Jubin (1977, 214) finds James using this point to classify spatial relations as "intellectual." But this seems no greater a role for intellect than the "weaving" described in the previous subsection of this paper, as applied to spatial relations; intellect, or the discriminating power, notices relations. And in the *Principles* (PP 1890, 772), "muchness" and "littleness" are applied to spatial properties and to "times, numbers, intensities" and other qualities. Both works deny that intellectual (or associative) processes are themselves generative of spatial content, as opposed to operating on spatial content given in sensation. The chapter affirms: "it follows, for aught we can as yet see to the contrary, that *all spatial knowledge is sensational at bottom*, and that, as the sensations lie together in the unity of consciousness, no new material element whatever comes to them from a supra-sensible source" (793); compare (EPs 1879, 79): "underneath" various objective spatial constructions, "the subjective sensation itself persists, with all its parts, alongside each other, in the full spatial collaterality which nativists claim for them" (see also 80–81).
22. Recall that perception requires current sensory stimulation; other cases involving conception, such as thinking about a type of bird, rely on memory and imagination for their content, rather than current sensory perception (PP 1890, 652; PBC 1892, 19–20).

23. James does not make perceived size depend on perceived distance, as do other accounts, both older, including Descartes (Hatfield 1990, 292, n. 44), and newer (Palmer 1999, 315–318). Accordingly, his account of distance perception (PP 1890, 846–850) is only loosely related to his account of size perception.
24. In discussing sensations as signs that are eclipsed by a more "constant" perception, James comes close to allowing unnoticed phenomenal sensations that evoke perception. He struggled with this issue, and seems to have come to the position outlined in this paragraph (PP 1890, 850–853, 868–898).
25. Myers's (1986, 122–128) objections to James on the formation of a unified perceptual space bring out some points of unclarity in James. Myers reads the preceding quotation as saying that what is constructed is merely conceived and so not really perceived (124). I find, on the contrary, that, even if the line between perception and mere conception is not sharp, conception is part of perception. Accordingly, James includes the "fringes" of a current space as a perceptual content. I find support in his account of the constancies, which describes the farther-away plates as experientially *perceived*; but it must be perception based in conception. Further support: the influence of past experience is what distinguishes perception from sensation (PP 1890, 652–653), bringing in further "facts" about the objects of perception, including quality instances that do not at the moment affect the sense organs, such as the back side of a table (722–724).
26. James is explicit on this point: "We can usually recover anything lost from sight by moving our attention and our eyes back in its direction; and through these constant changes every field of seen things comes at last to be thought of as always having a fringe of *other things possible to be seen* spreading in all directions round about it. Meanwhile the movements concomitantly with which the various fields alternate are also felt and remembered; and gradually (through association) this and that movement come in our thought to suggest this or that extent of fresh objects introduced. Gradually, too, since the objects vary indefinitely in kind, we abstract from their several natures and think separately of their mere extents, of which extents the various movements remain as the only constant introducers and associates. More and more, therefore, do we think of movement and seen extent as mutually involving each other, until at last (with Bain and J. S. Mill) we may get to regard them as synonymous, and say, 'What is the meaning of the word extent, unless it be possible movement?'" (PP 1890, 823). Of course, unlike Bain, whom he cites nearby, he does not attribute the origin of spatial content (original voluminousness) to the possibility of movement.
27. James analyzed the ideas of geometrical objects (such as lines, planes, and parallels) in terms of "serial increase": "The farther continuations of these forms, we say, *shall* bear the same relation to their last visible parts which these did to still earlier parts" (PP 1890, 1251). Of course, Kant did not claim to hold in intuition an actually infinite space (although he did consider space to be singular); but that's another matter.

Bibliography

Bain, Alexander. 1855. *The Senses and the Intellect*. London: Parker.
Bain, Alexander. 1868. *The Senses and the Intellect*, 3d ed. London: Longmans, Green.
Bain, Alexander. 1875. *The Emotions and the Will*, 3d ed. London: Longmans, Green.
Bain, Alexander. 1894. *The Senses and the Intellect*, 4th ed. London: Longmans, Green.

Barlow, Horace. 1995. "The Neuron Doctrine in Perception." In *The Cognitive Neurosciences*, edited by Michael S. Gazzaniga, 415–435. Cambridge, MA: MIT Press.

Bowne, Borden P. 1886. *Introduction to Psychological Theory*. New York: Harper.

Dewey, John. 1886. *Psychology*. New York: Harper.

Gibson, James J. 1950. *The Perception of the Visual World*. Boston: Houghton Mifflin.

Gibson, James J. 1966. *The Senses Considered as Perceptual Systems*. Boston: Houghton Mifflin.

Gibson, James J. 1979. *The Ecological Approach to Visual Perception*. Boston: Houghton Mifflin.

Gundlach, Horst. 2017. "William James and the Heidelberg Fiasco." *Journal of Psychology and Cognition* 2: 44–60.

Harvard University. 1886. *Announcement of Courses Provided by the Faculty of Harvard College*. Cambridge, MA: Harvard University.

Hatfield, Gary. 1990. *The Natural and the Normative: Theories of Spatial Perception from Kant to Helmholtz*. Cambridge, MA: MIT Press.

Hatfield, Gary, and William Epstein. 1979. "The Sensory Core and the Medieval Foundations of Early Modern Perceptual Theory." *Isis* 70: 363–384.

Heft, Harry. 2001. *Ecological Psychology in Context: James Gibson, Roger Barker, and the Legacy of William James's Radical Empiricism*. Mahwah, NJ: Erlbaum.

Helmholtz, Hermann. 1924–1925. *Treatise on Physiological Optics*. Trans. James P. C. Southall, 3 vols. Rochester, NY: Optical Society of America. Originally published as *Handbuch der physiologischen Optik* (Leipzig: Voss, 1867).

Helmholtz, Hermann. 1974. "The Facts in Perception." In Helmholtz, *Epistemological Writings*, translated by Malcome F. Lowe, 115–185. Dordrecht, Reidel. Originally published as *Die Tatsachen in der Wahrnehmung* (Berlin, 1878).

Höffe, Otfried. 1994. *Immanuel Kant*. Trans. Marshall Farrier. Albany: State University of New York Press.

Jubin, Brenda. 1977. "'The Spatial Quale': A Corrective to James's Radical Empiricism." *Journal of the History of Philosophy* 15: 212–216.

Klein, Alexander. 2009. "On Hume on Space: Green's Attack, James' Empirical Response." *Journal of the History of Philosophy* 47: 415–449.

Klein, Alexander. 2020. "The Death of Consciousness? James's Case Against Psychological Unobservables." *Journal of the History of Philosophy* 58: 293–323.

Köhler, Wolfgang. 1947. *Gestalt Psychology: An Introduction to New Concepts in Modern Psychology*. New York: Liveright.

Ladd, George Trumbull. 1887. *Elements of Physiological Psychology*. New York: C. Scribner's Sons.

Leary, David E. 2018. *The Routledge Guidebook to James's Principles of Psychology*. London: Routledge.

McCosh, James. 1886. *Psychology: The Cognitive Powers*. New York: C. Scribner's Sons.

Mill, James. 1869. *Analysis of the Phenomena of the Human Mind*. Ed. John Stuart Mill. London: Longmans, Green, Reader, and Dyer.

Mill, John Stuart. 1865. *An Examination of Sir William Hamilton's Philosophy*. London: Longman, Green, Longman, Roberts, and Green.

Moran, Dermot. 2017. "Phenomenology and Pragmatism: Two Interactions. From Horizontal Intentionality to Practical Coping." In *Pragmatism and the European Traditions: Encounters with Analytic Philosophy and Phenomenology Before the Great Divide*, edited by Maria Baghramian and Sarin Marchetti, 272–293. New York and London: Routledge.

Myers, Gerald E. 1986. *William James: His Life and Thought*. New Haven, CT: Yale University Press.

Palmer, Stephen E. 1999. *Vision Science: Photons to Phenomenology.* Cambridge, MA: MIT Press.

Perry, Ralph Barton. 1935. *The Thought and Character of William James,* 2 vols. Boston: Little, Brown.

Sever, Charles W., ed. 1878. *Harvard University, 1878-79: Courses of Study in Harvard College.* Cambridge, MA: Charles W. Sever, bookseller.

Spencer, Herbert. 1870-1872. *Principles of Psychology,* 2nd ed., 2 vols. London: Williams and Norgate.

Wundt, Wilhelm. 1862. *Beiträge zur Theorie der Sinneswahrnehmung.* Leipzig: Winter.

Wundt, Wilhelm. 1874. *Grundzüge der physiologischen Psychologie.* Leipzig: Engelmann.

Wundt, Wilhelm. 1880-1883. *Logik: Eine Untersuchung der Prinzipien der Erkenntnis und der Methoden wissenschaftlicher Forschung,* 2 vols. Stuttgart: Enke.

Wundt, Wilhelm. 1894. *Lectures on Human and Animal Psychology.* Trans. J. E. Creighton and E. B. Titchener. London: Sonnenschein.

Wundt, Wilhelm. 1902. *Outlines of Psychology,* 2nd ed. Trans. Charles H. Judd. Leipzig: Engelmann.

Wundt, Wilhelm. 1902-1903. *Grundzüge der physiologischen Psychologie,* 5th ed., 4 vols. Leipzig: Engelmann.

Yuste, Rafael. 2015. "From the Neuron Doctrine to Neural Networks." *Nature Reviews Neuroscience* 16: 487-497.

CHAPTER 4

JAMES AND CONSCIOUSNESS

ALEXANDER MUGAR KLEIN

Introduction

WILLIAM James offered an evolutionary-psychological account of phenomenal consciousness. In his view, consciousness enables the active evaluation of what is in (or might be in) one's environment. James hypothesized that this evaluative capacity was selected (in the Darwinian sense) because it "regulated" (ECR 1875, 303; PP 1890, 147) the behavior of creatures with highly articulated brains.

James's work on consciousness is substantively interesting in that he offers us a well-developed alternative to more familiar, naturalistic accounts available today. But his work is also methodologically interesting in that he did not develop, and did not intend to develop, what contemporary philosophers of mind are often seeking: a direct explanation of first-person conscious experience. He did not try to deduce the existence or nature of consciousness from another set of facts—he did not, that is, treat consciousness itself as an *explanandum*.[1] In fact, James regarded as perniciously metaphysical what we now call the "hard problem" of explaining why *this* brain state produces a conscious experience with *that* kind of qualitative feel.[2]

Instead, what he sought to explain was a set of results in experimental physiology concerning apparently purposive behavior in, of all things, live decapitated frogs. These results were hotly debated in his day, and James thought them puzzling from an evolutionary-biological standpoint specifically. Thus, he did not offer a direct proof of his hypothesis about consciousness; instead, he (abductively) recommended the hypothesis because it would help explain an evolutionary puzzle about physiology. My aim in this chapter is to evaluate James's account of consciousness by showing how it would explain the physiological results he found puzzling.

The most important source for James's early, interactionist-dualist account of consciousness is a *Mind* essay entitled "Are We Automata?" (EPs 1879, 38–61).[3] The article represents the culmination of at least six years' reflection on the place of consciousness in nature, for James, starting with an unpublished 1872 essay in which he had actually defended epiphenomenalism.[4] By the time he wrote two important book reviews in 1874 and 1875, he seems to have reversed course, expressing sympathy for interactionism.[5] And in November of 1878, he offered an extensive defense of interactionism in a six-part lecture series at the Lowell Institute, entitled "The Brain and the Mind,"[6] the sixth installment of which would become "Are We Automata?"[7] My central concern will be with this latter essay, along with some physiological evidence James added to enrich his account in the 1890 *Principles of Psychology*.

In a letter to Shadworth Hodgson composed two months after he published "Are We Automata?" James wrote that this essay "was written against the swaggering dogmatism of certain medical materials [sic], good friends of mine, here and abroad. I wanted to show them how many empirical facts they had overlooked" (CWJ 1879, 5.44). In the second section, I will explore the vogue for epiphenomenalism against which James was reacting, along with some of the "empirical facts" mentioned in this letter, which were drawn largely from physiology. The third section reconstructs James's evolutionary hypothesis and offers a further examination of experimental results his account was meant to explain.[8] The fourth section briefly considers his Darwinian objection to epiphenomenalism.

A final caveat is in order. Although James would later claim that "consciousness," as the term is *normally* used, names a "nonentity" (ERE 1904, 3), I do not believe he ever backed away from the view that consciousness in this other sense *does* exist. Still, it is enough in the present chapter to focus on James's positive view of consciousness as he developed it in the earlier works just cited, from about 1872 to 1890. Consult Cooper (this volume) and Klein (2020) for examinations of how such a view squares with James's later "pure experience" metaphysics.

Epiphenomenalism and Physiology

Though James seems to have been the first to use the term "epiphenomenon" in its philosophical sense (PP 1890, 133, 139, 1186; see Robinson 2015), neither he nor his opponents used the word "epiphenomenal*ism*" in published work, typically employing the phrase "automaton theory" instead.[9] For convenience, I will use this latter phrase interchangeably with our more current "epiphenomenalism."

Hodgson characterized such a view as asserting that "states of consciousness are not produced by previous states of consciousness, but both are produced by the action of the brain" (Hodgson 1865, 278).[10] Huxley would offer a famous metaphor: like the relationship between the sound of a steam whistle and an engine, conscious states are always products of bodily states, but conscious states never in turn make a causal difference to bodily states, according to epiphenomenalism (Huxley 1874/1894, 240). This view portrays humans as automata in the sense that all behavior (indeed all bodily motion) is understood to be a mechanistic product of prior bodily states, with no causal intervention from consciousness. Consciousness thereby becomes "a simple passenger in the voyage of life," as James would put it, something "allowed to remain on board, but not to touch the helm or handle the rigging" (EPs 1879, 38).

Here is how James introduced the topic of epiphenomenalism in the 1879 piece:

> The theory itself is an inevitable consequence of the extension of the notion of reflex action to the higher nerve centres. Prof. Huxley starts from a decapitated frog which performs rational-seeming acts although probably it has no consciousness, and passing up to the hemispheres of man concludes that the rationality of their performances can owe nothing to the feelings that co-exist with it. This is the inverse of Mr. Lewes's procedure. He starts from the hemispheres, and finding their performances apparently guided by feeling concludes, when he comes to the spinal cord, that feeling though latent must still be there to make it act so rationally. Clearly such arguments as these may mutually eat each other up to all eternity. (EPs 1879, 39)

This is a curious passage—James portrayed the debate about epiphenomenalism as stemming from a controversy over decapitated frogs, a controversy that pitted Huxley against G. H. Lewes. Contending that their dispute had become stalemated, James went on to say he would adduce a set of "facts hitherto ignored in the discussion" which "wholly favors the efficacy of Consciousness" (EPs 1879, 40), a promise that resonates with the letter to Hodgson quoted earlier. But what do decapitated frogs have to do with epiphenomenalism?

James was referring to experiments on vertebrates that had been de-cerebrated in various ways, experiments that "occupied the attention of almost all physiologists who lived during the second half of the 19th century" (according to Fearing 1930/1964, 161).[11] Sometimes these animals were fully decapitated, and sometimes a more precise procedure called "pithing" was used (this is a technique in which experimentalists use a blunt needle to destroy a creature's brain in whole or in part, leaving the spinal cord intact; for a description, see Huxley 1872, 54–55). Physiologists pithed fish, birds, turtles, and dogs, but the common frog was the most popular vertebrate for this purpose (Fearing 1930/1964, 166).

One aim of such experiments was to get a grip on which brain structures enabled which specific behaviors. For instance, Huxley reported that the cerebellum is necessary for jumping, since frogs that are pithed below[12] this brain structure cannot jump (Huxley 1870, 3–4).

The preoccupation with these animals was not simply due to an interest in correlating brain structures with physiological capacity, though. In an 1853 book, Eduard Pflüger had reported a particularly controversial experiment on pithed frogs. It seemed to establish that pithed frogs exhibit *purposive behavior*, even when they have been pithed at the bottom of the brain stem.[13]

The experiment involved dripping acid on the knee of a living, decapitated frog (Pflüger 1853, 16). Such a frog reliably wipes the acid away, even though it lacks a brain. By itself, this result would not have been surprising—it was already well known that many vertebrates not only survive, but exhibit *reflex action* even after being decapitated, and the simple acid-dripping case seems but one such example.[14] What surprised

Pflüger's readers is what happens when one amputates whatever foot the decapitated frog habitually uses for wiping away the acid. If the acid-wiping behavior were a mere reflex performed non-consciously, one might expect the amputated frog to wave its stump around helplessly in response to the irritant. But that is not what happens.

The amputated frog actually chooses another limb to try to wipe the acid away. Or if a suitable foreign surface is nearby, the frog may maneuver its body to wipe the irritated skin against the surface. If one accepts such choosing-behavior as an instance of purposiveness, and if one thinks purposiveness is a mark of consciousness, then one can infer from this experiment that the decapitated frog is somehow conscious. This is just the sort of view one finds in Lewes, Pflüger's most visible British champion (e.g., Lewes 1877, 427–30).[15]

But Pflüger's experiment created a curious theoretical dilemma. If such purposive behavior is a mark of consciousness, then the brain cannot be the sole organ that gives rise to conscious experience (because the brainless frog apparently acts with purpose). This is Pflüger and Lewes's position—they argued that the *spinal cord* must also produce some measure of consciousness by itself (e.g., Pflüger 1853, 123–26; Lewes 1859; 1859–1860, vol. II, ch. ix, sec. 3; 1873). On the other hand, if purposive behavior is *not* a mark of consciousness (as critics like Huxley had contended), then the way is open for regarding conscious experience as epiphenomenal. For, suppose one assumes brainless frogs obviously *cannot* be conscious even though they still *seem* to act with purpose. It follows that purposiveness alone cannot establish conscious control of behavior even in *intact* vertebrates—indeed, even in intact humans (Huxley 1874/1894, 222–226).

But as the debate was then playing out, it turned on whether or not purposiveness was an acceptable mark of consciousness. And that was a question that had to be answered before one could interpret any of these experiments, it seemed, and thus was not a question the experiments themselves could settle (Klein 2018). This is the apparent stalemate to which James was referring in the "decapitated frog" passage reproduced above.

James's intervention in the debate worked like this. He rejected epiphenomenalism because he thought it highly implausible that consciousness could have evolved through any known mechanism if epiphenomenalism were true (as we shall see later, in the penultimate section of this chapter). But he also rejected the Lewes/Pflüger contention that de-cerebrated vertebrates were fully conscious. James's crucial insight was that although de-cerebrated vertebrates were in fact capable of purposive behavior, they differed from their cerebrated peers in a subtle way that suggested a lack of fully fledged consciousness: they were apparently unable to *evaluate*. I now turned to James's positive account.

James's Evolutionary Account

There is no one passage that lays out James's own explanation of the pithing results. But toward the end of "Are We Automata?" we get what comes close to a summary of his argument:

> We have found that the unaided action of the cerebral hemispheres would probably be random and capricious; that the nerve-process likely to lead to the animal's interests would not necessarily predominate at a given moment. On the other hand, we have found that an impartial consciousness is a nonentity, and that of the many items that ever occupy our mental stage Feeling always selects one as most congruous with the interests it has taken its stand upon. Collating these two results, an inference is unavoidable. The "items" on the mental stage are the subjective aspects of as many nerve-processes, and in emphasising the representations congruous with conscious interest and discouraging all others, may not Attention actually reinforce and inhibit the nerve-processes to which the representations severally correspond?
>
> This of course is but a hypothetical statement of the verdict of direct personal feeling.... (EPs 1879, 52)

James suggests we should be surprised that vertebrates with healthy cerebral hemispheres in fact behave in ways "likely to lead to the animal's interests." To explain this capacity for interested action, he makes what he characterizes as a "hypothetical statement"[16] or an abductive "inference": that consciousness (which always "selects" what accords with the animal's "interests") may steer the animal to behave in profitable ways by "reinforc[ing]" and "inhibit[ing]" mechanical brain processes. Two pages later he makes clear that he means to be offering an *adaptive* explanation, explicitly suggesting that consciousness likely had a positive survival value (EPs 1879, 54).

This passage does not give us James's entire account of consciousness, but it does suggest at least the general structure of his reasoning. If we are willing to fill in some gaps by looking outside of "Are We Automata?"—in particular, to his treatment of relevant physiological material in the *Principles*—then we find something like the following line in James:

1. Intact, healthy vertebrates are capable of "prudent" behaviors.
2. (1) is a surprising fact that demands an explanation, since *de*-cerebrated vertebrates are incapable of prudence.
3. Phenomenological Claim: consciousness typically involves engaging in a (nonphysical) process of evaluation.
4. Quasi-Mechanistic Hypothesis: phenomenal consciousness produces prudent behaviors *by* enabling evaluation.
5. Adaptive Hypothesis: phenomenal consciousness is an adaptation for producing prudent behavior.

As I unpack these steps in turn, I will offer textual bases for attributing each to James.

A word on the modal force of James's argument is immediately called for. James did not offer (and did not intend to offer) reasons for thinking his brand of interactionism is *necessarily* true. If my reading is roughly accurate, James's argument was fundamentally empirical—he was proposing a hypothesis for accounting for some surprising physiological observations, not offering conceptual reasons for thinking interactionism *must* be right. And as we will see in the penultimate section of this chapter, his attack on epiphenomenalism also was not purely conceptual—he did not take himself to have shown automaton theory to be incoherent, but rather empirically implausible.

Also, we will see that James's interactionism only does explanatory work in steps 4 and 5, where consciousness is part of the *explanans*, not the explanandum. Again, James is not explaining consciousness itself. He is suggesting that *if* a particular form of interactionist dualism were true, it *would* explain the surprising physiological results identified in step 1.

Step 1. Intact, Healthy Vertebrates Are Capable of "Prudent" Behaviors

Let us begin with this term "prudence." I draw the term from a passage in the *Principles* where James was fleshing out the notion of stable, profitable behavior. He wrote that "no animal without" cerebral hemispheres "can deliberate, pause, postpone, nicely weigh one motive against another, or compare. *Prudence*, in a word, is for such a creature an impossible virtue" (PP 1890, 33, my italics).

As James used the concept, genuinely *prudent* behavior has two components. First, it involves making choices of a robustly purposive cast (something Pflüger's frogs can do). And second, it involves making those choices by considering information other than what is directly presented by sensory stimuli at the time of choosing (something Pflüger's frogs *cannot* do). The debate over epiphenomenalism had largely relied on the first component as a mark of consciousness; one of James's key (albeit rarely noticed) innovations was the addition of the second. I will take each component in turn.

First, consider the faux, purposeless brand of "choice" a magnet might be said to make when it attracts iron but not brass filings (an example considered at James 1879, 8.n). The magnet's "choice" is produced by what James called a "*vis a tergo*," or a force from behind. The magnet happens to achieve some end, but only accidentally—only because of causal factors that determine its course of actions without anything like consideration of where those actions might lead.

In contrast, suppose one submerges a frog in water, and then traps it under a glass bell when it tries to surface. The frog "will not . . . perpetually press his nose against its unyielding roof, but will restlessly explore the neighborhood until by re-descending again he has discovered a path round its brim to the goal of his desires" (PP 1890, 20). The *frog's* end is achieved by what James called a "*vis a fronte*"—a force operating, so to speak, from the front. Unlike in the magnet case, there is an "ideal purpose presiding over the [frog's] activity from its outset and soliciting or drawing it into being" (PP 1890, 21). Thus James defined *vis a fronte* choosing as "*[t]he pursuance of future ends and the choice of means for their attainment*" (PP 1890, 21). One necessary component of prudent behavior is the exercising of *vis a fronte* choice—that is, the agent must be capable of trying different means to achieve an end she has in view.

But one more condition must be met as well. For James explicitly noted that decerebrated frogs often exhibit such *vis a fronte* choosing, as Pflüger had clearly established in his acid-drip experiment. Indeed, James noted that Goltz had shown something even more startling, that the task of escaping the inverted glass bell when emerging for air can also be performed by a de-cerebrated frog (PP 1890, 22).[17] So here is where we find James's distinctive intervention into the Huxley-Lewes debate. James contended that the capacity for *vis a fronte* choosing is necessary, but not sufficient, for the kind of prudence one only finds in vertebrates with intact cerebral hemispheres. Such prudence also involves a capacity to make choices that are not prompted by present sensory stimuli, he held, resting this second claim on a collection of pithing results I will now examine.[18]

As physiologists had become more adept at pithing, their awareness of which specific brain structures were responsible for which behaviors blossomed. Figure 4.1 gives a schematic diagram of a frog's brain from the era, along with a description of what behaviors are lost when each structure is knocked out through pithing.

What is most important for James's account of consciousness is what happens when the cut is made just below the cerebral hemispheres. In such cases, "an unpractised observer" might fail to notice anything unusual in the animal. A de-cerebrated frog can react to *present* stimuli largely in the way an intact frog reacts. It can even exhibit *vis a fronte* choice, e.g., managing to navigate by sight around obstacles, as Goltz (1869, 65) had shown. But what a de-cerebrated frog typically does *not* do, crucially, is *initiate* any genuine behavior that is not incited by some sensory stimulus.

Thus Goltz's de-cerebrated frog moves reflexively toward a light source, even hopping around a book placed in its path. But in this case the light source acts as a stimulus. Without any such sensory incitement, the frog will simply sit, noiseless and motionless. James saw the de-cerebrated frog's quiescence as evidence of an inability to consider anything but what is directly presented in sensation.

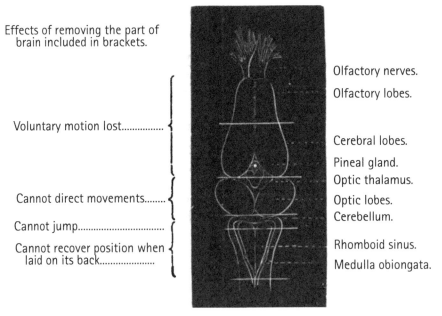

FIGURE 4.1. Diagram of a frog brain, with a summary of the effects of removing various structures (adapted from Brunton 1898, 227).

James offered an example to help crystalize his point about this second requirement for prudence:

> If I step aside on seeing a rattlesnake, from considering how dangerous an animal he is, the mental materials which constitute my prudential reflection are images more or less vivid of the movement of his head, of a sudden pain in my leg, of a state of terror, a swelling of the limb, a chill, delirium, unconsciousness, etc., etc., and the ruin of my hopes. But all these images are constructed out of my past experiences. They are *reproductions* of what I have felt or witnessed. They are, in short, *remote sensations*; and the *difference between the hemisphereless animal and the whole one* may be concisely expressed by saying that the *one obeys absent, the other only present, objects*. (PP 1890, 32; original italics)

This example of what James here calls "prudential reflection" is construed in terms of a special *kind* of *vis a fronte* choice, one that specifically employs *remembered*, and not merely presented, stimuli. It is not a choice between two presented objects, but a choice made partly by considering "absent" (remembered) objects. This capacity to consider absent objects is the second component of the sort of prudence James thought was distinctive to vertebrates with intact cerebral hemispheres.[19]

Now the word "prudence" did not appear in "Are We Automata?" But the concept is prefigured in that article nonetheless:

> The addition of the cerebral hemispheres immediately introduces a certain incalculableness into the result, and this incalculableness attains its maximum with the relatively enormous brain-convolutions of man. In the beheaded frog the legs twitch as fatally when we touch the skin with acid as do a jumping-jack's when we pull the string.... Even if all the centres above the cord except the cerebral hemispheres are left in place, the machine-like regularity of the animal's response is hardly less striking.... If I pinch [a de-cerebrated frog] ... under the arm-pits, he will croak once for each pinch; if I throw him into water, he will swim until I touch his hands with a stick, when he will immediately stop. Over a frog with an entire brain, the physiologist has no such power. The signal may be given, but ideas, emotions or caprices will be aroused instead of the fatal motor reply, and whether the animal will leap, croak, sink or swim or swell up without moving, is impossible to predict. In a man's brain the utterly remote and unforeseen courses of action to which a given impression on the senses may give rise, is too notorious to need illustration. (EPs 1879, 41–42)

Again, we see James contrasting the de-cerebrated frog, which reacts with "machine-like regularity" to stimuli, with intact vertebrates, which act from "remote and unforeseen" considerations. This is just the second condition of prudence that we have been discussing.

It may seem as though James believed the introduction of the hemispheres somehow broke apart the strict causal determinism that might be thought to govern a purely physical being. So before moving on, we must ask whether James was rejecting the very idea of a fully mechanistic physiology.

The answer is no, at least if one takes any physiological program that aims at lawlike generalizations about animal activity to count as mechanistic. James's interactionism would obviously violate a stronger form of mechanistic methodology according to which only *physical* mechanisms can appear in the explanans. But he saw his interactionism as fully compatible with a weaker form of mechanistic physiology.

One can see this in an 1879 letter to the psychologist J. J. Putnam. "Are We Automata?" had just been published:

> ... I did not pretend in my article to say that when things happen by the intermediation of consciousness they do not happen by law. The dynamic feelings which the nerve processes give rise to, and which enter in consciousness into comparison with each other and are selected, may in every instance be fatally selected. All that my article claims is that this additional stratum which complicates the chain of cause and effect also gives it determinations not identical with those which would result if it were left out. If a hydraulic ram be interposed on a water-course, a pendulum and escapement on a wheel-work the results are altered but still obey the laws of cause and effect. Free-will is in short, no necessary corollary of giving causality to consciousness. (CWJ 1879, 5.34)

James held that mental causes may permissibly appear in a strictly deterministic causal chain, and so appealing to consciousness need not undermine the goal of validating lawlike generalizations in physiology. However, James did not take consciousness to be a physical phenomenon, as we shall see in step 3, so again his interactionism obviously would violate the stronger form of mechanism mentioned earlier, a form of mechanism that Huxley himself perhaps favored (Greenwood 2010, 277).

There is evidence in the *Principles* that James saw the science of physiology as rightly aiming to model all bodily motion in terms of reflex action, by the way: "[t]he conception of *all* action as conforming to this type ['reflex action'] is the fundamental conception of modern nerve-physiology" (PP 1890, 35). So it seems that James did advocate a weakly mechanistic methodology for physiology, and apparently saw his own view of consciousness as compatible with this approach.[20]

Step 2. Step 1 represents a Surprising Fact That Demands an Explanation, Since De-cerebrated Vertebrates Are Incapable of Prudence

Why did James think we should be surprised that vertebrates with cerebral hemispheres exhibit behavioral prudence? Put simply, the answer is that vertebrates that *lack* cerebral hemispheres only exhibit "hair-trigger" (EPs 1879, 43) responses to stimuli. For example, we have seen that a pinch under the de-cerebrated frog's armpits produces a croak "as fatally . . . as do a jumping-jack's when we pull the string" (EPs 1879, 41).

So again, even though such frogs are capable of *vis a fronte* choosing, their behavior is characterized by a distinctive quiescence—by an apparent inability to act in response to anything *but* immediately presented stimuli. Goltz had reported that a de-cerebrated frog will sit in a warm bath with slowly increasing temperature even until it is killed by the heat (Danziger 1980, 100); and James takes this kind of case to show that de-cerebrated frogs have a diminished capacity for *spontaneous* action, action not directly generated by presented stimuli.

The discovery that the cerebellum is crucial for jumping prompts the question of just how the cerebellum accomplishes this trick. Similarly, James is suggesting that the hemispheres are crucial for enabling spontaneous action—the outward manifestation of the second aspect of prudence. What is apparently needed is an explanation of how they do this—of how the hemispheres help produce genuine prudence.

Step 3. Phenomenological Claim: Consciousness Typically Involves Engaging in a (Nonphysical) Process of Evaluation

James will propose that the hemispheres give rise to consciousness, and that consciousness in turn is a key factor in producing behavioral prudence. To start to understand his proposal, we first have to explore some phenomenological considerations he offered.

James claimed that where we find consciousness, we typically find unrelenting evaluation, and vice versa—where we find genuine evaluation, we typically find consciousness (EPs 1879, 46–51). He made this claim largely on the basis of introspection, further arguing that genuine evaluation cannot itself be a physical process, and that therefore consciousness cannot be physical either. Hence we get the main assertion of step 3.

Let us first consider James's claim that wherever we find consciousness we find evaluation.

> Looking back then over this review we see that the mind is at every stage a theatre of simultaneous possibilities. *Consciousness consists in the comparison of these with each other, the selection of some, and the suppression of the rest* by the reinforcing and inhibiting agency of Attention. The highest and most elaborated mental products are filtered from the data chosen by the faculty next beneath out of the mass offered by the faculty below that, which mass in turn was sifted from a still larger amount of yet simpler material, and so on. (EPs 1879, 51, my italics)

The italicized claim is quite strong. It suggests that one is phenomenally conscious *in virtue of* comparing "simultaneous possibilities" and continually using attention to select some for the basis of action. Suppose one allows this kind of selective attending to various possibilities, and perhaps to various aspects of the sensed environment, to amount to a form of evaluation (more on this point later). Then James's claim seems to be that "[c]onsciousness consists in" evaluating.

There are other passages that suggest a weaker connection between phenomenal consciousness and evaluation, though:

> There are a great many things which consciousness *is* in a passive and receptive way by its cognitive and registrative powers. But there is one thing which it *does*, *suâ sponte*, and which seems an original peculiarity of its own; and that is, always to choose out of the manifold experiences present to it at a given time some one for particular accentuation, and to ignore the rest. (EPs 1879, 46)

Here, James might be read as claiming that active choosing is *typical* of, but *not* essential to, consciousness. Evaluation is the only thing conscious states[21] do "*suâ sponte*"—of their own accord[22]—but they are also capable of passively registering a stimulus, according to this passage. So does James think we are conscious *in virtue* of evaluating, or not?

What James had in mind, I suggest, was that phenomenal consciousness is not *essentially* evaluative in any metaphysical sense, but that consciousness is *normally* evaluative, and indeed has evaluation as a proper etiological function.[23] This claim is compatible with the occurrence of the occasional conscious state that is not engaged in evaluation.[24]

Now, the important passage I have been discussing from (EPs 1879, 51) mentions "selection" and "comparison," but I have glossed these expressions as indicating a form of *evaluation*, which might seem stronger. Did James in fact think "selection" and "comparison" really amounted to a kind of *evaluation*? The answer is yes, and we can see this in nearby passages:

> Good involves the notion of less good, necessitates comparison, and for a drop of water either to compare its present state with an absent state or to compare its total self with a drop of wine, would involve <u>a process not commonly thought of as physical</u>. Comparison requires a *tertium quid*, a *locus*—call it what you will—in which the two outward existences may meet on equal terms. This forum is what is known as a consciousness. (EPs 1879, 43, my underline)

Consciousness involves a "comparison" between items, and here James construes this sort of comparison as issuing in distinctions between the "good" and "less good." As he would put it in the *Principles*, "consciousness" establishes value by "decree" (PP 1890, 144). Thus consciousness "evaluates" in the sense of *actively imposing* divisions between the more and less valuable *onto* the environment, for James. Evaluation can involve a comparison either between different things presented simultaneously in the environment or, crucially, between what is presented and "an absent state," as when I contemplate jumping over the snake I see or turning around and planning some other route through the woods.

The underlined sentence gives an important clue about why James held that an evaluating consciousness must be non-physical. What does the work, for James, is a tacit principle to the effect that value relations (better and worse, more or less important, and so on) are not physical relations.[25] Elaborating on this central idea, he wrote that *better* and *worse* in no way "pre-exist" a "consciousness [that] only discerns them" (EPs 1879, 46). Instead, consciousness in declaring ... superiority ... simply creates what previous to its fiat had no existence. The judge makes the law while announcing it: if the judge be a maggot, the suicide's brain will be best; if a king, the chancellor's. (EPs 1879, 45)

So, consciousness creates "by fiat" distinctions between "good" and "less good," and in that sense makes law. This is the process I am calling "evaluation."[26] But consciousness also enforces law in the sense of carrying out bodily action based on the "good" and "less good" divisions it itself has declared. Different consciousnesses (like the maggot's as compared with the king's) will harbor different interests, which is to say that each might assess the value of environmental conditions and possibilities—and then *act* on those conditions and possibilities—differently.[27]

In short, James apparently held that to be phenomenally conscious of some object o (whether o is presented in an occurrent sensation or represented in memory) with respect to a background b (whether b is presented in an occurrent sensation or represented in memory) typically involves *valuing* o with respect to b. To *value* means (1) to create an evaluation according to which o deserves more attention than b, and (2) to attend to o and ignore b (or make b peripheral) accordingly. As James would argue in the 1880 "Feeling of Effort" (reprinted in EPs), attending to o will then naturally trigger some bodily response or other, all things being equal (Klein forthcoming, part 4).

This neat formula undoubtedly puts James's position more abstractly than he would have liked, so perhaps it is better simply to say that for James, phenomenal consciousness typically involves *valuing*.

Step 4. Quasi-Mechanistic Hypothesis: Phenomenal Consciousness Produces Prudent Behaviors by Enabling Evaluation

We can see a happy synergy now between step 3 and the two that preceded it. If James is right that healthy, intact vertebrates exhibit a surprising ability to behave with prudence, and if we accept his claim that phenomenal consciousness typically involves evaluation, then it is natural to entertain the following hypothesis. Perhaps consciousness is what *produces* the cerebrated vertebrate's prudent choices, and perhaps it does so precisely by enabling evaluation.

We can get some purchase on the process James envisioned by briefly examining how the hemispheres might provide a locus for the supposed causal link between nonphysical consciousness and prudent behavioral patterns. He gives evidence that in humans at least, the hemispheres alone produce consciousness (PP 1890, 74). He also argues that the hemispheres play a key causal role in producing tendencies to react to physical stimuli in habitual (PP 1890, 112) or instinctive (PP 1890, 32) ways, not all of which actually benefit the organism.[28] He was proposing that consciousness then *selects* which of these temptations, if any, to act on or to perceptually focus on.

Sometimes this selection might involve foregrounding and backgrounding various aspects of the "blooming, buzzing confusion" that our sense-organs constantly register; and sometimes this selection might involve picking which of several reaction-temptations to actualize given a particular stimulus. Either way, Jamesean consciousness acts as a kind of filter or gate on our barrage of sensory stimulation, channeling an organism's active responses in prudent directions.[29]

I see no indication that James took himself to have directly *proved* that consciousness enables prudence. Recall the passage quoted earlier: this is a "hypothetical statement" only. Together with the adaptive claim I shall consider next, this statement is being recommended because it *would* help explain the physiological surprise we discussed in steps 1 and 2.

Step 5. Adaptive Hypothesis: Phenomenal Consciousness Is an Adaptation for Producing Prudent Behaviors

We can now see why James would suspect consciousness to be an adaptation.[30] *Prudent behavior* would likely help an organism survive and reproduce, and if he is right that consciousness is what produces this behavioral trait, then it stands to reason that consciousness might originally have proliferated because it produced this helpful behavior. In other words, it stands to reason that consciousness is an adaptation for producing prudence.

We can anchor this last step in the text. First, it is clear that James thinks consciousness itself is an adaptation (in the Darwinian sense), a trait that produces differential reproductive success by producing prudence:

> [G]ive to consciousness the power of exerting a constant pressure in the direction of survival, and give to the organism the power of growing to the modes in which consciousness has trained it, and the number of stray shots[31] is immensely reduced, and the time proportionally shortened for Evolution. It is, in fact, hard to see how without an effective superintending ideal the evolution of so unstable an organ as the mammalian cerebrum can have proceeded at all. (EPs 1879, 54)

James was suggesting that if consciousness has physical efficacy, then it might evolve as just one more, functional part of an organism's physiology. And this passage need not be read in a Lamarckian fashion, by the way.[32] He may simply mean that the organism grows to fit consciousness in the way that eyelids grow to fit eyeballs—in other words, the sense of "growing" here could be phylogenetic, not ontogenetic. Indeed, this fits with James's claim that consciousness "has been slowly evolved in the animal series, and resembles in this all organs that have a use" (EPs 1879, 40–41).

The next question is why James expected prudence to have survival value. We get a hint in the earlier suggestion that the cerebrum is an inherently "unstable . . . organ." James expected there to be an evolutionary trade-off between perceptual acuity and behavioral stability, and thus that a more articulated brain *should* simply produce a more varied, but less stable, array of perceptual reactions. He described nature's "dilemma" this way:

> [A] high brain may do many things, and may do each of them at a very slight hint. But its hair-trigger organization makes of it a happy-go-lucky, hit-or-miss affair. It is as likely to do the crazy as the sane thing at any given moment. A low brain does few things, and in doing them perfectly forfeits all other use. The performances of a high brain are like dice thrown for ever on a table. Unless they be loaded, what chance is there that the highest number will turn up oftener than the lowest? (EPs 1879, 43)

James associated prudence with behavioral regulation—with the ability to stabilize the superabundance of "hair-trigger" behaviors that might otherwise result from a highly articulated cerebrum.[33] As I read him, James thinks that a creature with a capacity for prudence is adaptively better off *because* it is better able to regulate its own behavior.

Let me illustrate the trade-off James envisioned between perceptual acuity and behavioral stability. On the one hand, some organisms survive and reproduce in relatively simple environments. For instance, yeast is a single-celled organism that metabolizes organic compounds in its environment. A yeast cell floating in a solution relatively homogenous with respect to nutrients has a limited need for either mobility or perceptual acuity—it can simply float free, taking up whatever nutrients happen to come into contact with its cell wall.[34]

But contrast this to the case of a field mouse that, let us suppose, eats a leaf whose characteristic pattern is mimicked by the skin of a local snake. If these mice react automatically and reflexively to occurrent stimuli—much like the armpit pinch elicits a croak without fail in the de-cerebrated frog—the mice might too quickly pursue every leaf-like color pattern they see, sometimes falling prey to the snake's mimicry.[35]

In other words, mice must have a capacity to react to a wide range of stimuli if they are to avoid predators and hunt for food. But if they respond instantly and unfailingly to every stimulus, they will go off half-cocked, so to speak, at every suggestion. In contrast, an organism perceptually attuned to a narrower band of stimuli might react "infallibly and certainly," but only at the cost of not being able to handle much environmental complexity, James would say (EPs 1879, 42–43). In short, James thought one would expect vertebrates with complex cerebral hemispheres simply to show ever more varied behavioral capacities, but to show increasing behavioral instability as well.

So we arrive at the second of James's conjectures. Suppose that the hemispheres give rise to an evaluating consciousness. Suppose such a consciousness in turn enables prudent behavior—that is, *purposive* behavior that takes account of *remote sensations* (like the mouse considering what *would* happen if it jumped at the color pattern). This kind of prudence would amount to a form of behavior regulation that might have a positive survival value, particularly for creatures with high perceptual acuity. Hence consciousness may have proliferated among ancestral vertebrates in virtue of performing this kind of regulating function, James was proposing—in virtue, that is, of enabling prudence.

AGAINST EPIPHENOMENALISM

We have just seen that James developed an interactionist conception of consciousness that would explain some puzzling physiological experiments. Thus his defense of his own interactionism has the form of an argument to the best explanation. Such arguments can be strengthened by demonstrating that competing explanations of the same phenomenon are likely to be false. And that is exactly what James did—he strengthened his case by providing independent reasons for rejecting Huxley-style epiphenomenalism.

It is useful to distinguish two related objections James raised. I will call the first objection "broad" and the second "narrow." The broad objection targets the notion that any conscious states could have been shaped by selection if epiphenomenalism were true. The narrow objection targets the notion that epiphenomenal pleasures and pains associated with "fundamental vital processes" could have been shaped by selection. The latter issue is now the more widely discussed.[36]

Here is the broad objection. Automaton theory depicts consciousness as something that could make no causal difference to an organism's behavior. But then consciousness "would be useless" from an evolutionary standpoint, in that it could not itself have contributed to any animal's reproductive success, and so could not have evolved via natural selection (EPs 1879, 41; also see PP 1890, 142).

The usual epiphenomenalist response (especially more recently; see, e.g., Jackson 1982) has been to speculate that consciousness could be an evolutionary by-product—a "spandrel" in the sense of Gould and Lewontin (1979)—rather than a trait that has been directly selected. As I read his narrow objection, however, James already forestalled this response by pointing to specific aspects of our conscious experience that bear hallmarks of natural selection's handiwork.[37] The particular band of experience in question is a subset of our phenomenal pleasures and pains—those associated with our "fundamental vital processes," as we shall see.

In "Are We Automata?," after considering some of the evidence concerning pithed vertebrates we have just discussed, James writes that there is "yet another set of facts which seem explicable on the supposition that consciousness has causal efficacy" and not explicable by epiphenomenalism (EPs 1879, 55; PP 1890, 146). The facts in question concern the link we typically find between what phenomenally *feels* good or bad and what *physically* benefits or harms us. He writes:

> *It is a well-known fact that pleasures are generally associated with beneficial, pains with detrimental, experiences.* All the fundamental vital processes illustrate this law.... An animal that should take pleasure in a feeling of suffocation would, if that pleasure were efficacious enough to make him immerse his head in water, enjoy a longevity of four or five minutes. But if pleasures and pains have no efficacy, one does not see... why the most noxious acts, such as burning, might not give thrills of delight,

and the most necessary ones, such as breathing, cause agony. (PP 1890, 146–147, italics original)[38]

Consider a subset of our phenomenal pleasures and pains—namely, those that natively go along with "fundamental vital processes." James's examples of vital pains include the experiences of being burnt, suffocated, or physically injured; his examples of vital pleasures include eating, drinking, and resting. Epiphenomenalists accept that these life-essential, phenomenal pleasures and pains are *effects* of the beneficial and harmful brain states with which they are natively associated. But epiphenomenalists *cannot* consistently say that they are *adapted* effects of those beneficial and harmful brain states. In other words, if epiphenomenalism were true, there can have been no selection pressure on any of the underlying bodily states to produce the particular, life-essential phenomenal pleasures and pains with which they are associated. This is because if epiphenomenalism were true, such pleasures and pains could have no "efficacy" and so (recall James's broad objection) could have made no difference to reproductive success.

But these phenomenal pleasures and pains have three features that *do* suggest that they were shaped by selection, for James: they are natively patterned[39] (they have a characteristic "*distribution*," he says); those patterns are systematically linked with underlying bodily states (this is the "*well-known fact*"); and the patterns are "universal" among humans. James concludes that epiphenomenalism cannot make sense of how our native distribution of life-essential, phenomenal pleasures and pains (with their systematic connections to underlying bodily states) could have evolved.

Concluding Remarks

James wrote such colorful descriptions of experience that he has earned a reputation as more poetic than empirical. But his literary flair can distract contemporary readers from the fertile, scientific context of his actual research.

I have argued that James sought to explain differences between the observed behaviors of intact versus pithed vertebrates, differences that had been recorded in a series of controversial experiments by Pflüger, Lewes, Goltz, and others. James suggested that what pithed vertebrates really lacked was a capacity for *prudent* behavior. He hypothesized that if the hemispheres give rise to phenomenal consciousness, and if consciousness is fundamentally an evaluating agency, then it would make sense of how intact vertebrates (but not their de-cerebrated peers) achieve prudent behavior. He further contended that since prudent behavior is stable behavior, and stable behavior might have positive survival value, consciousness might be an adaptation for this kind of behavior regulation.

James's hypothesis relied on an intriguing observation about an aspect of phenomenal consciousness that is rarely emphasized in contemporary discussions: when one is phenomenally conscious, James contended, one is continuously *evaluating* what is in one's environment, typically. In effect, he suggested that consciousness evolved as an appraisal system that helped our ancestors sift through the "blooming, buzzing confusion" of environmental details with which our perceptual apparatus puts us in touch.

In James's view, Huxley-style epiphenomenalism was the main rival to some form of interactionism like his own. But James argued that epiphenomenalism is likely false because it cannot give a satisfactory evolutionary explanation of phenomenal pleasures and pains.

So, James developed an account according to which *evaluating* is the proper etiological function of phenomenal consciousness. And he supported his account by arguing that it provided the best available explanation of some surprising experimental results in physiology.[40]

Notes

1. The idea that consciousness needs to be "explained" has been central in recent philosophy of mind (e.g., see Chalmers 1997, 9). Even those who are suspicious of the "hard problem" see consciousness as a proper *explanandum*, and the debate nowadays tends to focus on what kinds of things can serve as *explanantia* (e.g., see Dennett 2001; Carruthers 2001). For analyses of various senses in which people have sought to "explain" consciousness, see Van Gulick (1995) and Carruthers (1998).
2. James says the science of mind should not try to explain "how or why" conscious states and brain states "hang indubitably together," but should only attempt to document an "empirical parallelism" between the two, and to do so "provisional[ly]." This way "our psychology will remain positivistic and non-metaphysical . . . " (PP 1890, 182).
3. Parts of the essay were later used in chapters five and nine of James's opus, *The Principles of Psychology* (1890).
4. The essay can be found at MEN (1872, 247–256). For a recollection of the aims of this essay, see James's letter to C. A. Strong (October 21, 1889, quoted in Perry 1935, II.26).
5. See his 1874 review of William Carpenter's *Principles of Mental Physiology* (esp. ECR 274) and his review of Wundt's *Grundzüge der physiologischen Psychologie* the following year (esp. ECR 303). I thank Trevor Pearce for calling my attention to these reviews.
6. What remains of this manuscript can be found in *Manuscript Lectures* (1878, 16–43). Perry suggests James's lectures at Johns Hopkins in February of 1878 were similar to his Lowell series, citing a letter from Francis J. Child (who had hosted James during his stay in Baltimore) to the effect that the final Hopkins lecture had "offered reasons for not accepting the theory that we are automatons unreservedly" (RBP 1935, II.27). The documents that survive of that lecture series are also incomplete (ML 1878, 3–15).
7. See letter to Augustus Lowell, January 23, 1879 (CWJ 5.37).
8. There is surprisingly little literature on James's early defense of interactionism. For instance, this is one of the few major issues in James's writing barely touched on in the otherwise exhaustive (Myers 1986; see 54–58 for his brief discussion). Perry's chapter on the topic (Perry 1935, II.ch. 53) offers some revealing documentary evidence but is short on critical analysis. There is an idiosyncratic essay in the 1950s that mistakenly (see the 1879 letter quoted in the text, from CWJ 5.34) runs automatism together with determinism

(Capek 1954, esp. 274–276). Two more recent essays (Flanagan 1997; Reck 1972) are both concerned to reconcile James's early interactionist dualism with what he would later call his "philosophy of pure experience" (or what Russell termed "neutral monism"). As such, neither author makes much effort to unpack James's actual evidence for interactionism— Flanagan simply says James rejected epiphenomenalism on "'common-sensical' grounds" (Flanagan 1997, 31), and Reck makes a similar claim (Reck 1972, 29). James did regard interactionism as in accord with "common sense" (e.g., PP 1890, 139), but as we shall see he thought his view also accorded with extensive empirical evidence. Finally, there is a more recent literature on epiphenomenalism, some of which takes up one of James's key *objections* to this position (see n. 36, below), but none of which considers James's own positive view.

9. Indeed, James's usage is the first cited by the Oxford English Dictionary. James actually puts "epiphenomenon" in quotation marks (PP 1890, 133), seeming to attribute the term to Hodgson (1865), but I cannot find Hodgson using the term himself. In contrast, VRE (1902, 390), James attributed the term to Clifford. He presumably had in mind Clifford (1874/1886), but the word does not appear there, or anywhere else in Clifford's writings I can find. The OED cites a primary, older usage of the word that comes from medicine, and dates to the early eighteenth century. In medicine an "epiphenomenon" is a secondary symptom of an underlying condition, such as a fever caused by an infection. James had completed his physiology training in Harvard's medical school and was presumably adapting this medical usage in his discussion of consciousness. Finally, James actually did use "epiphenomenalism" in an unpublished notebook, dated 1903–1904 (MEN 52).

10. Hodgson articulated this view in 1865 (see Hodgson 1865, I.278 ff.), and James quoted from this work (PP 1890, 133). But Hodgson only actually espoused the view himself in Hodgson (1870, I.416 ff.).

11. I discuss these experiments at length in Klein (2018).

12. The frog brain was often depicted as a set of sub-structures connected serially, through the brain stem, to the spinal cord. For a diagram from the era, consult figure 4.1.

13. Pflüger says the frogs used in the experiment I describe in the text were pithed below the medulla oblongata (Pflüger 1853, 18).

14. James writes that reflex actions are "the result of outward discharges from the nervous centres" when "these outward discharges are themselves the result of impressions from the external world, carried in along one or another of our sensory nerves" (WB 1897, 91). A standard example would be wincing at an object moving toward the eye.

15. For an overview of Lewes's life and intellectual work, see Price (2014).

16. By calling his view a hypothetical statement of "direct personal feeling," he did not mean that the *evidence* for his hypothesis was personal feeling, but rather that he was offering a scientifically credible hypothesis that *agrees* with personal feeling (a point he made with some frequency; see above, n. 8). This is clear from the sentence following the passage I quote in the text: "But the intricate analysis by which it [viz., James's own hypothesis] has been reached gives it great plausibility" (EPs 1879, 52). The "intricate analysis" is not a simple appeal to common sense, but the physiological and evolutionary considerations I am analyzing here in the present section.

17. James did not give a citation, but he presumably had in mind (Goltz 1869, 70).

18. James was especially indebted to Goltz for the point that, despite their remarkable capacity for coordinated action, de-cerebrated frogs rarely act at all unless prompted by some overt stimulus. See Danziger (1980, 99–100) for a brief discussion, and for more on the controversy surrounding the pithing results generally, see Klein (2018, 897–898).

19. Let me emphasize that Jamesean prudence is not to be taken as an exclusively subjective concept. Both components of prudence involve objective, behavioral phenomena. Thus, James cashes out *acting on considerations of what is absent* as something observable in the intact frog, as when we find it "impossible to predict" (EPs 1879, 42) a response to a stimulus. And the same goes for *vis a fronte* choosing—one can simply observe whether this capacity is present, e.g., in a frog emerging for air that tries various means to reach its obstructed goal.

20. His subsequent work on will complicates this story somewhat, but I cannot explore this issue here. For more on how James's accounts of consciousness and will fit together, see Klein (forthcoming).

21. I read James's use of "consciousness" as shorthand for "conscious mental states." James held that psychology should resist the urge to postulate a *thinker* somehow standing behind our passing thoughts—the thinker *just is* the passing thought, for James (PP 1890, 328). So like in much contemporary philosophy of mind, when James uses the noun form "consciousness," this should be taken as shorthand for a property that only mental states (not whole creatures) can instantiate.

22. This phrase is usually used in connection with actions a court of law takes on its own accord, as opposed to actions it might take on motions brought by interested parties, as when a court by itself moves to dismiss a case (say, because of a lack of jurisdiction), rather than because an interested party has moved to dismiss.

23. On this terminology, see below, n. 30.

24. A trait that enables x-ing need not always be involved in x-ing in order to be an adaptation for x-ing. For instance, spatial pattern separation (the ability to remember distinct but similar spatial patterns) may be an adaptation for foraging (Mattson 2014, 5), even though we sometimes use this skill when not foraging (e.g., when playing various kinds of games). Similarly, consciousness could be an adaptation for evaluating, even though consciousness sometimes occurs without evaluation (perhaps in states of meditation, say). What is more, foraging is neither necessary nor sufficient for spatial pattern separation, obviously, even though the latter may still be an adaptation for the former; similarly, evaluation may be neither necessary nor sufficient for consciousness, even though the latter may still be an adaptation for the former.

25. In another memorable passage making a similar point, James wrote that an "electrical machine [n]ever get[s] restless because it can only emit sparks, and not hem pillow-cases like a sewing-machine" (PP 1890, 22). I take it the non-physicality of evaluation is James's central reason for resisting any account that portrays consciousness as *nothing but* prudent behavior, by the way, which is a purely physical activity. For James, consciousness is non-physical, so it may *cause*, but cannot therefore be identical with, behavioral prudence.

26. James sometimes writes about selecting objects "suited" to one's "private interests" (EPs 1879, 50).

27. It is not so much that all value is relative, for James held that *every* interest created by consciousness produces a prima facie demand to be satisfied (WB 1897, 148). Deliberation about value, for James, is not about figuring out what the *right* set of interests is. In some sense, *every* interest is "right," and none absolutely overrides any other. He was particularly keen to deny a kind of flat-footed evolutionary ethics that claimed survival to be an absolutely overriding interest, a view he associated with Spencer (Klein 2016, sec. 3). Instead, James thought ethical deliberation is about sorting out conflicts that will inevitably arise

between the mutually incompatible interests different conscious creatures will create—as he put it, ethics is about choosing *which* "interest out of several equally coercive shall become supreme" (EPs 1879, 51). This idea prefigures "The Moral Philosopher and the Moral Life" (1891), where James offers a naturalistic account of ethical evaluation in terms of the reconciliation of competing values. For discussions of James's treatment of value, see chapters by Marchetti, Bush, Talisse, and Throntveit and Kloppenberg in the present volume.
28. James wrote that the "materialist," or presumably anybody who denies the efficacy of consciousness, "is immediately confronted by the notorious fact that the strongest tendencies to automatic activity in the nerves often run most counter to the selective pressure of consciousness" (EPs 1879, 59).
29. Hence, "[c]onsciousness produces nothing, it only alters the proportions" (EPs 1879, 52).
30. I will follow Lloyd and Gould's definitions, according to which an adaptation is "a trait that has a direct proper (etiological) function." They define a proper, etiological function this way: "a trait has the *function* of x-ing, if x-ing increased fitness in recent evolutionary history . . . (over alternative, non-x-ing, versions of the trait), . . . increased fitness by x-ing, [and] explains the prevalence of the x-ing trait" (Lloyd and Gould 2017, 51).
31. The longer passage includes reference to "Mr. Darwin," who "regards animated nature as a sort of table on which dice are continually being thrown. No intention presides over the throwing, but lucky numbers from time to time fortuitously turn up and are preserved." For more on the dice metaphor, see the passage from EPs (1879, 43), reproduced immediately below.
32. Consult Pearce, this volume, on James and the evolutionary biology of his day.
33. A similar suggestion can be found at ML (1878, 26).
34. James would have been familiar with this example, which I adapt from Spencer (1873, I.295), and which I discuss in another connection in Klein (2016, 4).
35. James considers the related example of fish like "cunners and sculpins" that are easy for humans to catch because they "lack . . . all thought by which to weigh the danger against the attractiveness of the bait" (PP 1890, 34).
36. Some recent literature that takes up James's objection to epiphenomenalism includes Robinson (2007), Corabi (2008, 2014), and Robinson (2014). Another recent treatment is Wright (2015), which in some respects defends James's perspective.
37. For more detail on my reading of James's objection to epiphenomenalism, see Klein (2019).
38. The passage also appears at EPs (1879, 55–56), with minimally different wording.
39. By "native" I mean *inheritable*—I use the former term for linguistic convenience. The "distribution" of pleasures and pains at issue for James must be inheritable, since only inheritable traits can evolve.
40. I would like to thank Gary Hatfield for commenting on this chapter, along with Trevor Pearce and Elisabeth Lloyd, who both commented on early versions. I gave portions of this chapter as part of a lecture series at École Normale Supérieure in Paris. I would like to thank Mathias Girel, CAPHÉS, Labex, and the Centre de Cavailles for hosting me, and also the US-UK Fulbright Foundation for financial support during the 2016–2017 year when I was working out some of these ideas. That year I was in residence at the University of Sheffield, where conversations with Luca Barlassina and Jeremy Dunham particularly shaped the direction this research would eventually take. I finished work on this chapter, and this book, while supported by a Canada Research Chair at McMaster University.

Bibliography

Brunton, T. Lauder. 1898. *Lectures on the Action of Medicines: Being the Course of Lectures on Pharmacology and Therapeutics Delivered at St. Bartholomew's Hospital During the Summer Session of 1896*. London: Macmillan.
Capek, Milic. 1954. "James's Early Criticism of the Automaton Theory." *Journal of the History of Ideas* 15: 260–279.
Carruthers, Peter. 1998. "Natural Theories of Consciousness." *European Journal of Philosophy* 6 (2):203–222.
Carruthers, Peter. 2001. "Consciousness: Explaining the Phenomena." *Royal Institute of Philosophy Supplement* 49: 61–85.
Chalmers, David. 1997. "Facing Up to the Problem of Consciousness." In *Explaining Consciousness: The "Hard Problem,"* edited by Jonathan Shear, 9–32. Cambridge, MA: MIT Press.
Clifford, William Kingdon. 1874/1886. "Body and Mind." In *Lectures and Essays, by the Late William Kingdon Clifford*, edited by Leslie Stephen and Frederick Pollock, 244–273. London: Macmillan.
Corabi, Joseph. 2008. "Pleasure's Role in Evolution: A Response to Robinson." *Journal of Consciousness Studies* 15 (7): 78–86.
Corabi, Joseph. 2014. "The Misuse and Failure of the Evolutionary Argument." *Disputatio: International Journal of Philosophy* 6 (39):199–227.
Danziger, Kurt. 1980. "The Unknown Wundt: Drive, Apperception, and Volition." In *Wilhelm Wundt and the Making of a Scientific Psychology*, edited by R. W. Rieber and David K. Robinson, 95–120. New York: Plenum Press.
Dennett, Daniel. 2001. "Are We Explaining Consciousness Yet?" *Cognition* 79 (1–2): 221–237.
Fearing, Franklin. 1930/1964. *Reflex Action: A Study in the History of Physiological Psychology*. New York: Hafner.
Flanagan, Owen. 1997. "Consciousness as a Pragmatist Views It." In *The Cambridge Companion to William James*, edited by Ruth Anna Putnam, 25–48. New York: Cambridge University Press.
Goltz, Friedrich Leopold. 1869. Beiträge zur Lehre von den Functionen der Nervencentren des Frosches. Berlin: A. Hirschwald.
Gould, Stephen Jay, and Richard C. Lewontin. 1979. "The Spandrels of San Marco and the Panglossian Paradigm: A Critique of the Adaptationist Programme." *Proceedings of the Royal Society of London, Series B* 205 (1161): 581–598.
Greenwood, John. 2010. "Whistles, Bells, and Cogs in Machines: Thomas Huxley and Epiphenomenalism." *Journal of the History of the Behavioral Sciences* 46 (3): 276–299.
Hodgson, Shadworth Hollway. 1865. *Time and Space: A Metaphysical Essay*. London: Longman, Green, Longman, Roberts, and Green.
Hodgson, Shadworth Hollway. 1870. *The Theory of Practice: An Ethical Enquiry*. 2 vols. London: Longmans, Green, Reader, and Dyer.
Huxley, Thomas Henry. 1870. "Has a Frog a Soul? And of What Nature Is That Soul, Supposing It to Exist?" *Papers Read before the Metaphysical Society* (Privately Published): 1–7.
Huxley, Thomas Henry. 1872. *Lessons in Elementary Physiology*. 6th ed. London: Macmillan and Co.
Huxley, Thomas Henry. 1874/1894. "On the Hypothesis That Animals Are Automata, and Its History." In *Collected Essays: Method and Results*, 199–250. New York: Appleton.
Jackson, Frank. 1982. "Epiphenomenal Qualia." *Philosophical Quarterly* 32 (127): 127–136.
James, William. 1879. "Are We Automata?" *Mind* 4 (13): 1–22.

Klein, Alexander. 2016. "Was James Psychologistic?" *Journal for the History of Analytical Philosophy* 4 (5): 1–21.

Klein, Alexander. 2018. "The Curious Case of the Decapitated Frog: On Experiment and Philosophy." *British Journal for the History of Philosophy* 26 (5): 890–917.

Klein, Alexander. 2019. "William James's Objection to Epiphenomenalism." *Philosophy of Science* 86 (5): 1179–1190.

Klein, Alexander. 2020. "The Death of Consciousness? James's Case against Psychological Unobservables." *Journal of the History of Philosophy* 58 (2): 293–323.

Klein, Alexander. Forthcoming. *Consciousness Is Motor: William James on Mind and Action.* New York: Oxford University Press.

Lewes, George Henry. 1859. "The Spinal Chord a Sensational and Volitional Centre." In *Report of the Twenty-Eight Meeting of the British Association for the Advancement of Science; Held at Leeds in September of 1858*, 135–138. London: John Murray.

Lewes, George Henry. 1859–1860. *The Physiology of Common Life.* 2 vols. Edinburgh: W. Blackwood.

Lewes, George Henry. 1873. "Sensation in the Spinal Cord." *Nature* 9: 83–84.

Lewes, George Henry. 1877. *Problems of Life and Mind, Second Series: The Physical Basis of Mind.* London: Trübner & Co.

Lloyd, Elisabeth A., and Stephen Jay Gould. 2017. "Exaptation Revisited: Changes Imposed by Evolutionary Psychologists and Behavioral Biologists." *Biological Theory* 12 (1): 50–65.

Mattson, Mark P. 2014. "Superior Pattern Processing Is the Essence of the Evolved Human Brain." *Frontiers in Neuroscience* 8: 265.

Myers, Gerald E. 1986. *William James: His Life and Thought.* New Haven, CT: Yale University Press.

Perry, Ralph Barton. 1935. *The Thought and Character of William James.* 2 vols. Cambridge, MA: Harvard University Press.

Pflüger, Eduard. 1853. *Die Sensorischen Functionen Des Rückenmarks Der Wirbelthiere, Nebst Einer Neuen Lehre Über Die Leitungsgesetze Der Reflexionen.* Berlin: Hirschwald.

Price, Elfed Huw. 2014. "George Henry Lewes (1817–1878): Embodied Cognition, Vitalism, and the Evolution of Symbolic Perception." In *Brain, Mind and Consciousness in the History of Neuroscience*, edited by C. U. M. Smith and Harry Whitaker, 105–123. Dordrecht: Springer.

Reck, Andrew J. 1972. "Dualisms in William James's *Principles of Psychology*." In *Knowledge and Value: Essays in Honor of Harold N. Lee*, edited by Andrew J. Reck, 23–38. Dordrecht: Springer Netherlands.

Robinson, William S. 2007. "Evolution and Epiphenomenalism." *Journal of Consciousness Studies* 14 (11): 27–42.

Robinson, William S. 2014. "James's Evolutionary Argument." *Disputatio: International Journal of Philosophy* 6 (39): 229–237.

Robinson, William S. 2015. Epiphenomenalism. *The Stanford Encyclopedia of Philosophy.* Edited by Edward N. Zalta. Fall. Stanford, CA: Stanford University. http://plato.stanford.edu/archives/fall2015/entries/epiphenomenalism/.

Spencer, Herbert. 1873. *The Principles of Psychology.* 2nd ed. 2 vols, System of Synthetic Philosophy. New York: Appleton and Co.

Van Gulick, Robert. 1995. "What Would Count as Explaining Consciousness?" In *Conscious Experience*, edited by Thomas Metzinger, 61–79. Paderborn: Ferdinand Schöningh.

Wright, John. 2015. "On James's Argument against Epiphenomenalism." *William James Studies* 11: 69–85.

PART II
SCIENCE

CHAPTER 5

JAMES AND EVOLUTION

TREVOR PEARCE

JAMES was an evolutionary thinker who was critical of evolutionism; this chapter is an attempt to explain this strange state of affairs.[1] In the first section, I will sketch James's reaction to evolutionary ideas in the 1860s, especially those of Darwin: although he showed great interest, he stopped short of active endorsement. I will spend the bulk of the rest of the chapter detailing James's response to the work of Herbert Spencer, seen at the time as the most important philosopher of evolution. James argued against Spencer's evolutionism in the 1870s, but from the perspective of a broader naturalism. According to James, Spencer ignored important mental phenomena, in particular subjective interests and selective attention. Finally, I will briefly discuss how James deployed evolutionary ideas in his later writings on ethics and pragmatism. Although James opposed—often on scientific grounds—much of the philosophical work inspired by evolution, his philosophy was nevertheless built on its own evolutionary foundation.

EARLY ENCOUNTERS WITH DARWIN

As several generations of scholars have noted, someone coming of age intellectually in the 1860s and 1870s could hardly avoid the topic of evolution (Perry 1935, 1.463–493; Hofstadter 1944, 103–120; Wiener 1949, 97–128; Russett 1976, 47–81; Kuklick 1977, 5–27; Richards 1987, 409–450; Croce 1995, 83–148). James began his scientific education at Harvard in 1861, enrolled in the Lawrence Scientific School rather than the college. Darwin's *On the Origin of Species* (1859) had recently given new life to the idea of evolution. A series of discussions of the *Origin* in 1860 at the American Academy of Arts and Sciences involved not only Harvard naturalists such as Louis Agassiz and Asa Gray but also Francis Bowen, who taught philosophy at Harvard, and Chauncey Wright, a mathematician-philosopher who was later a friend and mentor to James (*Proceedings* 1860, 410–416, 432–433; Bowen 1860; Wright 1860).

Although studying chemistry at the Lawrence Scientific School, James still travelled to Boston to hear Agassiz's lectures on *Methods of Study in Natural History*. James was impressed by the Swiss naturalist: "he is an admirable, earnest lecturer, clear as day and his accent is most fascinating. I should like to study under him" (CWJ 1861, 4.41–43). Agassiz described these lectures, when they were published as a book, as entering an "earnest protest against the transmutation theory [i.e., evolution], revived of late with so much ability." He pulled no punches: naturalists like Darwin were "chasing a phantom," and there was "a repulsive poverty" in their explanation of life (Agassiz 1863, iii–iv). Apart from a short argument against Darwin's move from artificial to natural selection, however, the lectures themselves contained few criticisms of evolution. James was likely more fascinated by the content of Agassiz's lectures than their context: they covered everything from the general classification of organisms to the complex life cycles of marine invertebrates. James soon embraced the persona of budding naturalist, submitting a "future history" to his family in November: "1 year Study Chemistry, then spend one term at home, then 1 year with [the anatomist Jeffries] Wyman, then a medical education, then 5 or 6 years with Agassiz, then probably death, death, death with inflation and plethora of knowledge" (CWJ 1861, 4.52).

James started another year of chemistry at Harvard in 1862, but he switched to comparative anatomy the following fall to begin studying—a bit later than predicted—with Wyman. At this stage James was still unsure about his future profession and told his cousin that he had four alternatives: "Natural History, Medecine [sic], Printing, Beggary." He was drawn to natural history and bragged of working "in a vast museum, at a table all alone, surrounded by skeletons of mastodons, crocodiles, and the like." By December, however, he had chosen medicine—which seemed to combine his scientific interests with the necessity of making money—and he began attending medical lectures in 1864 (CWJ 1863, 4.81–87).

In September of 1863, when he was still deciding whether or not to pursue a career in natural history, James began reading and taking notes on Darwin's *Origin*. Unfortunately, these notes are lost (Richardson 2006, 57). Thus, our earliest hint of his opinion of evolutionary ideas comes in his very first publication, a review of Thomas Henry Huxley's *Elements of Comparative Anatomy* (1864). James did not endorse evolution in his review. However, referring to Huxley's *Evidence as to Man's Place in Nature* (1863), he did suggest that much of the opposition to it was emotional rather than scientific:

> [Huxley] jovially says that, if we admit the transmutation hypothesis at all, we must apply it even unto majestic man, and see in him the offspring of some great ape, pregnant with Futurity. Probably our feeling on this point, more than anything else, will make many of us refuse to accept any theory of transmutation. This is indeed not the place to discuss the question, but we think it could be easily proved that such a feeling has even less foundation than any other aristocratic prejudice.... Perhaps, by accustoming our imagination to contemplate the possibility of our ape descent now and then, as a precautionary measure, the dire prospect, should it ever really burst

upon us, will appear shorn of some of its novel horrors, and our humanity appear no less worthy than it was before.

James gave a list of recent converts to the evolution hypothesis, declared that it "cannot but be treated with some respect," and offered an amusingly reticent prediction as to its future success: "we may well doubt whether it may not be destined eventually to prevail" (ECR 1865, 198). Thus, when this review was written late in 1864, James was at least somewhat attracted to Darwin's views—perhaps not surprising given that his teacher Wyman supported evolution and had publically endorsed it the year before (CWJ 1864, 4.92–94; Appel 1988, 84–85; Croce 1995, 142).

Despite these sympathies, James would soon become an employee of evolution's fiercest critic: Agassiz. In April of 1865, a few months after the Huxley review was published, James was heading to Brazil as one of Agassiz's assistants—and one of the objects of the expedition was to find evidence against species evolution (Lurie 1960, 345).[2] During the voyage south, Agassiz gave a series of scientific lectures to James and the other assistants to prepare them for their work in Brazil. The last of these, on April 20, concerned "the development theory" (i.e., evolution). Although Agassiz was clearly critical, he ended by urging his students to let the facts speak for themselves:

> I bring this subject before you now, not to urge upon you this or that theory, strong as my own convictions are. I wish only to warn you, not against the development theory itself, but against the looseness in the methods of study upon which it is based. Whatever be your ultimate opinions on the subject, let them rest on facts and not on arguments, however plausible. This is not a question to be argued, it is one to be investigated. (Agassiz and Agassiz 1868, 43–44)

In a letter written the day after this lecture, however, James expressed skepticism that Agassiz was pursuing a "just the facts" approach, alluding to the religious motivation of his scientific views:

> Last Sunday, [Bishop Alonzo Potter] preached a sermon particularly to us "savans" as the outsiders call us, and told us we must try to imitate the simple child like devotion to truth of our great leader [i.e., Agassiz]. We must give up our pet theories of transmutation, spontaneous generation &c, and seek in nature what God has put there rather than try to put there some system wh. our imagination has devised &c &c. (Vide Agassiz passim.) The good old Prof. was melted to tears, and wept profusely. (CWJ 1865, 4.101)

The theological basis of Agassiz's position on evolution was obvious, according to James—"vide Agassiz passim" means "see Agassiz's works, throughout." As in the Huxley review, it was feeling and not fact that turned people away from transmutation.

James had great respect for Agassiz as a naturalist but thought him close-minded and biased when it came to evolution. In a letter to his brother Henry during the trip, James attributed this to a general character flaw: "[Agassiz] is doubtless a man of some wonderful mental faculties, but such a politician & so self-seeking & illiberal to others that it sadly diminishes one's respect for him" (CWJ 1865, 1.8). After returning home, James said the whole endeavor had been

> more profitable in the way of general experience than of Science.—For the manual labor of collecting and packing took so much time and energy that little was left for dissecting and studying specimens and "the principal light of modern science" [i.e., Agassiz] is not exceedingly communicative of his learning except in the way of damning the Darwinians, wh. though instructive is open to the charge of being monotonous. (CWJ 1866, 4.142)

Although James enjoyed poking fun at Agassiz's animosity toward Darwin's views, it is not obvious whether James counted himself among "the Darwinians" in 1866. Even in two reviews of Darwin's *Variation of Animals and Plants Under Domestication* (1868), James emphasized the probabilistic character of evolutionary reasoning: "it may never be any more possible to give a strict proof of it, complete in every link, than it now is to give a logically binding disproof of it" (ECR 1868, 239). Nevertheless, James had more respect for Darwin's position than for Agassiz's, as is apparent from a letter to his brother Henry:

> The more I think of Darwin's ideas the more weighty do they appear to me—tho' of course my opinion is worth very little—still I *believe* that that scoundrel Agassiz is unworthy either intellectually or morally for him to wipe his shoes on, & I find a certain pleasure in yielding to the feeling. (CWJ 1868, 1.38–39; see also CWJ 1870, 4.404)

This letter and several others (see below) indicate that James had embraced evolution by 1868—but it had taken him a while, especially when compared to friends like John Fiske and Chauncey Wright, who signed on almost immediately (Fiske 1860; Wright 1878, 43).

What is the significance of this delay? First, it helps to highlight certain subgroups among those involved in the famous "Metaphysical Club" of the early 1870s. Fiske and Wright had been committed to evolutionary ideas for over a decade when the club began meeting, and they had even corresponded with evolutionists such as Darwin and Spencer. Along with Francis Ellingwood Abbot, they were also both positivists in the broad sense; that is, they thought that science should remain agnostic about anything beyond the phenomena (Pearce 2015). James and Charles Sanders Peirce, in contrast, were sympathetic to religion and often critical of positivism—it is these views that may have made them reluctant to endorse evolution, at least initially. Second, the delay suggests that James may even at this early stage have been struggling to reconcile evolutionary ideas with more traditional accounts of human thought and action.[3] After briefly adopting a sort of narrow evolutionary empiricism in the late 1860s, James spent the rest of his life attempting to work out a broader compromise position—to construct a scientific and philosophical narrative that distinguished him from his positivist friends. Who better to cast as the villain than Fiske's hero, Herbert Spencer?

James and Spencer

Looking just at James's early book reviews and his journey with Agassiz, it might seem as if Darwin should be the main character in any story about James and evolution. But Herbert Spencer was the best known advocate of an evolutionary philosophy, and thus Spencer had the biggest impact on James, who saw himself more as a philosopher than a naturalist (Perry 1935, 1.474–493; Leary this volume). James later acknowledged the overwhelming influence of Spencer's multivolume *System of Synthetic Philosophy*, the first three parts of which were published in the 1860s and early 1870s:

> Who, since [Spencer] wrote, is not vividly able to conceive of the world as a thing evolved from a primitive fire mist, by progressive integrations and differentiations, and increases in heterogeneity and coherence of texture and organization? Who can fail to think of life, both bodily and mental, as a set of ever-changing ways of meeting the "environment"? (EPh 1903, 97)

The general idea of evolution—cosmic, organic, social—as a change from incoherent homogeneity to coherent heterogeneity was the centerpiece of *First Principles* (1862), a book that would soon be included on philosophy syllabi in the United States (*Harvard University Catalogue* 1879, 84; *Harvard University Catalogue* 1885, 95; *Calendar of the University of Michigan* 1886, 55; *Calendar of the University of Michigan* 1892, 61; ML, 146–177). Life as a correspondence between organism and environment—inner relations adjusting to outer relations—was the foundational commitment of both *Principles of Biology* (1864, 1867) and *Principles of Psychology* (1870, 1872).[4] This organism-environment dyad was linked to Spencer's progressive account of evolution: he saw science and civilization as crowning illustrations "of the truths, that Life is the maintenance of a correspondence between the organism and its environment, and that the degree of Life varies as the degree of correspondence" (Spencer 1870, 376).

James's reading of Spencer and other empirically oriented writers affected him both intellectually and personally (Richards 1987, 409–450). In the late 1860s, James told his friend Oliver Wendell Holmes, Jr. that he was "tending strongly to an empiristic view of life":

> I shall continue to apply empirical principles to my experience as I go on and see how much they fit. One thing makes me uneasy. *If* the end of all is to be that we must take our sensations as simply given or as preserved by natural selection for us, and interpret this rich and delicate overgrowth of ideas, moral, artistic, religious & social, as a mere mask, a tissue spun in happy hours by creative individuals and adopted by

other men in the interests of their sensations—how long is it going to be well for us not to "let on" all we know to the public? (CWJ 1868, 4.302)

This outlook was probably inspired by Spencer's *First Principles* (1862), which placed evolution in the background of our entire mental and social life.[5] In his diary at around the same time, James wondered how one might explain aesthetic appreciation "on utilitarian or Darwinian principles" (James 1868). He corresponded frequently with Thomas Wren Ward, a friend from the Agassiz expedition who had begun to question religion after "a casual reading of Herbert Spencer" (CWJ 1868, 4.322). Unfortunately, James's enthusiasm for the empirical perspective was accompanied by depression. As he wrote years later, probably thinking of his own case, "the purely naturalistic look at life, however enthusiastically it may begin, is sure to end in sadness" (VRE 1902, 119).[6] James told Ward that in the winter of 1866–1867 he had been "on the continual verge of suicide," and he was apparently having similar thoughts in the fall of 1868: "I am poisoned with Utilitarian venom, and sometimes when I despair of ever doing anything, say, 'why not step out into the green darkness?'" (CWJ 1868, 4.248, 4.347).

As is well known, James emerged from this depression guided at least in part by the work of the French philosopher Charles Renouvier.[7] That same fall, James had stumbled across Renouvier's long essay on nineteenth-century French philosophy, "De la philosophie du XIXe siècle en France" (CWJ 1868, 4.342). After reviewing the work of Henri de Saint-Simon and various forms of positivism and socialism, Renouvier criticized what all of these philosophical approaches had in common—not only a "belief in the natural and necessary progress of humanity," but also an "avowed determinism, the negation of freedom, and the substitution of the idea of evolution for that of fixed laws" (Renouvier 1868, 88). The "evolution school," said Renouvier,

> is forced to explain the constitution of apparent individualities by the action of environments [*milieux*] exclusively.... It must explain their faculties and their acts via suggestions coming from outside. Empiricism and sensualism work for this school to establish the laws of these suggestions, reducing almost to nothing the internally given. (Renouvier 1868, 92–93)

Although Renouvier only briefly mentioned Spencer, he did connect him to "ideas of development and progress," and it would have been natural for James to see him as part of the criticized "evolution school" (Renouvier 1868, 7).

As Spencer's work became more widely known in France, Renouvier and his collaborator François Pillon began to attack it in their new journal, *La Critique Philosophique*.[8] For example, Pillon argued that Spencer's psychology "systematically reduces innateness to the inheritance of acquired modifications" and thus represents "the negation of all mental nature, of all intellectual constitution, of all mental law, of all psychological specificity" (Pillon 1872, 214). James was happy to have found an alternative to the Spencerian approach, as he observed in a letter to Renouvier written a few months later:

> Over here, it is the philosophy of [John Stuart] Mill, [Alexander] Bain, & Spencer that presently carries all before it. This philosophy produces excellent works in psychology, but from the practical point of view it is determinist and materialist.... Your phenomenist philosophy seems well suited to make an impression on the elevated minds of the English empirical school. (CWJ 1872, 4.430–431)

By the early 1870s, James had moved away from Spencer's empirical outlook and adopted Renouvier's "phenomenist philosophy": "the knowable universe is ... a system of phenomena," but contains within it the possibility of freedom (ECR 1873, 266).[9]

James's opposition to Spencer's evolutionary empiricism began with Renouvier, but he soon found additional allies: Shadworth Hodgson and Wilhelm Wundt. In the work of these philosopher-psychologists, James discovered the two concepts that would frame his critique of Spencer: interest and attention. Hodgson had introduced the notion of interest in his book *Time and Space* (1865) as part of a chapter on "Spontaneous Redintegration"—the involuntary restoration of a past state of consciousness. When we have a new experience, it sometimes calls to mind a past experience. But why some particular past experience? According to Hodgson, redintegration has two stages: first, those parts of an experienced object that are uninteresting fade from consciousness; then the remaining interesting parts of the object combine with those past objects with which they have been habitually associated, yielding a new object. This cycle is ongoing:

> Scarcely has the process begun, when the original law of interest begins to operate on this new formation, seizes on the interesting parts and impresses them on the attention to the exclusion of the rest, and the whole process is repeated again with endless variety. (Hodgson 1865, 266–268)

Hodgson thus called interest the "secret spring" and "motive power" of spontaneous redintegration (Hodgson 1865, 266).

James was intrigued by the implications of Hodgson's "law of interest" for psychology generally, as it seemed to undermine Spencer's more passive account of the experiencing mind. The mind's active role was even more obvious in voluntary (rather than spontaneous) redintegration. As Hodgson wrote,

> it is impossible there to suppose consciousness to be a mere foam, aura, or melody, arising from the brain, but without reaction upon it. The states of consciousness are, in voluntary redintegration, links in the chain of physical events or circumstances in the external world. (Hodgson 1865, 280; quoted in ECR 1874, 273, and MEN 1872, 249)

James thought that Hodgson had identified a deficiency in Spencer's view—something it had missed. According to Spencer, feelings of pleasure evolved because "those species survived which came to have emotions of pleasure associated with experiences that were useful to them, whilst others perished" (ECR 1874, 272; cf. Spencer 1870, 280). But on this story, said James, "the purely *conscious quale* of the mental event seems to act as a determinant link in the chain of physical causes and effects," which contradicts Spencer's broader claim that "the links of the chain of conscious events" are mere "concomitants of those of the chain of successive physical phenomena" (ECR 1874, 271–272). Physical and mental events do not form two independent and parallel chains, as Spencer argued; they are at least sometimes links in the same chain. More specifically, the evolution of pleasure is an example, according to James, of how "quality of consciousness as such, instead of being discontinuous with all the facts of nerve vibration, may influence them in direction or amount" (ECR 1874, 273).[10]

This discussion of Hodgson's work appeared in a review of William Carpenter's *Principles of Mental Physiology* (1874). In that same review, James declared that Carpenter's chapters on sensation and perception were "very inadequate" in comparison to research "by German inquirers, among whom we may mention [Wilhelm] Wundt . . . and the immortal [Hermann von] Helmholtz in his Optics" (ECR 1874, 273).[11] Both of these authors emphasized the activity of the mind in perception. Helmholtz claimed that "the connection of the sensation with the idea of the object . . . depends in large part on acquired experience, and thus on mental activity," although he argued that most of this activity was unconscious (Helmholtz 1867, §26).[12] Wundt went even further in his *Grundzüge der physiologischen Psychologie* (Principles of physiological psychology):

> [Psychology] has tacitly presupposed that the course of sense-perceptions recapitulates immediately and essentially unchanged the temporal course of external impressions. But this is not so; rather, the way in which external events are pictured in our ideas is co-determined by the qualities of consciousness and attention. (Wundt 1874, 726)

The importance of consciousness and attention in experience would become a major theme in James's own psychology and the main weapon in his attack on Spencer.

James's 1875 review of *Grundzüge* contained almost all of his characteristic criticisms of Spencer, later presented in a series of journal articles (EPh 1878, 7–22; EPs 1878, 1–37; EPs 1879, 38–61).[13] In the book, Wundt's reaction time experiments had provided empirical evidence for the importance of attention. In particular, they showed that reaction time could be altered by manipulating attention (Wundt 1874, 727). As James summarized,

> the experimental circumstances which shorten the time of reaction are mainly those which define beforehand as to its quality, intensity, or time, the signal given to the observer, so that he may accurately expect it before it comes. The focusing of the attention takes place under these circumstances *in advance.*

In other words, if subjects are prepared for the signal, they react more quickly—not surprising perhaps, but now "mathematically" demonstrated (ECR 1875, 299–300).

After describing Wundt's experiments, James launched into a tirade against Spencer and the "a posteriori school," repurposing Hodgson's notion of interest:

> The *a posteriori* school, with its anxiety to prove the mind a *product, coûte que coûte* [whatever the cost], keeps pointing to mere "experience" as its source. But it never defines what experience is. *My* experience is only what I agree to attend to. Pure sensation is the vague, a semi-chaos, for the *whole* mass of impressions falling on any individual are chaotic, and become orderly only by selective attention and recognition. These acts postulate *interests* on the part of the subject,—interests which, as ends or purposes set by his emotional constitution, keep interfering with the pure flow of impressions and their association, and causing the vast majority of mere sensations to be ignored. It is amusing to see how Spencer shrinks from explicit recognition of this law, even when he is forced to take it into his hand, so to speak. (ECR 1875, 300)

James argued that subjective interests lead to selective attention, which in turn has a major role in determining our experience.[14] He thus defended a loose psychological analogue of Kant's famous Copernican turn: the mind is not a mere product, but itself shapes and orders experience (Kant 1998, Bxii–Bxviii; ECR 1875, 301). James criticized Spencer for ignoring the empirically demonstrated importance of the active mind.

A few months later, citing Wundt's teaching as a model, James proposed a new Harvard undergraduate course in psychology. He suggested in a letter to the president, Charles William Eliot, that the course would take a middle way between philosophy and physiology (CWJ 1875, 4.527–528). The course—Natural History 2: Physiological Psychology—was accepted, and James taught it for the first time in 1876–1877, using Spencer's *Principles of Psychology* as a textbook (*Harvard University Catalogue* 1876, 59; ML, xxxiv). As the Wundt review had indicated, James was unhappy with Spencer's account of the perceiving mind. Becoming more and more confident in his criticism, halfway through the class James pronounced himself "completely disgusted with the eminent philosopher" (CWJ 1876, 4.552). After delivering his final lecture, James sent a mocking letter to James Jackson Putnam, a clinical instructor in the medical school who specialized in diseases of the nervous system:

> Poor Spencer, reduced to the simple childlike faith of merely timid, receptive uncritical, undiscriminating, worshipful, servile gullible, stupid, idiotic natures like you and [John] Fiske! Would *I* were part of his environment! I'd see if his "intelligence" could establish "relations" that would "correspond" to me in any other way than by giving up the ghost before me! (CWJ 1877, 4.564)

Behind James's jokes lay a more serious point: the idea of a correspondence between relations in the mind and relations in the environment, so central to Spencer's psychology, was difficult to interpret. What counted as a better correspondence?

James tackled this question in his first published article, written in the fall of 1877: "Remarks on Spencer's Definition of Mind as Correspondence" (CWJ 1877, 4.587).

Spencer, as I have argued elsewhere, had popularized the idea of life as a relationship between two entities, organism and environment (Pearce 2010, 2014). The mind-environment dyad was merely a special case:

> Regarded under every variety of aspect, intelligence is found to consist in the establishment of correspondences between relations in the organism and relations in the environment; and the entire development of intelligence may be formulated as the progress of such correspondences in Space, in Time, in Speciality, in Generality, in Complexity. (Spencer 1870, 385)

For Spencer, the evolution of intelligence is just a progressively improving correspondence between mind and environment. But how would progress be assessed? For James, this story had as its implicit "teleological factor" Hodgson's notion of *interest* (EPh 1878, 15, citing Hodgson's "Spontaneous Redintegration" chapter). As James had already insisted in the Wundt review, "subjective interests" are "the real a priori element in cognition" and "precede the outer relations noticed" (EPh 1878, 11n). Thus, his main strategy, as Mathias Girel has shown, was to replace Spencer's two-place relation—organism-environment—with a three-place relation—organism-interests-environment (Girel 2000, 82). Only by adding this third element, which provides a kind of norm or end, are we able to judge whether a correspondence has improved. Spencer's account could not truly avoid this teleology, said James; it just assumed very specific interests, "those of physical prosperity or survival" (EPh 1878, 11).

So James's primary critique of Spencer, first presented in the 1875 review of Wundt and elaborated in the 1876–1877 course and the 1878 article, was that he ignored the importance of interests—"the very flour out of which our mental dough is kneaded" (EPh 1878, 18). When James sent his article to Renouvier, the French philosopher responded by dismissing not only Spencer but evolution in general:

> [Spencer's] great renown in Europe arises from his systematization of the theory of evolution. But evolution is a passing fad. It will last 15 or 20 years, and then we'll talk about it the way they talked about Lamarck's system in the age of Cuvier. So it goes. (CWJ 1878, 5.8)

James, in contrast, was happy with the evolutionary-naturalistic picture of the mind; he just thought that Spencer had left out key elements. He summarized his critique in another early essay, "Brute and Human Intellect": "Spencer, throughout his work, ignores entirely the reactive spontaneity, both emotional and practical, of the animal" (EPs 1878, 19).[15] According to James, Spencer's account of the mind as a "mere product" had absurd implications:

> If Spencer's account were true, a race of dogs bred for generations, say in the Vatican, would have characters of visual shape, sculptured in marble, presented to their eyes, in every variety of form and combination. The result of this reiterated "experience"

would be to make them dissociate and discriminate before long the finest shades of these particular characters. In a word, they would infallibly become, if time were given, accomplished *connoisseurs* of sculpture. The reader may judge of the probability of this conclusion. (EPs 1878, 19–20; repeated in PP 1890, 381)

That is, subjective interests—whether innate or acquired—inevitably shape our experience. Whereas we marvel at the sculpted agony of Laocoön, a dog cares only for "the odors at the base of the pedestals" (EPs 1878, 20). Spencer's theory, said James, could not explain this difference.

But was this really fair to Spencer? It is hard to imagine him denying Auguste Comte's claim, in an 1843 letter to John Stuart Mill, that "it is the organism and not the environment [*milieu*] that makes us men rather than monkeys or dogs" (Littré 1863, 411; quoted in Pillon 1872, 211).[16] After all, as Renouvier noted in his review of *First Principles*, Spencer had provided his own explanation for the innate features of organisms:

> Innateness [for Spencer] is nothing but inheritance, an inheritance that one must follow back through the ages along the series of ancestors of each man, and along the longer series of man's animal ancestors, to the first and evanescent origins of life. (Renouvier 1872, 15)[17]

Spencer's (imagined) reply is thus straightforward: the ancestral environment is the cause of the innate differences between humans and dogs. James would certainly have been familiar with this idea, as it appeared quite clearly in Fiske's *Outlines of Cosmic Philosophy*, a book he knew well: our minds are the product of "intercourse with their environment—both their own intercourse and that of ancestral minds" (Fiske 1874, 1.86).[18]

This apparent unfairness was probably the reason his friend Chauncey Wright was so frustrated with James's attack on the "a posteriori school." In the Wundt review, James had singled out Wright as one of the few empiricists who actually admitted the importance of the active mind in experience (ECR 1875, 300, referring to Wright 1873). Nevertheless, Wright was not happy and told Grace Norton that James had misunderstood empiricism:

> In a paragraph in which he distinguishes and compliments me among the "empiricists" he has so badly misapprehended what the experience philosophy in general holds and teaches, that the compliment to me goes for nothing in mitigation of my resentment. (Wright 1875a)

Wright complained to James himself a few days later that the compliment had been "made at the expense of my friends" (Wright 1875b). But Wright was no friend of Spencer and had even joked with Norton in the earlier letter about having recently revived his "old warfare with Spencerism" (see Wright 1865). So why was he upset? Wright probably thought that philosophers such as Mill and Bain, mentioned alongside Spencer in the review, had already embraced something like James's position. Bain, for example, had built his account of volition around the idea of "spontaneous activity": "our various organs are liable to be moved by a stimulus flowing out from the nervous centres, in the absence of any impressions from without" (Bain 1855, 289). Mill, for his part, had clearly acknowledged in *System of Logic* that people differed in their susceptibility to certain sensations:

> Differences of mental susceptibility in different individuals may be, first, original and ultimate facts, or, secondly, they may be consequences of the previous mental history of those individuals, or thirdly and lastly, they may depend upon varieties of physical organization. (Mill 1974, 8.856)

According to James, Bain and Mill were "desperately bent on covering up all tracks of the mind's originality" (ECR 1875, 301). According to Wright, this claim was simply false: just because Mill thought that "the German school of metaphysical speculation" had erred in failing to attribute mental differences "to the outward causes by which they are for the most part produced," that did not mean that he denied to such differences a role in shaping experience (Mill 1974, 8.859). Mill thought these differences were "for the most part produced" by the environment. Spencer simply extended this, arguing that even those differences that seem like "original and ultimate facts" could be viewed—from the perspective of evolution—as products of the ancestral environment.

Spencer, then, could appeal to evolutionary history to explain variation in interests within and across species—something Wright thought James should have acknowledged. But Spencer's explanation had a key weakness, according to James: it gave a misleading account of the origin of that variation. James claimed to have a better story: first, variation in interests, and thus in perception and experience, is influenced by consciousness; second, even when the environment does play a role, it merely preserves spontaneous variations.

James believed that consciousness helps determine one's interests. Recall the line from the Wundt review, repeated almost verbatim in later works: "*My* experience is only what I agree to attend to" (ECR 1875, 300; cf. EPs 1878, 19; PP 1890, 380). James was well aware that many critics of the a posteriori school were theologically motivated: they wanted to preserve consciousness as something linked to the supernatural (ML 1878–1879, 136; CWJ 1879, 5.34). But James had already stressed in the review of Wundt that his own approach to consciousness was strictly scientific. After all, Spencer's own evolutionism implied that consciousness must have a function:

> Taking a purely naturalistic view of the matter, it seems reasonable to suppose that, unless consciousness served some useful purpose, it would not have been superadded to life. Assuming hypothetically that this is so, there results an important problem for psycho-physicists to find out, namely, *how* consciousness helps an animal. (ECR 1875, 302)

James's answer was that it may make us more streamlined and efficient in our response to stimuli—that "much complication of machinery may be saved in the nervous centres ... if consciousness accompany their action":

> Might, for example, an animal which regulated its acts by notions and feelings get along with fewer preformed reflex connections and distinct channels for acquired habits in its nervous system.... In a word, is consciousness an economical *substitute* for mechanism? (ECR 1875, 302–303)

According to James, a mechanical response to a series of individual environmental stimuli might be unwieldy compared to a response regulated by consciousness—and this could be an explanation of why consciousness evolved in the first place. Thus, James accused Spencer of ignoring not only interests and attention but also the function of consciousness in experience.

These three notions came together in the 1879 essay "Are We Automata?" James repeated his earlier points about the active mind: "Whoever studies consciousness, from any point of view whatever, is ultimately brought up against the mystery of *interest* and *selective attention*" (EPs 1879, 46). Spencer, ignoring these two concepts, seemed to claim that a highly evolved mind would be exquisitely tailored and completely responsive to each and every aspect of its environment—this would be perfect correspondence. James's reply was that in fact

> the most perfected parts of the brain are those whose action are least determinate. It is this very vagueness which constitutes their advantage. They allow their possessor to adapt his conduct to the minutest alterations in the environing circumstances, any one of which may be for him a sign. (EPs 1879, 42)

According to James's own evolutionary account, the contribution of consciousness is to, "by its selective emphasis, make amends for the indeterminateness" of what is otherwise "a happy-go-lucky, hit-or-miss affair" (EPs 1879, 43, 56). Thus, the different aspects of James's critique of Spencer were linked: only by emphasizing the discriminating power of consciousness—"the mind's selective industry"—could we explain its evolution (EPs 1879, 49).

Spencer could have replied that James's own account of the evolution of consciousness relied implicitly on the ancestral environment: organisms with consciousness persisted and progressed because they coped with environmental challenges more successfully than those without consciousness. But in "Are We Automata?" James seemed to suggest that "ancestral choice"—and not only the ancestral environment—was an important factor in evolution:

> We may even, by our reasonings, unwind things back to that black and jointless continuity of space and moving clouds of swarming atoms which science calls the only real world. But all the while the world we feel and live in, will be that which our ancestors and we, by slowly cumulative strokes of choice, have extricated out of this,

as the sculptor extracts his statue by simply rejecting the other portions of the stone. Other sculptors, other statues from the same stone! Other minds, other worlds from the same chaos! Goethe's world is but one in a million alike embedded, alike real to those who may abstract them. Some such other worlds may exist in the consciousness of ant, crab and cuttle-fish. (EPs 1879, 51–52)

James was obviously enamored of this image, as he returned to it several times in later works (PP 1890, 277; P 1907, 119). It is consistent with his example of the dogs as well: the canine experience of a museum is different because dogs, like crabs and cuttle-fish, live in a different world. For James, one's world is the product not only of one's environment and that of one's ancestors but also of a long series of "cumulative strokes of choice."

It is difficult to determine exactly what role James was granting to consciousness and choice in evolution. He was not alone in considering the question. The paleontologist Edward Drinker Cope, a prominent American defender of evolution, had recently argued that "intelligent choice taking advantage of the successive evolution of physical conditions, may be regarded as the *originator of the fittest*, while natural selection is the tribunal to which all the results of accelerated growth are submitted" (Cope 1871, 259). The sculpture metaphor, with its emphasis on choice, suggests that James might have agreed with Cope on this point. Like Cope, he thought that consciousness could "immensely shorten the time and labor of natural selection" (EPs 1879, 53). On the other hand, he was also in the midst of developing a new critique of Spencer that downplayed the importance of direct adaptation to the environment and thus seemed to rule out any cumulative evolutionary effects of intelligent choice.

This new critique, first presented in the third version of James's Natural History 2 course (now rechristened Philosophy 4), claimed that Spencer had given an incorrect account of the origin of variation.[19] According to James, Spencer had failed to distinguish two independent causal factors in evolution: "the regulator or preserver of the variation, the environment, is a different part from its producer" (ML 1878–1879, 137). James pointed out that Darwin's phrase "spontaneous variation" was meant to capture the fact that variations usually stem from "unknown physiological conditions" (ML 1878–1879, 138). In Darwin's view, the environment does not normally directly shape organisms, but rather selectively preserves those that happen to possess beneficial variations.[20] Thus, he argued that "in most, perhaps in all cases, the organisation or constitution of the being which is acted on, is a much more important element than the nature of the changed conditions, in determining the nature of the variation" (Darwin 1868, 2.291). Spencer, in contrast, had argued that "the production of adaptations by direct equilibration" becomes more important as organisms become more active—in animals and especially in humans (Spencer 1864, 468). For Spencer, the environment was primarily a producer of variation; for Darwin, it was primarily a preserver of variation.[21]

Darwin and Spencer saw their debate as largely empirical, having to do with which sort of process was actually more prevalent in evolution. Both acknowledged that the other sort of process could and did occur.[22] So why was it so important to James? The full answer became clear only later, in *Principles of Psychology*. In the very last chapter of this book, James returned to these questions as part of a larger argument that "the experience of the race can no more account for our necessary or a priori judgments than the experience of the individual can" (PP 1890, 1216). To support this thesis, James needed his earlier distinction between the production and preservation of variation. He began with a concession: Spencer's environmentalist account of the mind is true, but only for the special case of "time- and space-relations":

> Here the mind is passive and tributary, a servile copy, fatally and unresistingly fashioned from without.... The degree of cohesion of our inner relations, is, in this part of our thinking, proportionate, in Mr. Spencer's phrase, to the degree of cohesion of the outer relations;... and we are, in so far forth, what the materialistic evolutionists would have us altogether, mere offshoots and creatures of our environment, and naught besides. (PP 1890, 1229)

James claimed that the evolution of this aspect of our intelligence, which we have in common with other animals, was equivalent to a steady improvement in the correspondence between relations in the environment and relations in our minds. That is, the "experience of the race" can account for judgments of this general sort. However, James thought Spencer's approach inadequate when it came to abstraction, classification, logic, aesthetic appreciation, and other more advanced forms of judgment. Referring to his broader critique of Spencer's account of evolution, discussed above, James argued that the external environment was not the direct cause of these judgments. Instead, proposed James, they may

> be pure *idiosyncrasies*, spontaneous variations, fitted by good luck (those of them which have survived) to take cognizance of objects (that is, to steer us in our active dealings with them), without being in any intelligible sense immediate derivatives from them. (PP 1890, 1228)

Sometimes, said James, experience directly teaches the mind by impressing its order upon it, as in the case of time and space relations. But more often, he suggested, what does the work are "indirect causes of mental modification—causes of which we are not immediately conscious as such, and which are not the direct *objects* of the effects they produce." Most of the interesting aspects of the human mind, according to James, stem from the latter kind of process:

> Our higher aesthetic, moral, and intellectual life seems made up of affections of this collateral and incidental sort, which have entered the mind by the back stairs, as it were, or rather have not entered the mind at all, but got surreptitiously born in the house. (PP 1890, 1225)

Thus, for James our higher mental life is the product of spontaneous variations, only some of which have been preserved.

But what determines which variations survive? The environment, at least in part: if they do not "steer us in our active dealings with [objects]," variations will not persist. Thus, "natural selection" of helpful thoughts should produce a rough correspondence between mind and environment, even without direct adaptation. However, as in his earlier critique, James claimed that our subjective interests—especially our need for system—also play a key role, undermining the correspondence:

> The popular notion that "Science" is forced on the mind *ab extra* [from outside], and that our interests have nothing to do with its constructions, is utterly absurd. The craving to believe that the things of the world belong to kinds which are related by inward rationality together, is the parent of Science as well as of sentimental philosophy. (PP 1890, 1260)

James insisted that this "rational order of comparison" is part of the selection process; thus it is not adequate to say that our knowledge is shaped by the environment, whether that shaping is direct or indirect.[23]

Despite James's critique of Spencer, he was indebted to the English philosopher's broader naturalistic approach and especially to his organism-environment framework. In a letter to Henry Holt, publisher of the *Principles*, James made this perfectly clear:

> So far am I from leaving out the environment, that I shall call my text-book "Psychology, as a Natural Science," and have already in the introduction explained that the constitution of our mind is incomprehensible without reference to the external circumstances in the midst of which it grew up. My quarrel with Spencer is not that he makes much of the environment but that he makes *nothing* of the glaring and patent fact of subjective interests which cooperate with the environment in moulding intelligence. (CWJ 1878, 5.24–25)

James made good on his promise: in Chapter 1 as published, he contrasted the fertility of Spencer's naturalistic approach with that of traditional psychology:

> On the whole, few recent formulas have done more real service of a rough sort in psychology than the Spencerian one that the essence of mental life and of bodily life are one, namely, "the adjustment of inner to outer relations." Such a formula is vagueness incarnate; but because it takes into account the fact that minds inhabit environments which act on them and on which they in turn react; because, in short, it takes mind in the midst of all its concrete relations, it is immensely more fertile than the old-fashioned "rational psychology," which treated the soul as a detached existent, sufficient unto itself, and assumed to consider only its nature and properties. (PP 1890, 19)

James's critique of Spencer was not that he was too naturalistic or scientific, but rather that he neglected certain facts about subjective interests, mental activity, and consciousness.

James often explicitly bracketed his own metaphysical stance when engaging in these arguments. Discussing his account of the evolution of consciousness, for example, James insisted that "free-will is in short, no necessary corollary of giving causality to consciousness. My phrase about choosing one's own character is perfectly consistent with fatalism" (CWJ 1879, 5.34). When he later applied his psychology to the topic of education, he encouraged his audience of teachers "to adopt with me, in this course of lectures, the biological conception, . . . and to lay your own emphasis on the fact that man, whatever else he may be, is primarily a practical being, whose mind is given him to aid in adapting him to this world's life" (TTP 1899, 24). In sum, although James was criticizing the "a posteriori school," he was doing it with respectably naturalistic arguments: "The antithesis between inner and outer may subsist on a purely natural plane and a Philosophy accentuating the inner element be true without in any sense being a supernatural Philosophy" (ML 1878–1879, 136). As he wrote in the last chapter of *Principles*, "the account which the apriorists give of the *facts* is that which I defend; although I should contend . . . for a naturalistic view of their *cause*" (PP 1890, 1216). Thus, James opposed Spencer's evolutionism from the viewpoint of a broader evolutionary naturalism.

James's Later Work

Evolution primarily functioned as a sort of background assumption in James's later work: we know that human beings have an evolutionary history, and we need to take that into account in our philosophy. In this section I will very briefly indicate the role of evolution in James's ethics and in his account of knowledge and reality.

In 1891, James published his first and only explicit discussion of ethics: "The Moral Philosopher and the Moral Life." He claimed in this paper that evolutionists in ethics were often concerned with "the historical *origin* of our moral ideas and judgments" rather than with our ethical obligations as such (WB 1897, 142).[24] Nevertheless, James's picture of ethics inspired the evolutionary approach of younger philosophers such as John Dewey, whose work James would later endorse. James's thesis in "The Moral Philosopher" was that "we all help to determine the content of ethical philosophy so far as we contribute to the race's moral life" (WB 1897, 141). Ethics, for James, stems from the wants and needs of real people rather than from some "abstract moral order": there is an ethical obligation whenever there is "a claim actually made by some concrete person" (WB 1897, 148).[25] The development of ethics has been the history of attempts to satisfy jointly as many demands as we can: "*Invent some manner* of realizing your own ideals which will also satisfy the alien demands—that and that only is the path of peace!" (WB 1897, 155). Ethical progress is experimental: radicals and conservatives alike

> are simply deciding through actual experiment by what sort of conduct the maximum amount of good can be gained and kept in this world. These experiments are

to be judged, not *a priori*, but by actually finding, after the fact of their making, how much more outcry or how much appeasement comes about. (WB 1897, 157)

That is, ethics is a series of human experiments in attempting to satisfy our diverse and often conflicting desires. This open-ended viewpoint, highlighting the endless struggle inherent in any attempt to achieve a broader satisfaction, contrasted with that of Spencer, who insisted on a final "perfectly-evolved condition" in which "all our virtue is to flow spontaneously from our natural constitution"—a kind of end of ethical history in which everyone takes supreme pleasure in altruism (ECR 1879, 351; Spencer 1879, 275).[26]

A few years later, Dewey—who was delighted by James's essay—would frame this humanistic, experimental approach to ethics in explicitly evolutionary terms (Dewey to James, June 3, 1891, in Hickman 1999–). Equally opposed to Spencer's "insipid millennium," Dewey reinterpreted James's "experiments" as ongoing attempts to adapt ethics to an ever-changing social environment (Dewey 1898, 333–335). The benefit of what Dewey called the "evolutionary method" in ethics was that it used history to understand how different moral norms responded to particular social problems, and thus helped explain the present success or failure of certain norms (Pearce 2017, 51–54). Like James, Dewey embraced the idea of ethics as the continual attempt to make things better—to seek "the richer and the more inclusive arrangement," in James's phrase (WB 1897, 157):

> It is the lack of adequate functioning in the given adjustments that supplies the conditions which call out a different mode of action; and it is in so far as this is new and different that it gets its standing by transforming or reconstructing the previously existing elements. (Dewey 1902, 368)

Whether James was happy to frame ethics in such evolutionary terms is not easy to determine. But he did note Dewey's "admirable writings on ethics" and praised the philosophy of Dewey and colleagues for being "an evolutionism" with a more sophisticated account of the organism-environment dynamic than that of Spencer (EPh 1904, 103). James even lamented a few years later that Dewey's articles on ethics would "never get the attention they deserve till they are printed in a book" (ERE 1905, 98n). Thus, although James was critical of Spencer's evolutionary ethics, he seems to have been willing to endorse Dewey's more nuanced approach.

James appealed to evolution more explicitly in his account of our knowledge of the world around us. In his defense of radical empiricism, James gave an evolutionary explanation of why our experience is always intellectualized and categorized rather than remaining in its "pure" state of "immediate flux":

> The environment kills as well as sustains us . . . . The tendency of raw experience to extinguish the experient himself is lessened just in the degree in which the elements in it that have a practical bearing upon life are analyzed out of the continuum and verbally fixed and coupled together, so that we may know what is in the wind for us and get ready to react in time. (ERE 1905, 47)

Along similar lines, James argued in *Pragmatism* that our common-sense categories "are discoveries of exceedingly remote ancestors, which have been able to preserve themselves throughout the experience of all subsequent time" (P 1907, 83). For instance, the idea of *kind* is merely a "colossally useful *denkmittel* [thought-aid]," which helps straighten "the tangle of our experience's immediate flux" (P 1907, 87–88). The theories of both science and common sense, James declared, "are *instrumental*, are mental modes of *adaptation* to reality" (P 1907, 94).

This story about our knowledge of the world grew from James's earlier focus, in his critique of Spencer, on the importance of interest and attention: our sensations, said James, are "undoubtedly beyond our control; but *which* we attend to, note, and make emphatic in our conclusions depends on our own interests" (P 1907, 118). As in his ethics, James saw reality as fundamentally open. We could, James suggested, imagine an account of reality "which it proves impossible to better or alter" and view the permanence of this impossibility as constituting the truth of that account (P 1907, 120). But in the end what is primary is our own active role in shaping experience and reality: "We plunge forward into the field of fresh experience with the beliefs our ancestors and we have made already; these determine what we notice; what we notice determines what we do; what we do again determines what we experience" (P 1907, 122). According to James, this open-endedness was what distinguished pragmatism from its competitors: "for rationalism reality is ready-made and complete from all eternity, while for pragmatism it is still in the making" (P 1907, 123). Thus, both pragmatism and radical empiricism embraced a kind of evolutionary metaphysics.

Conclusion

James developed as a thinker in the midst of discussions of evolution. Initially he was reluctant to embrace Darwin's ideas, but he seems to have done so by the late 1860s. He was greatly influenced by the evolutionary philosophy of Herbert Spencer and spent most of the 1870s responding in one way or another to Spencer's views. Although James argued that Spencer neglected the importance of the active mind, he inherited the English philosopher's organism-environment framework. Despite James's critique of Spencer's evolutionism, he ultimately developed his own evolutionary philosophy, pursuing an experimentalist approach to both knowledge and ethics that was grounded in his earlier psychology.

Notes

1. "[James] was Darwinian, but he was not a Darwinist" (Menand 2001, 141). I will only be able to scratch the surface of this exciting topic, which has lately been attracting renewed interest. Just in the past few years, several dissertations have been written in the area (Shaw 2010; McGranahan 2012; Brady 2013, ch. 2).

2. There is a large literature on the Agassiz trip and on James's involvement in it: see Winsor (1991, 66–80), Irmscher (1999, 236–281), Menand (2001, 117–148), Machado (2006), and Richardson (2006, 65–74).
3. Such struggles were not uncommon among those interested in both science and philosophy: George Herbert Mead is a similar case (Pearce 2016).
4. Spencer introduced this account of life to the English-speaking world after encountering a version of it in the work of Auguste Comte (Pearce 2010, 2014; see also Spencer 1864, 74n).
5. Although he emphasized the direct shaping of the organism by the environment—on which more below—Spencer also thought that natural selection was an important factor in evolution (Spencer 1862, 297–298; 1864, 443–463).
6. See Croce (2009) for more on this topic.
7. The full story is more complicated than a simple "Renouvier cure"; see Leary (2015).
8. James wrote a notice of this journal early in its existence (ECR 1873, 265–266; see also CWJ 1876, 4.542). He later dedicated *Principles of Psychology* to "my dear friend François Pillon, as a token of affection, and an acknowledgment of what I owe to the Critique Philosophique" (PP 1890, 3). Spencer's work was not well known in France until the 1870s (Becquemont and Mucchielli 1998, 257–274; Beck 2014, 49–64).
9. For more on James and Renouvier, see Perry (1935, 1.654–710), Viney (1997), Girel (2007, this volume), and Dunham (2015).
10. In the quoted texts, James and Hodgson were attacking and Spencer was defending what is now called epiphenomenalism, "the view that mental events are caused by physical events in the brain, but have no effects upon any physical events" (Robinson 2015). Hodgson attacked epiphenomenalism in *Time and Space* (1865, 273–283)—the text quoted here by James—but then embraced it in *Theory of Practice* (1870, 1:416–436); conversely, James seems to have supported epiphenomenalism only a few years before this explicit rejection of it (MEN 1872, 247–256; Perry 1935, 1.615). For more on James and epiphenomenalism, see Klein (this volume).
11. James had planned to study in 1868 with both Wundt and Helmholtz at the University of Heidelberg, but ended up leaving Heidelberg after less than a week, worried about his health (CWJ 1868, 4.292, 4.326–327).
12. On Helmholtz's psychology of visual perception, see Hatfield (1992, 165–234). Helmholtz placed much more emphasis on the active mind in his optics than in his account of musical hearing—he did not think the latter even required a psychology (Pearce 2008, 86–91).
13. Richards (1987, 433–435), McGranahan (2017, ch. 1), and Leary (this volume) also highlight the importance of this review and James's criticisms of Spencer.
14. See Bromhall (2015, ch. 3) and Prinz (this volume) for analyses of James's notion of attention.
15. Peter Godfrey-Smith nicely describes this as a contrast between Spencer's "externalism" and James's "internalism" (Godfrey-Smith 1996, 90–94).
16. James may have read Littré's *Auguste Comte* (1863), since his diary list of books read includes many of Littré's other works; he probably also read the Pillon essay in which it was quoted (James 1870 and n. 8 above). Comte's point was a response to Mill's claim that further "ethological analysis of the influence of external circumstances" was needed to determine the origin of differences between men and women (Mill to Comte, October 30, 1843, in Mill 1963, 13.605).
17. This anonymous review was attributed to Renouvier by Louis Foucher and was likely read by James (see Foucher 1927, XIII and n. 8 above).

18. James discussed Fiske's book with Wright, Peirce, and others shortly after its appearance (CWJ 1905, 11.94). The book was based on two sets of Harvard lectures (in 1869 and 1871) that Charles William Eliot had commissioned (Nelson 1977; Pearce 2015, 453).
19. Having used a different textbook for 1877–1878, James returned to Spencer's *Principles of Psychology* for the 1878–1879 academic year (*Annual Reports* 1880, 60; ML, xxxiv).
20. McGranahan (2017) describes how James generalized this Darwinian account of selection and applied it to psychology, sociology, and ethics. Relatedly, Richards (1987, 436) and Klein (2013, 418) have both claimed that James's epistemology was fundamentally evolutionary.
21. James repeated much of this discussion in the opening section of his 1880 paper "Great Men, Great Thoughts, and the Environment," later collected in *The Will to Believe* (see WB 1897, 167–169).
22. For this reason, I think characterizing James's late 1870s critique as an attack on Spencer's "Lamarckism" is anachronistic: all of the points James makes against direct adaptation are consistent with the inheritance of acquired characters, which most naturalists (including Darwin) accepted at the time. Thus, I think we should resist reading James's later critique of Lamarckian theories of instinct back into these earlier papers (PP 1890, 1270–1280). See also n. 23 below.
23. The relevant sort of inheritance here might be cultural rather than biological. However, it is worth noting that James did not criticize Lamarckism in the section described above, which was devoted to "the *theoretic* part of our mental structure." He only emphasized the contrast between Lamarck and Darwin when it came to the "practical parts of our organic mental structure," that is, "the origin of instincts" (PP 1890, 1270–1280). See also n. 22 above, and for a contrasting view, see Klein (2016, 9–17).
24. There were no changes between the 1891 version of the article and the version published in *The Will to Believe* (1897); thus, I will cite the latter.
25. Greg Priest (2017, 590–593) has suggested that James's view of ethics was directly indebted to that of Darwin.
26. Spencer thought this final state provided an "ideal code of conduct" for ethics. For more details as well as criticisms from some of James's contemporaries, see Pearce (2017, 45–47).

Bibliography

Agassiz, Louis. 1863. *Methods of Study in Natural History*. Boston: Ticknor and Fields.
Agassiz, Louis, and Elizabeth Cabot Agassiz. 1868. *A Journey in Brazil*. Boston: Ticknor and Fields.
Annual Reports of the President and Treasurer of Harvard College, 1878–79. 1880. Cambridge, MA: John Wilson and Son.
Appel, Toby A. 1988. "Jeffries Wyman, Philosophical Anatomy, and the Scientific Reception of Darwin in America." *Journal of the History of Biology* 21: 69–94.
Bain, Alexander. 1855. *The Senses and the Intellect*. London: John W. Parker.
Beck, Naomi. 2014. *La gauche évolutionniste. Spencer et ses lecteurs en France et en Italie*. Besançon: Presses universitaires de Franche-Comté.
Becquemont, Daniel, and Laurent Mucchielli. 1998. *Le cas Spencer: Religion, science et politique*. Paris: Presses Universitaires de France.
Bowen, Francis. 1860. "Darwin on the Origin of Species." *North American Review* 90: 474–506.

Brady, Michael. 2013. "Evolution and the Transformation of American Philosophy." PhD diss., Southern Illinois University, Carbondale.

Bromhall, Kyle. 2015. "James's Account of the Phenomena and Conditions of Action." PhD diss., University of Guelph.

Calendar of the University of Michigan for 1885-86. 1886. Ann Arbor: University of Michigan.

Calendar of the University of Michigan for 1891-92. 1892. Ann Arbor: University of Michigan.

Carpenter, William B. 1874. *Principles of Mental Physiology*. New York: D. Appleton.

Cope, Edward Drinker. 1871. "The Method of Creation of Organic Forms." *Proceedings of the American Philosophical Society* 12: 229-263.

Croce, Paul Jerome. 1995. *Science and Religion in the Era of William James*. Vol. 1. Chapel Hill: University of North Carolina Press.

Croce, Paul Jerome. 2009. "A Mannered Memory and Teachable Moment: William James and the French Correspondent in the *Varieties*." *William James Studies* 4: 36-69.

Darwin, Charles. 1859. *On the Origin of Species by Means of Natural Selection, or the Preservation of Favoured Races in the Struggle for Life*. London: John Murray.

Darwin, Charles. 1868. *The Variation of Animals and Plants Under Domestication*. 2 vols. London: John Murray.

Dewey, John. 1898. "Evolution and Ethics." *The Monist* 8: 321-341.

Dewey, John. 1902. "The Evolutionary Method as Applied to Morality." *Philosophical Review* 11: 107-124, 353-371.

Dunham, Jeremy. 2015. "Idealism, Pragmatism, and the Will to Believe: Charles Renouvier and William James." *British Journal for the History of Philosophy* 23: 756-778.

Fiske, John. 1860. Letter to Jonathan Ebenezer Barnes. Papers of John Fiske (mssFK 1-1661), Box 2. Huntington Library.

Fiske, John. 1874. *Outlines of Cosmic Philosophy, Based on the Doctrine of Evolution, with Criticisms on the Positive Philosophy*. 2 vols. London: Macmillan.

Foucher, Louis. 1927. "Bibliographie chronologique de Charles Renouvier." In *La jeunesse de Renouvier et sa première philosophie (1815-1854)*, I-XL. Paris: J. Vrin.

Girel, Mathias. 2000. "James critique de Spencer: d'une autre source de la maxime pragmatiste." *Philosophie* 64: 69-90.

Girel, Mathias. 2007. "A Chronicle of Pragmatism in France Before 1907. William James in Renouvier's *Critique Philosophique*." In *Fringes of Religious Experience: Cross-Perspectives on William James's The Varieties of Religious Experience*, edited by Sergio Franzese and Felicitas Kraemer, 169-199. Frankfurt: Ontos.

Godfrey-Smith, Peter. 1996. *Complexity and the Function of Mind in Nature*. Cambridge: Cambridge University Press.

Harvard University Catalogue, 1876-77. 1876. Cambridge, MA: Charles W. Sever.

Harvard University Catalogue, 1879-80. 1879. Cambridge, MA: Charles W. Sever.

Harvard University Catalogue, 1885-86. 1885. Cambridge, MA: Harvard University.

Hatfield, Gary. 1992. *The Natural and the Normative: Theories of Spatial Perception from Kant to Helmholtz*. Cambridge, MA: MIT Press.

Helmholtz, Hermann. 1867. *Handbuch der physiologischen Optik*. Leipzig: Leopold Voss.

Hickman, Larry A., ed. 1999-. *The Correspondence of John Dewey, 1871-1953*. 3 vols. Charlottesville, VA: InteLex.

Hodgson, Shadworth H. 1865. *Time and Space: A Metaphysical Essay*. London: Longman, Green, Longman, Roberts, and Green.

Hodgson, Shadworth H. 1870. *The Theory of Practice: An Ethical Enquiry in Two Books*. 2 vols. London: Longmans, Green, Reader, and Dyer.

Hofstadter, Richard. 1944. *Social Darwinism in American Thought, 1860–1915*. Philadelphia: University of Pennsylvania Press.

Huxley, Thomas Henry. 1863. *Evidence as to Man's Place in Nature*. New York: D. Appleton.

Huxley, Thomas Henry. 1864. *Lectures on the Elements of Comparative Anatomy: On the Classification of Animals and On the Vertebrate Skull*. London: John Churchill and Sons.

Irmscher, Christoph. 1999. *The Poetics of Natural History: From John Bartram to William James*. New Brunswick, NJ: Rutgers University Press.

James, William. 1868. Diary Entry (April 22). William James Papers (MS Am 1092.9), item 4550, vol. 1. Houghton Library, Harvard University.

James, William. 1870. Diary List of Books Read. William James Papers (MS Am 1092.9), item 4550, vol. 1. Houghton Library, Harvard University.

Kant, Immanuel. 1998. *Critique of Pure Reason*. Translated by Paul Guyer and Allen W. Wood. Cambridge: Cambridge University Press.

Klein, Alexander. 2013. "Who Is in the Community of Inquiry?" *Transactions of the Charles S. Peirce Society* 49: 413–423.

Klein, Alexander. 2016. "Was James Psychologistic?" *Journal for the History of Analytical Philosophy* 4(5): 1–21.

Kuklick, Bruce. 1977. *The Rise of American Philosophy: Cambridge, Massachusetts, 1860–1930*. New Haven, CT: Yale University Press.

Leary, David. 2015. "New Insights into William James's Personal Crisis in the Early 1870s." *William James Studies* 11: 1–45.

Littré, Émile. 1863. *Auguste Comte et la philosophie positive*. Paris: Hachette.

Lurie, Edward. 1960. *Louis Agassiz: A Life in Science*. Chicago: University of Chicago Press.

Machado, Maria Helena P.T., ed. 2006. *Brazil Through the Eyes of William James: Letters, Diaries, and Drawings, 1865–1866*. Cambridge, MA: Harvard University Press.

McGranahan, Lucas. 2012. "William James's Evolutionary Pragmatism: A Study in Physiology, Psychology, and Philosophy at the Close of the Nineteenth Century." PhD diss., University of California, Santa Cruz.

McGranahan, Lucas. 2017. *Darwinism and Pragmatism: William James on Evolution and Self-Transformation*. New York: Routledge.

Menand, Louis. 2001. *The Metaphysical Club*. New York: Farrar, Straus and Giroux.

Mill, John Stuart. 1963. *The Earlier Letters of John Stuart Mill, 1812–1848*. Collected Works, vols. 12–13. Toronto: University of Toronto Press.

Mill, John Stuart. 1974. *A System of Logic Ratiocinative and Inductive, Being a Connected View of the Principles of Evidence and the Methods of Scientific Investigation*. Collected Works, vols. 7–8. Toronto: University of Toronto Press.

Nelson, Clinton Eugene. 1977. "John Fiske's Harvard Lectures: A Case Study of Philosophical Lectures." PhD diss., University of Iowa.

Pearce, Trevor. 2008. "Tonal Functions and Active Synthesis: Hugo Riemann, German Psychology, and Kantian Epistemology." *Intégral* 22: 81–116.

Pearce, Trevor. 2010. "From 'Circumstances' to 'Environment': Herbert Spencer and the Origins of the Idea of Organism-Environment Interaction." *Studies in History and Philosophy of Biological and Biomedical Sciences* 41: 241–252.

Pearce, Trevor. 2014. "The Origins and Development of the Idea of Organism-Environment Interaction." In *Entangled Life: Organism and Environment in the Biological and Social Sciences*, edited by Gillian Barker, Eric Desjardins, and Trevor Pearce, 13–32. Dordrecht, the Netherlands: Springer.

Pearce, Trevor. 2015. "'Science Organized': Positivism and the Metaphysical Club, 1865–1875." *Journal of the History of Ideas* 76: 441–465.
Pearce, Trevor. 2016. "Naturalism and Despair: George Herbert Mead and Evolution in the 1880s." In *The Timeliness of George Herbert Mead*, edited by Hans Joas and Daniel R. Huebner, 117–143. Chicago: University of Chicago Press.
Pearce, Trevor. 2017. "American Pragmatism, Evolution, and Ethics." In *The Cambridge Handbook of Evolutionary Ethics*, edited by Michael Ruse and Robert J. Richards, 43–57. Cambridge: Cambridge University Press.
Perry, Ralph Barton. 1935. *The Thought and Character of William James*. 2 vols. Boston: Little, Brown.
Pillon, François. 1872. "L'innéité selon M. Herbert Spencer." *Critique Philosophique* 1: 209–215.
Priest, Greg. 2017. "Charles Darwin's Theory of Moral Sentiments: What Darwin's Ethics Really Owes to Adam Smith." *Journal of the History of Ideas* 78: 571–593.
Proceedings of the American Academy of Arts and Sciences. 1860. Vol. 4, May 1857 to May 1860. Boston: Welch, Bigelow.
Renouvier, Charles. 1868. "De la philosophie de XIXe siècle en France." *L'Année Philosophique* 1: 1–108.
Renouvier, Charles. 1872. "Review of Spencer, *Les premiers principes*, trans. Cazelles." *Critique Philosophique* 1: 12–16.
Richards, Robert J. 1987. *Darwin and the Emergence of Evolutionary Theories of Mind and Behavior*. Chicago: University of Chicago Press.
Richardson, Robert D. 2006. *William James: In the Maelstrom of American Modernism*. Boston: Houghton Mifflin.
Robinson, William. 2015. "Epiphenomenalism." http://plato.stanford.edu/archives/fall2015/entries/epiphenomenalism/.
Russett, Cynthia E. 1976. *Darwin in America: The Intellectual Response, 1865–1912*. San Francisco: W. H. Freeman.
Shaw, Elizabeth C. 2010. "William James on Human Nature and Evolution." PhD diss., Catholic University of America.
Spencer, Herbert. 1862. *First Principles*. London: Williams and Norgate.
Spencer, Herbert. 1864. *The Principles of Biology*. Vol. 1. London: Williams and Norgate.
Spencer, Herbert. 1867. *The Principles of Biology*. Vol. 2. London: Williams and Norgate.
Spencer, Herbert. 1870. *The Principles of Psychology*. 2nd ed. Vol. 1. London: Williams and Norgate.
Spencer, Herbert. 1872. *The Principles of Psychology*. 2nd ed. Vol. 2. London: Williams and Norgate.
Spencer, Herbert. 1879. *The Data of Ethics*. London: Williams and Norgate.
Viney, Donald Wayne. 1997. "William James on Free Will: The French Connection." *History of Philosophy Quarterly* 14: 29–52.
Wiener, Philip P. 1949. *Evolution and the Founders of Pragmatism*. Cambridge, MA: Harvard University Press.
Winsor, Mary P. 1991. *Reading the Shape of Nature: Comparative Zoology at the Agassiz Museum*. Chicago: University of Chicago Press.
Wright, Chauncey. 1860. "The Economy and Symmetry of the Honey-Bees' Cells." *Mathematical Monthly* 2: 304–319.

Wright, Chauncey. 1865. "The Philosophy of Herbert Spencer." *North American Review* 100: 423–476.
Wright, Chauncey. 1873. "Evolution of Self-Consciousness." *North American Review* 116: 245–310.
Wright, Chauncey. 1875a. Letter to Grace Norton (July 12). Letters received by the Norton family (MS Am 1088.1), item 310. Houghton Library, Harvard University.
Wright, Chauncey. 1875b. Letter to Grace Norton (July 18). Letters received by the Norton family (MS Am 1088.1), item 311. Houghton Library, Harvard University.
Wright, Chauncey. 1878. *Letters of Chauncey Wright, with Some Account of His Life*. Cambridge, MA: John Wilson and Son.
Wundt, Wilhelm. 1874. *Grundzüge der physiologischen Psychologie*. Leipzig: Wilhelm Engelmann.

CHAPTER 6

JAMES AND MEDICINE
Reckoning with Experience

PAUL J. CROCE

Young adult William James was a scientist. Medical study was the culmination of his first scientific work, which began in 1861 with courses in chemistry, anatomy, and physiology, at Harvard's Lawrence Scientific School. He transferred to the Harvard Medical School in 1864, which granted him his only degree, an MD, in 1869. This educational preparation helped him to get his first job in 1873, teaching physiology, also at Harvard. Medical study was his point of entry into his first career path in the new field of physiological psychology, which he began teaching in 1875. Throughout almost two decades when he identified as a scientist, he constantly also pursued his curiosity for a humanistic range of topics in religion, literature, the arts, and especially philosophy, with deep speculations about his own posture in the world and about the science of his vocation. By the end of his young adulthood, with his 1880 appointment as Assistant Professor of Philosophy, his reflective avocation would become his vocation as a philosopher, even as lessons from his medical and scientific studies endured.

James never did practice medicine beyond dispensing occasional advice to friends and family members; and in his medical comments and his own healing practices, he often strayed far from the work of his scientific training. He visited water cures, took homeopathic remedies, and explored mind cure, some of many alternative, or "sectarian," practices popular and influential before the increasing success and growing authority of scientific medicine by the early twentieth century.

For James, sectarian medicine represented not only alternative healing possibilities, but also ways of thinking that challenged the increasing scientific consensus about what qualified as empirical facts, and even about what constituted science itself. James neither fully accepted nor wholly rejected all these unorthodoxies, but he also approached mainstream science and medicine in the same way. Each approach to healing claimed truth to nature, even as they defined its character in different ways. This chapter explains, first, the competing medical systems during James's lifetime; second, James's own engagement with these medical practices; and third, the impacts of his little-known medical experiences on his well-known mature theorizing. His mediation of scientific and sectarian medicine encouraged his commitment to learning from contrasting theories and practices throughout his career.

AMERICAN HEALING PRACTICES IN JAMES'S TIME

While James was making vocational choices and extracting intellectual lessons from multiple medical perspectives, healing practices were going through tremendous changes, both inside the ranks of mainstream scientific medicine, and in its relation with the whole medical marketplace. Practitioners competed directly for patients and debated about the character and proper use of empirical facts and the nature of science.

In the early nineteenth century, most American doctors emphasized the "bedside manner" of clinical practices, with minimal research or study beyond brief apprenticeships. A perennial challenge was that the inner workings of the human body presented a veritable black box except for the clues provided by symptoms, secretions, and excretions. Doctors worried about the therapeutic uncertainties of medical practice, which encouraged many to turn to scientific research with hope that increased knowledge would bring improved practice (Warner 1986, 171).[1]

Clinical and laboratory innovations would increase doctors' ability to peer into the body's black box. From the late eighteenth century, mainstream clinical practices received a major boost from the work of French physicians who in turn were spurred by revolutionary democratic drives, with professional impulses for public service. French doctors worked in large hospitals and introduced statistical record-keeping for tracking symptoms. They emphasized increased attention to anatomical research, including through the use of autopsies, and technological innovations, such as stethoscopes, to increase the ability to peer into the body for improved understanding of particular causes of particular ailments. The many American doctors who visited France returned with enthusiasm for the scientific enhancements to clinical practice but were wary of the massive caseloads and impersonal assessment of conditions, which became known as French "routinism" (Warner 1986, 55; 1998, 254–255). American clinical practices remained focused on the primary duty to heal, and for that, even with increased attention to bodily facts, personal attention was key.

By mid-century, laboratory research offered the promise of still greater increase in the ability to understand the body's inner workings. Physiological experimentation explained organic tissue on a chemical and physical basis, which promised the possibility of identifying causes for medical pathologies, even though at this point laboratory research suggested few therapies. For example, in 1835, Johannes Müller's theory of specific nerve energies, which correlated specific nerve actions with particular sensory experiences, suggested the physical location of apparently immaterial feelings.

These findings supported psychophysical parallelism. Science would focus on material bodily factors, with the immaterial realms of mind and feelings left for philosophical reflections. This outlook involved methodological materialism (the belief that the work of science should only focus on material things), but did not require philosophical materialism (the belief that the world can be understood in exclusively material terms, with apparently immaterial parts of the world reducible to material things), although it did encourage this leaning.

In the winter of 1867-1868, James studied with Emil du Bois-Reymond, who supported the goal of establishing still more physical explanations of physiological functions, by using physics models to develop a picture of "the interior of the muscle" with "centers of electromotive action." When du Bois-Reymond himself was a young scientist researching in Müller's laboratory in the 1840s, he wrote "a solemn oath" eagerly signed by his fellow young research partners, including Hermann von Helmholtz, Ernst Brücke, and Karl Ludwig, who would all become influential laboratory researchers. They proposed that "no forces other than the common physical-chemical ones are active within the organism" (du Bois-Reymond 1852, 109; also see Boring 1929/1950, 30, 707; Wertheimer 1970, 44; Otis 2002, 120).[2]

Innovations in microscopes encouraged the turn from attention at the bedside to study of tissues. Clinical doctors objected because laboratory reports about physical factors applicable to all would mean less listening to each patient's own experiences; this undercut the "principle of specificity," the belief that the specific traits of each particular patient, and even of each particular geographic locale, were the driving determinants of health. The evolution from clinic- to laboratory-based medicine reinforced scientific commitment to physical causation with attention directed away from the whole person and toward the agency of particular body parts. While clinicians attended to the patient as a whole and to particular organs, laboratory researchers evaluated cellular functions. Focus on universal discrete parts, with emphasis on physical and chemical causation, was well suited to a society with a rapidly growing population and an emerging mass culture, and this turn away from evaluation of the whole person also supported professional specialization into sub-disciplines to deal thoroughly with those parts. Laboratory techniques promised to fulfill hopes that focus on the physical substance of the body would produce healing insights, even as this identification of medicine with research science would lead to less interaction with patients.

Mainstream doctors also disagreed over the effectiveness of therapies. Scientific medicine included the practice of bleeding and application of leeches, and the use of a pharmacopeia that included many chemicals, especially the bacteria-killing purgative calomel, which had harsh and even poisonous side effects. Because these methods did not often lead to decisive therapeutic benefits, many mainstream doctors turned toward practices of watchful waiting while only offering palliative care to ease patient burdens. Harvard physician Jacob Bigelow argued that most diseases are "self-limiting," meaning that "the physician is but the minister and servant of nature," with little more to do than "to remove obstacles out of her path" (Bigelow 1835, 34–35). James's own teacher at Harvard, Oliver Wendell Holmes, Sr., even declared in 1860, "if the whole materia medica [medical drugs], *as now used*, could be sunk to the bottom of the sea, it would be all the better for mankind,—and all the worse for the fishes" (Holmes 1861, 467; italics in original). When reformers advocated for inclusion of more laboratory research in Harvard Medical School's curriculum, Bigelow and Holmes warned against reducing the "practical significance" of clinical training (Holmes 1889/1899, 204; Harrington 1905, 2.855).

For Bigelow, Holmes, and other advocates of clinical care, "expectant medicine" along with attention to the specifics of each patient, offered more promise than did the invasive treatments. Fellow doctors, however, denounced this therapeutic scepticism as the "nature-trusting heresy," and derided reliance on the patient's own healing powers. These scientific doctors would not accept that those powers remained beyond medical comprehension and called for laboratory research (Warner 1977, 320–321; Warner 1986, 7, 58, 164, 189, 275).

Even the nature-trusting "heretics" supported widespread scientific hopes based on laboratory research to surpass medicines "as now used," even though these hopes remained largely unfulfilled until the last decades of the nineteenth century with the development of the germ theory of disease. Emerging from the physiological laboratory research that young James was studying and teaching, and using improved technologies to peer into smaller components of life, the field of bacteriology brought successful identification of the microscopic sources of major diseases. These innovations dramatically increased the medical authority of laboratory work and raised hopes that science would solve medicine's perennial challenge about the body's elusive black box. These approaches to medicine were particularly effective with diagnoses and treatment of acute illnesses. In fact, dramatic cures of deadly diseases solidified the alliance of science and medicine by the early twentieth century (Hansen 2009, 45–121).

As scientific medicine steadily grew in authority throughout the nineteenth century, alternative approaches to healing also maintained extensive support. The popular collective name for these alternatives, the "sectarians," points to their diversity and the depths of their commitment, with each based on theories and practices often believed in with fervor akin to, and for some derived from, religion. The supporters of mainstream medicine, eager to claim scientific superiority, thought of the sectarians as antiscientific, or more bluntly, "quacks," for retention of primitive thinking in deliberate defiance of science. The sectarians made empirical claims to effectiveness and called the mainstream just another competing sect, with its own assumptions and beliefs, and its own eagerness to defend its territory (Rothstein 1972, 302; Coulter 1973, 140–148).

The alternatives in medicine relied on an alternative view of science. Influential British philosopher William Whewell introduced the term "scientist" in the 1830s to describe the specialized researcher of the laboratory and field, who used rigorous verification by empirical facts, in keeping with the explanations rooted in physics and chemistry that du Bois-Reymond and his colleagues sought in their laboratories. The mainstream medical criticisms of sectarians embodied Whewell's view of unscientific speculations that remained mired in "empty abstraction and barren ingenuity" (Whewell 1837, I.7). By contrast, sectarians claimed that "science" referred not to the rigorously precise search for physical facts, but to a way of thinking that featured a great breadth of knowledge and a deep wisdom about a broad range of experience, a view of science with an ancient pedigree. Sectarian science included an empiricism attentive to the firsthand experiences of patients, without mediation by laboratory investigations. In other words, the sectarians claimed probative significance based on experiential empiricism, what modern scientists, however, call mere anecdotal evidence. Because of the competition of terminology and methods, both mainstream and sectarian medical practitioners claimed to be "scientific" and "empirical." In fact, sectarians were popularly called "empirics," or in the slurring words of mainstream doctors, "senseless empirics," in reference to their reliance on the subjective experience of patients, without verification according to the new emphases of scientific medicine (Warner 1986, 41–45).

The sectarians also claimed to be more natural than mainstream medical doctors. Their use of plant tinctures, water, and other natural substances readily supported their claims, especially by contrast with the overtly invasive and harsh features of scientific medicine. And sectarian appeal went still deeper. A consistent thread in mainstream medicine, from before to after its development of bacteriological therapeutics, was that nature alone, including the body's natural healing power, was unreliable, hence the need for contrasting agents and actions to achieve and maintain health. The nature-trusting heresy within the mainstream offered an opening for the sectarians to extend the heresy still further, by claiming trust in each person's natural power to maintain and improve health (Gevitz 1988; Haller 2010). Even William Osler, one of the founders of the Johns Hopkins School of Medicine and a leading advocate for scientific medicine, expressed a back-handed appreciation for the "lesson of homeopathy," in prodding awareness about the mainstream therapies that did "no good" (Rothstein 1972, 326, and see 299).

Sectarians maintained that the physical stuff of living matter contained a distinctive vitality; they avoided the mind-body dualism of scientific medicine and took little interest in the bodily focus of laboratory research. To sectarians, ill health was an expression of distortion in the living vitality manifesting not only in the material body, but also in immaterial emotions and thoughts. By contrast, the mainstream focused on physical explanations with body and mind considered separately, and increasingly treated by separate specialized professionals, with each condition of body or mind addressed on its own with little attention to their relation. While sectarians made use of a range of different therapeutic means, they all agreed that each particular symptom served as an expression of the general vitality of the whole person. They aimed to improve health by correcting the distortions in the whole, with each particular modality able to enhance the natural capacity to heal. This strengthening of the whole person, this increased vitality, would heal the patient's particular ailments, in effect, as an aside. In this way, with symptoms treated as part of the body's adaptive means for coping with diseases, sectarians showed even more fidelity to Darwinian theory than did mainstream doctors, who used nature-contrasting medical interventions to remove natural adaptations from the body's healing powers. For example, fevers serve as a person's natural defense for coping with an illness; within limits, the high temperatures are a part (an uncomfortable part) of the healing process. Countering this symptom brings short-term relief but does not address the source of the ill health and can even undermine health. To sectarians, every part of a person is a local manifestation of an integrated whole, so the symptom in one place is an indicator about the whole person's condition, and it is the person who needs mending, not primarily or only the local issue. This contrast is also a reminder that while mainstream medicine, especially with its technical and pharmacological interventions, offers quick relief, the sectarians called for patience with nature's paths, even as they promised more wholesale addressing of overall sources of problems.

The spectrum of health-care providers in James's lifetime spanned from the materialist scientific mainstream to an array of sectarians with degrees of material and immaterial commitments. James repeatedly visited mind-cure practitioners, even as he maintained skepticism about their explicitly anti-materialistic stance. Mind-cure advocates, especially in the Christian Science Church, founded by Mary Baker Eddy in 1879, believed in the mind's power over the body, including health. The Thomsonians were the most prominent of the herbal healers, with use of different plants to produce an array of physiological responses and emphasis on home remedies for average citizens.

James frequently attended water cures, which were more than spas for recreation. The healing system hydropathy depicted each person in a constant state of "appropriation and secretion," with congestion blocking the release of unhealthy substances occurring naturally with sweat and excretion (Rausse 1851, 5). Their multiple uses of water at different temperatures, including for drinking, immersion, wraps, and mud-poultices, would supplement the patient's own healing powers, making longer-enduring changes to the configuration of the blood vessels and other organs than conventional drugs would. In short, they argued, hydropathy supported processes already in place. James reported the effectiveness of the baths for "all sorts of chronic troubles" (CWJ 1868, 4.259); his word choice is a reminder that sectarian practices made less appeal for acute cases than for chronic ones that often eluded mainstream therapies.

The most sophisticated of the alternatives was homeopathy, developed in Germany in the late eighteenth century, and practiced in the United States from 1825, including by the James family. Its rapid growth led to the formation of the American Institute of Homeopathy in 1844, which spurred the establishment of the rival mainstream American Medical Association in 1847. Homeopathic commitments inspired the most fervent critical reactions from mainstream practitioners. Its Law of Similars, expressed as "like cures like" (hence the original name, "homoeopathy": from the Greek words for "same suffering"), meant that substances similar to the disease itself, ones that produce its symptoms, also help the body recover from that disease. And according to the Law of Infinitesimal Doses, they claimed that, once diluted, the remedy, even with substances harmful at full dose, actually increases its healing power, even when original substances would no longer be chemically detectable. Homeopaths engaged in scientific practices including systematic measurement of their remedies, careful testing of them and tracing of their impacts on patients; but that empirical rigor could not offset, for most mainstream doctors, the lack of homeopathic adherence to the philosophical assumptions of mainstream science with its prioritization of physical causality.

Mainstream doctors in the nineteenth century could dismiss most sectarians for their lack of education and reliance on folk traditions or variations on common sense and common hopes. Most homeopaths, however, emerged from the ranks of mainstream medicine itself. While many doctors maintained confidence in the emerging possibilities of laboratory-based innovation, the prevalent therapeutic uncertainties generated impatience with scientific medicine among both doctors and patients. For example, William Holcombe was the son of a mainstream doctor and received his medical degree from the University of Pennsylvania, where his teachers "denounced [homeopathy] bitterly"; but in practice, the slimness of effective therapies made him feel that doctors were "blind men, striking in the dark." During the 1849 cholera epidemic, he noticed "the cases which get well would have recovered without any treatment." With this tangible expression of the nature-trusting heresy, he tried "Hahnemann's medical moonshine" and observed improvement. After some more treatments with homeopathy, mostly with success, and after much re-thinking of his "education, . . . interest, . . . and habit" in the "old medical profession," he resigned from his mainstream medical society and became a homeopath, rising to the presidency of the American Institute of Homeopathy in 1874 (Holcombe 1877; quoted in Coulter 1973, 104–107). Such conversions of educated doctors from the social mainstream amplified the marketplace competition, with the public serving as decisive arbiters of medical choices. Mainstream doctors responded to the reductions in their popular support by setting standards for medical education and for the licensing of professional practice, with consultation clauses that prohibited doctors from even talking with sectarian practitioners (Rothstein 1972, 301–313; Coulter 1973, 206–219).

With their mutual hostility, homeopaths blamed any of their poor results on patients' prior treatments by mainstream doctors, and those doctors accused homeopaths of catering to public endorsement of their ways while secretly administering scientifically approved remedies to gain any of their achievements. Their competing arguments illustrate James's "sentiment of rationality," with the rational arguments of each set of practitioners beginning with the sentiments that shaped their commitments (EPh 1879, 32). To scientific doctors, use of their remedies and public gullibility were the only ways to explain the sectarian successes. Homeopathy defied basic principles of mainstream science. The infinitesimal doses lacked physical substance; and attention to the distinctiveness of each patient meant that no remedy could be tested for its universal causal impact. From the point of view of scientific medicine, homeopathy could be an agent for health only if, as one physician said pointedly in 1833, "the ordinary laws of nature were occasionally suspended" (Leo-Wolf 1835, 271).

Rather than focusing on physical causality, homeopaths carefully tracked symptoms, in enormous detail, as potential indicators of the character of each person's vital force. This is why mainstream doctors ridiculed the empirical cataloging of symptoms as "meaningless minutiae," in the dismissive words of one Yale professor and AMA vice president (Hooker 1850, 87). Despite the homeopathic adoption of the fact-gathering parts of scientific practice, to mainstream doctors, homeopathy was a derangement of science skating on the symptomology surface of health, overlooking the physical agents that caused the symptoms, and ignoring the promise of laboratory inquiries. While the mainstream did not want to give credence to this sectarian heresy through testing, the homeopaths did not even want to give credence to such testing because to them, the curative power was not in the remedy but in each distinct person, with even the same remedy having different impacts on different people.

Homeopathic thinking, as with sectarians in general, operated with an empiricism and a claim to science, but without privileging the most materially tangible of the sciences, physics and chemistry; instead they proposed that, as with the action of herbs and water in other sectarian modalities, their remedies acted energetically in resonance with the person's own vitality. Sectarians inverted mainstream thinking, emphasizing the degree of strength of the patient instead of the severity of the illness. While sectarians suggested that a person's general health, with periodic support, would prevent susceptibility to a host of potential problems, regular medicine depicted ill health as a problem or an invasion that needed to be quelled or attacked. In fact, the name "allopathy" for mainstream medicine, from the Greek words for *other* and *suffering*, emerged in contrast with the sectarians, especially homeopathy.

Through the 1860s and 1870s, when James studied medicine and identified as a scientist, and before the most sophisticated and influential impacts of scientific medicine, sectarians gained extensive public support, with homeopathy winning the most converts. Their successes stemmed from both the pull of their gentler approaches and the push away from the harsh therapies of the mainstream with few therapeutic benefits yet emerging from laboratory research. The more tolerant of the mainstream doctors pointed to the ancillary medical advice of the sectarians, for good general hygiene, as the source of any success they generated; and sectarians did in fact encourage healthy lifestyles more than the nature-contrasting allopaths. While the health-care providers debated, average citizens made choices, practicing what one sectarian called "curapathy," simply using whatever cured best in their own experiences with little attention to the fierce debates or the intellectual theorizing of the competing medical approaches (Coulter 1973, 119–124, 140–148; Whorton 2002, 307).

James's Engagement with Scientific and Sectarian Medical Practices

During the 1860s, as William James reached adulthood, he experienced the medical debates directly, first in his vocational choices. James family prosperity meant that he could end his 1863 list of "four alternatives" for future work with a joke: "Natural History, Medicine, Printing, Beggary" (CWJ 1863, 4.81). The humor reflected his frustration about his indecision over his many leanings; and yet, the rest of the list included a fairly accurate prediction of his first vocational steps. Two years later, he tried on a career in natural history when he joined Louis Agassiz's Thayer Expedition to Brazil (Croce 1995, 123–124; 2018, 53–68). While earning his medical degree, the printing reference showed his hope to write "for medical periodicals" (CWJ 1867, 4.243). He wrote dozens of reviews, starting in 1865, on topics related to his medical and scientific studies, which served as good training for the work of synthesizing and interpreting existing research as a background for his interpretive innovations—and for his emerging ability to express complicated ideas in popularly appealing prose. Robert Richardson identifies James's ability to adapt his writing for different professional and popular audiences (Richardson 2006, 360, 511–512).

Young James steadily followed his personal reflective interests into psychological and philosophical inquiries, while his medical studies provided physiological support for those reflections. Medicine would give him solid scientific credentials as the new field of psychology was applying physiological research to philosophical questions. From the perspective of his own lived experience in the 1860s, however, his work toward his MD was training to become a non-practicing research physiologist in keeping with the mainstream hope that improved medical diagnostics would bring better therapies. This was in fact the path of his colleague and friend Henry Bowditch, who became the first American doctor to work as a full-time research physiologist in 1871; and he enabled James to get his first job, teaching physiology in 1873. James declared in 1869, "purely scientific study . . . [is] the only satisfying work," which he also enthusiastically supported in Bowditch: "Go in old boy and drink deep [and] I, for one will promise to read yea, and *believe in*, all your researches" (CWJ 1869, 4.381; italics in original; Fye 1987, 106 and 110).

When James himself drank from the well of medicine, he was more self-deprecating, calling his final thesis a work of "no value," even though his whole education was quite robust (CWJ 1869, 4.378). He worked with the world-famous physiologist Édouard Brown-Séquard, who had grown up British in St. Mauritius, the son of a French mother and an American father, and who would command prominent university posts at Harvard and the Collège de France. He was rigorous in his laboratory research and such a passionate investigator that he would experiment on himself, once even paralyzing two fingers. Eager to promote the use of science within regular medical practice, Harvard Medical School directed "increased attention to the wants" of their new professor, and they gave him the honor of addressing the enrolling students in the fall of 1866, including James, who had recently returned from Brazil (Tyler and Tyler 1984, 1235). In his "Advice to Students," Brown-Séquard relayed the excitement he felt for the "complete revolution which is now taking place in every branch of the science of medicine." In particular, the study of physiology would offer "floods of new light . . . on the mysteries of disease"—that, he declared, was the way out of the "painful uncertainties of therapeutics." James was studying at the center of expectations that the black box of medical uncertainty was about to be opened through the work of laboratory physiology.

Urging laboratory investigation to supersede the authority of accepted theories based in clinical practice or the claims of sectarians, Brown-Séquard made a swipe at the experiential empiricism of these approaches, declaring that medicine "is now beginning at last to become rational, instead of being purely empirical as it was." James's coursework with Brown-Séquard included careful experimental research on cell physiology and the influence of chemicals on living muscles and nerves. This laboratory research supported the hope for rational therapeutics that would control medical scourges (Brown-Séquard 1867, 31, 10, 15).

The hiring of Brown-Séquard was a major step on the Medical School's path toward expanding its support of laboratory work, especially when Charles Eliot became university president in 1869. James had studied chemistry with Eliot starting in 1861 before his stellar administrative career, with the expansion of laboratory science serving as a centerpiece for promotion of professional rigor in the whole university. James's study of scientific medicine during this transition period included both laboratory and clinical work: he both studied with Brown-Séquard and was "anxious to get into the hospital." James held a kind of internship, serving as "acting house surgeon in the Mass. Gen. Hospital." He planned for the position of "House Pupil" in 1867 but turned it down, opting to go to Germany to study physiology and the impact of the nervous system on psychology (CWJ 1866, 4.148 and 143; 1867, 4.154). Even this first turn to psychology grew from his clinical visits to asylums; "of all departments of Medicine," he declared in 1863, that is "the most interesting" (CWJ 1863, 4.81).

During the 1860s, while James was studying the scientific medicine of clinic and laboratory, he also practiced alternative medicine extensively. He regularly visited water-cure baths for his persistent back, eye, and digestive problems and for his frequent depressed mood at least as early as 1867.[3] He understood these curative establishments in the language of energy use and depletion, outlooks that coincided with the diagnoses of neurasthenia, which he identified with for the rest of his life. In fact, he learned to manage this condition in ways that he first experienced in sectarian practice. Hard study would exhaust him and exacerbate problems, then water-cures would serve as filling stations to build up energy for more study. James's words about his care could have been taken from a hydropathic description of the effectiveness of a range of "sanatory exercises" for breaking through congestion in the body with the baths able to "remove 'exudations' f[ro]m sprained joints, old wounds &c, like a charm." And he added that they are "likewise of value in some nervous diseases"—particularly important for his depleting stores of energy. In short, "these baths were of great efficacity [sic] to me." However, he also compared the competing medical systems bluntly; mainstream doctors attacked problems immediately, whereas "the trouble with the water cure," and a challenge for all sectarians, "is that it takes such a h-ll of a time to produce its effects." In the 1860s, he was content to put aside his own impatience and "give the baths a fair chance of working" (CWJ 1868, 4.259–260, 338, 297).

In the fall of 1869, just a few months after James had completed his medical degree, when he was starting to slide into his darkest moods, he applied this same experimental approach to homeopathy. James John Garth Wilkinson, an English MD, who had turned to homeopathy from his own impatience with harsh chemical medicines, took his case. He had been a close James family friend since the early 1840s; in October of 1869, James's mother reported "Dr. Wilkinson's diagnosis & prescription" for William: "high dilutions of Rhus and Nux Vomica." To homeopathic physicians, Rhus Toxicodendron, a minimum dose of poison ivy, would have been indicated by his chronic back troubles, and

Nux Vomica, a strychnine tincture derived from poison nut, was frequently prescribed for those with digestion problems and an overworked nervous system. These symptoms were all ones that James repeatedly showed and therefore would have served as keynotes in Wilkinson's assessments of William's holistic remedy picture (CWJ 1869, 1.106; Mary to Henry James [Junior], September 21, 1869, James Papers).

Remedies often set patients back, at first. Homeopaths expected these aggravations; Hahnemann said remedies would make patients "medicinally ill, but only for a short time" (Hahnemann 1836, aphorism 29). Hydropaths called such temporary setbacks "crises"; and these were part of the extensive processes that tried the patience of those working with sectarians—including James. These processes also suggested a reason he used the word "crisis" so frequently and often without alarm: sectarian therapists even called acute crises "healing diseases," with these symptoms serving as part of each person's adaptive means for coping with troubles (Rausse 1851, 49). The patience called for with sectarian therapies extended also to expectation for more management of problems rather than complete cure.

James not only remained open to contrasting medical practices, but also studied them together. His friend, the scientist Nathaniel Southgate Shaler, early in 1868 urged him to consider "the degree of efficiency in [water cure] which is calculated to render it valuable for the Medical Profession" (CWJ 1868, 4.258). A few months later, James chose a topic for his thesis on "the physiological effects of cold," which drew upon his "thermal experiments" with water cure, but with scientific scrutiny (CWJ 1868, 4.52 and 1868, 4.346). While in medical school, he wrote in a private notebook about the hydropathic use of temperature variation, along with the Law of Similars in homeopathy, as some of "many remedies" worth studying; and he had corresponded with Henry Bowditch "about the therapeutics of Heat & Cold" (James papers, c. 1868–69; CWJ 1868, 4.260). James even proudly proclaimed, "the physiological effects of cold ... ramifies off into the whole of physiology almost, and suggests all kinds of openings" (CWJ 1868, 4.352). He used skills from his scientific training to scrutinize the evidence from lived experience. The thesis itself has not survived, but his later works supporting scientific inquiries into hypnotism, psychical phenomena, spiritual experiences, and many alternative healing practices suggest that his thesis advocated taking claims for the health implications of temperature seriously while calling for further study.

In order to earn his degree, James also needed to sit for an examination in the summer of 1869. James himself set the tone for the reputation of the exam as an informal ritual of little consequence when he reported that during the oral questioning, after his favorable response to one factual question from Holmes, his teacher then simply stopped the questioning in favor of a friendly chat. But this description from late in life, delivered with exaggeration and characteristic self-deprecation for encouraging students, referred at most to just one portion of the exam. And the story first emerged in James's son's biography of Harvard President Eliot, which emphasized his reforms for increased educational rigor begun that same year. The new president did indeed bring significant reforms, but James had already reaped his own version of these reforms during his study of physiology in Germany. The full examination was certainly more "laissez faire" than later ones, but it also included "a case to be reported on at the dispensary and . . . . . . written work to be handed in." And the oral examination itself included thorough demands in many areas of medicine; James was especially well prepared to display his extensive knowledge in the parts of medicine he had researched most (Kaltenborn 1907, 94; James 1930, 1.275–276). Before the exam, Bowditch wrote to James bluntly, speaking as a fellow specialized researcher, "don[']t let the Doctors bully you" with their own specialized questions; "if they try any game of that sort," his friend continued in recognition of James's learning in physiology, "knock them down with some of Helmholtz's latest views" (CWJ 1869, 4.365–366).

After his formal study of medicine, James would set his own course distinct from his work in medical school, but with constant reference to the methods of inquiry and the commitment to study of natural facts he had learned there. Reflective young James asked broad questions about his scientific work, about body and mind, and about natural facts and their causes. Before his first teaching job in 1873, his agitation over these questions was amplified by his early personal turmoil, which continued in degrees for the rest of his life. He had learned from the sectarians that the worst times, his "crises" like "healing diseases," were also opportunities for the deepest healing and growth. James emerged from these years not only with a commitment to assert his own free will, but also with an inclination to approach contrasts and dilemmas as both obstacles and opportunities. James was backing into philosophical thinking from the pressures of his own experiences.

Serious reckoning with both scientific and sectarian medical systems contributed to James's profound questioning of the relation of material and immaterial dimensions of life. Reflections on his education, both in and out of medical school, and discussions in the Metaphysical Club, encouraged his first major philosophical statements on what he called "The Sentiment of Rationality," with "psychological work on the motives which lead men to philosophize" (EPh 1879, 64). After training as a doctor, he became a psychologist with philosophical interests, and this is how he could say that "I never had any philosophical instruction, the first lecture on psychology I ever heard being the first I ever gave" (CWJ 1902, 10.590). That "first lecture" would have been when he developed a new course in 1875, "The Relations between Physiology and Psychology," which earned a $300 appropriation from the Harvard Treasurer for laboratory equipment. It was a striking innovation, but a small one. In fact, his student, G. Stanley Hall, who would become a significant organizer of the emerging field of scientific psychology, challenged James's priority, dismissing the Harvard laboratory as "a tiny room" with just a few "bits of apparatus" (Perry 1935, 2.13–14; Harper 1949, 170). James's experimental research, as with all his scientific and medical work, encouraged the orientation toward natural facts that animated all his philosophy. Harvard recognized James's intellectual turn with his appointment as professor of philosophy in 1880.

James's laboratory in psychology, along with his psychology courses, emerged in evolution from his study of physiology as a medical student. In December of 1875, James asked Charles Peirce in Paris to "bring me back an instrument or two" (CWJ 1875, 1.246). In 1878, Hall himself said that James's course in psychology was "the only course in the country where students can be made familiar with the methods and results of recent

German researches in physiological psychology" (Hall 1879, 97). Laboratory research was central to the increasing authority of professionalizing medicine and science, including the new science of psychology, with methodological materialism and the promise of identifying physical explanations about natural facts. James continued to support these scientific practices even as he raised questions about their assumptions and the extent of their reach.

From Medical Experiences to Philosophizing

As James turned to philosophizing, he incorporated his medical and scientific work through reflections on its meanings and implications. In fact, that was the philosophical character of his thinking, with philosophy serving less as a discipline than as a posture for questioning experience. Given his previous work, that meant questioning his experience as a scientist and the whole range of his encounters with healing. Diverse healing practices presented his first major confrontation with dramatically different ways of interpreting and dealing with the same facts, and his response would become a central feature of his theorizing: he turned heated debates into resources for both questioning and using the merits of each side. From scientific medicine, James adopted impulses to pay close attention to natural facts and to pursue constant inquiry for understanding them; and from the sectarians, he drew lessons about the importance of respecting lived experiences beyond the laboratory study of physical processes, even as he maintained the importance of understanding these experiences as further expressions of natural facts.

James's questions about science did not lead to withdrawal from its work; he spoke as an insider, urging enhancement of its practices. In his first publication, in 1865, James reviewed an icon of his field, Thomas Huxley, who had just published *Lectures on the Elements of Comparative Anatomy*. He began with praise for the book's "valuable contributions to almost every province of anatomical science." Then he turned philosophical with a distinction between "the two great intellectual tendencies" ever since "men began to speculate.... [S]ynthetists are theorists, who require their knowledge to be organized into some sort of a unity," while "analysts are actualists, who are quite contented to know things as isolated and individual." James offered a bold twist on Huxley's reputation as an avid man of factual science: in addition to Huxley's clear analytical coverage of anatomy, James argued, the British scientist had the heart of a synthesizer, ready to move beyond the empirical. In particular, Huxley used his zeal for scientific truth as a "battering-ram" to assert that the "phenomena of life . . . result directly from the general laws of matter." Huxley also brought to science his "love of coming rapidly to a definite settlement of every question, deciding either Yes or No" (ECR 1865, 197, 199, 202, and 198). James generalized his argument in the review into a "Program of the Future of Science," for promotion of scientific inquiry without reduction to physical causality, and without always expecting definite answers. But realizing the authority of science especially in his own academic circles, he was ready to use the "*perfect respectability*" of the more technical, scientific parts of the review "as a shield." (CWJ 1864, 4.93–94; italics in original). This stance explains his simultaneous openness to sectarian practices even while working within science, and it also displays a philosophical version of the sectarian emphasis on management rather than definitive solution.

James built his first philosophical work on his psychology, physiology, and medical training, and many of these essays became parts of his first book where he continued to peer across boundaries. *The Principles of Psychology* (1890) was a synthesis of the new physiological psychology, even as he reported on the field with philosophical reflections and introspective accounts of his experiences. The newly published text received backhanded praise from pioneering physiological psychologist Wilhelm Wundt: "It is literature, it is beautiful, but it is not psychology" (Steffens 1931, 149–150). James appealed to scientific readers by acknowledging and making use of the "strictly positivistic point of view" (PP 1890, 6), especially with his abundant references to laboratory research. He was working within a scientific field that relied on a dualist outlook, with separation of body and mind understood with the prevalent method of psychophysical parallelism, that is, with acknowledgement of both realms, but a methodological focus on the physical with no expectation that mental phenomena would provide any causal agency. Gerald Myers proposed that James adopted a "provisional dualism" in *Principles* (Myers 1986, 55, 192). Even in the text, however, James kept considering the inter-relation of physical and non-physical dimensions of experience (see Cooper and Klein, both in this volume).

In the *Principles*, James expressed impatience with reduction to physical causality more through critique of scientific certainty than with the presentation of alternatives—so in effect, he applied the skeptical scrutiny of positivism to science itself, by raising questions about the role of immaterial factors in psychology. For example, he approached even claims to "spiritual agents," including "Souls," as "pulses of consciousness ... affected by occurrences in the nervous centres." His descriptions recalled the energetic dynamics claimed by sectarian medicine, with forces "mysterious" existing "inside of both worlds," both body and mind. He avoided mention of such sectarian "unsafe hypotheses" and returned to the "provisional halting-place" of scientific psychology, with the "parallelism ... [of] positivism ... the wisest course." However, as with his scrutiny of alternative ideas in general, he called again for a future science when "things must some day be more thoroughly thought out." Meanwhile, he punctuated his scientific work with suggestions about interactions across the dualism, identifying "the tinge of mystery" within natural facts that even positivism could not dispel. James approached the dualism of his fellow scientific psychologists as a useful, if limited, tool for understanding mind and behavior, but not for final comprehension of psychology in general. He offered poetic expression for the simultaneous existence of the empiricism of physical science and the experiential empiricism of alternative approaches: "nature in her unfathomable designs has mixed us of clay and flame" (PP 1890, 181–82).

The openness that James maintained in *The Principles* to a range of experiences would also be a factor in his later philosophy. His pluralism is a formalized expression of this posture. James insisted in *A Pluralistic Universe* that "individuality outruns all classification" (PU 1909, 7), just as he witnessed in a plurality of medical modalities and learned from the sectarian attention to the unique specificity of each patient. The pragmatic focus on consequences included a call to liberate from claims to truth with authoritative pedigrees. Instead, pragmatism engaged experiences directly, not for acceptance of all, but to bring all to scrutiny for fidelity to natural facts and usefulness—the approach he had been using with different medical systems. Pragmatism brought curopathy to philosophy, with an "alteration in 'the seat of authority'" by "look[ing] forward into facts themselves," no matter their source (P 1907, 62).

When studying science in 1863, and well before developing his radical empiricism, James declared that "nature only offers Thing. It is the human mind that discriminates Things" (James Papers 1863, 59). He later called "Thing" "pure experience," the undifferentiated mass of data that nature offers, and from which the mind carves out, or discriminates, mental and physical objects. Consistent with his radical empiricism, James approached competing health systems as different ways of sorting the same health conditions according to the very different thoughts of scientific and sectarian medicine.

The significance of both a "thing and its relations" (ERE 1909, 45–47) in radical empiricism supplied still more mental tools for comprehending the range of medical thinking. James maintained the importance of scientific medicine for its ability to assess the physical "things" of health; meanwhile, sectarian medicine attended to the relations of health conditions. The holistic connections across parts of the body and spanning from body to realms of mind and emotions exemplify his theory of the reality of relations. And in practical terms, while the mainstream's close scrutiny of physical factors led to outstanding diagnostics and treatment of acute conditions, sectarians claimed more effectiveness with chronic conditions and preventive care, which were more likely to involve a network of factors in relation.

Just as James experimented with various health systems, he also circulated eagerly with unconventional people, ranging from Benjamin Blood, who promoted an "anæsthetic revelation" from drugs, to Charles Peirce himself, who, before his posthumous fame, was widely shunned (ECR 1874, 285; P 1907, 28–29). James also readily studied psychical experiences (see Sommer, this volume), and an eclectic range of spiritual figures (see Bush, this volume). As with his curopathic approach to healing practices, he took each lived experience as an empirical fact to be taken seriously and evaluated. In effect, he greeted each idea as its own eccentric, even regarding those from the mainstream in the same way, each worthy of inquiry. As with his approaches to religion, novel philosophies, psychic experiences, and even eccentric people, so with his exploration of sectarian healers: he welcomed each as an empirical artifact of human creativity, even as he called for deliberate scrutiny of each claim.

In his study of religious experiences, James readily included the perspectives of physical science, with its frequent secular or even anti-religious posture. He called this position "medical materialism" for its depiction of spiritual life as "'nothing but' expressions of our organic disposition" (VRE 1902, 19–20). James welcomed this attention to "religion and neurology" for highlighting the natural facts happening during religious experiences, but he insisted that this first step was not the last word. He continued with medical metaphors when naming different spiritual types, the "sick souls" and the "healthy minded." For religious commitments, as with curapathy, the genuine impact on lived experience would be his standard, not the ability to adhere to prior assumptions of reasonableness.

Shortly after publishing his justification of "The Will to Believe" in 1897, James received a spirited critical response from his friend, the writer John Jay Chapman, who scoffed at James's attempt to "bolster . . . faith," calling his position "immoral and dangerous." James thanked his friend for his "epistolary explosion" and shot back with his own hearty critique of such "positivistically enlightened scientific" scorn for mere belief unverified, especially when facts remain elusive or ambiguous. He then equated scientific dismissal of religious beliefs with the mainstream medical rejection of sectarian therapies, because they both display intellectual refinement "out of touch with genuine life," and he asserted that "homeopathic treatment, although you might not believe, really does good" (CWJ 8.253–254). James supported diverse beliefs, even when in conflict with each other. That is "my vocation," he stated plainly, "to treat of things in an allround [sic] manner and not make ex parte pleas [support of only one side]." He often patronized non-scientific healers, even as his scientific background colored his support for them: "Why seek to stop the really extremely important experiences which these peculiar creatures are rolling up?" (CWJ 8.253–255 and 348).

James's support of a range of human experiences did not reduce his firm commitment to the inquiries of mainstream science. He simply insisted that its good work did not preclude the addition of other inquiries that did not adhere to its assumptions. The materialist orientations of laboratory-based science restrict the range of experience suitable for inquiry and then establish tests set within those very limits. He assessed how selective attention, guided by "sentiment[s] of rationality," shape the direction even of scientific inquiries. Within those parameters, science produces very useful results, even as he maintained that those results will be shaped by the means used to achieve them.

James's simultaneous support for unconventional thinking, including in sectarian medicine, and also for mainstream science, put him in a position serenely above the controversies over medicine and more during his time—in theory. In practice, he noticed the rising authority of science and called for adjustment of the scales among the divergent approaches to science and medicine. With that even-handedness, he also critiqued the excesses of non-scientific believers. Brashly challenging such unquestioning beliefs, he said that "the northwest wind of science should get into them and blow their sickliness and barbarism away" (WB 1897, 7).

Just as alternative beliefs could benefit from science, James also insisted that science could benefit from a broadening of its attention to more realms of experience. In 1894, he vigorously critiqued a bill before the Massachusetts legislature that would restrict the practice of medicine to the work of mainstream doctors, which would effectively punish unorthodoxy. Because the sectarians produced facts "patent and startling" (ECR 1894,

148), James felt it was a misuse of science to disregard these experiences, which he hoped would soon be examined more carefully to enable greater scientific understanding.

When a similar measure emerged in 1898, James addressed the legislature in person to support the "enormous mass of experience" that pointed to "the efficacy of these remedies." Applying an argument from "The Will to Believe," he warned about a science so eager to "avoid error" that it would miss opportunities to seek out new truths (WB 1897, 24). Cautious avoidance of error means declaring, when meeting experiences outside of habitual channels, "'give me ignorance rather than knowledge.'" In his support of scientific inquiry, he critiqued a form of science that was willing to remain "partly blind" to whole swathes of natural facts. With greater openness to diverse experiences, mainstream medicine could grow into a "genuinely complete medical science" (ECR 1898, 57–58).

The year after his legislative testimony, James made a generalized warning about "A Certain Blindness in Human Beings," in critique of the tendency to treat one's own perceptions and assumptions as the norm (TTP 1899, 132–149). He applied the same message to the medical debates in maintaining that the mainstream and sectarian contenders are each "necessarily partly perceptive and partly blind"—adding sharply, "even the very best type is partly blind." This limitation resulted inevitably from the robust scale of experience whose enormity remained beyond the ken of any one person or any one system. So he had no patience for science-inspired practitioners who effectively told sectarians, "your experience... simply is n't fit to count" (ECR 1898, 60 and 57; and letter to James Jackson Putnam, March 2, 1898, CWJ 8.348).

James again experienced hostile reactions from the medical and scientific mainstream when he endorsed the Emmanuel Movement, a form of psychotherapy founded in 1906 emphasizing listening to each patient for moral re-education through psycho-social treatment of functional disorders. The therapy enlisted religion, alternative psychology, lay leadership, and modern science. To critics, however, the non-scientific features of the movement tainted the whole; James Jackson Putnam, an early advocate of psychoanalysis, even argued that "I do not think the success of the [Emmanuel] movement to be a warrant for its value" (quoted in Gifford 1997, 80). By contrast, James admired this therapy precisely for its practical achievements.

Later in life, James acknowledged that "when I was a medical student I feel sure that any one of us would have been ashamed to be caught looking into a homoeopathic book"—even though he repeatedly acted on just such curiosity (ECR 1898, 61). But he kept his openness to alternatives hidden behind the shield of respectability of his scientific schooling, just as he showed respect for psychophysical parallelism through most of *The Principles*. But in 1903 he blurted out, "I know homeopathic remedies are not inert, as orthodox medicine insists they neccessarily [sic] must be." He did not want homeopathy or any sectarian healing to displace the mainstream, but he believed they had a place in healing, especially to address cases allopaths found elusive. In particular, he maintained, "I always believed that homeopathy should get a fair trial in obstinate chronic cases," as he had recognized about sectarians in general since his days in medical school (to Henry Rankin, February 27, 1903, CWJ 1903, 10.208).

During James's lifetime, sectarian medicine became more marginalized as scientific medicine gained increasing success and influence. But he did not stop visiting sectarians—and he did not stop evaluating them critically. He took Roberts-Hawley lymph-compound, which contained an extract of bulls' testicles, and he reported in 1908, "I have had now an eight years [sic] experience of it and the results are perfectly uniform. In a week all symptoms begin to improve, fatigue diminishes, sleep improves, digestion ditto, courage & aggressiveness replace pusillanimity etc, etc." (LeClair 1966, 200). In 1909, when visiting a homeopathic doctor, James Taylor, James flippantly acknowledged mainstream views in calling him a "semi-quack." True to the holistic perspective, Taylor did not address problems in particular body parts, but rather "the 'pitch' at which a man lives"; this was a general expression of the homeopathic holistic constitutional profile. "I have been racing too much, kept in a state of inner tension," and as a result, "unnecessarily high pitch has produced arterial hardening." James knew that "any serious remodeling of one[']s tissues must require months or years," but as he had at water cures, he still groused about the "frightful patience" required (CWJ 1909, 3.376 and 386–387). James did indeed lose patience and resolved to "try Xian Science" again; he had been visiting mind-cure practitioners at least since the 1880s, but he repeatedly noticed more impact on friends and family than on himself, until 1906, when "for the first time in my life I practiced the Mind-cure philosophy rather successfully" (CWJ 1909, 12.356; Sutton 2012, 125).

James visited the Christian Science healer L. G. Strang with rising expectations. Although a "willing patient" through over twenty visits, James showed little improvement. Despite his respect for mind cure, he wondered if his intellectual posture was ill suited to such great trust in the powers of the immaterial parts of life, with this sectarian healing better suited to "only a part of mankind" (CWJ 1909, 12.387). Still, he reported that these visits brought some relief from his chronic heart condition, angina pectoris, a restriction of the blood flow to the heart that had hung over him since 1899. As with previous crises, he sought management of his troubles rather than full cure, but he could not stave off mortality, the ultimate chronic. And indeed, this heart condition was the immediate cause of his death in 1910.[4]

James's views of the experiences emphasized by mainstream science and by sectarian medicine, along with those of psychical research and religion, have some parallels with the role of Newtonian thinking in modern physics. Those early approaches are not wrong, but they are limited to particular bands of reality, where they still apply wonderfully. In the same way, James believed, mainstream medicine operates well and usefully on many aspects of health, even as unconventional medicine addresses other parts of health beyond the reach of laboratory inquiry. "Each attitude being a syllable in human nature's total message," he declared, "it takes the whole of us to spell the meaning out completely" (VRE 1902, 384). And with that openness, he insisted that all experiences be scrutinized thoroughly.

In 1868, when William James was thoroughly immersed in study of scientific medicine, he reviewed a book on alternative states of mind in sleep and hypnotism. He weighed the merits of both scientific and alternative perspectives, advising "take the remedy so long as it heals, [because] there should no more be an aristocracy of remedies than of physicians."[5] Mature James never practiced medicine, but he became a doctor of philosophizing retaining the spirit of scientific inquiry, with fidelity to natural facts in a range of human experiences, without assuming reduction to physical causality. The "curapathy" of the nineteenth-century marketplace of healing practices set the tone for much of his lifelong commitment to recognition of competing positions while learning from each side. The investigation of experience was his consistent goal, no matter the norms or commands of conventional authority.

Notes

1. See for example the prominent physician Morrill Wyman who, in "The Reality and Certainty of Medicine: An Address Delivered at the Annual Meeting of the Massachusetts Medical Society," pointed to the "peculiar certainty" of surgery, but with other medical interventions, "the degree of certainty diminishes" (30). He then criticized both "those with unbounded faith in imaginary remedies" and those who settled for "Nihilism," with "all disease... left to itself." The "Rational Physician" avoided each extreme, he argued, and "looks forward to the time when [the profession's] high aims and aspirations shall have been accomplished" (Wyman 1863, 40).
2. Du Bois-Reymond practiced methodological materialism but did not endorse philosophical materialism. He insisted that "it is and ever will remain utterly impossible to understand higher mental operations from the mechanics of the cerebral atoms" (du Bois-Reymond 1874, 28; see Finkelstein 2013).
3. James first visited a water cure in Teplitz, Bohemia; see William to Alice James (August 6, 1867, CWJ, 4: 185).
4. See James's letters to Alice Runnels and to Margaret James (December 15, 1909, July 5, 1906; CWJ 12.387 and 11.247). Also see Croce (2018, 131).
5. James writes, "prenez ce remède tant qu'il guérit"; my translation, from his review of Ambrose Liébeault, *Du Sommeil et des États Analogues* (ECR 1868, 245).

Bibliography

Archival References

William James Papers. 1863. "Notebook [3]: Reading Notes & Observations; sketches." Houghton Library, Harvard University, bMS Am 1092 (4497).

William James Papers. 1869. Mary to Henry James [Junior], September 21, [1869], Mary James letters, July 24, [1869]–April 27, [1873], files 93–5279. Houghton Library, Harvard University, bMS Am 1093.1 (34-36).

William James Papers. c. 1868–1869. "Similia similibus curantur [Like cures like]," Notebook 26, Houghton Library, Harvard University, c. 1864–1874, entry arranged not by page but alphabetically by entry title.

Published References

Bigelow, Jacob. 1835. *A Discourse on Self-Limited Diseases: Delivered before the Massachusetts Medical Society, at Their Annual Meeting, May 27, 1835*. Boston: Nathan Hale.

Boring, Edwin Garrigues. 1929/1950. *A History of Experimental Psychology*. 2nd ed. New York: Appleton-Century-Crofts.

Brown-Séquard, Édouard. 1867. *Advice to Students: An Address Delivered at the Opening of the Medical Lectures of Harvard University, November 7, 1866*. Cambridge, MA: Press of John Wilson and Son.

Coulter, Harris L. 1973. *The Conflict between Homoeopathy and the Ama: Science and Ethics in Medicine, 1800–1914*. In *Divided Legacy: A History of the Schism in Medical Thought*, 3 vols. Vol. 3. Washington, DC: McGrath.

Croce, Paul J. 1995. *Science and Religion in the Era of William James: Eclipse of Certainty, 1820–1880*. Chapel Hill: University of North Carolina Press.

Croce, Paul J. 2018. *Young William James Thinking*. Baltimore, MD: Johns Hopkins University Press.

Du Bois-Reymond, Emil. 1852. "On Animal Electricity: Being an Abstract of the Discoveries of Emil du Bois-Reymond," based on his *Untersuchungen über Thierische Elektricität* [Researches in animal electricity], edited by H. Bence Jones. London: J. Churchill.

Du Bois-Reymond, Emil. 1874. "The Limits of Our Knowledge of Nature." *Popular Science Monthly* 5: 17–32.

Finkelstein, Gabriel Ward. 2013. *Emil Du Bois-Reymond: Neuroscience, Self, and Society in Nineteenth-Century Germany*. Cambridge, MA: MIT Press.

Fye, Bruce. 1987. *The Development of American Physiology: Scientific Medicine in the Nineteenth Century*. Baltimore, MD: Johns Hopkins University Press.

Gevitz, Norman, ed. 1988. *Other Healers: Unorthodox Medicine in America*. Baltimore, MD: Johns Hopkins University Press.

Gifford, Sanford. 1997. *The Emmanuel Movement, Boston, 1904–1929: The Origins of Group Treatment and the Assault on Lay Psychotherapy*. Cambridge, MA: Harvard University Press.

Hahnemann, Samuel. 1836. *Organon of Homeopathic Medicine*. Allentown, PA: Academical Bookstore.

Hall, G. Stanley. 1879. "Philosophy in the United States." *Mind* 4: 89–105.

Haller, John S., Jr. 2010. *Swedenborg, Mesmer, and the Mind/Body Connection: The Roots of Complementary Medicine*. West Chester, PA: Swedenborg Foundation.

Hansen, Bert. 2009. *Picturing Medical Progress from Pasteur to Polio: A History of Mass Media Images and Popular Attitudes in America*. New Brunswick, NJ: Rutgers University Press.

Harper, Robert S. 1949. "The Laboratory of William James." *The Harvard Alumni Bulletin* 52: 169–173.

Harrington, Thomas F. 1905. *The Harvard Medical School: A History, Narrative and Documentary, 1782–1905*. Edited by James Gregory Mumford. 3 vols. New York: Lewis Publishing Company.

Holcombe, William. 1877. *How I Became a Homeopath*. New York: Boericke and Tafel.

Holmes, Oliver Wendell, Sr. 1861. *Currents and Counter-Currents in Medical Science: With Other Addresses and Essays*. Boston: Ticknor and Fields.

Holmes, Oliver Wendell, Sr. 1889/1899. *Medical Essays: 1842–1882*. New ed. Boston: Houghton.

Hooker, Worthington. 1850. *Lessons from the History of Medical Delusions*. New York: Baker & Scribner.

James, Henry, III. 1930. *Charles William Eliot: President of Harvard University, 1869–1909*. 2 vols. Boston: Houghton Mifflin and Co.

Kaltenborn, Hans von. 1907. "William James at Harvard." *Harvard Illustrated Magazine* 8: 93–95.

LeClair, Robert, ed. 1966. *The Letters of William James and Théodore Flournoy*. Madison: University of Wisconsin Press.

Leo-Wolf, William. 1835. *Remarks on the Abracadabra of the Nineteenth Century: Or, on Dr. Samuel Hahnemann's Homeopathic Medicine*. Philadelphia: Carey, Lea and Blanchard.

Myers, Gerald E. 1986. *William James: His Life and Thought*. New Haven, CT: Yale University Press.

Otis, Laura. 2002. "The Metaphoric Circuit: Organic and Technological Communication in the Nineteenth Century." *Journal of the History of Ideas* 63 (1):105–128.

Perry, Ralph Barton. 1935. *The Thought and Character of William James*. 2 vols. Cambridge, MA: Harvard University Press.

Rausse, J. H. 1851. *The Water-Cure Applied to Every Known Disease: A Complete Demonstration of the Advantages of the Hydropathic System of Curing Diseases: Showing, Also, the Fallacy of the Medicinal Method, and Its Utter Inability to Effect a Permanent Cure*. Translated by C. H. Meeker. 3rd ed. New York: Fowlers and Wells.

Richardson, Robert D. 2006. *William James: In the Maelstrom of American Modernism*. Boston: Houghton Mifflin.

Rothstein, William G. 1972. *American Physicians in the Nineteenth Century: From Sects to Science*. Baltimore, MD: Johns Hopkins University Press.

Steffens, Lincoln. 1931. *The Autobiography of Lincoln Steffens*. New York: Harcourt.

Sutton, Emma Kate. 2012. "Interpreting 'Mind-Cure': William James and the 'Chief Task . . . Of the Science of Human Nature.'" *Journal of the History of the Behavioral Sciences* 48 (2): 115–133.

Tyler, H. Richard, and K. L. Tyler. 1984. "Charles Édouard Brown-Séquard: Professor of Physiology and Pathology of the Nervous System at Harvard Medical School." *Neurology* 34 (9): 1231–1236

Warner, John Harley. 1977. "'The Nature-Trusting Heresy': American Physicians and the Concept of the Healing Power of Nature in the 1850's and 1860's." *Perspectives in American History* 11: 291–324.

Warner, John Harley. 1986. *The Therapeutic Perspective: Medical Practice, Knowledge, and Identity in America, 1820–1885*. Cambridge, MA: Harvard University Press.

Warner, John Harley. 1998. *Against the Spirit of System: The French Impulse in Nineteenth-Century American Medicine*. Princeton, NJ: Princeton University Press.

Wertheimer, Michael. 1970. *A Brief History of Psychology*. New York: Holt, Rinehart and Winston.

Whewell, William. 1837. *History of the Inductive Sciences, from the Earliest to the Present Times*. 3 vols. London: J.W. Parker.

Whorton, James C. 2002. *Nature Cures: The History of Alternative Medicine in America*. New York: Oxford University Press.

Wyman, Morrill. 1863. *The Reality and Certainty of Medicine: An Address Delivered at the Annual Meeting of the Massachusetts Medical Society, June 17, 1863*. Boston: David Clapp.

CHAPTER 7

JAMES AND PSYCHICAL RESEARCH IN CONTEXT

ANDREAS SOMMER

Introduction

JAMES is widely respected as a philosopher and regarded as a "founding father" of modern psychology. But not many like to talk about his unorthodox preoccupations with telepathy and other "psychic" phenomena, which tend to be viewed as an embarrassing stain on his otherwise progressive record. After all, modern curricula of psychology adhere to a prescription spelled out by Cornell psychologist Edward B. Titchener over a century ago, who declared in *Science* magazine: "No scientifically-minded psychologist believes in telepathy" (Titchener 1898, 897).

Titchener's article triggered a heated exchange with James as perhaps the most eminent though by no means only scientifically minded psychologist who did believe in telepathy.[1] This was not the first dispute between James and a psychological colleague over questions concerning "psychic" phenomena. In fact, his anger over Titchener was in part a hangover from a recent skirmish with another fellow psychologist, James McKeen Cattell, concerning Cattell's misrepresentation of a report on experiments with the Boston trance medium Leonora Piper by James's friend and fellow psychical researcher, Richard Hodgson (cf. EPR 1898, ch. 25). Discovered by James in 1885, Mrs. Piper was rigorously tested by himself, Hodgson, and various other investigators in the United States and England, most of whom agreed that the most rational counter-explanation for actual spirit communication in her case was not fraud or chance coincidence, but the assumption that benign "split personalities" appearing in her trances conformed to sitters' expectations by telepathically tapping the minds of the living to convincingly play the roles of spirits of the departed (cf. EPR 1890, ch. 12; 1909, ch. 37).

Mediums were rarely prepared to undergo the level of critical scrutiny endured by Mrs. Piper (whose trance state was tested through blistering, forced inhalation of ammonia, and other intrusive measures), but a more frequent complaint by James concerned the difficulty of finding experimenters willing to investigate them in the first place (e.g., EPR 1869, ch. 1; 1901, 195; 1909, 36; PP 1890, 1.374–375; PBC 1892, 190; EP 1890, 248–249). For example, in a letter to Cattell written shortly after his debate with Titchener, James stated that he had invited skeptical Harvard colleagues Hugo Münsterberg and Josiah Royce to freely examine Mrs. Piper at his house, only to receive blank refusals. What's more, James likened such colleagues who refused firsthand tests while publicly declaring heretical researchers dupes to the legendary "astronomers who wouldn't look through Galileo's telescope at Jupiter's moons" (CWJ 1899, 8.483).

Many will consider James's comparison of antipathies to research into stereotypically "supernatural" phenomena with the story of Galileo an affront to the secular and naturalistic tradition in which Western academics have been trained. After all, the installment of research groups investigating psychic phenomena at universities all around the globe since the 1930s notwithstanding (cf. Mauskopf and McVaugh 1980), associations of telepathy with gullibility and fraud are perhaps as widespread as the (now considered wrong) image of Galileo as an iconic quasi-martyr of modern secular science in the battle against religious dogmatism.[2] But the purpose of this chapter is not to engage in ongoing debates over the reality of telepathy. Instead, I will suggest that the supposedly long-running "naturalism" of contemporary science and Western academic culture at large is a retrospective construction of relatively recent vintage, built partly on unchecked, and ultimately problematic, ongoing historical assumptions.

With James as my obvious focus, it should be understood that he needs to be regarded as but one specimen among a considerable number of figures who are often assumed to have helped humanity make the critical shift from an unenlightened past to a progressive modernity, while at the same time appearing to sin against a basic modernist principle: at the very time when modern sciences began to emancipate themselves from theological interference through professionalization, James and other elite intellectuals actively contested the view that "naturalism" was a direct and inevitable outcome of the growth of scientific knowledge.[3] Sometimes adorned with the prefix "scientific," "naturalism" is now perhaps the most basic precondition for professionalized academic work, and yet an unambiguous definition of the term turns out to be surprisingly difficult. In fact, minimal definitions of *any* standard notion of ontological as well as methodological naturalism appear to be identical with the manner in which Thomas H. Huxley first used "scientific naturalism" in 1892, i.e., by mere contrast with a rather evasively construed "supernaturalism" (Huxley 1892, 35).[4]

Several authors have already outlined with varying accuracy what James's unorthodox science comprised of. However, no secondary text can be a substitute for James's original writings on the "supernatural" as compiled in *Essays in Psychical Research*. And while Robert McDermott's Introduction and editorial notes by Ignas Skrupskelis to *EPR* are important, much more needs to be said about the wider context to which James's corpus responded as a whole. Indeed, his open advocacy, practice, and various defenses of unrestrictedly empirical approaches to the "occult" still await to be rigorously situated within the context of his own time.[5] By providing a necessarily rough sketch of this wider context, I hope to offer a perspective which counters prevalent but unhelpful views that interpret *any* critical responses to "naturalism" as self-evident regress. On the contrary, I argue that if reconstructed on its own terms rather than through the epistemological filters of the present, James's psychical research can be reconciled with the progressiveness for which his canonical ideas are often regarded.

SCIENTISTS, MIRACLES, AND THE POLITICS OF DEGENERATION

As Paul Croce reminds us in his contribution to this volume, the word "scientist" is a fairly recent invention. Proposed in the 1830s by the English polymath William Whewell as a unifying label for members of the newly founded British Association for the Advancement of Science, the term was initially rejected and ridiculed by many science icons particularly in England, including, for example, Lord Kelvin, Lord Rayleigh (a colleague of James's at the Society for Psychical Research), and "Darwin's bulldog," Thomas Huxley (Ross 1962, 77–78). It was not until the 1890s, around the time when Huxley first used "scientific naturalism" roughly in the sense in which it is deployed today, that "scientist" became more widely accepted and commonly denoted an empirical worker committed to a "naturalistic" outlook which categorically excluded from the inventory of nature the kinds of debated anomalies of which James and fellow psychical researchers were trying to make sense.

While "scientist" was more readily accepted in the United States than in Britain, James would never completely embrace the term. In his writings, he often put the word in inverted commas, and to the vocal opponent of psychical research James McKeen Cattell he explained that he once used "*soi-disant* scientist" to deliberately "cast contempt on the *word* 'scientist', for which I have a dislike, though it is evidently doomed to acquire the rights of citizenship." To James, the word suggested "the priggish sectarian view of science, as something *against* religion, *against* sentiment, etc.," and he meant "to suggest the narrowness of the sort of mind that should delight in *self-styling itself* 'scientist,' as it proceeded to demolish psychical researchers" (CWJ 1898, 8.364, original emphases).

Back in England, Huxley's first use of "scientific naturalism" occurred a decade after another neologism was invented by a nephew of Whewell's, Frederic W. H. Myers. In November 1882, Myers, a co-founder of the Society for Psychical Research (SPR) and the man who was to become James's most significant collaborator in psychology, coined "telepathy."[6] In hindsight, it might be tempting to assume it was predestined from the start that "scientist" and "telepathy" were terms that would never go well together in the academies. Still, the making of modern psychology, for which James took such great credit, marked a short but historically significant period when a reconciliation of these terms did not seem entirely out of the question (cf. Sommer 2013a, 2013b). Moreover, Myers's neologism signifies a continuity of certain ideas and beliefs which, as fundamental revisions in current historical scholarship have revealed, had not simply been killed off through the growth of scientific knowledge during the Scientific Revolution and the Enlightenment (cf. Porter 1999; Sommer 2013a, ch. 1, 2014; Josephson-Storm 2017; Hunter 2020).

In England, for example, future physics Nobel laureate SPR members such as Lord Rayleigh and J. J. Thomson would follow with critical but sympathetic interest the unorthodox investigations of more active colleagues like the discoverer of thallium and collaborator with the Curies in the exploration of radioactivity, William Crookes (Marie Curie would join the SPR in 1911); the Professor of Experimental Physics at the Royal College of Science for Ireland, William F. Barrett; and the pioneer of electromagnetism research and radio technology, Oliver Lodge (Noakes 2019). With James's friends Edmund Gurney and Frederic Myers as the Society's most industrious workers, however, the major projects of the English SPR explicitly sought to contribute to the fledgling field of experimental psychology. In this regard it is also vital to acknowledge that James was by far the SPR's most active American representative. Indeed, modern psychologists writing histories of their discipline are prone to forget that most of James's own empirical and experimental contributions to psychology were published in the *Proceedings* of the American SPR (EPR 1886, chs. 3–4; 1889, ch. 10; 1890, ch. 12; EP 1886, 190–197, 200–203; 1887, 204–215; CWJ 1902, 10.1–2; Taylor 1996, 18–20).

Far from being attempts to scientifically prove life after death, however, James's experiments were mainly independent replications of studies of rudimentary "divided selves" in hypnotism and automatic writing, which directly tackled questions about the unity of the mind and cognitive capacities of its subliminal regions. With Gurney, Myers, Pierre Janet, Alfred Binet, Max Dessoir, and others, James actively contested German-style physiological psychology as the predominant mode of psychological science by turning induced automatisms and altered states of consciousness into instruments and domains of psychological experimentation. James cited some of his own results, along with related studies from France and Germany, throughout the *Principles of Psychology* and its abridged version. Moreover, these studies are also vital for an appreciation of the theoretical framework James applied in his lectures on abnormal psychology (ML 1895, 1896, ch. 5, and Appendix III; Taylor 1983) and in the *Varieties of Religious Experience*.

Much has been made of James's discovery of Mrs. Piper in the year he lost his infant boy Herman, which at first glance might suggest that James's prime interest in mediumship was in finding consoling evidence for an afterlife. However, James's studies of Mrs. Piper are long pre-dated by previous mediumistic experiments (cf. CWJ 1874, 4.496) and his first published critique of scientists refusing to investigate spiritualism (EPR 1869, ch. 1). Moreover, when James started to collaborate with the English SPR in the early 1880s, their work would actually inspire precious little hope that evidence for survival could be established at all, and on the contrary seemed to directly undermine it. In fact, the initially skeptical stance toward spiritualism particularly by psychologically oriented SPR leaders like Henry and Eleanor Sidgwick, Gurney, Myers, and Hodgson greatly annoyed spiritualists like the "other Darwin," Alfred Russel Wallace, who had converted to the belief that mediums indeed channeled spirits of the dead after studying the claimed marvels of spiritualism essentially as theoretically isolated anomalies.

In contrast to Wallace and other spiritualists, however, Sidgwick, Myers, and Gurney promoted psychical research as an integrative exploration that sought to establish theoretical continuities between the claimed extraordinary phenomena of spiritualism and cutting-edge psychological and medical knowledge of what the *embodied* mind could do. Grounding their studies of mediumistic trance productions in the state of the art of more conventional psychological research suggesting the occurrence of rudimentary "multiple selves" in dreams, hypnosis, and hallucinations in non-mediumistic samples, they offered explanations of mediumship and spirit-seership that did not actually require the "spirit hypothesis." Yet, rather than chiming in with contemporary mainstream theories, which reduced altered states and subliminal cognition to physiology or declared them inherently inferior to the ordinary capacities of the everyday waking self, Myers proposed an alternative model that was parsimonious and heretical perhaps in equal measure.

Mediumship, according to Myers, could in most cases be understood in terms of natural tendencies of the mind to create divisions in itself. The more unorthodox part of Myers's model consisted in its implication that the waking self, far from constituting the inherently superior part of the mind, was already just a partition of a more comprehensive whole. This "hidden self," according to Myers, was the origin of cognitive and creative capacities that were sometimes vastly superior to those of the habitual waking mind. What's more, the mind's subliminal regions were taken as the conduit of telepathic impressions, which Myers conceptualized in terms of "uprushes" into conscious awareness from a cosmic nexus perpetually connecting all beings. Hence, Myers argued, even when a medium provided highly specific details about a supposedly communicating deceased person, spiritualists were wrong to assume this in itself was sufficient proof for actual spirit identity (cf. Myers 1884, 1885). Myers would later convince himself that some cases of mediumship constituted genuine spirit communication. But when he first proposed his subliminal psychology, Alfred Russel Wallace and other spiritualists who had joined the SPR in the hope its work would confirm their beliefs felt betrayed. Many withdrew their support, and others fiercely attacked Myers and colleagues as dogmatic anti-spiritualists (Hamilton 2009, ch. 4; Sommer 2013a, 104, 165–166).

For a short but crucial period during the professionalization of modern psychology, the approach of Gurney and Myers—taken up by James and another founder of the psychological profession, Théodore Flournoy in Switzerland—seemed to advance into a serious rival of German-style physiological psychology commonly associated with Wilhelm Wundt (Shamdasani 1994; Sommer 2013a, ch. 3, 2013b). From the inception of the International Congresses of Psychology in 1889, members of the "Sidgwick group" (minus Gurney, who died in 1888) were actively involved in their organization, and in fact represented British psychology until Myers's death in 1901. At the first session in Paris, the Congress commissioned an international replication of a previous field study of "telepathic hallucinations" by the SPR, with James taking charge of the American portion (cf. EPR 1889–1897, ch. 11). Moreover, Henry Sidgwick served as president of the second session in London in 1892, with Myers organizing it (jointly with James Sully) as secretary. And while it has been remarked that the early SPR membership directories read like a Who's Who of Victorian physical sciences, they prominently featured early major representatives of modern psychology in particular, including not just James (Freud and Jung would join long after Myers's death), but especially French leaders of fledgling psychology such as Théodule Ribot, Pierre Janet and Henri-Étienne Beaunis.

To understand the centrality of hypnotism as a tool of experimentation in the psychological work of the SPR and James, it is vital to consider the concrete context into which psychology was born as a professionalized university discipline. After the practice and theory of mesmerism was deliberately but not altogether successfully purged of its occult phenomenology by figures like James Braid in England, Jean-Martin Charcot in France, and Rudolf Heidenhain in Germany, it began a partial rehabilitation in the guise of medical hypnotism as well as a method of "mental vivisection" in psychology. James's own hypnotic experiments and hypnotherapeutic efforts—e.g., in the treatment of the famous Ansel Bourne case of multiple personality—are not often elaborated on in histories of psychology. Yet, together with his studies in automatic writing and the psychology of trance, and his participation in research on hallucinations in the "sane," hypnotic inductions and treatments of divided strands of memory and volition by James and other psychologists were not as marginal as might be supposed today. Hypnosis formed part of a discrete integrative method of psychological experimentation, which James himself considered scientifically far more promising than experiments in physiological psychology.[7] Moreover, the supposedly inevitable evolution of mesmerism with its occult repertoire including thought-transference, clairvoyance, and spirit visions into a "naturalistic" hypnotism grounded in the principle of suggestion did not occur in a cultural vacuum. In fact, the "naturalization" of mesmerism was indicative of a larger trend that did not actually begin in medicine or the sciences, or even in the nineteenth century.

In Germany, for example, the rapid decline of mesmerism and Romantic *Naturphilosophie* (Fichte, Schelling, Hegel, and Schopenhauer were all convinced of the reality of mesmeric clairvoyance) cannot be understood without an acknowledgement of the war on the "supernatural" as a shorthand for Catholicism that was waged by political radical theologians, philosophers, writers, and scientists throughout the nineteenth century. Roughly since the days of the Reformation, Catholic miracle belief was widely held to be a necessary condition of theocratic despotism, and campaigns to root out "superstitions" associated with Catholicism were central in developments leading to the French Revolution and related upheavals, which spilled over into neighboring countries. In Germany, related major events like the March Revolution of 1848, the "debate concerning materialism" among naturalists and medics since the 1850s, and Bismarck's *Kulturkampf* during the 1870s lastingly shaped the way in which modern sciences started to organize themselves into secular professions (cf. Gregory 1977; Blackbourn 1993). Indeed, long before "naturalism" became a basic prescription for professionalized scientific practice, from the late 1830s a new generation of theologians spearheaded by David Friedrich Strauss more than paved the way for the "disenchantment" of nature when they demoted the biblical miracles from preambles of Christianity to vulgar heathen myths.

To say that the professionalization of psychology in Germany by Wundt and others took place in a climate that was not exactly conducive to investigations of occult phenomena would in fact be a gross understatement. After all, Wundt's inauguration of his experimental psychology coincided with the final phase of the *Kulturkampf* ("struggle for culture"), a virtual war on the Catholic Church throughout the 1870s. As in the days of the March Revolution, politicians and men of science with strong political leanings such as Rudolf Virchow and Darwin's "German bulldog," Ernst Haeckel, utilized an Enlightenment rhetoric that did a lot of polemical work in equating Catholic miracle beliefs with political corruption, bigotry, mental disease, and magical beliefs characteristic of the "lower races," lumping new occult movements like spiritualism readily into the mix.

Wundt himself attacked eminent scientific colleagues who seriously investigated spiritualism in a pamphlet that was published in the year he founded his psychological institute at Leipzig. And Wundt's polemic is one of many examples illustrating that the war on the "supernatural" by psychologists cannot be understood in simplistic terms such as materialism versus spiritualism, let alone science versus religion. For instance, Wundt and many other critics of spiritualism denounced it not by lamenting that spirituality and science were incompatible, but because for them spiritualism was just not spiritual *enough*. Charging mediumship researchers (including James's later philosophical hero, Gustav T. Fechner) of high treason against true science and true religion, Wundt in fact condemned spiritualism as a particularly revolting form of materialism. All that spiritualists did, Wundt argued, was to project grossly physicalist categories of space, time and matter upon the sacred realm of pure spirit (e.g., Wundt 1879, 592–593).[8]

Shortly before the second International Congress of Psychology took place under the aegis of SPR president Sidgwick in 1892, Wundt fired off another fusillade, now directed at the SPR, its French collaborators, and young German psychologists who had founded psychological societies in Munich and Berlin to emulate the SPR's and James's research program (Sommer 2013a, ch. 4, 2013b). What the "father" of German psychology had previously dismissed as an "aimless chase after wonders" (Wundt 1879, 593) was now threatening to compete with his own research program, and was represented by none other than his American counterpart James. Bypassing concrete methodological criticisms, Wundt dismissed experiments in the hypnotic manipulation of divided strands of the self as "nothing but an atavistic residue of those age-old ideas of possession," and he declared psychical research a "through and through pathological line of present-day science" (Wundt 1892, 38, 110, my translation).

Terms like "atavistic residue" may strike psychologists as obsolete today, but to simply filter them out in our reading of nineteenth-century sources is to miss their key function in the fight against "occult belief." Atavisms formed a prominent part within an arsenal of medical entities born out of the fear of degeneration—the flipside of nineteenth-century obsessions with mental and racial evolution, which long pre-dated the advent of Darwin's and Wallace's works. Nourished by deep worries that evolution and thus progress could be reversed, atavistic throwbacks served as standard explanations for madness, political unrest and indeed all sorts of ills, including deviations from social, political, and sexual norms, thus also laying the foundations for eugenics and associated race theories of the twentieth century (cf. Pick 1989; Shamdasani 2003, ch. 4; Porter 2018). Concepts of atavisms—spawned by political and metaphysical anxieties of anti-clerical anthropological and medical writers such as Adolf Bastian, E. B. Tylor, and Cesare Lombroso—became prominent weapons in the fight against the occult by many psychologists. Considered regrettable but normal in "savage" indigenous societies, belief in occult phenomena held by members of "superior" white races was widely explained and decried as a dangerous morbid atavistic relapse into lower stages of mental and racial development.

The professionalization of psychology in the United States and Britain did not see major religiopolitical upheavals comparable to events in Europe, which catalyzed medical and psychological theories of degeneration. Yet, particularly the German and French battles for secularization served as templates in ongoing British and American struggles to emancipate scientific work from dogmatically theological censorship. Mesmerism may officially have been "naturalized" into medical hypnotism. But fears of suggestive influence as quasi-witchcraft saturated mainstream theories of "crowd psychology," whose leading representatives such as Gustave Le Bon (1896) subsumed as instances of "mental epidemics" spiritualism along with religious fanaticism and political despotism.[9]

The famous physiologist William B. Carpenter, a particularly committed "enlightener" of the people in Britain, railed against a related shibboleth, "epidemic delusions." Carpenter belonged to a scientifically distinguished group of men including Michael Faraday, Huxley, John Tyndall, and others who fought for major educational reforms, and advanced the professionalization of science along the lines of secularization efforts in Germany. Faraday and Carpenter were devout Christians and did not see eye to eye with Huxley and Tyndall on religious grounds. But they all shared a central concern that guided their joint campaigns in what we might now call the "public understanding of science": belief in marvelous phenomena had to be rooted out once and for all, and by any means necessary (cf. Winter 1998).

A pious Unitarian, Carpenter believed in the immortality of the soul and stated he was raised in the faith that the biblical miracles were historical facts, but that the age of miracles had passed (e.g., Carpenter 1873, 132). When eminent scientific colleagues like Alfred Russel Wallace and William Crookes began reporting positive results of their experiments with mediums, Carpenter became their most aggressive antagonist, targeting them in his public lectures, popular articles, and academic writings as self-deluded victims of their undisciplined and un-Christian curiosity. Explaining belief in marvels observed in the practice of mesmerism and spiritualism as an "epidemic delusion" and "diluted insanity" (Carpenter 1875, 632–633), he merely expressed a standard view held by medical communities in Europe and the United States—a view, it should be stated, that was not arrived at through clinical tests, let alone was motivated by humanistic concerns over patient welfare (cf. Brown 1983; Shortt 1984; Williams 1985; Le Maléfan, Evrard, and Alvarado 2013).

When James reviewed Carpenter's *Principles of Mental Physiology*, he took issue with his dogmatic metaphysics of the will (the cultivation of which psychologists generally saw as the panacea to solve all sorts of social problems and religious differences), and noted the "running polemic against Spiritualism which seems to be the second great purpose of the book" (ECR 1874, 275). According to Carpenter's principles, his own son, the Sanskrit scholar, biblical critic and Principal of Manchester College at Oxford University, Joseph Estlin Carpenter, would have to be diagnosed as quasi-insane when he later put on record bafflement concerning his sittings with James's "white crow," the trance medium Leonora Piper. Like James, J. E. Carpenter openly confessed his conviction that Piper's trance states were as genuine as her capacity to tap the minds of the living to impersonate deceased loved ones (Hodgson 1898, 525–526, 528–529; CWJ 1894 7.619, 1898 8.617).

But critics of James's heretical science such as psychologist and *Science* editor James McKeen Cattell—who swept J. E. Carpenter's observations along with James's and many similar ones under the carpet in his review of the latest report on Piper (Cattell 1898; cf. EPR 1898, ch. 25)—had no use for such testimony. Cattell was part of the nascent American psychological profession whose members were deeply divided over specific metaphysical and religious positions, personal animosities, and methods and objectives of fledgling academic psychology. If there was something Cattell and several other psychologists could agree upon, however, it was this: not to impartially study what if anything was behind the alleged psychic phenomena, but, as E. B. Titchener put it in a letter to Cattell, to "stem the James tide."[10]

JAMES AND THE AMERICAN SOCIETY FOR PSYCHICAL RESEARCH REVISITED

James's psychical research cannot be understood in isolation from mainstream positions and theoretical frameworks of the contemporary human and medical sciences which we just sketched and which served to undermine the credibility of any empirical approach to the "occult" through a priori pathologization. Direct responses to what James saw as excessive applications of degenerationism in psychology and medicine were, for example, his 1896 Lowell lectures on exceptional mental states (Taylor, 1983, esp. lecture 8 on Genius) and other talks and lectures on abnormal psychology (e.g., ML 1895–1896, 56, 79–80, Appendix III, 517–518), reviews of the pertinent medical literature (e.g., ECR 1895, ch. 163–165), and of course his critique of sweeping pathologizations of mystical experiences throughout the *Varieties*.[11] An appreciation of this wider context also helps us understand why members of the "Sidgwick group" were James's most important allies in psychology.

James's priorities were no doubt different from those of Myers, whose primary aim was to find empirical evidence for postmortem survival within a theoretical framework of the mind that could incorporate mundane as well as extraordinary mental functionings. Yet, their assessment of the evidence for occult phenomena aside, the work of James and his English colleagues went against the grain of contemporary medical and human sciences in another rather fundamental regard: it appeared to refute the view that hallucinations, trance states, and automatisms like those observed in hypnosis and mediumship were inherently morbid (Taylor 1983; Williams 1985; Sommer 2013a, ch. 3). Examples are James's observations in the *Principles of Psychology* (e.g., in the chapter on self-consciousness) and his review of Myers's posthumous book, where James stressed that trance states and automatisms occurred in a large number of persons showing no other mental abnormalities (EPR 1903, 214).[12] One such person was James's "white crow," Leonora Piper.

James had published his initial experiments with Mrs. Piper in the first and only volume of the *Proceedings* of the original American SPR, which he had helped found in 1884. Yet, other ASPR members were not exactly happy about James openly coming out guardedly but unambiguously in favor of the reality of psychic phenomena. In fact, contrary to the standard view of the ASPR being the American "sister organization" of the English SPR (Knapp 2017, 2), it is no exaggeration to say that some of its most active members had joined not to promote but to police Jamesian psychical research. Leading among those working directly against James and the English SPR were the ASPR's first president, the astronomer and prime American popularizer of scientific naturalism, Simon Newcomb; the embryologist Charles S. Minot; and psychologists G. Stanley Hall and Joseph Jastrow (cf. Sommer 2013a, ch. 4).

Newcomb was one of the most vocal anti-occultism crusaders in the United States and joined the ASPR with one goal in mind—to save American science from being "infected" by spiritualism and other occult grassroots movements.[13] James's Harvard colleague at the ASPR, Charles S. Minot, in fact sought to publicly cement the priorities of the Society in this very sense during its formation in 1884. In an unsigned article in *Science*, Minot declared that "spiritualism is an evil in the world,—in America it is a subtle and stupendous evil; a secret and unacknowledged poison in many minds, a confessed disease in others,—a disease which is sometimes more repulsive to the untainted than leprosy," and he frankly conceded that "a stimulus to inaugurate the work of the American society" was the "hope that psychical research may liberate us from a baneful superstition" (Minot 1884, 369, 370).

Newcomb was no doubt motivated by worries that the advocacy of psychical research by famous physical scientists in Britain would hurt his own mission to secularize science in America. That he accepted the ASPR presidency to rid American science of investigations of what he saw as ridiculous old-wives' tales is also reflected in his public clashes with Gurney and James, which revealed Newcomb's rather superficial familiarity with the English research he derided.[14] Psychological colleagues of James—most notably Hall and Jastrow—joined the ASPR for similar reasons: Hall had publicly pilloried open-mindedness to psychic matters long before he served as an ASPR vice-president, and Jastrow published anti-spiritualist polemics while sitting on the ASPR council, declaring any belief in the occurrence of occult phenomena a morbid mental condition. Central in many of their polemics was again the concept of atavisms (e.g. Hall 1881,

1887, 1910; Jastrow 1886).[15] Moreover, Hall's writings in particular are replete with appeals to religion. In a review misrepresenting methodological standards and attitudes of the English SPR, for example, Hall declared spiritualism "the common enemy of science and true religion" (Hall 1887, 145), which along with many similar examples again indicates the inadequacy of simplistic science-versus-religion frameworks for an understanding of dominant responses to Jamesian psychical research.

Another suggestive instance along these lines is the involvement in psychical research by James's friend and colleague at Harvard, Josiah Royce. After playing a relatively active role in the ASPR between 1886 and 1889, in 1900 Royce defended James against newspaper allegations that his studies of Mrs. Piper indicated that James was mentally unsound. Taken together, these circumstances are occasionally assumed to demonstrate Royce's sympathetic interest in occult matters (e.g., Zedler 1974). However, Royce's psychical research publications are mainly limited to attempts at undermining the results of the English SPR. His refusal to follow James's invitation to investigate Mrs. Piper (CWJ 1894 7.611; 1899, 8.532), for instance, was long preceded by a dispute with Gurney in the journal *Mind* over the latter's study of "telepathic hallucinations," which James had applauded as a display of exemplary scientific qualities in a review in the previous year (EPR 1887, ch. 7). In his critique, Royce proposed that the whole idea of veridical hallucinations was in truth nothing but an erroneous inference from "*a not yet recognised type of instantaneous hallucination of memory, consisting in the fancy, at the very moment of some exciting experience, that one has* EXPECTED *it before its coming*" (Royce 1888, 245, original formatting). Gurney (1888) replied by politely reminding Royce that questions of timing in many of the roughly 700 analyzed cases were to varying degrees addressed through independent corroborations and thus Royce's criticism was not apt. Yet, instead of responding, Royce simply reprinted his argument verbatim in the ASPR *Proceedings* one year after Gurney's death, without mentioning the latter's rebuttal (Royce 1889, 366–370).

And two years after James's death, Royce summed up his views on psychical research this way:

> Man needs no miracles to show him the supernatural and the superhuman. You need no signs and wonders, and no psychical research, to prove that the unity of the spirit is a fact in the world. Common-sense tacitly presupposes the reality of the unity of the spirit. Science studies the ways in which its life is expressed in the laws which govern the order of experience. Reason gives us insight into its real being. (Royce 1912, 272)

He might as well have written this before he joined the ASPR.

The "Disenchanted" Absolute

It is hard to imagine that a solemn declamation like Royce's could ever emerge from James's pen. It is undisputed that James thought highly of his colleague as a friend and in many respects as a philosopher. Yet, Royce's sermon-style prose indicated just the kind of deliberate aloofness from the realities and indignities of life that James detested in countless similar declarations by fellow philosophers and scientists, and to which his work in psychology and philosophy responded as complementary strands of one project: to tear down system-building traditions and normative metaphysics that failed to do justice to the concrete experience of the individual, and which on the contrary downplayed if not censored experiences that deviated from highbrow ideals and supposed norms.

In absolute idealism as the dominating philosophical framework of his time (with Francis H. Bradley in Oxford and Royce at Harvard among its leaders), James opposed the aloofness of "high and noble" conceptions which tended to belittle human suffering as an illusion if not tacitly glorified it as a necessary byproduct of cosmic evolution, and he fervently attacked absolute idealism as "noble in the bad sense" and "inapt for humble service" in "this real world of sweat and dirt" (P 1907, 40). In science, James lamented that champions of "naturalism" typically shirked their scientific duties by refusing to impartially study anomalous experiences like those claimed by legions of practitioners of spiritualism and other occult grassroots religions, and instead reduced them to fraud and mental illness from a safe distance. In his obituary of Frederic Myers, for example, James noted that psychologists typically dismissed reports of anomalous phenomena using "vague terms of apperceptions" like "fraud," "rot," and "rubbish" (EPR 1901, 195). Without denying that separating the wheat from the chaff in occult matters was difficult business indeed, James insisted that Myers's unrestrictedly empirical research program signaled a stage in scientific psychology in which such dismissals "will no more be possible hereafter than 'dirt' is possible as a head of classification in chemistry, or 'vermin' in zoology" (loc cit).[16]

James shared tenets of Myers's quasi-Neoplatonism that had inspired his coinage of "telepathy," but differed from his colleague on the question of personal survival. While Myers's eventual conviction of continued individual mental activity after death was absolute, like Gurney and Sidgwick, James was prepared to consider what materialist and positivist fellow researchers like Charles Richet in France and Enrico Morselli in Italy postulated more explicitly: some "occult" phenomena were genuine scientific anomalies, but it was perfectly possible that they might have absolutely no inherent spiritual significance whatsoever (CWJ 1900, 9.164; EPR 1909, 369). Yet, as is obvious from countless references to psychic and mystical experiences in his writings and correspondence, James considered psychical research a prime arena in which to study manifestations of unchurched religious life in the concrete.

There is of course something that strikingly sets James apart from most other contemporary and current writers on religion: a refusal to proselytize any specific religious doubts or theological doctrines of his own. Not that it would be easy to specify what James's faith actually comprised of. In letters to friends and colleagues he disavowed Christian faith more than once (e.g., CWJ 1886, 6.124; 1901, 9.501), and as he was working out his pragmatist and radical empiricist philosophy, he would insult the orthodox sensibilities of many fellow philosophers and psychologists by hypothesizing a deity that was imperfect or "finite" (e.g., CWJ 1898, 8.336) at best.

Other reasons should also prevent us from considering James a clear-cut theist, and his hostility to the practical "aloofness" of absolute idealism should not divert from the fact that his psychical research still presupposed a certain theoretical congruence particularly with Bradley's metaphysics (cf. Kelly 2015, 521–526). For instance, in the *Principles of Psychology* James confessed: "I find the notion of some sort of an *anima mundi* thinking in all of us to be a more promising hypothesis, in spite of all its difficulties, than that of a lot of absolutely individual souls" (PP 1890, 328; see also EPR 1909, 374). James's own quasi-mystical and psychedelic experiences of a oneness of the self with the cosmos certainly informed and motivated the prominent place of altered states in his psychology long before the *Varieties* and statements of belief in a mental "cosmic reservoir" along the lines of Gustav T. Fechner (cf. John McDermott's Introduction to EP, xxxiii–xxxiv; Taylor 1996, esp. ch. 5 and 7).

Perhaps the fiercest antagonist of Bradley's was James's closest pragmatist ally, Ferdinand C. S. Schiller at Oxford, who like James was an anti-absolutist as well as an active psychical researcher.[17] Regarding James's growing enthusiasm about Fechner, Schiller once noted: "Apropos of what you say of Fechner & an all inclusive consciousness; the only argument for anything of the sort that ever seemed to me to have anything in it is that from telepathy etc. It wd. be amusing if we cd. drive absolutism back on that line of defence!"[18] On Royce's philosophical attitude to investigations of psychic phenomena we have already heard him speak for himself, and it is perhaps not surprising that Bradley also followed the work of the SPR. However, he did so apparently with greater sympathy than Royce. In a letter to James, Bradley in fact once accused Myers of failing to acknowledge his supposed debt to Hegel (CWJ 1897, 8.310–311). Over a decade later, Bradley became an SPR member (Society for Psychical Research 1909, 83) and confessed to James his guarded support for the Society's current work, which was now much more directly focused on assessments of mediumship for the "survival hypothesis" than before (CWJ 1909, 12.155).

Yet, as far as I'm aware Bradley never became practically involved in psychical research and seemed careful not to publicly express his moderate sympathies with it. And though he did not seem to share hostilities to the occult with other major proponents of idealism like Hermann Lotze in Germany[19] and Royce in the United States, his brand of idealism was still a rather different animal from the more overtly "mystical" systems of Fichte, Schelling, or Hegel. Whereas the Romantic idealists had typically viewed dreams, somnambulic trances and other altered states of consciousness as conduits for transcendental influxes from an all-connected world soul, less than fifty years later medicine along with fledgling anthropology and psychology dominated the discourse over magic and altered states by dismissing them as symptoms of morbid degenerative tendencies. Indeed, at the height of Bradley's influence, idealism had followed suit and undergone a programmatic "disenchantment" no less than large parts of theology.

The Right to Investigate: Pragmatism and Pathologies of Prior Belief

Once we familiarize ourselves with relevant primary sources, it's hard to escape the rather unpopular conclusion that vocal critics of Jamesian psychical research consistently employed strategies and methods that most of us would struggle to find particularly "scientific." Common to all were programmatic misrepresentations of James's and the Sidgwick group's work in their public conflations of elite psychical research with uncritical spiritualism and accusations of methodological incompetence. When critics like Carpenter, Wundt, Jastrow, and Hall deployed concepts like epidemic delusions and atavistic relapses, they consciously conflated belief in the very *possibility* of the occurrence of certain alleged phenomena with full-blown and supposedly inherently morbid spiritualist faith. Hardly conducive to differentiated analysis, the standard strategy of declaring those taking the phenomena seriously as quasi-insane was a sure way to inherently disqualify evident dupes along with hard-nosed investigators like James, who believed the occurrence of fundamental anomalies had been empirically established but struggled to interpret them theoretically. This is also the wider context in which to read one of James's most bitter public complaints about critics like Cattell, whom he accused of violating basic scientific standards in his misrepresentations of Richard Hodgson's second major report on Mrs. Piper (EPR 1898, ch. 25; CWJ 1989, 8.362–365): rather than offering dispassionate methodological critiques, James argued, Cattell and other public opponents of psychical research appeared to follow the principle that "in our dealings with the insane the usual moral rules don't apply. Mediums are scientific outlaws, and their defendants are quasi-insane. Any stick is good enough to beat dogs of that stripe with" (EPR 1898, 185).

Outspoken hardliners were no doubt personally as averse to anything smacking of magic as anybody could well be. But there was a tangible political dimension as well. Pioneers of the "new" experimental psychology in the United States and elsewhere struggled enormously to gain the public and institutional support they desperately needed to obtain laboratory space and funding for research, and to create permanent positions for themselves and their protégés. Seeing James as the leader of American psychologists openly investigating phenomena that were widely considered as the very epitome of backwardness, they felt he was sabotaging their efforts by severely damaging the public image of the "new" psychology (e.g., Coon 1992; Leary 1987). In this regard, not many psychological opponents of James's psychical research admitted as much in public as Cattell, who concluded his debate with James over Hodgson's report on the Piper mediumship by openly admitting that he had tackled James

> only because I believe that the Society for Psychical Research is doing much to injure psychology. The authority of Professor James is such that he involves other students

of psychology in his opinions unless they protest. We all acknowledge his leadership, but we cannot follow him into the quagmires. (EPR 1898, 186)[20]

Indeed, it turned out that the timing of Cattell's and Titchener's seemingly unconnected public attacks (which we mentioned earlier) was not accidental. It is unlikely that James would ever be aware of the private correspondence between the men, which reveals their attempts at shaping public opinion was orchestrated, in Titchener's already quoted phrase, to "stem the James tide"—that is to counterbalance what he and Cattell despised as "James' influence both in philosophy & psychology."[21] And perhaps unsurprisingly, James's philosophical work would sometimes be treated in the same undifferentiating manner as the unorthodox side of his psychology. In fact, the title of James's *The Will to Believe* promptly became akin to a dirty word in both psychology and philosophy, and often began to be used in slogan-like parlance to discredit his pragmatist philosophy along with his psychical research wholesale.

The purpose of most essays which comprised James's *The Will to Believe* was to offer a defense of the individual's right to believe in transcendental principles as long as such belief served tangible constructive functions and grounds for it were not conclusively refuted (see also Stephen Bush's chapter in this volume). Moreover, the book included the chapter "What Psychical Research Has Accomplished," which was one of James's defenses of members of the Sidgwick group against polemical attacks on their heretical research as self-evident "superstition" and vulgar obsession with "miracles." Indeed, those who began openly misrepresenting the meaning behind James's defense of the right to believe were often the same figures whose public portrayals of elite psychical research were little more than caricatures of what James and his collaborators at the SPR actually did. Psychological critics such as Jastrow, Hall, and Lightner Witmer did not engage with James's observations on the psychology of belief (e.g., ECR 1879, 355; PP 1890, chapter 21; WB 1897, *passim*; ERM 1905, 124–128), but began appropriating the phrase "will to believe" in their continuing public attacks on the occult to denote willful gullibility in the face of obvious counter-evidence, accusing James of irresponsibly providing his audience with a license to indulge in reprehensible superstitions (e.g., Jastrow 1900, 38; Hall 1908, 678, 683; 1910, xxxi; Witmer 1909, 43–44).

James was particularly grieved about an instance of simultaneous affronts on psychical research and pragmatism that came from Hugo Münsterberg, whom he had persuaded to leave Germany and run the Harvard psychology laboratory from 1892. This double attack on James's philosophy and psychical research occurred in Münsterberg's claim to have exposed the famous medium Eusapia Palladino as a fraud. Previous investigators who came to believe in the reality of some of her marvels had openly conceded that Palladino cheated whenever she was given the opportunity, but Münsterberg's specific claim of having caught her in the act has been accepted a little too readily as a historical fact (e.g., by Bjork 1983, 66–67; Bordogna 2008, 106; Knapp 2017, 294).

Apart from making evidently false claims about his alleged unmasking of Palladino, which conflicted with the minutes of the experiments in question he himself had signed (cf. Carrington 1954; Sommer 2012), Münsterberg more than just insinuated that her previous investigators, who had included materialists, positivists, and agnostics like the physician Enrico Morselli, the physiologists Richet and Filippo Bottazzi, and not least Marie and Pierre Curie, believed her phenomena were caused by spirits. Even more absurdly, and to the particular despair of James, Münsterberg implied that they were disciples of pragmatism (CWJ 1910, 12.432; Sommer 2012, 33).

Indeed, Münsterberg's article, which he entitled "My friends the spiritualists," and which lumped together spiritualism, psychical research, and pragmatism, reads like an advertisement for the kind of "naturalistic" standard position to which any psychological work had to conform if it was to stand a chance of receiving institutional support. A rejection of ontological materialism on the one hand, it was a simultaneous attack on "superstitions" like Jamesian psychical research and pragmatism: "Materialism," Münsterberg proclaimed, was "an impossible philosophy," which may be "necessary in natural science" as a merely methodological maxim but was "entirely unfit for an ultimate view of reality," which could be "given only by idealism" (Münsterberg 1910, 146). As a tacit explanation of what set him apart from elite scientists who unlike himself were unable to see Palladino as nothing but a fraud, Münsterberg stated, "I am not a pragmatist," and continued:

> With every fiber of my conviction I stand for idealism in philosophy, as far from materialism as from pragmatism. I believe that our real life is free will, bound by ideal standards which are absolute and eternal. The truth is such an eternal goal. We have to submit to it and not to choose it as the pragmatist fancies. But the obligation which truth forces on our will does not come from without as the materialist imagines; it is given by the structure of our own truth-seeking will. (Münsterberg 1910, 147)

Conclusion

Though the contexts outlined earlier are painted with a necessarily broad brush, their appreciation seems essential for a qualified historical understanding of James's heretical corpus. Placed back into their original circumstances, past controversies over occult phenomena to which James's work in psychology and philosophy responded throw fresh light on the significance of psychical research for James's canonical works.

Moreover, the story of James and fellow elite psychical researchers is a crucial yet remarkably understudied chapter in the history of scientific naturalism. Providing a convenient window into the past to help us reconstruct causes that have cemented "naturalism" in modern Western academic curricula, it shows that rather than being inherently secular let alone materialistic, notions of naturalism which are as axiomatic as they seem impervious to accurately historicized definitions have been nourished by many beliefs and anxieties. After all, squarely religious sentiments motivated the war on empirical approaches to supposedly "supernatural" phenomena during James's lifetime perhaps even more than did materialism. At the same time, contrary to received wisdom, open-minded approaches to alleged spiritualist and related marvels were practically outlawed not through careful, dispassionate scientific tests, but through polemical writings by often otherwise mutually opposed religious and irreligious figures.

Neither science nor philosophy were ever practiced in the proverbial ivory tower, and the boundaries of permissible academic inquiry were shaped and determined by conditions that were characteristic not of our time but of the nineteenth and early twentieth centuries. Fears over degeneration, and the complementary arch bogeys of "superstition" and "materialism," inextricable as they were from dramatic religio-political upheavals, may mean little to us today. But they positively occupied the minds of those who negotiated the curricula of the sciences as they became modern university disciplines. And it is no miracle that the professionalization of modern psychology as the "science of the soul" was particularly affected by these tensions.

Acknowledgments

I am grateful to the Wellcome Trust for funding my doctoral research on which part of this essay is based, and to Churchill College, University of Cambridge, for enabling me to conduct further research through a Junior Research Fellowship. Funding from Perrott-Warrick Fund, Trinity College Cambridge, has allowed me to finish work on this manuscript. I also wish to thank Gabriel Finkelstein, Bernie Lightman, and Troy Tice, who provided valuable feedback on a much longer previous version of this manuscript, and to Alexander Klein for his help in bringing it in its final shape.

Notes

1. For the James-Titchener controversy see EPR (1896–1899, ch. 22). I investigated the significance of Jamesian psychical research for the historiography of modern psychology in my doctoral thesis (Sommer 2013a), and will further develop arguments presented here in a book I'm currently working on.
2. On Galileo, see Shea and Artigas (2004), Numbers (2009).
3. For the history of scientific naturalism see, e.g., Turner (1974), Lightman (1987), Stanley (2015), Harrison and Roberts (2019).
4. Huxley simultaneously used and rejected Humean notions of supernaturalism tied to biblical miracles as self-evident violations of natural law. Spiritualists and psychical researchers were typically rather vocal in their own rejection of Humean pre-interpretations of certain phenomena as disruptions of laws of nature, yet Huxley referred to spiritualist phenomena as "supernatural" throughout his book. See Sommer (2018b) for the context of Huxley's first usage of "scientific naturalism." James himself overwhelmingly referred to alleged psychic phenomena by F.W.H. Myers's term "supernormal." Occasionally also using "supernatural," James never deployed the term in a Humean sense (cf. CWJ 1885 6.62; 1899, 9.86; EPR 1892, 99n2; WB 1897, 48, 50).
5. A recent historical study of James's heretical corpus (Knapp 2017) is remarkably uninterested in the contexts outlined below. For some other problems with the book, see Sommer (2018a).

6. For useful accounts of Myers, see Turner (1974, ch. 5), and Hamilton (2009).
7. For James's hypnotic experiments, and his hypnotherapeutic efforts regarding Ansel Bourne see, e.g., EPs (1886, 190–197; 1887, 200–203; 1890, 269), and Notes (with background information on Bourne, 372–373), and EPR (1886, 16–17; 1890, 82). On hypnosis as a tool of "mental vivisection" in French, German, and English experimental psychology, see Gauld (1992), Shamdasani (2003, 125–129), and Sommer (2013a, ch. 3).
8. For an interesting letter of Fechner to Wundt regarding his polemic, see Sommer (2013a, 226–227).
9. James critically reviewed Le Bon in the *Psychological Review* (ECR 1897, 533–535).
10. Titchener to Cattell, November 20, 1898, in Taylor (1996, 173).
11. The most thoroughly contextualized analysis of James's responses to degeneration theory has been offered by Sutton (2013, ch. 4, esp. 260–277).
12. It would take over a century for modern Western psychiatrists to abandon hallucinations and trance states as clear-cut indications of mental disease.
13. On Newcomb as a popularizer of secular science, see Moyer (1992).
14. See, for example, Newcomb's disputes with Gurney in *Science* (e.g., Newcomb 1884a; Gurney 1884; Newcomb 1884b), and James's reply to Newcomb's ASPR presidential address (EPR 1886, ch. 5).
15. Another psychologist deeply hostile to spiritualism, George S. Fullerton, served as both vice-president of the ASPR and Secretary of the Seybert Commission at the University of Pennsylvania, which was appointed in 1884 for the investigation of spiritualism following a bequest. Space constraints force me to reserve Fullerton's ASPR membership in the context of the Seybert Commission's refusal to investigate Mrs. Piper (cf. CWJ 1890, 7.107; 1894, 7.493–494; EPR 1901, 194) for separate treatment.
16. James voiced his view that Myers's framework was the "biggest step forward that has occurred in psychology" in the *Varieties* (VRE 1902, 402–403, n. 25, see also 191, 367, 403), but he had already made similar assessments in various previous writings that are now considered canonical, as well as in letters to his brother Henry and fellow psychologists (CWJ 1901, 3.156–157; 1901, 9.433; 1902, 10.92; Hamilton 2009, esp. ch. 5; Sommer 2013a, ch. 3.3.2).
17. Schiller would serve as the SPR's president in 1914. For an excellent study of Schiller that also addresses his psychical research, see Porrovecchio (2011). Apart from Sidgwick, James, and Schiller, other prominent philosopher presidents of the SPR were Henri Bergson (1913), L. P. Jacks (1917–18), Hans Driesch (1926–27), C. D. Broad (1935–36 and 1958–60), and H. H. Price (1939–41 and 1960–61).
18. Schiller to James, August 6, 1905, James papers, Houghton Library, Harvard University (bMS.Am.1092 [902]). This letter has only been calendared in CWJ (11.569–570).
19. Lotze was a friend and pupil of Fechner, but detested and ridiculed his heretical scientific interests (e.g., Lotze 1891).
20. In fairness to Cattell it needs to be pointed out that nobody forced his decision to reprint James's SPR presidential address in *Science*, or James's later obituary of Myers in the *Popular Science Monthly* (which was then also edited by Cattell). James in fact praised Cattell's editorial liberty, writing that "Thinking as you do about the spook business, it has always filled me with admiration to see how freely you gave me my head" (CWJ 1899, 9.3). In 1903, Cattell would even defend James against members of the National Academy of Sciences, who opposed his election on the grounds of his psychical research (Sokal 2010, 33; Sommer 2012, 36–37, n.3). Yet, these instances were not representative of Cattell's

position, and James, whom Cattell greatly admired personally, was the only psychical researcher he ever thought worthy of courteous treatment.
21. Titchener to Cattell, November 20, 1898, Library of Congress, Washington D.C., Cattell Papers (MSS15412/42/153).

REFERENCES

Bjork, Daniel W. 1983. *The Compromised Scientist: William James in the Development of American Psychology*. New York: Columbia University Press.

Blackbourn, David. 1993. *Marpingen: Apparitions of the Virgin Mary in Bismarckian Germany*. Oxford, UK: Oxford University Press.

Bordogna, Francesca. 2008. *William James at the Boundaries: Philosophy, Science, and the Geography of Knowledge*. Chicago: University of Chicago Press.

Brown, Edward M. 1983. "Neurology and Spiritualism in the 1870s." *Bulletin of the History of Medicine* 57: 563–577.

Carpenter, William B. 1873. "On the Psychology of Belief." *Contemporary Review* 23: 123–145.

Carpenter, William B. 1875. *Principles of Mental Physiology*. Second ed. London: Henry S. King & Co.

Carrington, Hereward. 1954. *The American Seances with Eusapia Palladino*. New York: Garrett Publications.

Cattell, James McKeen. 1898. "Mrs. Piper, the Medium." *Science* 7: 534–535.

Coon, Deborah J. 1992. "Testing the Limits of Sense and Science. American Experimental Psychologists Combat Spiritualism." *American Psychologist* 47: 143–151.

Gauld, Alan. 1992. *A History of Hypnotism*. Cambridge, UK: Cambridge University Press.

Gregory, Frederick. 1977. *Scientific Materialism in Nineteenth Century Germany*. Dordrecht: Springer.

Gurney, Edmund. 1884. "Psychical Research." *Science* 4: 509–510.

Gurney, Edmund. 1888. "Hallucination of Memory and 'Telepathy.'" *Mind* 13: 415–417.

Hall, G. Stanley. 1881. "Recent researches on hypnotism." *Mind* 6: 98–104.

Hall, G. Stanley. 1887. "*Proceedings of the English Society for Psychical Research*. From July, 1882, to May, 1887. *Phantasms of the Living*. By Edward [sic] Gurney, M.A., Frederick [sic] W. H. Meyers [sic], and Frank Podmore. Two Vols. 1886." *American Journal of Psychology* 1: 128–146.

Hall, G. Stanley. 1908. "Spooks and Telepathy." *Appleton's Magazine* 12: 677–683.

Hall, G. Stanley. 1910. "Introduction." In Amy E. Tanner, *Studies in Spiritism*, xv–xxxiii. New York: Appleton.

Hamilton, Trevor. 2009. *Immortal Longings: F.W.H. Myers and the Victorian Search for Life after Death*. Exeter, UK: Imprint Academic.

Harrison, Peter, and Jon H. Roberts, eds. 2019. *Science without God? Rethinking the History of Scientific Naturalism*. Oxford, UK: Oxford University Press.

Hodgson, Richard. 1898. "A Further Record of Observations of Certain Phenomena of Trance." *Proceedings of the Society for Psychical Research* 13: 284–582.

Hunter, Michael. 2020. *The Decline of Magic: Britain in the Enlightenment*. New Haven, CT: Yale University Press.

Huxley, Thomas H. 1892. *Essays upon some Controverted Questions*. London: Macmillan and Co.

Jastrow, Joseph. 1886. "The Psychology of Spiritualism." *Science* 8: 567–568.

Jastrow, Joseph. 1900. *Fact and Fable in Psychology*. Boston and New York: Houghton, Mifflin, and Co.

Josephson-Storm, Jason A. 2017. *The Myth of Disenchantment: Magic, Modernity, and the Birth of the Human Sciences*. Chicago: University of Chicago Press.

Kelly, Edward F. 2015. "Toward a Worldview Grounded in Science *and* Spirituality." In *Beyond Physicalism. Toward Reconciliation of Science and Spirituality*, edited by E. F. Kelly, Adam Crabtree, and Paul Marshall, 493–551. Lanham, MD: Rowman & Littlefield.

Knapp, Krister Dylan. 2017. *William James: Psychical Research and the Challenge of Modernity*. Chapel Hill: University of North Carolina Press.

Le Bon, Gustave. 1896. *The Crowd. A Study of the Popular Mind*. New York: Macmillan. (Original French edition in 1895.)

Le Maléfan, Pascal, Renaud Evrard, and Carlos S. Alvarado. 2013. "Spiritist Delusions and Spiritism in the Nosography of French Psychiatry (1850–1950)." *History of Psychiatry* 24: 477–491.

Leary, David E. 1987. "Telling Likely Stories: The Rhetoric of the New Psychology, 1880–1920." *Journal of the History of the Behavioral Sciences* 23: 315–331.

Lightman, Bernard. 1987. *The Origins of Agnosticism. Victorian Unbelief and the Limits of Knowledge*. Baltimore, ML: Johns Hopkins University Press.

Lotze, Hermann. 1891. "Anfänge spiritistischer Conjecturalkritik. Eine Geistergeschichte [1879]." In *Kleine Schriften von Hermann Lotze*, edited by David Peipers, 438–450. Leipzig: Hirzel.

Mauskopf, Seymour H., and Michael R. McVaugh. 1980. *The Elusive Science. Origins of Experimental Psychical Research*. Baltimore, MD: Johns Hopkins University Press.

Minot, Charles Sedgwick. 1884. "Psychical Research in America." *Science* 4: 369–370.

Moyer, Albert C. 1992. *A Scientific Voice in American Culture. Simon Newcomb and the Rhetoric of Scientific Method*. Berkeley, CA: University of California Press.

Münsterberg, Hugo. 1910. "My friends the spiritualists." In H. Münsterberg, *American Problems from the Point of View of a Psychologist*, 117–148. New York: Moffat, Yard and Co.

Myers, Frederic W. H. 1884. "On a Telepathic Explanation of Some So-called Spiritualistic Phenomena." *Proceedings of the Society for Psychical Research* 2: 217–237.

Myers, Frederic W. H. 1885. "Automatic Writing. Part II." *Proceedings of the Society for Psychical Research* 3: 1–63.

Newcomb, Simon. 1884a. "Psychic Force." *Science* 4: 372–374.

Newcomb, Simon. 1884b. "Psychical Research." *Science* 4: 410–411.

Noakes, Richard. 2019. *Physics and Psychics: The Occult and the Sciences in Modern Britain*. Cambridge, UK: Cambridge University Press.

Numbers, Ronald L., ed. 2009. *Galileo Goes to Jail and Other Myths about Science and Religion*. Cambridge, MA: Harvard University Press.

Pick, Daniel. 1989. *Faces of Degeneration. A European Disorder, c. 1848–c. 1918*. Cambridge, UK: Cambridge University Press.

Porrovecchio, Mark J. 2011. *F. C. S. Schiller and the Dawn of Pragmatism: The Rhetoric of a Philosophical Rebel*. Lanham, MD: Lexington.

Porter, Roy. 1999. "Witchcraft and Magic in Enlightenment, Romantic and Liberal Thought." In *Witchcraft and Magic in Europe. Volume 5*, edited by Bengt Ankarloo and Stuart Clark, 191–282. Philadelphia: University of Pennsylvania Press.

Porter, Theodore. 2018. *Genetics in the Madhouse: The Unknown History of Human Heredity*. Princeton, NJ: Princeton University Press.

Ross, Sydney. 1962. "*Scientist*: The Story of a Word." *Annals of Science* 18: 65–86.
Royce, Josiah. 1888. "Hallucination of Memory and 'Telepathy.'" *Mind* 13: 244–248.
Royce, Josiah. 1889. "Report of the Committee on Phantasms and Presentiments." *Proceedings of the American Society for Psychical Research* 1: 350–515.
Royce, Josiah. 1912. *The Sources of Religious Insight*. New York: Charles Scribner's Sons.
Shamdasani, Sonu. 1994. "Encountering Hélène: Théodore Flournoy and the genesis of subliminal psychology." In Théodore Flournoy, *From India to the Planet Mars*, edited by S. Shamdasani, xi–li. Princeton, NJ: Princeton University Press.
Shamdasani, Sonu. 2003. *Jung and the Making of Modern Psychology. The Dream of a Science*. Cambridge, UK: Cambridge University Press.
Shea, William R., and Mariano Artigas. 2004. *Galileo in Rome: The Rise and Fall of a Troublesome Genius*. Oxford, UK: Oxford University Press.
Shortt, S. E. D. 1984. "Physicians and Psychics: The Anglo-American Medical Response to Spiritualism, 1870–1890." *Journal of the History of Medicine and Allied Sciences* 39: 339–355.
Society for Psychical Research. 1909. "New Members and Associates." *Journal of the Society for Psychical Research* 14: 82–83.
Sokal, Michael M. 2010. "William James and the National Academy of Sciences." *William James Studies* 5: 29–38.
Sommer, Andreas. 2012. "Psychical Research and the Origins of American Psychology: Hugo Münsterberg, William James and Eusapia Palladino." *History of the Human Sciences* 25: 23–44.
Sommer, Andreas. 2013a. "Crossing the Boundaries of Mind and Body. Psychical Research and the Origins of Modern Psychology." PhD dissertation, University College London.
Sommer, Andreas. 2013b. "Normalizing the Supernormal: The Formation of the 'Gesellschaft für Psychologische Forschung' ('Society for Psychological Research'), c. 1886–1890." *Journal of the History of the Behavioral Sciences* 49: 18–44.
Sommer, Andreas, ed. 2014. "Psychical Research in the History of Science and Medicine." Special section, *Studies in History and Philosophy of Biological and Biomedical Sciences*, 48, 38–111.
Sommer, Andreas. 2018a. "Krister Dylan Knapp. *William James: Psychical Research and the Challenge of Modernity*." *Isis* 109: 410–411.
Sommer, Andreas. 2018b. "Materialism vs. supernaturalism? 'Scientific naturalism' in context." Available from https://www.forbiddenhistories.com/scientific-naturalism/.
Stanley, Matthew. 2015. *Huxley's Church and Maxwell's Demon: From Theistic Science to Naturalistic Science*. Chicago: University of Chicago Press.
Sutton, Emma. 2013. "Re-writing 'the Laws of Health': William James on the Philosophy and Politics of Disease in Nineteenth-Century America." PhD dissertation, University College London.
Taylor, Eugene. 1983. *William James on Exceptional Mental States. The 1896 Lowell Lectures*. New York: Charles Scribner's Sons.
Taylor, Eugene. 1996. *William James: On Consciousness beyond the Margin*. Princeton, NJ: Princeton University Press.
Titchener, Edward Bradford. 1898. "The 'Feeling of Being Stared At.'" *Science* 8: 895–897.
Turner, Frank M. 1974. *Between Science and Religion. The Reaction to Scientific Naturalism in Late Victorian England*. New Haven, CT: Yale University Press.
Williams, John P. 1985. "Psychical Research and Psychiatry in Late Victorian Britain: Trance as Ecstasy or Trance as Insanity." In *The Anatomy of Madness. Essays in the History of Psychiatry. Volume I*, edited by W. F. Bynum, R. Porter, and M. Shepherd, 233–254. London: Tavistock.

Winter, Alison. 1998. *Mesmerized: Powers of Mind in Victorian Britain*. Chicago: University of Chicago Press.

Witmer, Lightner. 1909. *Mental Healing and the Emmanuel Movement. An Editorial Criticism*. Philadelphia, PA: The Psychological Clinic Press.

Wundt, Wilhelm. 1879. "Spiritualism as a scientific question. An open letter to Professor Hermann Ulrici, of Halle." *Popular Science Monthly* 15: 577–593 (original German ed.: *Der Spiritismus. Eine sogenannte wissenschaftliche Frage. Offener Brief an Herrn Prof. Dr. Hermann Ulrici in Halle*. Leipzig: Wilhelm Engelmann, 1879).

Wundt, Wilhelm. 1892. *Hypnotismus und Suggestion*. Leipzig: Wilhelm Engelmann.

Zedler, Beatrice H. 1974. "Royce and James on Psychical Research." *Transactions of the Charles S. Peirce Society* 10: 235–252.

CHAPTER 8

PSYCHOLOGY AND PHILOSOPHY IN THE WORK OF WILLIAM JAMES

Two Good Things

DAVID E. LEARY

It is difficult to do two things at once, especially if they involve radically reconstructing both psychology and philosophy. That is precisely what William James undertook during the final three decades of his life. To make his task a bit less daunting, he tried to divide and conquer, as Alexander Klein (2008) has put it, first focusing primarily on producing his landmark psychological works on *The Principles of Psychology* (1890) and *The Varieties of Religious Experience* (1902) and only then turning most of his attention to producing his major philosophical works on *Pragmatism* (1907), *A Pluralistic Universe* (1909), and *The Meaning of Truth* (1909), not to mention his posthumously published *Some Problems of Philosophy* (1911) and *Essays in Radical Empiricism* (1912). But dividing the chore proved to be harder than he had anticipated, and neither his psychology nor his philosophy turned out to be independent of the other. Each was developed, however unevenly, over the entire thirty years; and each, in the end, was intricately implicated in and by the other.

That is not to say, as James initially feared, that the permeation of his psychology by philosophy, and his philosophy by psychology, necessarily spoiled two good things. In fact, his psychology and philosophy enriched each other in fundamental ways. If this means that James was guilty of "psychologism" in his philosophy, it is no less reasonable to accuse him of "philosophism" in his psychology.[1] Whether this indicates something damnably problematic, undercutting his remarkable achievements in either or both fields, each reader can decide. My own view is obvious in my characterization of the mutual *enrichment* of his psychology and philosophy. I ask only that persons with different inclinations consider the ways in which James's path-breaking psychology is related to his equally novel and consequential philosophy before reaching any final assessment.

Withholding precipitous judgments will almost certainly lead to greater understanding, deeper appreciation, and more nuanced conclusions regarding the nature and significance of his work.

Just as there are many ways in which James's psychology is related to his philosophy, there are many ways to characterize James's dual, sometimes shifting levels of commitment to psychology and philosophy. Some are rather prosaic; others more substantial. But even the more prosaic ways—reviewing James's indecision about his intended career, noting the changes over time in his professional titles, considering the courses he taught, and describing the nature and sequence of his articles and presentations—illustrate complex relations between his psychology and philosophy. It makes sense to begin with a matter-of-fact account of these matters before exploring the more substantive connections between his psychology and philosophy.

James as Psychologist and Philosopher

James's prolonged vocational crisis is more than amply documented. Having devoted himself to training as an apprentice painter in late 1860, he moved to Harvard in less than a year to study chemistry with Charles Eliot, and then anatomy and physiology with Jeffries Wyman, before transferring to Harvard's School of Medicine in 1864. Suspending his medical studies, he spent much of 1865 as a field naturalist in Brazil under the guidance of Louis Agassiz, and subsequently returned to Cambridge, Massachusetts, to continue his medical studies (including more work in anatomy and physiology) until he received his MD, the only academic degree he ever earned, in 1869.

Throughout this period James interrupted his formal studies for extended periods due to ill health, depression, and uncertainty about his prospects. He also engaged in a wide range of reading, including philosophy and psychology, and had protracted exchanges on scientific and intellectual matters with his friends Charles S. Peirce, Oliver Wendell Holmes, Jr., Chauncey Wright, and others. In addition, while recuperating in Europe in 1867–1868, he attended lectures and visited some laboratories to learn more about ongoing developments in experimental physiology, neurology, and psychology.

Receiving his MD did nothing to bring James's vocational vacillation to an end. Though he thought briefly about using his medical training to assist the mentally infirm, he never intended to serve as a day-to-day doctor. Instead, his thoughts—when he could marshal them to the task—zigzagged between anatomy and physiology, mental science, and philosophy. To the extent that he understood these fields to be fundamentally related, his vacillation was constrained, but real nonetheless. At bottom, his abiding and deepest interests revolved around philosophy, as reflected in his declaration in the mid-1860s that he would "study philosophy all my days" (CWJ 1865, 1.8). But it was psychology, still considered part of philosophy, that was at the center of his philosophic interests, especially as it was on the verge of being transformed in response to developments within the biological sciences. While convalescing in Berlin, he wrote that he was "going to try this winter to stick to the study of the Nervous system and psychology" (CWJ 1867, 4.199), observing that "perhaps the time has come for Psychology to begin to be a science" and that "Helmholtz & a man named Wundt," who were "strong on the physiology of the senses," were "working at it" in Heidelberg (CWJ 1867, 4.226). He became convinced that psychology would not be "*à la ordre du jour* until some as yet unforeseen steps are made in the physiology of the Nervous system" (CWJ 1868, 4.302). Meanwhile, he kept an eye on wider philosophical issues, asking Oliver Wendell Holmes to help him establish a "philosophical society" that would have "regular meetings and discuss none but the very tallest & broadest questions" when he returned to Cambridge (CWJ 1868, 4.245). (This "society" evolved into the famous Metaphysical Club of the 1870s.) Although his own approach was already aligned with "an empiricistic view of life," he could see "an ontological cloud of absolute Idealism waiting . . . far off on the horizon," promising a "fray" for which he presently felt "no passion" (CWJ 1868, 4.302). Committed to a Darwinian perspective, taking "our sensations as simply given or as preserved by natural selection" (CWJ 1868, 4:302), he reported "hovering and dipping about the portals of Psychology," with "a scientific life" as his "only ideal" (CWJ 1868, 4.346).

Even so, James was still rudderless more than two years after receiving his MD, when he accepted an offer to teach an undergraduate course in comparative physiology at Harvard. (In the intervening years, ill health, depression, and indecision had continued to plague him, as he worked on and off in his friend Henry Bowditch's Harvard physiology laboratory.) Now thirty-one, James had finally secured his first paid employment. His success at teaching led him to decide "to stick to biology for a profession *in case I am not called to a chair of philosophy*. . . . Philosophy I will nevertheless regard as my vocation and never let slip a chance to do a stroke of it" (James 1868–1873, February 10, 1873, entry, italics added). His concern, clearly, was not only the lack of immediate prospects for a job in philosophy—a field in which he had read and discussed a great deal but lacked any formal education—but also the tendency of philosophic rumination to stir up doubts and skepticism, exacerbating his mental condition. (Issues related to materialism, determinism, and scientism were among the cognitive sources of his frequent emotional distress.) Despite his seemingly firm decision "to stick to biology," however, he declined an offer to teach courses on both anatomy and physiology in 1873–1874, declaring that he had changed his mind and "resolved to fight it out on the line of mental science" (CWJ 1873, 1.194)! Even *he* had to admit his own "perplexity" at this flip-flop since permanent employment might well have followed upon the *other* line (CWJ 1873, 1.194); and sure enough, four days later he reversed course and accepted the "anatomical instruction" for the coming academic year, having concluded *now* that "philosophical activity as a *business* is not normal for most men, and not for me." Why? Because "to be responsible for a complete conception of things is beyond my strength" and would breed "hypochondria," even though "my deepest interest will as ever lie with the most general problems" (James 1868–1873, April 10, 1873, entry).

This quick summary highlights James's vacillations and insecurities, while revealing how seriously he took philosophy as an extension—even an intimate part—of his life, touching fundamental issues that disrupted his inner equilibrium: "As a professed philosopher pledges himself publicly never to have done with doubt on these subjects [having to do with 'the most general problems'], but every day to be ready to criticize afresh and call in question the growth of his faith of the day before, I fear the constant sense of instability generated by this attitude" would open "the abyss of horrors" and "imperil my reason." Alternatively, biological study would provide a means of collecting "concrete facts" that could "form a fixed basis from which to aspire" to "the mastery of the universal questions," while allowing him to "passively float, and tide over times of weakness & depression, trusting all the while blindly in the benefice of nature's forces, and the return of higher opportunities." A philosopher, James believed, had to renounce "the privilege of trusting *blindly*" (April 10, 1873, entry). As a result, the "wiser" if "tamer" decision, "for the present," was to "give myself to biology" by means of which "I can in a less penetrating way work out a philosophy in the midst of the other duties" (CWJ 1873, 1.203).

In the end, James did not teach at all in 1873–1874. Instead, he once again sought health and refuge in Europe. But when he returned to Cambridge, he taught anatomy and physiology in 1874–1875, and the continued success of his teaching opened an opportunity for him to offer the first graduate course in the United States on "The Relations Between Physiology and Psychology" in 1875–1876. In 1876, he was appointed Assistant Professor of Physiology, and in 1876–1877, while repeating his graduate course on physiology and psychology, he added a new undergraduate course on "Physiological Psychology," offered under the rubric of Natural History. When this latter course was given again in 1877–1878, its title was simply "Psychology" and it was listed—with the encouragement of Harvard's Board of Overseers—under Philosophy. (The course was innovative, at the forefront of both philosophical and scientific developments, and popular with students. Each of these characteristics made it relevant to the Overseers' desire to inject new life into Harvard's philosophical offerings.)

Thus, James got his foot into the doorway of Philosophy. In 1879–1880, when he offered his final courses on anatomy and physiology, he repeated his undergraduate course on "Psychology" and his graduate course on "Physiological Psychology," both listed under Philosophy. Coupled with the personal tempering that came with his marriage in 1878, his first substantive publications in 1878–1879, and his appointment as Assistant Professor of Philosophy in 1880, this marked the completion of James's unusual journey to the department in which he would teach for another twenty-six years. By 1882, after a year of traveling and discoursing with noted philosophers in Europe, he could report with confidence that "I really believe that in my way I have a wider view of the field than any one I've seen" (CWJ 1882, 5.302). The field he was talking about was philosophy, not psychology.

James remained a Professor of Philosophy until 1889, when he was appointed the Alford Professor of Psychology. He held this appointment until 1897, when his title was changed back to Professor of Philosophy, the professorial title he held until he retired from teaching in 1907. But titles aside, he taught many nonpsychology courses (e.g., "The Philosophy of Evolution," "Contemporary Philosophy," "English Philosophy," "Logic and Psychology," and "Ethics") during the 1880s as he worked on his *Principles of Psychology* (1890), and he continued to teach psychology throughout the 1890s, as he began to shift his attention to philosophy. In fact, James actually expanded his interest in abnormal psychology in the 1890s, doing experiments with students on unusual mental states and taking them for observational tours of local asylums, as he developed the ideas and convictions that he shared in his Lowell Lectures on Exceptional Mental States in 1896. Although he expanded his course offerings in philosophy (including courses on "Descartes, Spinoza, and Leibnitz," "Cosmology," "The Philosophy of Nature," "The Philosophy of Kant," and "Metaphysics") throughout the 1890s, it was only in 1903, after he had returned to Harvard from a three-year sabbatical in Europe, where he had prepared, delivered, and published his Gifford Lectures on *The Varieties of Religious Experience* (1902), that he finally directed his attention primarily to philosophy and, more particularly, to the elaboration of his own unique philosophical ideas, which he had been developing, in concert with his psychology, since the late 1870s.

A closer look at James's articles reinforces the claim that he was not a psychologist *first* and a philosopher *later*, nor a psychologist *in this article* and a philosopher *in that article*. Neither "Remarks on Spencer's Definition of Mind as Correspondence" (1878) nor "*Quelques Considérations sur la method subjective*" (1878) can be categorized as simply a work of psychology or philosophy. Nor can "Brute and Human Intellect" (1878) or "Are We Automata?" (1879) or "On the Function of Cognition" (1885). And the same can be said of articles like "Does 'Consciousness' Exist?" (1904), "The Experience of Activity" (1905), and "The Energies of Men" (1907), published in the final decade of James's life.[2] Despite James's greater emphasis upon psychology in his earlier years and his greater emphasis upon philosophy toward the end of his career, the preceding account makes it clear that he was both a psychologist and a philosopher throughout his career.

James's Psychology in Relation to His Philosophy

In the late 1870s, when James moved from teaching anatomy and physiology to teaching psychology and philosophy, the latter disciplines were closely linked with one another. (In fact, psychology was still considered one of the subfields of philosophy.) The revolution in psychology that James helped to spark and then worked to advance depended in the first instance *not* on changes within philosophy, though they would occur as well, but rather on the introduction of methods and ideas from the realms in which James had pursued his distinctive education. It was his reading and field experience in evolutionary biology, his formal training in anatomy and physiology, and his independent research into pioneering experimental work in sensory physiology and neurology that led him, as one of the first among others, to propose substantial modifications of both psychology and philosophy. He did so as the recipient, in 1878, of an invitation to produce a textbook on psychology for Henry Holt's American Science Series. Holt initially expected the manuscript within a year, but it took James a full twelve years of sustained effort to deliver his acknowledged masterpiece.

As James began working on his *Principles of Psychology*, he was already familiar with the leading-edge research of Gustav Theodor Fechner, Hermann Helmholtz, Wilhelm Wundt, Theodor Meynert, Emil Du Bois-Reymond, and many other sensory physiologists, anatomists, and neurologists, and—more to the point—he already saw the implications of their research for both psychology and philosophy. Perhaps the best way to indicate the kind of innovative insights that he drew from the work of these scientific researchers is to focus on the results of his reflections upon Helmholtz's physiological optics.

Helmholtz was, of course, a major force in the development of sensory physiology, which was then establishing the precise temporal, functional, and structural relations between initial sensory input, conscious experience, and motor output. James recognized early on that the facts being discovered through experiments in this field were essential to the development of psychology as a natural science. Helmholtz's magisterial *Handbook of Physiological Optics* (1867), in particular, offered an empirical, naturalistic foundation for understanding how the senses contribute to our perception, both of the *objects* in the world and of *their spatial relations* to one another and to us. These two topics, James knew, were relevant to many philosophical and psychological issues, including Kantian and post-Kantian propositions regarding innate forms of sensibility—innate, that is, to the knower's mind rather than to the external physical world. Hence, James was intrigued by Helmholtz's more than ample demonstration that, although the actual sensations of the retina are "to the last degree fluctuating and inconsistent," they nonetheless produce "exact and constant results" in what is seen by the observer. This led James to conclude, contrary to Helmholtz's own assertions about the role of "unconscious inference," that physiological sensations are actually "overlooked" by the mind so that *"things"* can be seen and become the actual "matter of knowledge" (ML 1876–1877, 128). This conclusion, based on James's assessment of the scientific evidence, was at the root of his philosophical realism.

Similarly, when James turned his attention to the perception of space, he once again followed the physiological evidence provided by Helmholtz and others to reach another distinctive conclusion, namely, that consciousness of spatial relations is *neither* the result of Kantian intuition *nor* the result of mental constructions as claimed by empiricists, but rather an immediate "given" within sensory experience. The experimental facts suggested to James that spatial relations are already *there to begin with*, along with all sorts of other relations, within the sensory "muchness" of immediate experience (EPs 1879, 62–82).

This and other related conclusions were significant in the development of James's thought, largely because they led to a fundamental premise of his psychology and eventually to a fundamental hypothesis underlying his metaphysical reflections. Experience or consciousness, James declared, appears *at the very start* as a unified whole. Once we have it, we may abstract various aspects or relations, including spatial relations, *out of* it; but consciousness itself *begins* as an undifferentiated unity. Years later, in his *Principles of Psychology*, James presented the classic statement of this basic insight in his celebrated chapter on "The Stream of Thought," in which he described the initially undivided mental state as "sensibly continuous," more like a flowing "river" than a linked "chain" (PP 1890, 231, 233). A few years after the publication of *Principles*, he characterized this entry point into psychological analysis as "the chief originality and service" of that entire work (EPs 1892, 275). And a little over a decade later, his insistence that we should begin psychology with the stream of thought was echoed in his contention that philosophers should begin metaphysical rumination with the premise of a similarly original, continuous, and undifferentiated state of affairs, which he called "pure experience," out of which we can abstract physical and mental phenomena (ERE 1904, 21–44; also see Cooper, this volume).

The significance for psychology of James's granting precedence to holistic consciousness became apparent in his early criticism of Herbert Spencer's (1855) psychology, which was being promulgated to great acclaim in the 1870s. This criticism provided the context within which James began to elaborate his own distinctive psychology. Like James, Spencer accorded priority to the facts of experience, but despite his allegiance to such facts, Spencer failed (as James noted) to base his psychology on the factual seamlessness of consciousness. Instead, he repeated Locke's mistake of rationally analyzing states of consciousness into their supposedly elemental "ideas" or "feelings" and then arguing that these inferred "elements" are the primal stuff from which experience is subsequently built up. Approaching the matter in this way, James observed, had forced Spencer (like Locke and his successors) to account for the building up or construction of the holistic conscious states that humans experience. Spencer had done so just as they had, by referring to a compounding of elements that supposedly govern the initial production as well as subsequent operations of consciousness. For James, who was seeking a radically consistent empiricism (which is to say, a thorough reliance on facts), the claim that consciousness, in its *original* form, is the result of a process of combination was empirically counterfactual: No one has ever *experienced* or *observed* mental elements being combined into an integrated whole. (On these matters, see EPh 1878, 20–22; EPs 1878, 14–16; and PP 1990, 160–164.)

In addition to this criticism, James was concerned that Spencer's way of using combination, like Locke's way of using the laws of association, to provide explanations all the way up and down the psychological scale conveyed an inaccurate—and very unfortunate—picture of mental life. Mental dynamics are *not*, he insisted, purely mechanical processes that automatically connect whatever elements happen to be in the mind, regardless of whose mind is undergoing these processes. To the contrary, James contended, observation suggests that mental life entails an active, selective shaping of experience in accordance with each person's distinctive interests.

James's contention that an individual's interests play a significant role in mental dynamics became a fundamental premise of his psychology and was directly related to the development of pragmatism as well as other aspects of his later philosophic formulations. His sensitivity to the role of human interests—and hence his awareness of the very personal nature of human consciousness—was apparent as early as 1875, in a review of Wilhelm Wundt's historically important *Principles of Physiological Psychology* (1874). In that review, after surveying some of Wundt's experimental research on attention, James asserted that he had focused on this particular topic because it demonstrated "what empiricists are too apt to ignore," namely, that there is a "thorough-going spontaneous mental element in determining even the simplest experiences." In their zeal to prove that the mind is a "product" of the environment, James said, "the a posteriori school" of psychologists, including Spencer, keeps pointing to "experience" as its source of evidence, yet "it never defines what experience is." "*My* experience," James affirmed, "is only what I agree to attend to." In fact, "the *whole* mass of impressions falling on any individual" is "chaotic" and becomes "orderly only by selective attention and recognition" as "interests ... keep interfering with the pure flow of impressions ... causing the vast majority of sensations to be ignored." In the face of clear evidence supporting his contention, James found it "amusing" that Spencer "shrinks" from acknowledging "this law" (ECR 1875, 300).

When James emphasized the pivotal role of interest, especially in relation to selective attention and memory, in his *Principles of Psychology*, he asked his readers to imagine four men sharing a tour of Europe:

> One will bring home only picturesque impressions—costumes and colors, parks and views and works of architecture, pictures and statues. To another all this will be non-existent; and distances and prices, populations and drainage-arrangements, door- and window-fastenings, and other useful statistics will take their place. A third will give a rich account of the theatres, restaurants, and public balls, and naught beside; whilst the fourth will perhaps have been so wrapped in his own subjective broodings as to tell little more than a few names of places through which he passed. Each has selected, out of the same mass of presented objects, those which suited his private interest and has made his experience thereby. (PP 1890, 275–276)

With this and other examples James underscored that even when humans share the same environments, each of them, from within commonly shared arrays of sensory givens, selectively notices and remembers different things, depending upon personal predilections and concerns. Even when multiple pairs of eyes and ears *take in* virtually the same physical stimuli, the mind connected to each pair will differentially select—that is, discriminate—different aspects from among the "simultaneous possibilities" offered by the same environment. Thus, each of James's tourists, after traveling through the same "real world," returned with a different "sense of reality," consonant with his own interests.[3] Several of James's first substantive publications strove to clarify the basic psychological procedures involved in such situations (e.g., EPh 1879, 32–64; EPs 1884, 142–167). As we shall see, the realistic yet individualistic point of view that James went on to develop, based upon these procedures, became equally significant for his philosophy (see Leary 2018 for elaborations of these and other points of connection).

Despite his criticisms of Spencer's psychology, James complimented Spencer for realizing the relevance of evolution and other nineteenth-century scientific advances for the reformulation of psychology. Specifically, he lauded him for accepting that humans, like other biological organisms, developed as a species and are developing as individuals in relation to their environments, and he agreed with Spencer's claim that the basic physiological reflex, connecting stimuli and responses, provides a useful template for many psychological explanations. In each case, however, he chided Spencer for going either too far or not far enough. For instance, Spencer went too far, in James's estimation, in attributing unqualified causal dominance to the environment. As illustrated by his four-tourists example, James felt that the environment *presents* stimuli but does not necessarily *impress* them ineluctably upon the human mind. In addition, individuals tend not only to notice and remember but also to *respond* in ways consonant with their previous experiences, interests, and aims. In doing so, they can *change* their environments, thus showing that the human mind is not a mere product of environmental influences, as Spencer had argued, but rather, an active, creative part of nature, spontaneously producing new insights and helping to realize novel possibilities. This basic insight figured prominently in James's ethical theory (see Leary 2009).

Similarly, regarding basic reflexes, James argued that humans are not simply bundles of automated reactions to stimuli. His knowledge of the rapidly advancing discipline of neurology allowed him to make empirically based conjectures about the evolutionary advantages conferred by highly developed, "unstable" brains in which impulses may be "reflected" and "channeled" in new ways (see Leary 2014). The willful formation of personal habits—basically *learned* reflexes—accounted in James's view for much of the variety as well as consistency in human thought and behavior. Opposing Thomas Huxley as well as Herbert Spencer, he emphasized that the learning of habits not only allows for but often depends upon the human will (see Leary 2013). His arguments for the reality of the human will involve what we might call the "intervening variables" between sensory input and motor output. Abetted by his knowledge of the brain and how it could serve the purposes of individualized cognition, James proposed that interests and attention could shunt neurological impulses in ways that initiate, inhibit, and modify actions according to individual character. All of this, along with insistence upon the personal character of consciousness, constituted steps toward James's personalistic philosophy.

Much more could be said about James's psychology in relation to his philosophy (e.g., see Leary 2018), but this review of some of the fundamental doctrines of his psychology should be sufficient to show how James's psychological insights and arguments frequently crossed over to his philosophical proposals and claims, as when his theory of perception led him to philosophical realism, his psychological doctrine of the original unity of consciousness morphed into his metaphysical doctrine of pure experience, his views on the selective character of human consciousness facilitated and supported his pragmatist inclinations, his convictions about the psychological possibility of novel understandings and actions enabled his ethical theory, and his neuropsychological views allowed him to resist the depersonalizing forces of materialism in defense of individualistic personality and proactive human will—which is to say, when these views provided the corporeal basis of his philosophical anthropology.

James's Philosophy in Relation to His Psychology

Four years before he was appointed an Assistant Professor of Philosophy at Harvard, James defined "philosophic study" as "the habit of always seeing an alternative, of not taking the usual for granted, of making conventionalities fluid again, of imagining foreign states of mind. In a word, it means the possession of mental perspective" (EPh 1876, 4). This focus on philosophical perspectivism was coextensive with James's psychological doctrine that each individual sees and understands from a necessarily unique position, and it remained a fundamental aspect of James's philosophical thought from that time onward. Even in his posthumous *Some Problems of Philosophy*, in which he shrunk the definition of philosophy to a bare Emersonian contention that it is simply "*man thinking*" (SPP 1911, 14), he made it clear that philosophy "is able to fancy everything different from what it is," seeing "the familiar as if it were strange, and the strange as if it were familiar" (SPP 1911, 11). These claims were related to James's conviction that human thought is fundamentally personal due to the influence of individual interests on cognition as well as perception. This conviction prompted his assertion that philosophy constitutes "a *weltanschauung*, an intellectualized attitude towards life" (SPP 1911, 10), and it lies behind the arguments he made throughout his career that "a philosophy is the expression of a man's intimate character, and all definitions of the universe are but the deliberately adopted reactions of human characters upon it" (PU 1909, 14). Perhaps nothing demonstrates the tight connection between James's philosophy and psychology more convincingly than his consistently held perspectivism and the closely related methods and doctrines associated with his philosophical pragmatism, pluralism, and radical empiricism.

Although James did not announce his commitment to pragmatism until 1898 (P 1898, 255–270), he had been developing and using his version of it since he first heard Charles Peirce speak about pragmatism in the early 1870s (e.g., see ML 1876–1877, 128). Contrary to Peirce's version, James's always had a psychological foundation. Indeed, James considered his 1885 article "On the Function of Cognition" to be the initial statement of his pragmatism (its "fons et origo," as he put it in CWJ 1907, 11.448), and he described this article, at the time of its publication, as "a chapter in descriptive psychology" (MT 1885, 14). The title alone of this article is revealing, highlighting as it does the *practical purpose* rather than the *theoretical nature* of cognition. This emphasis reflected James's background in the biological sciences, which prompted him (as a convinced Darwinist) to focus on the consequences rather than origins of cognitive processes—how they help or hinder us in the struggle for survival and in making our way through life, as we confront the various opportunities and challenges offered by our environment. This focus was also a natural result of a related contention that James expressed earlier (e.g., in EPh 1878, 20) and articulated later in his *Principles of Psychology*, namely, that "the pursuance of future ends and the choice of means for their attainment are . . . the mark and criterion of the presence of mentality" (PP 1890, 21). Humans, as James noted in 1878, have greater latitude than other animals in considering both future goals and the means to attain them, largely because our brains allow finer discriminations of the "similarities" between the things and properties encountered in widely different times and places. In other words, human cognitive capacities are not as restricted as those of other species by physical and temporal contiguity. This not only allows us to develop common-sense rules of thumb and more or less rigorous scientific laws; it also makes us "the only metaphysical animal[s]" that seek answers to the farthest-reaching existential questions (EPs 1878, 25).

Whether in everyday life, science, or philosophy, however, the proper function of cognition in James's estimation is to enable us to take appropriate action with respect to experienced objects (MT 1885, 23). And the way we can certify that we have done so—and that the meaning of our words and ideas is shared by others—is through observing whether or not we and they act similarly and as successfully toward the same known objects. This "practical point of view" regarding cognition, according to which we test our ideas by their utility in the conduct of our individual and social lives, appealed to James as a way in which "metaphysical cobwebs" could be brushed away from definitions, discussions, and conclusions (MT 1885, 24). Like Peirce, he hoped that this pragmatic approach to understanding meaning and truth, which he worked out more fully in *Pragmatism* (1907) and *The Meaning of Truth* (1909), would resolve philosophical as well as practical issues pertaining to our knowledge, behavior, and ever-ongoing adaptation to changing life circumstances.

James was not naïve about the likelihood of immediate acceptance of this novel approach to meaning, truth, and action. As previously discussed, he realized that the embracing of any philosophical system is facilitated or retarded by the possession of particular interests, character traits, or psychological temperament (see also P 1907, 9–26). Some individuals, with stronger empiricist sensibilities, are more comfortable viewing truth—and reality—as "in the making," whereas others, inclined more readily toward rationalism, prefer to believe in "ready-made reality" and hence seek absolute rather than probabilistic knowledge (P 1907, 123).

Given his psychological appreciation of human diversity, corroborated by his Darwinian sensitivity to variation within species, it should not be surprising that James espoused a thoroughly pluralistic as opposed to singular view of reality *as experienced*. But his pluralism was only partially based upon his recognition of the plurality of human knowers, each with his or her own past experiences, interests, and concerns. Complementing his awareness of the unlimited array of personal perspectives was his belief that the universe itself is thoroughly pluralistic—a "multiverse" of things that are not always and everywhere the same, or always and everywhere juxtaposed in identical ways. Even the "laws" of the universe might be subject to change over time, for all that we know! Meanwhile, new and unexpected things can and do occur, some of them unpredictable in principle, being outcomes of chance or indeterminate human action. As he put it early on, "all the evidence" about reality—evidence that can only arrive through human experience—"will not be 'in' till the final integration of things, when the last man has had his say and contributed his share to the still unfinished *x*" (James 1882, 84). More than twenty years later James formally explicated his pluralistic views in *A Pluralistic Universe* (1909).

Similarly, James argued for the plurality of moral states, asserting that the words "good" and "bad" describe actual and important matters of experience and noting that some things are liable to modification, for better or worse, whether through physical causality or human agency. In the world as he experienced and described it, real "possibilities," real "beginnings" and "ends," real "catastrophes" and "escapes," are always on the horizon (WB 1896, 6), prompting personal reactions and resistances. If life is not "a real fight" as it seems to be—a genuine contest with real outcomes hanging in the balance—then, he contended, our experience is illusory and life is a farce, a mere "game of private theatricals" (WB 1895, 55). But since he was convinced that the fight is real and that even physical reality can vary unpredictably at times, he concluded that our knowledge, opinions, and beliefs are always revisable, "ever not quite," never completed or final so long as we live and experience. In short, reality for James, not just our human experience and knowledge of it, is open-ended, unfolding, zigzagging, at times seemingly stable and at others disorientingly kaleidoscopic. The world, he proffered, is more like a mosaic than a solid block; there are gaps between its pieces, allowing the movement and even removal of old pieces and the insertion of new ones.[4]

The radical implications of James's pluralism as well as his pragmatism were lost on no one. His late-life writings on these topics stirred a hornet's nest of agreement and disagreement, praise and protest, prompting some to follow and others to criticize the path he had laid out (see Skrupskelis, this volume). What disturbed James were the critics who jumped straight to minute inspection and disapproval of secondary details in his works, without first stepping back and considering what he was getting at (see, e.g., CWJ 1909, 12.288). As a result, he felt, his primary "vision" was too often overlooked and the various things he hoped to accomplish by promoting pragmatism and pluralism were obscured. These included not only a propaedeutic cleansing of philosophical terms and issues, but also a humanistic enrichment of what might be called the anthropology of human persons and the promotion of personal responsibility for the physical and social world in which we live. If reality is really predetermined down to its final period, as monists of both the idealistic and materialistic varieties claimed, there would be no explanation or justification, he believed, for the experience of moral outrage: the compelling sense that the current state of affairs should be different (see Leary 2009). If one could do nothing about the way things are, there would be no reason for the basic and life-affirming experience of hope. If there was no chance for the improvement of one's lot in life through personally willful effort, resignation to fate would be the only reasonable response to life.[5]

These interrelated concerns had prompted James to draw upon his earlier psychological analyses of human cognition and agency (as asserted first in EPh 1879, 32–64, and EPs 1880, 83–124, and developed later in PP 1890, ch. 21 and 26) to produce the "essays in popular philosophy" that he assembled in *The Will to Believe* (1897). This book established his reputation as a philosopher among the American public. Also contributing to this reputation were his many addresses to teachers and students, some of which he published as *Talks to Teachers on Psychology and to Students on Some of Life's Ideals* (1899). Among these elaborations of his psychological insights were treatments of such topics as the significance of moral action (WB 1891, 141–162), the role of beliefs in the understanding and conduct of life (WB 1896, 13–33), the dignity of each individual person (TTP 1899, 132–149), the importance of mutual respect and communication in attempts at social amelioration (TPP 1899, 150–167), and the need to use psychological means in working toward social goals (ERM 1910, 162–173). Without a doubt, the desire to share his views on such topics with a wider audience kept James from developing his philosophy in a more technically precise manner. But even when he turned more purposefully to elaborating his philosophy in closer accord with professional standards, he continued to advance his thinking primarily by preparing and delivering lectures, thus lending a characteristically colloquial tone and a certain degree of conceptual looseness to the resulting works.[6]

Nonetheless, James's great hope throughout the final decade of his life was to flesh out his overarching philosophy of "radical empiricism" in a form that would assure its existence and development after his death. In an incredible burst of productivity, between mid-1904 and mid-1905, he published a series of articles, most gathered posthumously in *Essays in Radical Empiricism* (1912), that spelled out aspects of the innovative metaphysical and epistemological reflections he had been entertaining, as evident in his course notes, since the mid-1890s.[7] These reflections were foreshadowed by the nagging suspicion, expressed as early as 1888, that "states of consciousness," understood as metaphysical *entities* separate from the objects contained within them are fictitious (CWJ 1888, 6.409).[8] Instead, as he put it later, both "consciousness" and "matter" are simply different ways of construing something more basic, which James called "pure experience" (ERE 1904, 21–44). Everything there is in this world, and hence everything there is to know, whether known as "internal" conscious reality or as "external" material reality, is given in and selected from this pure experience, which itself is ontologically neutral with respect to what is taken to be mental and physical.

As an empiricist, James was committed to the foundational role of "facts," but as a *radical* empiricist, he insisted that *everything* is included in experience, not only substantive "things" but also the transitive "relations" among them, and he argued that any "conclusions concerning matters of fact," whether pertaining to "things" or "relations," are themselves "hypotheses liable to modification in the course of future experience" (WB 1896, 5). These conclusions were a direct consequence of his understanding of psychological dynamics, according to which (as we have seen) different individuals selectively notice and record different aspects of shared experiences. In the course of our own future experience as well as in the course of listening to the experiences and observations of others, we come—or *should* come, if we are paying adequate attention—to appreciate more fully the thick texture of reality and be persuaded that some ways of perceiving and conceptualizing reality are more effective and accurate than others, at least for this or that purpose. Thus, to summarize, if James's pragmatism had offered a way of defining and testing our concepts and his pluralism had acknowledged the multiple aspects and virtually limitless number of things and relations within reality, his radical empiricism articulated the metaphysical ground and epistemological consequences of his long-emerging *Weltanschauung*.

Paradoxically, James's innovative philosophical reflections, as published in "Does 'Consciousness' Exist?" (ERE 1904, 3–19), "A World of Pure Experience" (ERE 1904, 21–44), "The Continuity of Experience" (PU 1909, ch. 7), and other articles and chapters, represented both a next step in the development of his earlier psychology and a thoroughgoing revision of some of its underlying assumptions. In a kind of bootstrapping operation worthy of a pragmatic, pluralistic, and radical empiricist, he proposed, in outline, the new metaphysical foundation that he had previously acknowledged to be missing from psychology (PP 1890, 7; CWJ 1888, 6.409), thus leaving his psychology in need of serious reworking. Unfortunately, his death in 1910 foreclosed the possibility of his doing this renovation himself, just as it kept him from filling in the outline of his radical empiricism. As a result, both his philosophy and his psychology were left in need of further elaboration.[9] In essence, he had come full circle, back to the beginning—but a whole new beginning that put both philosophy and psychology on new paths. For a thinker committed to the proposition that theories and practices are in need of perpetual enhancement, through the collaboration of multiple individuals, it seems particularly appropriate that James had bequeathed to future philosophers and psychologists the challenge of exploring, enhancing, and extending the paths he had blazed.[10]

Excursus: James on Logic and the Nonlogical

A few words must be devoted to James's views on logic and his sometimes nonlogical ways of thinking, if only because his alogicality (and even antilogicality) has been a scandal and stumbling block for many thinkers who might otherwise have engaged, profited from, and built upon some of his views and propositions.[11]

James's good friend, Charles Peirce, was one of the preeminent logicians of modern times. Understandably, he often grew impatient with James who freely admitted, though with typically self-deprecating exaggeration, that he was "almost blind" with regard to logic (SPP 1911, 93). Peirce, with similar hyperbole, spoke regretfully of James's "intense hatred for logic" (Peirce 1931–1958, 6.128). It must be said, however, that Peirce also insisted the James was "about as perfect a lover of truth as it is possible for a man to be" and, beyond that, that James "seemed to comprehend" better than "scarce any [other] soul" the intellectual "mainspring" of his (i.e., Peirce's) thought (6.131). James, in short, got the "vision" behind Peirce's legendarily complex arguments even if he could not follow all the minute logical details.[12]

The key point here is not that James could reach or understand conclusions *despite* his lack of logical facility. Rather, what needs to be recognized is that James had an in-principle reason, not just a personal handicap, that motivated his eschewal of logic as a primary method of truth revelation. As James observed from time to time, logic demands universal definitions—"changeless to eternity"—whereas "the real world," in his estimation, is "incongruent" and "indeterminate" so that "the logical terms only mark static *positions* in a flux which no where is static" (CWJ 1909, 12.174). In other words, as he put it in *A Pluralistic Universe*,

> Reality, life, experience, concreteness, immediacy, use what word you will, exceeds our logic, overflows and surrounds it. . . . I prefer bluntly to call reality if not irrational then at least non-rational in its constitution—and by reality here I mean reality where things *happen*, all temporal reality without exception. I myself find no good warrant for even suspecting the existence of any reality of a higher denomination than that distributed and strung-along and flowing sort of reality which we finite beings swim in. That is the sort of reality given us, and that is the sort with which logic is so incommensurable. (James 1909/1977, 96–97)

This conclusion was a correlate of James's psychological claim that the things and relations in the world are perceived and understood differently by different individuals, some of their perceptions and understandings being more useful and truthful than others, but none being absolutely definitive or final. Any definition is necessarily limited to one perspective. Even—no, *especially*—when that perspective is abstract enough that it can be shared by others, it inevitably leaves out a variety of *other* ways in which the thing or relation, so defined, can be experienced. Definition *by definition* denies and makes us overlook the plurality of other aspects and uses to which phenomena can be subjected. In sum, no one version of a thing or relation can be said to be, or should be treated as, all that there is to say and do in relation to it. Although logic provides a nice tidy rendering of reality, it erases from consideration some of what actually *is* in the present and constricts our sense of what possibly *could be* considered in the future.

Attaching the label "vicious intellectualism" to this shrinking of reality into a simplified replica, with the varied shades of light and dark, colors and shadows, blurs and fringes eliminated from it, James reminded his readers that "the facts and worths of life need many cognizers to take them in. There is no point of view absolutely public and universal. Private and uncommunicable perceptions always remain over" (TTP 1899, 4). And when it comes to articulating those private and uncommunicable perceptions, James knew, our language—the terms upon which logic depends—is insufficient since there are always vaguely felt realities that are excluded by "conceptualization and verbalization."[13] Anticipating Ludwig Wittgenstein, James emphasized that "as long as one continues *talking*, intellectualism remains in undisturbed possession of the field." But "life" does not "come about by talking. It is an act. . . . The concepts we talk with are made for purposes of *practice* and not for purposes of *insight*" (PU 1909, 131). In short, we need to be actively pragmatic rather than passively logical.

As for understanding the sometimes obscure but pressing matters of life, James noted how individuals progress, experientially rather than logically, up various "faith ladders," each rung of which represents a living achievement rather than a strictly logical conclusion. Over and over, daily progress toward useful concepts and beliefs reveals "life exceeding logic" (PU 1909, 148). For James, the thick "particulars of life" were and always will be wider, deeper, messier, and more significant than any ordered set of "thin logical considerations" (PU 1909, 149).

This is not to say that we cannot or should not bring logic to bear upon our life and thought. It is simply that reasoning should serve the shifting needs of life rather than submit life to Procrustean rules of thought. There is more than one way to be reasonable as well as more than one way to be unreasonable. As Horace Kallen noted, "there are exactitudes and exactitudes" (1937, 76). James was remarkably exact in describing the *in*exact things and relations that surround us. Even D. C. Williams, a very capable logician, noted of James that "few persons have surpassed him in astute analysis," though he added "when he was in the mood." Nonetheless, Williams observed, "James's philosophical practice" with regard to logic "was vastly better than his preaching" (1942, 122). He was not, in other words, alogical simply for the sake of being alogical. And one can wonder, as Williams did, how James might have felt about later logical canons that are more flexible. For instance, one recent work (Shapiro 2014) deals with "logical pluralism" and "logical relativism," and touts the ability of newer logical maxims to deal with "vagueness" and "continuity," both of which were significant concerns that pushed James to criticize logic as he knew it.

However that may be, James preferred to live within and think about "free wild Nature," with all the drama and confusion entailed in doing so, rather than retreat to "an Italian Garden" in which the full array of natural possibilities have been artificially pruned and all messiness and conflict have been systematically eliminated (CWJ 1906, 11.241). And he wanted a psychology and philosophy that acknowledged, celebrated, and worked within the larger and freer domain of reality as it is perceived and conceived, pluralistically, by the full range of humankind. In sum, singular logic for James had to take a back seat to the revelations of multiple perspectives.

Conclusion

Although James's life and work are often discussed as if he had developed his psychology first and then turned his attention to philosophy, the relations between his psychology and philosophy were considerably more complicated than that. In essence, this chapter amplifies Ralph Barton Perry's observation that James's "philosophical and psychological interests were synchronous and interrelated" (1935, 1.x), showing that his premises, doctrines, and methods were also synchronous and interrelated.

James himself, in the first half of his scholarly life, would have been discomfited by this fact. In his *Principles of Psychology*, he claimed with apparent pride to have kept so "close to the point of view of natural science," using only "the data assumed by psychology," that his psychology was "strictly positivistic" and thus free of "metaphysics" (PP 1890, 6).

Although he granted that metaphysics is an important endeavor—ultimately necessary to keep psychology from producing "a confusion and a muddle" (CWJ 1888, 6.409)—he insisted that it "falls outside the province of this book" and resigned himself to the fact that, at such an early stage of psychology's development, "even in the clearest parts of Psychology our insight is insignificant enough" (PP 1890, 6 and 1280).[14]

James's attempt to keep psychology and philosophy apart was apparently motivated by his hope that a temporarily *a*philosophical science of psychology, relying upon descriptive "laws of coexistence" rather than imputing causal relations between brain states and psychological phenomena, would allow him and others to circumvent the seemingly endless debates that occupied empiricists and idealists, not to mention materialists and spiritualists, in his time. The fear that paralleled this hope for a temporary cease-fire was that the premature application of metaphysical reflection to psychology, in a way that would be "fragmentary, irresponsible, and half-awake," would spoil "two good things," both psychology and metaphysics. That was why he was offering the world a psychology that was "mainly a mass of descriptive details, running out into [but not answering] queries which only a metaphysics alive to the weight of her task can hope successfully to deal with." The fulfillment of that philosophical task, he conjectured, "will perhaps be centuries hence; and meanwhile the best mark of health that a science can show is this unfinished-seeming front" (PP 1890, 6–7).

It took several years of critical responses from Charles Peirce, Josiah Royce, George Trumbull Ladd, George Stuart Fullerton, and others to persuade James that he had failed to achieve his goal of keeping philosophy out of his psychology. Thank goodness he had failed! As this chapter shows, the intertwining of psychology and philosophy in his work—in his philosophy as much as his psychology—enriched both endeavors. Rooted in anatomy, physiology, and neurology as much as or more than in the empirical psychology and rational philosophy of old, James's foundational premises, doctrines, and methods—and the versions of psychology, pragmatism, pluralism, and radical empiricism that he based upon them—have provided many provocative and valuable insights into the human mind, self, person, world, knowledge, morals, and future possibilities. Rather than spoiling two good things, the integrated nature of James's work seems to have strengthened both, injecting the kind of vitality and novelty that come from grafting healthy sprigs onto related but different stock. Despite subsequent decades of epithet hurling, charges of psychologism and what I have called philosophism have diminished over time and have, in any case, failed to kill the vibrant offspring of James's work. Today, in fact, more than at any point since the institutional divorce of psychology and philosophy, there are psychologists looking to philosophy, and philosophers looking to psychology, for theoretical and practical ideas—in short, for premises, doctrines, and methods—that might be useful in formulating better answers to current questions as well as better hypotheses regarding emerging problems, especially those of an interdisciplinary sort.[15] Wherever such developments lead, this state of affairs seems a good thing ... and something James himself would have approved, based on lessons learned in his own life and work.

Notes

1. I use "psychologism" to indicate a view of philosophy as dependent in any of a variety of ways (semantic, epistemic, metaphysical, and/or methodological) upon psychology (see George 1997, 236–238)—and "philosophism" in a parallel way, not to indicate something false or deceitful (one of the dictionary definitions of "philosophism").
2. These articles appear, variously, in EPh, EPs, ERE, ERM, and MT, but they could well appear in different volumes of the Harvard edition of *The Works of William James* than they do. Albeit to lesser degrees, each could be called, as Suckiel has called PP 1890 and VRE 1902, "classics" in both philosophy and psychology (2006, 31).
3. James used another metaphor to further illustrate his point: "The mind . . . works on the data it receives very much as a sculptor works on his block of stone. In a sense the statue stood there [within the stone] from eternity [which is to say, from the very beginning]. But there were a thousand different ones beside it. . . . Other sculptors, other statues from the same stone!" (PP 1890, 277). James thus emphasized that the human mind is a proactive agent, making sense of itself and the world around it by selecting relevant aspects from the stream of consciousness, and only *then* associating these aspects according to their "similarity" or their "contiguity" in space or time.
4. For James's critique of "the block universe" to which all monists—both materialists and idealists—are either explicitly or implicitly committed, see PU (1909, esp. 145–148).
5. The difference between living with hope and living with resignation was crucial for James. He concluded VRE 1902 asserting: "No fact of human nature is more characteristic than its willingness to live on a chance. The existence of the chance makes the difference . . . between a life of which the keynote is resignation and a life of which the keynote is hope" (414).
6. Both P 1907 and PU 1909 were first delivered as series of lectures. Even so, as discussed in the next section, some "imprecision" in these works was purposeful, deriving from James's belief in an indeterminate world and his related aversion to "logic-chopping."
7. Fittingly, James developed his radically empiricist ideas in his lectures on "the philosophical problems of psychology" (ML 1897–1898, 234–259).
8. Another important precedent was "The Knowing of Things Together" (EPh 1895, 23–31), originally delivered by James as his 1894 Presidential Address to the American Psychological Association.
9. See Leary (2018), especially its final chapter, for suggestions about the direction his psychology would have taken, had James had world enough and time to revise his *Principles* at the end of his life.
10. Of course, no psychologist or philosopher accepted and followed all aspects of James's legacy, and philosophers in general turned in a very different direction in the decades after his death. But recent references to James's work, in both psychology and philosophy, demonstrate his continuing relevance as well as renewed interest in different aspects of his work.
11. Though critical of logic for many years, James explicitly rejected it as a primary tool for reaching conclusions about reality in PU 1909, where he famously wrote that "I have finally found myself compelled to *give up the logic*, fairly, squarely, and irrevocably. It has an imperishable use in human life, but that use is not to make us theoretically acquainted with the essential nature of reality" (96). I realize that this passage refers to James's rejection of the principle of identity and hence his rejection of logic in *one specific context* in which he wanted to allow for the compounding of consciousness, but as I will show,

James's hesitations about logic extended to its use in other contexts and in general. Davis (2005) has addressed James's "new way of thinking about logic" in ways consonant with my own understanding of it.

12. Peirce was both amazed and frustrated that James could reach "the right conclusions in most cases" and could "impart to audiences as near to the exact truth as they are capable of apprehending" while he (Peirce) was "like a miser who picks up things which *might* be useful to the right person at the right time, but which, in fact, are utterly useless to anybody else, and almost so to himself" (letter to James, June 13, 1907, quoted in Perry 1935, 2.437).

13. As James put it, "philosophers have always aimed at cleaning up the litter with which the world apparently is filled" (PU 1909, 26). A good example is provided by Peirce's (1904) admission that deductive or demonstrative reasoning is concerned with the "ideal states of things" or things "ideally conceived" as "some sort of diagrammatic, that is, iconic, representation of the facts, as skeletonized as possible." Such reasoning varies from induction, he noted, in that "it does not deal with a course of experience, but with whether or not a certain state of things can be imagined" (PU 1909, 428). James was not interested in idealized forms of reality.

14. As James averred, "a psychologist's merit seems to me, in the *present* condition of that science, to consist much less in the *definitiveness* of his conclusions, than in his suggestiveness and fertility" (CWJ 1892, 7.353). The same, I submit, could be said for James's merit as a philosopher.

15. The interest of psychologists in the relevance of philosophical analyses can be gleaned from the chapters in Martin et al. (2015). The converse interest of philosophers in the results of psychological investigations is apparent in recent contributions to naturalized epistemology and cognitive science as well as other recent attempts to fathom the nature as well as functions of perception, learning, moral cognition, consciousness, attention, free will, memory, and the like. An interesting survey of the "rather dramatic shift" in philosophical studies from work based upon "a priori methods" to work based upon "empirical studies" is provided by Knobe (2015). Also see Prinz (2008) on empirical and experimental philosophy. For an old yet timely discussion of the relation between psychology and the normative disciplines of logic, ethics, and aesthetics, see Angell (1903). Consonant with Angell's argument is Margolis's observation that "'psychologism' is no longer a central philosophical concern" (1997, 291).

Bibliography

Angell, James Rowland. 1903. "The Relations of Structural and Functional Psychology to Philosophy." *Philosophical Review* 12(3): 243–271.

Davis, Philip E. 2005. "William James and a New Way of Thinking About Logic." *The Southern Journal of Philosophy* 43(3): 337–354.

George, Rolf. 1997. "Psychologism in Logic: Bacon to Bolzano." *Philosophy and Rhetoric* 30(3): 213–242.

Helmholtz, Hermann von. 1867. *Handbuch der physiologischen Optik*. Leipzig: Leopold Voss.

James, William. 1868–1873. Diary 1. In William James Papers, Houghton Library, Harvard University, Cambridge, MA. (Catalogued as MS Am 1092.9 [4550])

James, William. 1882. "Rationality, Activity and Faith." *Princeton Review* 2(2): 58–86.

Kallen, Horace M. 1937. "Remarks on R. B. Perry's Portrait of William James." *Philosophical Review* 46(1): 68–78.

Klein, Alexander. 2008. "*Divide Et Impera!* William James's Pragmatist Tradition in the Philosophy of Science." *Philosophical Topics* 36(1): 129–166.

Knobe, Joshua. 2015. "Philosophers Are Doing Something Different Now: Quantitative Data." *Cognition* 135: 36–38.

Leary, David E. 2009. "Visions and Values: Ethical Reflections in a Jamesian Key." *Journal of Mind and Behavior* 30(3): 121–138.

Leary, David E. 2013. "A Moralist in an Age of Scientific Analysis and Skepticism: Habit in the Life and Work of William James." In *A History of Habit: From Aristotle to Bourdieu*, edited by Tom Sparrow and Adam Hutchinson, 175–206. Lanham, MD: Lexington Books.

Leary, David E. 2014. "Overcoming Blindness: Some Historical Reflections on Qualitative Psychology." *Qualitative Psychology* 1(1): 17–33.

Leary, David E. 2018. *The Routledge Guidebook to James's Principles of Psychology*. New York: Routledge, 2018.

Margolis, Joseph. 1997. "Late Forms of Psychologism and Antipsychologism." *Philosophy and Rhetoric* 30(3): 291–311.

Martin, Jack, Jeff Sugarman, and Kathleen L. Slaney, eds. 2015. *The Wiley Handbook of Theoretical and Philosophical Psychology: Methods, Approaches, and New Directions for Social Sciences*. Hoboken, NJ: Wiley.

Peirce, Charles Sanders. 1904. "Reasoning." In *Dictionary of Philosophy and Psychology*, edited by James Mark Baldwin, Vol. 2, 426–428. New York: Macmiallan.

Peirce, Charles Sanders. 1931–1958. *Collected Papers*. Edited by Charles Hartshorne, Paul Weiss and Arthur W. Burks. 8 vols. Cambridge, MA: Harvard University Press.

Perry, Ralph Barton. 1935. *The Thought and Character of William James*. 2 vols. Cambridge, MA: Harvard University Press.

Prinz, Jesse J. 2008. "Empirical Philosophy and Experimental Philosophy." In *Experimental Philosophy*, edited by Joshua Knobe and Shaun Nichols, 189–208. Oxford: Oxford University Press.

Shapiro, Stewart. 2014. *Varieties of Logic*. Oxford: Oxford University Press.

Spencer, Herbert. 1855. *The Principles of Psychology*. London: Longman, Brown, Green, and Longmans.

Suckiel, Ellen Kappy. 2006. "William James." In *A Companion to Pragmatism*, edited by John R. Shook and Joseph Margolis, 30–43. Malden, MA: Blackwell.

Williams, Donald Cary. 1942. "William James and the Facts of Knowledge." In *In Commemoration of William James, 1842–1942*, edited by Herbert Wallace Schneider and Brand Blanshard, 95–124. New York: Columbia University Press.

Wundt, Wilhelm. 1874. *Grundzüge der physiologischen Psychologie*. Leipzig: Engelmann.

PART III
VALUE

CHAPTER 9

HORTATORY ETHICS

SARIN MARCHETTI

An Overview of James's Moral Outlook and Works

ETHICS was one of the leitmotivs of James's intellectual biography, as his early, middle, and late production is invariably infused with a pronounced moral tone.[1] Writings touching upon one ethical theme or another and giving voice to his moral views can be found in all the phases into which we might want to slice James's life and *oeuvre*. The young, troubled William was consumed by ethical dilemmas, such as the choice of his career and role in society or the very existence of free will, dilemmas to which he struggled to find a philosophical answer. The eager, newly appointed Dr. James dedicated the best part of his energies to developing a pragmatist methodology capable of rephrasing and addressing crucial ethical issues, including those of moral motivation, heroism (as in exemplarity), and normativity. And the late-career Professor James was equally enmeshed in a variety of philosophical investigations of the ethical landscape, spanning from the ever-debated relation between ethical conduct and religious practice to the most pressing socio-political questions of his time, such as the democratization of society and the deconstruction—or rather transformation—of the American imperialistic policy and mindset.

Testimonies of his life-long, earnest engagement with moral issues are scattered throughout his writings, published and unpublished, public and private alike. In a revealing and dramatic diary entry, written at the pitch of a personal and intellectual crisis, the twenty-eight-year-old James remarked:

> Today, I about touched bottom, and perceive plainly that I must face the choice with open eyes; Shall I *frankly* throw the moral business overboard, as one unsuited to my innate aptitudes, or shall I follow it, and it alone, making everything else mere stuff for it? (MS Am 1092.9 [4550])

In the light of an unbroken concern for ethical matters, both philosophical and personal, we can safely conclude that James opted for the latter, taking the "moral business" seriously and making it the critical focus of his life and thought. In a blending of inward confession and overt commitment, James added:

> Hitherto I have tried to fire myself with the moral interest, as an aid in the accomplishing of certain utilitarian ends of attaining certain difficult but salutary habits. I tried to associate the feeling of moral degradation with failure, and add it to that of the loss of the wished for sensible good end—and the reverse of success. But in all this I was cultivating the moral interest only as a means & more or less humbugging myself. Now I must regard these useful ends only as occasions for my moral life to become active. (MS Am 1092.9 [4550])[2]

Here we find, *in nuce*, the key elements of James's radical views on ethics—namely, the centrality of habituation and dishabituation in moral affairs, the emphasis on self-cultivation and care as prime ethical practices, and the prioritization of activity (pragmatism) over thought (rationalism) and sensibility (empiricism)—which I shall be discussing in the central sections of this chapter.

Other aspects could be—and have been—highlighted as pivotal to his moral outlook, with alternative reconstructions of his ethics foregrounding different parts of his work. Despite these disagreements, there is little doubt that James took ethics to be at the very core of his concerns, both personal and philosophical. Besides James's most recognizable ethical essays (such as those included in WB 1897), his pioneering works on psychology and psychical research (PP 1890 and EPR), his imaginative studies into the anthropological and scientific dimension of the religious life (VRE 1902), his revolutionary pragmatist methodology and conception of truth (P 1907 and MT 1909), and his passionate public speeches on education, culture, and politics (TTP 1899, ERM, EPh, ECR) are also variously filled with ethical references and animated by a moral interest and zeal that made James a moral philosopher through and through. To this wealth of published and unpublished material, we should add the many diary entries and the hundreds of letters James wrote to a most diverse pool of interlocutors, in which he variously summarized his views on ethics and sometimes explored them in novel directions (MEN, CWJ).[3]

This multitude calls for a taxonomy of both James's moral writings and the moral themes and ideas there conveyed. There are indeed only very few things James wrote for publication, for teaching purposes, for public occasions, or for personal record that are free of moral considerations or unrelated to them; that said, some writings carry more weight than others in the quest of looking for James's ethics.

As a first stab at sorting out such an impressive body of work, we can distinguish, within James's writings, different kinds of moral considerations informing his overall picture of ethics. Beyond texts expressly dedicated to the discussion of moral *issues*, we have texts whose *intentions* are ethical, and finally texts with moral *implications*.

The philosophical surveys of various considerations at stake in reasoning about what shape to give to one's thoughts and conduct are instances of the first kind of text. These include "The Moral Philosopher and the Moral Life," "The Will to Believe," and (at least) the chapters on "Habit" and the "Will" of the *Principles*, where James variously relates moral deliberation to the fashioning of one's self rather than grounding moral deliberation in the observation of and respect for already established principles and rules.

An example of the second kind of text is the account of some deep-seated epistemological attitudes and tendencies explored in key chapters of *Pragmatism* and *The Meaning of Truth*, as well as in "Remarks on Spencer's Definition of Mind as Correspondence," where James denounces the picture of experiencing as passive mirroring of a detached reality. This epistemological attitude informs his treatment of the moral blindness toward aspects of the world—including aspects of the self, as in the best teachings of the Romantics and the Transcendentalists—in which the active exercise of one's subjectivity is called for. He also speaks about these issues at length in "On a Certain Blindness in Human Beings" and "What Makes a Life Significant."

Finally, as a specimen of the third kind of text, the discussion of the availability of a number of metaphysical and religious options is assessed with reference to the ethical implications for our lives, in texts like "The Dilemma of Determinism," in his "Introduction to *The Literary Remains of the Late Henry James*" (collected in EPh), and throughout *The Varieties of Religious Experience*. Even though we should not think of these three options and their representative texts as mutually exclusive, since quite often in his writings James productively juxtaposes them and creates theoretical short-circuits between them, this rough classification is useful to give the reader a glimpse of James's composite understanding of the purposes and uses of philosophical ethics.

To these variegated *ethical considerations*, we should also add the *moral preoccupation* informing James's biography throughout, which inevitably spilled over into his philosophical work. James rarely shied away from a moral problem and was seldom afraid to question his own moral fiber, employing and putting to the test the tools of philosophy—even though his own occasional blindness toward issues of race and gender was hardly exculpable. Being a strong advocate of articulating a philosophy suiting one's temperament, expressing it, and even improving it, James philosophized out of personal materials, weaving together intellectual sensitivity and ordinary reflection for practical bearing.

However, we would take a step too far if we reduced James's philosophical views on ethics to the sheer vindication of his particular moral convictions, as in this way we would delegitimize the inbuilt reflective dimension of his moral writings and turn them into more or less dogmatic pontifications.[4] While the sources of his philosophical investigations in ethics are indeed the very ordinary experiences and events he faced in his kaleidoscopic and adventurous life, themes that were developed with a distinctive personal tone in his writings,[5] there is also for James an activity of reflective elaboration *on* ethics whose register and strategies are irreducibly philosophical in that they try to speak to the reason and imagination of his audiences rather than merely attempting to convince them of one particular moral option he would have endorsed himself. Even if it is thus one's moral improvement that James is trying to affect via his work, rather than to change one's mere philosophical opinion about morality, it is still through piecemeal philosophical critique rather than through strokes of moral preaching that he sees the path forward.

Orthodox Versus Heterodox Readings

Confronted with this plentitude of moral writings and themes, James's readers tried to fathom the lineaments and meaning of his work in ethics as a whole. The brief articulation sketched above gives but a hint of the difficulties involved in this task, and it is thus no wonder that the most diverse interpretative keys to figuring out the riddle of James's moral philosophy have been offered. As a way of classification, the main options in the literature solidified around the two extremes of inconclusiveness and systematization. While the "inconclusivists" have vociferously rejected the very idea that there is an articulated philosophical defense of a moral position in his writings, the "systematizers" have attempted its very reconstruction. The inconclusivists have tried to show, in various ways and with different emphases and goals, either the theoretical weakness or the intended sporadic character of James's philosophical reflection on ethics, whereas the systematizers have argued in favor of its theoretical solidity and organic articulation. This general classification calls for a series of subtler distinctions.

Among the inconclusivists, some—the "hardcore inconclusivists" (e.g., Otto 1943; Garrison and Madden 1977; Diggins 1994; Aikin and Talisse 2011)—dismiss his moral considerations as unconvincing, passing thoughts, while others—the "mild inconclusivists" (e.g., Edel 1976; Lentricchia 1988; Franzese 2008)—defend the intentionally unsystematic character of his moral thought or its calculated deference to anthropological, historical, or sociological considerations.

The systematizers themselves give different and diverging expositions of his work, which however can be brought down to three general classes. The "theorists" (e.g., Boyle 1998; Gale 1999; Cooper 2003; Lekan 2012) deem "The Moral Philosopher and the Moral Life" as the key ethical text, in which James is supposed to have laid down the theoretical blueprint of his moral theory, widely considered as an eclectic version of consequentialism. This position is supposed to have been more or less consistently reprised in his other moral writings, even if some interpreters detected in it shades of deontologism which would resonate with said writings (e.g., Brennan 1961; O'Connell 1992; Schrader 1998). The "moralists" (e.g., Perry 1935; Roth 1965; West 1989; Cotkin 1994; Albrecht 2012) downsize the importance of "The Moral Philosopher and the Moral Life," pointing to its occasional inadequacies and shortcomings. This group focuses their attention on *The Principles of Psychology, Talks to Teachers on Psychology,* and on such essays as "The Energies of Men" and "Great Men and their Environment," where James is supposed to have defended a version of moral individualism and heroism resistant to theorization. And the "synthesizers" (e.g., Suckiel 1996; Lamberth 1999; Slater 2009; Pihlström 2009) read James's ethics in the light of the broader metaphysical and religious considerations and commitments articulated in "The Will to Believe," in *Varieties*, and in *Essays in Radical Empiricism*, turning ethics into a (central) branch or department of an ontological investigation of the world—secular or otherwise.

While the inconclusivists have been doubtful that the diverse parts of James's philosophical ethics resist any harmonic synthesis, the systematizers diverged precisely in the characterization of such a weaving. But despite their sometimes stark differences, both options are representative of what I shall label the *orthodox* reading of James's moral philosophy. The systematizers and the inconclusivists share a picture of philosophical ethics as an inquiry into the proper shape of a morally good life as well as into the strategies for its sound implementation and promotion.

Orthodox readers measure James's success as a moral thinker according to an understanding of philosophical ethics as aimed at giving a theoretical foundation for the moral life. However, against this very assumption, a growing number of *heterodox* readers suggest to radically revising our understanding of the nature and goals of James's philosophical ethics. On this reading, James is taken to have encouraged a radical shift in the meaning and practice of ethics in the direction of its de-intellectualization and de-trascendentalization. Overlooking such a shift lies at the basis of the many interpretative epicycles postulated by the orthodox readers to make sense of his work. As a result, heterodox readers claim, James's ethics has been forced in directions he himself was highly skeptical of, and skeptical of for philosophical reasons, thus betraying his most fertile views and teachings. According to this family of heterodox interpretations, the value of James's work as a moral philosopher should be assessed with reference to his novel yet underappreciated understanding of ethics: an alternative that has both a *pars destruens*, consisting in the criticism of the orthodox picture of ethics, and a *pars construens*, consisting in a replacement of such a picture with a heterodox one. Even within this camp we appreciate important distinctions: hence the need for one more classificatory layer and final round of nomenclature.

For the "moderate" heterodox readers (e.g., Franzese 2008; Cormier 2011; Throntveit 2014; Pihlström 2016; Lekan 2018)[6] James's ethics consisted in a *new*, exploratory (vs. justificatory) way of addressing the *old*, directive question of how to recognize and lead a good life. For the "resolute" heterodox readers (e.g., Putnam 2004; Stroud 2012; Marchetti 2015; Koopman 2017) James's ethics embodied a *new* ameliorative (vs. prescriptive) way of addressing the *new* therapeutic and transformative (vs. foundational) question about how we envision ourselves partaking in the moral life in the first place and at all—as opposed to how such a life should be portrayed and justified from without. The adjectives *old* and *new*, as I will be employing them, refer to the philosophical lens through which James's work has been (mis)read rather than to how ethics has been historically thought of in the Western philosophical tradition. What I label as the *new* therapeutic and transformative question has in fact deep roots in the ancient philosophical world and mindset, while the *old* directive question is a relatively recent acquisition of modernity. James's project, in the resolute heterodox reading I defend, is that of giving the ancient, therapeutic question novel transformative currency in a post-foundationalist, *modernist* world and mindset—a move shared by philosophers as diverse as Nietzsche, Wittgenstein, and some of their contemporary heirs—Michel Foucault, Stanley Cavell, and Richard Rorty being among the most prominent figures.[7] I suggest that *this* is the sense in which pragmatism, in James's hands, amounts to "A New Name for Some Old Ways of Thinking," as the famous subtitle reads.[8]

Moderate heterodox readers depict James as variously engaged in an elaborate rethinking of philosophical ethics as a tool suited to address the difficulties of the moral life once it drops its justificatory pretensions. Yet these readers still think that the outcome of such critical inquiry should be (translatable in) some sort of moral judgment about what needs to be done and why. Resolute heterodox readers agree about James's battle against the justificatory ambitions of moral system-building, whose foundationalist spell he sought to exorcize by means of historicized philosophical critique. Yet, unlike moderate readers, resolute heterodox readers characterize James's positive understanding of ethics as a philosophical elucidation of our very involvement with the moral life, which would eventually lead to self-scrutiny and reconfiguration. Moderate heterodox readers still give metaphilosophical currency to the *old* philosophical task of offering us positive criteria and solutions to sort out recognizable and agreed upon moral problems, which James would have fulfilled by elaborating a pragmatist methodology of problem-solving (or, occasionally, problem-dissolving) hinged on a historicized picture of the human sources of value and normativity. In contrast, resolute heterodox readers interpret James as dispensing with this very quest altogether, focusing rather on the *new* philosophical task of a therapeutic elucidation of the very posture we might assume toward morality as a whole and hence of the self-conduct springing from this transformative questioning. According to the latter understanding and course, ethics is not about the assessment of the content and character of one's particular thoughts and deeds concerning morality's dictates (which we can either respect or fail to respect); instead, ethics has to do with the deepening of one's overall stance and presence to oneself when taking morality in (or failing or refusing to).

In the remainder of this chapter I will be presenting the particular version of the resolute reading I consider to be at once the most congenial for making sense of what James wrote and also the most profitable for us doing ethics in his wake: namely, *hortatory ethics*.[9] According to this particular resolute heterodox reading, James's ethics hinges upon an understanding of philosophical critique as an activity of personal clarification and experimentation issuing in a peculiar kind of *moral exhortation* aimed at the amelioration of the moral life from within that does not amount either to an account of the moral order as we happen to find it (of the kind provided by descriptive ethics) or to the recommendation of one particular formula for solving moral conflict (as prescriptive ethics advocates).[10] The outcome of hortatory ethics is moral understanding and adaptation, which in turn are the result of an acquired reflective sensibility and imagination James is encouraging us to cultivate and experiment with by means of philosophical critique, rather than the consequence of the dispassionate application of a philosophical theory handed to us from without. That being so, the focus and centerpiece of James's work in ethics would be a radical rethinking of the credentials and very task of the moral philosopher.

BEYOND SYSTEM AND THEORY: AN EXHORTATIVE COURSE FOR ETHICS

For better or worse, at the dawn of the twentieth century philosophers were growing tired of the great systems of the past four hundred years, from Hobbes to Spencer. Sidgwick was a transitional figure, at once the last great systematizer and the first moral theorist. The great modern philosophical systems offered sweeping accounts of the moral life under the form of moral metaphysics (largely rationalistic) and moral psychology (empiricist in the main). With system-building under attack from several corners—Nietzsche being the most glaring example in the nineteenth century, Wittgenstein in the twentieth—philosophical ethics had to change its skin as well. Pragmatism, analytic philosophy, and phenomenology—the three great movements that renewed the intellectual and cultural scene across the Atlantic—took off by breaking with the modern philosophical tradition, with their respective moral philosophies being no exception. By prioritizing either moral *practice, language,* or *experience*, the three movements shifted away from systematic moral investigation.

Moral philosophers started to work on ethical problems in isolation from metaphysics and psychology, and got specialized in the business of telling fellow philosophers and laypeople what morality looked like and how to best implement it. Moral philosophy started to build its own theories, alongside those of the epistemologists and the logicians. The most successful version of moral theorizing was that pursued by the analytic tradition, which suddenly became the dominant model for philosophizing across the board. Philosophical ethics has since been customarily divided into meta-, normative, and applied. Meta-ethics investigates the nature of the central moral predicates and their relationship with allegedly non-moral ones (e.g., those pertaining to scientific or religious discourse and practice) in order to shed light on the core concepts of morality. Normative ethics analyzes the structure of moral reasoning (of moral reasons, incentives, and goals) for the sake of judgment and action. Finally, applied ethics deals with the moral permissibility of the principles and codes ruling the various disciplines (e.g., economic, technological, medical).

Despite its acquired familiarity, this way of conceiving of philosophical ethics hardly carves nature at its joints. Quite the contrary, this division was the result of a change in metaphilosophical paradigm and sensibility which, in the English-speaking world, took place sometime between 1874 (the first edition of Henry Sidgwick's *The Methods of Ethics*) and 1903 (the publication of G. E. Moore's *Principia Ethica*). This new way of organizing the intellectual work of the moral philosopher was motivated by the desire to get rid of the systems of the past, which relied either on a burdensome metaphysics of the cosmos or on a psychology of the individual, so as to finally offer a firm neutral basis for sound moral reasoning and judgment.[11]

James was reacting against both moral system-building and moral theorization, trying to emancipate moral philosophy from the older foundational project of systematic ethics as well as to differentiate it from the newer Archimedean course of ethical theory.[12] James sought an ethics that would be unsystematic without being either partisan or neutral: an ethics that would affect the moral life without determining its substance or subject matter ahead of first-hand, localized practice. The opening of "The Moral Philosopher and the Moral Life" launches such an alternative course, acknowledging an internal connection between moral philosophizing and moral living:

> The main purpose of this paper is to show that there is no such thing possible as an ethical philosophy dogmatically made up in advance. We all help to determine the content of ethical philosophy so far as we contribute to the race's moral life. In other words, there can be no final truth in ethics any more than in physics until the last man has had his experience and said his say. In the one case as in the other, however, the hypotheses which we now make while waiting, and the acts to which they prompt us, are among the indispensable conditions which determine what that "say" shall be. (WB 1897, 141)

A completed moral system must await the unfolding of the moral life. And yet we must reflect deeply, if unsystematically, about our ongoing practical deeds. The very capacity for such moral reflection is portrayed as a function of our personal contribution to the moral life, and our choice of an ethics is expressive of the moral selves we are and might become. What is more truly dangerous, for James, is the supposition that moral philosophers and philosophies do not simply speak from a perspective (say, as schoolmasters) that is up to us to elaborate, but rather that they exert temporal power over our minds and lives (as pontiffs). Writes James:

> All one's slumbering revolutionary instincts waken at the thought of any single moralist wielding such powers of life and death. Better chaos forever than an order based on any closet-philosopher's rule, even though he were the most enlightened possible member of his tribe. (WB 1897, 155)

> The ethical philosopher . . . whenever he ventures to say which course of action is the best, is on no essentially different level from the common man. "See, I have set before thee this day life and good, and death and evil; therefore, choose life that thou and thy seed may live"—when this challenge comes to us, it is simply our total character and personal genius that are on trial; and if we invoke any so-called philosophy, our choice and use of that also are but revelations of our personal aptitude or incapacity for moral life. (WB 1897, 162)

James is here remarking on the ceaseless shuttling back and forth from moral thinking to moral practice, shifting, in so doing, the ethical focus from the choices and behaviors allegedly dictated by moral theorizing to the deepening and widening of the concepts one lives by, also to be checked against the teachings of the great ethical ideas of the past. Moral cultivation and progress are depicted as options activated by our willingness to engage the moral life, to make one's life the field of moral interrogation, and to question the answers offered by the tradition or our fellow beings as options with which to experiment.

In his pedagogical lectures on psychology, James further explores the connection between philosophical reflection and the work on the self:

> The science of logic never made a man reason rightly, and the science of ethics (if there be such a thing) never made a man behave rightly. The most such sciences can do is to help us to catch ourselves up and check ourselves, if we start to reason or behave wrongly; and to criticize ourselves more articulately after we have made mistakes. (TTP 1899, 15)

What moral philosophy can do for us is to facilitate work on the self, which is open-ended in scope and never-ending in purport. No solutions on offer, then, but rather the encouragement to check our own positioning in the moral life: moral philosophy is at its best when reminding us that our own genius is on trial when reasoning something out of a problematic situation. What is most dangerous is not, for James, to give the *wrong answer*, but rather to give *no personal answer* at all, relying instead on formulas. This is nothing short of a wholesale reconfiguration of ethics around the quality and presence of the self to itself: an idle as against a mobile self—a self ready-made of theory, as against a self in the making.

Now, if philosophical ethics is primarily concerned with the care and transformation of the self, its very register should change accordingly. Ethics needs to *spur* us from the actual or possible moral deadlocks into which unreflective thought, talk, and conduct slip, rather than pretend to *uplift* us to morally secure vistas the philosopher would somehow know better than the layperson thanks to insight or acquaintance with the true sources of goodness. James rejoins in this regard:

> The philosopher . . . *quâ philosopher*, is no better able to determine the best universe in the concrete emergency than other men. . . . His books upon ethics, therefore, so far as they truly touch the moral life, must more and more ally themselves with a literature which is confessedly tentative and suggestive rather than dogmatic—I mean with novels and dramas of the deeper sort, with sermons, with books on statecraft and philanthropy and social and economic reform. Treated in this way ethical treatises may be voluminous and luminous as well; but they never can be *final*. (WB 1897, 158–159)

It is in this context that James marks the "deepest difference, practically, in the moral life of man ... between the easy-going and the strenuous mood": between those for whom the "ruling consideration" is the "shrinking from present ill" alone, and those who are not afraid to test their moral fiber to achieve a "greater ideal" (WB 1897, 159–160). This is no categorical distinction between individual *kinds* (the good, the righteous, or the virtuous vs. the evil, the sinful, or the vicious), but rather a practical alternative open to each and all of us to test our moral fiber as beings *in the making*. Besides reminding us of the tragedy of letting go of transcendental banisters to which we secure ourselves in the course of living morally, James sees philosophy's hortatory task as that of making us uncomfortable with the moral certainties we still allow ourselves. James ploughs a middle path between doubt and confidence, between skepticism and assurance.

If he is right, then our moral life is not threatened by temptation or by a fall into immorality so much as by the drift into demoralization[13]—a matter of living only half awake or not at all. Philosophy should not point to the good or construct the good for us where it is not in view, but rather should spur us to experiment ourselves with our understanding and practice of the good. What we are badly in need of, according to James, are neither descriptions of, nor prescriptions for, the good life, but rather exhortations to take care of it and to make it our own. Philosophical activity has to do with the elucidation of our historical present for transformation, the point of a pragmatist approach being that of showing us the consequences of the standpoint we currently occupy and the prospects of its reconfiguration or even abandonment. We need moral philosophies that prove to be enabling rather than disabling: philosophies congenial and leading to imaginative exercises of transformative self-questioning, rather than signposts for already configured characters and choices.

Moral Midwifery

The pulsing moral problem that motivated James's shift in philosophical orientation was the loss of moral conviction that affected generations of Americans nurtured in the wake of Darwin and the Civil War—that is, the crumbling of theological and political certainty.[14] The lesson to be drawn from these epochal happenings is that order—natural and social alike—is never given but rather always to be won and paid for, as it is the result of negotiation, agreement, and rupture. James contrasts the pragmatist option with the intellectualist one, for which sound, undistorted knowledge would put us in touch with how things really are. But "the pragmatism or pluralism which I defend has to fall back on a certain ultimate hardihood, a certain willingness to live without assurance or guarantees ... to live on possibilities that are not certainties" (MT 1909, 124). For pragmatism,

> truth grows up inside of all the finite experiences. They lean on each-other, but the whole of them, if such a whole be there, leans on nothing. All "homes" are in

finite experiences; finite experience as such is homeless. Nothing outside of the flux secures the issue of it. It can hope salvation only from its own intrinsic promises and potencies. (P 1907, 125)

Despite that more than a century has elapsed, with major socio-economic changes and scientific-technological leaps, I claim that our current situation is not significantly different in this respect, and hence both the moral problematic and the philosophical maneuver to best address it suggested by James still hold the stage. We are still very much working—and struggling to come to terms—with a culture of risk following the demise of certainty. We post-representationalists are still learning how to successfully navigate reality once we give up the master concept and activity of faithfully copying it.

It is in this context that James explicitly employs the very term "hortatory ethics." In the pivotal chapter on "Habit" of the *Principles*, speaking of the "*ethical implications of the laws of habit*," James lists several features of this key mechanism, some morally empowering and others morally detrimental. As for the empowering side of habit, James mentions its role as a facilitator of action and reaction, which would in turn become more accurate and effortless so as to strengthen our very sense of self. As for the detrimental side of habit, it makes us blind and deaf to novelty and variation, condemning us to that very identity it helped us to craft in the first place. Given this moral duality, James offers a practical maxim for habit—what we might call the cultivation of the habit of the unhabitual—aimed at making the best of it:

> *Keep the faculty of effort alive in you by a little gratuitous exercise every day*. That is, be systematically ascetic or heroic in little unnecessary points, do every day or two something for no other reason than that you would rather not do it, so that when the hour of dire need draws nigh, it may find you not unnerved and untrained to stand the test. . . . So with the man who has daily inured himself to habits of concentrated attention, energetic volition, and self-denial in unnecessary things. He will stand like a tower when everything rocks around him, and when his softer fellow-mortals are winnowed like chaff in the blast. (PP 1890, 130)

James continues:

> The physiological study of mental conditions is thus the most powerful ally of hortatory ethics. The hell to be endured hereafter, of which theology tells, is no worse than the hell we make for ourselves in this world by habitually fashioning our characters in the wrong way. Could the young but realize how soon they will become mere walking bundles of habits, they would give more heed to their conduct while in the plastic state. We are spinning our own fates, good or evil, and never to be undone. Every smallest stroke of virtue or of vice leaves its never so little scar. (PP 1890, 130–131)

Morality, on this picture, has to do with *morale*, that is with *what* we do with ourselves as much as with *how* we act. The hortatory dimension of ethics focuses on the heroic and ascetic component of self-care and transformation, which should characterize our most humble ordinary activities—such as our taking notice of the immediate effects of our eating choices on the environment—as well as the most glaring ones—say, the risking of one's life for a political ideal.

The theme is reprised in James's later *Talks to Teachers* (1899), where he relates habit to daily effort and moral growth. He writes:

> We forget that every good that is worth possessing must be paid for in strokes of daily effort. We postpone and postpone, until those smiling possibilities are dead. . . . By neglecting the necessary concrete labor, by sparing ourselves the little daily tax, we are positively digging the graves of our higher possibilities. . . . According as a function receives daily exercise or not, the man becomes a different kind of being in later life. (TTP 1899, 51–52)

These passages share the celebration of the good *of*, and *in*, activity as against the stiffening and petrification of one's thoughts and deeds.

This theme resonates in James's treatment of attention, belief, will, and necessary truths in the *Principles*, where the life of the mind is portrayed in light of a tension between inactivity and mobilization. But it is also at work in his later writing on pragmatism and radical empiricism, where activity is related to personal and moral growth:

> Our acts, our turning-places, where we seem to ourselves to make ourselves and grow, are the parts of the world to which we are closest, the parts of which our knowledge is the most intimate and complete. Why should we not take them at their face-value? Why may they not be the actual turning-places and growing-places which they seem to be, of the world—why not the workshop of being, where we catch fact in the making, so that nowhere may the world grow in any other kind of way than this? (P 1907, 138)

This is experimentalism at its finest: at once a call for the mobilization of the self and the downplaying of moral fixity. This is no optimism or pessimism about our alleged human nature or the very structure of reality, but rather *meliorism* about our mindedness and worldliness: namely, the idea and hope that things will play out for the better if we put effort in them, since in so doing we are reconfiguring the world—and ourselves through it—as a place hospitable to moral significance and progress.

In this sense hortatory ethics *ameliorates* us without either directing or enlightening us. By insisting on the importance of the care and transformation of the self as a primal moral activity, James draws a path of moral progress hinged on what we make of ourselves amidst uncertainty and repetition. If "authenticity" is perhaps too grand of a word, then perhaps the slightly humbler, more pragmatic one of "ductility" would do as the goal of a hortatory, ameliorative ethics. Moral exhortations are not to be understood as *arguments* for or against the validity of a moral order; rather, they are *invitations* to checking moral practice as we go along.

Philosophy understood and practiced in this way should thus abandon its *explanatory* ambitions and stick to *clarification* and *transformation* alone. As in the best practice of philosophical and moral midwifery of Greek ancestry, James seeks to put us back in touch with the often-overlooked nuances of our practices so as to renew or rather disown them. In this sense, philosophical reflection, far from being a discipline investigating problems without reference to their personal relevance and import, becomes an activity whose goal is that of *making a difference* in one's practical and reflective life. James was interested in changing our very expectations and assumptions about what moral reflection might do for our moral life. If this is the case, his originality needs to be assessed not so much with reference to the solutions he would have offered to the various moral problems we stumble upon in our ordinary and reflective lives but with reference to the methodology he invited us to explore and put to work to best tackle them, ourselves, *in deed*. Acquired sensibility and imagination, rather than sound casuistry, would then be the Jamesian path to moral critique, cultivation, and progress.

Looking Ahead

In the past century, this understanding of ethics, which as I claimed can be thought of as a contemporary reprise of the ancient tradition of the art of living, witnessed a variety of embodiments, pragmatist and otherwise. The dissatisfaction with moral theorizing, and in particular with the prescriptive and foundational thrust of orthodox ethics, led a number of thinkers and traditions to distrust top-down approaches to moral matters, and to craft or rediscover bottom-up ones hinged on the edificatory task of taking care of moral practice by taking care of what the self makes of itself. To name but a few names, besides later embodiments of pragmatism (Richard Rorty, Richard Bernstein, Michele Moody-Adams, James Wallace), approaches as diverse as ethical anti-theory (Bernard Williams, Annette Baier, John McDowell), the tradition of spiritual exercises (Pierre Hadot, Michel Foucault), and moral perfectionism (Stanley Cavell) share a call to work on the self as a primary ethical activity and dimension of the moral life. James could then be seen as partaking in this feast of heterodox ethics, with his hortatory option as a radical and still underplayed model of, and source for, moral thinking.[15]

Notes

1. There is no clear-cut, meaningful difference, in James, between ethics and morality. I shall then use the two terms as rough synonyms. That said, what we find in James is a general if unsystematic preference to refer to ethics (and cognate terms) to mean the "personal" dimension of one's thoughts, words, and conducts, and to morality (and cognate terms) for their "social" aspect. If so, then both ethics and morality can be equally reflective, and equally unreflective, practices.

2. We find evidence of James's moral concerns dating back to his teens, when for example he challenged his dear friend Edward Van Winkle about the very meaning of life: "What ought to be everyone's object in life? To be as much use as possible" (CWJ 1858, 4.11).
3. The late *Pluralistic Universe* is also full of moral insights, and yet what we find in it is an attempt at systematizing ideas James developed in his earlier works related to the value and possibility of pluralism as both world-picture and mindset—even though the emphasis shifted somewhat significantly (and for the worse, in my opinion) from an agential to an experiential account of meaning and value, marking a not-so-little distance between the earlier and the later work. For such a shift, see e.g., Koopman (2014) and Marchetti (2019).
4. Ralph Barton Perry takes things too far in this way, in his monumental and influential work on James (Perry 1935 II, 250ff), a move that has sedimented in some of the literature. Despite being a perceptive reader and continuator of James along lines congenial to the one defended in the present chapter, Dewey himself has sometimes contributed to this interpretative fashion, as for example when he famously commented that "James did not need to write a separate treatise on ethics, because in its larger sense he was everywhere and always the *moralist*" (2008, 92, emphasis added).
5. On the intertwinement of style and content, voice and method, and literature and philosophy in James's work, see Marchetti (2014).
6. In my classification, Franzese, Lekan, and Pihlström all figure as both orthodox and heterodox readers, since in their respective reconstructions of James's ethics we can appreciate aspects of the two interpretative lines.
7. On modernism as a philosophical category conceived along these lines, see Donatelli 2018, to which my own understanding of heterodox ethics is very much indebted; on pragmatism and modernism, see Schoenbach (2011) and Grimstad (2013); and on James and modernism, see Evans (2017).
8. The dedication of his philosophical manifesto to J. S. Mill as pragmatism's spiritual leader, a thinker similarly engaged in giving new currency to the old tradition of the art of living, is indeed telling and still very much overlooked. Pragmatism, so understood, would then not simply be a radicalization of Mill's already qualitatively enriched empiricism, but also and foremost a furthering of a tradition, within moral philosophy, skeptical of systematization and hinged on the notion of self-transformation.
9. For a more articulated defense of this option, and for a broader assessment of the competing readings mentioned above, see Marchetti (2015 and 2018).
10. While prescriptive ethics currently represents the orthodoxy in moral theorizing (metaethical, normative, and applied alike), descriptive ethics could be considered as part of the family of heterodox understandings of ethics, along with hortatory ethics. For a recent overview of descriptive ethics, see Hämäläinen (2016).
11. This is an admittedly skinny (and perhaps caricatural) description of a vastly rich and complex shift in philosophical and ethical axes, and yet it hopefully catches in its essentials the historical unfolding, and current self-understanding, of mainstream moral philosophy. For the greater philosophical narrative, of which this excerpt is but a fragment, see Baghramian and Marchetti (2017). For the ethical case, see Marchetti (in progress).
12. James was not alone in this task, of course, as both fellow (Deweyan) pragmatists and also selected (Heideggerian) phenomenologists and (Wittgensteinian) analysts fiercely resisted moral theorizing and reshaped ethics accordingly, if differently from each other. For a classical statement of the shape and limits of the ethical orthodoxy, see Williams (1985).

13. Myers (1986, 51) first drew the connection between *moral* and *morale* in the context of James's correspondence with his wife Alice, where James repeatedly contrasted morality with the weakness of will issuing in idleness and personal crises. Unfortunately, the parallel gets lost when Myers goes on to account for James's moral writings. For a congenial elaboration of this important if overlooked insight, see Koopman (2016).
14. For an overall recounting of the birth and unfolding of pragmatism along these lines, see Menand (2001); on James's distinctive elaboration on, and reaction to, the "intellectual sonnambulance" of American society, see Cotkin (1994); Franzese (2008) spoke of an "age of energy" as the background of James's ethics of activity.
15. Heartfelt thanks to Alex Klein for having invited me to contribute to this timely volume, and for his truly extraordinary patience and care as an editor. This piece witnessed, and eventually survived, three jobs in as many cities, fatherhood, and a number of philosophical adjustments.

References

Aikin, S. F., and Robert Talisse. 2011. "Three Challenges to Jamesian Ethics." *William James Studies* 6: 3–9.

Albrecht, J. M. 2012. *Reconstructing Individualism: A Pragmatic Tradition from Emerson to Ellison*. New York: Fordham University Press.

Baghramian, Maria, and Sarin Marchetti. 2017. *Pragmatism and the European Traditions: Encounters with Analytic Philosophy and Phenomenology before the Great Divide*. London & New York: Routledge.

Boyle, Deborah. 1998. "William James's Ethical Symphony." *Transactions of the Charles S. Peirce Society* 34 (4): 977–1003.

Brennan, Bernard P. 1961. *The Ethics of William James*. New York: Vintage Books.

Cooper, Wesley. 2003. "William James's Moral Theory." *Journal of Moral Education* 32 (4): 411–422.

Cormier, Harvey. 2011. "Comment on Talisse and Aikin." *William James Studies* 6: 10–17.

Cotkin, George. 1994. *William James: Public Philosopher*. Chicago and Urbana: University of Illinois University Press.

Dewey, John. 2008. *The Middle Works of John Dewey, Vol. 6: Journal Articles, Book Reviews, Miscellany in the 1910–1911 Period, and How We Think*. Carbondale: Southern Illinois University Press.

Diggins, J. Patrick. 1994. *The Promise of Pragmatism*. Chicago: The University of Chicago Press.

Donatelli, Piergiorgio. 2018. *Il lato ordinario della vita. Etica ed esperienza comune*. Bologna: il Mulino.

Edel, Abraham. 1976. "Notes on the Search for a Moral Philosophy in William James." In *The Philosophy of William James*, edited by W. R. Corti, 245–260. Hamburg: Felix Meiner Verlag.

Evans, David, ed. 2017. *Understanding James, Understanding Modernism*. London: Bloomsbury.

Franzese, Sergio. 2008. *The Ethics of Energy: William James's Moral Philosophy in Focus*. Frankfurt: Ontos Verlag.

Gale, Richard. 1999. *The Divided Self of William James*. Cambridge: Cambridge University Press.

Garrison, George R., and Edward H. Madden. 1977. "William James—Warts and All." *American Quarterly* 29 (2): 207–221.

Grimstad, Paul. 2013. *Experience and Experimental Writings: Literary Pragmatism from Emerson to the Jameses*. Oxford: Oxford University Press.
Hämäläinen, Nora. 2016. *Descriptive Ethics*. London and New York: Palgrave Macmillan.
Koopman, Colin. 2014. "Conduct Pragmatism." *European Journal of Pragmatism and American Philosophy* 6 (2): 145–174.
Koopman, Colin. 2016. "Transforming the Self amidst the Challenges of Chance: William James on 'Our Undisciplinables.'" *Diacritics* 44 (4): 40–65.
Koopman, Colin. 2017. "The Will, the Will to Believe, and William James: An Ethics of Freedom as Self-Transformation." *Journal of the History of Philosophy* 55 (3): 491–512.
Lamberth, David. 1999. *William James and the Metaphysics of Experience*. Cambridge: Cambridge University Press.
Lekan, Todd. 2012. "A Reconstruction of James's Normative Ethics." *William James Studies* 9: 144–167.
Lekan, Todd. 2018. "Who Are Moral Philosophers? Ethics William James Style." *The Pluralist* 13 (1): 81–96.
Lentricchia, Frank. 1988. *Ariel and the Police: Michel Foucault, William James and Wallace Stevenson*. Madison: University of Wisconsin Press.
Marchetti, Sarin. 2014. "Style and/as Philosophy in William James." *Journal of Philosophical Research* 38:339–352.
Marchetti, Sarin. 2015. *Ethics and Philosophical Critique in William James*. London and New York: Palgrave Macmillan.
Marchetti, Sarin. 2018. "William James on Metaphilosophy, Ethics, and the Moral Life: Replies to Dianda, Goldman, Pryba, and Voparil." *Syndicate Philosophy*, August, (https://syndicate.network/symposia/philosophy/ethics-and-philosophical-critique-in-william-james/).
Marchetti, Sarin. 2019. "Jamesian Liberalism and the Self." *Acta Philosophical Fennica* 95:193–202.
Marchetti, Sarin. In progress. *Ethics after Pragmatism*.
Menand, Louis. 2001. *The Metaphysical Club: A Story of Ideas in America*. New York: Farrar, Straus and Giroux.
Myers, G. E. 1986. *William James. His Life and Thought*. New Haven: Yale University Press.
O'Connell, R. J. 1992. "'The Will to Believe' and James's 'Deontological Streak.'" *Transactions of the Charles S. Peirce Society* 28 (4): 809–831.
Otto, Max M. 1943. "On a Certain Blindness in William James." *Ethics* 53 (3): 184–191.
Perry, Ralph B. 1935. *The Thought and Character of William James, Vol. 2: Philosophy and Psychology*. Boston: Little, Brown and Company.
Pihlström, Sami. 2009. *Pragmatist Metaphysics: An Essay on the Ethical Grounds of Metaphysics*. London and New York: Continuum.
Pihlström, Sami. 2016. "William James." In *International Encyclopedia of Ethics*, edited by Hugh LaFollette, 2820–2827. Malden (MA) and Oxford: Blackwell.
Putnam, Hilary. 2004. "Philosophy as a Reconstructive Activity: William James on Moral Philosophy." In *The Pragmatic Turn: Contemporary Engagements between Analytic and Continental Thought*, edited by W. Egginton and M. Sandbothe, 31–46. Albany: SUNY Press.
Roth, J. K. 1965. *Freedom and the Moral Life. The Ethics of William James*. Philadelphia: The Westminster Press.
Schoenbach, Lisi. 2011. *Pragmatic Modernism*. Oxford: Oxford University Press.
Schrader, D. E. 1998. "Simonizing James: Taking Demands Seriously." *Transactions of the Charles S. Peirce Society* 34 (4): 1005–1058.

Slater, Michael. 2009. *William James on Ethics and Faith*. Cambridge: Cambridge University Press.
Stroud, Scott. 2012. "William James and the Impetus of Stoics Rhetoric." *Philosophy and Rhetoric* 45 (3): 246–268.
Suckiel, Ellen K. 1996. *Heaven's Champion: William James' Psychology of Religion*. Notre Dame: Notre Dame University Press.
Throntveit, Trygve. 2014. *William James and the Quest for an Ethical Republic*. London and New York: Palgrave Macmillan
West, Cornel. 1989. *The American Evasion of Philosophy: A Genealogy of Pragmatism*. Madison: Wisconsin University Press.
Williams, Bernard. 1985. *Ethics and the Limits of Philosophy*. London: Fontana.

CHAPTER 10

JAMES AND RELIGION

STEPHEN S. BUSH

WILLIAM James is a towering figure in the history of American religious thought. He made signal contributions to the philosophical and psychological study of religion. His pluralistic, individualistic sensibility remains relevant to popular religiosity today, in no small part because as a preeminent public intellectual and widely read author, he has played a significant role in shaping American religious culture. James's two greatest contributions to the study of religion are his defense of the permissibility of religious beliefs and his methodological focus on individuals' religious experiences. However, he has important things to say on various other topics, including the relation between religion and other aspects of culture, such as ethics, politics, science, and philosophy. This chapter will discuss these themes by paying special, though not exclusive, attention to his two most influential writings on religion, "Will to Believe" (WB 1897) and *Varieties of Religious Experience* (VRE 1902).[1]

THE RIGHT TO BELIEVE

James's "Will to Believe" is known as a defense of the claim that it can be permissible (morally and epistemically) to hold religious beliefs. But his argument has a broader scope than just religion. He is concerned with the more general question of whether it is ever permissible to believe something that does not have conclusive evidence in support of it (provided there isn't conclusive evidence against it). According to the evidentialist view, one should not believe a proposition unless one has adequate supporting evidence. A notable proponent of evidentialism is mathematician and philosopher W. K. Clifford (1845–1879), and in "Will to Believe," James quotes Clifford's essay "The Ethics of Belief" (1947):

> Belief is desecrated when given to unproved and unquestioned statements, for the solace and private pleasure of the believer.... Whoso would deserve well of his fellows

in this matter will guard the purity of his belief with a very fanaticism of jealous care, lest at any time it should rest on an unworthy object, and catch a stain which can never be wiped away.... If [a] belief has been accepted on insufficient evidence [even though the belief be true, as Clifford on the same page explains], the pleasure is a stolen one.... It is sinful, because it is stolen in defiance of our duty to mankind. That duty is to guard ourselves from such beliefs as from a pestilence, which may shortly master our own body and then spread to the rest of the town.... It is wrong always, everywhere, and for anyone, to believe anything upon insufficient evidence. (WB 1897, 17–18)

James would acknowledge that for the great many cases in which observational evidence is available and conclusive, we should indeed affirm what the evidence indicates. It would be wrong not to. He accepts the scientific methodology of experimentation and observation to gather evidence so that one might confirm or disconfirm hypotheses. He is scientifically minded himself, as an academic psychologist and author of a landmark text in psychology, *Principles of Psychology* (PP 1890). He welcomes the use of evidence in shaping knowledge more generally, outside scientific inquiry. However, he worries that a strict reliance on observable evidence would leave us intellectually and practically impoverished in crucially significant domains of life, in particular, social interaction, morality, and religion. In those domains, we can only achieve certain highly valuable goods if we are willing to endorse beliefs for which there is no conclusive evidence. "Will to Believe" makes a case that we are permitted to do so.

Many interpreters have understood James's essay as involving a distinction between epistemic reasons to believe a proposition and (non-epistemic) practical reasons to believe a proposition. An epistemic reason is one that implies the truth of what is believed (Adler 2002, 28). For example, a basketball player's poor free-throw percentage, field-goal percentage, rebounds per game, and assists per game are evidence in support of the belief that he is not a good player. A good player would have much better statistics in one or more of these areas, so the poor statistics are epistemic reasons to accept the belief. A non-epistemic practical reason to believe does not imply the truth of what is believed, but consists in a beneficial consequence stemming from adopting the belief, in light of our goals and interests. Oftentimes it is clear that such reasons do not justify the belief in question.[2] Consider a father who regards his daughter as a good basketball player, despite the statistical evidence to the contrary, and does so because of how important it is to his happiness that his children be skilled athletes. The fact that he derives happiness from skilled progeny does not imply that his children are so.

We seem to find some support for the presence in "Will to Believe" of a distinction between epistemic and practical grounds for belief in James's distinction between what he calls our "merely logical intellect" (WB 1897, 13) and our "non-intellectual nature," "willing nature," or "passional nature." The argument he will make in "Will to Believe" is that our willing nature has a proper role to play in the formation of beliefs in certain conditions. Our willing nature consists of, in addition to "deliberate volitions as may have set up habits of belief," "all such factors of belief as fear and hope, prejudice and passion, imitation and partisanship, the circumpressure of our caste and set" (WB 1897, 18–19). Our disposition to accept beliefs independently of those factors, strictly in accordance to conclusive reasons and evidence, is what he has in mind when referring to our "merely logical" or "pure" intellect (WB 1897, 13, 28). It is tempting to think of the logical intellect as corresponding to epistemic reasons to believe and the willing nature as corresponding to non-epistemic, practical reasons to believe. But one of the things that James accomplishes in "Will to Believe" is to muddy up the distinction between epistemic reasons and practical ones. We see this right in his description of the willing nature. It includes not just desires and aversions, but also beliefs that we inherit from our peers. "Imitation and partisanship, the circumpressure of our caste and set" speaks of those beliefs we adopt on the basis of the testimony of others, our parents, teachers, colleagues, and compatriots. But epistemologists, including evidentialists, regard some testimony as an epistemic ground for belief (Adler 2002, ch. 5). It would be absurd to refuse every assertion that one's professor makes in Physics 101 without witnessing firsthand the supporting experimental evidence. The assertion of a principle of physics by a competent professor is in itself an epistemic reason to accept the proposition. So our willing nature (as James construes it) includes dispositions to believe that are clearly epistemic in nature.

Furthermore, James goes on to say, scientific and philosophical inquiry, the hallmarks of the epistemic reasoning of our intellect, are themselves dependent on our willing nature. "Our belief in truth itself for instance, that there is a truth, and that our minds and it are made for each other—what is it but a passionate affirmation of desire, in which our social system backs us up. We want to have a truth; we want to believe that our experiments and studies and discussions must put us in a continually better and better position towards it" (WB 1897, 19). James takes seriously the sceptic's challenge that we might be wholly deceived in all our beliefs. The sceptic entertains the possibility that the sensory evidence that we use as the basis of so much of our beliefs is itself illusory, systematically in error, and out of touch with reality. To what evidence could we appeal to refute the sceptic? Any such evidence to which we would appeal is what is in question. We opt against scepticism not because there is evidence or reason to refute the doubting hypothesis, but because our inquiries, scientific and otherwise, and indeed our human projects more generally, presuppose belief in truth. Belief in truth, that we are correct in many of our assertions, is fundamental to how we regard ourselves as thinking, acting beings. We attach great value to our belief in truth and the activities that depend on it, and James regards the value we attach to it as a legitimate ground to believe in it. So epistemic considerations themselves require practical ones.[3] We cannot apply any simple distinction between epistemic belief-forming processes and practical ones to James; things are far more "mixed-up" than any such distinction would allow (WB 1897, 20).

The fact that epistemic matters and practical ones are "mixed-up" does not for James license us to believe just anything we would like. In most matters, James would have us proceed just as the evidentialist would say we should. If the evidence in favor is conclusive, believe the proposition; if the evidence against is conclusive, disbelieve it; and if the evidence is mixed or lacking, suspend judgment. And this is so no matter how badly one would like to believe the proposition and no matter what personal benefits one would derive from it.

This is the way things should go in most matters. However, in certain cases, James argues that it is permissible to believe in the absence of conclusive evidence. What are the conditions under which one is permitted to believe? First, the belief must be what James calls "live." It must strike the believer as a plausible candidate for adoption. This plausibility is relative to the epistemic agent. For various reasons, a candidate for belief might be live for one person but not the next. For many of James's original audience of the "Will to Believe" essay, but not for all, Christianity is a live option. Whether or not they subscribe to the Christian faith, they regard its tenets as at least plausible, something worthy of their consideration and evaluation. James thinks his audience regards agnosticism as a plausible option, too, whether or not they subscribe to it. Islam, on the other hand, is not something James thinks is a live option for his audience (WB 1897, 14), just as Christianity would not be a live option to most Muslims. For a belief to be live, it must cohere with the subject's other beliefs. "Living options," James says in "Will to Believe," "never seem absurdities to him who has them to consider" (WB 1897, 32). And we regard things as absurdities when they contradict other beliefs we hold to be true. (This does not mean that James subscribes to a coherentist epistemology, since the question at stake with liveness has to do not with the justification of the belief, but its initial plausibility to the subject.) The need for coherence as a criterion of liveness rules out a lot of wishful thinking situations. James denies, for example, that religious faith is the permission to "believe something that you know ain't true" (WB 1897, 32).[4]

The second condition that must be in place for one to believe absent conclusive evidence is that the situation in respect to the belief must be what James calls "forced." A situation is forced if suspending belief about the proposition, neither accepting nor rejecting it, results in patterns of thought and behavior that are in important respects indistinguishable from disbelief, whereas believing results in quite different patterns of thought and behavior. Believers in God, James thinks, will commit themselves to religious practices, while both agnostics and atheists will not. The question is forced: will you avow the belief or not? Both suspension of belief and outright rejection are a refusal to commit to it. Finally, the belief in question must be momentous, not trivial. The stakes must be exceedingly high. One might think that a chemist's decision to spend a year investigating a hypothesis is a high-stakes commitment; that's a lot of time and resources he could have devoted to other pursuits. But no, this does not count as momentous, since "no vital harm" results if the experiments fail and he rejects the hypothesis (WB 1897, 15). The examples of momentous matters that James gives are a life-risking Arctic expedition, one's commitment to society, and one's commitment to a moral or religious life. Only matters that are existential in import or involve a commitment of one's very life to a high-stakes project count as momentous.

If a belief is, for a subject, live, forced, and momentous (and there is not conclusive evidence for or against it), James thinks it is permissible for the subject to avow it, and also permissible not to do so. In his view, it is as much a matter of our willing nature to refuse to avow it as it is to avow. Clifford would say there is a presumption in favor of not adopting the belief, but James thinks this is an expression of personal preference, not a universal epistemological rule. If one takes Clifford's cautious route of not adopting such beliefs, one is doing so out of a "horror of being duped" (WB 1897 25), that is, a preference for minimizing error. But in one's caution, one misses out not just on false beliefs, but a good many true ones too, and also on the benefits that come from believing them. A more permissive approach to belief adoption risks more errors, but also allows one to enjoy more truths. There should not be a general presumption either for or against adopting live, forced, and momentous beliefs that lack sufficient evidence. Whichever stance the subject adopts is epistemically allowable.

James then turns to the domains of morality, sociality, and religion to argue that important beliefs in these domains are, for many of his peers, live, forced, and momentous, and so they are within their epistemic rights to avow them or not to do so. (He has already, as we have seen, stated that he thinks the belief in truth that inquiry presupposes is also live, forced, and momentous.)

In terms of morality, James thinks that scientific and empirical research are incapable of grounding our moral beliefs. Science tells us what is, "what exists." Morality tells us what ought to be, "what is good" (WB 1897, 27). Even for cases in which humans treat certain things as good, for example, their own survival or happiness, science can tell us only that they actually do regard these things as good, not that survival or happiness actually is good or should be regarded as such. What is more, science has the distinct potential to undermine our moral beliefs. Scientific research could provide a strictly biological account of the origin of our moral beliefs, reducing morality to biology: "Are our moral preferences true or false, or are they only odd biological phenomena, making things good or bad for *us*, but in themselves indifferent" (WB 1897, 28). If this is so, then no amount of sensible evidence could possibly provide any sort of grounding for moral beliefs. James takes moral scepticism seriously, and thinks that many of his peers do too. "Moral scepticism can no more be refuted or proved by logic than intellectual scepticism can. When we stick to it that there *is* truth (be it of either kind), we do so with our whole nature, and resolve to stand or fall by the results" (WB 1897, 28). There is no conclusive evidence for the legitimacy of our moral discourse, then, but James nevertheless thinks it is permissible, indeed, advisable, to believe in moral value. If our moral conduct depends on our affirmation of moral value, the issue is forced. Our lives, projects, and communities would be unintelligible to us if morality is but an illusion, and thus, the question is momentous.

In social life, we often have to extend trust to strangers and assume that they trust us. Forming friendships and engaging in cooperative endeavors requires trusting strangers who have not yet given evidence that they are trustworthy, James says. Without a belief in their trustworthiness, many of the societies, communities, relationships, and cooperative undertakings that we value so highly would be unattainable (WB 1897, 28–29). Taking our peers as trustworthy, then, is forced and momentous.

Finally, James turns to religion. Importantly, he defines religion here as primarily a matter of value, a matter of the "best things," not of deities. Religion affirms two things, first, "The best things are the more eternal things, the overlapping things, the things in the universe that throw the last stone, so to speak, and say the final word." And second, "We are better off even now if we believe [religion's] first affirmation to be true" (WB 1897, 29–30). He does go on later in the essay to specify that for most of his peers, religion involves belief in a personal god, but this is not essential to religion as he conceives it. Whether a personal god is involved or not, the religious adherent is committed to a type of value that transcends the transient, impermanent values of merely human activities. This sort of value is superior in kind to merely human values and persists through history even as items of human value come and go. In whatever form it takes, this value is available for human apprehension.

James does not say a great deal in "Will to Believe" as to what he thinks the specific beneficial consequences of practicing religiosity are. Religion is a "vital good," he says, of sufficiently high stakes to count as momentous (WB 1897, 30). And for those who subscribe to belief in a personal god, there are benefits of relational communion with God, though he does not detail them (WB 1897, 31). In "Will to Believe," he does not say that religion makes people happier, makes them better adjusted, helps them cope with suffering, increases altruism, mitigates their fear of dying, or any such thing, and so he does not make a case, in this essay, that those sorts of benefits are what makes religious belief permissible. For the purposes of "Will to Believe," James is content to let his audience determine for themselves what their religion affords them. However, if we read "Will to Believe" in light of some of James's other writings, it becomes clearer what for him, at least, is at stake with religious belief.

"Will to Believe" is in significant ways a companion piece to his prior essay, "Is Life Worth Living?" James delivered both as speeches in the space of a year and developed "Will to Believe" in part as a reply to criticism of the earlier essay (WB 1897, 311). In the early piece, we get a more explicit understanding of the importance James assigns to religious belief. "Is Life Worth Living?" both reflects and responds to the threats of meaninglessness, pessimism, and nihilism that James and many of his peers acutely felt. As science steadily displaced traditional religion as an intellectual authority over the nineteenth century, many of the educated class responded to the prospect of a strictly natural universe with despair; for a good number of them, despair to the point of suicide.[5] So many in James's circles considered suicide that a colleague of his at Harvard could muse, "I wonder if anybody ever reached thirty-five in New England without wanting to kill himself" (Townsend 1996, 33). James, no stranger to the suicidal impulse himself, writes "Is Life Worth Living?" and "Will to Believe" with these concerns very much in mind. When pondering the cruelties, disorders, and sufferings of existence, religious persons can take comfort in "the old warm notion of a man-loving Deity," but the non-religious person must face the prospect that existence is, at root, "an awful power that neither hates nor loves, but rolls all things together meaninglessly to a common doom" (WB 1897, 41). A few years later, James would write of the same worry:

> For naturalism, fed on recent cosmological speculations, mankind is in a position similar to that of a set of people living on a frozen lake, surrounded by cliffs over which there is no escape, yet knowing that little by little the ice is melting, and the inevitable day drawing near when the last film of it will disappear, and to be drowned ignominiously will be the human creature's portion. The merrier the skating, the warmer and more sparkling the sun by day, and the ruddier the bonfires at night, the

more poignant the sadness with which one must take in the meaning of the total situation. (VRE 1902, 120)

What is at stake then in the naturalistic hypothesis is religious, moral, and existential. Religiously, naturalism denies that there is an "unseen order" of transcendent value that the human can access (WB 1897, 48). Morally, it casts doubt on the reality of all of our mundane values as well: in respect to a world without higher purpose, "we can establish no moral communion; and we are free in our dealings with her several parts to obey or destroy, and to follow no law but that of prudence in coming to terms with such of her particular features as will help us to our private ends" (WB 1897, 43). The result is an existential crisis. The world appears, in a fundamental way, meaningless, and human life and all its projects seem insignificant. Religion, then, affords not just access to transcendent values, but also a response to ward off moral skepticism and suicidal nihilism. Religion provides a grounding for the beliefs that morality is real and life is worth living, and perhaps it is the best or only such grounding available. "Faith in an invisible order is what inspires those efforts and that patience which make this visible order good for moral men. Our faith in the seen world's goodness (goodness now meaning fitness for successful moral and religious life) has verified itself by leaning on our faith in the unseen world" (WB 1897, 55). What James is saying here is that he thinks that religious beliefs provide epistemic support for the truthfulness of moral beliefs, though he does not take the support to be conclusive. To return to our earlier discussion of epistemic and practical grounds for belief, James's case for religious belief here is both epistemic and practical. Religion is a case in which, as he says in "The Sentiment of Rationality," "Intellect, will, taste, and passion co-operate" in the adoption of the belief (WB 1897, 77). Not everyone is disposed to take naturalism as involving a nihilistic threat, and to those who do not, there is no need for the religious hypothesis (WB 1897, 35–36). But for those who do take nihilism seriously, religion is a legitimate intellectual and practical commitment. These, then, are the sorts of benefits that religion brings for James and many of his peers, and these benefits render religious belief momentous. Since they are also forced, for those for whom the beliefs are live, it is permissible to hold them.

In certain respects, it is difficult to assess the legacy and plausibility of James's "Will to Believe" argument. In the time since James's day, epistemology has developed a technical vocabulary that allows for making a variety of distinctions in respect to the nature of evidence and justification that James and his peers were not in a position to make. It would be a speculative undertaking to attempt to rationally reconstruct James's arguments in terms of today's vocabulary. We can note, though, that a number of recent and contemporary philosophers have defended a more permissible standard of rationality in respect to religious beliefs, for example, Wolterstorff (1983), Adams (1987), Alston (1991), and Stout (2005), some of them with explicit reference to James's "Will to Believe." On the other hand, certainly Clifford has his heirs today, evidentialists who declare that religious belief is irrational for lack of sufficient evidence. The debate continues.

Varieties of Religious Experience

James's most extensive treatment of religion comes in his classic text, *Varieties of Religious Experience*, published in 1902 after being delivered as the prestigious Gifford Lectures in 1901 and 1902. As the title promises, the book reflects on a range of different sorts of religious experiences, and he incorporates into the book numerous and at times quite lengthy accounts of experiences by the subjects themselves. In speaking of religious experiences, James is referring to episodes of subjective awareness in which subjects take themselves to be conscious of something divine or transcendent in nature. *Varieties* is an important example of the study of religion from a non-confessional standpoint at a time when Christian theologians were conducting much of the academic study of religion. Many interpreters have regarded the book as an example of a scientific approach to the study of religion, and James himself presents it in this light at times. But it is important to appreciate the normative aims that James has. The testimonies he presents and the way he presents them are designed to show that religion, when understood in his individualistic and experiential way, has an ongoing psychological, cultural, and moral role to play, even in a scientific era. As he puts it in a letter describing his intent for *Varieties*, he wants to show that "although all the special manifestations of religion may have been absurd (I mean its creeds and theories) yet the life of it as a whole is mankind's most important function" (CWJ 1900, 9.185–186).

This helps make sense of his famous definition of religion in *Varieties*: "Religion, as I now ask you arbitrarily to take it, shall mean for us *the feelings, acts, and experiences of individual men in their solitude, so far as they apprehend themselves to stand in relation to whatever they may consider the divine*" (VRE 1902, 34). Later in the book, he describes religion as "the belief that there is an unseen order, and that our supreme good lies in harmoniously adjusting ourselves thereto" (VRE 1902, 51). In these formulations, as is the case in "Will to Believe," James is deliberately vague, trying to cast as wide and inclusive a net as possible. He does not want to restrict religion to any traditional form of theism, or theism at all. What people consider as divine could be a personal god, nirvana, the cosmos, or even the world itself, regarded as imbued with transcendent worth.

By the contemporary standards of the academic study of religion, *Varieties*' definition of religion, even granting that it is stipulative, is seriously deficient for its focus on individuals in their solitude. Religion for the vast majority of its practitioners is a matter that is social, discursive, communal, and institutional, not solitary and individual (Lincoln 2003, chap. 1). It only exacerbates the problem that James not only depicts religion as most importantly experiential, he gives causal priority to experiences over and against beliefs and practices: "Personal religion will prove itself more fundamental than either theology or ecclesiasticism. Churches, when once established, live at secondhand upon tradition; but the *founders* of every church owed their power originally to the fact of their direct personal communion with the divine. . . . So personal religion should still seem the primordial thing" (VRE 1902, 33).[6] James's explicit and considered decision to focus on the experiential aspects of religion instead of the institutional, then, significantly misrepresents religion. That is, it does so insofar as his aim is descriptive (as many interpreters have taken it to be). If, on the other hand, his aim is not only descriptive but also prescriptive, to present an unconventional version of religion that is well suited for his peers in the intellectual class, then his option for an experiential definition makes sense. He minimizes the institutional and doctrinal to focus on the sort of religiosity that he wants to promote: one that is individualistic and critical, as opposed to one that is institutional and deferential to authority. Recognizing the prescriptive agenda in *Varieties* is not to nullify its descriptiveness. But whatever the merits of James's descriptive analyses, and they are many, we should be cognizant of the limitations inherent in his individualistic methodology, which at times leads him to disembed particular religious actors from their social and institutional context.

The individualism in *Varieties* gives it some interesting political implications. Most interpreters of the text have not remarked on these, though that is starting to change as of late (Coon 1996; Carrette 2013). Of those who have explicitly addressed the question, influential figures have read *Varieties* as apolitical (Jantzen 1995; Taylor 2002). They have thought that James's individualistic approach in *Varieties* renders religion, in his understanding of it, politically inert. One version of this criticism involves the claim that Jamesian individuals who go about seeking personal ecstasies in their own private life are practicing a form of religiosity that leaves social and political power structures untouched (Jantzen 1995, 346), whereas feminists and others committed to social justice should want to see a form of religion that recognizes power relationships and challenges injustice. However, in respect to religion, as is the case more generally throughout his corpus, James's individualism is a political response to what he views as the primary political danger: the harm that large and powerful institutions wreak, when populated by docile and deferential people (Koopman 2005). "I am against bigness and greatness in all their forms," he writes in a letter to a friend, "and with the invisible molecular forces that work from individual to individual.... The bigger the unit you deal with, the hollower, the more brutal, the more mendacious is the life displayed" (CWJ 1899, 9.546). Individualism, whether in respect to political, economic, or religious institutions, is for James a challenge to the unquestioning and uncritical conformism that institutions tend to instill in their members. James locates religion in individuals' experiences as opposed to the external authority that is expressed in creeds, rituals, and institutions in order to place the onus of responsibility on individuals, as opposed to hierarchical authority figures, whether persons, traditions, or texts. He has severe concerns about the tendencies of religious institutions to dominate. They do so by what he calls the "ecclesiastical spirit," the operation of institutional power over both believers and outsiders, and the "spirit of dogmatic dominion," the tendencies in religious traditions to control what their adherents believe. People who regard themselves and their own experiences as authoritative over their practices and beliefs will, James thinks, be less apt to perpetuate the evils associated with ecclesiastical and dogmatic dominion (VRE 1902, 271).

James starts *Varieties* by asking his readers to evaluate religious experiences by their consequences, not their causes. He argues against those he calls "medical materialists," whose approach to religious experiences is to provide a naturalistic explanation of how an experience comes about. Then, because the experience is strictly natural (in contrast to what the experiencer typically believes), the medical materialist discounts any value to the experience. James's response is to say that regardless of the cause of the experience, whether natural or supernatural, we should still be sensitive to the consequences of the experience, whether good or ill. Experiences that bring about good consequences are to be appreciated for doing so (VRE 1902, 17–29). Eventually, James will go on to offer his own take on the causal origins of religious experiences. He thinks of them as arising from the subconscious. He asks his readership, regardless of their theological stance, to agree with him on that much. For those who are atheists and naturalists, only natural causes are in play, but there is still much to study, understand, and appreciate about the subconscious processes and the religious experiences that break forth from them into our conscious lives. The theologically or metaphysically minded person, though, can see the subconscious as itself open to transcendent influences beyond the individual's consciousness (VRE 1902, 402–404).

What, then, are the consequences of religious experiences that give them such important value, for James? Religious experiences produce a variety of different sorts of effects, and they do so in significant part depending on the particular psychological and personal characteristics of the experiencer. However, one sort of effect in particular is of preeminent concern for James, and that is the way that religious experiences sustain the moral life. In *Varieties* and throughout his corpus, James thinks of morality as demanding a "strenuous mood" (WB 1897, 160). Morality demands that we devote ourselves to others and to society at large, whereas our personal interests oftentimes exercise a powerful influence upon us to put our own needs ahead of others'. Because of this, he thinks that the moral life requires a firm resolve to undergo personal loss. Over the long haul, most people will not be able to sustain such resolve. "The moralist must hold his breath and keep his muscles tense; and so long as this athletic attitude is possible all goes well—morality suffices. But the athletic attitude tends ever to break down" (VRE 1902, 45). Where a non-religious commitment to morality fails, religious experiences provide the motivational resources necessary to sustain one's willingness to live for the sake of moral goods. James thinks religious beliefs accomplish this as well, and his discussion of the need for religion to sustain the moral life in "Moral Philosopher and the Moral Life" highlights the way that belief in God (again, not necessarily the God of traditional theism) energizes moral action (WB 1897, 160–161). In *Varieties*, though, James wants to emphasize the zeal to carry on that religious experiences supply. This is especially so in those moments of despair and bitter defeat, when it seems as though our best efforts have come to naught. "Religious feeling is thus an absolute addition to the Subject's range of life. It gives him a new sphere of power. When the outward battle is lost, and the outer world disowns him, it redeems and vivifies an interior world which otherwise would be an empty waste" (VRE 1902, 46). Throughout this discussion, James speaks of morality, but his conception of that in *Varieties* and in "Moral Philosopher and the Moral Life" is broad, encompassing political and social values as well as more narrow personal ones (VRE 1902, 292–293; WB 1897, 156–157). Religion, then, for James, plays an essential role in motivating and sustaining active commitment to political goods such as social justice as much as it does for personal moral goods. "How *can* religion on the whole be the most important of all human functions?" James asks, and then he immediately goes on to affirm that this in fact his "final contention," because religion's motivational role in relation to moral and political goods makes it "vindicated beyond dispute" (VRE 1902, 48–49).

Having identified what he thinks is religion's most important consequence, he goes on to analyze this and other consequences of religious experiences as they occur in relation to different personality types. Just as there is no one type of religious experience, there is no one type of religious experiencer. One important way to categorize experiencers, according to James, is as healthy-minded or sick-souled. Healthy-minded people are those who are psychologically disposed to see the good in the world as more fundamental and salient than evil (VRE 1902, 109). When they practice religion, they tend to regard God not as a harsh and exacting judge, but as the "animating Spirit of a beautiful harmonious world," James says, quoting Francis W. Newman (VRE 1902, 73). Religious experiences, for this type, tend to be unitive with divinity (VRE 1902, 72). God is good, people are good, and so no obstacles stand in the way of a joyful encounter between the two. There is no need for a "miracle of grace, or abrupt creation of a new inner man" (VRE 1902, 88). For the sick-souled folk, though, things could not be more different. Their attention is on the cruelties and sufferings of the world. The cosmos is shot through with evil; they are shot through with anxiety, fear, sorrow, and depression. Human nature is itself a tainted fountain, a source of harm and error that cannot fix itself. The sort of religiosity that this person practices sees the divine as something standing over and against the world. The action of the divine is needed to correct a world—and a human race— gone wrong (VRE 1902, 114). James calls these sick souls the twice-born. For the healthy-minded, one birth, their natural birth, suffices. For sick souls, a second, spiritual birth is needed to set things right and bring happiness: conversion.

James's assumption in discussing conversion is that human personality is in general characterized by stability. We acquire the habits that constitute our character through socialization, and we achieve a sort of psychological equilibrium (PP 1890, ch. 4). This is not to say that all of our drives, desires, and beliefs are harmonious, but even when there are tensions among them, we eventually incorporate that tension itself into fairly predictable routines of thinking, emoting, and behaving. A religious experience, springing forth from our "subconscious life," can disrupt this stable "equilibrium." It is a "sudden emotional shock" to the intellectual and practical dispositions that make up our personality (VRE 1902, 163–164). In the wake of the disruption, it is possible that a new arrangement of habits would take shape and stabilize. This is conversion. For the sick soul, once converted, the person can achieve reconciliation with the divine and come to appreciate that even if the natural universe is evil, a transcendent realm of goodness exists that is accessible through religious experiences. The collection of habits that is our personality includes our moral habits, that is, our moral character, so conversion is a moral event as much as a religious one. Once again, then, we see that the intertwinement of religion and morality is a central feature of *Varieties*, a fact many commentators have missed (but see Slater 2009, ch. 5).

For some, religion forms their moral character in such a way that what James calls "spiritual emotions," those emotions oriented toward transcendent values, become the "habitual centre" of the personality (VRE 1902, 219). These are saints, and others come to esteem such figures as exemplars. They express their sainthood in "strength of soul," purity, charity, and asceticism (VRE 1902, 221). James discusses each of these qualities, and admits frankly that many saints take them to excess. Strength of soul in excess leads to fanaticism, intolerance, and persecution (VRE 1902, 274). Purity reflects a desire to be untainted by non-religious life, and in excess, it leads to complete withdrawal from the surrounding society, rendering religion ineffectual (VRE 1902, 283). Charity in excess leads to non-resistance that lets evildoers go unchallenged (VRE 1902, 284). Asceticism in excess leads to self-mortification for mortification's sake (VRE 1902, 288). Having admitted the ways that saints can and do take their religiosity to inappropriate and harmful lengths, James insists that overall, even when judged by purely human standards, the positive contributions of the saints to human society has been evident. He enjoins his readers to find their own non-excessive forms of saintliness: "Let us be saints, then, if we can . . . Each of us must discover for himself the kind of religion and the amount of saintship which best comports with what he believes to be his powers and feels to be his truest mission and vocation" (VRE 1902, 299).

In his discussion of saintliness, James speaks of religion as having a role to play in the advancement of "social righteousness," that is, the alleviation of socially caused miseries such as poverty (VRE 1902, 277). We see this understanding of religion advanced in *Pragmatism* as well. There he distinguishes between pessimism and optimism, faulting both attitudes for eliciting passivity, the one because things will turn out poorly no matter what I do and the other because things will turn out well no matter what I do. James's pragmatism endorses meliorism instead: the active commitment to bettering society that is a precondition of the possibility of social improvement, but not a guarantee (P 1907, 137). In *Pragmatism*, James expresses the spirit of melioristic religion in these terms:

> Suppose that the world's author put the case to you before creation, saying: "I am going to make a world not certain to be saved, a world the perfection of which shall be conditional merely, the condition being that each several agent does its own 'level best.' I offer you the chance of taking part in such a world. Its safety, you see, is unwarranted. It is a real adventure, with real danger, yet it may win through. It is a social scheme of co-operative work genuinely to be done. Will you join the procession? Will you trust yourself and trust the other agents enough to face the risk?" (P 1907, 139)

In the closing chapters of *Varieties*, in which he discusses mysticism and philosophy, James returns to the question that occupies "Will to Believe": under what conditions is it permissible to hold religious beliefs? Mystical experiences, James tells us, are a subset of religious experiences that involve these four characteristics: ineffability, noetic quality, transiency, and passivity. Such an experience is significantly dissimilar to other sorts of experiences in that "no adequate report of its contents can be given in words." It has a quality that has to be directly experienced. This quality is noetic, despite its lack of propositional content, because it confers "insight into depths of truth unplumbed by the discursive intellect" (VRE 1902, 302–303). Mystical experiences are unitive: "The overcoming of all the usual barriers between the individual and the Absolute is the great mystic achievement. In mystic states we both become one with the Absolute and we become aware of our oneness." James thinks that this sort of experience occurs across time and religious tradition: "This is the everlasting and triumphant mystical tradition, hardly altered by differences of clime or creed" (VRE 1902, 332). It is worth noting that the view that there is a universal type of religious or mystical experience, popular in James's day, has come under severe criticism in the philosophy of religion in the time since (Katz 1978; Proudfoot 1985).[7]

In "Will to Believe," James treats religion as though there were not decisive evidence for it. In *Varieties*, however, he affirms that for some people the evidence could *seem* conclusive. Mystical experiences are one such example. In these cases, James regards the subjects as rational in their beliefs (though of course they still could be mistaken). For the outsider, however, the experiences of another person are not in and of themselves decisive grounds for belief (VRE 1902, 335–336). They can serve to outsiders as evidence for "hypotheses," which they can investigate or not. The experiences of the world's religious adepts are a body of evidence that suggests to the non-experiencer the "possibility" of transcendent value. The possibility is enough to ensure the permissibility of religious belief, as outlined in "Will to Believe," provided the criteria discussed earlier are met, but the evidence is not conclusive enough to engender "compulsion" for the outsider to believe (VRE 1902, 339).

For the person inclined to investigate the religious hypothesis, what would such an investigation involve? James thinks of such an investigation as a "critical Science of Religions" (VRE 1902, 359), which employs reason and philosophy to inquire into the status of religious truth-claims.[8] Reason in and of itself is incapable of proving God's existence. James has no use for the various attempts of theologians and philosophers to demonstrate the existence of God strictly through logical argumentation. Reason's role in relation to religious belief is critical, not generative. The material on which it exercises its critical operation is the testimonies of religious experiences. The experiences of the world's religions give rise to beliefs, and critical students of religion can assess these beliefs in light of the moral and scientific standards to which they subscribe. "Both from dogma and from worship [philosophy] can remove historic incrustations. By confronting the spontaneous religious constructions with the results of natural science, philosophy can also eliminate doctrines that are now known to be scientifically absurd or incongruous" (VRE 1992, 359).

After sifting through the data of the world's religious experiences, what does such a critical science of religions conclude? Nothing firm, James thinks. It proposes the hypotheses that there is a higher realm of value and significance that humans can access and that accessing it is the highest human good (VRE 1992, 382). It establishes that there is a wider self than our conscious self, though it is tentative as to whether this wider self is just our subconscious self or whether it connects to higher forms of consciousness than human consciousness (VRE 1992, 402–405). The data, James thinks, indicate that these religious hypotheses are possible, but not that they have been conclusively verified. What the individual philosopher of religion does with that possibility is, in keeping with "Will to Believe," an "exercise of our individual freedom" according to which we "build out our religion in the way most congruous with our personal susceptibilities," intellectual and emotional (VRE 1992, 405). For his part, James exercises his will to believe by affirming that a realm of higher value does exist and can be experienced: "The whole drift of my education goes to persuade me that the world of our present consciousness is only one out of many worlds of consciousness that exist, and that those other worlds must contain experiences which have a meaning for our life also" (VRE 1902, 408, 411–412).

In both "Will to Believe" and *Varieties*, James thinks that respecting others' right to believe religiously means we should be tolerant of their religious beliefs when they conflict with our own perspective. And not just the sort of tolerance that begrudgingly puts up with views one quietly detests, but rather a tolerance that has "tenderness" to others, "so long as they are not intolerant themselves" (VRE 1992, 405; see also WB 1897, 33). James's reflections on religion, then, are animated by his hope that people will practice a form of religion that is individualistic, conducive to pluralistic democracy, and critically fallible, but that nevertheless has enough substance to give believers the sort of confidence in the meaningfulness of life that will impel them to a life of moral and political action, whatever hardships may come.

Notes

1. I defend my interpretation of "Will to Believe" and *Varieties* at greater length in Bush (2017).
2. For a discussion of whether there are cases in which non-epistemic practical reasons do ever support beliefs, in relation to James's "Will to Believe," see Jackman (1999).
3. For further considerations on the way that epistemic considerations involve practical ones, see Harman (1999, ch. 4).
4. Though James does not say so explicitly in "Will to Believe," I would claim that the liveness criterion is best understood as involving a coherentist epistemic criterion. Both prior to and subsequent to "Will to Believe," James would endorse coherentist principles. In "Sentiment of Rationality," written some years before "Will to Believe," he speaks of confirming a hypothesis, whether moral or scientific, by examining whether it "fits" or is in discord with the facts already known (WB 1897, 86). In 1902's *Varieties of Religious Experience*, James speaks of our tendency to define the divine "in ways that harmonize" with our other beliefs (VRE 1902, 359). And in *Pragmatism*, published a decade after "Will to Believe," he speaks of the need to evaluate the hypothesis of God in relation to other beliefs "so that it will combine satisfactorily with them" (P 1907, 143). "Living options," James says in "Will to Believe," "never seem absurdities to him who has them to consider" (WB 1897, 32). And we regard things as absurdities when they contradict other beliefs we hold to be true. This is not to say that we should identify James, at any point of his career, as a thoroughgoing epistemological coherentist. For the coherentist, fit with one's other beliefs is the sole criterion for

determining the rationality of any given belief. James does not say coherence is his exclusive principle, but coherence is one epistemic principle to which he subscribes. And it is a significant one.
5. For more on the nihilistic tendencies in James's culture, as they pertain to "Will to Believe," see Klein (2015, 82–86) and Levinson (1981, 25–32).
6. James's view that experiences are the fundamental aspect of religion—that they give rise to beliefs and practices—is problematic. For a challenge to this account of the causal relation between practice and interiority, which argues that practices are what give rise to interior states such as emotions and experiences, as opposed to vice versa, see Mahmood (2005, chs. 4 and 5) and Mauss (1979).
7. For an overview of the developments in the academic study of mysticism and experience since James's time, see Bush (2014).
8. For differing assessments on the relation between the epistemic criteria for science versus that for religion in James, see Klein (2015); Misak (2013, ch. 4); and Hollinger (2013, ch. 5 and 6).

Bibliography

Adams, Robert Merrihew. 1987. "Moral Arguments for Theistic Beliefs." In *The Virtue of Faith and Other Essays in Philosophical Theology*, edited by Robert Merrihew Adams, 144–63. New York: Oxford University Press.

Adler, Jonathan Eric. 2002. *Belief's Own Ethics*. Cambridge, MA: MIT Press.

Alston, William P. 1991. *Perceiving God: The Epistemology of Religious Experience*. Ithaca, NY: Cornell University Press.

Bush, Stephen S. 2014. *Visions of Religion: Experience, Meaning, and Power*. New York: Oxford University Press.

Bush, Stephen S. 2017. *William James on Democratic Individuality*. Cambridge, UK: Cambridge University Press.

Carrette, Jeremy R. 2013. *William James's Hidden Religious Imagination: A Universe of Relations*. New York: Routledge.

Clifford, William Kingdon. 1947. "The Ethics of Belief." In *The Ethics of Belief, and Other Essays*, edited by Leslie Stephen and Frederick Pollock, 70–96. London: Watts.

Coon, Deborah T. 1996. "'One Moment in the World's Salvation': Anarchism and the Radicalization of William James." *Journal of American History* 83 (1): 70–99.

Harman, Gilbert. 1999. *Reasoning, Meaning and Mind*. Oxford, UK: Oxford University Press.

Hollinger, David A. 2013. *After Cloven Tongues of Fire: Protestant Liberalism in Modern American History*. Princeton, NJ: Princeton University Press.

Jackman, Henry. 1999. "Prudential Arguments, Naturalized Epistemology, and the Will to Believe." *Transactions of the Charles S. Peirce Society* 35: 1–37.

Jantzen, Grace M. 1995. *Power, Gender and Christian Mysticism*. Cambridge, UK: Cambridge University Press.

Katz, Steven T. 1978. "Language, Epistemology, and Mysticism." In *Mysticism and Philosophical Analysis*, edited by Steven T. Katz, 22–74. London: Sheldon Press.

Klein, Alexander. 2015. "Science, Religion, and the 'Will to Believe.'" *HOPOS: The Journal of the International Society for the History of Philosophy of Science* 5 (1): 72–117.

Koopman, Colin. 2005. "William James and the Politics of Personal Freedom." *Journal of Speculative Philosophy* 19 (2): 175–86.
Levinson, Henry S. 1981. *The Religious Investigations of William James.* Chapel Hill: University of North Carolina Press.
Lincoln, Bruce. 2003. *Holy Terrors: Thinking about Religion after September 11.* Chicago: University of Chicago Press.
Mahmood, Saba. 2005. *Politics of Piety: The Islamic Revival and the Feminist Subject.* Princeton, NJ: Princeton University Press.
Mauss, Marcel. 1979. "Body Techniques." In *Sociology and Psychology: Essays*, translated by Ben Brewster, 95–123. London: Routledge & K. Paul.
Misak, C. J. 2013. *The American Pragmatists.* Oxford: Oxford University Press.
Proudfoot, Wayne. 1985. *Religious Experience.* Berkeley: University of California Press.
Slater, Michael R. 2009. *William James on Ethics and Faith.* Cambridge, UK: Cambridge University Press.
Stout, Jeffrey. 2005. *Democracy and Tradition.* Princeton, NJ: Princeton University Press.
Taylor, Charles. 2002. *Varieties of Religion Today: William James Revisited.* Cambridge, MA: Harvard University Press.
Townsend, Kim. 1996. *Manhood at Harvard: William James and Others.* New York: W.W. Norton.
Wolterstorff, Nicholas. 1983. "Can Belief in God Be Rational If It Has No Foundations?" In *Faith and Rationality: Reason and Belief in God*, edited by Alvin Plantinga and Nicholas Wolterstorff, 135–86. Notre Dame, IN: University of Notre Dame Press.

CHAPTER 11

PLURALISM AND TOLERATION IN JAMES'S SOCIAL PHILOSOPHY

ROBERT B. TALISSE

INTRODUCTION: JAMES AS A SOCIAL PHILOSOPHER

WILLIAM James wrote almost nothing that would count today as political philosophy.[1] However, it is clear that much of his work is animated by rather profound concerns with our social lives. One might say, then, that James's philosophy is a thoroughly *social* philosophy. To cite one obvious case, James introduces his pragmatism by way of an anecdote in which he employs the pragmatic maxim to resolve a "ferocious metaphysics dispute" (P 1907, 27) among an otherwise friendly group of campers concerning a squirrel. Following James's pragmatist intervention, the group that had turned "obstinate" was able to abandon the "threadbare" dispute and return to its prior sociable state (P 1907, 27–28). This image of pragmatism as a philosophical means by which one could settle "disputes that otherwise might be interminable" (P 1907, 28) and thereby "smooth out misunderstandings" and "bring in peace" (P 1907, 259) runs throughout James's pragmatist writings. In fact, given James's analysis of the "present dilemma" in philosophy with which his *Pragmatism* lectures begin, it is fair to say that the central motive behind James's pragmatism is *conflict resolution*. And James is keenly attuned to both the personal/internal and interpersonal/social faces of intellectual conflict.

James's attunement to social life emerges in other writings as well. Recall that the ultimate upshot of his famous "The Will to Believe" is that a properly empiricist stance with respect to matters of faith not only bars scientific "vetoes" of religious commitment, but also fosters a "spirit of inner tolerance," by which we each fully embrace—rather than merely *endure*—one another's "mental freedom" (WB 1897, 33).[2] Although the details of his argument are notoriously obscure, the core of James's "will to believe" doctrine runs as follows: Once it is recognized that, with respect to certain questions, "the universe will have no neutrals" (WB 1897, 89), the empiricist *must* not only *allow* but *insist upon* the intellectual respectability of a broad range of believing attitudes, including those attitudes that involve accepting a hypothesis *so that* the evidence in its favor (should there be any) could be revealed. James holds that the empiricist must therefore protect the social space where the full range of permissible religious experiments may be conducted; religious beliefs, he says, must be afforded the liberty to "live in publicity" where they can be openly and fully tested in the lives and experiences of those who adopt them (WB 1897, 8).

In this way, we find in James a concern not simply with conflict resolution and the corresponding "live and let live" attitude that contributes to conflict avoidance; his view also involves a positive commitment to a certain kind of social and political order, namely one in which contending ideals and commitments—including, crucially, opposed moral and religious commitments—are lived. To put the matter in more current jargon, the "right to believe" (SPP 1911, 111) that James envisions is a *positive* right, a right *to* certain social resources, not merely a *negative* right, an entitlement *against* obstruction.

Thus far, I have been drawing out some of the social commitments that are merely implicit in James's writings. Insofar as it could be claimed that James proposes a social philosophy, it seems to be one that is abidingly individualistic, concerned strictly with the social requirements for individuals to live in accordance with moral and religious ideals that are, according to a Jamesian empiricism, epistemically respectable. But individualism is only part of James's story. Consider James's popular moral essays. These seem at first glance to fix on the strictly individual aspects of morality, such as the significance of one's own life (TTP 1899, 150–167) and, indeed, the question of whether life is worth living at all (WB 1897, 34–56). Yet even here his concern ultimately lies with the interpersonal and communal. For the lesson of many of James's examinations of the "meaning of life" is that in order to live well, we must join with others in large-scale struggles (TTP 1899, 154) and fights (WB 1897, 54) to redeem, or at least improve, the world. It is, according to James, our participation with others in "the everlasting battle of the powers of light with those of darkness" (TTP 1899, 153) that provide the distinctively moral content of human nature, the very possibility of living well or badly. Accordingly, in these writings James is often found lamenting the comforts and pacifications of modern bourgeois society and the "irremediable flatness" (TTP 1899, 154) and "unmanly ease" (ERM 1910, 172) that they bring to individual lives. Although his unforgettable invocations of "the strenuous mood" are most often indexed to the inner lives of individuals, it is no accident these are frequently coupled with mentions of overarching and "imperative" social ideals and loyalties, including justice and freedom (WB 1897, 159–160).

This general strand in James's thinking turns to topics that are decidedly political with the central proposal of his 1910 essay on "The Moral Equivalent of War." He longs for a "reign of peace" (ERM 170) and a future in which "acts of war shall be formally outlawed," but thinks that the "martial virtues" of "intrepidity, contempt of softness, surrender of private interest, obedience to command" and "patriotic pride" (ERM 171) must be preserved. The task, according to James, is to develop social institutions that supply occasions for fostering the martial virtues while sparing the need for actual carnage. For this, James proposes a "conscription of the whole youthful population to form for a certain number of years a part of the army enlisted against *Nature*" where soldiers would work on large-scale public service projects—James mentions work on iron mines, freight trains, and fishing fleets and tasks such as road-building and tunnel-making, among others (ERM 1910, 172).

It is important to note that the central political thought driving James's proposal is that there's something worthy of indignation (at least to "reflective minds") in the fact that "by mere accident of birth and opportunity" some citizens are doomed to lives of "toil and pain" while others "natively no more deserving" are spared any discomfort at all (ERM 1910, 170–171). This thought will be familiar to contemporary political philosophers familiar with ongoing debates about "luck egalitarianism," according to which the fundamental task of social justice is to ensure that each individual's holdings of whatever benefits and burdens political institutions have to distribute reflect her choices rather than her (good or bad) luck.[3] And James here seems to fall in squarely with the central luck egalitarians: There is something objectionable in the fact that gross social inequalities emerge out of morally irrelevant and desert-insensitive contingencies. It is, James holds, part of the political task to mitigate these inequalities, and he holds that the way to do so is to create institutions by which privileged citizens (James refers to a "luxurious class") would no longer be able to remain "blind" to the hardiness and travail that plague the lives of their disadvantaged fellows. A regime of compulsory social service, James thinks, would not only knock the "childishness" out of privileged youth but would also foster in them "healthier sympathies and soberer ideas" (ERM 1910, 172).

It seems, then, that although James is by contemporary standards not a political philosopher, his thought manifests a familiar (and attractive, it seems to me) social vision according to which individuals must be afforded the mental and physical freedom to pursue publicly their life projects (including their religious projects), under the stipulation that they remain internally tolerant of others' similarly tolerant practices. As was noted earlier, James sees the requisite freedom as involving a positive dimension; that is, he insists upon social conditions that enable, rather than merely allow, a broad range of individual pursuits. And this requires a political and social environment that fosters within each citizen a kind of fellow-feeling and "civic temper" (ERM 1910, 172) that, in a way, endorses and affirms the experiences, commitments, projects, and experiments of others, including those others whose lives embody ideals alien from one's own. For ease of expression, let us call this general collection of commitments James's doctrine of *social toleration*.

To repeat, social toleration forms the central plank of a very attractive social and political philosophy. But it is of course not unique to James (or to pragmatism). Similar themes lie at the heart of historical expressions of progressivist social thought, such as is found in Wilhelm Von Humboldt (1792/1854) and John Stuart Mill (1859/1991). Moreover, the kind of social toleration that James advocates is a highly general expression of the core ideals of liberal democracy as expressed, in varying ways, by contemporary political philosophers such as John Rawls, Ronald Dworkin, and Martha Nussbaum (Rawls 1999; Dworkin 2006; Nussbaum 2008).

What is distinctive, though, is James's proposed philosophical route to his social toleration doctrine. Rather than arguing from utilitarian or social contractarian premises, James proposes to base social toleration on his pluralist conception of value.

The aim of this chapter is to evaluate James's value pluralist argument for social toleration. Ultimately, I will argue that James's value pluralism does not provide a stable basis for social toleration. But I will also argue that James has at his disposal a far more promising *epistemic* argument for social toleration that he left largely undeveloped.

The remainder of the chapter proceeds as follows. The next section is devoted to discerning the general contours of James's value theory. In the third section, I will raise some criticisms of James's value pluralism, focusing particularly on James's proposed argument from value pluralism to social toleration. In the fourth section, I will propose an argument rooted in Jamesian *epistemological* commitments for a kind of social toleration. The chapter ends with a brief conclusion.

James's Value Theory

In two of his most profound essays, "The Moral Philosopher and the Moral Life" and "On a Certain Blindness in Human Beings," James develops the distinctively pluralist conception of moral value that he claims underwrites his doctrine of social toleration.[4] In the former essay, James begins from a pragmatic analysis of fundamental normative concepts, contending that "Goodness, badness, and obligation must be *realized* somewhere in order really to exit"; he then asserts that the "only habitat" of these moral properties is "a mind which feels them" (WB 1897, 145). Hence moral terms apply to certain states of mind, such as feelings and desires. "[T]he words 'good', 'bad', and 'obligation' " refer not to "absolute natures" of acts but instead are "objects of feeling and desire" that "have no foothold or anchorage in Being, apart from the existence of actually living minds" (WB 1897, 150).

Consequently, James holds that "nothing can be good or right except so far as some consciousness feels it to be good or thinks it to be right" (WB 1897, 147). To say that *x is good* is to report that someone in fact thinks it good or actually desires it. The same goes for obligation. A moral obligation arises, James says, only when "some concrete person" actually makes a claim or a demand that something or other should be done (WB 1897, 148). Indeed, "The only possible reason there can be why any phenomenon ought to exist is that such a phenomenon actually is desired" (WB 1897, 149).

James concludes that "the essence of good is simply to satisfy demand" (WB 1897, 153).[5] Hence he identifies the meaning of moral claims such as, *One ought never to lie*, as expressing a *demand* that one might make to always be told the truth; one makes such a demand on the basis of one's *desire* to not be lied to. The good is the satisfaction of desire.

Now, despite possible appearances, James's view is not a variety of ethical egoism. The egoist ties moral value to one's own interests, but James recognizes the moral status of *any* demand, even those issued by others. Whereas the egoist identifies the right action in any given context with that action that best furthers the interests of the agent, James acknowledges that "every . . . claim creates in so far forth an obligation" (WB 1897, 148). Consequently, on James's view, the interests of others can be the source of our obligations, regardless of whether satisfying those interests benefits us. In this way, James's value theory involves an egalitarian component: Every demand and every interest, no matter whose demand or interest it may be, morally counts. From this, James infers a *maximization* thesis. He holds that as the satisfaction of demand *as such* is "the essence of good," then a state of affairs in which more demands are satisfied must be better than one in which fewer are satisfied. Consequently, James bids us to satisfy "as many demands as we can" (WB 1897, 155); this policy amounts to the imperative to improve the world to that degree we are able. This injunction to satisfy as many demands as possible is James's *meliorism*.

All of this might suggest that James is a utilitarian. Yet he is not. Utilitarianism in all of its forms employs a paradigmatically monist conception of value, whereas, as I have already indicated, James holds a pluralist conception of value. The distinction is crucial. To get a grip on it, consider a simplistic version of utilitarianism, the "classical" or "hedonistic" version of the view found in Bentham and others. The centerpiece of the classical utilitarian's conception of value is the monist claim that there is but one thing of intrinsic value, namely pleasure. And the utilitarian's monism has a close corollary: Seeing all valuable things as either quantities of pleasure or variously efficient means of producing quantities of pleasure, the classical utilitarian is also committed to the claim that all goods are commensurable. This is the thesis that for any two values, A and B, it is necessarily the case that either one is better than the other, or else they are equally good.

The pluralist denies that there is a single intrinsic value to which all other values are reducible, and thus denies that there is a common measure by means of which different goods can be rank-ordered. Instead, the pluralist countenances "an exuberant mass of goods with which human nature is in travail," and holds that "there is hardly a good which we can imagine except as competing for the possession of the same bit of space and time with some other imagined good" (WB 1897, 155–156). Holding that goods are heterogeneous, the pluralist denies that for every two values, it *must* be the case that either one is better than the other or else they are equally good. Consequently, the pluralist countenances some moral conflicts that admit of no morally optimal resolution. In fact, the pluralist claims that some moral conflicts are such that *no* morally comfortable resolution is possible; with respect to conflicts of this kind, there is no third value to which someone may appeal in deciding how to choose. To put the point in a different way, for the pluralist, *nothing* plays the role that pleasure plays in hedonism; the pluralist contends that there is no summum bonum in light of which conflicts can be resolved. Thus moral choice is frequently tragic: We must choose between incommensurable goods, without the guidance of reason or principles, and we inevitably suffer a moral loss. As James explains, "there is always a *pinch* between the ideal and the actual which can only be got through by leaving part of the ideal behind" (WB 1897, 153).

From Pluralism to Social Toleration?

I trust that the sketch provided in the previous section suffices to convey the complexity of James's value theory. To employ some contemporary nomenclature, Jamesian ethics combines the following elements:

1. A *subjectivist* conception of the good, according to which the good is a certain state of a person's mind, namely the satisfaction of felt desire, expressed as a demand.
2. A *pluralist* view of the nature of value, according to which desires and their satisfactions are heterogeneous, that is, different not only in degree or intensity, but in kind.
3. A *content neutral* view of moral obligation, according to which the satisfaction of every desire is to some degree good, and the satisfaction of every demand is to some degree obligatory.
4. A *maximizing consequentialist* or meliorist view of right action, according to which the right action is the one that satisfies as many demands as possible under the given conditions.

My task in this section is twofold. First, I will ask whether this combination of elements is internally coherent. Then I will turn to whether James's value theory supplies a plausible basis for social toleration.

It is not clear that the commitments at the heart of Jamesian ethics are internally coherent. As was shown previously, James thinks that as the "essence of good" is the satisfaction of desire, and as desires and their satisfactions are heterogeneous and therefore incommensurable, the "guiding principle for ethical philosophy" is "simply to satisfy at all times as many demands as we can" (WB 1897, 155). I can see no way that James's meliorism is consistent with his subjectivism and his pluralism. Here's why. If demands and their satisfactions are, as James's pluralism would have it, heterogeneous, then there is no sense at all in which a state of affairs in which more demands are satisfied is *better than* one in which fewer are satisfied. A state of affairs in which twenty demands are satisfied cannot be *better than* one where only ten demands are satisfied unless a world in which more demands are satisfied is a world in which there is *more good*. But, again, the central pluralist premise of James's ethics is that desires (and the demands that express them) are heterogeneous states with "no common character" (WB 1897, 153); thus, the satisfaction of a greater number of demands does not cause there to be a greater *quantity* of good, only more *goods*. More good in the world is surely better than less good; but what is the value of there being more goods? In short, on a pluralist view of things, more goods is not necessarily better. In fact, on James's view, there can be no moral sense in which the satisfaction of more demands is better. But if more is not better, then there is no way to draw the meliorist result from James's implicit premises.

Contrast James's view on this point with a familiar utilitarian perspective. The utilitarian is a monist about the nature of value, holding that every good is either a quantity of pleasure or an instrument for producing a quantity of pleasure. Once pleasure is held to be the single thing that is intrinsically valuable, maximizing consequentialism follows easily: If pleasure is the only thing that is good in itself, a state of affairs in which there is more pleasure must be morally better than one in which there is less pleasure. Hence, the utilitarian contends, we should act always to bring about that state of affairs which contains as much pleasure as possible. This notoriously simple but undeniably compelling argument goes a long way in explaining the longevity of utilitarianism as a mainstream moral philosophy. But it is driven by the utilitarian's monist (therefore commensurabilist) conception of the nature of value. As pleasure is according to the utilitarian a homogeneous phenomenon, one can derive a sum of pleasure across an entire population. This is precisely what a pluralist view of the nature of value precludes. If demands are indeed heterogeneous, there is no sum of good to which each satisfied demand contributes. Again, James's prescription to "satisfy as many demands as possible" is, to say the least, unmotivated. In fact, it is not clear that any prescription regarding "the guiding principle for ethical philosophy" follows from James's premises.

Perhaps I've misconstrued the matter by presuming that James's meliorist conclusion was intended to follow from his premises? One could read James as simply *recommending* that, given his subjectivism and pluralism, the only sensible upshot is to attempt to act so as to satisfy as many demands as possible. The force of the maximizing consequentialist conclusion, that is, might be construed as less of an entailment and more of a piece of advice. Put otherwise, we might read James as claiming that the combination of subjectivism and pluralism suggests that there is no "guiding principle of ethical philosophy" in the usual sense, and so perhaps our best strategy (in some sense of "best") is to maximize the number of satisfied demands.

My sense is that this is the best reading of James. So let us grant that even if James's four commitments regarding ethics do not fit happily together philosophically, his aim lies elsewhere, namely in providing practical guidance in the face of the realization that moral philosophy, traditionally construed, is unable to guide us. Now the question becomes whether James is correct to think that his pluralist view of value is able to recommend social toleration.

James's "On a Certain Blindness in Human Beings" contains his most sustained attempt to draw the implication from his pluralism to social toleration. James articulates his pluralism as the view that "neither the whole of truth nor the whole of good is revealed to any single observer.... No one has insight into all the ideals" (TTP 1899, 149). He thinks that this entails that we ought to promote, rather than simply permit, as many ideals as possible.

To illustrate this point, James tells of his experience of squatters' cabins in North Carolina. He paints a scene of "unmitigated squalor," with the forest destroyed by girdled trees, zizags of fences, and ramshackle cabins plastered with mud. At first, he sees it as "hideous, a sort of ulcer ... Ugly, indeed, seemed the life of the squatter" (TTP 1899, 133–134). However, he later finds that he had overlooked the goods internal to that life and that landscape. "When *they* looked on the hideous stumps, what they thought of was personal victory.... [T]he clearing ... was to them a symbol redolent with moral memories and sang a very pæan of duty, struggle, and success" (TTP 1899, 134). He concludes that given our limited purview, we have "a certain blindness" which prevents us from seeing the goods that constitute others' lives. He holds that, consequently, no life or situation can instantiate all of the available goods. There is not enough time, space, or resources for them all to flourish, or even exist. We must then live our life in the face of a moral uncertainty of what answers are proper in the face of moral conflict. James thinks that what is called for is a life of "sweat and effort," "struggle," a life that is lived bravely in the face of this uncertainty. But, importantly, James holds that this struggle must be waged in a way that affords to our fellows the requisite latitude to pursue their own vision of the good. In this way, James sees his pluralism as supplying the basis for social toleration. He thinks that once we recognize that goods are many and heterogeneous, we will see that we must "tolerate, respect, and indulge those whom we see harmlessly interested and happy in their own ways, however unintelligible these may be to us" (TTP 1899, 149).

It should be noted here that James is not the only philosopher to have endeavored to derive a commitment to social toleration from value pluralist premises. In his seminal "Two Concepts of Liberty," Isaiah Berlin famously argued from his version of value pluralism to a conception of negative liberty that is designed to protect individuals' freedom to choose for themselves their own paths in life (Berlin 2002). But, as I have argued in other work (Talisse 2012; Talisse 2015), Berlin's attempted entailment from value pluralism to negative liberty is doomed to fail. I will not rehearse the details, but Berlin's arguments all feature—and, I contend, cannot avoid featuring—an illicit inference from a claim about *the nature of value* to a claim about *what is of value*.

The Jamesian version of the inference from pluralism to social toleration suffers a similar defect. In brief, it is not clear how tolerance, respect, and non-interference are supposed to follow from the claim that values are heterogeneous and thus plural. One may ask: What, precisely, is wrong with the thought that *because* the world contains an "exuberant mass of goods" which are in competition and conflict, one should most of all attempt to secure the conditions under which one's own preferred values prevail? Why not draw from pluralism the lesson that one must achieve hegemony for one's favorite goods? James could respond that this kind of moral imposition would serve to make others unhappy, or would be unfair, or would be oppressive. And surely James would be correct to say this. But what in his pluralism allows him to hold that individual happiness is paramount or that unfairness and oppression must be avoided? How could such a claim be sustained without forcing James to lapse into the monist view that individual happiness is the summum bonum, or the view that the obligation to be fair and avoid oppression is overriding?

The same thought can be pressed from a different direction. As value pluralism is a thesis about the nature of value rather than a thesis about what is of value, someone could with consistency be a value pluralist and a tyrant. Let us stipulate that the tyrannical value pluralist is someone who recognizes a plurality of objective incommensurable values, but embraces a conception according to which power, control, domination, hegemony, stability, and the humiliation of others are values. Those of us who oppose tyranny would surely disagree with the value pluralist tyrant, but our disagreement would be focused on the question of *what is* of value, not necessarily *the nature* of value. However, as there is no inconsistency in the idea of a tyrant who embraces pluralism, there is no entailment from pluralism to social toleration. This argument generalizes. There is no inconsistency in combining pluralism about the *nature* of value with any particular menu of *what is* of value. Thus, James is incorrect to suggest that, given his pluralism about value, "the first thing to learn in intercourse with others is non-interference with their own peculiar ways of being happy"; he is simply mistaken to assert that the fact that goods are many "is the basis of all our tolerance, social, religious, and political" (TTP 1899, 150). His value pluralism is consistent with the wholesale rejection of social toleration.

Once again, one might offer a relaxed reading of James on these points. One could say, as earlier, that James's idea is that value pluralism can offer, not an entailment or a basis, but instead a kind of support for social toleration for those who are already inclined to a broadly liberal social order. This seems correct, as far as it goes. The trouble, of course, is that it does not go far at all. To see this, consider a distinction noted by Thomas Nagel (2001) between two kinds of value conflict that the pluralist must countenance. We can say that two values are incompatible when the realization or pursuit of one precludes the pursuit of the other. In cases of conflict between incompatible values, one realizes that one must choose at most one to realize; however, one may recognize in such cases that both values are, indeed, valuable. But note that there are also conflicts between values that are in opposition. When two values are opposed, embracing one involves the condemnation of the other. Religious conflicts provide handy, albeit hackneyed, examples of value opposition. Several sects of Christianity are bound to regard non-Christian religions as mere idolatry, really not "religion" at all. Proponents of such species of Christianity cannot see the demands following from the non-Christian doctrines as in any respect worthy of satisfaction. To take a different kind of case, a Millian experimenter in living is bound to regard as "the chief danger of the time" the fact that "so few now dare to be eccentric" (Mill 1859/1991); however, the follower of Matthew Arnold's traditionalism is bound to see the Millian experimenter as nothing short of a barbarian, an opponent of "sweetness and light" (Arnold 1869/1993). Neither can see the other as an issuer of demands that it would be good to satisfy.

Now, the Jamesian view can provide some support to a policy of toleration in cases of conflict between incompatible values. With James, I can easily see the North Carolina squatters as engaged in the pursuit of a unique, though perhaps alien, good. But differences like these are, as we say, easy to tolerate. When it comes to the squatters, there is no cost to me in adopting James's advice: "Hands off" (TTP 1899, 149). We hardly need a conception of toleration for dealing with such cases. It is toleration in the face of conflicts between opposing values that we most need; this is where an account of toleration's value and importance is urgent if we are to avoid escalating hostility. Yet James's view offers us no help here. His prescription of social toleration extends only to cases in which it is possible to see the other's values as merely idiosyncratic, strange, or alien. When it comes to cases in which, given one's own values, one must regard the other's value commitments as illusory, depraved, wicked, sinful, or deformed, Jamesian pluralism offers no assistance whatsoever. It counsels only that we tolerate the tolerable.

It seems, then, that James's value theory is internally less stable than it first appeared. More important, his attempt to support his doctrine of social toleration by appeal to his value pluralism looks hopeless. Pluralism is consistent with the rejection of social toleration, and so there's no entailment from pluralism to toleration. Moreover, insofar as it provides any kind of motivation for toleration at all, Jamesian pluralism suggests only a thin and ultimately impotent toleration, toleration only in the cases in which toleration is costless.

A Moral-Epistemic Case for Social Toleration

I began this chapter with a very brisk review of some leading Jamesian themes that I allege suggest that James should be regarded as a social philosopher, even if not a full-bore political philosopher. I then argued that James's own philosophical account of his social vision is not successful. In this section, then, I draw on some alternative Jamesian resources that suggest a different philosophical path to social toleration.

Part of what motivates James to adopt his value pluralism is his reflection on a salient trait of what might broadly be called *moral experience*. As was mentioned earlier, James's grand conclusions in "On a Certain Blindness in Human Beings" that "neither the whole of truth nor the whole of good is revealed to any single observer" and "No one has insight into all the ideals" (TTP 1899, 149) is arrived at by a sustained exploration of experiences in which one confronts clashes between purported values, including clashes between familiar and seemingly alien purported values. And James is surely right about this much: In our struggles to live morally fulfilled and truly human lives, we inevitably confront situations in which indeed it looks as if "some part of the ideal must be butchered" (WB 1897, 154); and we experience such cases as tragic, instances in which we must abandon something that is not only authentically good, but also truly and uniquely precious, something whose loss cannot be compensated for by moral gains elsewhere. In fact, we sometimes confront cases in which it seems that unique and irreplaceable goods conflict, leaving us in a condition in which *no matter what we do, we do wrong*. Moreover, we tend to think that there's something stunted, unserious, shallow, and immature about a life without experiences of struggles of this tragic kind.

The question is what *philosophical* conclusion one should draw from the pervasiveness of such experiences. And here it seems to me that James has overplayed things. Rather than adopt a pluralist value theory that locates the source of such experiences in the structure of value itself, James might have begun with the following more modest, but I think also more potent, *moral-epistemological* thesis: Life often confronts us with conflicts among goods that we are bound to regard as authentic, and yet do not know how to commensurate. It is important to note that this claim declines to embrace the pluralist view that some values are indeed incommensurable, and also withholds ascent from the monist view that commensurability is a necessary condition for valuehood; it rather treats the question of value commensurability as a matter for further investigation.[6]

Importantly, this moral-epistemological thesis enables one to affirm that, since getting morality (including the question of whether all goods are commensurable) right is extremely important for our individual lives, we ought to uphold the social conditions under which the needed further investigation could proceed. And here's why. It is plausible to think that progress in moral inquiry is best enabled under conditions in which a broad range of experiments, projects, and commitments are afforded the social space required for their enactment in individuals' lives. This is because moral investigation, like scientific inquiry, is a *social* and *collaborative* undertaking, requiring large-scale coordination and cooperation among diverse and differently-situated individuals. One might say, then, that our individual moral projects (including the moral project of trying to adequately understand morality) are intrinsically *dependent* on those of others. To draw out the analogy with scientific inquiry, moral investigation can be conducted properly by an individual *only* within a broader community of investigators, and our individual investigations—scientific or moral—must be protected by social norms of non-obstruction, expressive freedom, autonomy, and the like. In short, part of what is required for moral investigation to commence is a policy of social toleration roughly of the kind that James proposes.

To be sure, I have provided only the slightest sketch of a moral-epistemic case for social toleration. However, this sketch suggests a view that is decidedly Jamesian in spirit. For one thing, it overtly begins from the recognition that our moral knowledge is incomplete, but could be completed with further inquiry. It thus perches somewhat precariously between a moral-epistemic optimism that holds that we know the good (and simply must muster the fortitude to do it), and a moral-epistemic pessimism according to which moral inquiry is futile or impossible. In this way, the view suggested earlier holds open the possibility of moral progress. Furthermore, the view accommodates many of the Jamesian thoughts about the centrality of struggle and the "strenuous mood" for moral life (WB 1897, 159–161). It recognizes that we do not (yet) adequately understand the full nature of morality, but still must live a life; from this, it draws the conclusion that striving to understand better, to gather more data, to broaden one's moral vision, is an essential part of the project of living a moral life. And, although there is nothing as strong as an entailment at work, the view promotes a kind of moral-epistemic humility that rides alongside its exhortation for further moral inquiry. In recognizing the need for continuing inquiry, we also recognize that our current commitments could be better informed, corrected, fortified, confirmed, and revised in light of new results. This humility is a natural cognitive counterpart to familiar understandings of toleration, open-mindedness, diversity, inclusion, and the rest. Importantly, it does not depend on an individual's readiness to see alien value commitments as nonetheless somehow good; it allows one to see one's neighbor's conception of the good as decidedly wrong, mistaken, perverted, and even depraved. However, the view also enables one to see even those who are deeply and seriously wrong as epistemic resources, victims of failed yet possibly instructive experiments, people stuck in the potholes along the road of inquiry, and hence deserving of leeway. Again, the proposed moral-epistemic view may not entail social toleration, but it does provide a compelling reason—an "inducement," perhaps—to adopt such a policy.

Conclusion

I have argued here that although James's own philosophical path to his doctrine of social toleration is unsuccessful, there is a more promising track provided by James's moral epistemology. Again, a lot more would need to be said in order to make this moral-epistemological proposal look philosophically viable. I leave it to contemporary Jamesians who seek to rescue and redeem James's social philosophical vision to pursue this line of research. I realize that the Jamesians among my readers might here conclude that the moral-epistemic view I just sketched is no innovation at all, but simply James's view properly understood. If so, then so much the better for James. Other Jamesians might demur from a different direction; they might complain that the proposal makes James an advocate of a rather familiar liberal progressivism of the kind canonically articulated in Mill's *On Liberty*. In response, I refer readers to the dedication of James's *Pragmatism*, and say, again, so much the better for James.

Notes

1. One important exception is his 1910 essay "The Moral Equivalent of War," which will be discussed later in this section.
2. Compare James's discussion in his "Is Life Worth Living?" (WB 1897, 52–53), and in his 1906 follow-up to "The Will to Believe," "Faith and the Right to Believe" (SPP 1911, 111–117), which was intended for his (unfinished) *Some Problems of Philosophy*.
3. The literature on luck egalitarianism is mountainous. For a helpful review of the issues (and a distinctive luck egalitarian proposal), see Tan (2012). See also the essays collected in Knight (2011).
4. The following two sections draw from Aikin (2011).
5. James uses "desire" and "demand" more or less interchangeably. I cannot here explore the issues this raises, but it strikes me that on James's view, a "demand" is simply the outward expression of a desire.
6. As I suggest in my concluding section, this moral-epistemic view strikes me as a profitable way to reconstruct James's writings in moral philosophy. To be sure, the epistemic interpretation of pluralism requires significant massaging of some of James's claims; and, moreover, the epistemic reading runs against the grain of James scholarship. See the special issue of *William James Studies*, which is devoted to a debate about James's moral philosophy (Vol. 6, 2011), as well as subsequent papers by Todd Lekan (2012) and Mark Uffleman (2012) for affirmations of the non-epistemic reading of James.

Bibliography

Aikin, Scott F., and Robert B. Talisse. 2011. "Three Challenges to Jamesian Ethics." *William James Studies* 6:3–9.

Arnold, Matthew. 1869/1993. *Culture and Anarchy and Other Writings*. Edited by Stefan Collini. Cambridge: Cambridge University Press.

Berlin, Isaiah. 2002. *Liberty: Incorporating Four Essays on Liberty*. Edited by Henry Hardy and Ian Harris. New York: Oxford University Press.

Dworkin, Ronald. 2006. *Is Democracy Possible Here?: Principles for a New Political Debate*. Princeton: Princeton University Press.

Humboldt, Wilhelm. 1792/1854. *The Sphere and Duties of Government*. Translated by Joseph Coulthard. London: J. Chapman.

Knight, Carl, and Zofia Stemplowska, eds. 2011. *Responsibility and Distributive Justice*. Oxford: Oxford University Press.

Mill, John Stuart. 1859/1991. "On Liberty." In *On Liberty and Other Essays*, edited by John Gray, vol. 35, 592. Oxford: Oxford University Press.

Nagel, Thomas. 2001. "Pluralism and Coherence." In *The Legacy of Isaiah Berlin*, edited by Mark Lilla, Ronald William Dworkin, Robert B. Silvers and Aileen Kelly, 105–112. New York: New York Review Books.

Nussbaum, Martha Craven. 2008. *Liberty of Conscience: In Defense of America's Tradition of Religious Equality*. New York: Basic Books.

Rawls, John. 1999. *Political Liberalism*. Revised ed. New York: Columbia University Press.

Talisse, Robert B. 2012. *Pluralism and Liberal Politics*. New York: Routledge.

Talisse, Robert B. 2015. "Value Pluralism: A Philosophical Clarification." *Administration & Society* 47 (9): 1064–1076.

Tan, Kok-Chor. 2012. *Justice, Institutions, and Luck: The Site, Ground, and Scope of Equality*. Oxford: Oxford University Press.

CHAPTER 12

JAMES AND POLITICS
The Radical Democracy of a Radical Empiricist

TRYGVE THRONTVEIT AND
JAMES T. KLOPPENBERG

WILLIAM James never developed anything resembling a comprehensive political philosophy. The radically pluralist epistemology and metaphysics for which "pragmatism" became his shorthand represented a revolt against all closed systems of thought. Yet James's very resistance to certainty and finality led him to participate actively in the civic life of his day, in order to promote both popular appreciation and practical opportunities for social experimentation and growth. Varying from context to context, this activity was consistently guided by James's pragmatist accounts of individual experience, moral obligation, and social interdependence, which to him implied a collective, ongoing responsibility to balance freedom, justice, and order amid complexity and change. Though providing no detailed blueprint for achieving and maintaining that balance, James's writings suggest a suite of practices and institutions that, in various forms and to varying degrees, have proven effective in the past and deserve continued trial. Equally important, his writings articulate a regulative ideal by which to evaluate all such working models of politics: an ideal of popular participation in all levels of social ordering that James described toward the end of his life as "radical democracy" (CWJ 1909, 12.291).

That ideal might sound ethereal, especially to ears ringing from the massive collapse of social equality and incessant clang of political dysfunction in many advanced democracies. Yet even from the distance of a century, it speaks with uncanny force to just those problems. Consequently, despite James's own lack of interest in articulating a self-contained and authoritative political philosophy, contemporary scholarly interest in his exploratory and provocative political philosophizing is mounting (e.g., Smith 2007; Stob 2011; Throntveit 2014; Kittlestrom 2015). Such interest is not unprecedented, but its revival is overdue. James's efforts to explain and promote his radically democratic ideal inspired some of the most consequential political thinkers and reformers of the early twentieth century in the United States (Kloppenberg 1986; Throntveit 2014;

Throntveit 2017). Yet few participants in the pragmatist revival that began in the 1970s have addressed the political implications of James's version of pragmatism, and despite renewed attention they remain widely ignored or misunderstood.

The reasons are not mysterious. James famously and frequently described his philosophy as "individualistic" (e.g., TTP 1899, 4), and that is how most interpret it (Otto 1943; West 1989; Danisch 2007). Yet James also denounced the free rein of "egoistic interests" (CWJ 1909, 12.291), instead advocating expansive, equal, and effective freedom for all people regardless of economic, social, or political status. As he wrote in 1905, the "best commonwealth" is that which cherishes the "residual interests," and "leaves the largest scope to their peculiarities" (ECR 1903, 97). This practical association of personal autonomy with the social obligation to promote its widespread enjoyment is central to James's radically democratic ideal, and responsible for his opacity to anyone seeking a neatly organized schedule of ethical and political goods. Human flourishing, as James understood it, requires both democratic deliberation and existential choice; respect for norms and suspicion of them; close-knit communities and idiosyncratic thinkers who challenge their conventions. When or how heavily to weigh some factors versus others in any given context is a matter for negotiation, and James's insistence that democracy lies in the quality and sustainability rather than the specific outcomes of such negotiations resulted in political writings as variegated as the events they addressed. Yet collectively those writings exhibit a philosophical richness, organic consistency, and breadth of application rarely achieved by the formal rigor of dominant liberal and communitarian theories (e.g., Walzer 1984; Rawls 1993; cf. Williams 2005).

Indeed, James's deepest relevance to the study of politics stems from his concern, not with the logical form, but rather the central problem facing modern political theory: the problem of plural values, especially in cases of individual or minority interests at odds with more powerful or popular agendas. Abjuring any attempt to solve that problem for his fellow citizens, James outlined the features of a polity equipped to ameliorate it, contain it, and even exploit its agitating effects: a pragmatist polity, with powers and authority calibrated to the dynamic and diverse historical experiences of its members yet employed to optimize freedom of thought and action across social space and time. More than a set of constitutional and legal forms, the pragmatist polity depends on virtues of deliberation, experimentation, historical reflection, and empathic reasoning to animate them. Nevertheless, the practice of those virtues must be encouraged and negotiated through institutions that foster tolerant exchange, promote mutually intelligible norms of reasoned discourse, and model the same awareness of interdependence that prompts their creation, all while remaining accountable and adaptable to public demand. Rather than "displacing" politics (Honig 1993), these institutions, formal and informal, should create "free spaces" in which political activity, including conflict, is equally, broadly, and fruitfully engaged—thus giving winners and losers alike a stake in their continued existence (Evans and Boyte 1986; see also Phillips 1991; Keane 2009).

THE ETHICAL REPUBLIC

James's pragmatist politics, including his vision of "radical democracy" and his interventions to advance it, emerged from his efforts to formulate a pragmatist ethics: a practical guide to conduct in an unfinished and irreducibly complex universe. James never attached any label to his guide, but he captured its nature in an arresting metaphor expressing his ethics in terms of its purpose: an "ethical republic" (WB 1897, 150; cf. Throntveit 2011, 2014). Ethics, pragmatically conceived, is not a fixed program or ranking of ideals. Rather, it is itself an ideal, of private and public interests converging—an ideal derived from experience, yet suggesting at every moment the terms and consequences of its own realization. In James's view, it is an empirical fact that all individuals have unique ideals, requiring cooperation or acquiescence from other individuals for realization. Thus all individuals, through their ideals, impose hypothetical obligations on others. The *practical* validity of ideals and obligations, however, can only be established in the course of moral life, as their consequences are considered and judged by the community. Thus while *an* ethical republic is an inescapable fact of experience, *the* ethical republic of each day depends for its scope and character on its members' interventions and interactions in it. The purpose of pragmatist ethics is to help people reflect on, test, and revise their ideals to accord with the republican reality of moral life, while also helping them alter that reality to accommodate as many other ideals as possible. "We all help to determine the content of ethical philosophy so far as we contribute to the race's moral life," James asserted in his seminal essay, "The Moral Philosopher and the Moral Life." "In other words, there can be no final truth in ethics any more than in physics, until the last man has had his experience and said his say" (141).

What guidance does James provide? If, as he asserts, our personal moral course through life affects the moral character of the universe we inhabit, we had best clarify the meaning and probable consequences of the goods we conceive before committing to their realization. That requires clarifying the meaning of "good" itself. James argued that the necessary consequence of conceiving any particular "good" is to lay an obligation upon someone, somewhere (even if only the original conceiver), to realize it (145–147). In other words, every imagined good entails a concrete demand that certain circumstances obtain over others; contrary to Kantian (and many modern liberal) formulas, there can be no obligation to abstract principles divorced from specific demands and consequences. As James wrote, "*we see not only that without a claim actually made by some concrete person there can be no obligation, but that there is some obligation wherever there is a claim.*" Therefore, he concluded, "*the essence of good is simply to satisfy demand*"—demand not just for pleasure, but for "anything under the sun" (148, 153).

Confidently as James stated it, this conclusion presents the obvious difficulty that demand cannot always be satisfied. For that reason, some scholars have characterized James's ethics as tragic (e.g., Kloppenberg 1986, 116). Indeed, James himself deemed the question of demand "most tragically practical," for "the actually possible in this world is vastly narrower than all that is demanded." Any answer to what he termed "the casuistic question" in ethics promised to confirm rather than avert this tragedy, for the very need of a "scale of subordination" to prioritize divergent demands—a "casuistic" scale—proved that with every moral choice, "part of the ideal must be butchered" (WB 1897, 154). Thus, as James told his students, demand alone is "too wavering and fallible a thing upon which to found a definitive system of ethics. Its data must themselves be compared, discussed and judged. But how?" (ML 1888–89, 183–184).

As so often, James found the clue to his philosophical puzzle in human psychology. From his functionalist perspective, our impulses to identify and align our personal interests with a larger good can be interpreted as versions of a species-generic and ethically crucial impulse: the search for a system to harmonize *all* ideals, in accordance with the mind's ceaseless efforts to organize experience in general (Throntveit 2014, 93–99). "*Invent some manner* of realizing your own ideals which will also satisfy the alien demands," James theatrically enjoined in "The Moral Philosopher and the Moral Life"; "... that only is the path of peace!" (WB 1897, 155).

Actually, James did not believe this meta-ideal of moral organization could deliver us from the daily toil of moral butchery. He did believe, however, that it could serve an invaluable function. Its prevalence and persistence across history should inspire us to "throw our own spontaneous ideals, even the dearest, impartially in with that total mass of ideals which are fairly to be judged." It should impel us to risk a collective experiment to determine which ideals are most compatible and which must be discarded, and to adopt as the "guiding principle" of moral life the duty "to satisfy at all times *as many demands as we can*" (WB 1897, 151, 155).

Sacrifice—or at least our willingness to risk it—is thus the price of fullest freedom in the ethical republic. We must recognize our particular ideals as subordinate to the meta-ideal of moral harmony, which finds its imperfect realization in a collective process of winnowing and organizing demands. Despite his slippery phrasing, however, James did not conceive this process as crudely utilitarian (cf. Myer 1986, 398–399). Although he did state, confusingly, that the "best act" is that "which makes for the *best whole*, in the sense of awakening the least sum of dissatisfactions," James stated in the same essay that every "end of desire" is "exclusive of some other end of desire," making mathematical nonsense of any effort to satisfy the greatest number of desired goods (WB 1897, 155, 154). Alternatively, if goods are not arithmetically equivalent but rather, as James asserted, share "a common essence" such as demand, "then the amount of this essence involved in any one good would show its rank in the scale of goodness," and thus its fitness for preservation (WB 1897, 152).

Thus, it is not the *number* of demands, but the *amount* of demand satisfied that should matter most to our moral calculations. And some demands are weightier than others. If "utopia" for millions required "that a certain lost soul on the far-off edge of things should lead a life of lonely torture" (WB 1897, 144), would not some, at least, of the saved revolt against the bargain? Even if their revulsion were culturally conditioned, such deference to tradition indicates a deep-seated interest in values with no immediately discernible individual or social benefit other than a reputation for yielding, over time, "the maximum of satisfaction to the thinkers taken all together"—*thinkers*, not demands (WB 1897, 156). Put briefly, when James, resigned to the necessity of "victory and defeat" in moral life, "prayed" for the triumph of "the more inclusive side," it was not on behalf of abstract ideals but of the living persons holding them (WB 1897, 155).

That inclusivity of persons is the hallmark of a healthy ethical republic, and the prism through which James's "ultimate principle" of demand-satisfaction must be interpreted.[1] Thus emerges a dialectic of freedom and unity in moral life. Our free, subjective inquiries into the nature of that life both trace and rearrange its existing conjunctions to enhance their congruence with our interests. Our will to believe in a more personally satisfying world obliges us to think relationally—to inquire into the myriad and protean ideals that shape our social environment, in order more adroitly to pursue and even reconceive our own so that others can tolerate and sustain them. Crucially, both for critics of "high liberalism" (Galston 2010, 385) and for its own inclusive imperative, this dialectic is neither arbitrarily selected nor culturally specific. Rather, the mutually constitutive goodness of freedom and unity is implicit in our universal drive to manipulate both our personal behavior and our external environment, in order to bring them into more satisfactory relation. At the same time, the contingency of such negotiations implies that any prescriptions based on their results are open to testing by every individual asked to accept them (*pace* Roth 1969, 72, 77).

James's entire oeuvre suggests that our principle means of such testing should be what today we might term "deliberation"—the open-minded exchange, comparison, and negotiation of ideas and ideals (cf. Dewey 1916; Barker et al., 2012). Indeed, the collective process of articulating, testing, and reflecting on moral hypotheses and their consequences constitutes both James's ethical ideal and the program of its realization: a good desired for its practical service to desire itself. As James wrote in *Pragmatism*, "one great use of knowing things is to be led not so much to them as to their associates, especially to human talk about them" (P 1907, 105). The reason, of course, is that what we know is valid, and thus valuable, only in its practical application to our irreducibly social existence; "human talk" supplies the clues to, and ultimately passes judgment on, the validity and utility of our ideas. Thus, we ought always to believe and act in ways that human experience writ large has "funded," while recalling that our beliefs and conduct—whether fruitful or frustrated—add to the "sum total of experience" both we and others will consult in the future (P 1907, 107). The goal of deliberation, in this Jamesian sense, is not necessarily to reach consensus, but to gain a "leveling insight" permitting responsible and legitimate action: action that demonstrates care for the inclusivity and sustainability of the deliberative process itself, and in that way promises "some stable gain" for the "religion of democracy" (TTP 1899, 156; cf. Singer 1973; Gutmann and Thompson 1996; Dryzek 2001).

Of course, to identify both the long-term interest of a community and the actions likely to promote it is a tall order, however deep our contemplations and conversations. James, however, endorsed three individual virtues to aid such inquiry: experimentalism, historical reflection, and empathic reasoning.

Ethical experimentation can cause conflict, but can also test, refine, or displace conventional and sub-optimal means of maximizing freedom. James described the phenomenon in organic terms as early as 1880, explaining the innovative socio-political perspectives of "great men" as spontaneous variations of social thought which the community's aggregate judgments either conserve or extinguish (WB 1897, 163–189). More than fifteen years later, James articulated the same basic argument in explicitly political language, declaring that the "mental freedom" of an "intellectual republic" was essential to the healthy growth of human communities (WB 1897, 33). The "active faiths of individuals... freely expressing themselves in life, are the experimental tests by which they are verified, and the only means by which their truth or falsehood can be wrought out," James declared a year later. The moral knowledge that enhances freedom depends equally for its creation upon individual assertion and social assent; therefore all "ought to live in publicity, vying with each other" (WB 1897, 8).

This running moral experiment could be chaotic. Yet as James explained in "The Moral Philosopher and the Moral Life," historical reflection on the practical needs and contingent factors driving it in the past could supply wisdom to discipline innovation without discouraging it in the present. Over generations, James argued, societies perform an "experiment of the most searching kind," and each day's initial casuistic scale should put "customs of the community on top" (WB 1897, 156). Certainly, some people are "born with a right to be original"—or at least a penchant for it—and at any time, deeply rooted as society's norms might be, "revolutionary thought or action may bear prosperous fruit." Still, such fruit is harvested "only through the aid of the experience of other men," and its value determined the same way (WB 1897, 157). James recapitulated this argument in *Pragmatism*, insisting that many ideas now considered routine or even fundamental are, in fact, "*discoveries of exceedingly remote ancestors, which have been able to preserve themselves throughout the experience of all subsequent time*" (P 1907, 83). That our "common sense" comprises the innovations of "prehistoric geniuses" reminds us that no truth is eternal and bold thinking drives the progress of knowledge. But it also cautions that even highly originative ideas take effective form only through widespread social testing, against both current exigencies with historical roots and contemporary values that are historically conditioned. Moral innovators are crucial to social development. But history and the societies it shapes provide resources from which all experimenters draw, and impose constraints under which they operate.

Arguably the highest of James's pragmatist virtues is that of empathic reasoning, for it alternately galvanizes and moderates the practice of the other two. A basic respect for the moral lives of others is logically implied by James's psychological account of ideals and the obligations they entail; as he wrote in *The Principles of Psychology*, "A thing is important if anyone *think* it important" (PP 1890, 1267). Yet insufficient interest in others' feelings often handicaps our quest for moral unity and the enhanced freedom it brings. James conveyed the gravity of this debility in his famous essay, "On a Certain Blindness in Human Beings," stating pointedly that judgments made in ignorance of others' feelings are "sure to miss the root of the matter" and "possess no truth" (TTP 1899, 133). Fortunately, most of us at some point (and some of us at many points) experience a "gleam of insight" into "the vast world of inner life" beyond our own. At such instances "the whole scheme of our customary values gets confounded" and "a new center and a new perspective must be found" (TTP 1899, 138). James interpreted such moral recalibrations as signs that we should *search out* alien ideals, to help realize the potentially greater goods waiting upon our creative inquiry. Rather than shirking our "practical" duties to ourselves (TTP 1899, 138), seeking meaning in the ideals of others enriches our personal moral worlds.

Such seeking will go astray if guided only by good intentions or shallow relativism. Actually to *see* deep meaning in the lives of others requires that we scrutinize our own idiosyncratic and culturally inculcated values through a pragmatist lens. Empathy is impossible if we cannot reflect critically on the unexamined assumptions guiding our conduct and, in the process, learn to "tolerate, respect, and indulge" those of our fellows "harmlessly interested and happy in their own ways" (TTP 1899, 149). Yet the keyword just stated is "harmlessly." Tolerance, pragmatically understood, is a means of maximizing freedom, not a euphemism for apathy; it is not tolerance of everything, but "tolerance of whatever is not itself intolerant" (TTP 1899, 4). Certainly, the main benefit of empathy is the "humility" it fosters: a broadened perspective yielding "a certain inner joyfulness at the increased importance of our common life" (TTP 1899, 165). In the interest of that common life, however, we must avoid condoning moral novelties without carefully consulting our interpersonally forged and culturally transmitted values—without attempting, as it were, to empathize with the race as a whole and to imagine how our judgment will affect it.

In short, moral reasoning is at once an inter-subjective, empirical activity and an existential exercise. Conflicts will arise among well-meaning factions; mavericks will scorn the status quo; and "in the struggle that follows, the whole of us get dragged up after a fashion to the advanced position" (MEN 1899–1901, 313). But whose position, and with what consequences, none can reliably foretell. Moral courage lies in choosing sides, battle after battle, despite the risk of disaster. Moral wisdom lies in choosing deliberately, considering the historical needs and demands of the community that sustains and constrains us. Even then, to choose ignominy (or worse) over conformity remains our prerogative. As James wrote, "it is at all times open to any one to make the experiment, provided he fear not to stake his life and character upon the throw" (WB 1897, 156).

From Ethical Republic to Radical Democracy

The political implications of metaphysical pluralism, psychological voluntarism, and ethical republicanism, if never crisply drawn by James, were powerfully apparent to him. His account of consciousness as autonomous, efficacious, and relational posed the problem of agency versus order at every level of human activity. As he wrote to fellow philosopher and future biographer Ralph Barton Perry, "the moment one *thinks* of other thinkers at all," the leap from "solipsism" to "reasoned faith in radical democracy" has been made (CWJ 1909, 12.291).

The contrast with solipsism is instructive. Cognitively, "radical democracy" entails the recognition that other people are essential, active, and dynamic elements of the larger reality our thoughts and acts must accommodate. Politically, it implies a society that resists domination by narrow interests and instead values diverse perspectives, broad and effective participation, and adaptation to change. But what does radical democracy look like in practice? How do we translate "reasoned faith" in its value into practical action in its behalf?

On an individual level, James's answer is straightforward: Practice the virtues of ethical republicanism. "Republicanism is of course the political corollary of free-will in philosophy," James wrote in his early thirties (ECR 1873, 266), and throughout his life he preached a gospel of "civic courage," calling each citizen to approach politics, like ethics, with as much concern for the moral commonwealth as for him- or herself (ECR 1888, 129; ERM 1897, 72). Human egoism makes it impossible to meet that standard fully. But the "democratic manners" (paraphrasing P 1907, 44) refined by pragmatism and its ethos of communal inquiry can, as James suggested to Perry, bring us to see others more clearly as equal partners in a creative process, whom we should get to know as well as we can and learn to work with as closely as possible if we want to build a decent public life.

Yet mere exhortations to ethical republicanism tell us little about how to organize its individualized practice in the service of radically democratic politics. Indeed, James is often portrayed as personally and intellectually indisposed to the kind of collective practice that politics entails (Kuklick 1977; Feinstein 1984; West 1989; Menand 2001; Danisch 2007). James bears much of the blame for these misconceptions. In a widely quoted letter of 1899 he declared himself "against bigness and greatness in all their forms, and with the invisible molecular moral forces that work from individual to individual." The "bigger the unit you deal with," he continued, "the hollower, the more brutal, the more mendacious is the life displayed." Thus James declared himself opposed to "all big organizations as such, national ones first and foremost," favoring instead "the eternal forces of truth which always work in the individual and immediately unsuccessful way, underdogs always, till history comes after they are long dead, and puts them on the top" (CWJ 1899, 8.546).

There is no doubt that James decried the trends toward monopoly capitalism and extraterritorial imperialism that shaped American life at the turn of the twentieth century. But to make too much of his polemic against "bigness and greatness in all their forms" is to ignore a large portion of his writings. The truth is that various strands, ranging from anarchy to social democracy, were woven through James's thought (Coon 1996; Kloppenberg 1986). As a pragmatist, James recognized that the problem of freedom and order takes different forms in different contexts. "Only in the free personal relation is full ideality to be found," he wrote in 1899 (CWJ 1899, 9.41), and few philosophers, psychologists, or laypersons would dispute that the deepest forms of moral understanding occur in contexts of intimate acquaintance.[2] A decade later, however, when contemplating the balance of freedom and order on a national scale, James asserted that "utopia," interpreted practically, could only mean "some sort of a socialistic equilibrium" (ERM 1910, 170). In the interim he described himself to a friend as "an anarchist" so far as his "ideas" were concerned, but applauded her "socialistic work" as more "practical" (CWJ 1903, 10.191).

That appreciation for the practical ends and constraints of politics is as common in James's writings as is his critique of bigness. Indeed, James frequently invoked organized social action as a counterweight to narrow interests that threatened the broad enjoyment of individual autonomy. James's most famous political cause—his protest against American suppression of the Philippine insurgency after the Spanish-American War—is a case in point. Widespread public support for the war left James feeling isolated, "more and more an indiv[id]ualist and anarchist," chafing under a government and culture that seemed incapable of viewing the insurgents as moral equals with claims to be considered. Yet his proposed remedy was not to abandon representative democracy. Rather it was to organize a global opposition to its imperialist captors, "a league for the purpose of fighting the curse of savagery that is pouring into the world" (CWJ 1900, 9.362). Indeed, besides feeling sympathy for the Filipinos, James worried that the smothering of self-government abroad signaled its constriction at home. As he saw it, certain Americans had bullied others into ignoring the "unsophisticated verdict" of their "plain moral sense," so that an ostensibly democratic polity was now "crushing out" another people's effort "to attain the possession of itself, to organize its laws and government, to be free to follow its internal destinies according to its own ideals." Worship of "a national destiny which must be 'big' at any cost" had resulted in the "impotence of the individual" in Cambridge as surely as in Luzon, while every soul destroyed in battle with the Filipinos destroyed a part of the "ancient soul" of America, too (ECR 1899, 156–158).

A high price indeed for bigness. And yet in seeking an antidote to his nation's pathological impulse toward "aggrandizement" (CWJ 1901, 9.526), James looked not to the ungoverned conscience but to the activated collective. "In a democracy the country belongs to each of us," he once jotted privately, but in the United States, it seemed, only "the selfish interests" had "organized." "Shall not the ideal ones"? (ERM n.d., 202). James's "ebullitions of spleen" against bigness were provoked not by scale or complexity per se, but by "the more brutal, the more mendacious" arrangements of life; by violence to the particular truths of experience. Homogenization, not organization, was anathema to James; a more "systematically unified moral truth" remained, for him, the predicate and product of an expanding moral freedom (WB 1897, 161). Given the importance James accorded to experiment and interpersonal discourse in that process of moral growth, it is no wonder he was attracted to a method of social analysis he once described as "anarchy in the good sense": a method assuming that "the smaller and more intimate" units of society gave the "truer" insights into its realities and possibilities. Yet in the same breath of praise for "anarchy" James equated its "good sense" with "democracy," and asserted that the "common life is realized" through struggles for "order" (quoted in Perry 1935, 2.383).

At least from James's perspective, it seems well-mannered anarchists and well-mannered democrats share the same pragmatist habits. Both look to the lives of their fellows when seeking patterns in which to better fit their own. Both resist abstraction and stagnation, conceiving order to mean capacity for complexity and growth. Both, in Tocquevillian fashion, view the everyday, interpersonal, local practice of communal inquiry and participatory problem-solving as antecedent rather than antithetical to the happier organization of large and diverse populations (cf. Pateman 1970; Evans and Boyte 1986).

Not surprisingly, the "radical democracy" that James envisioned in the context of America's diverse and protean citizenry differs significantly from the direct rule of citizen elites associated with ancient Athens. Nevertheless, James's writings suggest a meaning of "radical democracy" that is capacious yet still does justice to the phrase's classical roots: a form or structure of power (Greek *kratos*) generated, sustained, and observed by the people (Greek *demos*) that form its root (Latin *radix*). It is an organic structure that can take many shapes, but which had evolved, by James's day, certain basic organizing features, or institutions, vital to translating radically democratic consciousness into radically democratic practice. James believed that such institutions should serve not only to organize private quests for moral growth into collective action toward common goals, but also to maintain a form and degree of order that protects individual autonomy and permits collective retreat and revision.

James was not particularly creative in identifying his candidates for that dual task. In the spirit of pragmatism, he looked first to tools of proven value, at least when in good repair: popular government; social equality; rule of law; education; and finally, despite his hatred of violence, military service. Where James was bold, and the originality of his pragmatism evident, was in his vision of the social purposes these institutions could and should achieve.

For James, popular government meant more than plebiscites on the decisions of professional politicians. Above all, it meant citizen input in the business of state (cf. Barber 1984; Cohen 1989). As the Philippine fiasco showed, any form of "freedom" designed by self-styled experts and imposed on subjects was "sheer illusion, and can only mean rottenness and ruin" for the latter (CWJ 1899, 8.480). For this reason James was deeply critical of the American people (including himself) for their complacency in the run-up to the Philippine–American war (Throntveit 2014, 115–118). For the same reason he was generally disgusted with both major political parties in the late nineteenth century. Stocked with "pecuniary corruptionists" and "unscrupulous" partisans, they were too often "blind to the real life of the country," gulling its people with "dead shibboleths" and paralyzing its politics by their "hatred and prejudice." These "fossil" organs were deaf to the letters, pamphlets, speeches, rallies, and votes through which citizens sought to counsel their leaders and each other. Well ahead of the progressive movement, therefore, James called for "a new national party" to infuse greater "intellectual character and purposes" into American politics, with an eye not only to "civil service and economic reform" but "perhaps ultimately to certain constitutional changes of which we are in pressing need" (CWJ 1884, 5.505).

James never explained exactly what changes he envisioned, but it is certain he never saw them. Even after aligning himself with the Democratic Party's progressive wing in 1900 he criticized the "very mongrel kind of reform" they pursued (CWJ 1900, 9.357). Again James stayed silent on the specific details of his preferred platform, but it is safe to say that increased social equality would have been among its goals. James was convinced that the trenchancy and political efficacy of citizen deliberation depends on a broad and broadly equal participatory base. For much of his philosophical career he worried that economic disparities were constricting that base and eroding the nation's democratic habits. In 1899 he observed that divergent material circumstances were dividing the moral forces of society, and that "the distribution of wealth has doubtless slowly got to change" (TTP 1899, 166). By 1910, the year he died, he had grown more radical, identifying a "socialistic equilibrium" as central to his pragmatist political ideal (ERM 1910, 170).[3]

James was perhaps even more disturbed by racial inequality. He could indulge in casual racism, as in an 1897 letter relating his encounter with "the darkey" Booker T. Washington and the "good old darkey" veterans of the Massachusetts Fifty-fourth Regiment (CWJ 1897, 3.9). Yet in that same letter James praised Washington's eloquence in describing black Americans' efforts to educate and empower themselves. Some years later he publicly celebrated both Washington and the prominent African American social critic W. E. B. Du Bois as national political heroes, lauding both for embodying (in their different ways) the dual commitment to autonomy and reciprocity that radical democracy entails. Indeed, James warned, for African Americans to turn from or fail in their quest for equality would be "a national calamity" that "would turn our civilization into an irrevocable caste-system" (ECR 1909, 193).

The importance of social equality to James's pragmatist politics explains his deep commitment to another political institution, one often equated with conservatism rather than radicalism: the rule of law (Miller 1997, 25–26, 53). James did not just commend black Americans for demanding equal and humane treatment, but insisted that the laws assuring such treatment be followed and enforced. Above all, he decried the hideous practice of lynching. It was not just the dead and their kin who suffered from the violence. Countless others were prevented by fear from participating in deliberative political and social processes that depend for long-term success on inclusivity. Meanwhile, the farce of all-white juries acquitting murderers who gloated over their crimes undermined the whole legal and moral structure of ostensibly free communities. As James wrote in 1903, "the slightest loophole of licensed exception" could tear the seal of social order, especially in cases "where the impulse is collective." James thus had an answer to the home-rule logic of Jim Crow apologists. Southerners, white and black, were part of a larger commonwealth whose millions of individual destinies were linked. Lynching was not just a "homicidal custom" peculiar to the South, but a "manifestation of anarchy" that threatened the nation and deserved a harsh response (ECR 1903, 171–173).

James's frustration with Americans' failure to respect the rule of law helps explain his thoughts on the purpose and importance of education. James viewed education as a social process of knowledge production rather than an individual process of knowledge absorption. Its largest purpose is to foster habits of inquiry that refine our impulses into judgments informed by facts, then translate our judgments into action tailored to context (cf. Dewey 1916; Pateman 1970; Barber 1984; Fishkin 1991). In James's pragmatist polity, education comprises any and all tools and processes that facilitate this "sifting of human creations" (ECR 1907, 107); what one scholar dubs his "science of human nature" was meant to be a popular rather than arcane practice (Bordogna 2008, 10). That said, James recognized the value of specialized educational institutions to promoting that science (despite lamenting the over-professionalization of many disciplines, e.g., ECR 1903, 67–74). Indeed, he accorded one such institution a particularly important (and for some, controversial) role in promoting radical democracy—the modern college curriculum. He did not think highbrows and "prigs" (as he put it) should rule the country (ECR 1907, 108), nor did he call for an expert class to translate popular ideals into practical achievements (cf. Christiano 1996). Rather, he argued, the college-bred must fully embrace the spirit of the liberal arts, tabling assumptions and looking past stereotypes in order "to scent out human excellence" and bring it to society's attention (ECR 1907, 108). In short, they must adopt the mantle of social critic, executing the American university's mission of revealing the polity's character to itself (cf. Jewett 2012).

Rather than special privileges or power, then, James conferred upon the college-bred "aristocracy" an *obligation*: to promote the "rule of the best" whatever, wherever, and whoever the best may be. They must open their ranks to all who exhibit the "higher, healthier tone" of life that defines membership in their class, and they must count themselves students of those they seek to engage and instruct (ECR 1907, 111). Their calling is to inquire "how diverse the types of excellence may be, how various the tests, how flexible the adaptations," so that, through their curious and humble example, their fellows, too, can "gain a richer sense of what the terms 'better' and 'worse' may signify" (ECR 1907, 108). Dispersing any lingering whiff of elitism, James declared any education "a calamity" that does not develop a "sense for human superiority" capable of penetrating station and circumstance. "Democracy is on its trial," he cautioned, and if its product is mediocrity, low-born or well-born, the world will condemn it. It can triumph only by producing citizens alert to its flaws yet "bound not to admit its failure"—citizens through whom it conceives itself, in a pragmatist spirit, both as it *is* and as it *ought* to be (ECR 1907, 108–109).

That humbly aristocratic vision of democracy—as precious, even fragile, yet capable of greatness if our best selves do the work—inspired James's boldest idea for a pragmatist political institution: a "moral equivalent of war." Though pacifistic by inclination, James thought military training and combat cultivated many of the virtues he treasured, and reckoned the baser instincts that war inflamed impossible to extinguish. Rather than excoriate the military as a hopeless evil or aberrant excrescence, therefore, James sought to replicate its best features in a civil institution that might ultimately transform its parent and the polity: a national service corps, conscripting "the whole youthful population" in an "army enlisted against Nature" (ERM 1910, 171). James had no romantic attachment to force: violence of any sort, he wrote in "The Moral Equivalent of War" (1910), entails too high a cost to be justified by its "ideal fruits" alone, and inter-group violence especially is a high-risk and nearly zero-reward affair (ERM 1910, 162). Nevertheless, the stubborn fact of human nature remains: war appeals to our natural "pugnacity," a trait that partakes of both our drive to control our environment and our desire for others' esteem (ERM 1910, 164). But here James saw the glimmer of a solution, for war, as organized pugnacity, taught our ancestors to seek the esteem of *groups*. Over time it had "trained societies to cohesiveness" (ERM 1910, 164), and the world's militaries had refined this training till it approached a science. "Martial virtues" mix the egotistical and social instincts into the "enduring cement" of political life, and therefore "remain the rock upon which states are built" (ERM 1910, 170).

But war is not the only field in which to learn and practice those virtues. "All the qualities of a man acquire dignity when he knows that the service of the collectivity that owns him needs them," James wrote (ERM 1910, 169); the qualities need not be belligerent, nor the service violent. Thus James proposed the reform and gradual transformation of the military and the nation through a new kind of service corps, dedicated to universal training and concrete expressions of "civic passion." Invoking the contingency of ideals and the social purpose of moral inquiry, he insisted that any vision of collective achievement might serve as a "spark" around which patriots could rally. If enough people were given practical experience in "constructive" collective activities—ameliorating pain and suffering, building better public spaces, harnessing resources for the economic relief and spiritual recreation of fellow citizens—the allure of social justice and its morally enriching effects would increase. Universal service would instill "hardihood and discipline" in the nation's youth while revealing to the eyes of privilege their "relations to the globe"—including the "hard and sour foundations" of the comforts they take for granted (ERM 1910, 171–172). Despite disconcerting some later readers with his rhetoric of a manly army conquering nature (Martin 1987), James in fact challenged his nation to obviate aggression and destruction through promotion of inclusive, constructive causes. The moral equivalent of war did not consist in the specific tasks of a civilian corps, but in the continuous effort of a free commonwealth to enlarge its effective membership, supplanting the volatile "morals of military honor" with a robust "morals of civic honor" (171; cf. Kaag 2009, 119–121; Throntveit 2018). As with popular government, social equality, rule of law, and education, James sought not to design radically democratic institutions himself, but to project the basic contours of radical democracy on an institutional canvas that others, alerted to the radical potential contained in life's familiar materials, would fill. "Strenuous honor and distinterestedness abound," James asserted; only an "alteration in public opinion" stands between the present and "utopia" (ERM 1910, 173).

Nowhere did James draw a map of his own utopia—and fittingly so. "Faiths and utopias are the noblest exercise in human reason," he once wrote (ECR 1907, 109), but their nobility inheres in their eternally aspirational character and inspirational function. Nevertheless, James did have some sense of how a pragmatist polity aspiring to radical democracy would operate. Appropriately, his most revealing illustration was an extended reference to historical experience.

On Decoration Day in 1897, in a speech dedicating Boston's Robert Gould Shaw Memorial, James eulogized Colonel Shaw, along with the all-black Massachusetts Fifty-fourth Regiment he commanded in the Civil War, as models of the boldness, circumspection, empathy, and sacrifice that radical democracy requires of citizens. Shaw and most of his regiment were slaughtered in an assault on South Carolina's Fort Wagner, but James was not interested in the Fifty-fourth's battle record. He recounted its tale as a lesson in the virtues of the ethical republic, and as a reminder of the highest object of political life: securing freedom through enhancing solidarity. That object was "embodied" in the very "constitution" of the Fifty-fourth, a battalion of the oppressed marching not for their own freedom merely, but as "champions of a better day for man." From its beginnings the republic they fought for had been an "anomaly," a "land of freedom" with "slavery enthroned at the heart of it." Although slaveholders claimed liberty to organize their communities without northern interference, any liberty so wholly destructive of others' freedom imperiled what James considered the nation's defining faith: that "common people can work out their salvation well enough together if left free to try" (ERM 1897, 65–66).

To save this faith, James continued, had required imagining what better form it might take, reflecting on what that new form required, and acting to bring it about. It was just such an "experiment" in ethical republicanism that James meant to commemorate: the bold decision, by Massachusetts Governor John Andrew, Colonel Shaw, and the soldiers of the Fifty-fourth, to fight for a more integrated society with a more integrated army (ERM 1897, 67). Praising their boldness, James also noted the historical rationale behind it. By the 1860s, "law and reason" were under perpetual threat from a practice that was not only antithetical to democracy but that decades of "policy, compromise, and concession" had failed to arrest (ERM 1897, 66). Finally, James conveyed Shaw's empathy for the enemy and the increase of moral unity that he and his troops achieved. He quoted a Confederate officer who praised the gallantry of the "negroes" even as his very uniform denied their humanity, and he explained how the callous mass burial of the Fifty-fourth's dead in fact "bore witness to the brotherhood of Man," as Shaw's body was "united with the forms" of his comrades (ERM 1897, 71).

James was careful not to exalt destruction along with the destroyed. Instead of glorifying the martial exploits of his subjects, he suggested that their highest virtues, those of the ethical republic, could have prevented war had more Americans shared them. These virtues instilled the "lonely courage" to look beyond one's narrow interest, and the "civic courage" to act for the greater good of a community. Perhaps no passage in James's writings better encapsulates both the ambiguity and power of his political ideal than this equation of "lonely" with "civic," and of "courage" with "saving day by day." For James, the patriot is the citizen committed to "speaking, writing, [and] voting reasonably," maintaining "good temper between parties," and resisting the influence of "rabid partisans and empty quacks." Through such daily acts the deliberative citizens of healthy democracies can reduce conflict and realize the ethical republic. "Such nations," James wrote, "have no need of wars to save them" (ERM 1897, 72–73).

Nevertheless, war had come, and its arrival illustrates the single most important feature of James's democratic theory. Democracy, for James, denotes a people's collective capacity for conceiving, discussing, and addressing problems deliberatively; it does not describe a set of eternally effective or perfectly efficient institutions. It thus empowers citizens at the cost of imposing a burden on them: the burden of deciding, with no sure knowledge of the consequences, when their particular forms of democracy have failed the ideal, and their current deliberative processes have exhausted their use. Neither theory nor history provides a formula for making that decision; as James put it, "Democracy is still upon its trial." Certainly, citizens of "civic courage" can enhance its power and resilience, cultivating habits of "disciplined good temper" toward those who respect its principles and "merciless resentment" toward those, like the "Slave States," who subvert them (ERM 1987, 74). Yet these remain habits, not precise formulas. Our practices and institutions are means of approximating a radically democratic ideal of inclusivity, creativity, and collaboration in public life; they have no independent claim on our loyalty. Sometimes other means are necessary. When, and of what sort, James did not say. As in our moral lives, uncertainty is the price of a politics accommodating both individual and collective freedom. Only in the "zone of insecurity"—"the zone of formative processes, the dynamic belt of quivering uncertainty, the line where past and future meet"—can we join in the work of ordering rather than stifling difference and change (WB 1897, 192).

James and Modern Political Theory

However essayistic and incomplete, William James's century-old writings on politics continue to inspire as well as challenge a variety of efforts to revive pragmatism as a public philosophy.[4] Less explored is the way James's writings speak directly to contemporary projects in academic political theory.

James's political thought is perhaps most congruent with what William Galston (2010) (among others) has identified as a "realist" trend in political theory, one taking politics as it *is* as the starting point for inquiry into what it *can* and *ought* to be. In response to John Rawls, Ronald Dworkin, and other prophets of a "high liberalism" (Galston 2010, 386) seeking to eliminate conflict by appeal to an ultimate principle or universal interest, realists from Bernard Williams, Glen Newey, and John Gray to Bonnie Honig, Judith Shklar, Jeremy Waldron, and Stephen Elkin insist that no particular interest (e.g., Rawlsian justice) can be peremptorily and eternally established above all others without endangering the negotiation and ordering of interested pursuits that defines the essence of politics. Instead, political theory must identify "distinctively political" principles and methods by which persons wielding power can seek public warrant for doing so: principles and methods not imported from a temporally or logically prior morality, but derived from the essential character of politics as orderly contestation (Galston 2010, 388–389; cf. Williams 2005). To permit contestation in an absence of standards is to abandon politics to the power relations it is meant to regulate. To judge contestation from a prior moral standard, however, is to preempt politics and invite the same result.

In their quest to save political theory from practical irrelevance Galston's realists adopt several Jamesian commitments. These include "a moral psychology that includes the passions and emotions; a robust conception of political possibility and rejection of utopian thinking; [and] the belief that political conflict—of values as well as interests—is both fundamental and ineradicable" (Galston 2010, 385). Less clearly but still plausibly Jamesian is their "emphasis on the evaluation and comparison of institutions and regime-types, not only principles," in advancing political theory and practice (Galston 2010, 385, 408). Yet Galston identifies other features of realism that James's politics of radical democracy might enhance or outperform. First is the lack of a "coherent affirmative alternative" to the "liberal utopianism" that realists criticize, including some means to identify the "line dividing adversarial relations from all-out enmity." Legitimate conflict, by (realist) definition, is conflict that respects and invigorates the polity in which it occurs, and proceeds on the basis, however narrow and deeply buried, of "some idea of agreement and endorsement" (Galston 2010, 408). But what that basis is, or how citizens can build, reshape, relocate, and reestablish it in the course of the polity's conflictual evolution, is unclear in the realist literature. Second, realists quite reasonably insist that "ought implies can"—that "if a political proposal simply cannot be realized, it loses normative force"—but tend, less justifiably, to assume a narrow scope for human psychological and moral adaptation (Galston 2010, 408–409). Together, those commitments circumscribe the universe of political ideals, practices, and institutions open to theoretical inquiry and—if instantiated in political structures—to democratic discussion and experiment. The danger is not just theoretical impoverishment but political stagnation and illegitimacy.

James's writings suggest solutions to these problems that emerge from another difference between him and the realists: his refusal to draw sharp lines, either between political and moral life or between moral life and the rest of the pluralistic universe. In James's ethical republic, moral principles and virtues emerge from the same type of dynamic contests and negotiations that realists identify with politics. Because membership in an ethical republic is an inevasible condition of life for all human beings, whose selfhood and self-creation depend upon recognition and cooperation from their fellows, these contests and negotiations proceed on the assumption (however dimly recognized) that actions calculated to destroy the republic are illegitimate. James's radical democracy is an effort to identify and describe the virtues of the most widely satisfactory moral communities and promote them on the scale of modern societies. Thus the standards for legitimate public claims in a democratic polity are those of the ethical republic: embodiment of concrete demand; consideration of social consequence; submission to public criticism and judgment; and implementation through collectively endorsed procedures. The agreement to observe these standards as often and as carefully as possible creates the field upon which legitimate conflict is engaged and from which naked domination is prohibited. Finally, the very need for such a field of orderly conflict speaks not to a fixed psychology or moral capacity but to the limitless and unpredictable fecundity of individual human consciousness: an ever-evolving, idiosyncratic engagement with an ever-changing, subjectively apprehended world of pure experience.

None of this is to say that human beings invariably or even usually prefer legitimated claims to their own unrefined demands. Nor is it to deny that novel ideas and ideals are often just as limited by ignorance, prejudice, and selfishness as familiar ones. The point is that human beings *can* esteem the public good as highly as (or higher than) their narrow interest, and *do* at times imagine new goods and arrangements that scrutiny reveals to be feasible, but do so *rarely and ineffectively* unless the system encourages and facilitates it. In thus emphasizing the internal rather than imported character of political morality James moves even closer than the realists to their goal of aligning "ought with can," in the process resolving a troubling and longstanding paradox of political studies: the paradox of a "liberal" project aimed at promoting the right of rational or virtuous individuals to govern themselves responsibly, but frequently producing evidence of irrational or base individuals thwarting one another repeatedly (Purcell 1973; Ricci 1984). James's pragmatist approach obviates this existential threat, suggesting that democracies do not depend on rationality so much as seek to create it. Rationality and virtue are not political externalities, to be exploited by political systems. They are *inherently* political. They are relative measures of the success with which wilful people, embedded in society, contextualize, prioritize, and pursue their interests in satisfactory ways. To be sure, it is critical to determine the capacities for reason and virtue that a given democracy fosters and supports. But to limit democracy to its current achievements in those realms is, from a Jamesian perspective, tautological. Worse, it is tyrannical, firmly fixing the moral, social, economic, and political stations of democratic citizens so as to strip the label of all meaning.

Conclusion: Radical Realism

Here lies much of the power of James's regulative ideal of radical democracy. It permits the democrat to assert that the cure for the ills of democracy is indeed more democracy—just not *more of the same* democracy. In this sense it resembles the ideal of James's fellow pragmatist John Dewey, who insisted that the very concept of a theory of democracy implies "the need of returning to the idea itself, of clarifying and deepening our sense of its meaning to criticize and re-make its political manifestations" (Dewey 1927, 144). In Dewey's view, as in James's, there is no single means or set of means "by which a scattered, mobile and manifold public may so recognize itself as to define and express its interests" (Dewey 1927, 146; cf. Rogers 2009). If there were, we would have no need of democratic theory or even democracy. The experience of asserting, discussing, and peacefully negotiating diverse plans for associated life is exactly what fosters the "genuinely shared interest in the consequences of interdependent activities" which defines a democratic culture (Dewey 1927, 155). Democracies are rooted in democracy.

Equally powerful, however, is the supra-realistic strain in James's radical conception of democracy. Like his broader radical empiricism, it assumes a subject that in scope, variety, and novelty exceeds our apprehension, comprehension, and predictive capacity. The very existence of politics itself is explained by this impossibility of certainty. If certainty were possible, there would be no need for distinguishing and promoting legitimate versus illegitimate public claims and conflicts. Claims would simply be true or false, and those divining the truth would be bound, in the public interest, to ignore or suppress those too ignorant or sociopathic to grasp or accept it. James, by contrast, insisted that our claims on and about reality, however reasonable they seem at any given moment, are eternally subject to obviation or outright falsification by experience. This supra-realistic scepticism is particularly compelling in the case of public claims, which frequently demand choices and sacrifices so immediate as to make consensus—a potential proxy for certainty in some epistemic contexts—a practical impossibility. By disavowing certainty, Jamesian democrats can look instead to legitimacy in managing their unpostponable conflicts, responsibly eschewing correctness and agreement for reasonableness and provisional assent—presuming, of course, that the broadest possible community of inquiry is engaged in the process and invested in mitigating its failures.

After all, is that not what every empirical democratic community seeks, ideally, to embody in its institutions? James thought so. The embrace of uncertainty as both discipline and spur to action, as a call to "moral service" in "wider tribal ends," is "the civic genius" that James dubbed the "only bulwark" of democracy (ERM 1897, 72, 74). It must express itself in habits and institutions, and James had clear ideas about what some of those, at least in his day, should look like. But whatever form a democratic system takes, it must never contain or dispel the "inner mystery" of the ethical republic—the mystery of a world demanding both realism and radicalism from its human inhabitants (ERM 1897, 74). Everyone is "ready to be savage in *some* cause," James wrote in 1895, and we invite disaster if we fail to consider the concrete consequences of the savagery as well as the cause itself (CWJ 1895, 8.109). It is just as risky, however, to defer the ideal, and whatever "impotent row" against the system it demands, to a distant, impossible future free of uncertainty (CWJ 1903, 10.339). True democracy implies a contingent kind of progress, its standards subject to revision and achieved by the bold yet humble efforts of its collective creators and benefactors, "stumbling through every error till its institutions glow with justice and its customs shine with beauty"—and resuming their stumbling march whenever the glow fades and the shine dulls (ECR 1907, 109).

Notes

1. By contrast, Robert Talisse, in this volume, argues that James's description of goods as necessarily entailing demands that exclude other goods makes the goal of satisfying as much demand as possible non-sensical. This argument ignores James's view that a given good excludes *some* other goods, but nowhere close to *all* of them; as well as his view that there are qualitative differences among goods and varying levels of demand attached to them,

both of which must be ascertained through communication among the individuals who experience them.
2. This is not to say that intimate acquaintance guarantees deep moral understanding; when one or more parties view proximity as a threat rather than an opportunity, the reverse is often true.
3. Like Robert Dahl (1985), James suggested that more intimate and cooperative relations among workers and employers were as important to advancing democracy as a more equitable distribution of wealth; "blind to the internal significance of the other," James wrote, the laboring and capitalist classes could only regard one another as "dangerously gesticulating automata" (TTP 1899, 166).
4. Given space limitations, we can only gesture toward this topic and direct readers to major relevant texts. See Rorty (1982, 1989), Bernstein (1998, 2005, 2010), Habermas (2000, 2003), Misak (2000, 2008), McGilvray (2004), Talisse (2005).

Bibliography

Barber, Benjamin R. 1984. *Strong Democracy: Participatory Politics for a New Age*. Berkeley: University of California Press.
Barker, Derek W. M., Noëlle McAfee, and David W. McIvor, eds. 2012. *Democratizing Deliberation: A Political Theory Anthology*. Dayton, OH: Kettering Foundation.
Bernstein, Richard J. 1998. "Community in the Pragmatic Tradition." In *The Revival of Pragmatism: New Essays on Social Thought, Law, and Culture*, edited by Morris Dickstein. Durham, NC: Duke University Press.
Bernstein, Richard J. 2005. *The Abuse of Evil: The Corruption of Politics and Religion since 9/11*. Malden, MA: Polity Press.
Bernstein, Richard J. 2010. *The Pragmatic Turn*. Malden, MA: Polity Press.
Bordogna, Francesca. 2008. *William James at the Boundaries: Philosophy, Science, and the Geography of Knowledge*. Chicago: University of Chicago Press.
Christiano, T. D. 1996. *The Rule of the Many: Fundamental Issues in Democratic Theory*. Boulder, CO: Westview, Press.
Cohen, Joshua. 1989. "Deliberation and Democratic Legitimacy." In *The Good Polity: Normative Analysis of the State*, edited by Alan Hamlin and Phillip Pettit. New York: Blackwell.
Coon, Deborah J. 1996. "'One Moment in the World's Salvation': Anarchism and the Radicalization of William James." *Journal of American History* 83(1): 70–99.
Crick, Bernard. 1962. *In Defense of Politics*. Chicago: University of Chicago Press.
Cunningham, Frank. 2002. *Theories of Democracy: A Critical Introduction*. London: Routledge.
Dahl, Robert, 1985. *A Preface to Economic Democracy*. Berkeley: University of California Press.
Danisch, Robert. 2007. *Pragmatism, Democracy, and the Necessity of Rhetoric*. Columbia: University of South Carolina Press.
Dewey, John. 1916. *Democracy and Education: An Introduction to the Philosophy of Education*. New York: Macmillan.
Dewey, John. 1927. *The Public and Its Problems*. New York: Henry Holt and Company.
Dryzek, J. S. 2001. "Legitimacy and Economy in Deliberative Democracy." *Political Theory* 29: 651–669.
Evans, Sara M., and Harry C. Boyte. 1986. *Free Spaces: The Sources of Democratic Change in America*. Chicago: University of Chicago Press.

Feinstein, Howard M. 1984. *Becoming William James*. Ithaca, NY: Cornell University Press.
Fishkin, James S. 1991. *Democracy and Deliberation: New Directions for Democratic Reform*. New Haven, CT: Yale University Press.
Fung, Archon. 2012. "Continuous Institutional Innovation and the Pragmatic Conception of Democracy." *Polity* 44(4): 609–624.
Galston, William A. 2010. "Realism in Political Theory." *European Journal of Political Theory* 9(4): 385–411.
Gutmann, Amy, and Dennis F. Thompson. 1996. *Democracy and Disagreement*. Cambidge, MA: Belknap Press of Harvard University Press.
Habermas, Jürgen. 2000. "Richard Rorty's Pragmatic Turn." In Robert Brandom, ed. *Rorty and His Critics*. Oxford, UK: Oxford University Press. 31–55
Habermas, Jürgen. 2003. *Truth and Justification*. Trans. Barbara Fultner. Cambridge, MA: MIT Press.
Honig, Bonnie. 1993. *Political Theory and the Displacement of Politics*. Ithaca: Cornell University Press.
Jewett, Andrew. 2012. *Science, Democracy, and the American University: From the Civil War to the Cold War*. Cambridge, UK: Cambridge University Press.
Johnson, James, and Jack Knight. 2011. *The Priority of Democracy: The Political Consequences of Pragmatism*. Princeton, NJ: Princeton University Press.
Kaag, John. 2009. "A Call to Arms?—Militarism, Political Unity, and the Moral Equivalent of War." *The Pluralist* 4(2): 108–124.
Keane, John. 2009. *The Life and Death of Democracy*. New York: Simon & Schuster.
Kittlestrom, Amy. 2015. *The Religion of Democracy: Seven Liberals and the American Moral Tradition*. New York: Penguin Press.
Kloppenberg, James T. 1986. *Uncertain Victory: Social Democracy and Progressivism in European and American Thought, 1870–1920*. New York: Oxford University Press.
Kloppenberg, James T. "Pragmatism: An Old Name for Some New Ways of Thinking?" *Journal of American History* 83(1): 100–138.
Kuklick, Bruce. 1977. *The Rise of American Philosophy: Cambridge, Massachusetts, 1860–1930*. New Haven, CT: Yale University Press.
MacGilvray, Eric. 2004. *Reconstructing Public Reason*. Cambridge, MA: Harvard University Press.
Martin, Jane Roland. "Martial Virtues or Capital Vices? William James's Moral Equivalent of War Revisited." *Journal of Thought* 22(Fall 1987): 32–44.
Menand, Louis. 2001. *The Metaphysical Club: A Story of Ideas in America*. New York: Farrar, Straus, Giroux.
Miller, Joshua I. 1997. *Democratic Temperament: The Legacy of William James*. Lawrence: University Press of Kansas.
Misak, Cheryl. 2000. *Truth, Politics, Morality: Pragmatism and Deliberation*. London: Routledge.
Misak, Cheryl. 2008. "A Culture of Justification: The Pragmatist's Epistemic Argument for Democracy." *Episteme* 5(1) (Feburary): 94–105.
Myers, Gerald E. 1986. *William James: His Life and Thought*. New Haven, CT: Yale University Press.
Otto, M. C. 1943. "On a Certain Blindness in William James." *Ethics* 53(3): 184–191.
Pateman, Carole. 1970. *Participation and Democratic Theory*. Cambridge, UK: Cambridge University Press.

Perry, Ralph Barton. 1935. *The Thought and Character of William James*. 2 vols. Boston: Little, Brown, and Company.

Phillips, Anne. 1991. *Engendering Democracy*. University Park: Pennsylvania State University Press.

Purcell, Edward A. Jr. 1973. *The Crisis of Democratic Theory: Scientific Naturalism & the Problem of Value*. Lexington: University Press of Kentucky.

Putnam, Hilary. 1991. "A Reconsideration of Deweyan Democracy." In *Pragmatism in Law and Society*, edited by Michael Brint and William Weaver, 217–247. Boulder, CO: Westview.

Rawls, John. 1993. *Political Liberalism*. New York: Columbia University Press.

Ricci, David M. 1984. *The Tragedy of Political Science: Politics, Scholarship, and Democracy*. New Haven, CT: Yale University Press.

Rogers, Melvin L. 2009. *The Undiscovered Dewey: Religion, Morality, and the Ethos of Democracy*. New York: Columbia University Press.

Rorty, Richard. 1979. *Philosophy and the Mirror of Nature*. Princeton, NJ: Princeton University Press.

Rorty, Richard. 1982. *Consequences of Pragmatism: Essays, 1972–1980*. Minneapolis: University of Minnesota Press.

Rorty, Richard. 1989. *Contingency, Irony, and Solidarity*. Cambridge, UK: Cambridge University Press.

Roth, John K. 1969. *Freedom and the Moral Life: The Ethics of William James*. Philadelphia: Westminster Press.

Singer, Peter. 1973. *Democracy and Disobedience*. Oxford, UK: Clarendon Press.

Smith, Andrew F. 2007. "Communication and Conviction: A Jamesian Contribution to Deliberative Democracy." *Journal of Speculative Philosophy* 21(4): 259–274.

Stob, Paul. 2011. "Pragmatism, Experience, and William James's Politics of Blindess." *Philosophy and Rhetoric* 44(3): 227–249.

Talisse, Robert. 2005. *Democracy After Liberalism: Pragmatism and Deliberative Politics*. New York: Routledge.

Throntveit, Trygve. 2011. "William James's Ethical Republic." *Journal of the History of Ideas* 72.2: 255–277.

Throntveit, Trygve. 2014. *William James and the Quest for an Ethical Republic*. New York: Palgrave Macmillan.

Throntveit, Trygve. 2017. *Power without Victory: Woodrow Wilson and the American Internationalist Experiment*. Chicago: University of Chicago Press.

Throntveit, Trygve. 2018. "Civic Renewal: James's Moral Equivalent of War." *William James Studies* 14(1): 120–141.

Walzer, Michael. 1984. *Spheres of Justice: A Defense of Pluralism and Equality*. New York: Basic Books.

West, Cornel. 1989. *The American Evasion of Philosophy: A Genealogy of Pragmatism*. Madison: University of Wisconsin Press.

Williams, Bernard. 2005. *In the Beginning Was the Deed: Realism and Moralism in Political Argument*. Ed. Geoffrey Hawthorn. Princeton, NJ: Princeton University Press.

PART IV

MEANING, TRUTH, AND PRAGMATISM

CHAPTER 13

JAMES ON PERCEPTS, CONCEPTS, AND THE FUNCTION OF COGNITION

JAMES R. O'SHEA

CENTRAL to both James's earlier psychology and his later philosophical views was a recurring distinction between *percepts* and *concepts*. The distinction evolved and remained fundamental to his thinking throughout his career as he sought to come to grips with its fundamental nature and significance. In this chapter, I focus initially on James's early attempt to articulate the distinction in his 1885 article "The Function of Cognition." This will highlight a key problem to which James continued to return throughout his later philosophical work on the nature of our cognition, including in his famous "radical empiricist" metaphysics of "pure experience" around the turn of the century. We shall find that James grappled insightfully but ambivalently with the perceptual and conceptual dimensions of the "knowledge relation" or the "cognitive relation," as he called it—or what, following Franz Brentano, philosophers would later call our object-directed thought or *intentionality* more generally. Some philosophers have once again returned to James's work for crucial insights on this pivotal topic, while others continue to find certain aspects of his account to be problematic. What is beyond dispute is that James's inquiries in this domain were both innovative and of lasting significance.

PERCEPTS AND CONCEPTS IN "THE FUNCTION OF COGNITION" (1885)

Five years prior to the publication of his monumental two-volume work, *The Principles of Psychology* (1990), James published one of his most important early philosophical articles, "On the Function of Cognition" in the journal *Mind* (1885). Parts and revisions of this article would reappear in the *Principles*, and then two decades later the article would be reprinted, largely unchanged but with some important notes added by James, as Chapter 1 of his 1909 "sequel" to his 1907 *Pragmatism*, entitled *The Meaning of Truth* (MT 1909, 13–32).[1] In what follows, I want to suggest that this probing and insightful but in some respects perplexing early article is important for understanding both the continuities and the development of James's thought on the nature of knowledge and intentionality in general, and in particular on the nature of our most basic perceptual knowings.

In "The Function of Cognition," James made the terminological decision to use the word *feeling* as his general term "to designate generically all states of consciousness considered subjectively, or without respect to their possible function" (MT 1909, 13). Five years later in his *Principles*, James broadened this terminological choice to "feelings and thoughts," and in 1909 James added a sentence to his 1885 text at this point indicating that the reader "may substitute" for "feeling" the term *idea* taken in John Locke's broad sense, or else "state of consciousness" or "thought" (MT 1909, 13). James's terminological indecisiveness, I think, in part reflects his hesitation to use any *one* term (e.g., "feeling") to cover both percepts and concepts. In his final book, the unfinished and posthumously published *Some Problems of Philosophy* (1911), James explicitly devotes three chapters to exploring various aspects of his key distinction between percepts and concepts. On the terminological question, he there writes:

> In what follows I shall freely use synonyms for these two terms [i.e., for "percept" and "concept"]. "Idea," "thought," and "intellection" are synonymous with "concept." Instead of "percept" I shall often speak of "sensation," "feeling," "intuition," and sometimes of "sensible experience" or of the "immediate flow" of conscious life. Since Hegel's time what is simply perceived has been called the "immediate," while the "mediated" is synonymous with what is conceived. (SPP 1911, 48*n*)

(Hegel's distinction reflects his own critical reshaping of Kant's famous distinction between concepts as "mediate" cognitions and (sensory) intuitions as "immediate" or direct cognitions of the objects of our experience. What James is primarily concerned to investigate is this: What is the particular *functioning* of any mental state or state of consciousness such that it amounts to the cognition or intending of some object? The distinction between immediate cognition (feeling, sense perception, intuition) and mediated cognition (thought, conception) eventually emerges from his analysis, through several successive reformulations of an initial thesis that he proposes about the function of cognition as such.

The primary model for a feeling or thought that James begins with in the "Function" paper is what he describes as a certain qualitative mental state or feeling "q," "such as fragrance, pain, hardness" (MT 1909, 14). His concern is to investigate what gives "the feeling of q" the cognitive or "self-transcendent function" of referring to some reality other than itself. James's initial proposal is this: "For the feeling to be cognitive" there must be "*a reality outside of it* to correspond to its intrinsic quality q," and if the "reality *resemble* the feeling's quality *q*, I say that the feeling may be held by us *to be cognizant of that reality*" (MT 1909, 14, 15). James then develops and revises this initial thesis by considering what amount to four possible objections to it.

The first objection he entertains is reminiscent of one of Berkeley's fundamental objections to Locke: as James puts it, "How *can* a reality resemble a feeling?" James "evades" this particular objection by remarking that he will leave "it free to anyone to postulate as the reality whatever sort of thing he thinks *can* resemble a feeling—if not an outward thing, then another feeling like the first one" (MT 1909, 16). In both this and later works, James thus sometimes discusses the relation of cognition as something that obtains between items both of which are mental (for instance, between a concept and a sensory percept). But at other times, he discusses the relation in more realist or "dualist" terms (to use his term for this), as that between a mental state and a physical reality. His present inquiry, however, concerns the relation of cognition itself, not the nature of its relata, whatever they may be.

The first objection thereby evaded, James moves on to consider a second objection to his account of the simple conscious feeling, *q*, and its alleged cognitive functioning via resemblance. This time, the objection is from the side of those "relationist" philosophers, as he calls them—"those who claim to walk in the footprints of Kant and Hegel"—"to whom 'thought,' in the sense of a knowledge of relations, is the all in all of mental life; and who hold a merely feeling consciousness to be no better . . . than no consciousness at all" (MT 1909, 17). For reasons to be discussed, today we might add to the ranks of these Kantian and Hegelian "relationist" critics those who follow Wilfrid Sellars, on broadly Peircean, neo-pragmatist or later-Wittgensteinian grounds, in rejecting what Sellars famously characterized as the *myth of the given* (Sellars 1956). This is the myth, very roughly—it comes in different forms (cf. O'Shea 2007, ch. 5)—that there could be cases of basic or "direct" knowledge or cognition, or more broadly reference or intentionality in general, that do not presuppose that one possesses any *other*, inferentially related knowledge or conceptual abilities that one could call upon in support or justification of that (allegedly presuppositionless) direct or "immediate" cognition.

According to the Kantian–Hegelian or Sellarsian-pragmatist critics of the idea that any cognition is just "given" immediately or in isolation in the sense just stated, all representation or cognition of an object necessarily takes place within some wider "space of reasons," some normative network of connections.[2] This wider normative "space" can be inferential and logically structured, or (as Sellars 1981 extended the idea to animal cognition in general) it can be biologically natural and purposive due to evolutionary considerations. The point is that on this view the given occurrence, in order to be any kind of cognition or "knowing" at all, must in virtue of its embedding within such a logical or purposive "space" be evaluable normatively in terms of how it *ought* to function or "operate" (to use James's term) in relation to objects of the given kind and in relation to one's other mental states. On this view, words, for example, represent whatever they represent in virtue of how they are normally used in particular situations and inferences, that is, in virtue of shared (but, of course, malleable) norms of usage. Analogously, the active instincts, cognitive states, and organs of animals are what they are in virtue of how they *ought* to function in general, teleologically considered, for the sake of various adaptive ends, whether or not they successfully *do* so function in any particular case. Without this wider normative dimension of "ought-to-be"s or proper functioning, no sense of *mis*representation or *mal*functioning, and hence no sense of successful intentional representation or cognition, would be possible.

Something like the approach just outlined is how we might spell out today what James calls the Kantian–Hegelian "relationist" objection to his opening thesis that a "little feeling" having "its intrinsic quality q," considered in isolation "as an entirely subjective fact," could nonetheless have "a cognitive function" as long as there exists "*a reality outside of it*" that "*resemble[s]* the feeling's quality q." In such a case, against the Kantians and Hegelians, James insists, "I say that the feeling may be held by us *to be cognizant of that reality*" (MT 1909, 181).

This important second objection is not really, as we saw James overstate it three paragraphs back on the objectors' behalf, that a qualitative state of consciousness q by itself is "no consciousness at all." Rather, the real objection is that the feeling or sensory state q, considered either just by itself, or merely as resembling or being caused by other states or realities, is insufficient to account for q's being a cognitive state, a state of mind that succeeds in having the function of referring to or being *about* something other than itself. The Kantians, Hegelians, and Sellarsians argue, for example, that cognitive or intentional states—including our non-inferential or "direct" perceptual responses—presuppose the implicit ability to think and infer in terms of concepts (or proto-concepts), however crude.[3] By contrast, "our little supposed feeling," James admits, "knows q, if q be a reality, with a very minimum of knowledge. It neither dates nor locates it. It neither classes nor names it. It is, in short . . . a most dumb and helpless and useless kind of thing." It is this sort of characterization that raises the objections of the "relationists" Kant and Hegel, and (later) of the anti-givennist Sellarsians. As James himself asks on behalf of the objectors: if the feeling-state "can say nothing *about* itself or *about* anything else, by what right" can it be said to be cognizant of or refer to any reality other than itself?

At this point in the "Function" article, James now offers what he evidently takes to be an answer to that second objection: "In the innocent looking word 'about' lies the solution of this riddle" (MT 2009, 17). The solution that James develops here and repeats in the *Principles* is that "*there are two kinds of knowledge* broadly and practically distinguishable," namely, "*knowledge by acquaintance* and *knowledge about*" (PP 1890, 216–218; MT 1909, 17–19; James refers the distinction to Grote 1865, 60). To illustrate knowledge by acquaintance, he writes: "I know the color blue when I see it, and the flavor of a pear when I taste it . . . but *about* the inner nature of these facts or what makes them what they are, I can say nothing at all. . . . I cannot *describe* them, make a blind man guess what blue is like," and so on (PP 1890, 217).

However, just as James previously overstated what the "relationist" objectors were maintaining when he portrayed them as insisting that the conscious sensation or feeling q by itself is *nothing* ("a psychical zero," MT 2009, 17), whereas what the objectors really maintained was that q by itself is not sufficient for an instance of knowledge or intentionality, here, too, James overstates by portraying his objectors as insisting that for anyone to have a minimally adequate perceptual cognition or knowledge of the color blue, they must be able to have knowledge of its "inner nature," or of "what makes" blue what it is. But what the Kantian, Hegelian, and Sellarsian objectors in fact typically contend is that for anyone to have even the most simple perceptual knowledge of a blue object as such, or to know simply that something is blue—as opposed to someone's simply undergoing or having a sensation of the kind typically caused by blue objects, as a newborn infant might, for instance—is for one to have at least a minimal competence and (for human beings) a gradually acquired grip on the general sorts of situations in which one can and cannot reliably "tell the colors of things by looking," as it is put. Or again, our perceptual intentionality on this view arguably requires having standing cognitive resources sufficient to represent or to think of things as having their qualities independently of our perceiving them, and thus also (if only implicitly) as persisting over time, being located somewhere in space, being at least crudely but intelligibly re-identifiable, and so on.

In ordinary life, such conceptual abilities and presuppositions would typically find expression in one's minimal competence to say, or to think, in the right sorts of circumstances, that "this is blue," and to be able to respond with minimal competence to doubts that happen to arise ("Blue? In *this* lighting it only *seems* blue."). Such simple recognitional abilities would not require knowing the "inner nature" of blue, or being able to describe "what makes" blue the color it is. We need not at this point enter further into or pre-judge the ongoing debates concerning the "myth of the given," in this case in the form of James's appeal to an alleged knowledge of things by (entirely nonconceptual) "acquaintance," or by mere sensation or sensory consciousness alone, in order to make the present point that James has not here offered an adequate representation of the anti-givennist and anti-nonconceptual-knowledge-by-acquaintance considerations put forward by "those who claim to walk in the footprints of Kant and Hegel" (MT 2009, 17). In other contexts, as we shall see, James shows himself to be more keenly aware of the serious and complex issues that are at stake in his attempts to make the distinction he is attempting to make.

In introducing the distinction between knowledge by acquaintance with an object, as opposed to (conceptual) knowledge "about" that object, James contends that the former simply *gives us* the object as "the *what*" or the *it*, or *that*, and thus the subject or object *about* which judgments, predications, and descriptions can be made (MT 1909, 19; PP 1890, 217–218). So the first upshot, as James frames it in this 1885 piece, is the thesis that "all qualities of feeling, *so long as there is anything outside of them which they resemble, are feelings of* qualities of existence, and perceptions of outward fact" (MT 1909, 20). However, the further objections that James himself now goes on to consider in the article, in the process of revising that initial crude statement of his thesis (i.e., the thesis as to how a simple "feeling" is able to be "self-transcending" or cognizant of an object), serve to bring out his understanding of the complex problems that are involved in the seemingly obvious distinction between the direct, non-conceptual perceptual "acquaintance" with objects (or at least with "this" or "that"), and our conceptual thinking or knowledge "about" those objects (MT 1909, 20–32).

The third objection James now considers, then, is that a mere feeling or sensation q by itself gives no indication of *which* other resembling reality or object, q, it is "about" or "intends" or "knows," in cases in which there is more than one such candidate object. How does the feeling "show us which q it points to and knows" (MT 2009, 21)? It does so, James argues, in terms of the "*practical consequences*" that follow upon the feeling's operations or functions, perhaps initially in terms of further related "feelings" within the mind itself, but most importantly and ultimately in terms of leading to actions or operations that either directly or indirectly affect or "act upon" the particular reality or object q in a given *context* (MT 2009, 21–23). James's general thesis about cognition is thus refined so as to add a further necessary condition: "*The feeling of q knows whatever reality it resembles, and either directly or indirectly operates on*. If it resemble without operating, it is a dream; if it operate without resembling, it is an error" (M 2009, 24).

The last sentence suggests, for example, that if the mental image one has of a dog is not appropriately connected "operationally" by way of past and potential future actions that directly or indirectly affect or are affected by a given real dog, then no matter how much the mental image might in fact "resemble" that dog, it cannot refer to it or be "about" it. And conversely, James here suggests, no sensorial image or feeling-instance, q, can by itself succeed in being *about* any reality unless it not only operates upon but resembles that reality. His claim here is, for example, that the mental image of a black poodle is not of such a nature as to be able to perceptually represent, "intend," or make one directly acquainted with a white husky, no matter how systematically that image might operationally arise from and lead to a given white husky. Although James does not spell it out, the questions that might arise concerning this latter claim are such as to lead naturally to the final objection he considers, and thereby to the role of *concepts* in our knowledge "about" objects.

The fourth and final objection James thus considers is that his thesis, as so far developed, is such that

> the only cases to which it applies are *percepts*, and that the whole field of symbolic or conceptual thinking seems to elude its grasp. Where the reality is either a material thing or act ... I may both mirror it in my mind and operate upon it ... as soon as I perceive it. But there are many cognitions ... which neither mirror nor operate on their realities. (MT 2009, 26–27)

James explains that in "symbolic thought" we "intend" or know "particular realities, without having in our subjective consciousness any mind-stuff that resembles them even in a remote degree. We are instructed about them by language," where the words "are made intelligible by being referred to some reality that lies beyond the horizon of direct consciousness, and of which I am only aware as of a terminal *more* existing in a certain direction to which the words might lead but do not lead yet" (MT 2009, 27). Thus in a last revision of his thesis, we come finally to James's full 1885 distinction between percepts and concepts (or "conceptual feeling," which basically means "concept" in the following passage given the all-inclusive use that James has given "feeling" in the 1885 article):

> *A percept knows whatever reality it directly or indirectly operates on and resembles; a conceptual feeling, or thought, knows a reality, whenever it actually or potentially terminates in a percept that operates on or resembles that reality, or is otherwise connected with it or with its context.* The latter percept may be either sensation or sensorial idea; and when I say the thought must *terminate* in such a percept, I mean that it must ultimately be capable of leading up thereto—by way of practical experience, if the terminal feeling be a sensation; by the way of logical or habitual suggestion, if it be only an image in the mind. (MT 2009, 27–28)

Consider again the mental image that one might have of a dog. This percept, when functioning as the sense perception of (or immediate "acquaintance" with) a given dog, will typically arise directly, as we have seen, in a particular environmental context involving some practical engagement or other with the dog that it resembles or "mirrors," and to which the percept thereby refers. The same "sensorial idea" or image might also function as a memory of the dog in its context. A *concept* of the dog, on the other hand, is for instance either the same sensorial idea, or more likely a particular use or occurrence of the word *dog* in speech or thought (e.g., "My dog is in the neighbor's yard."), *functioning as* a "symbolic thought" or sign of the dog "by being referred to some reality that lies beyond the horizon of direct consciousness" (MT 2009, 27). Depending on the context, the word or symbol *dog* so functions in my thinking and in my actions as to "terminate," for example, in either my memory-idea of having very recently seen my dog in my neighbor's yard, or in my subsequent verification of this reality by direct sense perception (i.e., by looking and seeing), or in a train of inferential reasoning that leads me from my neighbor's firm promise to look after the dog, to my forming an image or a thought of my dog as in her yard.

But how exactly do words, images, and other symbols function so as to have these referential and classificatory capacities? In the next section, I will briefly clarify what I take to be James's important and innovative views on the cognitive role or "function" of concepts in our experience of objects, properties, and kinds. I will then turn in the concluding section to some critical reflections on James's contrast between percepts and concepts, both as it has arisen earlier in this chapter and also pointing ahead to James's later philosophical treatments of the distinction.

JAMES ON THE NATURE AND FUNCTIONING OF CONCEPTS IN HUMAN COGNITION

When James focuses on explaining the nature of *conceptual* cognition in his various works throughout his career (e.g., in PP 1890, ch. IX and XII; P 1907, Lec. V; or SPP 1911, ch.IV–VI), he offers an account in terms of which concepts, as embodied or realized in words or in various other mental and physical media, serve to abstract and "substitute for" various particular aspects of the perceptual "flux," by functioning as "signs" of further realities also exhibiting that "same" aspect. That is, as a result of naturally and socially acquired habits of association and action, such words or other experienced items function as symbols or "substitute" in our thinking by exhibiting, as James variously puts it, a "felt tendency" to "lead to" further instances of that aspect or kind in other experienced particulars within the ongoing "stream" or flux of experience. The flux or "chaos" of our immediate sensory experience, as James ubiquitously describes it throughout his works, is itself continuously changing. Although in ordinary life we are primarily aware of the relatively stable objects for which we have concepts and which we can thus re-identify or meet again as the "same" thing or quality, James argues that the actual chaotic or flux-like nature of all our immediate sensory experience can be known indirectly to *be* such a flux by scientific experiments and by philosophical arguments, as well as more directly by careful phenomenology.[4] The *sameness* of the various objects, qualities, and kinds that we thus re-experience and re-identify over time (tables, colors, molecules, people, et al.) is itself strictly correlative to—both partly a product of, and partly revealed by—the activity of conceptualization itself. All of the various "worlds" or aspects of reality in which we take any practical or theoretical *interest*—the worlds of mathematics, ethics, common sense, theoretical physics, and so on—are the objects and products of our conceptual thinking in this sense.

By using the phrase "objects *and products*" of our concepts, I am attempting to capture a delicate balancing act of James's own with respect to fundamental questions concerning the objectivity or mind-independence of empirical reality. On the one hand, there is James's professed *epistemological realism* or "dualism," that is, his view that the empirical objects of the physical world exist as they are independently of our knowledge of them. This is what James assumes from the perspective of both his psychology and his famous pragmatism, while leaving various further metaphysical questions open as important philosophical domains of inquiry and hypothesis (e.g., MT 2009, 9, 102–106, 115, 144–145). His own "radical empiricist" metaphysics is intended to be consistent with this epistemological realism, too, as we shall see in the final section.

On the other hand, we have James's interest-based, teleological view of the nature of all cognition or mentality, which stresses that our ever-present practice of conceptualizing the flux of experience into objects, qualities, and kinds is fundamentally designed to suit our "purpose, that of *naming* the thing" to serve our particular interests (including our more "theoretical" interests in prediction and in systematicity); while meanwhile "the reality overflows these purposes at every pore." Our conceptual classifications, according to James, consequently "characterize *us* more than they characterize the thing," but "we are so stuck in our prejudices" that we take the kinds that our concepts thus sort out in order to suit our interests as if they were the real "essences" of the realities thereby known. We take it, for example, that to conceive ordinary objects according to their common kinds is "the only true way," but in fact, James contends, those ways "are no truer ways of conceiving them than any others; they are only more important ways, more frequently serviceable ways" (PP 1890, 961–962). James's pragmatism stresses these aspects of his thinking.

But again, in this very same context, James explains this purpose-relative conception of our concepts of objects in terms that are consistent with epistemological realism. For example, he indicates that while in principle "this world *might* be a world in which all things differed," or "a world in which no concrete thing remained of the same kind long, but all objects were in a flux," the fact is that "our world is no such world," but rather one in which the world's kinds themselves have proven by ongoing experience (so far) to be suited to our conceptualization:

> [Ours] is a very peculiar world, and plays right into logic's hands. *Some* of the things, at least, which it contains are of the same kind as other things; *some* of them remain always of the kind of which they once were.... *Which* things these latter things are we learn by experience in the strict sense of the word. (PP 1890, 1246–1247; cf. 961–962)

A "conceptual scheme is a sort of sieve in which we try to gather up the world's contents," says James (PP 1890, 455). What James thus takes his teleological view of cognition to imply is neither anti-realism (as we would put it today) nor relativism, but rather a pluralism of conceptual schemes that is nonetheless supposed to be consistent with realism.

In this regard, it should be noted that James argues in strong and explicit terms (e.g., in *Pragmatism* 1907, Lec. V) that there are multiple, even *conflicting* or contradictory conceptual schemes each of which nonetheless successfully reveals different aspects of reality in their different vocabularies and by differing standards, with no likelihood and no demonstrable requirement, for James, that these plural, reality-revealing schemes must in the end be reducible to one, final, all-inclusive conceptual framework. For James, as he puts it, "the only real truth about the world, apart from particular purposes, is the *total* truth" (PP 1890, 961–962*n*). That is, the overall truth would be the sum of all the various particular, purposive schemes and experiences that will have proven their worth within the totality of human experience on the whole and in the long run, without any justifiable requirement ("intellectualist" philosophers notwithstanding) that there must in the end be a single, over-arching and unifying logical systematization of reality in terms of concepts. I will not pause on this occasion to explore further or to assess James's uniquely pluralist realism, though I have examined the internal tensions in this pluralist view of "the *total* truth" elsewhere.[5] As should become clear, however, it is James's complex but elusive distinction between percepts and concepts that lies at the very heart of his metaphysical pluralism.

As far as the nature of our specifically *conceptual* intentionality is concerned, James's discussions throughout his works exhibit two primary ways he has of describing the various mental and physical cognitive relations that obtain between the embodied concepts, symbols, or signs that constitute our conceptual thinking, on the one hand, and the corresponding objects or ideal realities they are "about," on the other. He describes them as *feelings of relation*, and thus in terms of various phenomenologically accessible *felt tendencies* (or "directions," "fringes," or "halos") in our thinking. And he also describes them in terms of the behavioral and associational *functions* (or "leadings-to," "operations," or "experienceable workings") that have as their end or purpose actually "terminating" in a percept or image of that object or reality. James does not distinguish sharply between these two ways of attempting to describe the relation of intentionality or cognition, that is, in terms of a *feeling* of "direction" or in terms of functional "leadings" to the object. But whatever problems or challenges there might be for James's account in this respect,[6] his investigations arguably have the merit of attempting to explain substantively what such a relation of knowledge or intentionality might actually consist in, or pragmatically be "known-as" (to use a favorite phrase of James's), as opposed to having recourse to an "*actus purus* of Thought, Intellect, or Reason, all written with capitals" (PP 1890, 238). Later in his 1904 "radical empiricist" article, "A World of Pure Experience," James nicely sums up his view of the nature and importance of our conceptual cognitions this way:

> The towering importance for human life of this [conceptual] kind of knowing lies in the fact that an experience that knows another can figure as its representative, not in any quasi-miraculous "epistemological" sense, but in the definite practical sense of being its substitute in various operations, sometimes physical and sometimes mental, which lead us to its associates and results. (ERE 1904, 31)

In this way we see that James, both early and late in his career, sought to explain our conceptual cognition functionally or operationally in a way that was intended to rely only upon entirely non-mysterious psychological (associational, inferential) and physical causal relations. In such practical terms, James thus attempted to describe the seemingly mysterious capacity by which our particular ideas and words, so to speak, "reach out" or "mentally point" or "transcend" themselves in our thought and knowledge of distant objects existing beyond our immediate perceptual consciousness. James offered this in a way that was, for example, explicitly designed to eschew the posit of a special mode of "intentional inexistence" for the objects or contents of our thoughts and other mental or "intentional acts." The latter was a conception of our mentality having deep roots in medieval and Cartesian philosophy, a conception of which James was well aware from his reading of Brentano, and one which has subsequently exerted a powerful influence in both phenomenology and analytic philosophy.[7] While as noted earlier there are indeed aspects of James's thought that have important affinities with later phenomenological thinkers, I believe that in relation to his views on the nature and functioning of our thought and cognition James was attempting to stake out different ground.[8]

However, despite his firm recognition of the importance and indispensability for us of our conceptual thinking, James also argues in different ways across his corpus, both as a scientific psychologist and as a metaphysical philosopher, that our conceptual thinking and our language not only omit, but also falsify and mislead us about certain fundamental truths concerning both mind and reality. In such cases, or at such a level, "language works against our perception of the truth" (PP 1890, 234); or as James puts it in his last work, *Some Problems of Philosophy*: "concepts are secondary formations, inadequate and only ministerial; ... they falsify as well as omit, and make the flux impossible to understand" (SPP 1911, 45). And yet he also stresses that it is by means of our *conceptualized* "*whats*" that "we apperceive all our *thises* [i.e., percepts]": "Percepts and concepts interpenetrate ... Neither, taken alone, knows reality in its completeness. We need them both, as we need both our legs to walk with" (SPP 1911, 34).

In the final section, I want to reflect on some of the issues that have arisen in both of the earlier sections concerning James's account of the complex interaction between our concepts and our percepts in our cognitive relationship to the world.

Some Reflections on James on the "Interpenetration" of Percepts and Concepts

As we have seen, James holds that there "are two ways of knowing things, knowing them immediately or intuitively" in our percepts, "and knowing them conceptually or representatively" by means of some "outer chain of physical or mental intermediaries connecting thought and thing. *To know an object* [conceptually] *is to lead to it through a context which the world supplies,*" or *would* supply (MT 2009, 33, 34–35).[9] In the first section we saw James in 1885 begin with an isolated quality-feeling or percept, q, and then consider, in light of a series of objections, what is involved in our taking q to be cognizant of or to "intend" some other reality. James went on to refine and modify his basic percept/concept distinction in his later works, as we have already seen.[10] But I think that certain pivotal issues anticipated earlier in the first section continued to present challenges for James, as indeed they continue to present challenges for us today; and these issues continued to rise to the surface in James's later philosophical works, despite important changes in his view.

Common to James's various accounts of our cognition or "knowings" of objects, we have, on the one hand, the demand for immediacy or directness in our perceptual cognition of reality; and on the other hand, in relation to both perception and conceptual thinking, we have James's innovative and detailed attempts to account for what he calls the *cognitive relation* between our conscious mental states and the objects known (whether the latter be interpreted as another mental state, or, as I will assume for ease of exposition, a physical object). It is in his ongoing attempts to account for our percepts as immediate cognitions of reality that I think James struggled to find a satisfactory view, though with insight and fully aware of the difficulties involved.

In the early "Function" article, we saw James object to the views of the "relationist" Kantian and Hegelian philosophers. What he objected to in particular is "this everlasting slip, slip, slip, of direct acquaintance into [conceptual] knowledge-*about*, until at last nothing is left about which the knowledge can be supposed to obtain," in which case "does not all 'significance' depart from the situation?" (MT 1909, 19). The problem raised by the Kantians, Hegelians, and Sellarsians, however, is that when one attempts to strip away all of the conceptual or proto-conceptual thinkings about what one is immediately experiencing in perception, it is—not surprisingly—unclear what one is left with. In the "Function" article, James attempted to strip all the way back, suggesting that a given intrinsic feeling-quality, q, only *accidentally* stands in a cognitive relation to any "resembling" external reality to which it is related. As far as the feeling q is concerned, the "self-transcendent function of cognition," in relation to some other resembling reality q that it knows, "is accidental ... and falls outside of its being" (MT 2009, 20). As we saw, this leads James to consider the various "*practical consequences*" (MT 2009, 22), including conceptual "leadings" to the (thereby signified or "represented") object, q, that in practice show us *which* object we are knowing, and tell us (so to speak) *what* it is.

However, *before* he thus adds the functional dimensions of operative action and conceptual representation, James still seemed to want the isolated qualitative feeling q itself to be in some sense intrinsically directed:

> A feeling feels as a gun shoots. If there be nothing to be felt or hit, they discharge themselves *ins blaue hinein* [i.e., "into the blue"]. If, however, something starts up opposite them, they no longer simply shoot or feel, they hit and know. (MT 2009, 20)

But by James's own reckoning two pages later, as we saw, the only way to have a feeling q that is *about* anything in particular is to bring in the "functional" (or "relational") dimensions of practice and conceptual signification that constitute the feeling as a feeling *about* the given thing or kind: "as a matter of fact, every actual feeling *does* show us, quite as flagrantly as the gun, which q it points to; and practically in concrete cases the matter is decided by" the practical "leadings to" the object, by means of the "definitely experienceable workings" that James then goes on to describe (MT 2009, 22, 23). The idea that the isolated feeling q first—that is, by its own nature or considered by itself—"feels as a gun shoots," and only needs to then find some objects to determine which sorts of things the feeling *feels about* (or shoots at), should be incoherent by James's own reckoning in the rest of the "Function" article. For as we saw earlier, James immediately goes on to draw out the need for "practical consequences" and conceptual determination if intentional reference to any particular objects is to be possible in the first place. But as far as the cognition of any reality is concerned, the latter requirement on intentional reference of practical and conceptual determination is effectively to concede to the Kantian–Sellarsian "relationists" their "slip, slip, slip of direct acquaintance into knowledge-*about*," that is, into conceptual-pragmatic "leadings" to the particular kind of object that is thus "felt" or perceived (or "shot").

Let us suppose for the sake of argument the correctness of something similar to James's account of conceptual representation (or "knowing in absence") as discussed in the previous section, that is, as a systematic functional "leading to" the object. On this Jamesean functionalist view, in conceptual or "representative knowledge there is no special inner mystery, but only an outer chain of physical or mental intermediaries"—reflected systematically, for instance, in our standing logical and causal inferences, and in our actions and reactions—"connecting thought and thing. *To know an object is here to lead to it through a context which the world supplies*" (EPh 1895, 74; in MT 2009, 34). In the case of percepts, that is, the direct perceptual knowledge of some reality ("knowing in presence"), the difficulty confronting James is to explain, without introducing any mysterious "intentional *inexistence*" of the object "in" the mind, both (a) the "*cognitive relation*" between the knowing mental state and the object known, and (b) the *immediacy* or un-mediated nature of such direct "acquaintance" with the object in perception. So far, I have suggested that in the 1885 "Function" article James fails to give an intelligible account of direct perceptual cognition, except to the extent that he in effect brings conceptual representation into the story, which thus appears to concede to the Kantians, Hegelians, and Sellarsians that sensory intuitions without concepts are blind (cf. Kant 1787/1997, A51/B75).

The latter philosophers hold that concepts (or proto-concepts) are already involved in constituting anything that can properly amount to the cognition of an object in direct perceptual experience. As noted in the first section, the key for such "relationist" philosophers is to understand how our conceptualized perceptions are in one sense unmediated—they are non-inferential, directly evoked by the object as qualitatively experienced—and yet also the same mental state is conceptually mediated, as reflected in the "space" of inferences that constitutes such conceptual content. I'll put my cards on the table: I think these philosophers are correct, and that James ought to have taken his own view that "concepts and percepts interpenetrate" the further step just outlined, as indeed his own writings sometimes suggest. In this I follow the Kantians, Hegelians, and Sellarsians (and I think, Peirce, Wittgenstein, and many neo-pragmatists, too) in rejecting the Myth of the Given, which I think can be done without sacrificing either the richness or the cognitive functioning of our qualitative experiences.

Other pragmatists disagree.[11] Many philosophers both past and present, and from many different philosophical perspectives, would argue that we ought to follow James's own primary tendencies on this matter of "immediate knowledge," rather than follow "the relationists" with their "slip, slip, slip, of direct acquaintance into knowledge-*about*." As usual, James himself went on to pursue several lines of thinking on the matter that succeeded in anticipating some of the most influential views about immediate perceptual knowledge held by later philosophers. Here I can only add just a few brief hints as to what lay ahead in James's own rich philosophical work after 1890, adding a few critical reservations.

James's 1895 article, "The Knowing of Things Together" (cf. note 7 in this chapter) represented an important transitional stage in his thinking. In particular, it represented a step toward James's later "radical empiricist" metaphysics of "pure experience" (cf. Klein 2015), which eventually came to be characterized as a "neutral monism" stretching from Ernst Mach, through James, to Bertrand Russell and beyond.[12] In that article, James indicates that he was mistaken to hold as he did in his *Principles of Psychology* that the science of psychology can and should refrain from introducing any metaphysical views concerning "the knowledge relation." In particular, he now introduces the idea, key to his later doctrine of pure experience, that *to know immediately or intuitively is for mental content and object to be numerically identical*. Thus in the following passage James asks us to consider "the case of immediate or intuitive acquaintance with an object," and to "let the object be the white paper before our eyes":

> [I]f our own private vision of the paper be considered, . . . then the paper seen and the seeing of it are only two names for one indivisible fact which, properly named, is the datum, the phenomenon, or the experience. The paper is in the mind and the mind is around the paper, because paper and mind are only two names that are given later to the one experience, when, taken in a larger world of which it forms a part, its connections are traced in different directions. [WJ's footnote: "What is meant by this is that 'the experience' can be referred to either of two great associative systems, that of the experiencer's mental history, or that of the experienced facts of the world. Of both of these systems it forms part."] *To know immediately, then, or intuitively, is for mental content and object to be identical.* (EPh 1895, 74–75; MT 1909, 36)

But what does *that* mean? It turns out not to be easy to say.

For if we consider this immediate phenomenon, datum, or (pure) experience to be the experience of a table (a physical object) "before our eyes," as James put it—as surely we do throughout the "natural realism" of ordinary life—then once again we are already considering the experience as conceptualized within some wider inferential or "associative" context of spatio-temporal and causal relations. And similar questions arise in relation to James's further remarks in this context, that is, if we consider these "ultimate data" of experience as falling within one's own psychological history; or if we consider "someone else's experience" of the same object; or if we consider the "hidden molecules" that make up the objects we experience. James stresses that all of these are instances of conceptualized knowledge, in which "the things known" are "absent experiences," "a case of [non-present] tigers in India again," not a case of our "states of immediate acquaintance" or "ultimate data" themselves (EPh 1895, 75; MT 1909, 35).

James both here and in his later *Essays in Radical Empiricism* accordingly tends to describe these immediate, neutral, pure experiences in terms that simply express various *intrinsic quality-contents*, as we might characterize them. For example, what we have immediate acquaintance with or direct perception of is not the physical white paper itself, it seems, but "the whiteness, smoothness, or squareness of this paper" (EPh 1895, 75; MT 1909, 35), out of which either my perceiving of the physical paper, or the physical paper-object itself, are functionally built up and conceptually represented despite their "absence" to my strictly "present" conscious "datum." But then *what is* this strictly present datum, this "presentation, the experience, the *that* in short (for until we have decided [i.e., conceptually] *what* it is it must be a mere *that*)" (ERE 1904, 8)? And is *it* (or is the *that*) somehow, as James indicates, itself "subjective and objective both at once" (ERE 1904, 7); or is *it* perhaps, in its own actuality, *neither*, as James sometimes also indicates: "*That* pen, virtually both objective and subjective, is at its own moment actually and intrinsically neither" (ERE 1905, 64)? I can subsequently functionally classify (e.g., conceptually represent) a given pure quality-datum *as mine*, that is, as taking place in my consciousness, or you can classify it as in *yours*, if it is felt or represented by you *as* yours: "But it is felt as neither *by itself*, but only when 'owned' by our two several remembering experiences, just as one undivided estate is owned by several heirs" (ERE 1905, 66). By themselves the quality-contents or pure experiences are like the original isolated feeling, q, with which James started in the 1885 "On the Function of Cognition" article, only now q "*by itself*" is not assumed to belong to any state of consciousness per se.

Much ingenuity was subsequently applied by Russell and other philosophers in attempting to explain both (a) how the "neutral datum" should itself be characterized or understood, and (b) how we are to "construct" out of the "neutral" or "pure" basis the shared worlds of psychology, common sense, physics, and other minds. Sometimes neutral monism in various thinkers (and, at times, in James) has seemed clearly to slide into a form of phenomenalism, with actual and possible sensations or perhaps "sense-data" serving as the basis for the constructions of the various ordinary and scientific worlds. At other times, however, philosophers have continued to attempt to read James's account of pure experience as a direct perceptual realism or "natural realism" (see, e.g., Putnam 1990).[13] It will be worth concluding with a brief look at Banks's (2014) helpful attempt to reconstruct and defend the neutral monism or "Realistic Empiricism" that he finds in Mach, James, and Russell, a metaphysics that on Banks's account is a *physical realism* as well.

James himself is clear on the goal: "To be radical, an empiricism must [not] admit into its constructions any element that is not directly experienced" (ERE 1904, 22). But again, when one looks to the details of the sympathetic reconstructions of James's neutral pure experiences interpreted as a form of direct realism, puzzles continue to arise. For example, when Banks in his substantial chapter on "William James's Direct Realism: A Reconstruction" explains in neutral monist terms how "James thinks that when I am actually in the room, I perceive the room and the book themselves as they *really* exist, and *not* indirectly through intermediary images or ideas," Banks inevitably appeals to a "neutral bit of pure experience [which] can be taken as real merely by taking it to be the complex of colored blobs, squiggles, and flashes that it is." And "taken in itself like this, it is neither a physical object, nor is it a sensation. *It is just exactly the neutral collection of blobs and flashes it seems to be*" (Banks 2014, 92; italics added). But in response to this, the "relationist," anti-Givennist philosophers will object (or ought to object) that when one sees a room full of books, nothing visually "seems" to one to be, or directly visually presents itself as, a "collection of blobs, squiggles, and flashes," whether "neutral" or otherwise.

There are of course classical phenomenalist and sense-datum accounts that encourage precisely that slide, but for good reason that is not supposed to be Banks' directly realist James. Neither does careful phenomenology reveal the squiggles, flashes, and blobs. It is, of course, open to a scientific *theory* of perception to hypothesize that in our ordinary perspectival perception of a room full of books, various non-conceptual arrays of sensory "information" are involved in the process, and which help to explain how the books *do* appear to us as they do in the given situation. (This was in fact Sellars's own move, for instance, in his explanatory postulation of qualitatively rich non-conceptual sensory representations, while firmly rejecting the myth of the sensory-epistemic Given). But I can see no plausible way of attempting to scrape away from my direct experience of the room the concepts (or proto-conceptual "animal" representations) of *books, room,* and so on, which are what make it possible for there even to *seem to me* to be those objects in the relevant sense in the first place, and which represent or present the objects that I *do* directly perceive in the experience. "A bunch of blobs and flashes, even if they look exactly like Memorial Hall . . ." (Banks 2014, 93)—here I want to say that we are already inevitably on the slide to implausible phenomenalist or quasi-phenomenalist dead-ends, however much Banks and (in his better aspects) James wanted to avoid them.

The better route, I suggest, would be to give up the quixotic quest for the impossibly "neutral" immediate given, and to follow the more pragmatic-functionalist side of James into a more thorough embrace of his own views on the ubiquitous "interpenetration" of concepts and percepts. However, in his final book published during his lifetime, *A Pluralistic Universe* (1909), James heroically dug in further and not only granted but prioritized and celebrated the ineffability of our immediate non-conceptual intuitions of reality, which he there argues provide the deepest of metaphysical insights into the nature of things. But even if we cannot follow James cheerfully into that particular ineffable region of his thinking,[14] I hope it has been clear throughout that James's innovative and evolving views on the nature of our perceptual and conceptual cognitions represented an exceptionally fertile source of enduring insights.[15]

NOTES

1. Page references to "On the Function of Cognition" will be to its 1909 reprinting as chapter one of *The Meaning of Truth* (MT), "The Function of Cognition," but the reader should bear in mind the earlier 1885 date of its initial publication.
2. It is crucial to note that Sellars is not rejecting as a myth the idea that there is such a thing as direct or "immediate," non-inferential perceptual knowledge of physical objects. In fact, his own view of perceptual cognition is just such a view. One key to avoiding the myth, for Sellars, is to see that our non-inferential perceptual responses to objects are directly *about* those objects, not about any mediating sensory processes that might be involved (and for Sellars the latter *are* importantly involved, but they are recognized as such on theoretical or scientific rather than epistemological grounds). On Sellars's view, our perceptual "takings," like Kant's perceptual cognitions, are *directly about* the objects in terms of which such perceptions are constitutively *conceptualized* (or "proto-conceptualized," in the case of Sellars [1981] on animal cognition). However, as involving concepts, such perceptual knowings for Sellars will presuppose the acquisition or possession of wider conceptual abilities (the "space of reasons") in a way that is inconsistent with the sort of immediate, presuppositionless knowledge of "the given" that is assumed in various guises by both traditional empiricists and rationalists.
3. Again, in the case of non-human animals, their cognitive states (e.g., "animal beliefs," perceptual tracking abilities, instinctual drives) are on some views thought to involve representational functions or "proto-concepts" that play roles analogous to concepts, thanks to

their natural biological "proper functioning" due ultimately to time-extended evolutionary processes (cf. O'Shea 2014, §IV).

4. See, for example, the various considerations that James adduces at PP (1890, 224–230), in defence of his thesis that "*Thought*," understood in James's experiential sense (i.e., as the "stream of consciousness"), "*is in Constant Change.*"

5. For my elaboration and assessment of James's conceptual scheme pluralism, see O'Shea 2000. In what I have said here I take myself to agree in large part with Steven Levine's recent discussion of this issue in Levine (2013, e.g., 125–128), and in particular with his account of how James can intelligibly hold that "while knowers partially create the reality that they come to know, they are nonetheless constrained by this reality in coming to know it" (2013, 125; Klein 2015, 163–164, also raises this problematic issue). However, I am not as convinced as Levine seems to be that James's views on pluralism and on the matters I am discussing in this chapter are unproblematic as far as the "myth of the given" is concerned, for reasons to be noted briefly in the next section (and in O'Shea 2000 and 2014). See Levine (2013, 128–130) for his contention that James does not fall afoul of that myth.

6. I have offered my own analysis of the tensions in James's views on intentionality in O'Shea (2014); and for further helpful and sympathetic investigations of James's views in this area, see especially Jackman (1998). See also Steven Levine's chapter in this volume for the important phenomenological aspects of James's approach to human cognition and action.

7. As James puts it as only he can (here referring to our present knowledge of the distant tigers in India): "A great mystery is usually made of this peculiar presence in absence; and the scholastic philosophy, which is only common sense grown pedantic, would explain it as a peculiar kind of existence, called *intentional inexistence*, of the tigers in our mind. At the very least, people would say that what we mean by knowing the tigers is mentally *pointing* towards them as we sit here" (MT 1909, 33–34). This passage is from James's "The Tigers in India," which is itself an excerpt from his 1895 "The Knowing of Things Together" published in the *Psychological Review*, which was then published in full in James EPh (1895, 71–89). More on the latter article in the next section. As far as the term "*intentional inexistence*" is concerned, it had been used by Brentano in his *Psychologie* of 1874 (Brentano 1973, 88–89), a work that James cites favorably in his own *Principles of Psychology*, but not in relation to the notion of intentional inexistence.

8. For further thoughts on the significance of James's account of intentionality from this broad perspective, including his rejection of "intentional existence" and his attempt to offer a new alternative in broadly functional and causal terms, see for example Banks (2014) and O'Shea (2014). Banks attempts to reconstruct and defend James's account of "pure experience" as a *neutral monism* with strong affinities to those of Ernst Mach and Bertrand Russell, whereas I stress the kinship of James's views with a line of broadly functionalist and inferentialist thinking that stretches from Kant, Peirce, and C. I. Lewis to the later Wittgenstein and Sellars.

9. James of course recognizes that most of our conceptual thinkings "intend" or refer to their non-present objects—for example, to the tigers existing in India—without *actually* leading us up to them, and are supported rather by our counterfactual readiness to act and infer in appropriate ways: supported, for example, by our "rejection of a jaguar, if that beast were shown us as a tiger," or by "our ability to utter all sorts of propositions which don't contradict other propositions that are true of the real tigers" (MT 1909, 34).

10. In reprinting "On the Function of Cognition" article twenty-four years later for *The Meaning of Truth* (1909), James added a "Note" listing six assertions that he has continued to hold, but also identifying four "defects" in the earlier account (MT 1909, 32).

11. See Scott Aikin (2009) for a vigorous and helpful presentation and defense of arguments that can be marshalled *against* the idea that pragmatists are in danger of falling victim to the alleged "Myth of the Given." Aikin concludes: "It seems clear that pragmatism's anti-foundationalism needn't itself entail a rejection of the doctrine of the Given, as the doctrine is clearly implicated in inquiry as pragmatists consider it. The Given ain't a myth, and that's not just something that pragmatists can live with, it's something they *must*" (Aikin 2009, 25). For a contrasting view, I provide a sympathetic account of Sellars's attack on the Given—both what I call the "epistemic given" and the more basic "categorial given" (or the cognitive given)—in O'Shea (2007, ch. 5).

12. "Neutral" insofar as the fundamental elements of the system—"pure experiences" for James, "sensations" or "percepts" for Mach and Russell—are held to be themselves neither mental or physical, but to serve as the neutral, immediately given data of experience out of which the domains of the mental and the physical are constructed (roughly, according to the laws of psychology and physics, respectively). Strictly speaking, in the 1895 article, James places his view within "the idealistic philosophy ... that began with Berkeley," holding that "things have no other nature than thoughts have, and we know of no things that are not given to somebody's experience" (EPh 1895, 72). Later, in "A World of Pure Experience," however, it is for James "impossible to subscribe to the idealism of the English school. Radical empiricism has, in fact, more affinities with natural realism than with the views of Berkeley or of Mill" (ERE 1904, 37). For a recent historical overview, reconstruction, and defense of neutral monism, see Banks (2014). For a sympathetic treatment of James's neutral monism from a Deweyan and cognitive scientific perspective, see Rockwell (2013), and in relation to recent radical embodied cognitive science, see Silberstein and Chemero (2015). For an overview of both traditional (Mach, James, Russell) and more recent neutral monist views, see Stubenberg (2016). An extended treatment of James's metaphysics of pure experience with a view to how it relates to the vital role in his philosophy of social and religious ideas is provided in Lamberth (1999). The collection of papers in Alter and Nagasawa (2015) shows what a live contender "neutral monism" has once again become in recent debates in metaphysics and the philosophy of mind, some versions of which might help to illuminate James's own radical empiricism.

13. Putnam (1990, 249–250), as well as Lamberth (1999), rightly stresses the importance of the fact that by the time of his later radical empiricism James now recognizes non-perceived but (presently) merely *conceived* objects, properties, universals, and kinds, as "a co-ordinate realm of reality," that is, as "pure experiences" along with the domain of our percepts (ERE 1904, 9–14; SPP 1911, 32–36, 40–41, 55–58; PU 1909, 122; MT 1909, 32 "Note"). But I cannot see that this helps with the particular issues I have raised. Putnam himself concedes in relation to this particular aspect of James's metaphysics of pure experience that a "metaphysics in which reality consists of intentional objects which are 'natures' of bits of 'pure experience' is, I confess, too rich for my battered digestive system" (1990, 250). (Putnam's digestive system was subject to frequent changes over time, however).

14. Cf. O'Shea (2000, 2014). But see Jackman 1999 for a clear and sympathetic account of James's so-called rejection of logic in *A Pluralistic Universe*. And see Levine (2013, 123–124) for an equally clear and helpful defense of James against my charge (e.g., in O'Shea 2000) that James in these later views falls afoul of the Myth of the Given. I am not convinced, however, and James's views in PU and earlier works on ineffable metaphysical intuitions

still strike me as a paradigm case of one form of the Myth, roughly the givennist idea that something can allegedly be *immediately reality-revealing* without it or its object being available for effable conceptualization. Unfortunately, I must leave an adequate response to Levine's defense to another occasion.

15. I am grateful to Alex Klein, Steven Levine, and Tony Chemero for their comments and suggestions.

Bibliography

Aikin, Scott F. 2009. "Pragmatism, Experience, and the Given." *Human Affairs* 19, 19–27.
Alter, Torin, and Yujin Nagasawa, eds. 2015. *Consciousness in the Physical World: Perspectives on Russellian Monism*. Oxford: Oxford University Press.
Banks, Erik C. 2014. *The Realistic Empiricism of Mach, James, and Russell: Neutral Monism Reconceived*. Cambridge: Cambridge University Press.
Brentano, Franz. 1874/1973. *Psychology from an Empirical Standpoint*. London: Routledge.
Grote, John. 1865. *Exploratio Philosophica: Rough Notes on Modern Intellectual Science*. Cambridge: Deighton, Bell, and Company.
Jackman, Henry. 1998. "James' Pragmatic Account of Intentionality and Truth." *Transactions of the C.S Peirce Society* 34: 155–181.
Jackman, Henry. 1999. "James's naturalistic account of concepts and his 'rejection of logic.'" Meeting of the Society for the Advancement of American Philosophy. Available at http://www.yorku.ca/hjackman/papers/james-logic.html.
Kant, Immanuel. 1787/1997. *Critique of Pure Reason*. Paul Guyer and Allen W. Wood, tr. Cambridge: Cambridge University Press.
Klein, Alexander. 2015. "Hatfield on American Critical Realism." *HOPOS: The Journal of the International Society for the History of Philosophy of Science* 5: 154–166.
Lamberth, David C. 1999. *William James and the Metaphysics of Experience*. Cambridge: Cambridge University Press.
Levine, Steven 2013. "Does James Have a Place for Objectivity? A Response to Misak." *European Journal of Pragmatism and American Philosophy* 5(2). http://ejpap.revues.org/551.
Levine, Steven. forthcoming. "The *Principles of Psychology*: The Phenomenological Reading.".
O'Shea, James R. 2000. "Sources of Pluralism in William James." In *Pluralism: The Philosophy and Politics of Diversity*, edited by Maria Baghramian and Attracta Ingram, 17–43. London: Routledge.
O'Shea, James R. 2007. *Wilfrid Sellars: Naturalism with a Normative Turn*. Cambridge: Wiley/Polity Press.
O'Shea, James R. 2014. "A Tension in Pragmatist and Neo-Pragmatist Conceptions of Meaning and Experience." *European Journal of Pragmatism and American Philosophy* 6(2), December 2014. http://ejpap.revues.org/297.
Putnam, Hilary. 1990. "James's Theory of Perception." In *Realism with a Human Face*, edited by James Conant, 232–251. Cambridge, MA: Harvard University Press.
Rockwell, Teed. 2013. "Representation and Radical Empiricism." *Intellectica* 60: 219–240.
Sellars, Wilfrid. 1956. "Empiricism and the Philosophy of Mind." In *Minnesota Studies in the Philosophy of Science*, vol. 1, edited by Herbert Feigl and Michael Scriven, 253–329. Minneapolis: University of Minnesota Press.
Sellars, Wilfrid. 1981. "Mental Events." *Philosophical Studies* 39: 325–345.

Silberstein, Michael, and Anthony Chemero. 2015. "Extending Neutral Monism to the Hard Problem." *Journal of Consciousness Studies* 22: 181–194.

Stubenberg, Leopold. 2016. "Neutral Monism." *The Stanford Encyclopedia of Philosophy* (Winter 2016 Edition), Edward N. Zalta. ed. https://plato.stanford.edu/cgi-bin/encyclopedia/archinfo.cgi?entry=neutral-monism.

CHAPTER 14

JAMES, INTENTIONALITY, AND ANALYSIS

HENRY JACKMAN

Introduction

THROUGHOUT his career, William James was gripped by the problem of how our thoughts come to be about the world, and the question of intentionality (sometimes referred to by him as the relation of "knowing" or as the "truth processes") was never far from his mind.[1] His concern with this problem was expressed particularly vividly in his early (1885) review of Josiah Royce's *The Religious Aspect of Philosophy*:[2]

> The more one thinks, the more one feels that there is a real puzzle here. Turn and twist as we will, we are caught in a tight trap. Although we cannot help believing that our thoughts *do* mean realities and are true or false of them, we cannot for the life of us ascertain how they *can* mean them. If thought be one thing and reality another, by what pincers, from out of all the realities, does the thought pick out the special one it intends to know? (ECR 1885, 386)

Later, in his *The Principles of Psychology* (1890), he claimed that "the *relation of knowing* is the most mysterious thing in the world. If we ask how one thing *can* know another we are led into the heart of *Erkenntnisstheorie* and metaphysics" (PP 1890, 212). This early interest continued throughout his life and (in a letter to his brother) James complained that his *Pragmatism* (1907) was widely misunderstood because people failed to appreciate that "it really grew up from a more subtle and delicate theoretic analysis of the function of knowing, than previous philosophers have been willing to make."[3]

Nevertheless, in spite of the importance he placed on it, James's account of knowing is typically, if unjustly, neglected. This is at least in part because coming up with a sympathetic reading of James's account requires appreciating that James's approach to analyzing a phenomenon is very different from that which most contemporary philosophers have found natural.

Prototypes and Philosophical Analysis

In particular, philosophers and non-philosophers alike often understand phenomena in terms of the concepts by which they are designated, and think of these concepts in "definitional" terms.[4] They thus picture an adequate analysis of a phenomenon as providing necessary and sufficient conditions for the corresponding concept's satisfaction. Consequently, they assume that one can criticize another's analysis of a phenomenon by showing that the resulting conceptual criteria includes things that the associated term doesn't apply to, or fails to include things to which it does.

If one treats James as trying to provide such an analysis of intentionality (that is to say, one takes him to be trying to provide necessary and sufficient conditions for a thought's being about an object), his account will seem not only rather slapdash, but also subject to embarrassingly obvious counterexamples. Fortunately for James, however, he was not aiming for this sort of analysis of intentionality. In particular, he was not aiming to provide any sort of *conceptual analysis* of the phenomenon. Rather than trying to capture the *essence* of the category by providing necessary and sufficient conditions for *every* case of a thought's being about an object, James starts his analysis with the core/prototypical/paradigm cases, and works out from these, supplementing this analysis of the core with additional remarks about how the less prototypical cases could be understood in terms of their relations to (and similarities with) the paradigm.[5] If one analyzes something in this way, marginal cases do not count as "counterexamples" simply because they lack properties that are prominent in the characterization of the prototypical ones. Their lack of these properties merely explains why they are marginal rather than prototypical. James is quite explicit about the prototypical nature of the sorts of cases he focuses on, claiming, for instance, to be interested in the "originals and prototypes of the truth-process" and that other types of intentional relations can be understood in terms of their relation to the prototypes.[6]

James was not, then, attempting to provide anything like a traditional "definition" of what it was for a thought to be about something else. James was aware that he was occasionally read as attempting to provide such definitions, and he insisted that criticisms based on that assumption (such as Russell's) were unfair. As he puts it:

> A mathematical term, such as *a, c, x, y,* sin, log, is self-sufficient, and terms of this sort, once equated, can be substituted for one another in endless series without error. Mr. Russell . . . seem(s) to think that in our mouth also such terms as "meaning," "truth," "belief," "object," definition" are self-sufficient with no context of varying relations that might be further asked about. What a word means is expressed by its definition, isn't it? The definition claims to be exact and adequate, doesn't it? Then it can

be substituted for the word—since the two are identical—can't it? Then two words with the same definition can be substituted for one another, *n'est-ce pas*? Likewise two definitions of the same word, *nicht war*, etc., till it will be indeed strange if you can't convict someone of self-contradiction and absurdity. (MT 1909, 148)

Definitions are fine for the terms of artificial languages of math and logic, but when providing an analysis of the "natural" language terms such as "meaning," "truth," and "belief," one should not expect such neatness.

It is important to stress that his pursuing this kind of analysis needn't represent any lack of rigor on James's part. Prototype-driven analyses are not reserved for those too lazy to roll up their sleeves and work out the required sets of necessary and sufficient conditions. Studies of human categorization provide strong evidence that many, if not most, of our categories simply *can't* be adequately captured by sets of necessary and sufficient conditions.[7] Prototype-centered accounts may thus be the only way to provide empirically adequate analyses of our categories, since there simply may be *no* set of properties that all and only the things that fall within a category possess.

Since this last point about categorization is fairly crucial for this reading of James, I will digress a bit on it here.

The mechanism by which a prototype-centered category gets its extension is very different from that traditionally associated with concepts. According to the traditional story, a concept's extension was made up by all and only those objects that possessed the properties that were characteristic of the concept. Every object either does, or does not, fall within the extension of the concept, and no instance of a concept is any more central to it than any other. To take an (all too familiar) example, if a "bachelor" is defined as an "unmarried adult male," then everything either would, or would not, be a bachelor in virtue of their having (or lacking) the properties of being an adult male and being unmarried (and no one who had both those properties would be a better or worse example of a bachelor than any other).

Things are very different when categories are understood as displaying prototype effects, and the following example from traditional Dyirbal (an aboriginal language of Australia) should make this clear.[8]

In Dyirbal classification every object in the world falls into one of four categories, *bayi, balan, balam, bala*, and speaking Dyirbal correctly requires using the right classifier before each object. The members of the four categories include the following:

1. *Bayi*: men, kangaroos, possums, bats, most snakes, most fishes, some birds, most insects, the moon, storms, rainbows, boomerangs, some spears, etc.
2. *Balan*: women, bandicoots, dogs, platypus, echidna, some snakes, some fishes, most birds, fireflies, scorpions, crickets, the hairy mary grub, anything connected with water or fire, sun and stars, shields, some spears, some trees, etc.
3. *Balam*: all edible fruit and plants that bear them, tubers, ferns, honey, cigarettes, wine, cake.
4. *Bala*: parts of the body, meat, bees, wend, yamsticks, some spears, most trees, grass, mud, stones, noises and language, etc.

The project of trying to find necessary and sufficient conditions for membership in these four groups is hopeless because their membership is determined very differently from what the classical picture of categories presupposes. Instead of being determined by the possession of a fixed group of properties, class membership in Dyirbal has the following characteristics.

Centrality: Categories have certain central members. For *Bayi*, the central members are (human) males and animals. (Willy wagtails and the moon are less central members.) For *Balan* the central members are (human) females, water, fire, and fighting. (Stinging vines, gar fish, and the hairy mary grub are less central members.) For *Balam*, the basic members are non-flesh food. In each case, the central member will be "better" and "less problematic" examples than the others, and this will be reflected in the speed, ease, and certainty to which people apply the category in various cases. (We see a similar phenomenon with our own use of words such as "bird," "table," or "game.")

Chaining: Complex categories are structured by chaining. Central members of a category are linked to other less central members, which are linked to still others, and so on. These "chains" often incorporate specific knowledge (including certain idealized models of the world, such as knowledge of mythology) which overrides general knowledge in such cases. Birds, for instance, even though they are animals, fall into category 2 (rather than category 1) because, in Dyirbal mythology, they house the spirits of dead females. Other more mundane knowledge can also affect the chains. For example, women are mythologically linked to the sun (while men are linked to the moon, which thus falls into category 1), which is linked to sunburn, which is linked to the hairy mary grub (the grub produces a painful rash that feels much like sunburn). It is by virtue of such a chain that the hairy mary grub is thought to be in the same category as women. The chains are mythologically motivated (women to the sun), causally motivated (the sun to sunburn), and experientially motivated (sunburn to the hairy mary grub). In none of these cases are common objective properties being picked out by both instances of the term. There is nothing "objectively" "masculine" about the moon or "feminine" about the sun (the gender roles of the two heavenly bodies are reversed in cultures with different mythologies—as with Apollo and Artemis in Greek mythology), and the extension of the term to the hairy mary grub relies on contingent facts about our own embodiment (a creature who didn't have a sunburn-like reaction to its contact would see no connection between the grub and the sun).

No Common Properties: Categories on the whole need not be defined by common properties. There is no reason to believe that the Dyirbal find anything in common between women and hairy mary grubs. Nor do they assume, so far as is known, that there is anything feminine about fire or danger, or anything fiery or dangerous about women. The lack of common properties is most clearly seen with the fourth category, *Bala*, which seems to simply include everything not in the other classes.

Dyirbal classification may be an unusually vivid case, but these basic phenomena of centrality, chaining, and lack of common properties are widespread, and they are reflected in James's account of intentionality. James's implicit assumption that an adequate analysis of intentionality should have such a prototypical structure is very plausible. For James, cases in which we actually see and/or manipulate the objects of our thought provide the prototype of "knowing," and other cases are understood in terms of their relation to the prototype even if they lack properties that are crucial to the prototypical cases.[9]

Both the classically definitional and the prototype-centered analyses of categories can, in some sense, be understood as trying to get at what is "essential" to a category/phenomenon, but each brings with it a different conception of what "being essential" involves. In the former case, the essential properties must be shared by all members of the category. In the latter, the essential properties need not be possessed by everything which falls under the term, but the intelligibility of the category depends upon the essential cases because the peripheral cases are understood as members of the category in virtue of their relation to the more basic ones.

James's Basic Account of Intentionality: Immediate and Mediate Knowing

James wanted to provide a naturalistic explanation of how one piece of "flat content . . . [with] no self-transcendency about it" came to be "about" something else:[10]

> We are not to ask, "How is self-transcendence possible?" We are only to ask, "How comes it that common sense has assigned a number of cases in which it is assumed not only to be possible but actual? And what are the marks used by common sense to distinguish those cases from the rest?" In short, our inquiry is a chapter in descriptive psychology—hardly anything more.[11] (MT 1909, 14)

James's method was to look at the clearest cases in which we *treat* our thoughts as being about the world and provide an analysis of what is going on in them. His account of "knowing" thus has a strong descriptive/phenomenological component, and so it is perhaps not surprising that the story he ends up with has a clear prototype structure.

James thought, plausibly enough, that the prototypical cases of our thoughts being about objects in the world involved their "operating" on those objects (either by our *perceiving* them, *handling* them, or both), and so his discussion of "operation," especially in its perceptual form, provides the foundation for his account.

While the material from *Essays in Radical Empiricism* (published in 1912, but primarily collecting material from 1904 to 1905) focus on perception as the core case from which the other cases of intentionality are understood, it is noteworthy that his earlier work on the topic, particularly in "The Function of Cognition" (1885) and *The Principles of Psychology* (1890), also put considerable emphasis on our ideas "operating" on (or "affecting" (MT 1909, 32)) the realities we take them to be about.[12]

> Now by what tests does the psychologist decide whether the state of mind he is studying is a bit of knowledge, or only a subjective fact not referring to anything outside itself?
>
> He uses the tests we all practically use. If the state of mind *resembles* his own idea of a certain reality; or if without resembling his idea of it, it seems to imply that reality and refer to it by operating upon it through the bodily organs; or even if it resembles and operates on some other reality that implies, and leads up to, and terminates in, the first one,—in either or all of these cases the psychologist admits that the state of mind takes cognizance, directly or remotely, distinctly or vaguely, truly or falsely, of the reality's nature and position in the world. (PP 1890, 213.)

Or, as he put it in "The Function of Cognition": "*The feeling of q knows whatever reality it resembles, and either directly or indirectly operates on.* If it resemble without operating, it is a dream; if it operate without resembling, it is an error" (MT 1909, 26).[13]

James was happy enough with this basic account for him to republish "The Function of Cognition" in his *The Meaning of Truth* (1909), and while he appended a note to the reprinted version to add that the earlier paper suffered from a "possibly undue prominence given to resembling" (MT 1909, 32), James never takes back this emphasis on the importance of operating on objects.[14]

Nevertheless, for James, like many others, the clearest cases of the knowing relation can be found in perception, where we are directly acquainted with the object of our thoughts.[15] Nevertheless, it is instructive to compare James and Russell (or at least the Russell of *The Problems of Philosophy* [1912]) on this matter. While both philosophers assigned a primary role to what we were "acquainted" with in (among other things) perception, the sense in which acquaintance is the "foundation" for other types of "mediated" knowing is very different in James than it is in Russell.[16] In particular, while Russell contrasted immediate "knowledge by acquaintance" with the more mediate "knowledge by description," acquaintance was "foundational" for Russell in the very robust sense that "knowledge by description" could be *reduced* to logical compounds of items known by acquaintance.[17] By contrast, acquaintance was, for James, foundational only in the sense that other types of knowing were ultimately *understood in terms* of it. Our "knowledge about" an object was not, however, *reducible* to what we knew by acquaintance. "Knowledge about" objects involves "causal/external" rather than "logical/conceptual" relations to what was known immediately.

In particular, James extends the paradigm of perceptual reference by arguing that one's ideas can know objects outside of one's perceptual field by *leading* one through a series of experiences that *terminate* in an actual percept of the object referred to. For instance, James's "Memorial Hall" idea may just be a dim image in his mind, but if this image allows James to go to the hall and recognize it, then "we may freely say that [he] had the terminal object 'in mind' from the outset, even altho *at* the outset nothing was there in [him] but a flat piece of substantive experience like any other, with no self-transcendency about it" (ERE 1904, 29). Our ideas about objects outside of our perceptual field need not *share* all the properties of the core cases of perception, but they bear a "chaining" relation to them:

they are ideas that lead one to the actual percept. Indeed, such cases can be considered the "prototype" of *conceptual* reference for James. The prototypical case of having "knowledge about" an object involves being led to direct acquaintance with that object. As he puts it, "Following our mental image of a house along the cow-path, we actually come to see the house; we get the image's full verification. *Such simply and fully verified leadings are certainly the originals and prototypes of the truth-process*" (P 1907, 99).

James's initial account of the intentionality of our thoughts, in which our ideas are about objects because they lead us into perceptual contact with (or some other type of operation on) those objects, faces a number of problems if viewed as a conceptual analysis of the form: *P's idea x is about object O if and only if x leads P to come into perceptual contact with or otherwise "operate" on O*. Among such problems are:

1. It suggests that one can't have thoughts about objects until one has *actually* tracked them down. For instance, my "Paris-thought" isn't actually *of* Paris until I actually make it to the city, and so if I never visit Paris, I will have never actually thought about it.
2. It ignores the "social" character of language and cognition, and suggests that I couldn't have thoughts about things that I couldn't recognize.
3. It would seem to make reference to unobservable entities impossible.
4. By making non-perceptual cognition dependent upon how we track things down in the future, it suggests that we couldn't have thoughts about the past.
5. It suggests that I could never *mis-identify* an object, since whatever object I picked out would become the one I "had in mind."

However, all of these problems are manageable once we realize that James typically keeps his discussion close to the core of the subject. While these would be problem cases if intentionality were simply *equated with* the prototype, they can be incorporated into James's account since they can still be *understood in terms of* the prototype. As James puts it, "Experience offers indeed other forms of truth-process, but they are all conceivable as being verifications arrested, multiplied or substituted one for another."[18]

Virtual Knowing and the Potentially Verified

Starting with the first of the issues just listed, an apparent (and immediate) problem with James's account of intentionality is that while it allows that my idea of Memorial Hall counts as having always referred to the hall once it *actually* leads me to it, common sense suggests that our idea refers to the hall *before* this happens, or even if I *never* track the building down. Indeed, it might seem that a large and significant portion of my thought is outside even James's initial extension of the prototype to non-perceptual cases. I can have thoughts about Barack Obama, Bucharest, or the Basilica of St. John the Baptist, but none of these ideas may ever reach the stage of "face-to-face" verification characteristic of the prototype.

James responds to this worry by arguing that in cases in which we haven't actually tracked down the purported objects of our thoughts, we can still be understood as "virtually" referring to them.

> The key to this difficulty lies in the distinction between knowing as verified and completed, and the same knowing as in transit and on its way. To recur to the Memorial Hall example lately used, it is only when our idea of the hall has actually terminated in the percept that we know "for certain" that from the beginning it was truly cognitive of *that*. Until established by the end of the process, its quality of knowing that, or indeed of knowing anything, could still be doubted; and yet the knowing really was there, as the result now shows. We were *virtual* knowers of the hall long before we were certified to have been its actual knowers, by the percept's retroactive validating power. Just as we are "mortal" all the time, by reason of the virtuality of the inevitable event which will make it so when it shall have come. (ERE 1904, 34; MT 1909, 67.)

But, of course, there are not only cases in which we have not tracked down the objects of our thoughts *yet*, there are also many cases in which the relevant objects are *never* tracked down. Our eventual tracking down of objects lacks the inevitability of our eventual demise, so the comparison to "mortal" may not seem entirely apt. James recognizes this, and he goes on to claim that "the immensely greater part of all our knowing never gets beyond this virtual stage" (ERE 1904, 34; MT 1909, 67). James assumes that his "transcendentalist" opponent will object that "by first making knowledge to consist in external relations" and "then confessing that nine-tenths of the time these are not actually but virtually there," he has "knocked the solid bottom out of the whole business, and palmed off a substitute of knowledge for the genuine thing" (ERE 1904, 35; MT 1909, 68). James, however, argues that as long as we *can* find the object of our thoughts, we need not always *actually* do so, and "where potentiality counts as actuality in so many other cases, one does not see why it may not so count here" (MT 1909, 91). After all, as James stressed, as long as this "virtual knowing" could be cashed out whenever it needs to be, there would be no *practical* difference between a theory which says that we are virtually referring to objects most of the time and one that claims that we are *completely* doing so. After all, what practical difference would it make if we were to "completely" rather than "virtually" refer to these items?[19] Since virtual knowing plays the same practical role as "completed" knowing in most cases, it is justifiable to extend "knowing-talk" to these cases that remain virtual. There is nothing about our practice of "about" talk that is dependent upon knowing being "non-virtual" all (or even most) of the time.

Even if most of our knowledge were virtual, these "virtual" cases would still be understood in terms of their relation to the non-virtual prototypes. It is precisely in virtue of their potential to become like the prototype that the ideas in question count as "knowing" the objects that they do,[20] so a given dog-idea is "cognitive" of a real dog because "the actual tissue of experience is constituted [so that] the idea *is capable of leading into a chain of other experiences . . . which go from next to next and terminate at last in vivid sense-perceptions of a jumping, barking, hairy body.*"[21] Virtual knowing is still a type of knowing, and with it, James's account of intentionality expands its focus from the most central cases of *verification* to the broader notion of *verifiability*. The verification-processes is still, as James puts it, "essential," but this means only that we can't understand verifiability independently of verification.

Of course, one might still wonder why James can't give a more traditional definition of aboutness by making a direct appeal to potential verifiability, and, indeed, he may seem to be doing just this when he claims that "*A percept knows whatever reality it directly or indirectly operates on and resembles; a conceptual feeling, or thought, knows a reality, whenever it actually or potentially terminates in a percept that operates on or resembles that reality, or is otherwise connected with it or with its context*" (MT 1909, 27–28).[22] This sort of disjunction is a useful way to summarize the accounts, but such rough presentations aren't definitions, and would still be open to other counterexamples (say, about the past and unobservables) that the full account will cover.

THE SOCIAL CHARACTER OF LANGUAGE

James is frequently criticized for taking an overly "individualistic" approach to philosophical questions, so it is not surprising that he has also been accused of missing out on the *social* character of language and cognition.[23] Indeed, it is easy to see how one might get such an impression from James's writings, since the prototypical cases of intentionality (at least for James) *are* individualistic. However, even if the presentation of acquaintance and the prototypical cases of "knowledge about" objects is focused exclusively on the individual's perceptions and operations, the analysis of the more extended cases of non-perceptual intentionality can still do much to accommodate the social aspects of language and cognition.

In the core cases that James focuses on, we are always able to, on our own, *recognize* what we are ultimately referring to. Consequently, if one takes all the characteristics of the core to be essential, it can seem that in order to refer to something, one must at least be able to locate or recognize it on one's own. If an idea is *unable* to lead one to a particular object, then it isn't cognitive of it. James highlights this issue himself in his discussion of Memorial Hall.

> For instance, if you ask me what hall I mean by my image, and I can tell you nothing; or if I fail to point or lead you towards the Harvard Delta; or if, being led by you, I am uncertain whether the Hall I see be what I had in mind or not; you would rightly deny that I had "meant" that particular hall at all, even though my mental image might to some degree have resembled it. The resemblance would count in that case as coincidental merely, for all sorts of things of a kind resemble one another in this

world without being held for that reason to take cognizance of one another. (ERE 1904, 28; MT 1909, 62.)

James here seems to be suggesting that, if the individual himself couldn't locate or recognize the object, he couldn't have thoughts about it. This would be, however, unduly restrictive since we frequently credit people with thoughts about objects or types of things which, if left entirely to their own devices, they would be unable to locate or identify.[24] After all, I certainly think that *I* can refer to Memorial Hall, but I wouldn't be able to recognize it if I were taken to Boston and asked to pick it out from a group of buildings standing in front of me.

Nevertheless, James can accommodate such cases, since it is crucial to his account that knowing an object involves being led to it "through a context which the world provides."[25] Being able to *actually* locate the objects of our thoughts does not require being able to distinguish them from all others in a context-independent way. My ability to locate, say, my copy of Henry James's *Washington Square* is based largely on the fact that it is the only copy of the novel to be found on the bookshelf in my living room, rather than my knowledge of perceptual features that distinguish it from all other copies of that book.[26] Our being embedded in particular contexts thus turns out to be essential to our ability to locate the particular objects of our thoughts. However, once we admit that our context is important in this way, there seems little reason to think that such an account can't include our *social* context as well. After all, I couldn't find Memorial Hall on my own, but given my social context, I would have no trouble locating the building if I were placed in Cambridge. I would only need to find a map of the city, or ask people around me until I found someone who was able to lead me to it. Indeed, even in the passage about failing to identify Memorial Hall quoted earlier, James allows that the knowing function does not require our being able to find the hall on our own, rather, it counts us as knowing the hall if we can "recognize" it after being led to it by our peers (ERE 1904, 28; MT 1909, 62).[27] It is only if, after getting such help, that we still insist that we aren't sure that the hall in front of us is what we had in mind, that James entertains doubts that we were really thinking about it.

I refer to what I do by many of my terms because, given my social context, the people I rely on would lead me to some objects and not others. If I were in a different social context, many of my ideas would be cognitive of different things.[28] How a term is used in one's social surrounding can thus affect what one's own ideas are about. I am treated as referring to Memorial Hall by "Memorial Hall" even if I cannot uniquely pick it out myself, because I can rely on others to do so for me. As long as *somebody* can be relied upon to know where the building actually is, the system works. Such a picture of our "trading truths" with others brings to mind, of course, what is today frequently referred to as the "division of linguistic labor,"[29] and James stresses this "cooperative" aspect of language use in the following:

> The untrammeled flowing of the leading-process, its general freedom from clash and contradiction, passes for its indirect verification; but all roads lead to Rome, and in

the end and eventually, all true processes must lead to the face of directly verifying sensible experience somewhere, which somebody's ideas have copied. (P 1907, 103)

The "division of labor" metaphor is especially apt for James, and his claim that "truth lives... on a credit system" (P 1907, 100) applies equally well to intentionality.

This division of labor thus accounts for how social usage can help determine what we are talking about when we are ambivalent or uncertain about a term's conditions of application, and James can allow for such social contributions even when our dispositions are not indeterminate (as when I'm initially disposed to pick out Elliot Hall as "Memorial Hall"). If an idea refers to the object that brings its workings to a satisfactory terminus, then social factors can affect what we are talking about to the extent that they affect which objects we ultimately find satisfactory. The "satisfaction of hearing you corroborate me"[30] is part of what we often look for in a successful case of knowing, and so one of the desiderata for a successful case of knowing is to get one's conversational partners to agree that what one has picked out is indeed what one was talking about. What might otherwise "work" for the individual may turn out not to be satisfactory because it would involve picking out as the referent of his term something different from what his compatriots would.

Why such corroboration should be important to us is clear. First of all, we want our utterances to be understood by others. Furthermore, the utterances of others are much more likely to be useful to us as sources of information about the world if we mean what they do by the same words. If we go our own way with the meanings of our words, we can lose our grip on a tremendous amount of information that would otherwise be available. James stresses this in a passage that highlights the importance of treating our language as a shared, temporally extended, practice:

> All human thinking gets discursified; we exchange ideas; we lend and borrow verifications, get them from one another by means of social intercourse. All truth thus gets verbally built out, stored up, and made available for everyone. Hence, we must *talk* consistently just as we must *think* consistently: for both in talk and in thought we deal with kinds. Names are arbitrary, but once understood they must be kept to. We mustn't now call Abel "Cain" or Cain "Abel". If we do, we ungear ourselves from the whole book of Genesis, and from all its connections with the universe of speech and fact down to the present time. We throw ourselves out of whatever truth that entire system of speech and fact may embody. (P 1907, 102–103)

James here spells out the pragmatic justification for the idea that each speaker typically understands themselves as a "reference preserving link" (Evans 1973) in a continuous chain of use for the terms in a shared language. Objects which don't lie at the beginning of such chains tend to be "intellectually less satisfying" than those that do because they frustrate this presupposition and disconnect us from the testimony of others.

Once again, the basic explanation is individualistic, as in the core cases, but our desire to refer to what other people do by their words allows reference in non-core cases to be socially determined. If my conception of sofas, or arthritis, were idiosyncratic, I might still refer to what my fellows did by these terms because my intention to use my words in line with social usage may ultimately make the socially determined referents more "satisfactory" for me.

Unobservables

This brings us to the case of "unobservables," those items which we could not, perhaps even in principle, have perceptual contact with (quarks, another's thoughts, etc.). Such cases obviously cause at least prima facie problems for an account of intentionality that grounds so much in perceptual contact with the objects referred to. Of course, those who play up James's "instrumentalism" might suggest that he would simply bite the bullet here and deny that we can refer to unobservables. This would, however, be a mistake. Even if one can read James as denying the existence of, say, the theoretical posits of the sciences of his day, that sort of instrumentalism isn't grounded in general worries about unobservables, and it would be much harder to read him making similar claims about, for instance, the mental states of others.[31]

However, if James doesn't deny that such reference to unobservables is possible, then how can he explain it? First of all, one should also note that while reference to unobservables is more problematic for some of the exclusively perception-grounded talk about knowing in the *Essays on Radical Empiricism*, it is less of a worry for the earlier, and more recognizably pragmatist, account in *The Principles of Psychology* and "The Function of Cognition," which stresses the importance of our thoughts "operating" on objects in a non-perceptual sense as well. This commitment to "operation" is never given up by James, so even in his "A world of pure experience," we find him insisting that:

> Where direct acquaintance is lacking, "knowledge about" is the next best thing, and an acquaintance with what actually lies about the object, and is most closely related to it, puts such knowledge within our grasp. Ether-waves and your anger, for example, are things in which my thoughts will never *perceptually* terminate but my concepts of them lead me to their very brink, to the chromatic fringes and to the hurtful words and deeds which are their really next effects. (MT 1909, 69; ERE 1904, 36)

Even if we can't directly observe sub-atomic particles, we can manipulate them in ways that allow our thoughts to be understood as "cognitive" of them. Much the same could be said of the thoughts of others. We can't perceive them directly, but we do feel their effects (those "hurtful words and deeds") and can operate on them as well. We don't just hear our interlocutor's angry words, but we are also (if all goes well) capable of acting in ways that can reduce their anger, change their beliefs, etc. It's not just a matter of being *close* to the unobservable, it's a matter of being able to affect its behavior and tailor our behavior to it.

Furthermore, even when we start with the "perceptual" rather than "operational" paradigm, we can see how James's account could be extended to such cases. Examples of virtual knowing discussed earlier have involved a thought's being about something even though no perceptual contact is ever *actually* made, and by focusing on some of the phenomenal features of such cases, particularly how the virtually known typically coheres well with the rest of our knowledge, James can explain why we extend the application of "knowing" to those cases in which perceptual contact could not even *possibly* be made. We thus make a move from the merely *unobserved* to the *unobservable*. After all, James characterizes virtual cases for observables as follows:

> The immensely greater part of all our knowing . . . is never completely nailed down. I speak not merely of our ideas of imperceptibles like ether-waves or dissociated "ions" or other "ejects" like the contents of our neighbors' minds; I speak also of ideas which we might verify if we would take the trouble, but which we hold for true altho unterminated perceptually, because nothing says "no" to us, and there is no contradicting truth in sight. (MT 1909, 67; ERE 1904, 34)

Once we admit the standard cases of virtual reference and allow that "*to continue thinking unchallenged is, ninety-nine times out of one hundred, our practical substitute for knowing in the completed sense*" (MT 1909, 67; ERE 1904, 34), reference to unobservables can be admitted as well.[32]

Non-actualized cases of virtual knowledge generally have the "freedom from clash and contradiction" that passes for "indirect verification"[33] and this characteristic could be shared by our thought about unobservables.[34] Standard cases of virtual knowledge count as "knowing" in virtue of having the potential to become like the prototype; reference to unobservables counts as "knowing" in virtue of sharing the evidential characteristics (that freedom from clash and contradiction) of the virtual cases.

Thinking about the Past

Still, even when developed in these ways, James's account of intentionality seems to remain forward-looking, and this raises potential problems for providing an account of our thoughts about the past.[35] Indeed, reference to the past is frequently taken to be the most serious problem with James's theory of truth,[36] and it poses a similar problem for his account of intentionality.[37] We typically understand ourselves as being able to refer to historical figures like Caesar, but how is this to be explained on James's account? Certainly not in terms of our tracking him down, or for that matter, even being able to be led into his immediate environment.

However, this will be another case in which James can appeal to the fact that "*to continue thinking unchallenged is, ninety-nine times out of one hundred, our practical substitute for knowing in the completed sense*" (MT 1909, 67; ERE 1904, 34). While Caesar and his immediate environment are not available, there are other items associated with Caesar (manuscripts, statues, etc.) that we can be connected with.

> Caesar *had* and my statement *has*, effects; and if these effects in any way run together, a concrete medium is provided for the determinate cognitive relation.... The real Caesar, for example, wrote a manuscript of which I see a real reprint and say "the Caesar I mean is the author of *that*." (MT 1909, 121)

We can't directly perceive or operate on items from the past, but as long as our words get a grip elsewhere, they can extend from their more secure base. In particular, James has plenty of room to add something like Russellian "denoting" to his account, and so could always claim that some (past) items could be known "by description." James distinguishes "knowledge of acquaintance" from "knowledge about" (PP 1890, 216–217), and this distinction is frequently compared to Russell's knowledge-by-acquaintance knowledge-by-description distinction.[38] Nevertheless, it should be noted that while James's "conceptual knowing" is often informed by "knowledge about," it is not knowledge "by description" (since what our knowledge about leads us to track down may not be what the associated descriptions are true of). As a result, something like knowledge by description can still be added to James's account, and while Russell's descriptions needed, ultimately, to be composed of elements that we were directly acquainted with, James could include items that are only virtually known among the ingredients that can go into the descriptions. So, for instance, I can denote Caesar as "the author of *The Gallic Wars*," while the book itself is referred to in virtue of my ability to track down a copy, rather than in virtue of further identifying descriptions.

Of course, if James makes such a move, he may still face the problems typically associated with descriptive accounts—what if, say, Caesar didn't really write *The Gallic Wars*?[39] This worry about our descriptions picking out people who we aren't intuitively talking about highlights a similar problem with the non-denotational cases: namely, what should we say if the object we would (collectively) track down isn't the object that we are "intuitively" understood as talking about? This general problem of "misrepresentation" will be the subject of the following section.

Misrepresentation (and Truth)

A particularly pressing source of potential problems for James's basic account are misidentifications. For James, our being led to an object does not merely *indicate* that we had always been thinking about it. Rather, the leading relation is supposed to be *constitutive* of the intentional one. The objects our practices ultimately end up "operating" on are thereby the ones our ideas refer to. As James puts it:

> The percept here not only *verifies* the concept, proves its function of knowing that percept to be true, but the percept's existence as the terminus of the chain of

intermediaries *creates* the function. Whatever terminates the chain was, because it now proves itself to be, what the concept "had in mind".[40] (MT 1909, 64; ERE 1904, 31)

The "direction of fit" between what we are referring to and our attempts to locate such referents thus seems to be the opposite of what is commonly supposed. What we are referring to appears to be beholden to our investigations rather than the other way around.

This makes the problem of misrepresentation pressing, since people can occasionally pick out things that their words and ideas intuitively don't seem to refer to. If I go out to find Memorial Hall, and wind up at Eliot House instead, it seems wrong to claim that Eliot House was what my "Memorial Hall" idea had been referring to all along (which it would seem to be if the tracking down *created* the knowing function). Fortunately, as the discussion of language's social character suggested, James has the resources to account for such cases.

In particular, while the termination of the chain creates the knowing function, whether or not a chain has, in fact, been *terminated* is not something about which we are infallible, and mis-identification involves us thinking that a chain is terminated when it is not. Briefly put, mis-identifications are understood in terms of identification that are corrected by *future* experience. As James famously puts it with respect to truth:

> The "absolutely" true, meaning what no farther experience will ever alter, is that ideal vanishing-point towards with we imagine that all our temporary truths will some day converge.... Meanwhile we have to live to-day by what truth we can get to-day, and be ready to-morrow to call it falsehood.... The present sheds a backwards light on the world's previous processes. They may have been truth processes for the actors in them. They are not so for one who knows the later revelations of the story. This regulative notion of a potential better truth to be established later, possibly to be established some day absolutely, and having powers of retroactive legislation, turns its face, like all pragmatist notions, towards concreteness of fact, and towards the future. (P 1907, 106–107)

Questions of truth and intentionality are deeply connected for James (as is seen in his willingness to talk about the "truth" of names and concepts), and just as James talks about "absolute" and "temporary" truth, there are objects that our thoughts are "temporarily" cognitive of, and those that they are about "absolutely." Cases of mis-identification can thus be understood as those in which the "temporary" and "absolute" extensions of one of one's terms come apart. The chain can appear to be finished even when it isn't, but such cases can still leave the knower with ("virtual") "absolute" knowledge of the correct objects. So, for instance, I can still count as "virtually" referring to Memorial Hall with my "Memorial Hall" thoughts even as I identify Eliot House as what I was thinking of. Of course, were the tissue of experience set up so that no correction of this initial judgment were possible (say, I'd steadfastly refuse to withdraw my claim that Eliot House was "Memorial Hall" no matter what evidence I was subsequently given), then James would have to say that Eliot House was what I was referring to in the fuller sense as well. However, if things really were that way, then James might be right to doubt that there was much sense to be made of the claim that I was "really" referring to anything else. (In such a scenario, I would certainly be referring to Eliot House by "Memorial Hall" *eventually*, so the question would be how far back these attributions can be legitimately made.)

Conclusion

In spite of its attracting comparatively little attention during its time (or since), James's account of intentionality played a central role in his thinking, and while his account is not without its problems, it's arguably superior to most of the alternatives offered in James's day. This lack of attention may be in part due to its missing the (definitional) form that philosophers typically expect from an account, but James not only rejects the common assumption that theories must have such a form, but provides an account that undermines that very assumption. If intentionality worked through some sort of "copying," then one might expect every category (including those relating to truth and reference) to have necessary and sufficient conditions associated with it, since those are the conditions which would give the criteria by which objects "fit" the relevant terms. On the other hand, if intentionality is ultimately based on our having the potential to *operate on* the objects of our thoughts, then the tidiness of our categories (and thus of our accounts of intentionality and truth) is less of an issue. James's account of intentionality thus supports his approach to analysis, and so feeds into his account of truth not only because constraints on what we can talk about are bound to affect the truth conditions of our claims, but also because what sort of account we can give of truth will depend in part on how we think that the word "truth" itself comes to pick out whatever it does. James's writings on truth often have the comparatively unsystematic quality that his writings on intentionality also display, but if his writings on intentionality are on the right track, then this lack of systematicity need not be a bad thing.

Notes

1. Thanks to Alex Klein, Jim Conant, Richard Gale, and members of the audience at The University of Guelph for comments on earlier versions of this paper. Note that when I quote James, italics, unless stated otherwise, are always James's.
2. Royce (1885). In this book Royce presented what James called an "original proof of Idealism" based on the question, "How can a thought refer to, intend, or signify any particular reality outside itself?" (ECR 1885, 384, 385). For a nice summary of how James understood Royce's argument and its importance, see his 1888 letter to Charles Renouvier (CWJ 1888, 6.358–360).

3. Letter to Henry James, September 8, 1907 (CWJ 1907, 3.344).
4. I should note that James often speaks of *concepts* in just this way. But in James's case this is combined with a skepticism about the extent of the match between our concepts and the realities that they purport to represent, and he takes this mismatch between how we conceive of things and how we refer to them to underwrite a type of skepticism about the "conceptual method" in philosophy. (For further discussion, see Jackman 2018.)
5. For a discussion of James's general tendency to focus on concrete examples and lack of interest in providing necessary and sufficient conditions, see Gale (1998, 38, 52), Seigfried (1990, 148–151), and Putnam (1997).
6. P 1907, 99. The "truth process" here is more tied to intentionality than propositional truth, with the example James discusses being about how "a mental image of a house" could lead us to follow a cow path until we encounter the real house.
7. Rosch (1975) and Lakoff (1987).
8. This example adapted from Lakoff (1987, 96).
9. This may have some affinities to Wittgenstein's point that "meaning" and "reference" are "family resemblance" terms (Wittgenstein 1953, section 67). (For more on this connection, see Boncompagni, this volume.)
10. Much of the material in this section is discussed in more detail in Jackman (1998). Quoted from MEN (1903–1904, 17). See the chapters by Levine and O'Shea in this volume for additional discussion of this issue.
11. See Bordogna (2008, 157) for a discussion of how this approach related to boundary disputes between philosophy and psychology in James's time.
12. Strong (1904) gives a useful exposition of this early stage of James's work, arguing that for James "operate" is an "inexact expression" that has "to do with causal relations, but not necessarily with causal relations that influence the object" so that "act with reference to" or "adjust our relations to" (as in the case when we encounter a tree and turn out of our initial path to avoid walking in to it), might be a more accurate way of characterizing the relation (Strong 1904, 256, 257).
13. This reading thus differs from that of O'Shea (this volume), who claims that James is here suggesting that "no sensorial image or feeling-instance, q, can by itself succeed in being *about* any reality unless it not only operates upon but *resembles* that reality." However, this requires a thought's being an "error" to amount to a failure to be *about* the object at all, while I'm more inclined to think that James endorses Royce's insight that the very possibility of error presupposes the ability of the thought to still be about whatever reality it is in error about.
14. While he does regret the "undue emphasis laid upon operating on the object itself," the regret is about the emphasis on the *object itself* rather than the *operation*, since he later realized that operation on the object itself is often "replaced by operations on other things related to the object" (MT 1909, 32). This expanded base will be crucial in letting his account deal with thoughts about "unobservables" and the past.
15. During the period of his focus on radical empiricism, perception often displaced operation as the explicit focus of his account of knowing, since for the radical empiricist, to perceive an object, or to know it immediately, "is for mental content and object to be identical" (MT 1909, 36; see also MT 1909, 35, 61–62) so that "[t]he external and the internal, the extended and the not extended fuse and make an indissoluble marriage" (ERE 1905, 265). See Lamberth (1999), Putnam (1998), and Putnam (1999).

16. Further, for Russell, the justification for giving pride of place to such "immediate" knowing was primarily epistemic (though perhaps not in a purely "foundationalist" way—see Klein [2017]), while for James the motivation was primarily metaphysical and phenomenological.
17. For instance we know about Caesar through "some description which is composed wholly of particulars and universals with which we are acquainted" (Russell 1912, ch. 5), and "[e]very proposition which we can understand must be composed wholly of constituents with which we are acquainted" (Russell 1910–1911/1918, 219).
18. P 1907, 99. Original in italics.
19. Hence his rhetorical question "What then would self-transcendency affirmed to exist in advance of all experiential mediation or termination, be *known-as*? What would it practically result in for *us*, were it true?" (ERE 1904, 36; MT 1909, 68).
20. James makes a similar point about truth itself when he claims:
    We let our notion pass for true without attempting to verify. If truth means verification-processes essentially, ought we then to call such unverified truths as this abortive? No, for they form the overwhelmingly large number of the truths we live by. Indirect as well as direct verifications pass muster. Where circumstantial is sufficient, we can go without eye-witnessing.... The verification of the assumption here means its leading to no frustrations or contradiction.... For one truth-process completed there are a million in our lives that function in this state of nascency. They turn *towards* direct verification; lead us into the *surroundings* of the objects they envisage; and then, if everything turns out harmoniously, we are so sure that verification is possible that we omit it, and are usually justified by all that happens. (P 1907, 99–100)
21. See MT (1909, 74); ERE (1905, 101, italics mine).
22. See also ERE (1904, 27).
23. The suggestion that James generally neglects "the social" can also be found, among others, in Gale (1998, 29, 165), Thayer (1975, xxii), McDermott (1986, 53), Otto (1943, 189), Morris (1970, 143, 151), and Scheffler (1974, 124, 145–146).
24. This should all be familiar from the cases discussed in Putnam (1975) and Burge (1979).
25. See MT (1909, 35, original in italics).
26. For a related discussion, see Evans (1982, 278–280).
27. James's famous discussion of our being able to think about tigers in India (EPh 1894, 72–74; MT 1909, 33–35) also involves a situation in which one must rely on the expertise of others to have a realistic hope of making it from Cambridge, Massachusetts, to those parts of India where one might encounter those "striped rascals" (MT 1909, 34; EPh 1894, 74).
28. James recognizes this possibility explicitly when he notes that "If a different intermediation, leading to a different real terminus, should occur, we should say, even were the initial state of mind identical, that now it had a different 'object'" (MEN 1903–1904, 17).
29. See Putnam (1975).
30. See MT (1909, 118).
31. See Jackman (2018).
32. Such an account would also allow us to refer to things like the number 26, though James didn't devote much attention to such cases.
33. See P (1907, 103).
34. One should note, however, that for James many of the theoretical entities posited by the scientific theories of his day would not be candidates for "knowing" of this sort. This was precisely because he took them *not* to be free from such "clash and contradiction" when

they were extended beyond the very restricted domains where they proved useful (see Jackman 2018).
35. Specifically, the distant past that we never experienced. James takes reference to things from our own past to be relatively unproblematic, and that in cases where we have had past perceptual contact with an object, we can always succeed in referring to it in a retrospective way (MT 1909, 26).
36. Such a view is shared by early critics of James such as Royce and Bradley and contemporary (sympathetic) expositors of James such as Putnam and Gale (Gale 1998, Putnam 1997).
37. James flags the problem himself in a frustratingly enigmatic footnote to his unfinished manuscript *The Many and the One*: "Knowledge of the past immediately occurs to one as incompatible with such an account. Less so than appears, however; but this question is just one of those that are postponed" (MEN 1903–1904, 17).
38. See, for instance, Misak (2016, 54).
39. All familiar from Kripke (1980).
40. See also MT (1909, 63); ERE (1904, 29).

Bibliography

Bordogna, F. 2008. *William James at the Boundaries*. Chicago: University of Chicago Press.
Burge, T. 1979. "Individualism and the Mental," in *Midwest Studies in Philosophy IV: Studies in Metaphysics*, edited by Peter A. French, T. F. Uehling and H. K. Wettstein, 73–121. Minneapolis: University of Minnesota Press,. 1979.
Evans, G. 1973. "The Causal Theory of Names," in *Collected Papers*, edited by G. Evans. New York: Oxford University Press, 1985.
Evans, G. 1982. *The Varieties of Reference*. New York: Oxford University Press.
Gale, R. 1998. *The Divided Self of William James*. New York: Cambridge University Press.
Jackman, H. 1998. "James's Pragmatic Account of Intentionality and Truth." *Transactions of the Charles S. Peirce Society* XXXIV (1).
Jackman, H. 2018. "William James's Naturalistic Account of Concepts and his 'Rejection of Logic'." in *Philosophy of Mind in the 19th Century*, edited by S. Lapointe, 133–146. New York: Routledge.
Klein, A. 2017. "Russell on Acquaintance with Spatial Properties: The Significance of James," in *Innovations in the History of Analytical Philosophy*, edited by S. Lapointe and T. Pincock. New York: Palgrave McMillan.
Kripke, Saul A. 1980. *Naming and Necessity*. Cambridge: Harvard University Press.
Lakoff, G. 1987. *Women, Fire and Dangerous Things*. Chicago: University of Chicago Press.
Lamberth, D. 1999. *William James and the Metaphysics of Experience*. New York: Cambridge University Press.
McDermott, J. 1986. *Streams of Experience: Reflections on the History and Philosophy of American Culture*. Amherst: University of Massachusetts Press.
Misak, C. 2016. *Cambridge Pragmatism: From Peirce and James to Ramsey and Wittgenstein*. New York: Oxford University Press.
Morris, C. 1970. *The Pragmatic Movement in American Philosophy*. New York: George Braziller.
Otto, M. 1943. "On a Certain Blindness in William James." *Ethics* 53: 184–191.
Putnam, H. 1975. "The Meaning of 'Meaning.'" Reprinted in H. Putnam, *Mind Language and Reality*, 215–271. New York: Cambridge University Press.

Putnam, H. 1997. "James's Theory of Truth" in *The Cambridge Companion to William James*, edited by R. A Putnam. New York: Cambridge University Press.

Putnam, H. 1998. "Pragmatism and Realism" in *The Revival of Pragmatism*, edited by M. Dickstein. Durham, NC: Duke University Press.

Putnam, H. 1999. *The Threefold Cord: Mind, Body, and World*. New York: Columbia University Press.

Rosch, E. 1975. "Family Resemblances: Studies in the Internal Structure of Categories." *Cognitive Psychology* 7 (4) (October): 573–605.

Royce, J. 1885. *The Religious Aspect of Philosophy*. Boston: Houghton Mifflin.

Russell, B. 1910–1911/1918. "Knowledge by Acquaintance and Knowledge by Description." In B. Russell, *Mysticism and Logic: And Other Essays*, 209–232. London: George Allen & Unwin.

Russell, B. 1912, 1997. *The Problems of Philosophy*. New York: Oxford University Press.

Scheffler, I, 1974. *Four Pragmatists*. New York: Humanities Press.

Seigfried C. H. 1990. *William James's Radical Reconstruction of Philosophy*. Albany, NY: SUNY Press.

Strong, C. A. 1904. "A Naturalistic Theory of the Reference of Thought to Reality." *The Journal of Philosophy, Psychology and Scientific Methods*, 1(10) (May 12): 253–260.

Thayer, H. S. 1975. "Introduction" to W. James, *The Meaning of Truth*. Cambridge, MA: Harvard University Press.

Wittgenstein, L. 1953. *Philosophical Investigations*, 3rd edition. Oxford, UK: Blackwell.

CHAPTER 15

WHAT WAS JAMES'S THEORY OF TRUTH?

TOM DONALDSON

INTRODUCTION

In the second lecture of *Pragmatism*, William James promised his audience a "theory of truth" (P 1907, 32–33, 37). However, many of his readers have struggled to find James's theory among his various metaphors, his anecdotes, and his criticisms of his "intellectualist" rivals.[1] These quotations should give you some sense of the challenge that confronts a sympathetic reader of James's work on truth:

(1a) Our account of truth is an account of truths in the plural . . . having only this in common, that they *pay*. (P 1907, 104)
(1b) I am well aware of how odd it must be for some of you to hear me say that a belief is "true" so long as to believe it is profitable for our lives. (P 42)
(2a) The "absolutely" true, meaning what no farther experience will ever alter, is that ideal vanishing-point towards which we imagine that all our temporary truths will some day converge. (P 106–107)
(2b) Truth absolute, he [the pragmatist] says, means an ideal set of formulations towards which all opinions may in the long run of experience be expected to converge. (MT 1909, 143)
(3) True ideas are those that we can assimilate, validate, corroborate and verify. False ideas are those that we cannot. (P 97)

(1a) and (1b) suggest that, for James, a belief is true just in case it is beneficial to the believer. But this seems hopeless. It may benefit a shy person at a job interview to believe that he is the best person for the job—even if he isn't. So a belief can be beneficial even if it is not true. Conversely, by memorizing the digits of the decimal expansion of the square root of seventeen, you can acquire many beliefs that are true but not beneficial.

(2a) and (2b) suggest that James had a somewhat more complex theory. In these passages, James seems to imply that all disagreements are temporary. In the long run, opinion will converge on a single consensus position, an "ideal set of formulations." A belief is true just in case it is an element of this ideal set.[2]

The standard objection to this proposal is the "buried secrets" problem, as follows. Consider:

(a) Richard III killed the princes in the tower.
(b) Richard III did not kill the princes in the tower.

It may well be that all the relevant evidence has been destroyed, in which case it will forever be unsettled whether Richard III was the murderer. In this case, neither (a) nor (b) is an element of the "ideal set of formulations towards which all opinions may in the long run of experience be expected to converge." In this case, James's theory seems to imply that perhaps neither (a) nor (b) is true—a surprising conclusion, to say the least.[3]

In quotation (3), James apparently claimed that a belief is true if and only if it can be verified. On this reading, James's account of truth will again have the perhaps objectionable implication that it may be that neither (a) nor (b) is true, since it may be that neither is verifiable.[4]

Even if we can find some way around the buried secrets problem, there remains the further problem that proposals (1), (2), and (3) apparently contradict one another: a belief may benefit the believer even if it is not verifiable; a belief may be verifiable *now* even if in the future it will not be verifiable and so will not end up in the "ideal set of formulations"—and so on.

On the basis of considerations like these, many of James's contemporaries concluded that his "theory" of truth was just a dog's breakfast. James typically responded to his critics by protesting (with obvious frustration) that he had been misunderstood. For example, he vigorously insisted that he had *not* meant to say that a belief is true just in case it is useful to the believer (MT 1909, 126, 128).

These protestations did little to silence his detractors. In *Pragmatism* James really does *seem* to endorse the claim that a belief is true if and only if it benefits the believer. His later pronouncements to the contrary only added to the impression that his position was inconsistent and muddled.[5]

It seems to me, however, that we should not accept the conclusion that James's work on truth was a dog's breakfast unless we can first convince ourselves that no more charitable interpretation of the text is available. And so we face an exegetical challenge: *Can we find a charitable interpretation?*

I contend that *Pragmatism* should be central in discussions of James's theory of truth. James's earlier writings on truth are not as well-developed as *Pragmatism*, and his later writings on truth are largely responses to *Pragmatism*'s critics. In the sections of this chapter "Pragmatism and Common Sense," "James's Critique of the Copy Theory of Truth," and "Beyond the Copy Theory," I will give an (inevitably partial)[6] survey of Lectures V and VI of *Pragmatism*. In the section "Did James Have an Account of the Nature of Truth?" I consider the suggestion that it is a misunderstanding of James's project to say that he sought a theoretical account of the nature of truth. In the section "What Was James's Theory of Truth?" I offer my own response to the accusation that James's theory was a dog's breakfast.

Pragmatism and Common Sense

I begin this section with a discussion of James's metaphysics of pure experience—a view that he presented in a series of papers published around 1904[7] and that is an important part of the philosophical backdrop of *Pragmatism*. Sadly, we do not have space for a thorough discussion, so a quick sketch will have to do. For more, see Cooper's, Dunham's, and Inukai's contributions to this volume.[8] Having looked at James's metaphysical views, we will consider James's discussion of the goals of inquiry in Lecture V of *Pragmatism*, "Pragmatism and Common Sense."

Let us start with a question: what is the difference between a physical ball and an imaginary one? One's first thought might be that they are made from different materials. The physical ball will be made of steel, or rubber, or wood, or some other physical stuff. The imaginary ball, one wants to say, can't be made of any such physical material, precisely because it is not a physical thing. Physical things are made of physical stuff; mental things are made of mental stuff.

James disagreed. He claimed that both mental and physical things are composed of the same "primal stuff or material" (ERE 1904, 4). Indeed, for James, there need be no *intrinsic* difference between a mental thing and a physical thing; what makes something mental, or physical, is not its intrinsic features, but how it relates to other things:

> We find that there are some fires that will always burn sticks and always warm our bodies, and that there are some waters that will always put out fires; while there are other fires and waters that will not act at all. The general group of experiences that act, that do not only possess their natures intrinsically, but wear them adjectively and energetically, turning them against one another, comes inevitably to be contrasted with the group whose members, having identically the same natures, fail to manifest them in the "energetic" way. I make for myself now an experience of blazing fire; I place it near my body; but it does not warm me in the least. I lay a stick upon it, and the stick either burns or remains green, as I please. I call up water, and pour it on the fire, and absolutely no difference ensues. I account for all such facts by calling this whole train of experiences unreal, a mental train. Mental fire is what won't burn real sticks; mental water is what won't necessarily (though of course it may) put out even a mental fire. Mental knives may be sharp, but they won't cut real wood. Mental triangles are pointed, but their points won't wound. (ERE 1904, 17)

For James, a thing can be both mental *and* physical. Suppose, for example, that you accurately see a cricket ball. Then the ball is at once a perception, a part of your mental world, and a physical thing that could cause a bruise if it struck someone's forehead.

James's view therefore differs greatly from "indirect realist" theories of perception, according to which the things we perceive are mental copies of physical things. For James, the ball that you perceive is not a mental simulacrum of the physical ball; rather, the physical ball and the perception are one and the same.

James's word for the "primal stuff or material" from which both mental and physical things are made was "pure experience." The term has the potential to mislead, for it is natural to think that every experience must have a subject—a person who *has* the experience. But this was certainly not James's view. He wrote:

> We at every moment can continue to believe in an existing beyond. It is only in special cases that our confident rush forward gets rebuked. The beyond must, of course, always in our philosophy be itself of an experiential nature. If not a future experience of our own or a present one of our neighbor, it must be a thing in itself in Dr. Prince's and Professor Strong's sense of the term. (ERE 1904, 43)

Strong's definition of "thing in itself" was this:

> By "things-in-themselves" I understand realities external to consciousness of which our perceptions are the symbols. (Strong 1903, ch. 10)

So James's claim was that there are things "of an experiential nature" that are nevertheless "external to consciousness"—that is, there are "subject-less" experiences, experienCES without experienCERS. For example, consider a rock on some distant unpopulated planet. From a Jamesian point of view, this rock will (like terrestrial rocks) be composed of experiences. But if it happens that no sentient creature ever visits the planet, it may be that these experiences never have a subject.

At this point, it is tempting to complain that James's "pure experiences" shouldn't be called "experiences" at all—perhaps they should be called "basic objects" or something similar instead. Perhaps this is right, but I will stick to James's term.

James believed that the experiences of a newborn baby are a chaotic mess—a "blooming, buzzing confusion" as he eloquently put it (PP 1890, 462). James's goal in Lecture V of *Pragmatism* was to explain the components of the common-sense "conceptual system" (P 1907, 84) that we adults use to "[straighten] the tangle of our experience's immediate flux and sensible variety" (P 1907, 87).[9]

James thought that the newborn baby does not think of its experiences as experiences *of* physical objects that persist even when they are not perceived:

> A baby's rattle drops out of his hand, and it has "gone out" for him, as a candle-flame goes out; and it comes back, when you replace it in his hand, as the flame comes back when relit. (P 1907, 85)

As we get older, we learn to "interpolate" persisting physical objects between their "successive apparitions" (P 1907, 86). These physical objects can then be arranged into "kinds": some of the objects are balls, others are cups, others are trees, and so on (P 1907, 88).

Common-sense geometry is another component of our common-sense conceptual system. James thought our "primitive perceptions of space" (PP 1890, 787) include perceptions of the sizes of different experiences. "The entrance into a warm bath gives our skin a more massive feeling than the prick of a pin," he wrote (PP 1890, 776). What's more, our primitive perceptions of space include certain spatial relations—relations of distance and adjacency, for example.[10] However, James emphasized that these primitive perceptions are in many ways muddled and incomplete. We do not perceive distances between objects that cannot be perceived simultaneously. Less obviously, the perceptions of the different senses may conflict with one another: the cavity that remains after a tooth has been extracted feels enormous when explored with the tongue but looks small when seen in a mirror (PP 1890, 781). What's more, James thought, we do not directly perceive distances between experiences of different senses (PP 1890, 819). Thus, he wrote, "primitively our space-experiences form a chaos" (PP 1890, 819). However, as adults we learn to combine our space-experiences "into a consolidated and unitary continuum," (PP 1890, 819) a single "cosmic space" (P 1907, 87) that persists as physical objects move around through it.[11]

Our common-sense conceptual system also includes a temporal component. The newborn baby has experiences of duration and temporal order. However, the baby has to learn to think of events as distributed along a single timeline:

> That one Time which we all believe in and in which each event has its definite date, that one Space in which everything has its definite position, these abstract notions unify the world incomparably. (P 1907, 87)

I hope that the general outlines of James's account of our common-sense conceptual system are now sufficiently clear. James thought that our "primitive" experiences are "chaotic" or "tangled" and that we use the "conceptual system" of common sense to systematize the flux of sensations.

It is noteworthy that the account of common sense that James offers here is very similar to his discussion of philosophical and scientific inquiry in his "The Sentiment of Rationality":

> Our pleasure at finding that a chaos of facts is at bottom the expression of a single underlying fact is like the relief of the musician at resolving a confused mass of sound into melodic or harmonic order. The simplified result is handled with far less mental effort than the original data; and a philosophic conception of nature is thus in no metaphorical sense a labor-saving contrivance. (EP 35–36)

To help summarize all of this, I will introduce a new term. Let's say that an "experiential fact" is a fact that could possibly be perceived, independently of the conceptual innovations of common sense or science. For example, the fact that two particular experiences are adjacent would be an experiential fact. By contrast, *that there are two phones three inches apart* would not be an experiential fact—for the concepts *phone* and *inch* are part of our common-sense conceptual system. James's proposal, then, was that the goal of both common-sense and scientific inquiry is to *systematize* or *organize* the experiential facts, which otherwise constitute an unmanageable knotted mess.

James's Critique of the Copy Theory of Truth

James told his audience that "any dictionary will tell you" that truth means "agreement with reality." James accepted this dictionary definition but then claimed (correctly, I think) that the dictionary definition is of little value in the absence of some further discussion of "agreement" and "reality" (P 1907, 96). James went on to say that one "popular" way of developing this dictionary definition is to say that a true idea is a *copy* of what it represents (P 1907, 96). I will call this the "copy theory" of truth. James presented his evaluation of the copy theory at the end of Lecture V and the beginning of Lecture VI of *Pragmatism*.

Our discussion in the previous section of James's metaphysical views, and his views about the goals of enquiry, should already lead you to expect James to reject the copy theory—at least as a fully general account of truth. For one thing, we have already seen that, for James, a perception is not a *copy* of something in one's environment: it *is* something in one's environment. For another, we have seen that, according to James, our beliefs about, for example, "cosmic space" are not a copy of anything found in experience; rather, they are a tool that we use to organize the otherwise chaotic "primitive perceptions of space."

And indeed, James argued that the copy theory is not correct in all cases, though he was willing to concede that there may be some cases in which our true beliefs are copies:

> Our true ideas of sensible things do indeed copy them. Shut your eyes and think of yonder clock on the wall, and you get just such a true picture or copy of its dial. (P 1907, 96)

James continued his discussion of the clock by providing a simple counterexample to the copy theory:

> Your idea of [the clock's] "works" (unless you are a clock-maker) is much less of a copy. (P 1907, 96)

Let's suppose, for example, that one of James's audience members believed, truly, that the clock was powered by a descending weight. Nevertheless, the audience member might have been completely unable to form an accurate visualization of the clock's mechanism. In this case, there is a true belief about the clock that is not a copy of the clock, except perhaps in some extended or metaphorical sense. This is a straightforward, compelling counterexample to the copy theory.[12]

Another one of James's objections to the copy theory is much harder to interpret. The objection first appears in "Humanism and Truth," an article which slightly predated *Pragmatism*.[13]

> As I understand the pragmatist way of seeing things, it owes its being to the breakdown which the last fifty years have brought about in the older notions of scientific truth.... Up to about 1850 almost everyone believed that sciences expressed truths that were exact copies of a definite code of non-human realities. But the enormously rapid multiplication of theories in these latter days has well-nigh upset the notion of any one of them being a more literally objective kind of thing than another. There are so many geometries, so many logics, so many physical and chemical hypotheses, so many classifications, each one of them good for so much and yet not good for everything, that the notion that even the truest formula may be a human device and not a literal transcript has dawned upon us. (MT 1909, 40)

James's argument in this passage seems to be this. Modern science in some cases presents us with radically different theoretical accounts of a single subject matter. Since these theories are radically different from each other, they can't *all* be copies or duplicates of the reality that the represent—but even so they are true. And so truth is not duplication.

The argument is puzzling. A proponent of the copy theory may simply reply that the diverse scientific theories James has in mind are not true in the strict sense—though they may be in some sense approximately true.[14]

A slightly different version of the argument appears at the end of Lecture V of *Pragmatism*. James contrasted our common-sense *Weltanschauung* and the world view of the hard sciences. James suggested that common sense and the hard sciences are incompatible. In particular, common sense tells us that secondary qualities (including colors) are real, but science disagrees. Science tells us that secondary qualities are unreal; what are real are "her atoms, her ether, her magnetic fields, and the like" (P 1907, 90).

James was cautious in responding to this problem. He expressed sympathy for a form of instrumentalism, according to which scientific unobservables are unreal.[15] However, James finished the chapter by tentatively recommending a more radical way of reconciling the common-sense and scientific world views. He wrote:

> The whole notion of truth, which naturally and without reflexion we assume to mean the simple duplication by the mind of a ready-made and given reality, proves hard to understand clearly.... It is evident that the conflict of [the scientific and common-sense worldviews] obliges us to overhaul the very idea of truth, for at present we have no definite notion of what the word may mean. (P 1907, 93–94)

This is another puzzling passage, but James's suggestion seems to have been this. The common-sense and the scientific positions are both true, even though they seem to conflict with one another. Since these two theories are so different from one another, they can't *both* be copies or duplicates of reality. So there must be something wrong with the copy theory. James finished his discussion of the point with a question, "May there not after all be a possible ambiguity in truth?" (P 1907, 94). Apparently, James was suggesting that there is more than one sort of truth—that is, he was recommending the position that is today called "truth pluralism."

James returned to this theme at the beginning of Lecture VII:

> *The* Truth: what a perfect idol of the rationalistic mind! I read in an old letter—from a gifted friend who died too young—these words: "In everything, in science, art, morals, and religion, there *must* be one system that is right and *every* other wrong." How characteristic of the enthusiasm of a certain stage of youth! . . . [T]he question "What is *the* truth?" is no real question. (P 1907, 115–116)

These are difficult passages, to be sure, so we must be cautious in our interpretation. My own tentative proposal is that James's suggestion was that there are several truth properties. Our common-sense beliefs have one truth property; the findings of the hard sciences have another. So understood, James's discussions of the copy theory of truth dovetail neatly with his discussion of the goals of inquiry, which I considered in the section "Pragmatism and Common Sense." As I said, for James, it is the goal in both common-sense and scientific inquiry to *systematise* the experiential facts, which are otherwise an unmanageable knotted mess. In the passages just quoted, James suggested that common sense and science have reached two variant systematizations, which are individually useful but which cannot be combined. I will return to this theme presently—first, I would like to look at James's presentation of his positive account of truth.

Beyond the Copy Theory

James began his presentation of his theory with the following pithy statement, which I have already quoted:

> True ideas are those that we can assimilate, validate, corroborate and verify. False ideas are those that we cannot. (P 1907, 97)

He then went on to explain his position in more detail. The claim just quoted, then, was not a presentation of James's final position—it is rather a "first pass" summary of the position that James presented to his audience to prepare them for the more detailed discussion that followed.

James explicitly distinguished "absolute truth" from "relative truth." He illustrated the distinction by listing cases of discredited theories: "ptolemaic astronomy, euclidean space, aristotelian logic, [and] scholastic metaphysics" (P 1907, 107). These theories, he argued, were relatively true in their day, but have subsequently turned out not to be absolutely true. James also referred to the relative truths as "half-truths," which suggests that, for James, relative truths need not, strictly speaking, be truths at all—the relative truths are beliefs that one can reasonably *take* to be true, given one's evidence (Putnam 1997).

For James, relative truth and absolute truth are both important, though for rather different reasons. He stressed the remoteness of the absolute truth, saying that "[i]t runs on all fours with the perfectly wise man" (P 1907, 107); in consequence, our actions must be based on relative truths. "[W]e have to live to-day by what truth we can get to-day, and be ready to-morrow to call it falsehood" (P 1907, 107). The absolute truth, by contrast, acts as a "regulative notion" (P 1907, 107). "To admit, as we pragmatists do, that we are liable to correction," James explained, "involves the use on our part of an ideal standard" (MT 1909, 142).

Some readers find James's terminology confusing. Henry Jackman writes:

> Whether or not they accept James's gloss on the nature of absolute truth, most philosophers still insist that such "objective" truth is the *only* kind of truth, and that James's insistence on referring to our temporary beliefs as *truths* of any sort is just perverse. A *temporary* truth is standardly taken to be no more a *kind* of truth than a *purported* spy is a sort of spy. (Jackman 2008)

Perhaps so—but this is a terminological complaint only, not a substantive objection to James's position.

In the remainder of this section, I will discuss James's account of relative truth, and then turn to his account of absolute truth.

James claimed that as we search for relative truths, we are subject to three constraints (he called them "realities"). First, our theories must be consistent with "the flux of sensations" (P 1907, 117). Second, James said, our ideas must be consistent with the "relations that obtain between our sensations or between their copies in our minds" (P 1907, 118). James stressed that these include "mutable and accidental" relations such as spatial and temporal relations, but he also included "relations of ideas" in something like's Hume's sense. He gave examples:

> It is either a definition or a principle that 1 and 1 make 2, that 2 and 1 make 3, and so on; that white differs less from gray than it does from black; that when the cause begins to act the effect also commences.[16] (P 1907, 100–101)

Third, James argued that in our theorizing we are constrained by previous theories. He claimed that we must create new theories by making *small* changes to existing theories:

> Our theory must mediate between all previous truths and certain new experiences. It must derange common sense and previous belief as little as possible. (P 1907, 104)

James stressed that it is extremely difficult to find theories that meet these three constraints. "Between the coercions of the sensible order and those of the ideal order," he wrote, "our mind is thus wedged tightly" (P 1907, 101).

However, he thought that when we *can* find more than one theory that meets the three constraints, we should break the tie by appeal to pragmatic considerations:

> Our theories are wedged and controlled as nothing else is. Yet sometimes alternative theoretic formulas are equally compatible with all the truths we know, and then we choose between them for subjective reasons. We choose the kind of theory to which we are already partial; we follow "elegance" or "economy." Clerk Maxwell somewhere says it would be "poor scientific taste" to choose the more complicated of two equally well-evidenced conceptions; and you will all agree with him. (P 1907, 104)

In effect, James's claim was that finding relatively true theories is a constrained optimization problem. We must respect the three constraints, but otherwise we try to optimize our theory with respect to pragmatically desirable characteristics such as economy and elegance.[17]

Having discussed relative truth, James then explained what "absolute truth" is in the following words, which I have already quoted:

> The "absolutely" true, meaning what no farther experience will ever alter, is that ideal vanishing-point towards which we imagine that all our temporary truths will some day converge. (P 1907, 106–107)

James's suggestion seems to have been this. It may be that *now* there are several inconsistent theories that accommodate all the available evidence and are tied with respect to all relevant pragmatic considerations. However, eventually, once enough evidence has been gathered and enough reasoning has been carried out, opinion will converge on a single ideal theory that is superior to all competitors.

This is puzzling, because James gave no argument for the conclusion that there is such an ideal theory. What grounds have we for ruling out the possibility that there are several different theories that will be forever tied for the title "best theory"? What's more, James's use of the definite article in this passage (*the* absolutely true) seems to conflict with his endorsement of truth pluralism.

I will return to these puzzles presently. For now, I would like to put this point to one side, to admire how neatly James's theory of absolute truth dovetails with his views about the goals of inquiry, which I described in the section "Pragmatism and Common Sense." As I said, James thought that in constructing our belief system, our goal is to *systematize* the otherwise chaotic morass that is the "flux of our sensations." As inquiry advances, our systematizations improve. The limiting point of this process (the absolutely true) is the optimal systematization.

Did James Have an Account of the Nature of Truth?

Now that we've looked at the text, we can return to the exegetical puzzle presented in the Introduction: can we find a charitable interpretation of James's work on truth, or are we stuck with the conclusion that it was a dog's breakfast?

In this section I consider two writers who have argued, in different ways, that the exegetical problem arises only because we mistakenly assume that James's goal was to give an account of the *nature of truth*, that is, an account of *what truth is*—when in fact James did not have this goal at all.

Denis Phillips argued that James's goal was not to explain what truth is, but rather to give us a method for finding truths:

> [Moore] failed to appreciate the problem James was concerned with: How do we come to *ascribe* truth to an idea, that is, what experiences lead us to recognize that an idea is true . . . James accepted the correspondence theory as a *definition* of truth, but . . . he also regarded this as fairly unenlightening. So, his interest was elsewhere; he wanted to establish a *criterion* of truth, to establish a procedure for identifying "tue ideas." (Phillips 1984, 424)[18]

There is something to this: in his discussions of *relative* truth, James *was* giving an account of "how we come to ascribe truth to an idea." However, when he gave his account of *absolute* truth as the "ideal vanishing point," James seems to have been attempting to explain what truth is, and not merely how it is recognized. James explicitly rejected Phillips's reading in "The Pragmatist Account of Truth and Its Misunderstanders," in which he presented as one of the "misunderstandings" of his theory the claim that "pragmatism explains not what truth is, but only how it is arrived at" (MT 1909, 108).

Richard Rorty's approach is rather different (Rorty 1982, ch. 9).[19] Rorty claimed that many philosophers who have written about truth have supposed that truth has an *essence*, and that it is the goal of the philosopher to produce a *theory* that reveals this essence. However, for Rorty, James's goal in his discussions of truth was very different. According to Rorty, James believed that truth has no essence, and so there is no need for a *theory* of truth at all. James's goal was to redirect our attention away from pointless theorizing about the essence of truth and toward more fruitful topics. Rorty believed that James's critics have failed to understand this:

> Let me illustrate this by James's definition of "the true" as "what is good in the way of belief." This has struck his critics as not to the point, as unphilosophical, as like the suggestion that the essence of aspirin is that it is good for headaches. James's point, however, was that there *is* nothing deeper to be said: truth is not the sort of thing which *has* an essence. (Rorty 1982, 162)

What are we to make of this? An extended discussion of Rorty's claim that James had no "theory" of truth is liable to degenerate into aimless squabbles about what would count as a "theory." Suffice it to say that James himself said that he was presenting a "theory" of truth (P, 1907 32–33, 37) and there is no evidence that these remarks were meant ironically. The case for Rorty's claim that James was anti-essentialist about truth is stronger. James talked about the "essence" of truth only once in *Pragmatism,* and when he did so he was paraphrasing an *objection* to his own views (P 1907, 105). However, even if Rorty was correct on this point, we can hardly stop here. We have yet to figure out what to say about the problem of buried secrets, and we have yet to understand James's truth pluralism. So let's move on.[20]

What Was James's Theory of Truth?

I would now like to offer my own response to the exegetical challenge that I presented in the Introduction to this chapter. I start with a word of caution. In a couple of places in *Pragmatism,* James talked about providing a "definition" of truth (P 1907, 42, 96). Philosophers trained in the analytic tradition may infer that James's goal was to provide an "analysis" of the word "true," analogous to the mathematical definitions of words like "prime" or "square." On this view, James's account of truth would take the following form, where $\varphi(x)$ does not contain the word "true" or any word which is defined in terms of truth:

> Given any belief x, x is true just in case $\varphi(x)$.

However, we should not assume at the outset that James's theory took this form. James rejected the analogy between his theory of truth and the definitions used in mathematics (MT 1909, 148–149).[21]

This cautionary note aside, let's get started. As I noted in the Introduction to this chapter, there are passages in *Pragmatism* in which James seems to endorse the crude claim that a belief is true just in case it benefits the believer. However, in his later writings he adamantly denied that he had ever made this claim. What are we to make of this? A simple solution is available: we should conclude that in those passages in which he appears to endorse the crude claim (as in sentences 1a and 1b, above), James was speaking, loosely, of *relative* rather than absolute truth. I have already explained that I think we should not take at face value James's claim that "true ideas are those that we can ... verify" (sentence 3, above; P 1907, 97)—this was a "first pass" statement of James's view only. I suggest, then, that James's core thesis was this, which I have already quoted several times:

> The "absolutely" true, meaning what no farther experience will ever alter, is that ideal vanishing-point towards which we imagine that all our temporary truths will some day converge. (P 1907, 106–107)

Two challenges remain. First, there is the problem of buried secrets. Second, there is the problem of squaring James's apparent truth pluralism with his claim that there is a *single* "ideal set of formulations" toward which the opinions of humanity are converging.

I'll start with the problem of buried secrets. To repeat, it is natural to think that one or other of these statements must be true:

(a) Richard III killed the princes in the tower.
(b) Richard III did not kill the princes in the tower.

However, it seems entirely possible that all of the relevant evidence has been destroyed. In this case, the opinions of humanity on this topic will not converge on this question, and so neither (a) nor (b) will end up in the "ideal set of formulations." And so James's theory of truth seems to imply that perhaps neither (a) nor (b) is true—and this consequence of James's theory seems objectionable. In short, James's theory of truth seems to conflict with the principle of bivalence in a counterintuitive way.[22]

In "A Dialogue," in *The Meaning of Truth* (MT 1909, 154–159), James addresses a version of the buried secrets problem. The two interlocutors in the dialogue were "Pragmatist" (who presented James's views) and "Anti-Pragmatist," who presented the following formulation of the buried secrets problem:

> Suppose a certain state of facts, facts for example of antediluvian planetary history, concerning which the question may be asked: "Shall the truth about them ever be known?" And suppose (leaving the hypothesis of an omniscient absolute out of the account) that we assume that the truth is never to be known. I ask you now, brother pragmatist, whether according to you there can be said to be any truth at all about such a state of facts. Is there a truth, or is there not a truth, in cases where at any rate it never comes to be known? (MT 1909, 154)

One point that Pragmatist was anxious to stress in his reply is that truth is a property of *beliefs held by people*. James had no time for the suggestion that truth is primarily a property of propositions, conceived of as abstract objects that exist independently of thinkers. It is a consequence of this position that if nobody ever forms a belief about the relevant portion of "antediluvian planetary history," then there are no truths about it. However, Pragmatist agreed that we may still talk, counterfactually, about the truth-values that such beliefs *would have* if they were formed. This caveat aside, Pragmatist's response is as follows:

> There have been innumerable events in the history of our planet of which nobody ever has been able to give an account, yet of which it can already be said abstractly that only one sort of possible account can ever be true. The truth about any such event is thus already generically predetermined by the event's nature; and one may accordingly say with perfectly good conscience that it virtually pre-exists. (MT 1909, 155)

James's position, then, was that the truth-values of beliefs about an event in "antediluvian planetary history" are "predetermined by the event's nature." Note that James did not insist that beliefs about antediluvian planetary history can only be true if sufficient evidence remains. I suggest, then, that James's response to my Richard III example would have been that either (a) or (b) is true even if insufficient evidence remains to settle the question. But how can we square this with the rest of James's account?

To answer this question, let us first recall that, for James, there are experiences that have no subject—experienCES without experienCERS. Once this claim has been accepted, it is natural to accept in addition that there are experiential facts that are never observed. For example, consider a pair of adjacent subject-less experiences. The fact that these two experiences are adjacent will be an experiential fact, in my sense, even if no sentient creature has ever, or will ever, observe it.[23]

Now recall that, for James, the goal of both scientific and common-sense enquiry is to systematize the otherwise tangled mess of experiential facts. Our predecessors have given to us theories that systematize many of their experiences. Working together, we modify these theories to accommodate our own additional observations. We also make conceptual innovations, finding newer, more elegant systematizations of the experiential facts. As time passes, then, we find ever better systematizations of ever more experiential facts. The ideal limit point of this process is a best possible systematization of *all* the experiential facts—including unobserved experiential facts. On this view, there will be truths about antediluvian rocks, and about whether Richard III killed the princes in the tower, even if these truths are epistemically inaccessible to us. Understood in this way, James's theory is not vulnerable to the buried secrets problem.[24]

Now let's turn to the challenge of squaring James's truth pluralism with his claim that there is a *single* "ideal set of formulations" toward which the opinions of humanity are converging. To see that there is a problem here, compare these two passages, which I have already quoted:

> The "absolutely" true, meaning what no farther experience will ever alter, is that ideal vanishing-point towards which we imagine that all our temporary truths will some day converge.' (P 1907, 106–107)
>
> The Truth: what a perfect idol of the rationalistic mind! I read in an old letter—from a gifted friend who died too young—these words: "In everything, in science, art, morals, and religion, there must be one system that is right and every other wrong." How characteristic of the enthusiasm of a certain stage of youth! . . . the question "What is the truth?" is no real question. (P 1907, 115–116)

As I said, the passages in which James defends truth pluralism are hard to interpret, and so our response to this exegetical problem must be somewhat tentative. My own view is this. I suggest that James *vacillated* on the question of whether there is a single optimal systematization of the experiential facts. When he spoke of "the" absolutely true, he assumed that there is one single "ideal set of formulations." In those passages in which he tentatively put forward truth pluralism, he was suggesting that there may be several different ideal sets, each of which corresponds to a variety of truth. These different ideal sets are internally consistent, but they may contradict one another. For example, there may be a "common-sense" set, which includes the belief that ripe bananas are yellow, and a "scientific" set, which includes the belief that colors are illusory. If so, then the belief that ripe bananas are yellow has the "common-sense" truth property but it lacks the "scientific" truth property.[25,26]

James's Theory of Truth Today

I conclude that James's theory of truth was not a dog's breakfast and that the naïve objections to James's theory, presented in the Introduction to this chapter, all fail. At the same time, I don't expect contemporary philosophers to find James's theory attractive. As Lamberth has stressed (Lamberth 1999, 207), James's views on truth were intertwined with metaphysical views that are out of favor today. However, James's work on truth is not without significance for contemporary philosophy. I will wrap up by mentioning two questions for further research.

(1) Truth pluralism, the claim that there are several different truth properties, has been much discussed recently.[27] However, a reader of the contemporary literature could easily end up with the impression that truth pluralism was first discussed in the 1990s—though as we have seen James had defended truth pluralism almost a century earlier.

If I'm right about James's version of truth pluralism, however, it was in one respect *far* more radical than more recent versions. As we have seen, in some places James seems to have accepted instances of the following schema:

φ has one truth property, and $\neg\varphi$ has a different truth property.

Thus, James's version of truth pluralism resembles dialetheism.[28] As far as I can tell, no recent writer on truth pluralism has discussed the very radical idea that two contradictory statements might both have a truth property. This is an important lacuna in today's literature on truth.

(2) To repeat, James's theory of truth is unlikely to appeal to philosophers today because it is entwined with his metaphysics of pure experience. It is an open question, however, whether James's theory of truth could be adapted to cohere with metaphysical views that are favored today. Could there be, for example, a physicalist version of James's theory of truth?

Notes

1. Olin (1992) has collected some important early critiques of James's work.
2. For a recent defence of a position of this kind, see Misak (2000).
3. The problem was first explained by Peirce (1878). This essay is reprinted in the first volume of Houser and Kloesel (1992).
4. It's worth noting that this "verificationist" position remains popular today, especially in the philosophy of mathematics. See for example Prawitz (1998).
5. For example, Moore (1907–1908) wrote:

   But it by no means follows that because a philosopher would admit a view to be silly, when it is definitely put before him, he has not himself been constantly holding, and implying that very view. He may quite sincerely protest that he never has either held or implied it, and yet he may all the time have been not only implying it but holding it—vaguely, perhaps, but really.

6. In particular, I will have nothing to say in this essay about James's notorious claim that "Truth *happens* to an idea. It *becomes* true" (P 1907, 97). For an excellent discussion of this aspect of James's position, see Schwartz (2012, ch. 6).
7. See in particular "Does 'Consciousness' Exist?" (ERE 1904, 3–20) and "A World of Pure Experience" (ERE 1904, 21–44).
8. For further discussion of this aspect of James's work, see Cooper (1990), Lamberth (1999), and Banks (2014).
9. James's discussion of the common-sense conceptual system in *Pragmatism* is brief, so in what follows I draw upon the *The Principles of Psychology*. One must be careful mixing quotations from these two books: there are large differences in opinion—as well as commonalities—between the two works. In particular, *The Principles of Psychology* assumes a *dualist* philosophy of mind, at odds with the metaphysics of pure experience that I describe in this paper. I hope to take advantage of the commonalities without being misled by the differences.
10. On the philosophical significance of the claim that *relations* are among our "primitive perceptions of space," see Klein (2009).
11. It's fascinating to compare James's *psychological* treatment of this issue with the *logical constructions* offered by Russell in "The Relation of Sense Data to Physics," in his *Mysticism and Logic* (1917). In a famous critique of such logical construction, Quine wrote:

    Why all this creative reconstruction, all this make-believe? The stimulation of his sensory receptors is all the evidence anybody has had to go on, ultimately, in arriving at his picture of the world. Why not just see how this construction really proceeds? Why not settle for psychology? (Quine 1969, 75)

    I suggest that James "settled" for psychology eighty years before Quine recommended it! Having said that, there are also deep differences between Quine's approach and James's. On this point, see Klein (2018).

12. Here is a further challenge to the copy theory. For an idea to be true, it does not suffice that it copy *something*, it must copy *its referent*. Thus, the copy theory is incomplete in the absence of a theory of *reference*. James was aware of this point, and discussed the theory of reference in detail. For a summary, see Jackman's contribution to this volume.

13. "Humanism and Truth" was originally published in *Mind* in 1904.
14. For a discussion of closeness-to-truth, see Oddie (2016).
15. He wrote, "Scientific logicians are saying on every hand that these entities [i.e. scientific unobservables] and their determinations, however definitely conceived, should not be held for literally real" (P 1907, 93). He went on to praise Mach, Ostwald, and Duhem, who were well-known opponents of atomism.
16. James discussed a priori truths more thoroughly in the final chapter of *The Principles of Psychology* (PP 1890, 1215–1280).
17. We should ask whether, for James, these pragmatically desirable characteristics vary from one person to another. Could it be that what's relatively true for you is relatively false for me because we have, so to speak, differing theoretical tastes? The following passage from the Lecture II of *Pragmatism* suggests a positive answer to this question:

    New truth is always a go-between, a smoother-over of transitions. It marries old opinion to new fact so as ever to show a minimum of jolt, a maximum of continuity. We hold a theory true just in proportion to its success in solving this "problem of maxima and minima." But success in solving this problem is eminently a matter of approximation. We say this theory solves it on the whole more satisfactorily than that theory; but that means more satisfactorily to ourselves, and individuals will emphasize their points of satisfaction differently. To a certain degree, therefore, everything here is plastic. (P 35)

18. See also Bybee (1984).
19. For related discussion, see Cormier (2001).
20. For further discussion of Rorty's reading of James's work on truth, see Gale (1999, 155).
21. On this point, see Schwartz (2012, 94) and Lamberth (2009).
22. Cheryl Misak has found an elegant solution to the problem of buried secrets in the writings of C.S. Peirce (Misak 2013, ch. 3). Robert Schwartz (2012, 110) in effect suggests that James *should* have responded to the buried secrets problem in the manner recommended by Misak's Peirce. Perhaps so—but I can find no textual evidence to support the claim that James *did* accept Peirce's solution.

    I discuss a challenge to the Misak/Peirce approach in Donaldson (2014). For another take on Peirce's theory of truth, see Hookway (2004).
23. I defined "experiential fact" by saying that an experiential fact "could possibly be perceived, independently of the conceptual innovations of common sense or science." It is crucial that the sense of "possibility" involved here is one that ignores certain practical limitations on what can be observed. There can be experiential facts that are so distant that nobody will ever observe them—in the same way that a substance can be water soluble even if (for some practical reason) it is impossible to put it in water.
24. Note that on this reading James's theory was in effect an "impure coherence theory" in the sense of Ralph Walker (1989). It is an important question whether James's theory is vulnerable to Walker's "master objection." For discussion of the master objection, see Wright (1995).
25. For further discussion, see Jackman (2008, 80–85).
26. Alternatively, one might propose that in the passages in which James endorses truth pluralism, he is concerned only with *relative* truth. On this interpretation, James is convinced that there is *one* best-possible systematization of the experiential facts—there is no "tie" between optimal systematizations—though he adds that (for the moment) our *relative* truths may come into conflict with one another. I disfavour this interpretation, for two

reasons. (1) I can find no *argument* in James for the bold claim that there is a single optimal systematization of the experiential facts. And it is far from clear what argument could be given for this claim. So this interpretation uncharitably attributes to James a strong thesis for which he had no justification. (2) There are passages that do not fit this interpretation. For example, in Lecture VII of *Pragmatism* James makes fun of the "rationalist" idea that there is a single "édition de luxe" of the universe, and then "various finite editions, full of false readings, distorted and mutilated each in its own way" (P 1907, 124). But on the proposed interpretation, this was James's own view!

27. Crispin Wright (1992) initiated the recent literature. For more recent work, see for example Lynch (2009) or Pedersen and Wright (2013).
28. See Priest (2006) for a recent defence of dialetheism.

References

Banks, Erik. 2014. *The Realistic Empiricism of Mach, James, and Russell: Neutral Monism Reconceived*. Cambridge, MA: Cambridge University Press.

Bybee, Michael. 1984. "James's Theory of Truth as a Theory of Knowledge." *Transactions of the CS Peirce Society* 20 (3): 253–267.

Cooper, W. E. 1990. "William James's Theory of Mind." *Journal of the History of Philosophy* 28 (4): 571–593.

Cormier, Harvey. 2001. *The Truth Is What Works: William James, Pragmatism and the Seed of Death*. Lanham: Rowman & Littlefield Publishers.

Donaldson, Thomas. 2014. "Review of *The American Pragmatists*, by Cheryl Misak." *Philosophical Review* 123 (3): 355–359.

Gale, Richard. 1999. *The Divided Self of William James*. Cambridge, MA: Cambridge University Press.

Hookway, Christopher. 2004. "Truth Reality and Convergence." In *The Cambridge Companion to Peirce*, edited by Cheryl Misak, 127–149. Cambridge, MA: Cambridge University Press.

Houser, Nathan, and Christian J W Kloesel, eds. 1992. *The Essential Peirce, Volume 1: Selected Philosophical Writings, (1867–1893)*. Bloomington: Indiana University Press.

Jackman, Henry. 2008. "William James." In *The Oxford Handbook of American Philosophy*, edited by Cheryl Misak, 60–86. Oxford: Oxford University Press.

Klein, Alexander. 2009. "On Hume on Space: Green's Attack, James' Empirical Response." *Journal of the History of Philosophy* 47 (3): 415–449.

Klein, Alexander. 2018. "In Defense of Wishful Thinking: James, Quine, Emotions, and the Web of Belief." *In Pragmatism and the European Traditions: Encounters with Analytic Philosophy and Phenomenology Before the Great Divide*, edited by Maria Baghramian and Sarin Marchetti, 228–250. London: Routledge.

Lamberth, David. 1999. *William James and the Metaphysics of Experience*. Cambridge, MA: Cambridge University Press.

Lamberth, David. 2009. "What to Make of James's Genetic Definition of Truth?" *William James Studies* 4:1–20.

Lynch, Michael. 2009. *Truth as One and as Many*. Oxford: Clarendon Press.

Misak, Cheryl. 2000. *Truth, Politics, Morality: A Pragmatist Account of Deliberation*. London and New York: Routledge.

Misak, Cheryl. 2013. *The American Pragmatists*. Oxford: Oxford University Press.

Moore, G. E. 1907–8. "Professor James' "Pragmatism"." *Proceedings of the Aristotelian Society*, New Series, 8:33–77.
Oddie, Graham. 2016. "Truthlikeness." In *The Stanford Encyclopedia of Philosophy* (Winter 2016 Edition), edited by E. N. Zalta. <https://plato.stanford.edu/archives/win2016/entries/truthlikeness/>.
Olin, Doris, ed. 1992. *William James: Pragmatism in Focus*. New York: Routledge.
Pedersen, Niolaj, and Cory D. Wright. 2013. *Truth and Pluralism: Current Debates*. Oxford: Oxford University Press.
Peirce, C. S. 1878. "How to Make Our Ideas Clear." *Popular Science Monthly* 12 (January): 286–302.
Phillips, Denis. 1984. "Was William James Telling the Truth after All?" *The Monist* 68 (3): 419–434.
Prawitz, Dag. 1998. "Truth and Objectivity from a Verificationist Point of View." In *Truth in Mathematics*, edited by H. G Dales and G. Oliveri, 41–51. Oxford: Clarendon Press.
Priest, Graham. 2006. *Doubt Truth to Be a Liar*. Oxford: Oxford University Press.
Putnam, Hilary. 1997. "James's Theory of Truth." In *The Cambridge Companion to William James*, edited by Ruth Anna Putnam, 166–185. Cambridge, MA: Cambridge University Press.
Quine, W. V. O. 1969. *Ontological Relativity and Other Essays*. New York: Columbia University Press.
Rorty, Richard. 1982. *Consequences of Pragmatism (Essays: 1972–1980)*. Minneapolis: University of Minnesota Press.
Russell, Bertrand. 1917. *Mysticism and Logic*. London: George Allen & Unwin Ltd.
Schwartz, Robert. 2012. *Rethinking Pragmatism: From William James to Contemporary Philosophy*. West Sussex: Wiley-Blackwell.
Strong, C. A. 1903. *Why the Mind Has a Body*. New York: The Macmillan Company.
Walker, Ralph. 1989. *The Coherence Theory of Truth: Realism, Anti-Realism, Idealism*. London and New York: Routledge.
Wright, Crispin. 1992. *Truth and Objectivity*. Cambridge, MA: Harvard University Press.
Wright, Crispin. 1995. "Critical Study: Ralph C.S. Walker, *The Coherence Theory of Truth: Realism, Anti-Realism, Idealism*." *Synthese* 103 (2): 279–302.

CHAPTER 16

JAMES AND PRAGMATISM
The Road Not Taken

PHILIP KITCHER

Radical Pragmatists

THE thought of human life as a journey, in which we may find ourselves in a dark wood where the straight way is lost, finds its classic expression in the opening lines of Dante's *Commedia*. Among many who have taken it up in subsequent centuries, William James, in the pivotal lecture at Berkeley where he first disclosed his enthusiasm for the pragmatism, or "practicalism" of Charles Sanders Peirce, adopted Dante's image to introduce his theme. The use of this image was not accidental. For almost two decades before the Berkeley lecture, James had been preoccupied with a cluster of questions he identified as the core agenda for philosophy, and that he addressed in "The Sentiment of Rationality" (1879, 1882), "Reflex Action and Theism" (1881), and "Is Life Worth Living?" (1895). In a world dominated by the achievements of natural science, and by the scientism of post-Darwinians like T.H. Huxley, Ernst Haeckel, and William Kingdom Clifford, James saw the predicament of humanity in much the way Dante had envisaged himself as a pilgrim. In the closing section of his most famous engagement with Clifford, "The Will to Believe" (1896), that vision is set in a different context (the snowy mountain summit rather than the dark forest), but the message is the same: humanity, both collectively and individually, is lost, and the task of philosophy is to help us find our way again.

The Berkeley lecture, "Philosophical Conceptions and Practical Results," opens with an explicit specification of what philosophy ought to accomplish:

> The words and thoughts of the philosophers are not exactly the words and thoughts of the poets—worse luck. But both alike have the same function. They are, if I may use a simile, so many spots, or blazes,—blazes made by the axe of the human intellect on the trees of the otherwise trackless forest of human experience. They give you somewhere to go from. They give you a direction and a place to reach. (P 1898, 258)

Although it's tempting, when we read James's *Pragmatism* of nearly a decade later, to divorce its contents from his earlier lectures and essays in "popular philosophy," I'm going to argue that the pragmatism of both James and Dewey is grounded in a determination to make philosophy relevant again to what they take, in their somewhat different ways, to be the central issues of human life. To normalize their forms of pragmatism, to set them in conversation with the professionalized Anglophone philosophy of the late twentieth century and the early twenty-first century, is, I claim, profoundly to distort their true importance. James and Dewey aimed to amend the pursuit of philosophy, to offer "Reconstruction in Philosophy" (in the title of the influential Dewey 1920), and it appeared, in the 1920s and 1930s, that the brilliant philosophical exiles from Vienna and Berlin were recruits for their pragmatist cause. Yet, as I hope to show, the concerns of the logical positivists and early logical empiricists, while closer to those of James and Dewey than to those of contemporary "analytic"[1] philosophers, were subtly different. James and Dewey marked out a path for the reform of philosophy. Professional Anglo-Saxon philosophy headed off, however, in a slightly different direction, and the pragmatist track turned out to be the road not taken.

Making a Difference

In the years between the Berkeley lecture and *Pragmatism*, James's most prominent work was the book that emerged from his Gifford Lectures, *The Varieties of Religious Experience*. It's no exaggeration to say that the entire project is driven by the felt need to understand how life can be given direction, infused with significance, in a world that appears, given our best scientific knowledge, to nullify any such aspiration. The predicament James had explored again and again in his early—"popular"—essays is described with a vivid image:

> For naturalism, fed on recent cosmological speculations, mankind is in a position similar to that of a set of people living on a frozen lake, surrounded by cliffs over which there is no escape, yet knowing that little by little the ice is melting, and the inevitable day drawing near when the last film of it will disappear, and to be drowned ignominiously will be the human creature's portion. The merrier the skating, the warmer and more sparkling the sun by day, and the ruddier the bonfires at night, the more poignant the sadness with which one must take in the meaning of the total situation. (VRE 1902, 120)

Using this image to crystallize the despair and pessimism felt by many people—including his own, carefully veiled, past self—James proposes that the "real core of the religious problem" is a cry: "Help! help!" (VRE 1902, 135). *Varieties* is James's attempt to show how philosophy, fully informed by empirical study of human experience, can answer that cry.

Pragmatism initially looks different, for it appears to offer a method that can be deployed to tackle (or dissolve) the traditional problems of philosophy. Many philosophers, including some who are most exercised by the alleged shortcomings of the pragmatist movement, view James and Dewey as competitors on their own turf, as bunglers who proposed dangerously misguided theories of the Really Central philosophical notions of Mind, Meaning, Truth, and Knowledge. Anyone who approaches the book in this way must suppose that the first lecture is merely another case of James's tiresome throat-clearing. For, in conformity with the approaches of his early lectures and essays, including the Berkeley lecture, James begins with the human project of finding one's way in the universe, and he identifies the "present dilemma" in philosophy, in just the way he conceived the core religious problem in *Varieties*:

> You want a system that will combine both things, the scientific loyalty to facts and willingness to take account of them, the spirit of adaptation and accommodation, in short, but also the old confidence in human values and the resultant spontaneity, whether of the religious or the romantic type. And this then is your dilemma: you find the two parts of your *quaesitum* hopelessly separated. (P 1907, 17)

Pragmatism is advertised as a method in philosophy that will enable people to undertake this fundamental project of reconciliation. In doing so, it will concern itself with "traditional" problems of philosophy only insofar as they are relevant to the primary purpose, or to some other end that the pragmatist method can endorse.

I recommend that we take James's announced intentions very seriously, and that we keep them in mind as we consider his characterizations of "the pragmatic method." Those characterizations come thick and fast in the second lecture of *Pragmatism*, and they are, to understate, not obviously equivalent to one another. The first version is easily connected to the theme of the first lecture, the idea that philosophy should make a difference to human life:

> The pragmatic method in such cases [metaphysical disputes: PK] is to try to interpret each notion by tracing its respective consequences. What difference would it practically make to anyone if this notion rather than that notion were true? (P 1907, 28)

James then tells us that we can understand the method better by tracing the history of pragmatism, and, returning to Peirce's explicit formulation, he elaborates the idea of making a practical difference in terms of human conduct and seems to hint at a general approach to meaning: "to develop a thought's meaning, we need only determine what conduct it is fitted to produce: that conduct is for us its sole significance" (P 1907, 29). After noting that, in the Berkeley lecture, he had revived Peirce's principle from a state of relative neglect, James suggests that the principle had been tacitly adopted by others, and, specifically, that it had pervaded Wilhelm Ostwald's approach to issues in the philosophy of science. Ostwald writes: "I am accustomed to put questions to my classes in this way: In what respects would the world be different if this alternative or that were true? If I can find nothing that would become different, then the alternative has no sense" (P 1907, 29).[2] In a further quotation from Ostwald, James provides a very specific interpretation to the notion of respects in which the world might be different—some disputes would never have begun "if the combatants had asked themselves what particular experimental fact could have been made different by one or the other view being correct" (P 1907, 30).

Having given these characterizations of the pragmatist method, James sums up with a paragraph that brings together, almost *verbatim*, three sentences that were separated in the more extended treatment of his Berkeley lecture.

> It is astonishing to see how many philosophical disputes collapse into insignificance the moment you subject them to this simple test of tracing a concrete consequence. There can *be* no difference anywhere that doesn't *make* a difference elsewhere—no difference in abstract truth that doesn't express itself in a difference in concrete fact and in conduct consequent upon that fact, imposed on somebody, somehow, somewhere and somewhen. The whole function of philosophy ought to be to find out what definite difference it will make to you and me, at definite instants of our life, if this world-formula or that world-formula be the true one. (P 1907, 30)[3]

The famous middle sentence of this paragraph can easily distract attention from the first and the last. Yet James's closing identification of the whole function of philosophy is as clear a recapitulation as we could get of his envisaged connection between philosophy and human life that pervades his work from "The Sentiment of Rationality" through the "popular essays" and *Varieties* to the first lecture of *Pragmatism*. Reading the first sentence in light of the third, it's evident that attention to the serious function of philosophy may entail dismissing certain traditional debates as irrelevant and insignificant—and that, in consequence, James may not be so much interested in using a new method to address the venerable questions as in reconstituting the agenda of philosophy.

In the space of three pages, he has offered us several formulations of pragmatism's central idea, and the middle sentence of his summation allows alternative readings. I envisage three main styles of interpretation, the last with two sub-versions:

- *Ontological Reading*. In responding to a philosophical doctrine, we should ask what difference would be made in the world if that doctrine were true.
- *Psychological Reading*. In responding to a philosophical doctrine, we should ask what difference would be made to a person's psychological state if that person were to accept that doctrine.
- *Semantic Reading* (Verificationist). The meaning of a philosophical doctrine is exhausted by the evidence that would confirm it.
- *Semantic Reading* ("Pragmatist"). The meaning of a philosophical doctrine is exhausted by the behavioral differences that would be produced by accepting it.

Many philosophers unsympathetic to pragmatism have supposed that the appropriate interpretation is the Verificationist version of the Semantic Reading, but the only passage in James's explanation that really suggests anything of this sort is the citation from Ostwald, seen through the lens of the explicit verificationism that logical positivists would use for understanding Ostwald's notion of "experimental fact." To be sure, later philosophers could forge an alliance between pragmatism and positivism by interpreting the pragmatist method in this way, but there's nothing in James's own prose that indicates anything of the kind. Nor, despite the fact that the citation of Peirce would make the "Pragmatist" version of the Semantic Reading a better candidate, is there any reason for supposing that James has any general interest in the theory of meaning. The quest for a theory of meaning is a philosophical project, and, in light of James's explicit account of the "whole function of philosophy," we ought to ask if providing a general theory of meaning contributes to that function. The obvious answer is that nothing so grandiose is required: it's simply enough to ask, of any philosophical question, what difference finding an answer would make to us. A philosopher whose agenda had been set by Gottlob Frege and Bertrand Russell might have seen semantics as central to philosophy, but James was not steeped in this tradition or in its concerns.[4] Indeed, I suggest that his use of the term *meaning* is entirely casual, that its central sense for him is bound up with what matters to people, with what is significant in human life. Like Dewey after him, James talks of "meaning" quite promiscuously, to mark out the ways in which human lives can be enriched or given direction.

We're thus left with two main readings, both of which do connect with the large project introduced in the opening lecture. Understanding how the Ontological Reading and the Psychological Reading can be viewed as different perspectives on the same basic idea is part of the project of reconciliation envisaged there. James offers both formulations, because the Ontological Reading, taken in isolation from psychological constraints, turns out to be empty, while the psychological version, released from any shaping by reality, becomes arbitrary and capricious.

These points can be clarified by considering how one might put the pragmatist method, read either way, to work in a concrete situation. As the later treatment of truth makes apparent, James is concerned with the proposals of his Hegelian contemporaries, who approach the issues in terms of "the Absolute." Imagine a dialogue in which James tries to wield the Ontological Reading of the pragmatist method to expose the insignificance of what the Hegelian metaphysician is saying.

WJ: What difference would it make in the world if your doctrine of the existence of the Absolute were true?
HM: There would be an Absolute.

The strategy is, of course, perfectly general: for any term F, you can turn back the challenge to say what the ontological "cash value" of "$(\exists x)Fx$" is by making the claim "Worlds with an F are different from worlds without an F"; effectively, this is a disquotational strategy. James wants to block the universal deployment of the strategy, and he does so by insisting on the psychological difference that must be made. You can only legitimately employ the disquotational strategy when you can specify a difference made to the psychological life of an agent by the acceptance of the claim.

Given this development of the Ontological Reading, you might think that James could simply dispense with the ontological part and rely on the Psychological Reading alone. Yet, taken in isolation, the Psychological Reading is itself inapt. Imagine round two of the dialogue with the Hegelian metaphysician.

WJ: What psychological difference would it make to someone to accept your doctrine of the existence of the Absolute?
HM: It would give that person a sense of order and comprehension—as it does for me.

This dialogue is equally unsatisfactory, and James's remedy is to insist that the psychological difference that is made stems from the admirable characteristics of the subject described in the first lecture—the tough-minded resolution not to invent a reality to suit one's prior hopes and the tender-minded concern to find significance in the world. James is never prepared to abandon the first to make life easy with the second. Throughout his decades-long examination of the tenability of religious belief, he never acquiesces in the thought that one can simply forget about scientific evidence because "affirming the universe" or identifying with the "last things" is more valuable than honoring the facts. Only when he has gone to great pains to argue that science has no bearing on a core religious idea does he endorse belief in a carefully circumscribed (and quite minimal) religious claim.[5]

In effect, the two readings are there to be used in different contexts, depending on the kind of mistake that the proponent of faulty philosophical doctrine is making. Some people, apparently pursuing rigorous chains of reasoning involving formidable abstractions, need to be recalled to the "whole function of philosophy," need to be challenged concerning the psychological differences their proposals would make. Others, attentive to the power of suggestive metaphor, have to be brought back to reality and our best methods of investigating it. The multiplicity of formulations of the pragmatist method is, I suggest, a recapitulation of the tendencies noted in the first lecture, and the application of the method requires an understanding of the ways in which we can be tempted to solve the problem of reconciliation by emphasizing one to the exclusion of the other.

Reconsidering Truth

Apart from the formulation(s) of the pragmatist principle, the sections of *Pragmatism* that have excited most philosophical attention are those that bear on the notion of truth. Many subsequent commentators have supposed that James was offering a theory of truth, a rival to the correspondence theory, and many of them have taken his "theory" to be profoundly unsatisfactory. By far the most frequent objection has been the charge that the pragmatist "theory" counts comfortable falsehoods as true—as when the committed religious believer announces that the elaborate dogmas of a particular religion "work in the way of belief." Any understanding of James's previous writings, and of *Pragmatism* in the context of those writings, should make it apparent that he is not committed to a consequence of this kind. The discussions of religion from "The Sentiment of Rationality" to *Varieties* and the opening lecture of *Pragmatism* could be radically truncated, if James could simply have availed himself of the premise "Religious dogmas work in the way of belief," and the inference from "*S* works in the way of belief" to "*S* is true." In fact, I think the critical error goes deeper, that James isn't interested in opposing the correspondence theory of truth but in understanding what might be right about it, and that, in accordance with his fundamental goals, he doesn't want a complete theory of truth, but enough grasp on the notion of truth to proceed with the really important questions.

The critical reaction is surely provoked by James's one-sentence slogan, italicized in the original, when that slogan is detached from the context in which it is set:

"The true", to put it very briefly, is only the expedient in the way of our thinking, just as "the right" is only the expedient in the way of our behaving. (P 1907, 106)

We can begin to restore context by adding the next sentence: "Expedient in almost any fashion; and expedient in the long run and on the whole of course: for what meets expediently all the experiences in sight won't necessarily meet all farther experiences equally satisfactorily." This sentence implicitly alludes to a subject of experience who changes his mind in light of the further course of experience. In emphasizing the need to respond to the long run, James must presuppose that a particular strategy of response is not available, to wit that of simply hanging on to prior belief come what may. Hence there are tacit psychological constraints on how "working" is to be assessed, and such constraints may debar the "working" of comfortable falsehoods. Indeed, in light of the first lecture and of our discussion of the pragmatist method, we ought to expect that the constraints *will* debar the exclusively tender-minded approach of retaining a belief because of the consolation it brings, even when experience presents a severe challenge.

This is only the first step, however, in understanding James's position. His approach to truth is articulated in response to a group of opponents he labels "intellectualists," whose positive doctrines only emerge sporadically and unsystematically in James's argument: they are, apparently, committed to an unexplained notion of correspondence (or "agreement") with reality, possibly to some notion of an Absolute, and to Reality as a source of imperatives for human belief (P 1907, 96, 109, 112). James's worries about the notions of agreement and reality, evident in his uses of scare quotes and his ironic capitals ("Truth," "Reality"), can easily lead readers to suppose that he rejects truth as correspondence and is suspicious of ordinary realist talk. In later responses to his critics, he insists again and again that he is not challenging common-sense views of the existence of objects: "both pragmatists and anti-pragmatists believe in existent objects, just as they believe in our ideas of them" (MT 1909, 6).[6] As he frequently pointed out in these replies, he had begun the discussion of truth with a clear statement of what was not in dispute.

> Truth, as any dictionary will tell you, is a property of certain of our ideas. It means their "agreement," as falsity means their disagreement, with "reality." Pragmatists and intellectualists both accept this definition as a matter of course. They begin to quarrel only after the question is raised as to what may precisely be meant by the term "agreement," and what by the term "reality," when reality is taken as something for our ideas to agree with. (P 1907, 96)

James's challenge doesn't propose to abandon the dictionary idea of truth as correspondence (or agreement) but to articulate it. The error of intellectualists is either that they fail to say anything about the central notions the idea presupposes—the notions of agreement and truth—or, when they do, they offer the vague suggestion that "ideas possess[ed] truth just in proportion as they approach to being copies of the Absolute's eternal way of thinking" (P 1907, 96).

Philosophers who want to recruit James as an ally in their opposition to *contemporary* correspondence theories of truth must surely reckon with the character of the positions against which he was reacting. Neither he nor his Idealist targets could approach the concept of truth by using the Tarskian framework, and they were thus unable to find the most satisfactory formulation of the correspondence idea. Yet once Alfred Tarski's apparatus is available, we can give James's approach to truth a clearer formulation than *Pragmatism* achieves.

Tarski shows how to provide a recursive definition of truth for sentences in a class of formal languages, where the base clauses ascribe relations of reference (between names and objects, between monadic predicates and sets of objects, and so forth). To satisfy James's pragmatic challenge, we need to explain the notion of reference and the status of the entities (objects, sets of objects, etc.) so that the differences made by the statements of semantic theory are apparent. If this explanation is to accord with his own discussions, then three important conditions must be satisfied.

1. The explanation should be compatible with common-sense realism.
2. The explanation should connect the notion of reference with the practical activities of language-users.
3. The explanation should honor James's frequent denial that reality sets an agenda for human cognition.

There is a version of the correspondence theory that meets all three constraints.

As I've already noted, James's responses to his critics make his endorsement of common-sense realism apparent. The way he understands the notion of correspondence, or agreement, is also easier to recognize in these responses. *Pragmatism* tells us only, rather vaguely, that agreement is "an affair of leading—leading that is useful because it is into quarters that contain objects that are important" (P 1907, 103). The earlier presentations hint at a navigational project that receives a much more elaborate account in *The Meaning of Truth*. There James considers how his use of the term *Memorial Hall*—or, in his own favored formulation, his image of Memorial Hall—comes to refer to a particular definite object. He suggests that reference would fail for a user who could not do anything in response to a query about the intended referent, and contrasts the inability to point or to lead with the successful case.

> On the other hand, if I can lead you to the hall, and tell you of its history and present uses; if in its presence I feel my idea, however imperfect it may have been, to have led hither and to be now *terminated*; if the associates of the image and of the felt hall run parallel, so that each term of the one context corresponds serially, as I walk, with an answering term of the other; why then my soul was prophetic, and my idea must be, and by common consent would be, called cognizant of reality. (MT 1909, 62–63)

Although somewhat indefinite, James's proposal is pregnant—and it has the capacity to deliver a pragmatist account of the notion of reference.

The assumed relation of reference (or "meaning") is revealed by the fact that it helps us see the imagined walk as a success. We can develop the example in a more stylized fashion. Suppose we are watching a person on whom we have already carried out the initial test: she has led us to Memorial Hall and confessed to that sense of "termination" to which James alludes; we're thus confident that, by "Memorial Hall," she refers to Memorial Hall. We now take this person to an unfamiliar part of the general neighborhood, and ask her to lead us back to Memorial Hall. We provide her with a map, and ask her, as she proceeds, to express openly the thoughts that are guiding her navigation. So we hear her connect symbols on the map with parts of the environment; we see her picking out particular chunks of independent reality (reality independent of her[7]). She uses her connections, together with the map, to direct her movements, even though she is constantly reckoning with things she has not previously seen. If the map is a good one, and if she is skilled at map-reading, then she eventually leads us to Memorial Hall. This success depends in part on a correspondence between the map and reality: it's because the various symbols correspond to parts of the environment, and because the relations among those parts are well depicted in the map, that her skilled reading of it works. (There's that "serial correspondence" that James notes.) The referential relations play a role in explaining her success.[8]

James seems to be aiming at something like this point in a discussion that follows soon after his "Memorial Hall" example. He writes:

> By experimenting on our ideas of reality, we may save ourselves the trouble of experimenting on the real experiences which they severally mean. The ideas form related systems, corresponding point for point to the systems which the realities form. (MT 1909, 65)

This idea of related systems, one of signs and one of things, corresponding point for point, needs to be given content: we need to be told just what difference it would make to us to accept that. The story James tells, and that I've elaborated, gives an answer. The thought of the correspondence can be used to explain behavior, and, in particular, to understand the successes of representation-coordinated behavior.

The stylized scenario exhibits the ways in which reference is manifested in action. Our imagined map user deploys her well-entrenched categories and cognitive habits to organize her experience of a reality independent of her.[9] As we follow her actions, we suppose that she is arriving at an organization much like the one we'd adopt. We can liberate the general approach to reference from the particular context of navigation, and envisage different kinds of activity that fix reference—finding your way is a vivid example, but is not essential.[10]

Yet the account I've outlined so far may seem at odds with a fundamental feature of *Pragmatism*: its rejection of any static notion of truth in favor of the proposal that "Truth *happens* to an idea" (P 1907, 97). Here I want to develop the third aspect of James's discussion, his denial that reality sets an agenda for human cognition and his corresponding commitment to a pluralism about the categories we legitimately adopt. *Pragmatism* recapitulates an analogy that James originally introduces in *Principles of Psychology*: even with respect to sensory experience, the subject plays a constructive role, because even though "[w]e receive . . . the block of marble, . . . we carve the statue ourselves" (P 1907, 119).[11] The world allows division into objects and categories of objects in many different ways, and we choose boundaries and class limits that suit our purposes (P 1907, 121).[12] Agreement with reality is subsequent to this initial decision: as James puts it, we make "additions" to sensible reality, and we can do so in many ways that "agree" with it (P 1907, 121). He is opposing the thought that there is a privileged structuring of what is independent of us into objects and categories of objects, to which any adequate language must answer. Human beings with different interests—and, more radically, other cognitive creatures with different capacities—would respond to the same independent reality in distinct ways, generating alternative schemes for dividing it up. Properly understood, there would be no incompatibility among the statements generated and accepted by the users of the rival schemes, simply differences in the ease with which the users could pursue their diverse projects.

I read the proposal that "Truth happens to an idea" in light of this pluralism. On the modest correspondence approach I've attributed to James, the relation between sentences and the world is static. Once a particular language has been fixed, the singular terms pick out certain chunks of independent reality, the monadic predicates pick out certain sets of chunks of independent reality, and so forth, and the truth of sentences is atemporally fixed by the inclusion relations together with the recursion clauses for connectives and quantifiers. So far, truth doesn't "happen to an idea." But, James insists, the obtaining of this static relation isn't the "essential" point—what really matters is whether the sentences we endorse can continue to play their guiding role (P 1907, 102). Hence, he withholds the ascription of truth from sentences couched in languages that cease to be adequate to our purposes; in his stronger sense, to say that a sentence is true is to affirm that the language in which it is couched continues to be adequate to our aims and that the static relation between this sentence and reality obtains. Because the first part of the affirmation is hostage to our evolving goals, the relation of truth is also dynamic, and truth can reasonably be said to "happen to an idea."

Religious Hypotheses

James's pluralism about categories is not just central to his thoughts about the abstract topic of truth, but also key to his closing lecture, in which he returns to the problem he had originally formulated. As so often, it's easy to read James's remarks out of context and to find them absurd or disappointing. Apparently, a sentence and a half, on the penultimate page, wrap up the difficulty of reconciling the scientific vision of the world with religious belief:

> On pragmatistic principles, if the hypothesis of God works satisfactorily in the widest sense of the word, it is true. Now whatever its residual difficulties may be, experience shows that it certainly does work. (P 1907, 143)

Taken in isolation, it's easy to read these words as the simplistic argument I've already rejected as a satisfactory view of his intentions: most people find that religious belief "works for them" (it uplifts them, gives them a direction in life, etc.); that kind of working suffices for truth, conceived in the pragmatist fashion; hence the God hypothesis is true. Yet James goes on immediately to note the problems in explicating religious claims, and he explicitly disclaims the project of giving a "whole theology" (P 1907, 143). Instead, he refers us to a previous book—*Varieties*—in order to rebut any charge that pragmatism is necessarily atheistic. Interestingly, that work already recognized the tremendous variety of religious hypotheses, and seems committed, from the outset, to rejecting a literalist monotheism. So we know, in advance, that the problem of explicating claims about "God" will be far from straightforward.

More importantly, James has led us to this point by a circuitous route that has associated pragmatism with a very specific religious attitude. This, he claims, derives from the pluralism that pragmatism encourages. We are all interested, James claims, in the salvation of the world (P 1907, 137). Traditional religions, and philosophy, treat salvation as assured, while pessimists (James cites Arthur Schopenhauer) take it to be impossible. Pragmatism, however, proposes meliorism, understood as a commitment to try to realize current ideals and to eliminate existing shortcomings piecemeal, where it is recognized that success isn't guaranteed. Allegedly, this provides a new type of religion, one that allows the reconciliation of the tensions of the opening lecture.

There's much that is obscure in these formulations, but I think we can make sense of James's strategy, despite reasonable doubt about its success. The languages people use evolve to adapt to their needs in inquiry—this is the message of the pluralism that underlies James's approach to truth—and we can ask whether the traditional language of religion is ripe for abandonment. Defenders of the tradition will claim that it is still needed to formulate truths about the universe, while post-Darwinian scientists will contend that standard claims to religious truth have been radically undermined. James is willing to concede that, as conventionally understood, religious doctrines have been called into question, but he thinks continued employment of religious language plays a valuable role in the essential human project of striving to make the world better. The advocates of scientism, and pessimists like Schopenhauer, are depriving themselves of important tools for going forward, piecemeal, in the attempt to realize ideals and work through conflicts of values. On the other hand, traditionalists who make literal claims about the existence of entities with extraordinary powers commit themselves to something far stronger than they need, something that is at odds with the tough-minded attitudes of thoroughly modern science. Pragmatists encourage pluralistic talk about what they call, with admitted vagueness, "the transcendent," for the purposes of advancing an enterprise to which nobody can be indifferent.

The obvious issue that arises for James, on this construal, is whether language that helps us in thinking about values, progress, and the improvement of the world needs to be specifically religious—and it tells in favor of my reading that James brings up the objection himself.

> Many people would refuse to call the pluralistic scheme religious at all. They would call it moralistic, and would apply the word religious to the monistic scheme alone. (P 1907, 140)

James's own reply is to acknowledge the opposition between surrender to the will of an all-powerful deity and active efforts to improve things, which, he thinks, lies behind the charge. He tries to commend the active attitude, and to link it to particular kinds of religious attitude.[13]

As I read him, James is moving toward a position that Dewey would articulate two decades later (in Dewey 1934). The difficulties and unclarities of James's discussion result from his residual hope that continued uses of religious language will eventually license some claims about "the transcendent" as true. Dewey, more firmly focused on the needs of human inquiry (understood in the broad fashion he shared with James), abandons this hope in favor of a sharper position. Recognizing the variety of ways in which the "unseen powers" have been envisaged, we should simply drop the practice of talking about them:

> there is nothing left worth preserving in the notions of unseen powers, controlling human destiny to which obedience, reverence and worship are due, if we glide silently over the nature that has been attributed to the powers, the radically diverse ways in which they have been supposed to control human destiny, and in which submission and awe have been manifested. (Dewey 1934, 7)

Yet this can be done, Dewey claims, without losing sight of the issue I interpreted as central to James's final lecture: the needs of human ventures in practical progress. Dewey takes this issue as seriously as James did, and his response to it is explicitly to re-conceive the continued use of religious language.

It is the claim of religions that they effect this generic and enduring change in attitude. I should like to turn the statement around and say that whenever this change takes place there is a definitely religious attitude. It is not *a* religion that brings it about, but when it occurs, from whatever cause and by whatever means, there is a religious outlook and function. (Dewey 1934, 17)

This is one place, but not the only place, in which Dewey makes explicit ideas toward which I take James to have been groping. In closing, I want to use Dewey—and the subsequent course of Anglophone philosophy—to sharpen James's philosophical project, and to crystallize what *Pragmatism* means and what Pragmatism might still mean for us.

The Revolution That Never Was

Here is a way of reading James's great book. The heart of philosophy is a small collection of human problems, problems that arise in different ways for different groups of people at different stages of human inquiry. For post-Enlightenment, post-Darwinian thinkers, the question of how to reconcile a scientific world view with values and ideals, and with the claims of religion, is prominent among these problems. Professional philosophy, however, tends to become ossified, focused on issues that have arisen from earlier attempts to address questions that were once live human concerns, and it pursues technicalities that are no longer relevant to the changed landscape in which people find themselves. When that occurs, philosophy needs renewal, and the pragmatist method is a wonderful tool for diagnosing trouble and inspiring a return to the genuine questions. Allegedly "central" areas in philosophy—epistemology and metaphysics, for example—are valuable only insofar as they enable us to address those genuine questions. To pursue them at great length because of their alleged intrinsic importance is comparable to becoming so enamored of the techniques for glass-blowing used in making the apparatus for experimental research that one spends a lifetime producing vessels with fantastic shapes that could serve no purpose in the laboratory.

This attitude is, I suggest, implicit in James's *Pragmatism*, and it becomes fully formulated in Dewey.[14] Dewey takes the core philosophical problem to be that of understanding how to live, both as individuals and in community, and he sees this problem as taking different forms in different eras, as people learn more about the world in which they find themselves.[15] In *Reconstruction in Philosophy*, he tells us that "the task of future philosophy is to clarify men's ideas as to the social and moral strifes of their own day" (Dewey 1920, 26). The point is recapitulated, in a way that generalizes James's question in the opening lecture of *Pragmatism*, in Dewey's own Gifford Lectures:

> The problem of restoring integration and cooperation between man's beliefs about the world in which he lives and his beliefs about the values and purposes that should

direct his conduct is the deepest problem of modern life. It is the problem of any philosophy that is not isolated from that life. (Dewey 1929/1981, 204)

Elsewhere, Dewey connected this problem to the "general theory of education" and to the project of improving democracy.[16] In all these modes, he consistently gives to the fields that contemporary Anglophone philosophers regard as central—epistemology, metaphysics, philosophy of mind, philosophy of language—a purely instrumental significance, viewing them as useful only insofar as they help with the really serious issues of ethics, social and political philosophy, religion, art, and education. Dewey turns the current map of Anglo-American philosophy inside out, and, in doing so, I take him to be following through the central tendency of James's *Pragmatism*.

James and Dewey both hoped for a reform of philosophy—and so, of course, did others. In the 1930s, American Pragmatism allied itself with Central European Logical Positivism, and there was apparently good reason for the union symbolized by the joint project of the *Encyclopedia of Unified Science*. Both movements insisted that traditional philosophical problems were not significant—but their common formulation was based upon an ambiguity. James and Dewey, uninterested in the theory of linguistic meaning, saw those traditional problems as not mattering to human lives, as questions whose answers would make no practical difference to anyone anywhere anywhen. Rudolf Carnap, Moritz Schlick, and others saw the questions as pseudo-problems, as literally failing to say anything. Moreover, in contrast to the expansive—purple?—prose of James, and the plain, but seemingly woolly language of Dewey, the positivists brought a shining new implement with which to carry out reconstructive surgery. Given the superficial precision of the verifiability criterion, was it really surprising that positivism became the dominant partner in the reform movement, and that the pragmatist concerns disappeared?

Yet, as their repeated efforts to state the verifiability criterion with complete logical precision were to reveal, the criterion was only superficial. Carl Gustav Hempel's landmark article on the struggles to formulate the criterion of cognitive significance closed with a retreat from the original positivist program of diagnosis and radical cure for the ills of philosophy (Hempel 1965). Henceforth, logical empiricism (positivism's heir) would devote itself to the analysis of those features that had made the natural sciences so strikingly successful, in hopes that, once recognized, the features could be imported into other parts of the intellectual landscape: the logic of science was no longer to be the whole of philosophy, but philosophy of science, directed at explicating "confirmation," "explanation," "law," and "theory" could still promise serious reform for the future. Half a century on, those general enterprises have proved as recalcitrant as the search for the criterion of cognitive significance: there is no serious hope that philosophers will supply precise formal methods that can be useful to those who hope to develop nascent sciences: even the most ardent Bayesian (or advocate of any rival mode of explicating any meta-scientific concept) must acknowledge the limitations of analytic machinery when confronted with the live debates of contemporary inquiry.[17]

For many different reasons, contemporary Anglophone philosophy has given up on the reform movement to which the positivists and their logical empiricist successors were committed. Today's professional philosophy finds room for projects in analytic metaphysics, analytic epistemology, and even analytic ethics and aesthetics, that are as technical and arcane as those that provoked the positivists of the 1930s—and their pragmatist predecessors. With respect to many of the questions currently regarded as "central" to philosophy, we'd do well to reflect on James's question: what practical difference would it make to anyone, anywhere, anywhen, if an answer to that question were found? Perhaps a defender of philosophical practice will offer an analogy with the natural sciences. Molecular biologists, after all, answer minute questions about individual molecules in organisms of little obvious interest. They do so, of course, in the hope that their answers will dovetail with those offered by different researchers, working on different problems or on different organisms, so that a collective project of understanding cellular metabolism or early development may be advanced.[18] Philosophy differs from molecular biology in that we typically lack methods for resolving even our most technical questions, and hardly ever build on the achievements of other members of our community in the way that typifies the mature sciences—as Richard Rorty rightly puts it "Philosophy ... is not a *Fach*" (Rorty 1982, 28).[19]

The present scene provides numerous examples of work that would survive the pragmatist challenge. There are philosophers working on concrete social problems of race, gender, and class; on the difficulties of democracy; on specific issues in normative ethics; in problems that arise from individual sciences (physics, biology, anthropology, economics, psychology, semantics, and so on); or from the arts. James and Dewey would, I think, also approve of nascent attempts to develop philosophical themes from works of literature and music, and I think they would find many contemporary studies in the history of philosophy sophisticated and illuminating. Yet all these healthy tendencies arise at what professional philosophy typically views as the periphery.

I draw an obvious moral. We need reconstruction in philosophy as much as James thought it was needed in 1907, as much as Dewey thought it was needed in 1920, and as much as the positivists thought it was needed in 1930. There were differences in the precise character of the reforms urged by pragmatists and positivists—although there were, of course, figures like Otto Neurath who shared many of Dewey's concerns, and, indeed, many of the early positivists would have sympathized with some of the pragmatists' goals. As it turned out, the attractions of positivist precision steered the reform movement away from the large human questions that worried James and Dewey, but, reading them again a century later, it is hard to resist the thought that they had identified the fundamental issues, issues that ought to be replaced at the center of philosophy today.

My title is taken from a famous poem by an American, Robert Frost. A traveler, arriving at a fork in a wood, peers down both paths, before choosing "the one less traveled by." That, Frost suggests, makes "all the difference." I propose that we return to the forking paths of positivism and pragmatism that lead to possible reform, and that this time we take the pragmatist track, the road not taken. Perhaps it will make "all the difference" to future philosophy.

Notes

1. I use scare quotes here because I find the term *analytic* problematic as a designation for the work of philosophers, many of whom reject the project of conceptual analysis on Quinean grounds. Nor is it reasonable to use language that restricts a particular style of philosophy to works written in English, given that today there are prominent ventures in philosophy in Scandinavia, Germany, Spain, and elsewhere that continue the Anglo-American tradition of the mid-twentieth century. So "analytic" in scare quotes will have to do.
2. James is quoting in his own translation from Ostwald (1905).
3. For the formulations in the Berkeley lecture, see P (1898, 260).
4. Peirce is much closer to the tradition we associate with Frege, Russell, and their successors. Hence, contrary to James's own views, I am separating his pragmatism from the approach articulated by Peirce. This is, however, closer to Peirce's own assessment of their relationship. For valuable discussions of the differences, I am indebted to Cheryl Misak, although she would probably defend a closer connection between Peirce and James.
5. This occurs both in "The Will to Believe" and, on a different and more extensive basis, in *Varieties*. For further discussion, see my essay "A Pragmatist's Progress" (Kitcher 2004).
6. See also MT (1909, 45, 104, 117–118, 127–128, 147).
7. Most of the things she identifies will be dependent on human activity of various sorts, but, unless she is very unusual, she won't have been involved in those activities.
8. I articulate and defend this point more fully in Kitcher (2002).
9. I've suggested elsewhere that this enables us to defend common-sense realism. See Kitcher (2001a, 2001b, 2011).
10. Even when we consider the totality of someone's actions, there may remain indeterminacies in referential relations, as W. V. O. Quine famously argued. On a pragmatist account these indeterminacies are unworrying, since they provide equivalent accounts of reality and of our language-guided interactions with it.
11. See also PP (1890, 274, 277). This analogy is tricky because James ought to admit that there are fault lines in the marble, and, to make the analogy go through, the fault lines have to depend on us.
12. Among James's examples is the grouping of stars into constellations. This recurs in the later debate between Nelson Goodman and Israel Scheffler—and with good reason, since Goodman's views in *Ways of Worldmaking* are close to those James is developing in this passage.
13. In particular to that strain of Puritanism that was willing to risk salvation (P 1907, 142).
14. Although Dewey develops it in a different way. In an obvious sense, he recognizes many kinds of philosophical questions, but insists, as James does, that they bear on human life and experience. Using a distinction made famous by Isaiah Berlin, Dewey is a fox, and James a hedgehog. I am grateful to Jennifer Welchman for urging me to make this difference more explicit.

15. He explores the ways in which the problem was posed for the ancient world, and for the architects of the new sciences in the seventeenth century. Even more imaginatively, he sometimes considers the ways in which it would have emerged in human pre-history, and how myths and religious beliefs responded to it.
16. See Dewey (1916/1944, ch. 24, esp. 328; 1927/1980, ch. 6, esp. 208).
17. These are points that should have been learned from Thomas Kuhn's *Structure of Scientific Revolutions* (Kuhn 1962)—ironically the last volume published in the *Encyclopedia of Unified Science*—and from some of the historical and sociological literature that it has inspired. To concede these points is not to abandon the ideal of scientific rationality, but simply to recognize the complexities of scientific reasoning. I have tried to show this in chapters 6–8 of *The Advancement of Science* (Kitcher 1993).
18. For my proposals concerning how these technical questions obtain significance, see chapter 6 of *Science, Truth, and Democracy* (Kitcher 2001b).
19. I used to think that Richard Rorty's response to Anglophone philosophy only applied to a small set of questions that twentieth-century philosophy had inherited, questions in metaphysics, epistemology, and philosophy of mind, and that much of the general work in these fields, as well as areas like philosophy of science and ethics, would emerge unscathed from his critique. I now believe that this was mistaken. The pragmatist challenge can cause embarrassment in almost any sub-field of philosophy.

References

Dewey, John. 1916/1944. *Democracy and Education: An Introduction to the Philosophy of Education*. New York: Free Press.
Dewey, John. 1920. *Reconstruction in Philosophy*. New York: Henry Holt.
Dewey, John. 1927/1980. *The Public and Its Problems*. Athens: Swallow Press.
Dewey, John. 1929/1981. "The Quest for Certainty." In *The Later Works, 1925–1953*, edited by Jo Ann Boydston. Carbondale: Southern Illinois University Press.
Dewey, John. 1934. *A Common Faith*. New Haven: Yale University Press.
Hempel, Carl G. 1965. "Problems and Changes in the Empiricist Criterion of Cognitive Significance." In *Aspects of Scientific Explanation and Other Essays in the Philosophy of Science*, edited by Carl G. Hempel, 101–119. New York: Free Press.
Kitcher, Philip. 1993. *The Advancement of Science: Science without Legend, Objectivity without Illusions*. New York: Oxford University Press.
Kitcher, Philip. 2001a. "Real Realism: The Galilean Strategy." *The Philosophical Review* 110 (2): 151–197.
Kitcher, Philip. 2001b. *Science, Truth, and Democracy*. Oxford: Oxford University Press.
Kitcher, Philip. 2002. "On the Explanatory Role of Correspondence Truth." *Philosophy and Phenomenological Research* 64 (2): 346–364.
Kitcher, Philip. 2004. "A Pragmatist's Progress: The Varieties of James's Strategies for Defending Religion." In *William James and a Science of Religions: Reexperiencing the Varieties of Religious Experience*, edited by Wayne Proudfoot, 98–138. New York: Columbia University Press.
Kitcher, Philip. 2011. "Scientific Realism: The Truth in Pragmatism." *Poznań Studies in the Philosophy of the Sciences & the Humanities* 101: 171–189.

Kuhn, Thomas S. 1962. *The Structure of Scientific Revolutions*. Chicago: University of Chicago Press.
Ostwald, Wilhelm. 1905. "Theorie Und Praxis." *Zeitschrift des Österreichischen Ingenieur- und Architekten-Vereines* Vortrage-Zyklus über moderne Chemie 57: 3–9.
Rorty, Richard. 1982. *Consequences of Pragmatism: Essays, 1972–1980*. Minneapolis: University of Minnesota Press.

CHAPTER 17

JAMES AND EPISTEMIC PLURALISM

IGNAS KĘSTUTIS SKRUPSKELIS

WHILE in Oxford delivering the Hibbert Lectures, published as *A Pluralistic Universe* (PU 1909), William James, on May 24, 1908, met with Bertrand Russell, and some hours later prepared what amounts to a memo of their disagreement. Two major points emerge. First: James's conception of truth is a pluralistic one. He writes: "instead of there being one universal relation *sui generis* called 'truth' between any reality and an idea, there are a host of particular relations varying according to special circumstances and constituted by the manner of 'working' or 'leading' of the idea through the surrounding experiences of which both the reality and the idea are part." Second: only in special cases are "working," "leading," and similar terms to be understood in a narrow utilitarian sense (CWJ 12.18). Russell had entered the fray in October of 1907 with a talk to several hundred undergraduates—later published as "Transatlantic 'Truth' "—claiming that if the pragmatic account of truth is itself to be useful, it should be possible to establish that a belief pays without knowing that it is true (Russell 1908).[1]

Two allies had warned James that Russell was his most formidable opponent. Ferdinand Canning Scott Schiller, whose humanism came closer to intellectual anarchism than James's pragmatism, was present for Russell's talk. Schiller had a low opinion of his opponents: the American critics are "stupid," the English, "vicious." But in his letter of October 25, 1907, he made clear that Russell was neither: Russell's was "a very fine paper ... full of fine points & subtle misconceptions, but with some unexpected concessions & in a friendly tone" (CWJ 11.468). Horace Meyer Kallen, studying at Oxford while a graduate student at Harvard, offered a fuller report. On November 6, he boasted that in spite of arriving late, he became the center of the discussion: "When I finished I became immediately the target for all sorts of questions and it seemed Russell was forgotten." But Russell was kind, invited Kallen to his home, and they trashed the matter out for six hours. Kallen concluded that Russell "is an important and dangerous man" (CWJ 1907, 11.473–474). Thus, James reached Oxford forewarned that he would be called upon to defend pragmatism and his view of truth. It is less clear that he was prepared to confront a mind more analytically inclined than his own. Unfortunately, all that survives of the confrontation is James's memorandum.

It is important to understand that the controversy was public, by no means confined to academic journals, with the reputations of universities and perhaps countries at stake. Russell's title, "Transatlantic 'Truth,'" suggested by the editor, draws attention to this (Russell 2014, 5.465). Some Europeans dismissed pragmatism as the product of a nation so given to business as to be incapable of philosophy, and indeed, James's more colorful phrases lend themselves to caricature. Kallen in turn dismissed Oxford as a "middle-class paradise." Thus, an interpreter must remember that James rarely worked out a position in the quiet of his study. On the contrary, he often wrote in the heat of controversy, and at times, while defending the intellectual respectability of his allies.

A second caution emerges. The controversy was not restricted to the single matter of the definition of truth, but extended to a broad range of philosophical issues. In fact, at issue was a whole outlook arising out of Darwin and the new physiology of the brain and nervous system. James worked out its foundation in *The Principles of Psychology* (PP 1890) by arguing that it is the brain that thinks—that is, by developing a psychology without a soul. The surviving notes, sketchy and often unintelligible, for his philosophical psychology courses of the 1890s testify to his efforts to uncover the philosophical implications of the rising neurological sciences (ML 1891–1898, 206–259). In the late 1890s he began to systematize his philosophical outlook under the name of radical empiricism.[2] And in a 1903 text we read: "The essential consequence to remember is that, if experiences ... are the minimal world-factors, absolute 'substances' in the old dualistic sense of 'material masses' on the one hand, and 'souls' or 'spirits' on the other, cannot be allowed to be real" (MEN 1903, 21).

If free will is possible only for spiritual beings and it is only souls that struggle after truth, beauty, and goodness, as has been held by many Western philosophers and in many religions, a naturalistic psychology, one without a soul, cannot help but be reductive, seeing human life as nothing more than the surface play of unseen forces. By contrast, James, and Dewey in particular, were nonreductive naturalists, striving not to dismiss but to reinterpret what the Western tradition has seen as most human and valuable.[3] Thus, in his 1878 Lowell lectures, after declaring materialism to be unscientific, James writes: "I trust that you ... will go away strengthened in the natural faith that your delights & sorrows, your loves & hates, your aspirations & efforts are real combatants in life's arena, & not impotent, paralytic spectators of the game" (ML 1878, 30). It is significant that in his 1905 essay "The Thing and Its Relations," James contrasted not rationalism and empiricism, but rationalism and naturalism. For the rationalist, "to understand is simply the duty of man," but for the naturalist, understanding is the struggle to isolate the elements in experience that "have a practical bearing upon life," to discover "what is in the wind for us and get ready to react in time" (ERE 1905, 47). This kind of naturalism is open to the possibility that free will is a fact in nature, a power which some organisms have.

The nonreductive linking of Darwinism and epistemology forms the background of James's account of truth. In his psychology the minimum mental unit is the reflex, with the brain selecting the response in cases where the linkage of stimulus and response is not mechanical (see Klein, this volume). For James, the function of the brain is to select reactions.[4] Since the brain and the nervous system are organs of reaction, every sensory stimulus evokes some response. But, as we mature, we learn how to control ourselves and not allow the response to develop into a full-fledged action.

The pragmatists responded creatively to the rising biological sciences for which man is an organism in nature, facing similar problems and working under similar constraints as other organisms. I would also argue that pragmatism, while not intended for such a career, for many reasons became the public face of radical empiricism. But these arguments are much too broad to be developed here. The essential point is that for James philosophy cannot be divorced from psychology nor can psychology be divorced from physiology (see Leary and Levine, both in this volume).

Setting aside broader issues, I will confine myself to the modest task of pulling together the varieties of truth recognized by James, something that he himself did not do.[5] However, I must first sketch out the radical empiricist account of relations, because truth is a relation.

Two claims are important. First, radical empiricism cannot "admit into its constructions any element that is not directly experienced." Second, distinguishing radical empiricism from the halfway empiricism of Berkeley, Hume, and others—"*the relations that connect experiences must themselves be experienced relations*" (ERE 1904, 22; see Inukai, this volume). It follows that what we eventually come to call the knower is a "piece of experience," while the known is another, and the two are connected by actual or possible "tracts of conjunctive transitional experience" (ERE 1904, 27). Thus, in the case of one kind of knowledge, that of "sensible realities," knowing is "experience from point to point of one direction followed, and finally of one process fulfilled." That, James continues, "is all that knowing (in the simple case considered) can be known-as, that is the whole of its nature, put into experiential terms" (ERE 1904, 29).[6]

James borrowed the phrase "known-as" from the British philosopher Shadworth Hollway Hodgson and repeated it often. In fact, in a somewhat jocular New Year's greeting to Hodgson, he states that Peirce and "S.H.H. with his method of attacking problems by asking what their terms are 'known-as'" are the two sources of his pragmatism (CWJ 1910, 12.400).[7] While James never explained what the phrase means, its use underscores his interest in describing our experiences of truths, a task that Russell never pursued. And for James, to experience truths is to experience different kinds of satisfactoriness.

Everything begins decades before pragmatism, with James's attempt to refute the argument from the possibility of error proposed as the foundation of absolute idealism by Josiah Royce in *The Religious Aspect of Philosophy* (Royce 1885). Royce argues that error appears to be impossible, because a thought can be in error only about its intended object, while one can intend only what one knows and one cannot be mistaken about what one knows. But if the Absolute steps in to link thought and object, error is possible. As James put it in "On the Function of Cognition" (1885), Royce "maintained that the notion of referring involved that of an inclusive mind that shall own both the real q and the mental q, and use the latter expressly as a representative symbol of the former." But "any definitely experienced workings would serve as intermediaries quite as well as the absolute mind's intentions."[8]

Royce makes intention the foundation of any account of knowledge. And James was impressed: "there is a real puzzle here." In his review of Royce's book, he writes: "If thought be one thing and reality another, by what pincers, from out of all the realities, does the thought pick out the special one it intends to know?" (ECR 1885, 386).[9] Royce invokes the Absolute, while James develops the idea of experienceable intermediaries.

In putting together *The Meaning of Truth*, James violated chronology by beginning with "The Function of Cognition" and an excerpt under the title of "The Tigers in India" from an 1895 paper. This has to be understood against the background of the pragmatism controversy: pragmatists were often depicted as intellectual anarchists and even as advocates of the useful lie. Thus, Russell objected that for pragmatism the belief that something exists can be deemed true even when in fact the thing does not exist (Russell 1908/2014). In response, in "Two English Critics," James characterized Russell's criticism as the "usual slander" (MT 1909, 147). The two early papers show that for James, a belief works, in one important sense, when reality is found to be what we expect it to be.

"The Tigers in India" deals with the problem of reference, and in "The Relation between Knower and Known" (1904) he is still preoccupied with Royce's claim that resemblance between idea and object is not enough to constitute truth. But the upshot of the earlier article is this: "There are tigers in India," when the tigers are not immediately present, is true if and only if there are experienceable paths which if followed out would place us in the immediate presence of the "striped rascals" (MT 1909, 34). In the later paper he uses Harvard's Memorial Hall to the same purpose, putting his point this way: "In this continuing and corroborating, taken in no transcendental sense, but denoting definitely felt transitions, *lies all that the knowing of a percept by an idea can possibly contain or signify*" (MT 1909, 63). In the former case he is describing what he calls "representative knowledge," in the latter—"knowledge-about." Neither term is made precise, but his examples indicate a large class of claims to the effect that objects of a given kind exist. These could be called referential assertions, which are true when the reference is successful, that is, when we follow out an experienceable path and find what we expected to find. In this case, the following captures James's position: a statement that *p* exists is true, if and only if, there are experiencable paths which if followed out would place us in the presence of *p*. In this, rather than in a narrow utilitarian sense, they can be said to work or pay.

He handles historical claims in a related way. Obviously, assertions about past existents "admit of no direct or face-to-face verification." Yet truth is still a matter of leading, in this case to the "present prolongations or effects of what the past harbored" (P 1907, 103). While James does not elaborate, his meaning is the ordinary one that, for example, bones in a cemetery are a "present prolongation" of the past.

In James's "web of belief" conception of knowledge, referential assertions serve as anchors, keeping our inclinations at bay. They compel belief, regardless of whether belief is pleasing or profitable. James calls these experienceable paths "objective reference" and insists that for him truth means agreement with reality. Note the exasperation by the failure of critics to recognize this: "I apprehended no exclusively subjectivist reading of my meaning. My mind was so filled with the notion of objective reference that I never dreamed that my hearers would let go of it" (MT 1909, 128). In another text, after insisting that for pragmatism to be true a statement must agree with "some such reality," he writes: "Reference then to something determinate, and some sort of adaptation to it worthy of the name of agreement, are thus constituent elements in the definition of any statement of mine as 'true'" (MT 1909, 117–118). Misunderstandings could have been avoided had he been this explicit in *Pragmatism* (1907). But the idea of reality as constraining our beliefs is there: "Between the coercions of the sensible order and those of the ideal order, our mind is thus wedged tightly" (P 1907, 101).

While agreement can consist of resemblance, "agreement" should not be understood as a synonym for "resemblance." He writes: "To copy a reality is, indeed, one very important way of agreeing with it, but it is far from being essential.... Any idea that helps us to *deal*, whether practically or intellectually, with either the reality or its belongings, that doesn't entangle our progress in frustrations, that *fits*, in fact, and adapts our life to the reality's whole setting, will agree sufficiently to meet the requirement" (P 1907, 102). Being guided, dealing, fitting, will not be found in any dictionary of philosophy. But they serve James's purpose of getting us to recreate in our imaginations some of our various truth-seeking experiences.

Thus, it is a mistake to think of the pragmatic and the correspondence accounts of truth as alternatives. For James, correspondence is a special case of the former. In "Humanism and Truth," he explains why correspondence has come to play a prominent role in philosophical conceptions of truth. It is because of the importance of prediction: "It is easy to see from what special type of knowing the copy-theory arose. In our dealings with natural phenomena the great point is to be able to foretell" (MT 1909, 51). Prediction depends on our ability to duplicate mentally—provide an "exact copy"—of sequences in reality. And the copy need not be a picture: often symbolic representations are more helpful. For James, there are different ways of corresponding.

Given the polemical context, his preoccupation with Royce and the defense of pragmatism against accusations of subjectivism, it is understandable that most of his attention should be devoted to referential assertions. I am not aware of any attempt to generalize to all statements. But his brief treatment of relations of ideas suggests that a generalized notion of leading would be involved. In *Pragmatism* he writes: "In this realm of mental relations, truth again is an affair of leading." He does not elaborate and provides no examples, but warns against misreadings: "Our ready-made ideal framework for all sorts of possible objects follows from the very structure of our thinking. We can no more play fast and loose with these abstract relations than we can do so with our sense-experiences. They coerce us; we must treat them consistently, whether or not we like the results" (P 1907, 101). This passage has a Kantian ring, hinting as it does at categories. And in fact, in *Pragmatism*, James provides a list of categories, although treating them not in a Kantian but in a Darwinian manner. The categories—he lists eleven, including "Thing," "One Time," and "One Space"—are not fixed structures utilized by all discursive reasoners, but discoveries of our remote ancestors that have preserved themselves through thousands of years of experience (P 1907, 83–85).[10] They are revisable, but maintain themselves as long as they work. Thus, one may conclude that for James, statements such as "Every event has a cause" are true in that they lead us to connect experiences in fruitful ways.

So far we have examined the various truth-relations that James thinks hold between reality and referential assertions, a class that includes historical assertions, predictive claims, and categorical statements. What relation constitutes the truth of a scientific theory, acording to James?

James was not a philosopher of science. Many of his early comments remain on the level of introductory texts, to the effect that scientific claims must be clear, well-reasoned, and verified. At the same time, from the beginning, he emphasizes the role of "subjective marks." Thus, in the 1879 paper "The Sentiment of Rationality," he argues that philosophers prefer that conception of things which is marked by a "strong feeling of ease, peace, rest" (EP, 32).[11] While the later controversy over pragmatism raged, James read extensively in current philosophy and noticed a broad movement away from a realistic interpretation of scientific truths, a movement in line with his own reflections and deserving of his support. At the forefront stood his allies, Schiller and Dewey. Thus, in *Pragmatism*, after a sketch of recent developments in the sciences, he writes: "Riding now on the front of this wave of scientific logic Messrs. Schiller and Dewey appear with their pragmatistic account of what truth everywhere signifies" (P 1907, 34). A colorful account of the new wave is found in his 1904 paper, "Humanism and Truth": up to about 1850 it was believed that the "anatomy of the world is logical, and its logic is that of a university professor." He then mocks the idea that it is the soul that knows and, considerably simplifying the history of thought, links the soul theory with a realistic conception of scientific laws: "all were supposed to be exact and exclusive duplicates of pre-human archetypes buried in the structure of things, to which the spark of divinity hidden in our intellect enables us to penetrate" (MT 1909, 40).

But after 1850, according to James, in a phrase borrowed from Karl Pearson, more and more, scientific laws came to be seen as mere "conceptual shorthand."[12] One formulation is said to be superior to another, not because of its "literal 'objectivity,'" but because it is more useful, elegant. In *Pragmatism*, he places much stress on the problem of fitting novel facts into the system of established beliefs. Because being conservative we prefer to disturb our beliefs as little as possible, we "hold a theory true" when it "marries old opinion to new fact so as ever to show a minimum of jolt, a maximum of continuity" (P 1907, 35). Thus, according to James, a scientific theory is held to be true if and only if it fits the facts, can be integrated into our system of established beliefs with minimum disturbance, and is simpler and more fruitful than any alternative.

At this point we enter into murky waters, with James providing little guidance. In *Pragmatism*, after insisting that his is an "account of truths in the plural," he writes: "Truth for us is simply a collective name for verification-processes. . . . Truth is made, just as health, wealth and strength are made, in the course of experience" (P 1907, 104). Perhaps, by truth being made he means something like the following. Before Darwin, for example, there were no "pre-human archetypes buried in the structure of things" for him to detect. It was Darwin who by, devising a conceptual shorthand, created a new fact, the fact of natural selection.

But this seems to erase a distinction that James wants to maintain, the difference between a theory *being* true and *believing* that a theory is true. After admitting that he had erred in this way, on September 13, 1907, James wrote Arthur Oncken Lovejoy: "Consequences of true ideas per se, and consequences of ideas *qua believed by us*, are logically different consequences" (CWJ 11.444).[13] But how can they be different if only the proposing of a theory brings into existence the facts themselves and initiates processes of verification for which truth is only a collective name? We can try to preserve the distinction by setting aside such consequences as, for example, usefulness in getting tenure and research grants as *extrinsic* to a scientific theory's meaning, and therefore as establishing only the utility of the theory "*qua believed by us.*" What James calls subjective factors—simplicity, economy, fertility—may then be regarded as *intrinsic* to the meaning of a theory, and thus as helping establish the theory's truth.

Such subjective factors come into play only when a theory is proposed and the processes of verification are initiated, however. That would mean that the distinction between the *truth of* and *belief in* arises only after a theory has been discredited, that is, is possible only in retrospect. But before a theory has been relegated to a museum, the claim that a theory is true can mean no more than that those who hold it experience no discord.

Some of the difficulties for pragmatism arise because of entanglements with religion and James's association with the will to believe. Thus, writing to James on July 22, 1909, Russell confessed: "The pragmatic difference that pragmatism makes to me is that it encourages religious belief, & that I consider religious belief pernicious" (CWJ 12.294). In his turn, James thought that Russell's "atheistic-titanic confession of faith" was a splendid example of the will to believe. And he complained to Schiller on December 4, 1909, that Russell is "rabid on the subject" and sees it where it does not exist: "Where in the M. of T. is the will to believe defended?" (CWJ 12.244, 12.379).

Writing to Kallen on August 1, 1907, he attempts to separate the account of truth from the justification of belief in the absence of decisive evidence in those cases where action cannot be delayed: "Truth is constituted by verification actual or possible, and beliefs, *however* reached, have to be verified before they can count as true. The question of whether we have a right to believe anything before verification concerns not the question of truth, but the policy of belief" (CWJ 11.404).

Unfortunately, some of the clearest texts are found in private correspondence. But early in 1908 he published a short paper, reprinted in *The Meaning of Truth* as "The Existence of Julius Cæser," which should have prevented some misreadings: "My account of truth is purely logical and relates to its definition only. I contend that you cannot tell what the *word* 'true' *means*, as applied to a statement, without invoking the *concept of the statement's workings*" (MT 1909, 120).

Russell's remark that pragmatism encourages religious beliefs shows how difficult it was to isolate the question of the meaning of truth from ideological biases. He fears that

James's account of truth will serve to cover superstitions with a cloak of intellectual respectability. In effect, he asks what prevents a believer in biblical chronology, for example, from deflecting criticism by claiming that the belief is true because it satisfies him? And there are texts which Russell could cite. After all, in *Pragmatism* James asserts that one's philosophical outlook reflects one's temperament, that the tender-minded are religious, while the tough-minded depend on facts and are irreligious (P 1907, 13).

Finally, this brings us to religious truths. It is not possible in the space available fully to analyze James's accout, to set out both his development and his mature view. But a convenient summary is found in *Varieties*. Here, James claims that to be true, religious opinions must satisfy the conditions of "philosophical reasonableness," "immediate luminousness," and "moral helpfulness." Because of the first condition, religious opinions cannot be in conflict with facts and scientific theories. Because of the second, they must bring "immediate delight" and carry a "sense of inner authority and illumination." Because of the third, they must serve our "moral needs" (VRE 1902, 21–23).

In theory, religious truths must satisfy more conditions than scientific truths. But in practice, in most cases, to distinguish the true from the false we have to fall back on the third condition. This is so, because many incompatible beliefs satisfy the first condition, while the authority of luminousness remains private, because James associates it with mystical states. This leaves only the lives of believers, upon whom the burden of proof thus falls. He writes: "In the end it had to come to our empiricist criterion: By their fruits ye shall know them, not by their roots" (VRE 1902, 25).[14]

James accepted the common view, that in science we find mostly verified beliefs, with problematic ones only on the fringes, of course, leaving open the possibility that the status of a particular belief will change. But in religion the case is otherwise. Of the vast number of religious assertions, while some have been discredited, most remain available for belief. Because of this, James's approach is dominated by fears that dogmatic attitudes would block the discovery of important truths: "I fear to lose truth by this pretension to possess it already wholly" (VRE 1902, 268). In this spirit, motivated by the wish not to impoverish human experience, he opposed medical licensing laws, supported the mind-cure movement, and engaged in psychical research.

Beginning with blood sacrifice, in the chapter on "The Value of Saintliness," he describes many religious attitudes that we now find abhorrent or puerile. For example, Saint Teresa of Avila, "one of the ablest women," was so absorbed in her relations with God, to the exclusion of everything else, that it is a "pity that so much vitality of soul should have found such poor employment." For similar reasons, a God who keeps a "pedantically minute account of individual shortcomings... is too small-minded a God for our credence." But in the end, James decides in favor of some religious attitudes because "life, more life, a larger, richer, more satisfying life, is in the last analysis the end of religion" (VRE 1902, 277, 278, 399).

So it is not that in religion we are entitled to ignore intellectual standards. It is that religion involves many "over-beliefs," beliefs that are underdetermined by evidence. In such cases, we can adopt satisfying beliefs at our own risk, like St. Teresa who risked and lost, in the hope that this will enrich human experience and eventually resolve the matter. In this way, James's pluralistic account of truth includes religious truths, by identifying a distinctive kind of satisfaction.

James ultimately offers too many formulations, and not while seeking philosophical precision, but for literary effect. As I have argued, he is primarily interested in three kinds of truth relations: those that involve referential assertions, scientific theories, and religious claims. It is fitting to end with a passage that reminds us of the realistic spirit with which James discussed all these varieties of truth: there is "no *room* for any grade or sort of truth outside of that jungle of empirical workings and leadings, and their nearer or ulterior terminations, of which I seem to have written so unskillfully." But so that we do not lose our way in the jungle, we have to keep in mind that "there can be no truth if there is nothing to be true about" (MT 1909, 89, 106).

Notes

1. Reprinted as "William James's Conception of Truth" in Russell (1910) and in Russell (2014).
2. As he explains in MT (1909, 6–7), radical empiricism consists of a postulate ("the only things that shall be debatable among philosophers shall be things definable in terms drawn from experience"), a statement of fact ("the relations between things, conjunctive as well as disjunctive, are just as much matters of direct particular experience, neither more so nor less so, than the things themselves"), and a generalized conclusion ("therefore the parts of experience hold together from next to next by relations that are themselves parts of experience"). For my argument, what is important is the doctrine that relations are matters of experience. The hypothesis of pure experience is something different. In the end, James himself found it troubling (see PU 1909, 94–95, and the Miller-Bode objections published at MEN 1905–1908, 65–129).
3. In the end the controversy revolves around the question of free will. It would have helped if they had tried to show the evolutionary advantages of free will. But I can only find hints in this direction, more in Dewey than in James.
4. In 1910, as his contribution to the pragmatism controversy, Dewey published a collection of essays under the title of *The Influence of Darwin on Philosophy*, noting that the pragmatic notion of "practice" should not be understood as "utilitarian in some narrow sense." According to many interpreters (e.g., Johnston 2014, 46), Dewey's 1896 paper "The Reflex Arc Concept in Psychology" marks a major milestone in his movement from idealism to naturalism.
5. And he was aware of his failure. In commenting on Russell in his letter to Kallen of February 12, 1908, he writes: "Much truth *is* useful in the narrower sense, so is much falsehood; but much truth 'pays' without being useful in *that* sense. A developed pragmatism will have to discriminate the various types of truth-making satisfactoriness" (CWJ 11.539).
6. James used the same texts in two related articles—in 1904's "A World of Pure Experience," collected in ERE, and in an extract of the latter essay that James titled "The Relation Between Knower and Known" and that he included in MT.
7. For references to Hodgson, see MT (1909, 171). That James and Russell moved in different philosophical universes is shown by the fact that in volume 5 of *Collected Papers of Bertrand Russell*, covering the years 1905–1908, the years of the controversy over truth, Hodgson is never mentioned.

8. Reprinted in MT (1909, 23n). I have dealt with this dispute in Skrupskelis (2000).
9. "The Function of Cognition" is some months earlier than the review of Royce's book, but James was familiar with the argument before the book was published.
10. The importance of Kant is shown by James's interleaved and heavily annotated copy of the Adickes (1889) edition of the *Critique of Pure Reason* preserved in Harvard's Houghton Library. I barely scratched the surface in Skrupskelis (1989).
11. James's formulation has an affinity with Peirce's "The Fixation of Belief," which was published in 1877.
12. For the reference to Pearson see SPP (1911, 148).
13. Also see his letter to Kallen of September 29, 1907 (CWJ 11.452).
14. James is arguing against "medical materialism," the effort to discredit religious beliefs by pointing to their origin in pathological mental states.

Bibliography

Johnston, James Scott. 2014. *John Dewey's Earlier Logical Theory*. Albany: State University of NY Press.
Royce, Josiah. 1885. *The Religious Aspect of Philosophy: A Critique of the Bases of Conduct and of Faith*. Boston: Houghton, Mifflin and Company.
Russell, Bertrand. 1908. "Transatlantic 'Truth': Review of William James, *Pragmatism*." *Albany Review* 2: 393–410.
Russell, Bertrand. 1908/2014. "William James's Conception of Truth." In *The Collected Papers of Bertrand Russell*, edited by Gregory H. Moore, 465–486. London: George Allen & Unwin.
Russell, Bertrand. 1910. *Philosophical Essays*. London: Longmans, Green, and Co.
Russell, Bertrand. 2014. *The Collected Papers of Bertrand Russell*. Edited by Gregory H. Moore. 36 vols. Vol. 5. London: George Allen & Unwin.
Skrupskelis, Ignas K. 1989. "James and Kant's Second Analogy." *Kant-Studien: Philosophische Zeitschrift der Kant-Gesellschaft* 80(2): 173–179.
Skrupskelis, Ignas K. 2000. "James's Pragmatism and the Problem of Reference." In *Pragmatismus: Ein Neuer Name Fur Einige Alte Wege Des Denkens*, edited by Klaus Oehler, 165–183. Berlin: Akademie.

PART V
LATER METAPHYSICS

CHAPTER 18

JAMES'S RADICAL EMPIRICISM

Sensation and Pure Experience

WESLEY COOPER

Introduction

WILLIAM James put psychology on a scientific footing in his great book, *The Principles of Psychology* (1890), then went on to develop a radical-empirical metaphysics in essays that were collected in the volume *Essays in Radical Empiricism* (1912).[1] What is the relationship between James's early scientific work, notably the *Principles*, and his later metaphysics? There are interpretations that play up the science at the expense of the metaphysics, notably those that esteem his contribution to the beginning of psychology as a natural science. There are also interpretations that do the opposite, dismissing the *Principles* as largely a mistake and praising James's metaphysics as an anticipation of phenomenology (e.g., Wilshire 1968, 1969).

I will pursue the line that it is above all a relationship of continuity, wherein the methodological dualism between the mental and the physical—the official position of the *Principles*—is later dissolved, and the two erstwhile categories are presented afresh in a unitary world of pure experience. What makes this a matter of continuity is the *Principles'* protean concept of sensation, which is capable of signifying something inner and psychological, something outer and physical, and something neither inner nor outer. This latter is the *prima materia* that is at the origin of mind and body, according to his later metaphysics.

Sensation

James announces his methodological dualism in the Preface of the *Principles*, as a matter of what any natural science does, insofar as it assumes its data without prejudice to further ("metaphysical") inquiry that would explain these data or call them into question.

> I have kept close to the point of view of natural science throughout the book. Every natural science assumes certain data uncritically, and declines to challenge the elements between which its own "laws" obtain, and from which its own deductions are carried on. Psychology, the science of finite individual minds, assumes as its data (1) *thoughts and feelings*, and (2) *a physical world* in time and space with which they coexist and which (3) *they know*. Of course these data themselves are discussable; but the discussion of them (as of other elements) is called metaphysics and falls outside the province of this book. (PP 1890, 6)

The scientific search for laws correlating the mental and the physical is not replaced when James walks through the portal of his psychology into his pure-experiential metaphysics. He takes all that with him. How can this be? Like empiricists before him, James thought that the contents of the mind are built up from sensations; this is the sensationalism of the *Principles*. But for him this interior location is secondary to sensation's first location, which is exterior to the mind.

This point is hidden in the *Principles*. I use the term "hidden" advisedly. It is hidden, for one thing, because a full accounting of sensation's exteriority would be too metaphysical in the context of an exposition of the brain's functions. Specifically, that would require putting aside the methodological dualism of the *Principles*, placing sensation in a world of both physical and mental events. In contrast, the neutral monism of the later metaphysics is a world that is neither mental nor physical. The privacy of the mind and the brute externality of the physical world are eliminated, as we will see.

One can detect the hidden duality of sensation, for example, in James's discussion of a child touching a flame. In his diagram, there are two physical things—a flame and an infant. The infant (see the diagram at PP 1890, 37) contains both interior sensational and physical cerebral processes. As James develops his view, specifically in Chapter 17, "Sensation," he is explicit that the child at first experiences the pain, just as much as the flame, as something objective, "out there." James admits in the Preface that some parts of his book are more metaphysical than others. If objective sensation is hidden in Chapter 2, in conformity with his official "positivistic" point of view, as he calls it, evoking Auguste Comte's distinction between science and metaphysics, Chapter 17's discussion of sensation is on the very cusp of his metaphysics.

There, he denies that sensations at first appear to us as subjective or internal and then get "extradited" or "projected" so as to *appear* located in an outer world. He also denies a corollary of this view, that our sensations are originally devoid of all spatial content. Subjective consciousness, aware of itself as subjective, does not at first exist. Pain is at first experienced as something objective and as having volume, a spatial quale:

> We often hear the opinion expressed that all our sensations at first appear to us as subjective or internal, and are afterwards and by a special act on our part "extradited"

or "projected" so as to appear located in an outer world.... It seems to me that there is not a vestige of evidence for this view. It hangs together with the opinion that our sensations are originally devoid of all spatial content, an opinion which I confess that I am wholly at a loss to understand. As I look at my bookshelf opposite I cannot frame to myself an idea, however imaginary, of any feeling which I could ever possibly have got from it except the feeling of the same big extended sort of outward fact which I now perceive. So far is it from being true that our first way of feeling things is the feeling of them as subjective or mental, that the exact opposite seems rather to be the truth. Our earliest, most instinctive, least developed kind of consciousness is the objective kind; and only as reflection becomes developed do we become aware of an inner world at all. Then indeed we enrich it more and more, even to the point of becoming idealists, with the spoils of the outer world which at first was the only world we knew. But subjective consciousness, aware of itself as subjective, does not at first exist. Even an attack of pain is surely felt at first objectively as something in space which prompts to motor reaction, and to the very end it is located, not in the mind, but in some bodily part. (PP 1890, 679)

Only after the outward encounter does the developing child *import* the pain as subjective, interior to the mind, while the flame itself remains something external. The pain is internalized as part of the infant's image of the flame, which takes its place in the subjective contents of that mind. And so? And so these objective sensations, neither subjectively mental nor objectively physical, are suited to be items of pure experience, as are the flame and the candle. Sensations are comparable in part to Berkeley's "ideas," but in James's psychology their interiority and exteriority are differentiated by their role in the economy of the mind.

In his radically empiricist metaphysics, the economy of the mind will become the economy of the world. The law-governed dualism of mind and body persists, even if these categories are anachronistic from a metaphysical viewpoint. The world of pure experience retains the nomic structure introduced in the *Principles*, and as such it is not autonomous from the physical. The physical is rendered pure-experiential, but its relationship to the mental, also now rendered pure-experiential, remains governed by scientific law. If the categories of mind and body are bathwater—disposable postulates of James's psychology—the nomic connections between brain and mind, now conceived as collections of pure experience, are the baby that toddles across the bridge from psychology to metaphysics. The pursuit of laws between mind and body is not invalidated but rather circumscribed.

Sensation is the primary link between James's early positivistic psychology and his later radical empiricist metaphysics. In the *Principles* he writes:

The first sensation which an infant gets is for him the Universe. And the Universe which he later comes to know is nothing but an amplification and an implication of that first simple germ which, by accretion on the one hand and intussusception on the other, has grown so big and complex and articulate that its first estate is unrememberable. In his dumb awakening to the consciousness of *something there*, a mere *this* as yet (or something for which even the term this would perhaps be too discriminative, and the intellectual acknowledgment of which would be better expressed by the bare interjection "lo!"), the infant encounters an object in which (though it be given in a pure sensation) all the "categories of the understanding" are contained. (PP 1890, 657)

Sensation is of a pair with perception. The latter always involves sensation, and sensation in adult life always is colored in some way by perception. Sensation is "knowledge by acquaintance" with a fact, perception is "knowledge about" a fact. In sensation we come to know "bare immediate natures" by which various objects are distinguished (PP 1890, 653).

The Cerebralism of the *Principles*

In the *Principles,* James's sensationalism is tied to his cerebralism. His theory of the brain and the mind-brain relationship is provided in the imposing chapter entitled "The Functions of the Brain," which is largely given over to an analysis of what he calls "the Meynert scheme," after Theodor Meynert, who was instrumental in providing in James's generation the minute anatomy and the detailed physiology of the brain (PP 1890, 27). It hypothesizes that the brain is a reflex mechanism both in its lower centers and its upper hemispheres, though the latter is somewhat "instable" (PP 1890, 35). The remark about instability foreshadows the discussion of this topic in Chapter 5, "The Automaton Theory," where consciousness is invoked to "load" the "dice" of the brain in favor of preferred ends (PP 1890, 143). Exactly how this loading-of-the-dice is subsumed by the nomic dependence of the mental on the cerebral is never explained, but whether this amounts to a contradiction or is accounted for in the over-arching teleology is an open question.

This background to "Functions" perhaps explains why James begins the chapter by bringing up an issue that he later drops, namely whether the brain is an automatism to which consciousness is an idle bystander, or whether consciousness is sometimes implicated in the brain's activity. In "The Automaton Theory" he will plump for a crucial role for consciousness that is limited to the upper hemispheres, but he may be bringing up the matter here in order to make a reminder that the grand debate between mechanism and teleology is at stake, behind all the physiological minutiae of "Functions."

His discussion of the frog's nerve centers leads him to several conclusions, among them the hypothesis that the lower centers act from present sensational stimuli alone, whereas the hemispheres act from perceptions and considerations (PP 1890, 32). Consequently the latter are viewed as the seat of memory. James emphasizes that this difference between the lower and the upper does not alter the fact that the brain might be a reflex mechanism from top to bottom.

How is this consistent with his insistence in "The Automaton Theory" that the instability of the hemispheres allows consciousness to load the dice of the brain? This is a crucial question, with implications for James's view about free will, the will to believe, and so forth. Does he mean that the difference in degree permits the influence of consciousness while retaining the brain's broadly reflex type of organization? Apparently so. But this suggests that the brain is a little bit non-reflexive, which may put one in mind of being a little bit pregnant. This analogy is unfair, arguably, if the upper brain is to be understood as a causal mechanism, albeit more subtle than the habit-molded parts of the brain. Instability is not the same thing as indeterminism, which is surely ruled out, at least on methodological principles, by James's law-seeking approach to the brain. Nor is it the same as unpredictability, since a good person predictably chooses virtuous conduct, even if that individual's brain, in the absence of consciousness, would be just as likely to choose evil. Loading the device of the brain, consciousness must still have a neural correlate upon which it is dependent: "No psychosis without neurosis" (PP 1890, 133).

This dictum means rejection of a Cartesian, indeterminist conception of volition; and it must be rendered wholly consistent with the metaphysics of pure experience that James develops later, in *Essays in Radical Empiricism*. If neurons and volitions are "made of the same stuff," as the metaphysics says, the contribution of consciousness will be made within the world of pure experience. Any further explanation will count as "innocent over-belief" and symbolic expression of it, as James called it in *The Varieties of Religious Experience*, not to be taken literally.[2]

Under the rubric "The Education of the Hemispheres" in *Principles*, James blocks out the relationship between reflex acts in the lower centers and corresponding ideas in the hemispheres. All ideas being at bottom reminiscences, he writes, his question is, How can processes become organized in the hemispheres which correspond to reminiscences in the mind? He addresses his question by making four "inevitable" assumptions:

1) The same cerebral process which, when aroused from without by a sense-organ, gives the perception of an object, will give an idea of the same object when aroused by other cerebral processes from within.
2) If processes 1, 2, 3, 4 have once been aroused together or in immediate succession, any subsequent arousal of any one of them (whether from without or within) will tend to arouse the others in the original order. [This is the so-called law of association.]
3) Every sensorial excitement propagated to a lower center tends to spread upward and arouse an idea.
4) Every idea tends ultimately either to produce a movement or to check one which otherwise would be produced. (PP 1890, 36)

In this way he sets the stage for his celebrated chapter "Habit," as well as rejecting phrenology, pouring scorn on the latter in the next section, "The Phrenological Conception." Modern science extrapolates from these assumptions to the hypothesis that brain and mind alike consist of simple elements, sensory and motor. "There is a complete parallelism between the two analyses," James writes. "The same diagram of little dots, circles, or triangles joined by lines symbolizes equally well the cerebral and mental processes: the dots stand for cells or ideas, the lines for fibres or associations. We shall have later to criticise this analysis so far as it relates to the mind..." (PP 1890, 41).

Notably, he criticizes it in Chapter 6, "The Mind-Stuff Theory," which rejects the atomism about the mental in the empiricist tradition, in favor of the view that the mental emerges from groups of corresponding physical states. His discussion of an experiment of A. Fick illustrates his view memorably.

> He made experiments on the discrimination of the feelings of warmth and of touch, when only a very small portion of the skin was excited through a hole in a card, the surrounding parts being protected by the card. He found that under these circumstances mistakes were frequently made by the patient, and concluded that this must be because the number of sensations from the elementary nerve-tips affected was too small to sum itself distinctly into either of the qualities of feeling in question. He tried to show how a different manner of the summation might give rise in one case to the heat and in another to the touch. "A feeling of temperatures," he says, "arises when the intensities of the units of feeling are evenly gradated, so that between two elements a and b no other unit can spatially intervene whose intensity is not also *between* that of a and b. A feeling of contact perhaps arises when this condition is not fulfilled. Both kinds of feeling, however, are composed of the same units." But it is obviously far clearer to interpret such a gradation of intensities as a brain-fact than as a mind-fact. If in the brain a tract were first excited in one of the ways suggested by Prof. Fick, and then again in the other, it might very well happen, for aught we can say to the contrary, that the psychic accompaniment in the one case would be heat, and in the other pain. The pain and the heat would, however, not be composed of psychic units, but would each be the direct result of one total brain-process. So long as this latter interpretation remains open, Fick cannot be held to have proved psychic summation. (PP 1890, 153–154)

Appeal to the like of "one total brain-process" is James's preferred source of explanations, rather than atomic psychic units, but also rather than the innate ideas posited by rationalist psychology, which is the grand enemy of his approach, and rather than the cranial lumps and associated "faculties" favored by the phrenological conception.

He affirms however that the brain has native tendencies that account for our emotions and instincts; it is not the "virgin organ" which the Meynert scheme called them (PP 1890, 83).

Pure Experience

Taking a deep breath, let us move from the cerebralism of the *Principles* to his pure-experiential metaphysics, specifically the essays "Does 'Consciousness' Exist?" and "A World of Pure Experience," in which he presents the view that "there is only one primal stuff or material in the world, a stuff of which everything is composed" (ERE 1904, 4). His aim is not only to debunk the idea of a spiritual substance, but also to show how the functions for which it has been invoked, such as knowing the world, can be explained by the relations among items of pure experience. This primal stuff, to repeat, is neither mental nor physical but is fit to *be* either, and fit as well to explain a person's knowledge of the world without invoking a nullity like the soul, but instead by tracing a relationship between two portions of pure experience.

James offers a helpful illustration to bring forward the radically empiricist metaphysical difference between external reality and the stream of thought. Speaking of a room in a house, he writes:

> The room thought-of, namely, has many thought-of couplings with many thought-of things. Some of these couplings are inconstant, others are stable.... We call the first collection the system of external realities, in the midst of which the room, as "real," exists; the other we call the stream of our internal thinking, in which, as a "mental image," it for a moment floats. (ERE 1904, 12)

James has pressed his enquiry beyond the assumptions that define scientific psychology, namely, that a physical world exists; that thoughts and feelings exist; and that individual minds know the physical world in virtue of their thoughts and feelings. Such deepened enquiry, which is what he calls metaphysics, shows that consciousness does not exist in the same sense that the physical world does not exist. So he is not an 'eliminative materialist', one who affirms the existence of a physical world while rejecting consciousness as a superstition, the product of a false theory (so-called folk psychology). James accepts both folk psychology and folk physics as sound theories within their restricted domains. But neither thoughts nor physical objects belong to the ultimate things in the universe.

In this, he largely follows Berkeley, for whom both an apple and a train of thought about an apple are collections of ideas. But there are differences. For instance, whereas three-dimensionality, such as the volume of a pitcher of apple juice, is constructed from two-dimensional images in Berkeley's system, James presents "voluminous" sensations as given, as discussed earlier with regard to an infant's pain upon touching a flame, their three dimensions immediately experienced without inferential construction.

Pure experience retains four of what the *Principles* had characterized as five of the essential characteristics of the mental:

1) Every thought tends to be part of a personal consciousness.
2) Within each personal consciousness thought is always changing.
3) Within each personal consciousness thought is sensibly continuous.
4) It always appears to deal with objects independent of itself.
5) It is interested in some parts of these objects to the exclusion of others, and welcomes or rejects—*chooses* from among them, in a word—all the while. (PP 1890, 220)

The pure experience view rejects only the first item in this list. In this way, minds become continuous with each other, for they are fundamentally pure-experiential, and pure experience is not part of a personal consciousness. Indeed minds become continuous with the physical world, since the latter is a construct out of pure experience.

Terms like "construction" and "built up," with their teleological connotations, are appropriate in this context, for James, since he speculates that chaotic pure experience is primeval, whereas mind and body are evolutionary constructions (ERE 1904, 18). The mechanism and laws of causal dependence of the mind on the brain are left behind in the metaphysics, which opens the way for various teleological/religious conceptions of the universe.

> If one were to make an evolutionary construction of how a lot of originally chaotic pure experiences became gradually differentiated into an orderly inner and outer world, the whole theory would turn upon one's success in explaining how or why the quality of an experience, once active, could become less so, and, from being an energetic attribute in some cases, elsewhere lapse into the status of an inert or merely internal "nature." This would be the "evolution" of the psychical from the bosom of the physical, in which the esthetic, moral and otherwise emotional experiences would represent a halfway stage. (ERE 1904, 18–19)

James never fully explains the nature of this evolutionary guidance, though he notes that a thoroughgoing interpretation of the world in terms of mechanical sequence is compatible with its being interpreted teleologically, for the mechanism itself may be designed (WB 1897, 66).

It is important to note that even in the *Principles,* duality for James is not a duality of substances, but of functions;[3] *this very* pure-experiential item can function either in relationship to the world, in which case its primary virtue is as a guide to the "curious stubbornness" of fact,[4] or in relationship to the person's biography, in which case its primary virtue is coherence with the rest of the stream of thought.

This is an important juncture. In terms of Derek Parfit's more recent distinction between reductive and non-reductive theories of personal identity, James is a reductionist like Parfit and Robert Nozick, though the details are dramatically different (see Nozick 1981; Parfit 1984). They all reject a substantial "I" or "ego," the unchanging persistence of which guarantees personal identity, and so they reject Descartes's theory as well as many religious conceptions.

This account denies both that experiences are self-intimatingly mental and that they represent an external, non-experiential reality. At its evolutionary origins, James suggests, experience may have been "external" and "active": the fire there would burn me. Gradually a class of experience would evolve which is passive and of an internal nature: my idea of fire does not burn me.

To return to "Does 'Consciousness' Exist?" James concludes that essay with a diagnosis of the "I think" that Kantians allege to accompany each thought: it is nothing more than the breathing that accompanies thinking. "The stream of thinking ... consists chiefly of the stream of my breathing. The 'I think' which Kant said must be able to accompany all my objects, is the 'I breathe' which actually does accompany them" (ERE 1904, 19). With this provocative remark James signs off by promising further clarity about "a world of pure experience" in his essay of that name, to which I now turn.

James named his metaphysics radical empiricism because it defined everything, including relations, within the realm of experience. "For such a philosophy, *the relations that connect experiences must themselves be experienced relations, and any kind of relation experienced must be accounted as 'real' as anything else in the system*" (ERE 1904, 22).

So the relation of a conscious state to the self that is in that state must be understood as a relation among pure experiences. All the more, the relation between that state, such as an experience of pain, to the consciousness of it must be construed as a relation among pure experiences. There is no place in this philosophical system for a self or a consciousness that does not get explained without remainder by reference to pure experience and relations inside it. These "connective" relations, he argues, distinguish radical empiricism from other empiricist accounts, which emphasize rather the "disjunctive" aspect of self and world (ERE 1904, 22–23).

In this way he hopes to capture the grain of truth in the rationalist pursuit of the non-experiential and the transcendent, but without going there. James's world is purposive without a "purposer" (ERE 1904, 24).

He is impressed by the co-conscious transition "by which one experience passes into another when both belong to the same self," but he wants to avoid an "experiencer." Instead he recognizes this transition as high on the scale of connective relations. For him, "There is no other *nature*, no other whatness than this absence of break and this sense of continuity in that most intimate of all conjunctive relations, the passing of one experience into another when they belong to the same self" (ERE 1904, 26).

The cognitive relation, too, is to be understood in this austere way: there is no "knower" apart from this relation between experiences: either a "self-same" experience in different contexts, accounting for knowledge by acquaintance or representative perceptual knowledge (its visually seeming that there is a blue expanse, or verily seeing a blue sky or blue wall); or else two actual experiences of the same subject with definite tracts of conjunctive transitional experiences between them (my memory now of doing such-and-such then); or finally "the known is a *possible* experience either of that subject or another, to which the said conjunctive transitions *would* lead, if sufficiently prolonged" (I know that this car would start if I turn the ignition; ERE 1904, 27).

The affinity of radical empiricism with pragmatism, even if the former stands on its own feet, is manifest:

> Unions by continuous transition are the only ones we know of, whether in this matter of a knowledge-about that terminates in an acquaintance, whether in personal identity, in logical predication through the copula "is," or elsewhere. If anywhere there were more absolute unions realized, they could only reveal themselves to us by just such conjunctive results. These are what the unions are *worth*, these are all that *we can ever practically mean* by union, by continuity. Is it not time to repeat what Lotze said of substances, that to *act like* one is to *be* one? (ERE 1904, 30)

Radical empiricism and pragmatism work well together, so well that one might have doubts whether pragmatism can function without a world of pure experience. If reality is external to our experience of it, pragmatic considerations are bound to leave something out, namely, the remainder when experienced reality is subtracted from reality.

James's doctrine of over-belief, developed late in his career in the *Varieties* and sketched earlier, allows James's radical empiricism to countenance such possibilities despite the strictures of his pragmatism, even deities and substantial selves that are transcendent to experience. Radical empiricism accommodates the transcendent as having symbolic value for this or that culture, even if such entities lack real existence as defined by the radical-empiricist world of pure experience. In this respect, the over-belief idea is generous where pragmatism is less so. For himself, James seems to have found his God within a radical-empiricist world, as the purposiveness (without a "purposer") of the cosmos, analyzed according to his metaphysics as an evolution of pure experience into a physical world and streams of thought. He discerns a pure-experiential cosmos driven by purpose, though he allows that others, justified by his doctrine of over-belief, may see different worlds.

Notes

1. For a more detailed interpretation along the lines pursued here, see my *The Unity of William James's Thought* (2002). And for a broad historical introduction to brain science and its philosophical aspects, read Churchland (1986).
2. Various religions may legitimately postulate more than can be found in the austere empiricist world that grounds James's metaphysics, he writes, but these are optional add-ons to, or "buildings-out from," the obligatory basics that the world of pure experience provides (VRE 1929, 422).
3. These are evolutionary functions, as James states in several places, by which primeval, chaotic pure experience is guided into physical constructs (the physical world) and mental constructs (streams of consciousness). This metaphysical functionalism generalizes and adapts the functionalism of his scientific psychology. This latter, as Charles Stangor notes, is a view about psychological characteristics that derived from Darwin and, in turn, gave rise to evolutionary psychology.

   > ... the goal of William James and the other members of the school of functionalism was *to understand why animals and humans have developed the particular psychological aspects that they currently possess....*
   >
   > James and the other members of the functionalist school were influenced by Charles Darwin's (1809–1882) theory of natural selection, which proposed that the physical characteristics of animals and humans evolved because they were useful, or functional. The functionalists believed that Darwin's theory applied to psychological characteristics too. Just as some animals have developed strong muscles to allow them to run fast, the human brain, so functionalists thought, must have adapted to serve a particular function in human experience. (Stangor 2015, 30)

4. Royce's phrase, borrowed with approval by James at ERE (1904, 12).

Bibliography

Churchland, Patricia Smith. 1986. *Neurophilosophy: Toward a Unified Science of the Mind/Brain.* Cambridge, MA: MIT Press.

Cooper, Wesley E. 2002. *The Unity of William James's Thought.* Nashville, TN: Vanderbilt University Press.
Derek Parfit. 1984. *Reasons and Persons.* Oxford, UK: Oxford University Press.
Goodman, Russell. 2003. William James. *The Stanford Encyclopedia of Philosophy.* Edited by Edward N. Zalta. Spring ed. http://plato.stanford.edu/archives/spr2003/entries/james/.
Nozick, Robert. 1981. *Philosophical Explanations.* Cambridge, MA: Harvard University Press.
Stangor, Charles. 2015. *Introduction to Psychology.* Washington, DC: Flatworld Knowledge.
Wilshire, Bruce. 1968. *James and Phenomenology.* Bloomington: Indiana University Press.
Wilshire, Bruce. 1969. "Protophenomenology in the Psychology of William James." *Transactions of the Charles S. Peirce Society* 5: 25–43.

CHAPTER 19

JAMES AND THE METAPHYSICS OF INTENTIONALITY

Royce, Bergson, and the Miller-Bode Objections

JEREMY DUNHAM

IN this chapter, I argue that from the 1880s to the very end of James's life, the central developments in James's metaphysics were driven by the aim of providing an adequate response to the problem of intentionality highlighted by the American idealist philosopher Josiah Royce (1855–1916) and his "argument from error." In the first section, I demonstrate that James's earliest attempt—in "The Function of Cognition" (1885)—aimed to answer the problem from a "phenomenist" perspective inspired by the French "neo-criticist" philosopher Charles Renouvier. In the second section, I show that James's radical empiricist defense of "conjunctive relations" was in part motivated by the attempt to improve on the inadequacies he eventually saw in Renouvier's philosophy and the latter's attempt to solve the problem of intentionality. In the third section, I argue that the reason why the objections levied at James's radical empiricism in 1904 by Dickinson S. Miller and Boyd Henry Bode caused him so much mental trouble is that they showed why his philosophy did not provide the solution to Royce's problem that he thought it did. In the fourth section, I argue that it was by means of James's "Bergsonian conversion" that he solved this problem and produced the satisfactory answer to Royce he spent the best part of his career trying to find.

Royce, Renouvier, and "The Function of Cognition"

Royce's argument from error is a stunning attempt to prove the existence of an Absolute Mind from human error.[1] As Kenneth Winkler (forthcoming) has noted, it's the sort of argument that should be taught in every introduction to philosophy course. It's fascinating, elegant, and hard to escape. In fact, the argument—conclusion and all—is not without contemporary defenders.[2] The crux of the argument—and the part that enthralled James—is about intentionality. First, it aims to prove that without a full-bodied intentional relationship we cannot explain error; then, second, that the necessary condition for full-bodied intentionality is the existence of an "Absolute Mind." James did not want to accept the existence of an Absolute Mind, and he wasn't even sure that such a mind would solve the problem of intentionality. However, he did think that the problem was a very real one that he must solve.

Why, for Royce, does the existence of error require us to explain intentionality? This is because of the link between error and misrepresentation. Error, for Royce, *is* misrepresentation. But what are the conditions for the possibility of misrepresentation? Our judgment about an object *x* misrepresents if (and only if) our judgment fails to be an accurate representation of *x*. However, for a representation to fail to represent *x* accurately, *x* must be something other than our representation of it (it cannot be a mere subjective state), and we must have *intended* to represent that *x*. For example, our judgment of a tower as round only misrepresents the square tower if we had intended to make a judgment about *that* square tower. The tower as we perceived it *was* round and we cannot make an error about that. Since it is impossible to err about our perception of the tower as round, it must be possible to explain the connection between the perception in our mind (the tower as round), and the intended object (the square tower), otherwise error is impossible *tout court*. Royce attempts to show that the only way that we can account for the intentional relationship and, therefore, error, is by means of the existence of the "Absolute"; a higher inclusive organism of thought that is somehow constitutive of both the false (the tower is round) and true (the tower is square) judgments. Without the postulation of the absolute there is too much distance between mind and external object to explain the intentional relationship.

James admitted many times in correspondence and in print that he believed that the argument "caught [him] in a tight trap" (ECR 1885, 384; cf. CWJ 1887, 6.204). The problem that caught him is this: how can an empiricism that sticks strictly to the phenomena give a satisfactory explanation of the relationship between our ideas and the objects that they represent without introducing a relationship between them and a mysterious "beyond"?

James's first attempt to answer to Royce is found in his 1885 *Mind* article "On the Function of Cognition" (MT 1909, 13–31). This was written before Royce had yet published his argument, but James knew it from his discussions with him (MT 1909, 23 n.6). James's response was written when he was still heavily influenced by the French philosopher Charles Renouvier (1815–1903) and the latter's *phenomenist* trail is clearly evident.[3] Renouvier referred to his philosophy as "phenomenism" because it asserts that the only reality we can ever know is phenomenal (i.e., revealed to us by our phenomena). He claims that phenomenism starts from the "point of view of knowledge," that point of view which sticks to the phenomena. The contrasting, "point of view *without* knowledge" is the position that argues for unknowable metaphysical substances as the ultimate ground of this phenomena. Starting from the point of view *of* knowledge means giving up theoretical reason's pretentions to absolute certainty and its use of a priori reasoning. But, Renouvier argues, scepticism's great lesson is that any truth theoretical reason attempts to prove as certain by the "natural light of reason" can be doubted. This means that the attempt to discover foundational indubitable truths leads to *universal incertitude*. Once we give up on reason's claims to certitude, we must recognize that all our beliefs are subject to doubt. In fact, "belief," for Renouvier, *means* the possibility of doubt (ECG II.ii.20). Nevertheless, this does not reduce all truth to ungrounded subjective opinion. It is only once we recognize that all *certitude* is merely "belief" or "faith," he claims, that any kind of *certitude* is possible at all.

Renouvier's position differs from both simple fallibilism and simple phenomenalism through the defense of a fallibilist practical a priori—a series of practical postulates. He claims that the pursuit of knowledge must begin with philosophical faith in these postulates. These postulates require faith because they cannot be indubitably demonstrated without begging the question and must be believed through an act of free volition. However, it is subjectively necessary that we believe in them if we want to engage in scientific inquiry. Since the deliberation and judgment necessary to choose to believe in these postulates require free will, the first and most fundamental postulate is that we will freely. After that we must postulate that: (i) we exist as a "subject"; (ii) there is an external world; (iii) this world is of such a nature that it is possible for our phenomena to know it (the world in some way *resembles* our phenomena); and, (iv) our faculties are capable of knowing.

Renouvier insists that this new "phenomenist" method does not depend on upholding these postulates without scrutiny. They work for us because they enable us to engage both with nature and a community of scientific inquirers. It is for him a movement away from the dogmatism of a priori reason and toward the "critical method": "This method," he writes, "is sustained reflection, constant research, healthy critique, the elimination of harmful passions, the satisfaction of just instincts, the observed equilibrium between knowledge, which often eludes us, and the will ready to suppose or feign knowledge; it is ... the wise exercise of freedom" (ECG II.ii.95–96).

James also relies on the use of postulates at various stages in his career (see, e.g., PP 1890, 6). The most famous example is his claim that the "first act of free-will, in short, would naturally be to believe in free-will" (PP 1890, 948).[4] However, the crucial postulates for "The Function of Cognition" are (ii) and (iii). In reference to (ii) he tells us that " 'Reality' has become our warrant for calling a feeling cognitive; but what becomes our warrant for calling anything reality? ... The only reply is—the faith of the psychologist, critic, or inquirer" (MT 1909, 16). And for (ii) he allows the reader the freedom to postulate as the "Reality" whatever sort of thing they think *can* resemble a feeling.

James's first answer to Royce is one that attempts to account for the problem of misrepresentation on the basis of phenomenism and these Renouvierian postulates. He shows that although the "mysterious" mind-to-world relationship cannot be explained on the basis of phenomenism, we can provide a perfectly plausible explanation of misrepresentation on purely practical grounds—one that can tell us all that we can practically *mean* by the intentional relationship—so that any further metaphysical speculation about intentionality is unnecessary.

For the early James, successful or unsuccessful representation is merely a case of verification. Our thought that the "tower is square" will misrepresent the reality if it fails to lead, actually or potentially, to an experience of an object that is actually a square tower. If the thought leads us, for example, to a round tower, we know the thought to have been in error. However, if it successfully leads us to a square tower, we can say that the thought "knew" the tower was square. This, argues James, is a fully acceptable account of what we mean when we say that someone *knows* x. There is no need to go into further metaphysics to explain the relationship between object and idea:

> It would practically be a case of *grübelsucht*, if a ruffian were assaulting and drubbing my body, to spend much time in subtle speculation either as to whether his vision of my body resembled mine, or as to whether the body he really *meant* to insult were not some body in his mind's eye, altogether other from my own. The practical point of view brushes such metaphysical cobwebs away. (MT 1885, 24)

To return to the square tower example, there is no point speculating over whether the tower that I experience in close quarters is the same one I thought was round from one hundred meters. Practically, I am certain that it is, and that is enough for the everyday inquirer.

However, James was not satisfied with the first answer for long. On February 6, 1887, he wrote to Carl Stumpf that "I have vainly tried to escape from it [Royce's problem]... but I frankly confess that I am unable to overthrow it" (CWJ 6.204).

JAMES'S RADICAL EMPIRICISM

Why was James unsatisfied with his first attempt to solve Royce's problem? We can find the reason by returning to Renouvier. Thanks to James's suggestion that he read Royce's *Religious Aspect of Experience*, Renouvier wrote a two-part article dedicated to the work in his journal *La Critique philosophique* (1888).[5] Renouvier, like James, was struck by the book. He wrote to James that it "has been a long time since any philosophical book has interested me and won me so completely as this, by the profundity of its thought and the originality of its execution" (Perry 1935, I, 700–701). Nonetheless, his article was strongly critical of the argument from error.

For Renouvier, the main problem is that Royce treats an experience as relationless. For Royce, according to the common-sense understanding of assertion, a judgment picks its object and asserts something about it. But the problem is that to pick out an object and make a judgment about it, the knower must already know it. One, therefore, cannot make a mistake about an as-yet unknown object. I pick out an object in my experience—a round tower—and the object of my experience *really is round*. Then, I walk closer toward the tower and I pick out an object in my experience—a square tower—and this object of my experience *really is square*. We think that common sense permits us to say that the second judgment supersedes the first. But why does it permit this? A past thought and a present thought are separated by a gulf just as unbridgeable as the two thoughts and the tower itself. "An assertion is true or false apart from any other assertion or thought. Alone, as a separate fact, a judgment has no intelligible object beyond itself" (Royce 1885, 393). To say that the first and the second thought are directed at the same object, our thoughts must be "an organic part of [i.e., related by] a reflective and conscious larger self which has [all of] those objects immediately present to itself" (1892, 378).

In contrast to Royce, Renouvier believes that the experience of relation is a fundamental aspect of any phenomenon. The idea of an experience freed from relations is pure fiction. To experience an object *as an object*, we experience it as something that behaves according to laws and thus in a constant and relatively predictable way from one phenomenon to the next. I cannot assert in an isolated experience that what I am experiencing is an apple; rather, I can assert, on the basis of several related experiences, that what I am experiencing is an apple because it behaves in predictable "apple-like" ways. The idea that we can have a singular experience of an apple, Renouvier argues, follows from the view that what we do when we perceive an apple is have a direct experience of something like a stable "substance." However, such a view involving unknowable substances follows from the point of view *without knowledge*. From the point of view of knowledge, all we can experience are groups of phenomena connected in a lawlike manner. Our ideas about the apple will be "correct," if the sensations we receive from it are those that we expect to, and we will err if they are not. In his earlier work, the *Traité de psychologie rationnelle*, Renouvier cited Helmholtz approvingly: "the representation of an object is correct when it allows us to determine in advance the sensible impressions that we will receive from this object" (ECG II.ii.58).

So far all of this sounds relatively in tune with James's own thinking. The Helmholtz passage says almost exactly what James will later say in "The Function of Cognition." In fact, underneath this passage in his copy of Renouvier's book, James has written: "i.e. the relation of truth is not between the idea and the thing in itself, but between the present representation and an absent one."[6] James clearly saw Renouvier's (and Helmholtz's) ideas as anticipating the theory of truth that he would first publish just as few years later. Nonetheless, he was not satisfied with Renouvier's response. Why? He makes this clear in a letter to Renouvier from March 29, 1888:

> It seems to me that you understand the absolute Mind to be needed for the sake of *ascertaining* the error, of *verifying* the truth of the judgments which the finite individual's mind may make. Of course all *verification* must take place in another consciousness (another act of consciousness at least) from that whose deliverances are on trial. But that is not what Royce means. He means that a superior consciousness to the one on trial is needed to *constitute* as well as to verify the truth or error of the latter's judgments. (CWJ 6.359)

What Renouvier has shown is that *verification* of one's representations is possible by a latter "act of consciousness." My idea of a square tower can be shown to be correct if it led me to the sensible impressions I expected to experience when in the close vicinity of a tower and I could see and feel its corners. The latter conscious act, therefore, verifies the earlier one. However, the relationship of constitution is more complicated. This is the relationship that makes our idea *about* a particular object in the world. What permits us to say that my first judgment, made from a distance, that "the tower is square," is an error, once I have approached the tower and found that it has no corners at all, rather than a judgment about a different tower? James's first answer to Royce, like Renouvier's, had also focused on the verification problem and did not answer this constitution problem. This is why he could not be satisfied with it.

James ended the letter by telling Renouvier that he was sure that the solution to the problem would involve "your system of relations *de proche en proche*" (CWJ 6.360). This turned out to be correct, and when James finally developed an account of the constitutive relation, it would include Renouvier's verification account, but he would also build on it in a subtle and ingenious way. Nonetheless, this new construction was one that Renouvier himself would not have fully approved. One of the issues that James had with Renouvier's philosophy is that he admitted only *disjunctive* relations. One phenomenon follows another in a lawlike manner, but he agrees with Hume that between the phenomena themselves we experience no "connexion," no causal force, no transition. There is simply one phenomenon and then the next (*de proche en proche*). He believed that if there were continuity between phenomena, the determinateness of discrete individuals would be lost and rational classification would be impossible.[7] Such orderly succession between phenomena is the result of well-defined laws and a kind of "pre-established harmony."

James, in contrast, became a defender of the experience of a "felt transition between one experience and the next." He was unconcerned with Renouvier's criticism and replied that what we understand to be the discreteness of phenomena is merely the result of selective attention and abstraction (CWJ 1894, 5.525). This is the main distinction between his "radical" empiricism and the "ordinary" empiricism of Locke, Hume, and, in this case, even Renouvier. Radical empiricism "*does full justice to conjunctive relations*" (ERE 1904, 23):

> What I do feel simply when a later moment of my experience succeeds an earlier one is that tho they are two moments, the transition from one to the other is *continuous*. Continuity here is a definite sort of experience. (ERE 1904, 25)

But why does continuity help with the constitution problem? To answer that, I must first explain another key "radical empiricist" revision. This is the understanding of "subject" and "object" or, as James refers to them, "knower" and the "known."

One of James's key aims in his radical empiricist writings is to persuade us that there is no real duplicity of subject and object but rather subject and object are simply functions of the same experience treated in one way or another. One thing to recognize when trying to make sense of this claim is that when James talks about an object, he is talking about the object of experience, but, at the same time, he believes that the *esse* of this object is its *percipi*. As James says in an earlier paper:

> What, then, do we mean by "things"? To this question I can only make the answer of the idealistic philosophy. . . things have no other nature than thoughts have, and we know of no things that are not given to somebody's experience. When I see the thing white paper before my eyes, the nature of the thing and the nature of my sensations are one. Even if with science we supposed a molecular architecture beneath the smooth whiteness of the paper, that architecture itself could only be defined as the stuff of a farther possible experience, a vision, say, of certain vibrating particles with which our acquaintance with the paper would terminate if it were prolonged by magnifying artifices not yet known. (EP 1895, 72–73; cf. ERE 1904, 7)

For James, definite "things" or "objects," such as paper, water, or even animals, exist *as* definite things or objects only to perceiving humans. However, this does not mean that, like Berkeley, he rejects the existence of the material. Rather he claims that:

> In physical nature, it is universally agreed, a multitude of facts always remain the multitude they were and appear as one fact only when a mind comes upon the scene and so views them, as when H-O-H appear as "water" to a human spectator. (EP 1895, 71)

This follows from James's argument in the earlier *Principles of Psychology* and the *Briefer Course* that entities cannot "sum" unless there is some external combiner. Without "a medium or vehicle," James argues "the notion of combination has no sense"; worse still, it is "logically unintelligible" (PBC 1892, 177).

> No possible number of entities (call them as you like, whether forces, material particles, or mental elements) can sum *themselves* together. Each remains, in the sum, what it always was; and the sum itself exists only *for a bystander* who happens to overlook the units and to apprehend the sum as such; or else it exists in the shape of some other *effect* on an entity external to the sum itself. (PP 1890, 161)

James writes this in the context of his attack on mental "elementarism."[8] This is the position of the associationist psychologists and philosophers who regard our complex mental states as made up of simple ideas or elements. However, James is making an even stronger claim here. It is not just mental elements that cannot combine without a combiner, *no entities* can. Therefore, the "water" that we perceive *as water* rather than "H-O-H" only exists insofar as it has the effects we expect water to have on other entities. The pen I perceive is the pen only insofar as I experience it as a pen. Beyond my perception of it, or the effect it has on the paper that I am writing on, it is just a collection of "molecules or what not" (MEN 1907, 106). However, this does not mean that the pen I experience is in any sense illusory or the *mere appearance* of molecules—my experience of the pen really is the pen (it is its *esse*)—so crucially this experienced pen is just as real as the molecules out there in the world (see PP 1890, 310, n.1)

So how does all this help James's answer to Royce's problem? In Renouvier we had a solution to the *verification* problem but not the *constitution* problem. James's radical empiricism, through the introduction of conjunctive relations, allows a real continuity between (i) the thought *about* the object and (ii) the object *thought about*. Royce's explanandum was the relation between the thought about the object "the tower is round" and the object itself "the square tower." For James, conjunctive relations provide us a way to bridge the chasm without introducing the absolute, because they allow there to be a real link, made during the course of experience, between the original judgment and the tower itself. Royce's presumption was that the intentional relationship had to be instant. The judgment "the tower is square" had somehow to be directly and instantly connected with the tower in the world. However, for James the relationship of aboutness does not need to be instant. I can judge that "the tower is square," and what *makes* that judgment ultimately *about that* tower is that there is a continuous chain of experiences—continuous because of the conjunctive relationships between experiences—that leads from the original subjective judgment to the very object itself: the square tower. "That percept," in this case the percepts resulting from our eyes being squarely fixed on, and our hands touching, the square tower,

> was what I *meant*, for into it my idea has passed by conjunctive experiences of sameness and fulfilled intention. Nowhere is there jar, but every later moment continues and corroborates an earlier one.... Wherever such transitions are felt, the first experience *knows* the last one. Where they do not, or where even as possible they cannot, intervene, there can be no pretence of knowing. (ERE 1904, 29)

Because each experience, from the initial judgment to the final percept (the object *perceived* and thus what it is in *esse*), is joined by a conjunctive experience, it follows that the two are connected by an unbroken line. So there is an internal relation between the original judgment and the final percept of the ultimate tower, which is in itself partly constituted by the original perception. This means that the final percept can have "retroactive validating power," such that it ratifies our claim to know the tower and makes it actual. Prior to this we *knew* the tower *virtually*, just as we are *actually* mortal because of the *virtuality* of the event that will finish us off on the day we die.[9]

The Miller-Bode Objections

In March 1905, Boyd Henry Bode published a critical comment on James's radical empiricist theory of intentionality for the *Journal of Philosophy*. Initially James was not too concerned about his objections. In a letter to Bode from March 5, 1905, he wrote that it is "much the most pointed contribution to the discussion of Humanism from the adverse side, that has so far appeared" (CWJ 10.561). However, he was confident that the objections could be faced easily enough and hoped that Bode's mind would be changed once he had read his more recent articles.

James wrote a short response to Bode which was published less than two months afterward. The response is interesting because it shows, on the one hand, the direction in which James would have to develop his philosophy to solve the problem Bode raises, but, on the other, that James has not yet grasped the severity of the problem for his philosophy. Bode raised two objections. The first is that radical empiricism ends up being *solipsistic*, and the second is that it cannot provide a version of the world in which *two minds can know the same thing*.

As I read Bode's first objection, the point he is trying to make is that radical empiricism is a *solipsism of the present moment*. Consider James's attempt to solve what I have been calling the constitution problem. The relationship of intentionality is constituted in experience because there is a smooth unbroken line leading all the way from the original idea to the specious present, so that in the final experience we have created a real relation between the first term, the original idea, and the object it was about, the square tower. Royce had suggested that between two mental states, there is a chasm as unbridgeable as between our experience of the world and the world itself. James thinks, by means of conjunctive relations, that he has now shown this to be untrue.

Bode objects that if James's solution is to work, the final experience must somehow be a composite experience—it must contain (i) the original judgment; (ii) the percept of the object; and, (iii) the relation between (i) and (ii). This wouldn't cause a problem for some empiricists, but it does for James because, as we have seen in the second section, James *denies the possibility of mental composition*. "Distinct mental states," he writes in the *Briefer Course* "cannot 'fuse'" (PBC 1892, 177). This means that just as the taste of lemonade is not a composite of lemon *plus* that of sugar, but an altogether new "psychic fact" that is in some respects *like* lemon and sugar, an experience cannot be a composite of *earlier mental states*, but rather an altogether new one that is in some respects *like* the earlier ones. "Each pulse of cognitive consciousness, each Thought," James writes, "dies away and is replaced by another" (PP 1890, 322; cf. CWJ 1909, 12.278).[10] The final "knowing" experience, therefore, cannot be a composite of the original judgment, the percept, and its relations, and Royce's chasm remains unbridged. Bode's objection is ingenious and James's first attempt to solve it almost suggests that Bode knew James's philosophy better than James knew it himself.

In James's first reply, he suggested that Bode was trying to use rationalist abstract categories where radical empiricism was a position altogether opposed to them. The very notion of individual terms and distinct relations between them is an "attempt to substitute static concepts of the understanding for transitions in our moving life" (ERE 1904, 121). But this just shows why James had failed to fully grasp the problem, and why it would vex him so badly when he did. Bode had not argued that his radical empiricism was incompatible with rationalism, a rationalism James could easily reject, rather, he had shown that it was incompatible with *James's own theory*: his psychology of mental states. This psychology would be much harder for James to turn his back on.

Bode's second objection follows from the same incompatibility. Bode claims that "[u]nless each percipient is to dwell in a world apart, there must be points in his experience which are not precisely similar to, but numerically identical with, corresponding points in the experience of other percipients" (Bode 1905, 131–132). However, again this seems impossible given James's psychology. There could only be identical points in two people's experiences if these experiences could in some sense share an identical component. However, this is impossible on James's psychology because each experience is an indecomposable unit. One of the crucial points Royce made was that if one person makes a judgment that "the shield is red all over" and another says "the shield is yellow all over," we can only assume that one is right and the other wrong if we know that they are talking about the same shield. James's problem as highlighted by Bode is that it seems as if he can't account for this. Person 1 perceives a shield, the *esse* of that shield is its *percipi* by person 1. Person 2 perceives a shield, the *esse* of that shield is its *percipi* by person 2. Now, the "molecules or what not" that are the basis of these perceptions are the same, but this is irrelevant since they in no way form parts of the experience. Person 1's and person 2's shields are different shields *in essence* and rational disagreement and debate over the true nature of "the" shield is impossible.

It was this second objection that really bothered James. In fact, between 1905 and 1908, he dedicated a notebook to trying to solve the problem and to modify radical empiricism so that it could show how two minds could know the same thing.[11] James opens the notebook with his summary of the problem:

> In my psychology I contended that each field of consciousness is entitatively a unit, and that its parts are only different cognitive relations which it may possess with different contexts.
>
> But in my doctrine that the same "pen" may be known by two knowers I seem to imply that an identical part can help to *constitute* two fields.
>
> Bode & Miller both pick up the contradiction. The fields are not then entitative units. They are decomposable into "parts," one of which at least is common to both, and my whole tirade against "composition" in the psychology is belied by my own subsequent doctrine! (MEN 1905, 65)

James had never been convinced by Royce's solution to his problem. He believed that the cost of positing an Absolute Mind was that the individual minds have no true reality. The many is subsumed by the one. However, he came to believe that the Miller-Bode objections showed that his solution fared no better than Royce's, because he had precisely the *opposite* difficulty: "If the parts are all the experience there is," he writes in the notebook, "how can the whole be experienced otherwise than as any of them experiences it?" (MEN 1905, 71). Royce's problem is "how can we account for a world of individuals in a monist whole"? James's problem is "how can we account for the whole in a world of isolated individuals?"

James's "Bergsonian Conversion"

Despite his protracted struggle with the problem evidenced in the Miller-Bode notebook, James eventually realized that, to solve the problem, he would have to give up on his objection to the compounding of consciousness. But what made him object to it in the first place? The reason is in part empirical and in part logical. On the empirical side, as we have already seen, when we drink lemonade, we don't experience elements, i.e., the taste of pure sugar *plus* the taste of pure lemon, as we might expect if the elementarist picture were correct. We experience some different "whole" flavor, which is in some respects *like* the taste of sugar and *like* the taste of lemon. On the logical side, if it were true that the taste of sugar and taste of lemon were *parts* of the taste of lemonade, the experience of the lemonade would be, at once, the taste of the "many" individual parts (*sugar* plus *lemon*, etc. . . .), and, at the same time, the "whole." However, as the many, this experience *is* the taste of sugar and the taste of lemon, etc. . . , but as a whole it does not taste of sugar and lemon (because it tastes of lemonade), which means that to assert that this taste were composed of parts would be to assert that the experience was both the taste and not the taste of sugar and lemon, which would be absurd. It would be to:

> throw away the logical principle of identity in psychology, and say that, however, it may fare in the outer world, the mind at any rate is a place in which a thing can be all kinds of other things without ceasing to be itself as well. (PP 1890, 175)

When James reports on what plagued him during this period in his 1909 *A Pluralistic Universe* lectures, he emphasizes the logical side of the problem. The problem of composition, he told his audience:

> is the general conceptualist difficulty of one thing being the same with many things, either at once or in succession, for the abstract concepts of oneness and manyness must needs exclude each other. (PU 1909, 127)

On September 12, 1906, James made an entry into the notebook in which he suggested that maybe his whole problem had come from being too concerned with this "conceptualist difficulty." "May not my whole trouble," he wrote "be due to the fact that I am still treating what is really a living and dynamic situation by logical and statical categories?" (MEN, 104). As James re-states his problem, the question of whether or not we can know the same pen rests on the issue that when I experience the pen and you experience the pen, because the pen is not composed of elements, my pen and your pen are different pens. However, by thinking about the problem in this way, he has been treating these experienced pens as fixed, static entities: "did n't [sic] I," he asks himself,

> stick to "pen," "me," and "you," and the relations "co" and "ex," in a purely static manner? Did n't [sic] I treat them as so much flat "content," immediately given, and, as such, fixed for the time being? Did n't [sic] I leave the mechanism of their givenness behind the scenes? Ditto the mechanism of their change, in the sense of their being superseded by new contents given? Substituting the kinetoscopic for the continuous view of the world? which is the living common sense view? (MEN 104)

The example of the kinetoscope is key. A kinetoscope was an early cinematic device in which an individual could look through a peephole and see a motion picture produced by a series of images on a strip of film. The illusion of motion is the result of a quick succession of static images. James was concerned that he had been treating experience in the same way, i.e., he treats experience *as a noun*, rather than as a continuous process, i.e., *as a verb*.[12] However, through reading Bergson, James started to realize that this might not be the right way to think about experience, and that rather than think of experience *as one experience and then another*, we should consider it as a verb in the active voice. We should understand it not as *presented to* as if it were like a static block, but rather as *lived through*. In the same entry, he writes:

> wouldn't the remedy lie in making activity a part of the content itself, reintroducing agents, but not leaving them behind the scenes? Vivify the mechanism of change! Make certain parts of experience do work upon other parts! Since work gets undeniably done, and "we" feel as if "we" were doing bits of it, why, for Heaven's sake, throw away that naif impression, and banish all the agency and machinery into the region of the unknowable, leaving the foreground filled with nothing but inactive contents? For the conjunctive relations, as I have talked of them so far, are inactive, they do but represent the fruits of relating activities elsewhere performed. (MEN 104)

The distinction he makes here between two ways of understanding experience comes from his reading of Bergson's (1903) *Introduction à la métaphysique*. Bergson uses the example of watching an arm rise through geometrical space. Although when I watch your arm rise up, I represent it as moving through defined spatial positions, and it is as if I could cut up each of these positions into distinct moments (like the images in a kinetoscope), the same is not true of my experience of moving my own arm up in the air. As I lift my arm, I do not experience distinct replaceable moments, but a continuous process in which the past (the intention) continues to live on throughout until my arm reaches the desired position. As *lived through*, we understand it as one single continuous process with concrete duration, even though as *presented to* (from the outside), the lifting of an arm looks as if it is merely a succession of individual static moments. For Bergson, when we understand experience as lived through, we shift our focus away from the "*already-made*," the "*being-made*" (CE 238, 259). The "being made" is not a series of entitative units, one replacing the other, but rather a "continual flux." In this continual flux, we do not experience one discrete moment being replaced by another (although this is how we must understand it when we reflect upon it), but rather a pure continuity in which every moment extends into every other. This is what Bergson calls "real duration."

> Our duration is not merely one instant replacing another; if it were, there would never be anything but the present—no prolonging of the past into the actual, no evolution, no concrete duration. Duration is the continuous progress of the past which gnaws into the future and which swells as it advances. (CE 4–5, 6–7)

If James were able to free himself from the kinetoscopic perspective and take on the Bergsonian understanding of *duration*, he would have an answer to Bode's first problem. From the kinetoscopic perspective, the experience of "knowing" the square tower cannot *include* the original idea of the tower, because each experience is only an "entitative substitute" of the former one. However, from the Bergsonian point of view, there really is a continuous process; the idea lives on into the specious present. There is a continuous experience that links idea to object. But, there is an obvious problem. Bergson can answer Bode's problem because he was not concerned by the conceptualist problem that bothered James. If the past is gnawing on into the future, it must live on in the present as a kind of element; there *is* a "fusing" of psychic states. As James writes in his entry from two days later:

> B[ergson] gets the permanent agency that common sense gets by his supposition of a mind with its memories. This can be translated into phenomenal terms, if we restore dynamic form to the phenomenon. The phenomenal mind is a subconscious reserve growing in time by addition & intussusception of new memories; passing into attentive consciousness and acting from moment to moment, in obedience to desire; calling, and effectively calling, on new parts of experience to come, while other new parts come without being called. (MEN, 106)

Although it is clear in these 1906 entries that James was already tempted to simply give up on this conceptualist worry altogether and go with the "naif" impression of activity, it wouldn't be until he read Bergson's 1907 *L'Evolution créatrice* that he would finally have the confidence to do so. This work was crucial for James because he believed that in it "the beast intellectualism" had been "killed absolutely *dead!*" (CWJ 1907, 11.378). What is this beast? Roughly, *intellectualism* (or conceptualism) is the doctrine that we understand the underlying nature of the world by means of static intellectual concepts. It is the view that the *intellectual* or *logical* has ultimate priority over other forms of comprehending the world. For James, Bergson showed him that his claim that one thing cannot be at the same time many things was intellectualist because it, in Peircean language, put a roadblock in the way of inquiry: no matter what experience might tell you, the logic is clear and cannot be contradicted.

The key claim of *L'Évolution créatrice* is that if the intellectual is given this priority, evolution cannot be understood. The intellect thinks the world through mathematics—especially geometry. It does this because it is *practically useful* to do so. Our mathematical conception of space allows us to plan our possible interactions with the world. But, nonetheless, such a geometrical space is not something we could ever *perceive*, but only *conceive*. It is "an idea that symbolizes the human tendency of the human intellect toward fabrication" (CE 157, 173). As I watch your arm rise, and represent it as moving through geometrical space, I catch this movement in a conceptual net. The positions I represent your arm moving through, however, are not *real* positions that actually exist, but rather *suppositions*. The problem is that because it is practically useful to *think* space mathematically, scientists end up over-emphasizing the spatiality of objects and they start to think of them as they are *in themselves* in terms of discrete measurable units. They substitute the signs they have developed to *comprehend* these beings for the original beings themselves.

This is especially problematic, Bergson argues, when time is considered in the same way, and thought of as "spatialized," i.e., cut up into a succession of discrete units. This *intellectualist* understanding of time could never explain how evolution could occur, since the latter "implies a real persistence of the past in the present, a duration which is, as it were, a hyphen, a connecting link" (CE 22, 27). Evolution, he claims, requires the continuation of the past into the present. Furthermore, to understand evolution we must account for the emergence of real novelty, and no matter how elaborate our mathematical formulae may be, Bergson insists, there is no way they could introduce the slightest bit of novelty into the world. All new moments would be mere rearrangements of past moments. Consequently, the intellectualist understanding of time fails to do justice to both the past and the future.

There is, however, an alternative. We can understand life and evolution through intuition. Intuition, Bergson claims, is disinterested instinct. It is instinct that has been able to free itself from everyday practicalities and reflect on its inward operations. Intuition brings us into direct contact with reality, since it is formed and molded by life. Through intuition—in the "depths" of our experience—we come into contact with pure duration, creative life, and the unceasing swelling of the "absolutely new"; an inner life of the mind that cannot be represented by images or concepts. This intuition requires us to turn away from the faculty of seeing and become one with the act of willing. This means turning away from the evidence of the "external senses," and focusing on the inner sense, because it is in inner sense that we can best understand our experience as an activity, as a verb in the active voice, as "continual flux."

In the intuition of pure duration, furthermore, we access the two essential elements of what it is to be a "person." These are "memory" and "will." There is memory because the pure continuity of duration means that every moment of the past continues to live on into the present (1903, 40). We know that this must be true in a limited sense, because we can only hear a series of notes as a melody because the experience of the previous notes lives on into the present. However, Bergson expands on this phenomenological truth to claim that all of the past must live on into the continually growing present state. For this reason,

> Every psychical state . . . reflects the whole of a personality. Every feeling, however simple it may be, contains virtually within it the whole past and present of the being experiencing it, and, consequently, can only be separated and constituted into a "state" by an effort of abstraction or of analysis. (1903, 31)

This "gathering of the past" is concurrent with the creation of the future—"a continual forward movement" (M 1914, 1065). This internal impulse or strain toward the future is what Bergson calls "will." It is a constant and essential part of what it is to be human. "To be a human being," he writes, "is in itself a strain" (M 1914, 1065). The will is also a "creative force" (M 1914, 1071) by which the human person "is capable of drawing out of himself more than is actually there" (M 1914, 1064; M 1916, 1203). Unlike material forces, which are limited to determinate quantities, the will is able to grow in its power so that the more one wills the greater it becomes. By means of this force the human being creates itself. The effort of our will is visible to consciousness in heightened situations when we "contract our whole being in order to thrust it forward" (CE 238, 259). But the will is not limited to such situations; it is co-extensive with our being, consciousness, or character. The will is the underlying effort of our being that is continually working against our organic predispositions and already-formed intellectual habits to both re-mold and re-create them so that they better suit our practical purposes. If we understand the world in terms of geometry, there can be no genuinely new creation. All we have is a continual rearrangement of pre-existing parts. However, the world of duration is different: "duration means invention, the creation of forms, the continual elaboration of the absolutely new" (CE 11, 14).

On June 13, 1907, after reading *L'Évolution créatrice*, James wrote to Bergson to tell him that he felt "rejuvenated" (CWJ 1907, 12.376). By means of his arguments for the rejection of conceptualism and the importance of the "intuition" of experience as active and continuous, Bergson had provided James with a means finally to provide a rock-solid solution to the problem raised by Royce back in the 1880s. James started to work this out most carefully in the final few entries in the Miller-Bode notebook, in February 1908. For James, the crucial point is that Bergson's critique of the "static" pertains even to the most instantaneous moment of reality:

> no element of it could be treated as a "piece" or stable grammatical subject, but that whatever *is* has the durcheinander character, meaning by that that when you say it is anything, it obliges you also to say not only that it is more and other than that thing, but that it *is not* that thing, both the is and the *is not* implying at bottom only that our grammatical forms, condemned as they are to staticality and alternation, are inadequate, if we use them as literal substitutes for the reality. (MEN, 123)

If we want to understand how this can be "without paradox," he writes, we can do so only by "awakening sympathy with it." While "logic makes all things static. As living … all radiate and coruscate in many directions" (MEN, 123).

James most clearly defends the importance of *intuition* as a method in the 1909 *A Pluralistic Universe* lectures. He tells his audience to "dive back into the flux itself" (PU 1909, 113), to "place yourself at a bound, or *d'emblée*, as M. Bergson says, inside of the living, moving, active thickness of the real" (PU 1909, 116), and to "put yourself in the making by a stroke of intuitive sympathy with the thing" (PU 1909, 117). However, for all these literary flourishes, the key thing James is doing is simply highlighting Bergson's distinction between the "already-made" and the "being-made." James says that "[w]hat really exists is not things made but things in the making," and what he means by "intuitive sympathy" is simply to put oneself from the perspective of the one raising their arm, rather than the one watching the arm being raised (PU 1909, 117). It's to experience oneself as becoming something that one is not—something new—while at the same time remaining what one was, and to experience the past being retained into the present through memory and will. In short, experience as a verb, rather than as a noun. Insofar as we recognize that we become what we are not, while remaining what we are, we have direct experience of "manyness-in-oneness" despite what the "logic of identity" might say. Therefore, "each of us actually is his own other," and "to that extent," James maintains, "livingly knowing how to perform the trick which logic tells us can't be done" (PU 1909, 115).

Since, according to the converted James, the past really does *gnaw* into the present, the first of Bode's criticisms—the solipsism of the present moment—has been successfully overcome. But what about the second answer? Is it now possible, according to James's metaphysics, for two minds to know the same thing?

The final entries into the notebook are crucial here and offer us great insight into his final metaphysics. In his radical empiricist works, the importance of the continued interaction between individuals was underemphasized, since the experienced object—the phenomenon—was always one step removed from the object itself. But the later James is at pains to emphasize the crucial role of reactions and willed actions in the formation of an individual. "All living things distinguish assert and maintain themselves as against their environment," he wrote on January 11.

> They actively create the relation. Interactions are *grounded in the real*. Reactions are one kind of interaction. . . but the case of living reactions is different, for these often enhance the action when it feels favourable. (MEN 1908, 122, my italics)

The italicized passage highlights an important shift. As we saw earlier, James followed Renouvier in believing that we are tied to phenomena and that we have no direct contact with "reality" itself. We start from the point of view of the subjective idealist, but must "postulate" the existence of an external reality for the sake of scientific inquiry. But what this passage shows is that James has become much more realist in his later years. Our willed interactions now put us in direct contact with reality. As he writes in his posthumous *Some Problems of Philosophy* "[t]he concept 'reality', which we restore to immediate perception, is no new conceptual creation, but a kind of practical relation to our Will, *perceptively experienced*" (SPP 1911, 60).

Since we now have direct contact with objects, their *esse* is more than their *percipi*. The pen *as a pen* (rather than as a pattern of molecules) is no longer isolated to my experience or yours, but rather a "continuum." Just as I become what I am through my living interactions with other beings, so too does the pen. Because I can experience what it is like to be something that continues to be what it is even while it becomes what it is not through such interactions, and thus be a "manyness-in-oneness," I can, through "living sympathy," understand what it is for a pen, or any other object, to do the same. James now understands the pen to be, a business centre, a "firm." It has many customers, my mind, e.g. and the physical world. To call it the *same* pen both times would mean that, altho my mind and the physical world can and may eventually figure in one and the same transaction, they need not do so, are not at all times fixed in that transaction, and that in respect of this particular pen experience neither *counts* in the transaction which the other is carrying on. Neither *is counted* by the other, neither is *for* the other. (MEN 1908, 126)

As a business center, "*it* is alive enough to carry on more than one business. It can *turn* inside of itself—which means that without ceasing to *be* itself, it can stand in many relations, of which being with the 'rest' is only one" (MEN 1908, 128). What this means for the problem of whether two minds can know the same thing is that my idea of a shield can now lead me either really or potentially to a physical interaction with the shield in which the shield itself will form a real ingredient. Your idea of the shield can also terminate in the very same shield. Although there will be perspectival differences, due to selective attention and prior experience, the shield itself is real and there is a fact of the matter over whether or not it is red all over or yellow all over, such that if I think the former and you the latter, then at least one of us must be in error.

In sum, in order for the radical empiricist account of the constitution of the intentional relation to work there had to be a real internal relation between the original idea and the object thought about such that a series of experiences could terminate in a fusion of both. Bergson convinced James that he could reject the intellectualist concerns that prohibited him from properly accounting for such a relation and consequently to rethink both the nature of experience and of objects. Once James had rethought both so that they could be conceived of as "remaining what they are, whilst turning into what they are not," it was possible both to think of an earlier idea becoming a constituent part of a latter one, and thus account for the intentional relation, and also to think of an identical object contributing to the experience of two subjects, and thus account for how two minds can know the same thing.

Conclusion

Let's recap James's (and my own) progress. I have argued that James's aim, i.e., to show that a solution to Royce's problem of error could be established without appeal to a metaphysical Absolute Mind, is a thread that leads all the way from 1885 to his very last work. At first, James saw this problem as one relating simply to *verification* and attempted to give a *purely* practical solution to this theoretical problem. However, he came to realize that the problem was stickier than that. The problem was not just about the *verification* of our ideas, but also about the very *constitution* of the intentional relationship that makes our ideas *about* an object in the first place. For my judgment "the tower is round" to be a false judgment about the square tower in the world, rather than a true report of my subjective state, there must be some form of relation between the judgment and the tower itself, and this is precisely what philosophical positions that refuse to go "beyond the phenomena" cannot provide, according to Royce. In his 1904–1905 *Radical Empiricism* essays, James attempted to provide a story about this intentional relation by means of conjunctive relations between our experiences such that there is a continuous chain of relations that leads from the original judgment concerning the tower to the terminating experience where we are in perceptual contact with it. If the original judgment about a round tower leads us to a square tower, then, by virtue of leading us to it, this is the tower it was about—so there is a constitutive relationship of aboutness—but insofar as the tower is square and not round, the judgment was in error. Royce stated his problem as follows: "If I aim at a mark with my gun, I can fail to hit it, because choosing and hitting a mark are totally distinct acts. But, in the judgment, choosing and knowing the object seem inseparable" (1885, 399). The success of the *Radical Empiricism* essays was to show that enough of a distinction can be made between choosing and hitting the mark to make misrepresentation possible. If we judge that the tower at which we aim is a "round tower," but when we arrive it turns out to be a "square tower," then we failed to hit what we had aimed for. The idea picked out an object, but the object was not as we thought it was.

Boyd and Bode, however, showed that this solution was not consistent with the further systematic commitments of James's philosophy. They showed that without a better explanation of our perceptual contact with the world than the one offered by the metaphysics of pure experience, James couldn't explain "hitting" at all. And certainly not how two shooters could hit the same target. Hitting requires that there be an internal relation between the original judgment and the terminating percept such that the two become one. However, James's long-held belief that elements cannot compose meant that such a fusion of judgment and percept is strictly speaking impossible. James struggled with this systematic incoherence for several years, but came to a solution partly through the inspiration of Bergson. James's belief that things could not compose was based on the logical principle that things cannot be both "one" and "many." Bergson's arguments against the priority of such logical principles in philosophy allowed James to reject the principle in favor of the data acquired from direct experience and life. Here in the "living thickness of the real" we experience beings perform the tricks which logic prohibits. In life and in our experience, each being becomes what it was not while remaining what it was. From the perspective of our own experience, this means that we are no longer stuck in a solipsism of the present moment. There really is a continuous relationship from one experience to the next such that the original judgment can be a constitutive part of the terminating percept. James realized that a more heavyweight metaphysics was necessary to account for the intentional relationship and he was finally willing to pay the price. From the perspective of beings, recognizing that they are both "one" and "many" is necessary for ensuring that this intentional relationship is one that can be maintained between one object and two different subjects. They are "business centres" able to enter into transactions with more than one customer. For this reason, it is possible for two different shooters to aim toward and even hit the same target, and, consequently, for there to be meaningful agreement and disagreement. In terms of the basic explanation of intentionality, therefore, James's late works are perfectly in tune with his 1904–1905 essays. The crucial difference is the form of metaphysics that underlies it.[13]

Notes

1. Royce published several different versions of the argument from error (1885, 1892, 1895, 1898, and 1900). James was aware of it before its first publication in his (1885) *The Religious Aspect of Philosophy*, but became even more concerned with it after it appeared in print. It is this version that we shall be primarily concerned with in this chapter. James provides very helpful summaries of Royce's argument in his review of the *Religious Aspect* (ECR 1885, 383–388), and in a letter to Renouvier (CWJ 1888, 6.358–361). On James and Royce, see Conant (1997), Oppenheim (1999), and Sprigge (1993: 25-30)
2. William Mander writes "I do not for my part see how the true answer... can be so very different from that which Royce proposes" (1998, 457).
3. For a different take on the James-Renouvier relation, see Matthias Girel's chapter in this volume. On an account of Renouvier's influence on James's "will to believe" doctrine, see Dunham (2015). For good overviews of Renouvier's philosophy, see Séailles (1905), Verneaux (1945), and Schamus (2018).
4. On the use of postulates in the *Principles*, see Klein (2010).
5. See Renouvier's letter to James, March 27, 1887 (Perry 1935 1, 700–702).
6. Reference WJ 675.61.4 at the Houghton library, Harvard. James wrote this note around 1875, a few years before the first version of his theory of truth appeared in print (see EPh 1878, 7–22).
7. See his letter to James, September 11, 1884 (Perry 1935 I, 696).
8. This position was called "elementarism" by Boring (1929). For more on James's rejection of "elementarism," see Klein (2020)
9. For a more detailed discussion and partial defence of this account of intentionality, see Jackman's chapter in this volume.
10. As James puts it: "If experience be a stream, the recognitive experiences are entitative substitutes of other experiences, are not one with them" (MEN 1905, 66)
11. On the Miller-Bode notebook, see Moller (1997, 2001, and 2008), Perry (1935 II, 393–394), and Sprigge (1993: 165–171).
12. As Pauline Phemister (2004) has insightfully pointed out, treating experience as a noun was common among the classical empiricists.
13. Thanks to Emily Herring and Neil Williams for comments on an earlier draft of this chapter. Special thanks to Alexander Klein for his comments on many drafts of this chapter.

Bibliography

Abbreviations

CE: Bergson, H. 1907 (2016). *L'Évolution créatrice*. Paris: PUF
Bergson, H. 1941. *Creative Evolution*. Translated by A. Mitchell. New York: The Modern Library.
ECG: Renouvier, C. B. 1912. *Essai de Critique générale. Deuxième Essai: Traité de psychologie rationnelle d'après les principes du criticisme*. 2 Vols. Paris: Librairie Armand Colin Cited by *Essai* and volume number.

M: Bergson, H. 1972. *Mélanges*. Paris: PUF.

Other Texts Cited

Bergson, H. 1903 (1912). *Introduction to Metaphysics*. Translated by T.E. Hulme. Cambridge, UK: Hackett.
Bode, H. 1905. "'Pure Experience' and the External World." *Journal of Philosophy* II (March): 128–33.
Boring, E. G. 1929. *A History of Experimental Psychology*. London: The Century Co.
Conant 1997. "The James/Royce Dispute and the Development of James's 'Solution.'" In *The Cambridge Companion to William James*, edited by R. A. Putnam, 186–213. Cambridge, UK: Cambridge University Press.
Dunham, J. 2015. "Idealism, Pragmatism, and the Will to Believe: Renouvier and William James." *British Journal for the History of Philosophy* 23 (4): 756–778.
Klein, A. 2010. "*Divide et Impera!* William James's Pragmatist Tradition in the Philosophy of Science." *Philosophical Topics* 36 (1): 129–166.
Klein, A. 2020. "The Death of Consciousness? James's Case against Psychological Unobservables". *Journal of the History of Philosophy*. 58 (2): 293–324
Mander, W. 1998. "Royce's Argument for the Absolute." *Journal of the History of Philosophy* 36 (3): 443–457.
Moller, M. S. 1997. *William James's Quandary*. Dissertation. Washington University, St. Louis, MO.
Moller, M. S. 2001. "James, Perception and the Miller-Bode Objections." *Transactions of the Charles S. Peirce Society* 37 (4): 609–626.
Moller, M. S. 2008. "'The Many and the One' and the Problem of Two Minds Perceiving the Same Thing." *William James Studies* 3.
Oppenheim, F. M. 1999. "How Did William James and Josiah Royce Interact Philosophically?" *History of Philosophy Quarterly* 16 (1): 81–96.
Perry, R. 1935. *The Thought and Character of William James*. Volume II Cambridge, MA: Harvard University Press.
Phemister, P. 2004. "'All the time and everywhere everything's the same as here': The Principle of Uniformity in the Correspondence Between Leibniz and Lady Masham." In *Leibniz and His Correspondents*, edited by P. Lodge, 193–213. Cambridge, UK: Cambridge University Press.
Renouvier, C. 1888. "La Haute métaphysique contemporaine, J. Royce." *La Critique philosophique*. 4 année. 3–4 (2): 4–24, 85–120.
Royce, J. 1885. *The Religious Aspect of Philosophy*. Boston: Houghton Mifflin.
Royce, J. 1892. *The Spirit of Modern Philosophy*. Boston: Houghton Mifflin.
Royce, J. 1895. *The Conception of God*. London: Macmillan.
Royce, J. 1898. *Studies in Good and Evil*. New York: D. Appleton and Company.
Royce, J. 1900. *The World and the Individual*. First Series. London: Macmillan.
Schmaus, W. 2018. *Liberty and the Pursuit of Knowledge. Charles Renouvier's Political Philosophy of Science*. Pittsburgh, PA. University of Pittsburgh Press.
Séailles, G. 1905. *La Philosophie de Charles Renouvier*. Paris: Félix Alcan.
Sprigge, T. 1993. *James and Bradley: American Truth and British Reality*. Chicago: Open Court.
Vernaux, R. 1945. *L'idéalisme de Renouvier*. Paris: Vrin.
Winkler, K. Forthcoming. *A New World. Philosophical Idealism in America*. Oxford, UK: Oxford University Press.

CHAPTER 20

JAMES AND MATH
On Infinite Totalities

FRANCESCA BORDOGNA

INTRODUCTION

IN Chapter 1 of his posthumously published *Some Problems of Philosophy,* William James drew a distinction between a broader and older conception of philosophy, according to which philosophy "must include the results of all the sciences," and a more recent and narrower conception of philosophy as the discussion of specific metaphysical problems. In the older sense philosophy could not "be contrasted" with the "special sciences," a phrase James used to refer both to empirical sciences, such as physics and psychology, and to "*a priori* sciences," such as logic and mathematics (SPP 1911, 19, 35). In the more recent and more technical sense of "metaphysics," instead, philosophy was "something contrasted with the sciences." James announced that the remainder of the book would be devoted to philosophy in this narrower sense and that he would "let . . . the results of the sciences alone" (SPP 1911, 19–20). In Chapter 7, however, as James dealt with the metaphysical question of whether novelty comes into being through continuous or through discrete processes, he broke his promise. James attacked "the new infinite"—a mathematical definition of infinity that had been offered by Bernard Bolzano in 1851 and resurrected, independently, by Richard Dedekind and Georg Cantor. He contended that the new definition could not be invoked to account for physical processes of change and used that argument provisionally to defend a discrete metaphysics of novelty. In doing so, he cast himself against leading mathematicians, logicians, and philosophers who made routine use of the "new infinite."

The technical nature of James's discussion of infinity in a work that was supposed to "let the results . . . of the sciences alone" seems to be out of place. Furthermore, although with *Some Problems of Philosophy* James "hoped . . . to round out" his metaphysical "system" (James, quoted in Hare 1979, xiii), the main purpose of the book was to introduce "beginners" to philosophy (Hare 1979, xix; SPP 1911, 10); yet James's analysis of mathematical topics in Chapter 7 was hardly tailored to the needs of beginners. Why then did James deal with mathematics in a book on philosophy "in the narrow sense"?

This paper answers this question by examining James's decades-long engagement with "the problem" or "question of the infinite." Among the many questions James asked himself concerning infinity, two were particularly important to him: is the notion of an infinite totality free from contradictions? And, if so, do infinite totalities exist?

In the thirty years that preceded the composition of Chapter 7 of *Some Problems of Philosophy* James periodically revisited those questions and, in the last years of his life, he engaged with a rich body of literature in mathematics, the philosophy of mathematics, and logic in order to best answer them. The exact chronology of James's thoughts about infinity cannot be determined, for the date of composition of some of the most relevant manuscripts is uncertain.[1] Nevertheless we know that, when James began addressing the problem of the infinite, he operated with traditional definitions of infinity as something endless, interminable, boundless. In light of such definitions, he rejected the notion of an infinite totality as self-contradictory and bracketed the question of the existence of infinite totalities. James likely encountered the new definition of infinity in January 1900, when he read the first volume of his colleague Josiah Royce's *The World and the Individual* from "cover to cover," including, presumably, the long "Supplementary Essay," in which Royce mathematized the Absolute as a "new infinite" (CWJ 1900, 9.127). However James did not elaborate on the new definition until a later date, perhaps the central years of the decade, or even the end of the decade. By then similarly to Royce, he had come to view infinite sets (or "systems" or "classes," as James also wrote) according to the new definition as actually infinite totalities, all the elements of which were given simultaneously. Although James came to accept with Royce and the new infinitists that the "new infinite" was not self-contradictory, he rejected both the extra-mathematical existence of infinite totalities and the claim that such totalities could be known or experienced by finite knowers.

In chapter 7 of *Some Problems of Philosophy* James re-cast questions concerning infinite totalities in logical terms as questions concerning ways of defining infinite sets. There James offered a bifurcated argument, as he considered two types of infinity, which he had long labeled the "growing infinite" (that is, infinite systems according to old definitions, such as endless series), and the "standing infinite" (such as, for example, the infinitely many stars, assuming there exist infinitely many stars).[2] The former were potential infinities, the latter actual infinities. Restating a position he had announced in 1880 and had never abandoned, he argued that an understanding of "growing infinities" as totalities was logically contradictory. Although he was unable to rule out as self-contradictory an understanding of "standing infinities" as totalities, he urged that standing infinities could not be experienced as totalities and should not be defined as such, and continued to ban them from his pluralistic universe.

James's dealings with mathematical and logical matters have attracted little attention, perhaps because of James's repeated confessions of his "mathematical and logical" blindness (e.g., SPP 1911, 93).[3] Moreover, the few authors who have addressed James's work on mathematics have focused mostly on his understanding of continuity, dealing with his thoughts on infinite totalities only insofar as they related to continuity.[4] This paper contends that James's engagement with questions concerning infinite totalities had important implications for the development of his metaphysics. In 1903 James told his students that "the whole consideration of the Infinite strengthens Pluralism, making it more probable, tending to allow us to explore beginnings" (Bechtel 1902–1903, notes for Jan. 13, 1903). This essay argues that James's reflections on infinite totalities led him to think in new ways both about his pluralistic empiricism and about the nature of the contrast between that type of metaphysics and Royce's absolutism. Once we realize the importance of questions of infinite totalities for James, it will become obvious that, despite his promise, in *Some Problems of Philosophy* James could not have left mathematics (or logic) alone.

James, Renouvier, and the Principle of Totality

James's interest in the problem of the infinite was sparked by his encounter with the writings of Charles Renouvier. Although the French philosopher was an important source for James throughout his career (*Some Problems of Philosophy* was dedicated to him), as Mathias Girel argues, James began distancing himself from Renouvier as early as 1880 (Girel 2007, 182. On the relationships between James and Renouvier see also Girel, this volume). In a letter to Renouvier, James raised questions about Renouvier's use of one of the philosopher's fundamental principles, the "*principe du nombre*," according to which "things that are, or any parts of things that are, always form numbers, that is, determined numbers, different from all other numbers" (Renouvier 1875, 46). The principle was incompatible with the notion of an infinite number, with the "thesis" of "the existence of an infinity of things," and with the idea of "an actual infinity," three notions Renouvier equated and dismissed (Renouvier 1875, 53–54).

James questioned Renouvier's use of the "principle of number" in demonstrating that space, time, and movement could not be considered as "subjects in themselves." In the case of time, for example, Renouvier reasoned that "if time is a thing in itself, it has parts in themselves." These "parts," or "durations," would be "composed of other durations, because their objective forms are divisible"; and those durations, in turn, would be composed of other durations, and so on "without end" (Renouvier 1875, 58). As a result, "no determined number of partial durations" could "reproduce the veritable and final number of the durations of time," an implication Renouvier found "absurd." Thus, Renouvier concluded, "time, divisible time, is not in itself" (Renouvier 1875, 59).

Never a fan of things in themselves, James nevertheless challenged the way that Renouvier had framed his argument. Complaining about the different treatment Renouvier reserved for space and time "in themselves" versus space and time as phenomena, he contended that space and time are "neither finite nor infinite, but simply *boundless* and *continuous*," that is, they "offer a standing condition for the formation of parts infinite in addition" (boundlessness) and "in subdivision" (continuity)[5] (CWJ 1880, 5.76–77).

James found nothing wrong with the notion of infinite divisibility. As for the boundlessness of space and time, he conceded that the notion was problematic, but only if one viewed space and time as "totalities."

How did James reach that conclusion? James, who at this time adopted the Kantian definition of infinity as "something that cannot be completed by successive synthesis," found that the notion of "totality," involving the idea of "limitation" and of "bounds," was incompatible with the notion of boundlessness (or "illimitation"). In short, the notion of a "boundless totality" was self-contradictory. To give an example, according to James's argument, the endless series N of the natural numbers, $1, 2, 3, \ldots, n, \ldots$, being "boundless," could not constitute a totality. James referred to the claim of the self-contradictory nature of the notion of a boundless totality as the "principle of totality."

According to James's principle, "space and time are given, but not as totalities." The "principle of totality," James suggested, would suit Renouvier's purposes better than the "principle of number" (CWJ 1880, 5.76–77). Renouvier, however, promptly rejected the suggestion, arguing that his principle of number was "exactly the same" as James's principle of totality (Charles Renouvier to William James, Jan. 18, 1880, in Perry 1935, 314.) What Renouvier did not appreciate was that, in contrast with the principle of number, the principle of totality did not imply a commitment to finitism and thereby clashed with a fundamental aspect of Renouvier's neo-criticism. James's principle of totality, similarly to Renouvier's principle of number, barred the notion of an infinite (boundless) totality, but, in contrast to the principle of number, it did not bar the possibility of the existence of infinitely many things, *provided those things did not constitute a totality*. In other words, the principle of totality allowed for the existence of infinite "multiplicities," a term I use in this essay to refer to pluralities of things that do not form, or cannot not be experienced by a knower as, totalities. That apparently technical condition turned out to be the pivotal point for much of James's subsequent metaphysical work.

More than twenty years later, James presented exactly that point to students attending his 1902–1903 course "Philosophy 3: The Philosophy of Nature," in the context of a critical discussion of Kant's analysis of the first mathematical antinomy, according to which it was possible to prove both that the world has a beginning in time and that it does not have a beginning in time. Michelle Grier explains that, according to Kant, the conflict derived from errors in a syllogism, the major premise of which was that, "if the conditioned is given, the entire series of all conditions [the unconditioned] is likewise given" (Grier 2006, 198). James interpreted the premise as signifying that "the present moment of time [the conditioned] must follow the totality of previous moments [its conditions]," that is, "the whole of past time," or the "unconditioned" (Bechtel 1902–1903, notes for Oct. 16, 1902, and Jan. 10, 1903). Kant found the premise illusory and stated "repeatedly" that "we are not entitled to assume that the totality of conditions is actually given" (Grier 2006, 196–198). James may have not fully understood Kant's argument, for he accused Kant of perpetrating a "fallacy": the German philosopher had made an unwarranted switch from the claim that "no condition can be lacking" to the claim that the totality of ("the whole of," "the sum of") the conditions must be given. The crucial claim that "no condition can be lacking," as James's student Edwin DeTurck Bechtel dutifully wrote under "Dictated," means that "ea[ch] several condition must be there [;] but if each is 'there' we are tempted to say 'then, all are there,'—then . . . the totality [of them] is there, and once having passed from the distributive to the collective manner of speaking we find ourselves believing that they just form a whole or total" (Bechtel 1902–1903, notes for Jan. 10, 1903).

In line with his old principle of totality, James again asserted that a "total" or a "whole" is "necessarily finite" and that, thereby, if past events formed a totality, they must be finite in number; but he did question the slippage in language that led to the conclusion that there was a "whole" to begin with: "We start by confirming correctly that if a condition be there, no single condition can be left out. We end by saying that the conditions form a whole." In the same passage Bechtel jotted down: "the problem is whether a collection of eaches can form an all," that is, whether a multiplicity can form a totality.

James's principle of totality provided a partial answer to the problem, for it implied, on logical grounds, that, if "infinite" means "endless," infinitely many eaches could not "form" an all, or, as James also put the point, that a "growing infinite" (an endless series) could not constitute a totality—a conclusion James never abandoned.

That in his 1903 lectures James developed the same line of thought, initiated in 1880, is illustrated by the fact that, after noting that Renouvier's "principle of number" was "best paraphrased by saying that if anything exists the whole of it must be there," he accused Renouvier of the same fallacy he ascribed to Kant (ML 1902–1903, 272). In direct contrast with Renouvier's principle of number, James then concluded that there may exist infinitely many things and that past time may well be infinite. This claim agreed with the principle of totality that, as we have seen, barred the existence of infinite totalities, but not that of infinite multiplicities (ML 1902–1903, 272). Whether infinitely many things existed or past time was infinite, similarly to the question whether the quantity of matter found in the universe was infinite, were questions of fact, to be answered by natural sciences such as physics, astronomy, and cosmology, not by logic. If, according to Renouvier, finitism was "logically necessary," to James it was only "a probable hypothesis," though an attractive one (Bechtel 1902–1903, notes for Jan. 13, 1903).

The argument James dictated in January 1903 can be found, in almost identical form, in Chapter 7 of *Some Problems of Philosophy,* where James, once again, accused Kant of switching from the distributive to the collective language, even though "the logical situation" did not call for that switch (SPP 1911, 83–84). By then James had long come to make the distributive and the collective languages into markers, respectively, of his pluralistic empiricism and of absolutist idealism. Furthermore, he had come to envision the contrast between those two types of metaphysics both in mathematical and in logical terms as a conflict between different types of infinity and between different ways of defining infinite classes. To understand how that happened, we need to examine James's continued efforts to grapple with Josiah Royce's mathematization of the Absolute as an infinite totality.

Royce and the "New Infinite"

Royce introduced his metaphysical uses of the "new infinite" in the "Supplementary Essay. The One, the Many, and the Infinite," a long appendix to Vol. 1 of *The World and the Individual*.

The essay conveys the excitement Royce felt when he encountered the new definition of infinity and discovered in Dedekind's theory of infinite systems the long-sought-after solution of two metaphysical issues that were vitally important to him: rescuing a conception of the Absolute as an actual infinity from accusations of absurdity and shedding light on the nature of the relationships between the One and the Many. Royce approached these problems by replacing traditional "negative" conceptions of infinity as something boundless, endless, indefinite, or incomplete, with the new "positive" definition of "an infinite system."

In 1888 Dedekind had stated that "a system S is said to be *infinite* when it is similar to a proper part of itself" (Dedekind 1901b, 63). In modern terminology, a set S is infinite if it can be mapped by a "one-to-one" function onto a proper subset S' of itself.[6] For example, the series N of the natural numbers, i.e. the system $\{1,2,3,\ldots n, \ldots\}$, is infinite because the function $h: N \to N$ mapping each natural number n to the natural number $2n$ is one-to-one, and because $h(N)$, i.e. $\{2, 4, 6, \ldots 2n, \ldots\}$, is a proper subset of N, since, e.g., 1 belongs to N, but does not belong to $h(N)$.

Royce was quick to see that the new definition not only cast the "problem of the infinite" in a decidedly new light, allowing for unprecedented "exactitude and clearness" in mathematics (Royce 1902–1903, 22), but could also be used to perform a kind of metaphysical work that neither "mystical" nor the customary "negative" definitions of the infinite could effect. The metaphysical fruitfulness of Dedekind's definition was brought into relief for Royce by Dedekind's proof of an existence theorem and by the properties of a mathematical structure (that of the "chain," or "*Kette*") with which all infinite systems, according to the new definition, were endowed.

The theorem stated that "there exist infinite systems." Dedekind proved it by proving that a certain system was infinite. The system in question was "*meine Gedankenwelt*" ["my own realm of thoughts"]—that is, "the totality S of all things, which can be objects of my thought" (Dedekind 1901b, § 66). The elements of this system included the thoughts that those objects can be thought. The latter type of thoughts were the elements of a subset S' of S. S was mapped onto S' by the function that mapped a thought s to the thought that "s can be object of my thought, itself an element of S." Dedekind proved that the function was one-to-one and that the image S' of S was a proper subset of S, because there were elements of S, such as, strangely enough, "my own Ego," which belonged to S, but did not belong to S' (Dedekind 1901b, § 66). Thus S was infinite according to the new definition. Dedekind's proof has been called into question since its publication. As Ansten Klev notes, today the main objection against the theorem is that it invokes non-mathematical notions, such as the *Gedankenwelt*

(Klev 2018). Yet Dedekind's use of the *Gedankenwelt* is precisely what made his theory philosophically important to Royce.

As for the "chain," it is, in modern notation, a structure (S, f) consisting of a system S and a function f mapping S onto a subset S' of S. If f is one-to-one and S' is a proper subset of S, S is infinite by definition. (For example the series N of natural numbers or, as Royce referred to it, "the whole number series," $\{1, 2, \ldots, n, \ldots\}$, is a chain under the function g mapping n onto $n + 1$, and it is an infinite chain because g is one-to-one and $g(N)$, i.e. $\{2, 3, 4, \ldots\}$, is a proper subset of N, for it does not include the number 1).

Royce referred to infinite chains as "internally self-representative systems." He was especially interested in infinite systems that were made into chains by recursive functions, that is by functions that recreated "their own occasion for application" (Royce 1900, 496), such as the function g that mapped a natural number n onto $n + 1$, and, upon a second application, $n + 1$ onto $[(n + 1) + 1]$, and so on ad infinitum (Royce 1900, 509). In Dedekind's terminology, such systems were "simply infinite"; they were "similar" to N and had the same type of order as N under its natural ordering "<", or "less than," a type of order Georg Cantor called "omega" (ω) (Dedekind 1901b, § 71–73, 132–133).[7] Especially relevant to Royce was that the order of such systems was "absolutely predetermined" by the definition of the recursive functions that made them into chains of that kind, and that it was "logically accomplished by means of one act" (Royce 1900, 532).[8]

Royce also emphasized that such systems were "well-defined" in Cantor's sense, that is, it was possible to distinguish precisely between objects that belonged to one such system and objects that did not belong to that system, membership being predetermined by the function (Royce 1900, 582). Furthermore, given any natural number n, the nth element of any infinite series M was predetermined by the definition of the function that made M into a chain, whether a human observer had been capable of computing that element or not (Royce 1900, 571). Indeed, according to Royce, the definition of the function "validly" predetermined "all the members of the series" "at once," defining them simultaneously (Royce 1900, 583). This point was important because, as E. A. Jarvis observes, it enabled Royce to convey the broader claim that simply infinite systems, and by extension all infinite systems, were "actually contained in their definition" (Jarvis 1975). As a result, a knower such as the Absolute would view an infinite series not only as an "endless succession," but also as an "actual infinity": to the Absolute and "in the Absolute" an infinite series, rather than a succession "of sundered successive states of temporal experience," was given "all at once," "totum simul," or "at one stroke" (Royce 1900, 546). Viewed as an endless succession, N could never be "completed" by a recursive procedure, such as counting, because it did not have a last element; for that reason, it had "no totality" (Royce 1900, 581–582). However, viewed as ideally given by the definition of the function that made it into a chain, it was an "infinite totality" and it could be treated as such by the mathematician and by the philosopher (Royce 1900, 514). This conclusion clashed directly with James's "principle of totality," according to which, as we have seen, the notion that an endless series could constitute (or be viewed as) a totality was self-contradictory.

Dedekind's and Cantor's work paved the way for Royce's mathematization of metaphysical problems, allowing him to conclude that an "ideal," "completed Self" contained a subset which had the same structure and type of order as N under its natural ordering "<." This is what Royce meant when he wrote that the whole number series N was the "bare, dried skeleton" of the "completed self," and that the "metaphysical fate" of such a self "stands or falls with the possibility of such [self-representative] systems" (Royce 1900, 513, 526–7, 578). The Absolute was "either a Self, and that concretely and explicitly," or "no Absolute at all"; it was a "self-representative ordered system or *Kette* [chain], of purposes fulfilled," an actually infinite totality which existed "*totum simul*" and all the elements of which were given "at once" and "at a stroke" (Royce 1900, 545, 580).

To Royce's mind, by demonstrating the existence of an entity that illustrated the new definition of infinity, Dedekind's existence theorem had proved the non-contradictory nature of that definition, thereby helping Royce make the case that a conception of the Absolute as an actually infinite totality was not self-contradictory.[9] Armed with the "new infinite," Royce also solved to his satisfaction the problem of the One and the Many, reconfiguring the relationship between the Absolute and the individual selves in terms of the ability of the Absolute, an infinite system, to be mapped by one-to-one functions onto (infinitely) many parts of itself, each of which stood for an individual self (Royce 1900, 514).

JAMES READS ROYCE

Although the "Supplementary Essay" has seldom factored into analyses of the James/Royce debate, James's familiarity with the essay colored his understanding of Royce's idealism. Furthermore, as I will also contend, Royce's mathematizing of the Absolute and of the problem of the One and the Many inspired James to turn to mathematical analogies in his own metaphysical work.

James viewed Royce's mathematized "Absolute self" as "the most trivial idol" he had "ever conceived of" (CWJ 1904, 10.377). Nevertheless, he was concerned about the use of the "new infinite" as a tool for developing a metaphysical understanding of the world and of human experience. Royce's use of infinite chains led James to conclude that Royce's idealism failed to do justice to a fundamental aspect of human experience—its temporality.[10] As we have seen, according to Royce, "all" the elements of a chain were "ideally given" (that is, given to the absolute knower) simultaneously and instantly by the definition of the chain, rather than emerging in a temporal succession as "your acts in counting" would (Royce 1900, 583). To James's mind Royce's mathematized metaphysics treated "the possible additions to an experience" as "realized" when that experience was "realized," rather than coming into being through time, thereby viewing the "possible additions" to an experience as elements of an actually infinite totality (MEN 1902–1910, 218). Thus it ruled out an understanding of the growth of experience as a process that unfolds through time (James undated, 582–583). From the perspective of Absolutism, James noted in his "Syllabus in Philosophy D: General Problems of

Philosophy (1906–1907)," "the future and the past were given in one," making the temporality of human experience illusory (ML 1906–1907, 411–412).

Royce's conception of the Absolute as a knower to whom, as we saw, an infinite series was given "all at once," rather than as a sequence "of sundered successive states of temporal experience" (Royce 1900, 546, 568), led James to question the Roycean Absolute's ability to know and experience through time, confirming his suspicion that the Absolute was "out of time" (ML 1906–1907, 408). As James jotted down, if "the infinite kette" is given to the Absolute, then the Absolute "must have for its experience . . . some Bradleyan non-successive form" (James undated, 585). This argument supported James's comment, in *A Pluralistic Universe*, that none of the "attribute[s] connected with succession" could be predicated of the Absolute or its experience (PU 1909, 22). The Absolute's inability to experience through time made it alien to human experience, which, instead, was "incurably rooted" in temporality (PU 1909, 23).[11]

Royce's mathematical arguments strengthened James's contention that absolutism was fatalistic. James agreed with Royce that the values of a mathematical function (or the results of a mathematical operation) were pre-determined by the definition of the function (or of the operation). "The hundredth decimal of π the ratio of the circumference to its diameter, is predetermined ideally now, tho no one may have computed it," James noted in *Pragmatism* (P 1907, 101). This sentence could have been written by Royce, so precisely it echoed the language of the "Supplementary Essay." However, James worried that, if applied to natural facts and human experience rather than to mathematical objects, the idea of the pre-determination of the values of a function would rule out the possibility of chance and genuine novelty. For James, modeling the growth of experience after a chain implied that the "possible additions to an experience" were "pre-included" in and "pre-determined" by that experience (MEN 1902–1910, 218). James saw clearly that the analogy between new experiences and the values of a function ruled out the possibility that the present could bifurcate into "two alternative futures . . ., both [of which] may now be really possible"—an idea central to James's philosophy of chance since at least 1884's "The Dilemma of Determinism" (WB 1897, 118).[12] Royce's use of the "new infinite" was among the reasons why, although James knew that Royce had made room for possibility and freedom, James argued that absolutism, including Royce's, "denies possibility," and that monism broadly writ was hostile to the idea that new experiences could come into being by chance processes (Bechtel 1902–1903, notes for Nov. 20, 1902).

The "Cardinal Infinite" Versus the "Ordinal Infinite"

Although James was concerned about Royce's metaphysical uses of the "new infinite," he responded positively to Royce's suggestion that metaphysicians "could learn" from mathematicians and that metaphysical work could benefit from mathematical ways of thinking (Royce 1900, 462; Royce 1904, 453). His engagement with the "Supplementary Essay" represented a turning point in James's metaphysical thinking because, more than any other work, it spurred James not only to read widely in mathematics, the philosophy of mathematics, and logic, but also to think mathematically about certain metaphysical problems.

In ms. 4437, "Infinity," James went as far as to reconfigure the contrast between Royce's idealism and his own pluralistic empiricism as a contrast between two different types of infinity: the "cardinal infinite" and the "ordinal infinite." Ms. 4437 consists of two texts. The editors of *Manuscript Lectures* indicate 1902–1910 as the probable date of composition of the entire manuscript, allowing for the possibility that the first text was composed in 1902, though they also concede it may have been written as late as 1910. James's use of language derived from Russell's *Principles of Mathematics* (1903) suggests that first text may indeed have been composed after October 1908, perhaps in May 1909, when James reported having spent much time over Russell, Cantor, and French philosopher Louis Couturat, or even as late as the following February.[13] James's presentation of the contrast between his and Royce's metaphysics in terms of different types of infinity was probably inspired by a contrast that Couturat, in his *De l'infini mathématique*, had identified between an "empiricist stance" (that of Renouvier and his followers), according to which the natural numbers "are given one by one and in a succession [*successivement*] similarly to playing cards," and the "rationalist theory" (Couturat's own, and then Royce's), according to which "all" natural numbers are given "at a stroke [*d'un seul coup*] with [*dans*] the law of formation, which is a general and uniform rule" (Couturat 1896, 468). Although James disliked the spirit of Couturat's book, Couturat's discussion may have been in the back of James's mind when, in ms. 4437, he contrasted a type of metaphysics that allowed only for "ordinal infinities" (his own empiricist metaphysics) with a type of metaphysics that instead was committed to "cardinal infinities" (Royce's) (MEN 1902–1910, 217–218).

This terminology was loosely derived from Georg Cantor, who had introduced transfinite cardinal numbers and transfinite ordinal numbers as free creations of the human spirit. From various sources James learned that the cardinal number of a set (its "cardinality") was the number of the elements of that set and that it was "the property of a class considered as a whole," that is, as a totality, rather than of its elements (Couturat 1904, 213). He knew that, according to Cantor, if the set was infinite, its cardinal number was a transfinite cardinal number and that Cantor denoted the cardinal number of the set of N of the natural numbers with the symbol $\aleph$ null (a symbol James replaced with "*a null*," for Aleph null). James understood that two infinite systems that could be put into a one-to-one correspondence had the same cardinality, and that an ordinal number expressed the type of order of a system under a certain ordering. Like Cantor he used the symbol "ω" to denote the smallest transfinite ordinal number—e.g., the order type of the whole number series N under its natural ordering "$<$." Thus, although James could not grasp some of Cantor's most important results (e.g., that the cardinality of the continuum was different from $\aleph$ null), he understood the basic aspects of Cantor's theory (SPP 1911, 91).

Nevertheless, James's use of the phrases "cardinal" and "ordinal" infinities to convey the nature of the contrast between Royce's idealism and his own pluralism was idiosyncratic. By a "cardinal infinite" James meant systems that satisfied the new definition of infinity. "Cardinal" infinities were infinite totalities; they were realized "at a stroke," rather than through time; "all" of their elements were given (that is, depending on the context of James's discussion, "existed" or "were experienced" or "known" by a knower) at once. James used the phrase "ordinal infinite" synonymously with "growing infinite," to refer to multitudes that were infinite in the traditional negative sense of being "interminable." Their infinity was potential, rather than actual: they were "infinite" in the sense ascertained by the pragmatist criterion of meaning, according to which "infinity simply means that more may come" (ML 1902–1903, 272). In contrast to "cardinal infinities," which "realized" themselves "immediately" in their definition, ordinal infinities realized themselves "by addition" (James undated, 582); that is, their elements would come into being (or would be given to a knower/experiencer) one after another, in a temporal sequence. Moreover, according to James, the kind of "self-realization by addition" of ordinal infinities was logically incompatible with the "immediate realization" of "cardinal infinites," for the same reason why, back in 1880, James had found the notion of a completed endless series to be self-contradictory (James undated, 582). Thus, as we will see below, according to James, "ordinal infinites" could not be treated as "new infinities."

Exactly what did James mean when he presented the "alternative of pluralism & monism" as the contrast between the ordinal and the cardinal infinities?

In the first place, that formulation of the alternative brought into relief pluralism's and monism's contrasting stances concerning the question of the existence of infinite totalities. By the time he wrote ms. 4437, James had come to agree with Royce that there was "nothing self-contradictory in the notion of [the] realization" of a (standing) infinite system as a totality realized "at a stroke" and that the new definition of infinity was free of contradiction (MEN 1902–1910, 217–218, 473). However, James insisted that, although the "partisans of the new infinite" had shown that "the realization of a cardinal infinite" was not "*impossible*," they had not proved yet its "real" (extra-mathematical) "existence" (MEN 1902–1910, 217–218; ML 1903–1904, 313).[14] Nor could they ever prove it, for the definition of a notion, even when non-contradictory, could not guarantee the extra-mathematical, "non-logical" existence of instances of that notion (James undated, 515, 582; MEN 1902–1910, 217; MEN 1903–1904, 313). From definition to existence, from "*what . . . to that*," in short, there was "a non-logical step" (ML 1904–1905, 340). Whether "cardinal" infinities (i.e., standing infinite totalities) had "real" existence, similarly to the question whether infinite multiplicities existed, was "a question of fact," one neither mathematics nor logic could answer (MEN 1902–1910, 217). How one answered that question depended on one's "view of the constitution of reality" (MEN 1902–1910, 218): in James's pluralistic universe, in contrast to Royce's monistic world, there was no room for the extra-mathematical existence of infinite totalities, for no such totalities were given to finite, human experience (MEN 1902–1910, 219).

Secondly, by associating his pluralistic empiricism with the "ordinal" infinite James conveyed both his pragmatist vision of an "unfinished universe" (ML 1902–1903, 271) and his philosophy of chance. In 1903 James started expressing his tychism, a type of metaphysics that considered chance to be real and to have real effects and, similarly to Renouvier's philosophy, allowed "for new beginnings," in mathematically inspired terms, describing the chance relationships between experiences as "additive" (ML 1903–1904, 302–303; Bechtel 1902–1903, notes for Jan. 13, 1903). In James's tychistic universe "the future may not be co-implicated with the past, but may be really *added* to it," though added "in one shape *or* another," rather than according to a rule (ML 1906–1907, 410–411; SPP 1911, 72). In ms. 4437 he associated the view according to which "experience joins experience by additive relations solely" to a stance according to which "the only realized infinity is that of growth, that of the ordinal type"—the type of infinity which, as we saw, according to James realizes itself "by addition" (MEN 1902–1910, 218).

James's discussions of tychism were linked to the ordinal, or "growing," infinite in yet another way. Between 1903 and 1910, as is well-known, James occasionally endorsed a discretist, rather than synechistic (continuist), form of tychism. When James wrote in his discretist mode, he denied the continuity of change and posited that experience (including novelty) grows by discrete, "finite," "successive increments" (ML 1902–1903, 272). He compared those increments to "drops" and to the discrete "minima sensibilia" by which, as evidenced by psychophysical experiments on the "threshold of perception," our perceptual experience changes, even when, as James knew, the physical excitation modifying our perception changes in a continuous way (SPP 1911, 80, 82; for experiments of this kind, see Bergson, 1889, ch. 1). When James sided with this discretist tychism, he linked his rejection of "continuous change" to his rejection of the notion of a completed endless series or, which to him was the same, the notion of the "realization at a stroke" of an ordinal infinite, as a logically contradictory notion, in accordance with his old principle of totality (ML 1902–1903, 272).[15]

To James's mind, the model of the "new" or "cardinal infinite" imposed dogmatically "the form of totality" onto reality, whereas that of the "ordinal" or "growing" infinite did not. In *Some Problems of Philosophy* James re-envisioned the contrast as one between two ways of defining infinite classes: definitions "by enumeration" and definitions "by intension." This point has hardly been noted, but it is important, for it shows that thinking with mathematics and logic had become for James a metaphysical practice. James's remarks on definitions by enumeration and definitions by intension were part of his discussion of the question whether novelty comes into being through discrete or continuous processes. In the first long part of Chapter 7 of *Some Problems of Philosophy*, James went to great pains to defend Renouvier's "discrete hypothesis." He did that by attacking the hypothesis according to which novelty comes into being through processes continuous according to "the mathematical definition" of continuity, which he incorrectly continued to identify with infinite divisibility (a necessary, but not sufficient condition of continuity), and associated with Dedekind cuts (SPP 1911, 94–95).[16] The main thrust of James's argument was that, as he had stated in 1903, "continuous change would give us the *completed* [growing] infinite," and that the notion that a "growing infinite" could be completed and be viewed as a totality, involved a "logical contradiction" (ML 1902–1903, 272; SPP 1911, 93).[17]

In the course of the argument James mobilized the latter claim against Bertrand Russell's solution of Zeno's paradox of Achilles and the Tortoise. In James's rendition of the classical paradox, under the assumption that a line is infinitely divisible—a necessary condition of continuity—if the Tortoise is given a head start of one inch, Achilles will never be able to overtake it, even though Achilles were to run twice as fast as the Tortoise. Russell had offered a simple solution of the paradox, by establishing a one-to-one correspondence between an infinite class (the series 0, 1, 1+ ½, 1+½+¼, . . . of the points to be traversed by Achilles) and a proper "part" (or, subset) of that class (the series 1, 1+ ½, 1+ ½+¼, . . . of the points to be traversed by the Tortoise). In James's understanding of Russell's solution, if both series of points were plotted against a common scale of time, the one-to-one correspondence between the two series ensured that "the paths to be traversed by the two runners" had "the same time measure," even though they did not have "the same length" (SPP 1911, 91), thereby allowing Achilles to overtake the Tortoise. The British logician insisted that his solution rested on a definition "by intension" rather than "by enumeration," both of the two infinite series in question and of the one-to-one relationship between the "whole" (the first series) and the "part" (the second series)—a relationship which, as we have seen, was central to Dedekind's definition of an infinite system (Russell 1903, § 342).

In Russell's *Principles of Mathematics* James read that definitions by enumeration defined a class by enumerating one by one each element of that class, whereas definitions by intension, or by "comprehension," or by "inclusion and exclusion," defined a class by a class-concept. For example, one could define the inhabitants of London by naming them, one by one, or by the class-concept "the inhabitants of London." James presented definitions by "enumeration" as definitions that made use of the terms "each" or "any"; in contrast, he identified definitions by intension (or, as he also called them, "abstract definitions," "definitions by inclusion and exclusion," or definitions by "an abstract predicate") with definitions that made use of the term "all." Definitions by "enumeration," he wrote, took a class distributively "to mean . . . *each* or *any* of its terms," whereas definitions by "intension" considered a class "collectively" "to mean *all* of its terms" (SPP 1911, 421). Elsewhere James associated the use of definitions by intension with the assumption of "the givenness all at once" of a class, implying that definitions by intension could not account for "sensible determinations" such as "successive existence" and "priority of elements over the whole," which, to his mind, were displayed by "the classes 'real' for humans" (ML 1903–1904, 313). To James, defining an infinite class by intension implied viewing that class as an infinite totality, in accordance with the "new" definition of infinity.

Russell had argued that, while finite classes could be defined either by extension or by intension, infinite classes could be defined only by intension, for, due to psychological limitations, "we cannot enumerate more than a finite number of parts belonging to a whole" (Russell 1903, § 71, § 330). The crux of James's argument against Russell's solution to Zeno's paradox was that "growing infinities"—such as the infinite discrete series involved in the paradox of Achilles and the Tortoise—could only be talked about "distributively" and defined "by enumeration" (SPP 1911, 84). James felt strongly that, "when Mr. Russell solves [Zeno's] puzzle by saying ... that 'the definition of whole and part *without enumeration* is the key to the whole mystery,'" Russell was "deliberately ... throw[ing] away his case" (SPP 1911, 93). Elsewhere James had rejected the use of the "collective" language to talk about the one-to-one correspondence between infinite series (James undated, 516). In *Some Problems of Philosophy* he argued that interminable series ("growing infinites") could not be defined by intension, because that would have amounted to defining something endless as a complete, a bounded total, a notion he continued to view as self-contradictory (SPP 1911, 88, 93).[18] James used this argument to conclude that "the new infinite need no longer block the way to the empiricist opinion," which he identified with Renouvier's hypothesis according to which "real processes of change," including the coming into being of novelty, should no longer be "treated" as "continuous, but as taking place by" discrete, "finite, non infinitesimal steps" (SPP 1911, 88, 93–94).[19]

James's contention that "growing infinities" could be viewed as infinite totalities only at the cost of a contradiction was identical to the argument James had given to Renouvier, back in 1880, in support of the principle of totality. Yet what if infinitely many things were already in existence? Suppose, for example, that there existed infinitely many stars, or that an event had been preceded by infinitely many events. Could such infinities—"standing infinities," as James called them—be defined by intension?

The general thrust of James's reflections on the "new infinite" suggests strongly that James would have been delighted to be able to answer a resounding "no" to those questions. By the time James was completing Chapter 7 of *Some Problems of Philosophy* he had encountered descriptions of new antinomies of infinity (the so-called "Cantorian antinomies"), such as the Burali-Forti paradox, which affected the class of all ordinal numbers, and Cantor's paradox, which affected the class of all classes (Russell 1903, § 100, § 344; Poincaré 1906, 303–304). The latter compromised the Roycean Absolute, which Royce appears to have identified precisely with the class of all classes (Kuklick 1972, 152–153). It is tempting to think that James may have hoped to find logical arguments against definitions by intension of standing infinities in the literature on the Cantorian antinomies. However, James, who died shortly afterwards, never offered such arguments. In *Some Problems of Philosophy* he stated that "the existence" of infinitely many things, such as infinitely many stars, "offers no logical difficulty" as "long as we keep taking such facts piecemeal, and talk of them distributively as 'any' or 'each,'" thereby implying that "the existence" of infinitely many things did present "logical" difficulties if one talked about those things "collectively" (SPP 1911, 86). However, he did not specify the nature of the difficulties.

To sum up: since the late 1870s/early 1880s James held that a conception of "growing infinites" as totalities was logically contradictory and vetoed the possibility of a "completed" growing infinite. A physical agent, such as Achilles, could not "complete" the infinite summation $1 + 1/2 + 1/4 + \ldots + 1/(2^n) \ldots$ (where n takes successive values in N), that is, the sum of the distances separating Achilles from the Tortoise. Analogously, in mathematics, though James accepted that 2 was the limit of that sum, he insisted that it could not be reached through the endless process of the growth of the variable n. Rather, he contended that the limit "gets itself into being independently of the series" (ML 1903–1904, 312).

As for standing infinities, James could not argue on logical grounds that the notion of a standing infinite totality was self-contradictory. For that reason, the question whether standing infinite totalities enjoyed "real" existence, in addition to mathematical existence, remained for him a question of fact, similarly to the question of the existence of standing infinite multiplicities. However, for James, while the latter question belonged to the natural sciences, the former fell in the domain of philosophy. In ms. 4437 James approached that question metaphysically, arguing that how one answered it depended on which metaphysical hypothesis one adopted: the monistic or the pluralistic, or "piecemeal." For James the pluralistic hypothesis, being rooted in human experience, was the better one. Because by the time he composed ms. 4437 James had come to identify reality with experience and because he viewed human experience as finite, he excluded the extra-mathematical existence of standing infinite totalities from his universe.[20] There is no reason to believe that in *Some Problems of Philosophy* he changed his mind.

James's skirmishes with Kant, Renouvier, Royce, and Russell on the use of the collective, rather than the distributive, language, were part of a broader attempt to hone his pluralism as a "distributive" vision of experience and of reality. This project was very important to him. Back in 1896, James had associated "radical empiricism" with the denial of the existence of any "possible point of view from which the world can appear an absolutely single fact" (WB 1897, 6). James's reflections on the mathematics of infinity and logic provided him with tools he used to deepen that initial understanding. In the May 1908 Oxford lectures, subsequently published as *A Pluralistic Universe*, James presented matter-of-factly the contrast between the "all-form" ("the form of totality") and the "each-form" (or "distributive form") as the fundamental difference between "the shape" in which reality is "experienced or realized" according to absolutism and that in which it "may exist" according to "our human form of experiencing the world" (PU 1909, 25–26, 62). In ms. 4437 he cast the contrast between monism and pluralism as a contrast between the cardinal and the ordinal infinities and, in *Some Problems of Philosophy*, he re-envisioned that contrast as a distinction between two ways of defining classes (by "intension" and by "extension" or "enumeration") and two ways of viewing classes (as totalities or as multiplicities). Pluralistic empiricism emerged from the latter text as a metaphysics that viewed both "standing" and "growing" infinities as multiplicities of "eaches" amenable only to definitions by enumeration. James presented it as a stance according to which "*piecemeal existence is independent of complete collectibility*" (which now he associated to definitions by intension) and "some facts, at any rate, exist only distributively, or in the form of a set of eaches which (even if in finite number) need not in any intelligible sense either experience themselves, or get experienced by anything else, as members of an all" (SPP 1911, 87, n. 9).

Dealing with the question of the infinite may or may not have helped James make his pluralistic empiricism "more plausible," as he had announced to his students in 1903.

Yet, James's growing familiarity with mathematical and logical literature, his awareness of the difference between "empiricist" and "rationalist" (or "idealist") stances toward the actual infinite and "the new infinite," and his annoyance at the dismissive way in which the new infinitists dealt with those "whom the notion of a completed infinite in any form still bothers" (SPP 1911, 88, 91) were all instrumental to a new and richer understanding of the fundamental differences between monistic idealism and "pluralistic empiricism."

When Royce prophesized that "metaphysics of the future will take fresh account of mathematical research," he may not have thought of his colleague William James (Royce 1900, 527). Yet James ended up fulfilling the prophecy.

Although, by the end of his life, thinking *with* mathematical analogies had become for James a metaphysical habit, he never offered a mathematized philosophy. For James nature was not mathematical, though it behaved "as if" mathematical descriptions of phenomena were "laws of nature" (ML 1903–1904, 280). The seemingly "pre-established harmony" between such "laws" and reality was a product of the fact that human beings projected mathematical notions onto reality and then read them back from reality, forgetting they had projected them onto it (Bechtel 1902–1903, notes for Oct. 21, 1902). James subscribed to an instrumentalist philosophy of mathematics, according to which mathematical concepts were useful tools. His engagement with the "question of the infinite" led James to view the "ordinal" or "growing" infinite as an excellent tool for deepening, through analogical thinking, his understanding of certain metaphysical problems, especially the problem of novelty. James also used that mathematical concept for bringing together in an economic way the main features of his pluralistic empiricism. By associating his pluralistic empiricism with the "ordinal," rather than the "cardinal" infinite, James conveyed, at once, all of the following: his commitment to a distributive ontology, which allowed for partial unity, but not for absolute unity; his preference for finitism; his temporalism; his rejection of an "all-knower"; his dismissal of Royce's claim that reality had been eternally "ordered" at a stroke; his emphasis on the methodological importance of beginning from parts (elements, individuals), rather than from wholes (systems, classes, social institutions); and his defense of indeterminism and individualism. The "ordinal infinite" thus functioned as a shorthand for all those aspects of James's pluralistic empiricism, allowing James to remind readers that they all stemmed from the same core.

For these reasons, in *Some Problems of Philosophy* James could not have ignored mathematics, despite his promise to "let the results of the sciences alone." Rather, in that book he seems to have reverted to an understanding of metaphysics that he had initially articulated in 1892, in the context of a discussion of the relationships between psychology and philosophy. Metaphysics, he had written at that time, was the forum in which the special sciences "must hold their assumptions and results subject to revision in the light of each other's needs" (PBC, "Epilogue"). In *Some Problems of Philosophy* James combined that insight with an understanding of metaphysics as "a science of hypotheses" (ML 1906–1907, 381), both metaphysical and scientific. Its task included, among others, that of identifying "absurd," "self-contradictory" "hypotheses," such as "the notion of anything made by the successive addition of infinitely numerous parts, and yet completed" (SPP 1911, 23).

By criticizing as self-contradictory the notion of a completed growing infinite and casting doubts on definitions by intension of standing infinities, James succeeded in illustrating, to his intended audience of beginning philosophers, how to carry out an important metaphysical task, while also furthering his own "distributive" metaphysical vision.

Notes

1. These included James's marginalia to Royce (1900); ms. 4437, "Infinity"; and later additions to James's original lecture notes for his 1903–1904 course, "Philosophy 20c: Metaphysical Seminary—A Pluralistic Description of the World."
2. James and Royce sometimes used "series" to indicate what today is called as a sequence (e.g., the endless sequence of the natural numbers $1, 2, 3, \ldots, n, \ldots$). I follow their use of the term.
3. According to mathematician Cassius Keyser, "our own beloved William James" "deeply regretted" his "mathematical ignorance" (Keyser 1922, 135).
4. See, e.g., Myers (1986), Grünbaum (1970), Salmon (1970). Hare (1979) is an exception.
5. James incorrectly considered infinite divisibility as a sufficient condition of continuity.
6. A few definitions can be recalled.

    A set S' is a subset of a set S ($S' \subseteq S$) if each element a of S' is also an element of S (or, what comes to the same thing, if a "is a member of S" or "belongs to S"). S' is a "proper" subset of S ($S' \subset S$, or $S \supset S'$) if there exists an element b which belongs to S, but does not belong to S'.

    A function, or "transformation," f mapping a system S to a system T (in modern notation: $f: S \rightarrow T$, to be read "f from S to T"), is a "law" (Dedekind's term) that assigns to each a in S an element $f(a)$ in T. The element $f(a)$ is called the image of a, and $f(S)$, that is, the set "of all $f(a)$ with a in S," is called the "image" of S (Kaplansky 1977, 14, 16). A function $f: S \rightarrow T$ is "similar" when $a \neq b$ implies that $f(a) \neq f(b)$, where a and b are elements of S (Dedekind's definition).

    Dedekind's definition of infinity relied on his definition of the similarity between two systems, according to which the systems S and T are "similar" if there exists a similar transformation $f: S \rightarrow T$ such that $f(S)=T$ (Dedekind 1901b, §32). If S and T are "similar" they have the same number of elements.

    A function $f: S \rightarrow T$ is "one-to-one" if $f(a)=f(b)$ implies $a=b$ for all a, b belonging to S. If a function is similar, it is also one-to-one (Dedekind 1901b, § 26); for that reason, I will use the phrase "one-to-one," instead of "similar," whenever that does not create ambiguities.

    A "correspondence" between S and T is a function from S to T that 1) is one-to-one and 2) is "onto," that is, every element of T is the image of some element in S (i.e., $T = f(S)$) (Kaplansky 1977, 15).

7. A "type of order" is a way of ordering a system. Both finite and infinite sets can be ordered in different ways, although for finite sets all the orderings are equivalent. For example. the set containing 1 and 2 can be ordered as {1,2} under the relationship "<", less than, and as {2,1} under the relationship ">", greater than, but the two ways of ordering are equivalent, with a first element followed by a second element.
8. Following Dedekind, Royce argued that a recursive function f that makes a system K into a chain defined instantaneously an order on that system by defining an infinite series of nested chains, in modern notation $K \supset f(K) \supset f(f(K)) \supset f(f(f(K))) \ldots$, each of which included all the elements of the chain that preceded it, with the exception of one element. The sequence of the successively excluded elements was the ordering induced by the function f onto K (Royce 1900, 531–532).

9. According to Royce, the word "existence" in the statement of the theorem "express[ed] existence within the realm of consistent mathematical definitions" (Royce 1900, 511).
10. For a different interpretation of the relationship between the Roycean Absolute and temporality, see Auxier (2013).
11. For a classical discussion of the centrality of temporality to James's pragmatism and radical empiricism see Wahl (1925, 162–169).
12. A well-defined function $f: S \to T$ assigns to an element of S one and only one element of T.
13. In an October 1908 letter to Russell, James referred to a non-existing chapter of Russell's "*Phil. of M.*" (i.e., *Principles of Mathematics*) on "truth," revealing he may not have been entirely familiar with Russell's book at that time (CWJ 1908, 12.102–3). Similar chronological considerations apply to an addition to James's "Notes for Phil. 20c, 1903–1904," suggesting the addition was probably written at the same time as Ms. 4437 (ML 1903–1904, 313).
14. An exchange between James and Harvard mathematician E. V. Huntington clarifies that James viewed the mathematical world as "a separate realm of realities" (ML 1908, 439–440). For example, according to James "the class of cardinal numbers has only so far a logical existence" and "to prove that 'a_o' [$\aleph$ null] or 'ω' have a 'real' existence, would require additional ontological reasoning" (ML 1903–1904, 313).
15. On James's synechistic version of tychism see, e.g., Wahl (1925, 79). Girel (2007), and Klein (2009, 436). On the importance of continuity in James's work more generally, see Bella (2019).
16. James alluded to Dedekind's arithmetization of the continuum and his construction of the number continuum through "cuts" (Dedekind 1901a; SPP 1911, 88–89).
17. James insisted that physical agents could not "traverse a continuum." However, I agree with Wesley Salmon that the import of James's argument was that "the mathematical account of continuity is inadequate for the description of temporal processes," whether physical or non-physical (Salmon 1970, 17). The difficulty was logical, rather than only physical.
18. James's suspicions about the arithmetical continuum, aside from its counter-intuitive nature, seem to rest on a similar argument: the construction of the continuum via Dedekind-cuts assumes that the "infinitely growing process" of making the cuts has been completed, thus treating a growing infinite as a standing infinite totality (SPP 1911, 90–91).
19. At the end of the chapter James returned to the possibility of the continuity of change, though not according to the "mathematical definition."
20. "If reality be experience & experience be finite then no reality corresponds to 'ω'" (MEN 1902–1910, 219). James used "ω" equivalently with $\aleph$ null.

References

Auxier, Randall E. 2013. *Time, Will, and Purpose. Living Ideas from the Philosophy of Josiah Royce*. Chicago: Open Court.

Bechtel, Edwin DeTurck. 1902–1903. Lecture notes for James's course Phil. 3 (1902–1903). HUC 8899.321. Pusey Library, Harvard University.

Bella, Michela. 2019. *Ontology after Philosophical Psychology: The Continuity of Consciousness in William James's Philosophy of Mind*. Lanham: Lexington Books.

Bergson, Henri. 1889. *Essai sur les données immédiates de la conscience*. Paris: Alcan.

Couturat, Louis. 1896. *De l'infini mathématique*. Paris: Alcan. WJ 614.89. Houghton Library, Harvard University.
Couturat, Louis. 1904. "Les principes des mathématiques." *Revue de Métaphysique et de Morale* 1212:211–240.
Dedekind, Richard. 1901a. "Continuity and Irrational Numbers." In *Essays on the Theory of Numbers*, translated by W. W. Belman, 1–43. First German ed. 1872. New York: Dovers.
Dedekind, Richard. 1901b. "The Nature and Meaning of Numbers." In *Essays on the Theory of Numbers*, 44–125. First German ed. 1888. New York: Dover.
Girel, Matthias. 2007. "A Chronicle of Pragmatism in France before 1907. William James in Renouvier's *Critique Philosophique*." In *Fringes of Religious Experience, Cross-Perspectives on James's The Varieties of Religious Experience*, edited by Sergio Franzese and Felicitas Kraemer, 169–199. Frankfurt: Ontos Verlag.
Grier, Michelle. 2006. "The Logic of Illusion and the Antinomies." In *A Companion to Kant*, edited by Graham Bird, 192–206. Oxford: Blackwell.
Grünbaum, Adolf. 1970. "Zeno's Metrical Paradox of Extension." In *Zeno's Paradoxes*, edited by W. Salmon, 176–199. Indianapolis: Hackett.
Hare, Peter. 1979. "Introduction." In James, *Some Problems of Philosophy*, xiii–xli. Cambridge, MA: Harvard University Press.
James, William. 1884. "The Dilemma of Determinism." In James, WB 114–140.
James, William. Undated. Marginalia to Royce, *World and the Individual. First Series*. WJ 477.98.6. Houghton Library, Harvard University.
Jarvis, E. A. 1975. *The Conception of God in the Later Royce*. The Hague: Martinus Nijhoff.
Kaplansky, Irving. 1977. *Set Theory and Metric Spaces*. New York: Chelsea Publishing Company.
Keyser, Cassius. 1922. *Mathematical Philosophy. A Study of Fate and Freedom. Lectures for Educated Laymen*. New York: E. P. Dutton & Company.
Klein, Alex. 2009. "On Hume on Space: Green's Attack, James's Empirical Response." *Journal of the History of Philosophy* 47:415–449.
Klev, Ansten. 2018. "A Road Map of Dedekind's Theorem 66." *HOPOS. Journal of the International Society for the History of the Philosophy of Science* 8 (2): 241–277.
Kuklick, Bruce. 1972. *Josiah Royce. An Intellectual Biography*. Indianapolis: Bobbs-Merrill.
Myers, Gerald E. 1986. *William James. His Life and Thought*. New Haven, CT: Yale University Press.
Perry, Joseph B. 1935. "Un échange de lettres entre Renouvier et William James." *Revue de Métaphysique et de Morale*" 42:303–318.
Poincaré, Henri. 1906. "Les mathématiques et la logique." *Revue de Métaphysique et de Morale* 1414:294–317.
Renouvier, Charles. 1875. *Essais de Critique Générale. Premier Essai. Traité de logique générale et de logique formelle. Second édition revue et considérablement augmentée*. Paris: Au Bureau de la Critique Philosophique.
Royce, Josiah. 1900. "Supplementary Essay. The One, the Many, and the Infinite." In Royce, *The World and the Individual. First series*, 473–588. New York: Macmillan.
Royce, Josiah. 1902–1903. "The Concept of the Infinite." *The Hibbert Journal* 1:21–45.
Royce, Josiah. 1904. "Sciences of the Ideal." *Science*, New Series 20:449–462.
Russell, Bertrand. 1903. *Principles of Mathematics*. Cambridge: Cambridge University Press.
Salmon, Wesley. 1970. "Introduction." In *Zeno's Paradoxes*, edited by W. Salmon, 5–44. Indianapolis: Hackett.
Wahl, Jean. 1925. *The Pluralist Philosophies of England & America*. London: Open Court.

PART VI
CONVERSATIONS, PAST

CHAPTER 21

JAMES AND HUME

Radical Empiricism and the Reality of Relations

YUMIKO INUKAI

JAMES introduces his version of empiricism at the beginning of "A World of Pure Experience," which is originally published in 1904:

> I give the name of "radical empiricism" to my *Weltanschauung*. Empiricism... lays the explanatory stress upon the part, the element, the individual, and treats the whole as a collection and the universal as an abstraction.... It is essentially a mosaic philosophy, a philosophy of plural facts, like that of Hume and his descendants. (ERE 1904, 22)

He then goes on to explain how his empiricism is different from Hume's:

> To be radical, an empiricism must neither admit into its constructions any element that is not directly experienced, nor exclude from them any element that is directly experienced. For such a philosophy, *the relations that connect experiences must themselves be experienced relations, and any kind of relation experienced must be accounted as 'real' as anything else in the system*.... Now, ordinary empiricism... has always shown a tendency to do away with the connections of things, and to insist most on the disjunctions.... Hume's statement that whatever things we distinguish are as "loose and separate" as if they had "no manner of connection"... are examples of what I mean. (ERE 1904, 22–23, original italics)

To be a *radical* empiricist, there are two constraints: (1) not to include anything in his system that is *not* experienced and (2) not to exclude anything in his system that *is* experienced. Hume's empirical methodology described in the Introduction to *A Treatise of Human Nature* conforms to (1). Hume explicitly declares that he is determined to remain within the boundary of experience in explaining the workings of human mind, not introducing anything that could not be established on "the only solid foundation," that is, "experience and observation" (T Intro. 7, SBN xvi).[1] Indeed, Hume goes even further to profess that any explanatory principles that go beyond experience ought "to be rejected as presumptuous and chimerical" (T Intro. 8, SBN xvii). However, Hume's empiricism still is not entirely *radical*, because it does not properly observe (2), since, according to James, it excludes the reality of connections in experience, which is implied by Hume's description of perceptions as "loose and separate."[2] James is quite adamant throughout his various works that Hume denies conjunctive relations in experience on the basis of the assumption that any factors in experience, if they are distinguishable, are in fact distinct and separate elements of experience. This point plays a major role in his criticisms against Hume, and what James calls "ordinary empiricism," "Associationis[m]," and "Sensationalism" in general. Separating himself from such "ordinary" empiricists and associationists as Hume, Berkeley, and the Mills by underscoring the experiential reality of conjunctive relations as well as any other relations, James believes that his empiricism does not leave "the universe of human experience" in any way incoherent or unintelligible (ERE 1904, 24) so that there would be no need to make "artificial correction" (ERE 1904, 23) to the unity of experience.

Now, the question is: Is James right about Hume? Is James fair to Hume in his critical descriptions of Hume's positions? My answer is both yes and no. James is right that Hume indeed takes perceptions to be discrete, separate constituents of human experience. But he is not right that Hume denies the reality of relations of conjunctive types altogether. There may be a good reason for James's unrelenting charge against Hume on the nature of human experience, which probably led him to call Hume "as much of a metaphysician as Thomas Aquinas" (PP 1890, 334). Nevertheless, the fundamental psychological mechanism involved in Hume's accounts of our ordinarily held beliefs (e.g., beliefs in external bodies and an identical self) reveals that he not only recognizes but also needs the immediate presence of some conjunctive relations in experience for his psychological explanations to work. Those psychological accounts of Hume's prove to be more similar to James's than James makes them out to be: Hume *is* a radical empiricist in some sense.

A similarity between James and Hume goes beyond the inclusion of conjunctive and disjunctive relations as the key factors in their accounts. A close look at how certain relations figure in their explanations of the self and external objects shows, I argue, that, for both James and Hume, the self as well as objects are constructions out of basic elements in their systems, namely, pure experience and perceptions, respectively. This move to collapse the inner and outer worlds of the subject and object into one world (of pure experience for James and of perceptions for Hume) may look rather obscure and unintuitive at first glance. However, this is exactly what they see as a way of preserving our ordinary sense of experience of objects: we do not perceive any mental replica of a physical hat, shoe, room, or book. We immediately perceive them.

Finally, I will suggest that there is an important kinship between James's and Hume's similar injunction to take seriously "the reader's sense of life" (ERE 1904, 8) and "the sentiment of the vulgar" (T 1.4.3.9, SBN 223).

James's Attitude Toward Hume

Although psychology as a separate, organized discipline was not yet existent in Hume's time, James classifies Hume as one of "The English writers on psychology" (PP 1890, 191) or "psychologists of the English empiricist school" (PP 1890, 380). For James, who conceives of psychology as "the Science of Mental Life" (PP 1890, 15), the existence of mental states such as feelings, desires, cognitions, reasonings, and so on is an undeniable fact. His scientific psychology relies in part on introspective observation to collect its material for investigation where thoughts and feelings need be dealt with just as they occur. These points are quite similar to important aspects of Hume's methodology described in the Introduction to *A Treatise of Human Nature*.[3] Hume calls his philosophy "the science of human nature" and states that "the only solid foundation we can give to this science itself must be laid on experience and observation" (T Intro. 7, SBN xvi). Any claim made in Hume's science of human nature must be grounded strictly on careful observation of "the operation of my natural principles" as they are manifested as impressions, ideas, passions, and so on in experience, and nothing else (T Intro. 10, SBN xix). A more apt description of Hume's project appears in *An Enquiry Concerning Human Understanding*: it is "mental geography," in which the different operations of the mind are delineated and properly classified (Hume 1748/1999, 1.13).

James considers Hume's theories relevant to his own projects of psychology as well as philosophy: he openly acknowledges Hume's legacy and contributions, both positive and negative, in the topics like personal identity, the constitution of conscious experience, the perception of reality, volition, causation, and of course, association. For instance, James admits the correctness of Hume's conception of belief as an idea occurring in a lively and forceful manner (PP 1890, 924) and of Hume's account of various principles of association (PP 1890, 1230). Most notably, James highly praises Hume for his empirical approach to the question of personal identity and his claim about diversity in perceptions, going so far as to call them "the imperishable glory" (PP 1890, 319) and "this good piece of introspective work" (PP 1890, 333), respectively. Hume's contributions are not just limited to these positive results but extend to problems or issues that his philosophy exposes, leaves unsolved, or creates. One of these problems is the psychological fact that we are often induced to believe something to be real when it itself lacks any compelling factor or power but is only associated with something else that has it (PP 1890, 931–932). Another is the view that we can observe only the outward effects of our volition and not hidden, secret inner "powers" (PP 1890, 1110; see Hume 1748/1999, 8.14). Still another is the question of personal identity. James writes, "Ever since Hume's time, it has been justly regarded as the most puzzling puzzle with which psychology has to deal" (PP 1890, 314).

Finally, the most significant problem that Hume's philosophy leaves for James's to deal with is his theory of perceptions; James disparagingly calls Hume "the hero of the atomistic theory" (PP 1890, 691). The attribution of the atomistic theory of perceptions to Hume is reasonable. Hume holds a simple-complex distinction about perceptions, complex perceptions being made up of simple ones. He argues that simple perceptions indeed satisfy the definition of substance some philosophers often provide: "*something which may exist by itself*" (T 1.4.5.5, SBN 233). Hume appeals to two principles—the Separability Principle, according to which "whatever objects are different are distinguishable, and that whatever objects are distinguishable are separable by the thought and imagination" (T 1.1.7.3, SBN 18), and the Conceivability Principle, according to which "Whatever is clearly conceiv'd may exist; and whatever is clearly conceiv'd, after any manner, may exist after the same manner" (T 1.4.5.5, SBN 233). Hume maintains that it is conceivable for a simple perception to exist separately from other things since it is distinguishable and thus separable by the imagination; that is, each simple perception can be thought of without anything else. Therefore, it is entirely possible that a simple perception exists by itself. From this possibility, he concludes that distinguishable simple perceptions are *really* separable from one another.[4] This is the point in Hume about which James is most critical.[5] About Hume's atomistic simples, "for the existence of which no good introspective grounds can be brought forward," James points out that "the continuous flow of the mental stream is sacrificed" (PP 1890, 195). Another problem with Hume's theory of perceptions is that Hume admits separation but not conjunction, both of which, James contends, are relations equally realized in experience. James sees that favoring one type of relation and disfavoring another is what makes Hume's empiricism create paradoxes and contradictions.

Throughout *The Principles of Psychology* (referred to as *Principles* hereafter), James criticizes Hume on these points, calling Hume's theory "ridiculous" (PP 1890, 246). Furthermore, James consistently keeps his own psychological findings as the foundation for his philosophical empiricism—Radical Empiricism—and it is this psychological foundation that ultimately differentiates James from Hume.

But, how different are James's theories from Hume's after all? As we saw above, Hume's professed methodology is not so different from James's method in psychology, especially when James's explanations are primarily concerned with mental states.[6] However, according to James, Hume ultimately does not follow through and ends up with a picture of experience that is fundamentally and significantly impoverished. James takes himself to have a richer account of experience, and thus more explanatory resources at his disposal for constructing empirically grounded theories. But is this really so?

RADICAL EMPIRICISM IN ACTION

In this section, I am going to discuss Hume's and James's theories of the self and the object in order to see whether (and if so how prominently) relations figure in their explanations. It is clear that Hume does not declare openly at the beginning, in the way that James does, that experienced relations are the key elements in various psychological phenomena. Rather, it has been widely acknowledged, mainly on the basis of his argument regarding causation, that Hume denies the existence of *real* ties among perceptions. James is one of those who have placed a strong focus on that claim of Hume's and emphasized Hume's atomist tendency, as I have already discussed above. Paying close attention to the role of relations in their actual accounts of the self and the object will show, I believe, that not only is James wrong in his unyielding charge against Hume's exclusion of conjunctive relations from experience but also there are interesting similarities between them.

Self

How the issues of the self are treated in *Essays in Radical Empiricism* (referred to as *Essays* hereafter) is different from the way that they were dealt with in *Principles* earlier. In *Principles*, James accounts for how we commonly come to conceive ourselves as a unified self with a specific identity by laying bare psychological factors including the structure of conscious experience. On the other hand, in *Essays*, James is more concerned with the existence, or rather the nonexistence, of consciousness as a fundamental entity, and how the self as a subject of knowledge is constituted out of what he calls "pure experience," which is undifferentiated, unqualified stuff. However, there definitely are continuing threads between the two works despite the obvious difference in their aims and purposes.[7] One important, common element in these works is James's insistence that "undeniably 'thoughts' do exist" (ERE 1904, 4).[8] It is also a familiar move of James's that different types of things that we ordinarily tend to distinguish as different kinds are explained by assigning different functions to one and the same thing. So, in both works, James attributes the function of knowing to "thoughts" and thereby eliminates the need to posit consciousness or a separate subject as a thinker or knower. James indeed refers to his explanation of the "passing thought" given earlier in *Principles* when he begins his discussion on pure experience in *Essays*, indicating that he has already shown that a thought itself functions as a knower.[9] This reference strongly suggests that James still maintains the account of a knowing, continuous self that he offered earlier from the viewpoint of the psychologist. Furthermore, although it was not explicitly invoked as such, the thesis of Radical Empiricism was already present noticeably in his descriptions and explanations of various psychological phenomena, in which the experiential reality of relations was emphatically insisted, especially in the chapter on "The Stream of Thought." In light of James's own references to the *Principles* account as well as the common threads between *Principles* and *Essays*, I take it that his psychological explanations of the stream-like continuity of thought and our accentuated sense of an identical knowing self in *Principles* complement his accounts of the subjective side of the split between a subject and an object in *Essays*.[10] Hence, my discussion of James's theory of the self, below, takes both works into consideration, although one may be conceived of as more psychologically inclined and the other as more metaphysically inclined.[11]

James's purpose in "Does Consciousness Exist?" is to argue that "consciousness" does not refer to any substantial entity but rather to a *knowing* function of pure experience.

James contends that the duality of the subject and the object does not exist in pure experience and that the split between them comes about when one and the same portion of pure experience takes on different functions, one knowing and the other known, in different contexts in which it is connected with different groups of associates. Thus, subjectivity becomes something that exists only in relation to something else, and not as an intrinsic property of anything in itself. A bit of pure experience, before it gets connected with some other portions in a particular context, therefore, is neither mental nor physical, since it itself is "a mere *that*" and not a "what" yet (ERE 1904, 8). He writes: "The instant field of the present is at all times what I call the 'pure' experience. It is only virtually or potentially either object or subject as yet. For the time being, it is plain, unqualified actuality, or experience, a simple *that*" (ERE 1904, 13). Let's take an example of a computer monitor. In the first instance, there does not exist either a physical monitor or my conscious experience of it, yet. A piece of pure experience gets to function as a mental perception of a monitor in my "field of consciousness" when it enters into my "personal biography" by being related to my "sensations, emotions, decisions, movements, classifications, expectations, etc." (ERE 1904, 8)—for example, to my current feeling of excitement, my past ambivalent decision to buy it, and my anxiety about its payments. Connections and relations it has with other states can be fluid and inconstant: "as a 'mental image,' it for a moment floats" (ERE 1904, 12). In this context, the portion of pure experience of the computer monitor is taken as a *subjective* state representing a physical monitor.

A piece of pure experience being a mental, subjective image of something is the function of knowing, for which, according to James, the notion of "consciousness" is invoked. A subjective experience of a computer monitor is a state in which the monitor is perceived and known.[12] The fact that it not just *is*, but *knows* something else is what the quality of "being conscious" is supposed to explain, and what is supposed to distinguish it from the physical. This is where knowledge-by-acquaintance occurs: "the kind of knowledge called perception ... in which the mind enjoys direct 'acquaintance' with a present object" (ERE 1904, 27–28). The knowing function of a bit of pure experience in this direct acquaintance with an object cannot be explained in terms of a transitional, cognitive relation into which two or more bits of pure experience enter, because it involves one and the same bit of pure experience functioning as the knower and the known.[13] James does not explain a relation between them in the case of knowledge-by-acquaintance much in *Essays* but he does earlier in "The Knowing of Things Together."[14] He acknowledges that the monitor being known and the knowing of it are "only two names for one indivisible fact which, properly named, is *the datum, the phenomenon, or the experience*" (EPh 1895, 75). James adamantly argues that pure experience contains no duality in it, and its subjectivity and objectivity only appear as its different functions in different contexts. Thus, clearly, even as a subjective state, there is no act-content distinction in it: it is just a mental presentation of the monitor. James claims in "The Knowing of Things Together": "*To know immediately, then, or intuitively, is for mental content and object to be identical*" (EPh 1895, 75–76). There is no relation more direct and immediate than identity. This idea paves the way to his later claim about knowledge by "acquaintance with a present object" within the framework of pure experience: that the subjective, mental monitor and the objective, physical monitor are really identical. As a mental state, the portion of pure experience whose content is the monitor plays the role of a direct perceiving and knowing of the physical monitor. That portion *is* a knower.

In James's view, nothing stands as a subject, a knower, or consciousness on its own, but rather, it comes into existence within a web of things that are connected through various relations. Connections and relations are integral parts of the existents that are "whats" in our world, including ourselves. This metaphysical account of the emergence of subject and object is consistent with his strong emphasis on the immediate presence of connections and relations in a stream of thought in *Principles*: our subjective, personal consciousness flows like a stream, in which we, as knowers, appear as concrete "whats."[15]

The fundamental materials with which Hume starts his inquires are perceptions, the mental. Thus, Hume's starting point is closer to the one at which James begins his psychological investigations in *Principles*. James positively acknowledges Hume as one of the first philosophers who made the questions about the self an empirical matter: "it is to the imperishable glory of Hume and Herbart and their successors to have taken so much of the meaning of personal identity out of the clouds and made the Self an empirical and verifiable thing" (PP 1890, 319). Given that undeniable data for a psychologist's investigations are thoughts and feelings, which we are directly, immediately, acquainted with, explaining how we come to believe we are persisting, single, thinking, and experiencing subjects becomes a puzzle. Since thoughts and feelings are all constantly flowing in a stream of thought, there is nothing in it that could directly point to such a being. James finds some resources in the stream: there are two types of relations on the basis of which we come to have the sense of persistence—*resemblance* and *continuity*, and an aspect of currently occurring conscious thought that grounds our sense of ourselves being a singular, unified subject of experiences. Just as he does in "Does Consciousness Exist?" James assigns the function of knowing to thought itself: a current "Thought," or what he sometimes calls a "judging thought," has the capacity to grasp and to appropriate certain parts of the stream as belonging to itself, and its activities are definitely experienced within the stream (PP 1890, 320–321). James identifies a presently existing self with a center of perspective in the present portion of the stream, which accompanies intimate, raw feels brought about by the bodily existence and thinking activity, which James characterizes as "the character of warmth" (PP 1890, 316). As elusive as those feelings may seem, they are phenomenal feels essential to our having a sense of the present self, which performs an appropriative act of forming connections among past selves and itself so as to yield a unified whole.

The two relations, *resemblance and continuity*, facilitate our sense of persistence over time and assist, as it were, the appropriative act of the judging thought. Resemblance relation works this way: when some parts of the current portion of the stream present past activities with the same feelings of warmth and intimacy as those accompanying the current Thought, or the present self, they are recognized as *my* activities and unified together. The present judging thought functions as the "herdsman," and the feelings of warmth and intimacy as the "herd-mark": "The animal warmth, etc., is their herd-mark, the brand from which they can never more escape. It runs through them all like a thread through a chaplet and makes them into a whole, which we treat as a unit, no matter how much in other ways the parts may differ *inter se*" (PP 1890, 317).

Another relation is *continuity*. In the specious present,[16] the Thought occupies a focal point of present awareness, to which an immediate past "I" (which is a Thought that occupied a focal point of experience in the immediate past) is phenomenally presented as an object of awareness. This allows the Thought to directly feel *continuity* between the immediate past "I" and itself, on the basis of which the Thought takes it to belong to itself, along with what the immediate past "I" has judged to belong to it. When such an experience of continuity is absent in a case as of the present self and a self of a month ago, the resemblance of the feelings of warmth and intimacy does the work. Although there are changes and variances in the stream of experience, the experienced relations of resemblance and continuity among portions of the stream make the present self connect itself with past selves to realize a unified whole.

The relations of resemblance and continuity play crucial roles in not only the generation of our sense of persistence over time but also the formation of a unified self in each moment. James's insistence on the experiential reality of relations proves to be critical at the psychological level, since it makes our sense of persistence and our belief that we are identical, unified selves empirically grounded. Despite the fact that there are various, distinguishable components in the stream, the self is experienced as unified in each pulse of consciousness; and, although there are obvious changes and diversities, we are not entirely deluded in thinking that we are identically persisting beings over time, according to James.

Let us look at Hume's explanation of our belief in a persisting self. Just like James, Hume first rejects the view that our sense of a persisting self is grounded in the immediate awareness of something with enduring, unchanging properties. He then attempts to explain how our belief in such a self arises nonetheless. What does Hume appeal to in order to explain such a common psychological phenomenon? If James is right about his charge of Hume's failure to recognize the experiential reality of conjunctive relations, Hume has only discrete perceptions.

Hume clearly resorts to something other than discrete perceptions to account for the activity of the imagination that results in the emergence of our belief in an identical self in the mind; that is, the associative principles of resemblance and causation. Hume explains that because of the imagination's general tendency, it mistakes a smooth and easy feel that arises in surveying a succession of associated perceptions for a feel that arises in viewing a persisting, identical thing. As a result, the imagination attributes an identity to a succession of merely associated, diverse perceptions. For Hume, a smooth passage of the mind facilitated by the relation of resemblance and causation is what association is.[17]

It is worth noting that Hume seems to recognize only two types of connections among perceptions: one is a *real* connection and the other a *felt* connection (i.e., association). Hume explicitly denies the existence of "real connexion" (T 1.3.14.27, SBN

168) or "real bond" (T 1.4.6.16, SBN 259) among perceptions and thereby affirms that the only connections among them are associative connections. However, associative connections do not really bind perceptions together; they are merely *felt* among them in the imagination.[18] Thus, denying *real* connections among perceptions, Hume leaves perceptions "loosen'd" and disconnected from one another (T App. 20, SBN 635). This, in conjunction of the real separability of perceptions explained above, lends strong support to James's criticism against Hume. What is real about perceptions for Hume seems to be discreteness.

Hume's strong commitment to the real discreteness of perceptions is clear: he is not willing to renounce it even when he recognizes that it poses a serious problem for his own account of personal identity (T App. 21, SBN 636). Hume would have to concede that perceptions of relations like "being next to" and "being after" are also distinct and separable if relations are as real as sensible qualities like color and taste. But this is absurd; how could a perception of a relation, "being next to," exist on its own, separated from perceptions of its relata? It is therefore reasonable to attribute to Hume the view that relations cannot be real features of perceptions. Nevertheless, a close look at his explanation of the associative mechanism shows that Hume not only allows (perhaps tacitly or unknowingly) but needs some relations to be immediately present among perceptions.[19]

The associative principles responsible for the generation of our belief in an identical self are those of resemblance and causation. Speaking of the relation of resemblance, Hume explains that we tend to retain the memory of a considerable number of past perceptions, which imposes a relation of resemblance on them (T 1.4.6.17, SBN 260–261). The memory, for Hume, is a faculty that produces less vivid ideas of past perceptions in the same order and structure as the past perceptions. Thus, the attribution of identity to a succession of perceptions by the imagination is facilitated by the presence of resemblance relations that are created by the memory's reproduction of past perceptions. Hume speaks of a relation grounding association as "that quality, by which two ideas are connected together in the imagination" (T 1.1.5.1, SBN 13). A quality of resemblance, therefore, must be present and thus experienced between objects of past perceptions and of memory-ideas for the imagination to slide through them.

A similar thing can be said about the relation of cause and effect. In his explanation of how the relation of cause and effect links "different perceptions or different existences" into a "system," namely, "the human mind," Hume loosely describes it in such ordinary causal words as "destroy, influence, and modify" (T 1.4.6.19, SBN 261). However, Hume has earlier analyzed causation as an association by the imagination induced by the constant conjunction of two contiguous objects or events, that is, the relation of spatial and temporal succession repeatedly experienced between a pair of objects or events. So, to be consistent, Hume must mean by causal patterns among perceptions that some perceptions have been repeatedly experienced together in succession; otherwise, no causal relation could be attributed to any pair of perceptions. For a *pair* of perceptions to be experienced in succession, for Hume, is for them to occur together in a temporal succession within the same bundle of perceptions. Now, *repeated* experience of a pair of particular perceptions in succession amounts to the multiple occurrences of the *resembling* pair of perceptions within the same bundle. Thus, not only do two perceptions have to stand in the relation of temporal contiguity but also they, as a pair, must stand in the relation of resemblance with other pairs of perceptions in the same bundle in order for them to be deemed as causally connected. So, again, the relations of temporal contiguity and resemblance must be present among some perceptions for the imagination to make a smooth transition through them, as a result of which an identity is attributed to them.

Unfortunately, Hume does not give any detailed explanation of how exactly causal associations among various perceptions are made in the way that can induce the imagination to attribute an identity to them. What is worse, he only describes his point about a causally unified self in the ordinary way with no reference to his own account of causation (T 1.4.6.19, SBN 261). His explanation of resemblance associations is no better. The relation of resemblance that Hume points to is the one between a past perception and its less vivid, carbon-copy idea. As James rightly points out, Hume usually identifies perceptions in terms of phenomenally distinguishable, determinate, substantive things like an apple, a globe, whiteness, and so on. There is no textual evidence, at least in Book One of the *Treatise*, that Hume might be thinking of subtle feels like "warmth and intimacy" suffusing some perceptions when explaining the resemblance relation for personal identity. Clearly, Hume's account of our belief in an identical self cannot fairly be compared with James's, especially given its lack of explanatory rigor and psychological details. However, Hume clearly allows some relations other than separation and distinction to be present among perceptions and, more importantly, recognizes that they are the ground for our belief in an identical self. Associations could not be facilitated, and so our belief in an identical self would not arise, unless the relations of resemblance and causation among perceptions were experienced in the first place.

James acknowledges that resemblance and temporal contiguity are conjunctive relations (ERE 1904, 23).[20] As we saw above, James himself takes resemblance relations and temporal contiguity or continuity to be relations grounding our sense of persistence over time and the appropriation of various parts of the stream into a unified, persisting whole, which is considered as the self. Despite the differences, it is nonetheless fair to say that Hume and James both recognize that some type of resemblance and continuity relations must be experienced in order for a belief in an identical, persisting self to arise in us. This is a considerable similarity between their accounts. Hume's explanation of the generation of our belief in an identical self corroborates, to some extent, James's assessment about Hume's atomist tendency: what Hume starts with are fleeting perceptions in constant flux. However, James is wrong about his charge of Hume's exclusion of conjunctive relations altogether.

External Objects

Unlike James, Hume does not explicitly concern himself with the question of how the subject-object split happens. However, unbeknownst to him probably, Hume's explanation of how we come to believe in the continued existence of body could be seen as an account of the emergence of external objects out of perceptions for us.

Hume contends that only internal, perishing perceptions are immediately present in, and thus directly available to, the mind. His empiricist methodology restricts him to treating ideas as needing to be derived from past corresponding impressions to be legitimate.[21] Accordingly, Hume maintains that we cannot have an idea of external existence as specifically different from perceptions:

> Now since nothing is ever present to the mind but perceptions, and since all ideas are deriv'd from something antecedently present to the mind; it follows, that 'tis impossible for us so much as to conceive or form an idea of any thing specifically different from ideas and impressions. . . . [W]e never really advance a step beyond ourselves, nor can conceive any kind of existence, but those perceptions. (T 1.2.6.8, SBN 67–68)

We cannot even form an idea of an external object that is an entity of a different species than a perception. He puts the same point thus: "we may well suppose in general, but 'tis impossible for us distinctly to conceive, objects to be in their nature anything but exactly the same with perceptions" (T 1.4.2.56, SBN 218). If an externally existing, material thing that is entirely different from perceptions is utterly inconceivable and incomprehensible to us, what are we thinking of as objects when we think of things like computer monitors and keyboards? Hume answers: "Generally speaking we do not suppose them specifically different; but only attribute to them different *relations, connexions* and *durations*. But of this more fully hereafter" (T 1.2.6.9, SBN 68; my emphasis). Hume's reference here is to the later section called "*Of scepticism with regard to the senses*" in which he discusses how we come to believe in the continued, independent, and external existence of bodies. This reference suggests that his explanation in "*Of scepticism with regard to the senses*" is supposed to show that bodies that we ordinarily believe to exist independently from us are not "specifically different" from perceptions, and they are the same as perceptions, only with different relations like continuity, identity, and externality attributed to them. In other words, it is *relations* and *connections* that turn momentary, diverse perceptions into continuous, identical "bodies" that we normally believe to exist outside us.

Having ruled out the senses and reason as inadequate for the task of attributing an external and continued existence to perceptions,[22] Hume, unsurprisingly, turns to the imagination. He explains that the imagination is facilitated by the relations of *constancy* and *coherence* among some perceptions to attribute a continued existence to them. How?

Coherence for Hume consists in regularity among perceptions. Suppose two types of perceptions have regularly occurred together in a temporal succession, for example, an auditory perception of a creaking noise and a visual perception of an opening door. Due to past experiences of their regular occurrences in succession, the imagination is naturally led to suppose the existence of an opening door (or, in Humean terms, produce an idea of an opening door) when only a creaking noise is heard and an opening door not seen. The imagination maintains the coherence of the present experience, in which only a perception of a creaking noise is present, with past experiences in which creaking-noise and door-opening perceptions regularly occurred together, by supposing that a door has been existent the whole time and that it was opened when the creaking sound was heard. To put it in Hume's terms, the imagination ascribes a continued existence to a perception of an opening door in order to reconcile the present situation with the regularity of the two perceptions experienced in the past.

Constancy is another relation which supplements coherence. Hume explains that our natural propensity to take, or rather mistake, resembling perceptions for an identically continuing perception even after an interruption is due to an error on the imagination's part: since the mind makes a smooth transition among resembling perceptions, the mind mistakes those perceptions for one "constant and uninterrupted perception" (T 1.4.2.35, SBN 204). But, when resembling perceptions are obviously interrupted by other perceptions, they would be considered distinct in reflection, which is contrary to the imagination's natural verdict on them as identical. Hence, to reconcile the contradiction between the experienced interruption and diversity of perceptions and the imagination's tendency to take them as identical and continuous, it performs another feat—inventing the continued existence of the perception, thus preserving an invariable existence of it throughout the interrupted succession.

In both cases of coherence and constancy, for the imagination to attribute a continued existence to perceptions is for the imagination to fill out gaps in an interrupted sequence, which *is* to take those perceptions to exist continuously even when they are not present to the mind, and thereby it takes them to be distinct from the mind. In this way, perceptions come to be considered as continuously existing objects that are independent from the mind, rather than as fleeting mental states, according to Hume. This activity of the imagination is a habit of the mind that comes to be developed due to regularities and resemblances among perception. After all, to say that there is the regularity of particular perceptions together is, for Hume, to say that there are resemblance relations among the particular pairs of those types of perceptions within the same bundle.

Perceptions are momentary, internal, mental items which are all that are to be allowed in Hume's system. However, coherence, constancy, resemblance, and temporal contiguity as well as interruption and diversity are all *relations*, which must be present, and *experienced*, in a sequence of perceptions as well, such as in a creaking noise and an opening door. Otherwise, none of the associative activities and feigning productions of the imagination could be naturally and prereflectively facilitated at all. External objects are also, strictly speaking, the same things as perceptions: yet they are not considered as perishing, mind-dependent entities but as persisting, independent, external entities in the context where perceptions are connected by the relations of coherence and constancy. Hume does not deny that bodies exist: he views them as the same kind of things as perceptions but differentiates them from perceptions by attributing "different relations, connexions and durations." Neither does James deny that bodies exist: he views them as made up of the same kind of stuff as what minds are made of, namely, pure experience. Hume and James both distinguish bodies from minds by citing the different kinds of relations that perceptions or pure experience enter into, although the specific relations they use to account for this differentiation are different.

We saw briefly above that James argues that the duality of the mental and the physical does not point to two different kinds of stuff but to different functions that portions of pure experience take on in different contexts. Recall that pure experience is the uncategorized, immediate field of the present living moment, "a *that*," which may be later categorized as physical or mental particulars, "*whats*." It is close to what James earlier called "one great blooming, buzzing, confusion" of an infant's experience in *Principles*. Categorization of pure experience into a physical computer monitor or a mental image of it is done by way of arrangements and relations in which a given pure experience stands. In other words, one and the same bit of pure experience stands in the intersection of two different processes or systems in which things are related and connected, say, the history of the room in which the computer monitor exists and my personal biography. The pure experience plays a different role in each system, either as a physical computer monitor or as my subjective, mental image of it, respectively. James gives an example of a "pen" to explain the difference:

> This "pen," for example, is, in the first instance, a bald *that*, a datum, fact, phenomenon, content, or whatever other neutral or ambiguous name you may prefer to apply. I called it in that article ["Does Consciousness Exist"] a "pure experience." To get classed either as a physical pen or as some one's percept of a pen, it must assume a *function*, and that can only happen in a more complicated world. So far as in that world it is a stable feature, holds ink, marks paper and obeys the guidance of a hand, it is a physical pen.... So far as it is instable, on the contrary, coming and going with the movement of my eyes, altering with what I call my fancy, continuous with subsequent experience of its "having been" (in the past tense), it is the percept of a pen in my mind. (ERE 1905, 61)

The way in which a "pen" is connected with other things in one context is very different from its relations with others in the other context. There definitely is some stability and determinacy in the context in which a "pen" is considered as a physical pen: ink is almost always in it, it is used to write something on a piece of paper, it has a determinate shape and length, and a certain amount of force must be applied to it to destroy it. On the other hand, relations and connections are more fluid, often momentary, and variable in the context in which a "pen" is taken as my mental image: it can come and go instantaneously, and its shape can be changed by the imagination alone.

Let's take our previous example of a computer monitor again. A physical computer monitor sits with other things like a keyboard, a mouse, and a lamp on a brown desk in the room here. It was produced in some factory somewhere some time ago, and it was purchased a year ago in Boston. It has been sitting on this desk only for a few weeks in this apartment, which is located in Cambridge, a city in the state of Massachusetts in the United States, since it was moved from my previous apartment a few weeks ago. These spatial relations (as well as temporal ones) that the computer monitor now has with the keyboard, the desk, the room, and once had with my previous apartment, and so on, are more or less stable or "stubborn" relations (ERE 1904, 12, 16, 18); it has a particular, definite position in the network of those things connected spatially and temporally. James calls the system in which it "coheres" with them "the system of external realities," in which the computer monitor exists (ERE 1904, 12). *This* computer monitor is an object that exists in the physical world, an object-being-perceived.

Relations and connections that make a portion of pure experience count as a physical object are regular, constant, stable, and coherent, maintaining a stronger and more definite "foothold" (ERE 1904, 12). As an illustration, James contrasts a physical fire and a mental fire (ERE 1904, 17). A mental fire can burn a mental stick even if it does not burn a physical stick; but it does not always have to. I can easily imagine that a fire burning a whole tree leaves the tree unharmed. On the other hand, a physical fire will always destroy a stick: there is the relation of constancy and regularity between a fire blazing and a stick burning in the physical world. Without that regularity, there would not be "the stable part of the whole experience-chaos, under the name of the physical world" (ERE 1904, 17)—that is, there would not be any external, physical objects. These are similar qualities of relations to those that Hume also recognizes.

The Vulgar

Both James and Hume attempt to account for ordinary experiences of objects that we have at the common-sense level of "the vulgar." Interestingly, they both reject the representative theory of perceptions, or in Humean terms, the philosopher's double existence of perceptions and objects, to preserve, as James puts it, "the reader's sense of life, which knows no intervening mental image but seems to see the room and the book immediately just as they physically exist" (ERE 1904, 8). Instead, they come up with views that ultimately collapse the inner and outer worlds into one world of pure experience or perception, in which the duality of subjects and objects that is ordinarily experienced is retained and yet a deep chasm between them is removed. It is precisely because they are so adamant not to allow the existence of anything like substance and a soul that is "mysterious and elusive" (ERE 1904, 7) or "obscure and uncertain"[23] to enter into their philosophical systems that they resort to things that are definitely experienced—thoughts, perceptions, sensible qualities, and *relations*—to account for the self, objects, and the distinction between the two.

James contends that relations are significantly lacking in Hume's system, which is perhaps the most important way for him to differentiate himself from Hume. However, I have attempted to show above that James is not entirely right on this point. Hume certainly not only allows but more importantly employs conjunctive relations so experienced in his explanations. Experienced relations are fundamental aspects of our experience that facilitate the imagination's associative activities to generate our naturally held beliefs about ourselves and the world. So, if an empiricist who takes both conjunctive and disjunctive relations to be experienced and thus uses them in his system is to be considered as a *radical* empiricist, Hume is as much of a radical empiricist as James.

The similarities between the two men are more striking and interesting than James recognizes: the roles of the relations of resemblance, temporal continuity, constancy, coherence, and regularity in their accounts of the self and the object, their rejection of the representative theory of perception, and their intentions of preserving our commonsense experiences and beliefs, to list only a few.

There is another similarity in their accounts of the self and the object in terms of pure experience and perceptions: these accounts are *drawn* from processes that cannot be found at the level of experience that we ordinarily have. For those processes give rise to our ordinary, "vulgar" experience in which a physical *object* is present to *us*. In our ordinary experience, the dualism of a subject and an object is already present and we think that we are aware of objects external to us. Pure experience, a simple "*that*," is not available at all at the level of our ordinary experience, because what we are aware of are already "*whats*" like a burning incense or my experience of its smell. We ordinarily experience things, either externally or internally, which have already been placed in a connected web to be either a physical object or a conscious state.

If pure experience cannot be *experienced* in the ordinary way, it must be experiencible at least in a different way; otherwise, James as a radical empiricist would not be allowed to include it in his system. Even if it may be experiencible in a different form of consciousness like a mystical state, it still cannot be described and specified as "*whats*." Problematically, pure experience seems like a "mysterious and elusive" metaphysical postulate after all, since it still cannot be known as such in our ordinary cognition for James. Something similar can be said about Hume's explanations. The imagination's activities in his accounts are the psychological underpinnings that the vulgar are not aware of but a scientist of human nature must be if she is to explain the origin of the vulgar's natural beliefs. But are these activities really available in experience and observations at least to a scientist of human nature? There seems to be no way of introspectively noticing interrupted perceptions *as* numerically discrete, separate perceptions; neither is there any way of recognizing the transformation of perceptions from interrupted perceptions to the continued existence of a computer monitor. Interrupted perceptions, which, in some cases, are purported to be continuously existing bodies, begin to look like "obscure and uncertain" metaphysical postulates after all.

James is right, to this extent, to call Hume a metaphysician regarding perceptions. But then Hume is "at bottom as much of a metaphysician as" William James.

Notes

1. References to Hume's *Treatise of Human Nature* will be shown in the text, coming in two parts. The first part is the Norton & Norton edition (2000), abbreviated as "T" followed by book, part, section, and paragraph numbers, or in the case of the Introduction, "Intro" and paragraph numbers. The second part is the L. A. Selby-Bigge and P. H. Nidditch edition (1978), abbreviated as "SBN" followed by page numbers.
2. James takes this description from Section 7 paragraph 27 of Hume's *An Enquiry concerning Human Understanding*, originally published after *A Treatise of Human Nature* in 1756.

3. James takes brain processes, or "brain-physiology," as indispensable conditions of mental states, so he contends that they must be included in psychology (PP 1890, 6–7, 18). Hume, on the other hand, does not admit into his explanations anything other than introspectively available perceptions (see also n. 8 later).
4. Baxter (2015, 53–57) gives a similar reading of the real separability of simple perceptions, by drawing on the passage at T 1.4.5.5 (SBN 233) and other passages where Hume appeals to the Separability Principle and the Conceivability Principle.
5. James calls this aspect of Hume's view "Hume's maxim" (PU 1909, 119). James describes it in the following way: "whatever things are distinguished are as separate as if there were no manner of connexion between them" (PU 1909, 119), or more concisely, "to be distinguishable ... is to be incapable of connexion" (PU 1909, 110). These formulations are rather too simple, and, moreover, there could be questions about what kind of connections Hume denies. (I will come back to this issue later.) But it is a fair description of Hume's view understood as an atomistic account of perceptions.
6. There is one crucial element in James's psychology that Hume does not consider in his inquiry—that is, brain processes. After he briefly goes through what he calls the "spiritualist" and the "associationist" explanations of different mental states and activities, James states: "Our first conclusion, then, is that a certain amount of brain-physiology must be presupposed or included in Psychology" (PP 1890, 18). Hume, on the other hand, takes questions regarding physical or brain processes that may precede the appearance of impressions of sensation to be questions for "anatomists and natural philosophers" (T 1.1.2.1, SBN 8). So this is a significant difference between James's psychology and Hume's science of human nature. However, this difference is not relevant to my purpose of the discussion on James and Hume here, since my main concern is with the role of *experienced* relations in their empiricist projects.
7. For an argument that there is substantial continuity between the conceptions of experience in James's earlier psychology and in his later radical empiricism, see Wesley Cooper (this volume); cf. Steven Levine's account (also in this volume) of the so-called phenomenological reading, which argues that James's later shift to metaphysics involves *abandoning* his earlier, scientific account of experience.
8. James, for example, says in *Principles*, "*the first fact for us, then, as psychologists, is that thinking of some sort goes on*. . . . If we could say in English 'it thinks' as we say 'it rains' or 'it blows,' we should be stating the fact most simply and with the minimum of assumption. As we cannot, we must simply say that *thought goes on*" (PP 1890, 219–220).
9. See the first footnote of "Does Consciousness Exist?" (ERE 1904, 4). Later, in "World of Pure Experience," James refers to *Principles* chapters on the Stream of Thought and on the Consciousness of the Self while explaining the continuity of one's personal biography (ERE 1904, 25).
10. The precise relationship between James's psychological accounts of the stream of conscious and of the self in *Principles* and his account of pure experience in *Essays* is a significant issue of debate. The continuity that I see is between the stream and the self in *Principles* and the mental, subjective side of the duality that appear once bits of pure experience have already been contextualized. For a more sustained, detailed discussion of the continuity of James's thoughts between his earlier and later works, see Cooper (2002).
11. Here is another controversy: is James's *Principles* through-and-through a psychological work in that it does not contain *any* metaphysics explicitly or implicitly in it, as he professes (PP 1890, 5–7)? Are his later philosophical works like the *Essays* entirely metaphysical? This

is another, perhaps more general, way of formulating a question regarding the continuity and relationship of James works. Wilshire (1969), for example, argues that a metaphysics creeps into James's understanding and description of mental states in his *Principles*, which anticipates the phenomenological investigation of the mind in Husserl. Flanagan (1991, 23–54), on the other hand, argues that James is a naturalist about the mind in that no "metaphysically odd properties" are attributed to mentality at all.
12. James distinguishes three different ways in which an experience functions as a knower of something, the first of which is immediate perception (ERE 1904, 27–28). For my purpose of comparing James with Hume, I restrict my discussion to James's views regarding perception here.
13. James describes the general structure of knowing at the beginning of "Does Consciousness Exist?" as follows: "knowing can easily be explained as a particular sort of relation towards one another into which portions of pure experience may enter. The relation itself is a part of pure experience; one of its 'terms' becomes the subject or bearer of the knowledge, the other becomes the object known" (ERE 1904, 4–5).
14. This was originally read as the President's Address before the American Psychological Association in 1894, and subsequently published in *Psychological Review* 2, no. 2 in 1895.
15. I am aware that *Principles* came before *Essays*, so I am not claiming here that James intended to connect those two works in this way. My point is mainly about the prominent place relations and connections occupy in James's psychology as well as philosophy.
16. James forcefully argues that our present awareness is not like a knife's edge; it is temporally extended, in which a just-past and a present are all phenomenally present. This fact of temporal extensiveness of a present awareness is what James calls "the specious present" (PP 1890, 573–574).
17. Association is not "an inseparable connexion" that binds perceptions together, but merely *felt* connections, or "a gentle force" between them (T 1.1.4.1, SBN 10). For example, a perception of my computer monitor and a perception of my keyboard may be spatially associated with each other; that is, when I see my computer monitor, I may immediately think of my keyboard. This association may happen in my mind without fail, but there is no necessity with it: I could be thinking about my keyboard, remembering that I have to buy some batteries for it, without having a slightest thought of my computer monitor at all.
18. In his discussion of personal identity, Hume asks whether there is "something that really binds our several perceptions together, or only associates their ideas in the imagination" when we attribute an identity to them (T 1.4.6.16, SBN 259). The former is what he calls "real bond" and the latter "association."
19. It has been historically argued that the commitment to the atomistic view of perceptions makes it impossible for Hume to hold that relations, for example spatial relations, are really presented in perception. For a detailed discussion of this line of criticism given by Green in his Introduction to Hume's *Treatise* and James's response to it, see Klein (2009). Hume argues that our ideas of space and time are copies of complex impressions of colored points and of notes, respectively, and not copies of something additional to the points or the notes (T 1.2.3.4, SBN 34; T.1.2.3.10, SBN 36–37). It seems, indeed, that Hume is trying to deny the existence of spatial and temporal relations along with particular colored points and sounds in simple impressions. However, there *is* something additional to colored points and notes in his explanations: complex impressions must be "dispos'd in a certain manner" (T 1.2.3.4, SBN 34; T 1.2.3.10, SBN 37). Lorne Falkenstein (1997, 181–190) discusses this point. I also argued elsewhere that Hume's accounts introduce relational properties

existing along with particular sensible qualities/objects within impressions, from which various ideas of, for example, space, time, and philosophical relations are produced, and on the basis of which the imagination associates ideas in terms of resemblance, contiguity in space and time, and causation. This, however, poses a problem for Hume, I argued, because it would violate the real separability and discreteness of perceptions. See Inukai (2010). For a similar point about the relationship between relations and the separability of perceptions, see Weinberg (1965, 114–116).
20. James ranks conjunctive relations according to "different degrees of intimacy" in "A World of Pure Experience": for instance, "with," "simultaneity," "time-interval," "space-adjacency," "similarity and difference," and "causal order" (ERE 1904, 23).
21. The so-called Copy Principle, according to which every simple idea is derived from a past corresponding impression, is Hume's methodological directive for investigating various ideas and concepts (e.g., ideas of necessary connection, substance, etc.). The Copy Principle, strictly speaking, applies only to simple ideas. Complex ideas may also be derived from past corresponding complex impressions, but that is not always the case, since the imagination can produce complex ideas by combining other ideas. However, all simple ideas constituting a complex idea produced by the imagination must be derived from past corresponding simple impressions.
22. It is Hume's contention that impressions of sensation themselves do not present anything as distinct or independent. He also recognizes, just like James, that the content of perceptions of sensation does not contain any feature pointing to the represented or the representing (T 1.4.2.11, SBN 191). Nor is reason capable of inferring the existence of body from that of perceptions. Inference from the existence of one thing to that of another can be made only on the basis of the relation of cause and effect, according to Hume. But we cannot observe the relation of cause and effect between objects and perceptions because only perceptions are present to the mind (T 1.4.2.47, SBN 212).
23. Hume often calls "obscure and uncertain" the philosopher's principles and ideas that are not based in experiences (see, for example, T 1.3.1.7, SBN 72; T 1.3.14.7, SBN 158; and T 1.4.5.1, SBN 232).

Bibliography

Baxter, Donald. 2015. "Hume on Substance: A Critique of Locke." In *Locke and Leibniz on Substance*, ed. Paul Lodge & Todd Stoneham, 45–62. London: Routledge.
Cooper, Wesley. 2002. *The Unity of William James's Thought*. Nashville, TN: Vanderbilt University Press.
Falkenstein, Lorne. 1997. "Hume on Manners of Disposition and the Ideas of Space and Time." *Archiv für Geschichte der Philosophie* 79(2): 179–201.
Flanagan, Owen. 1991. *The Science of the Mind*. Cambridge, MA: MIT Press.
Hume, David. 1739-40/1978. *A Treatise of Human Nature*. 2nd ed. Edited by L. A. Selby-Bigge and P. H. Nidditch. Reprint. Oxford: Clarendon.
Hume, David. 1739-40/2000. *A Treatise of Human Nature*. Edited by David Fate Norton and Mary J. Norton. Reprint. Oxford: Oxford University Press.
Hume, David. 1748/1999. *An Enquiry Concerning Human Understanding*. Edited by Tom L. Beauchamp. Reprint. Oxford: Oxford University Press.

Inukai, Yumiko. 2010. "Hume on Relations: Are They Real?" *Canadian Journal of Philosophy* 40(2): 185–209.

Klein, Alexander. 2009. "On Hume on Space: Green's Attack, James' Empirical Response." *Journal of the History of Philosophy* 47(3): 415–449.

Weinberg, Julius R. 1965. *Abstraction, Relation, and Induction: Three Essays in the History of Thought.* Madison: University of Wisconsin Press.

Wilshire, Bruce. 1969. "Protophenomenology in the Psychology of William James." *Transactions of the Charles S. Peirce Society* 5(1): 25–43.

CHAPTER 22

JAMES AND HEGEL
Looking for a Home

ROBERT STERN AND NEIL W. WILLIAMS

Introduction

THROUGHOUT his career, William James took G. W. F. Hegel and the British and American idealists influenced by him to be his primary philosophical opponents. His work is littered with references to, and criticisms of, these idealists. However, in the light of contemporary Hegelianism, James's critique might seem as quaint and outmoded as the forms of Hegelianism it is directed against. James paints Hegel as highly metaphysical, absolutist, anti-individualist and intellectualistic, in stark contrast to today's non-metaphysical, humanistic, liberal, and neo-pragmatic Hegel.[1] As a result, one might feel justified in brushing aside James's attacks as deserved punishment for the fact that he did not engage properly with Hegel's works, instead absorbing them second-hand through the distorting lens of his British and American idealist contemporaries.[2]

This impatient response is not entirely unjustified. James can appear cavalier, rhetorical, and downright ignorant in some of his comments on Hegel. In fact, James frankly admits that he is not a careful reader of Hegel's philosophy, in part due to the obscurity of his writing.[3] In a way that can frustrate modern readers, James spends more time engaging with absolute idealism as a broad metaphysical vision than he does criticizing the technical details of Hegel's philosophy. He does so for two reasons. James was often writing for popular audiences, and as such was wary of delving into the technical details of the philosophies he examined. But, more importantly, James was primarily interested in broad philosophical visions and their pragmatic consequences, rather than in the abstract minutiae of philosophical argumentation. As such, we generally find James engaging with the absolute idealist mindset as a whole, the set of values and presuppositions which support it, and the practical ramifications it entails.[4]

A second, connected problem with James's engagement with Hegel is that James generally leveled his criticism against absolute idealism as a whole movement, and was often broadly indiscriminate about which of the idealists his criticisms applied to. James did not see Hegel as an isolated intellectual figure, but as the origin (more so even than Kant) of a whole philosophical school, which at the time included most of the significant thinkers in America and Britain. It is therefore not really possible to study James's arguments against Hegel on their own, set as they are against the background of his engagement with American and British idealists such as W. T. Harris, Josiah Royce, F. H. Bradley, T. H. Green, and a host of related figures. James read Hegel through these figures, and often his criticisms seem more relevant to them than they do to Hegel himself. As we shall see, however, when James *does* make a distinction between Hegel and the other idealists, it is usually to the benefit of Hegel.[5]

With these problems in mind, it is easy to see James as a poor reader of Hegel, and his critique as an external and crude one. Indeed, James often appears to be setting up his own philosophy as diametrically opposed to Hegel, as he reads him. Hegel is presented as rationalistic, intellectualist, absolutist and monistic, in comparison to James's empiricist, experimentalist, fallibilist, and pluralistic position. Seen in this light, it may seem that there is little to be gained from the encounter between the two, as each side will simply largely talk past the other.

However, in this chapter we suggest that James's criticism in fact emerges from what he perceives as a common starting point, so that James offers something more like an *internal* critique of Hegel on the basis of what he saw as their shared project. This common ground is identified early on in *A Pluralistic Universe*, where James quotes Hegel as saying that "[t]he aim of knowledge is to divest the objective world of strangeness, and to make us more at home in it" (PU 1909, 10).[6] In this attempt to be at home in the world, James presents Hegel and the absolute idealists as being far closer to his own position than either materialism or theism (PU 1909, 16–19). And as "being at home in the world" is taken to be the aim of both idealism and James's empiricism, success or failure in reaching this aim is presented as a pragmatic test of the competing metaphysical visions. In what follows, we will attempt to unpack what this notion of "being at home in the world" amounts to for James, and argue that this common ground gives James's criticisms of Hegel a depth which they might otherwise seem to lack.

James's sustained and explicit criticism of Hegel himself appears in two essays written at either end of his philosophical career. The first is his essay "On Some Hegelisms," which was written in 1881, published in *Mind* in 1882, and reprinted with some alterations in *The Will to Believe and Other Essays* in 1897. The second appears in *A Pluralistic Universe*, published in 1909 and based on his Hibbert Lectures given in Oxford the previous year. The fact that both were originally presented as popular lectures and writings lends James's discussion of Hegel a breezy, rhetorical character. This is particularly true of "On Some Hegelisms," in which James addressed Hegel and his followers with a "superficiality" for which he would later apologize (WB 1897, 9). This chapter was delivered first to the Hegel class of George Herbert Palmer (1842–1933), a colleague of James's at Harvard. James's aim in giving it was apparently "to leave as disrespectful an impression [of Hegel] on the minds of the students as possible, Palmer having all the rest of the year to himself to wipe it out" (letter to W. T. Harris, CWJ 1882, 5.206). His goal in having it published in *Mind* was similarly to stir controversy, as the editor, G. Croom Robertson, happily acknowledged, while noting with disappointment afterward that it had failed to provoke the Hegelians into a response (letters from G. Croom Robertson, CWJ 1881-1882, 5.181–182 and 226–227). While considerably more measured and respectful, the treatment of Hegel in *A Pluralistic Universe* was still written to entertain an audience, though one for whom Hegel is seen as less of a wicked temptation and more as a dead (or at least dying) dog, allowing James to be more magnanimous in his tone (PU 1909, 7). Nonetheless, this is still far from a sober and sombre academic study, and at least one correspondent complained that "[y]ou take your Hegel impressionistically."[7]

Despite the rhetoric and jocularity, however, there seems little doubt that James intended his engagement with Hegel to be taken seriously. James's essential concerns with Hegel's idealism remain constant, and it is clear that his respect for him increased over time.[8] As will become evident in the next section, outside of these central texts, throughout his career James frequently returns to Hegel as a touchstone, as an opponent, and, very occasionally, as an ally.

The Roots of James's Criticism of Hegel

Throughout his career, James consistently presents philosophy's task as attempting to formulate an account of the universe so that it appears "rational." As philosophers, James suggests in "The Sentiment of Rationality," we aim to "attain a conception of the frame of things which shall on the whole be more rational than the fragmentary and chaotic one which everyone by gift of nature carries about with [them]" (WB 1897, 57). However, exactly what it means to find the world a rational place is more complicated than we might at first think. In his early papers, James is clear that the rationality of a conception is not a self-evident property of it, but is only recognized by "certain subjective marks," such as a "strong feeling of ease, peace [and] rest" (WB 1897, 57). These subjective marks indicate that we "feel at home" in the world (WB 1897, 96).

We should not be too concerned about James's appeal to subjective states as marks of what is rational. James is careful never to equate what is rational with what would give us subjective satisfaction, but rather only asserts that our subjective satisfactions are marks of a concept's rationality. This fits in with his broader pragmatism in two ways: the thought that the *working* of a concept is the best mark of its truth, understood as its agreement with reality (see, for instance, MT 1909, 106); and the broad pragmatist model of inquiry, shared with C. S. Peirce and John Dewey, which sees inquiry as the attempt to overcome real doubt, understood as a kind of unease or an incapacity to practically continue. With this in mind, we can make sense of James's picture of what philosophy is meant to achieve:

> [A]ny view of the universe which shall completely satisfy the mind must obey conditions of the mind's own imposing [. . .] Not any nature of things which may

seem to *be* will also seem to be *ipso facto* rational; and if it do[es] not seem rational, it will afflict the mind with a ceaseless uneasiness, till it be formulated or interpreted in some other and more congenial way. (WB 1897, 99–100)

The aim of our philosophical theorizing, then, is to find an account of the universe which will allow us a certain "fluency" of thought, rather than its interruption by doubt (WB 1897, 58). It is this picture of philosophy's task as finding the world to be a rational place which James takes himself and Hegel to share, and by which he assesses the latter. Being "at home" in the world, for James, thus seems to mean finding it rational in this sense: being able to live, act, and think in the world in a way that does not lead to us encountering severe disappointment, doubt, or other impediments.

James offers several different formulations of what would count as a rational philosophical account of the universe in his early papers. In "Reflex Action and Theism" (1881), James suggests that a rational account of the universe must appeal to the operation of sensation, conception, and action, as different facets of our engagement with reality, and that any philosophy which does not appeal to each of these in some regard would become, at best, "the creed of some partial sect" (WB 1897, 100). In "The Sentiment of Rationality" (1879/1882), James separates our practical and our intellectual needs in finding the world rational. The intellectual aspect finds satisfaction in simplifying the world and finding identities between apparently disparate things (WB 1897, 58), and the practical aspect aims to keep things distinct, and to be "acquainted with the parts rather than to comprehend the whole" (WB 1897, 59). Our aim should be to "balance" these two "cravings" (WB 1897, 59). Another formulation of what it is to find the world a rational place is found in "The Dilemma of Determinism" (1884). Here, James separates an idea or conception having rationality in the sense of meeting our logical or intellectual demands; rationality in the sense of meeting our mechanical, practical, or scientific needs; and rationality in the sense of meeting our moral requirements. None of these, thinks James, should have precedence, each demand being "quite as subjective and emotional as the other" (WB 1897, 116).

Though these formulations differ, several things remain constant. In each case, finding the world to be a rational place is understood as involving several different aspects of our natures, limited not merely to intellectual comprehension, but also involving a practical (and in the 1884 formulation, a moral) engagement with reality. In each formulation, James suggests that a good philosophy needs to provide an account which satisfies or balances all of these different needs. And in each account, Hegel is presented as an example of a thinker who does *not* aim for this balance, but instead privileges just one aspect of our engagement with reality: the intellectual.

By privileging the intellectual need, Hegel's "intellectualist" account results in several features, according to James. It privileges unity and simplicity over particularity and distinctness. It aims to satisfy our need to understand the world over our need to act within it. Further, it aims to understand the world "completely", for "if the universe is reasonable [...] it must be susceptible, potentially at least, of being reasoned *out* to the last drop without residuum" (WB 1897, 108). As a result, the aim of the intellectualist account is to provide a system whereby everything is unified in a whole, ending in the apprehension of a "universal concept" or "absolute datum" (WB 1897, 62; 63). Finally, such a philosophy has a tendency to see the universe as already complete, finished and perfect, and our own contribution to be merely that of bringing this rational whole to consciousness, rather than contributing at all to the makeup of reality (SPP 1910, 111). Our practical or moral engagement with reality will be seen, at best, as purposeful only insofar as it can further our theoretical comprehension of the universe (WB 1897, 109). As such, the intellectualist will tend to be a monist and a problematic rationalist, in ways which we will explore later. In this thought lies the core of James's critique of Hegel: according to James, Hegel privileges the intellectual, and denies the practical, in his account of how we are to find the world a rational place.

We will now consider in further depth how this issue underpins James's mature engagement with Hegel in *A Pluralistic Universe*, and consider how far James's critique of Hegel on this issue should be taken seriously. James's strategy in *A Pluralistic Universe* is twofold, and we shall then consider each aspect in turn. First, James attempts to negate arguments for the logical necessity of absolute idealism (see "Against the Logical Necessity of Absolute Idealism," below), and then James considers the plausibility of the concept of the absolute taken as a hypothesis, judged against the criterion of "feeling at home" (see "Rationalism and Monism," below). After this, we shall return to James's early papers to detail the differences between Hegel's and James's accounts of feeling at home in the world (see "Practicality and Contingency," below).

AGAINST THE LOGICAL NECESSITY OF ABSOLUTE IDEALISM

When James returns to seriously engage with Hegel in *A Pluralistic Universe* (1909), it is to contrast his own metaphysical system with Hegel's absolute idealism. James's "radical empiricism" is a vision of the universe which is pluralistic and empiricist, and so sharply distinct from what he takes to be the monism and rationalism of Hegel's system. The common criterion by which James compares these two metaphysical hypotheses is "intimacy"—a notion which has replaced the prior notion of "rationality" (PU 1909, 144–145). Intimacy is contrasted with "foreignness" and is a measure of how at home in the world a particular philosophy allows us to feel. This is not, for James, a merely abstract measurement, but one which carries serious pragmatic weight:

> From a pragmatic point of view the difference between living against a background of foreignness and one of intimacy means the difference between a general habit of wariness and one of trust.[9] (PU 1909, 19)

Early on in *A Pluralistic Universe*, James repeats his claim that both he and Hegel take philosophy's aim to be, in part, allowing us to feel at home in the world. Though he recognizes that "[d]ifferent men find their minds more at home in very different fragments of the world" (PU 1909, 10), we should not lose sight of this common aim:

> [A]ll such differences are minor matters which ought to be subordinated in view of the fact that [. . .] we are, ourselves, parts of the universe and share the one deep concern in its destinies. We crave alike to feel more truly at home in it, and to contribute our mite to its amelioration. It would be pitiful if small aesthetic discords were to keep honest men asunder. (PU 1909, 11)

This common aim not only unifies differing philosophies, but it also provides a criterion of assessment. James very quickly rejects materialism and theism as not meeting this criterion, and presents his own thesis and monistic idealism as the only accounts of reality offering sufficient intimacy. In this sense, James presents himself and Hegel as aligned in project and vision, and as differing only in the *form* which an intimate view of the universe should take. Whereas monistic idealism will hold that the true form of reality should be conceived of as a rational whole, to be accessed through reason alone, James's pluralistic empiricism will reject this notion of a rational whole or "all-form," and hold instead that reality is primarily accessed through experience. We will return to this broad distinction in the next section.

However, while James thinks that it is on the question of intimacy that the real issue between absolute idealism and radical empiricism turns, he recognizes that absolute idealists also offer a priori arguments for their position. So, before assessing the two metaphysical theses in light of the common criterion of intimacy, James must first defuse absolute idealism's apparent claim to be logically necessary.

In his lecture on "Monistic Idealism," James clearly lays out the common argumentative trajectory which he sees Royce, Bradley, Hermann Lotze, and all "post-Kantian absolutism" to have taken. These thinkers start from a position he is happy to share, but end in a position which holds the absolute as logically necessary:

> First, there is a healthy faith that the world must be rational and self-consistent. "All science, all real knowledge, all experience presuppose," as Mr. Ritchie writes, "a coherent universe." Next, we find a loyal clinging to the rationalist belief that sense-data and their associations are incoherent, and that only in substituting a conceptual order for their order can truth be found. Third, the substituted conceptions are treated intellectualistically, that is as mutually exclusive and discontinuous, so that the first innocent continuity of the flow of sense-experience is shattered for us without any higher conceptual continuity taking its place. Finally, since this broken state of things is intolerable, the absolute *deus ex machina* is called on to mend it in his own way, since we cannot mend it in ours. (PU 1909, 38)

Though James does not mention Hegel at this point, this line of thought is strikingly similar to one attributed by him to Hegel in "On Some Hegelisms" some twenty-seven years previously (WB 1897, 198 ff.). When James turns to Hegel in 1909, however, in the lecture titled "Hegel and His Method," he is careful to separate Hegel from the other absolute idealists in light of this passage. As such, it is worth dwelling on this paragraph in some detail, to bring out the ways that James differentiated between Hegel and his followers in his criticisms of absolute idealism.

The line of thought begins with the claim that we aim to find the world rational and self-consistent. This is merely the assertion of the philosophical project which James sees as unifying himself and the Hegelians.[10] However, things start to go wrong at the second step.

According to James, Hegel has two central features to his monistic idealism: "[t]he first part [is] that reason is all-inclusive, the second [is] that things are 'dialectic'" (PU 1909, 44). Perhaps surprisingly, James agrees with both when sufficiently limited. James takes the first point to be a commitment to holism, the claim that "[t]he full truth about anything involves more than that thing. In the end nothing less than the whole of everything can be the truth of anything at all" (PU 1909, 45). In "On Some Hegelisms," James held that a commitment to a modest holism was "an integral part of empiricism, an integral part of common-sense" and, we might add, an integral part of pragmatism (WB 1897, 206). The second, dialectical claim, on James's account, concerns a fundamentally empirical truth that within our experience nothing is ever perfectly stable or complete. James goes as far as to suggest that this is a great empirical truth to which Hegel brought philosophy's attention:

> What, then, is the dialectic method? It is itself a part of the hegelian vision or intuition, and a part that finds the strongest echo in empiricism and common sense. Great injustice is done to Hegel by treating him as primarily a reasoner. He is in reality a naively observant man [...]. He plants himself in the empirical flux of things, and gets the impression of what happens.[11] (PU 1909, 44)

As such, James approves of both central facets of Hegel's philosophy, when "taken in the rough" as empirical claims. The mistake comes, on James's view, when the Hegelian begins to interpret these empirical results conceptually.

It is this move from the empirical to the conceptual which marks the second step of our paragraph. Hegelians find sense experience insufficient for providing the kind of rationality they are looking for, which they think can only be found in a substituted conceptual order. Despite his keen observational sense, James thinks that Hegel was not satisfied with a merely empirical philosophy, but wanted to have his philosophy be a "product of eternal reason," to work via logic and a priori reasoning (PU 1909, 46). For James, this is a mistake for two reasons. Firstly, because experience *can* provide us with the unity we are looking for, as long as we do not have the desire for *total* unity. Secondly, because the idealist's treatment of concepts means that we further *dis*-unify our experience by treating it conceptually.

Let us begin with the first point. James's own metaphysics is built on the idea that we do not need to appeal to any non-experiential forces when giving a unified account of our reality. The universe of our experience is unified through conjunctive and disjunctive relations, which are themselves experiential (ERE 1904, 22). In this way, the universe "hangs together" by the edges, rather than being unified by one overarching substance, idea or agency.[12] Moreover, our experience taken in its immediacy is not simple, but already has a complexity and a connection to other "pulses" of experience. James suggests that in some way, we can see each portion of experience acting "as its own other," in the sense that "no part absolutely excludes another, but [. . .] they compenetrate and are cohesive" (PU 1909, 121). As such, James's assertion is that experience, treated correctly, can satisfy the (moderate) need for unity and the (moderate) need for holism that Hegel requires. It is only because the absolute idealists are intellectualists, and think that total or absolute unity is required for us to feel at home in the world, that Hegel and his followers think that the world of sense is not sufficient for meeting this need.

The second reason James thinks that it is a mistake to move from the experiential to the conceptual realm when seeking unity is that James thinks that the intellectualist is constrained to think of concepts as "mutually exclusive and discontinuous." As such, moving to a conceptual way of treating our experience results in less rather than more unity, as experiential elements which are conceptually distinguished are treated as being necessarily or essentially distinct. This is the third step of our paragraph. James calls the treatment of experience via concepts which are mutually exclusive and discontinuous the mistake of "vicious intellectualism" (PU 1909, 32). The mistake occurs when we assume "that a concept excludes from any reality conceived by its means everything not included in the concept's definition" (PU 1909, 52). Such reasoning, to take James's tongue-in-cheek example, results in suggesting that "a person whom you have once called an 'equestrian' is thereby forever made unable to walk on his own feet" (PU 1909, 32). As a result of treating the world conceptually in this way, Lotze, Royce, and Bradley are not able to account for how these conceptually distinct properties can ever be unified. This leads them to the fourth step of the line of thought presented earlier: the invocation of a kind of deus ex machina in the form of a trans-experiential agent of unity—the Absolute. On James's analysis, then, it is the conceptual separation of our experience into mutually exclusive and discontinuous parts which leads the Hegelians to the conclusion that the absolute is a logical necessity.

However, Hegel himself did not have precisely this problem, according to James. Hegel does not need to invoke a semi-divine absolute to unify our conceptualized experience, because Hegel moved past the logic of identity, which held that concepts could only be related by sameness, and moved onto the thought that concepts "are identical with themselves: but only identical in so far as at the same time they involve distinction" (Hegel 1873/1975, §115 Addition, 168; quoted by James PU 1909, 47).[13] Hegel's most profound originality, for James, lay in transporting his dialectical vision of empirical reality to the sphere of concepts:

> Concepts were not in his eyes the static self-contained things that previous logicians had supposed, but were germinative, and passed beyond themselves into each other by what he called their immanent dialectic. In ignoring each other as they do, they virtually exclude and deny each other, he thought, and thus in a manner introduce each other. (PU 1909, 46)

Hegel therefore does not require the invocation of an absolute mind to unify the world treated conceptually, because for Hegel it is the mutual exclusivity of concepts themselves which provide their own continuity. James sees Hegel as finding the unity he is searching for through their disunity, by a kind of determination by negation. By concepts excluding each other, they must refer to each other, and so in some sense include each other in their identities. As each concept does this, we unify the world into an absolute through their contradiction and negation (PU 1909, 52). In this sense, Hegel is meant to offer a unique, but vivid, example of vicious intellectualism, though one which does not require the agency of the absolute as a unifying mind. So the main difference between Hegel and the other idealists for James is that Hegel does not appeal to an absolute mind; rather, Hegel's absolute emerges from the dialectical movement of concepts.[14]

To sum up, James thinks that any a priori argument for absolute idealism fails because it makes two key mistakes: (a) it assumes that experience is not rationally satisfying; and (b), it assumes that concepts are at some level "mutually exclusive and discontinuous." In contrast, James thinks that experience is sufficiently unified and coherent, and that the shift to the conceptual level is not required. We can see this in James's interpretation of Hegel's holism and dialectical methodology as primarily empirical insights. So, James's analysis at this stage is supposed to serve two purposes: it defuses monistic idealism's claims to logical necessity, and it shows that the enterprise of monistic idealism is predicated on a certain suspect treatment of both experience and concepts.

How compelling is James's critique of Hegel in these respects? Firstly, considering (a), it may appear that James's worry is justified up to a point. It seems that, in Hegel's treatment of the relation between experience and conception, we often find him privileging the conceptual. In support of this reading, James quotes a passage from Hegel's discussion of the ontological argument in the *Encyclopedia Logic*, which he takes to give us a vital insight into Hegel's "central thought" and "vision":

> It would be strange if the Notion, the very heart of the mind, or, in a word, the concrete totality we call God, were not rich enough to embrace so poor a category as Being, the very poorest and most abstract of all—for nothing can be more insignificant than Being.[15] (quoted by James, PU 1909, 44)

And James might perhaps have continued by citing the rest of this passage as evidence for his interpretation (switching to a more recent translation):

> Only this much may be more trivial, namely, what one first imagines somehow with respect to being, such as an *external, sensory* existence like that of the paper here in front of me. But after all, no one will want to talk about the sensory existence of a limited, transient thing. (Hegel 2010, 101)

Here, it seems, we find expressed just the kind of lofty Platonic contempt for mere "external, sensory existence" that James identifies as typical of Hegel; and James could also have cited evidence for it elsewhere, had he wanted to. For example, in an important passage from *The Science of Logic*, Hegel writes that "[t]he idealism of philosophy consists in nothing else than in recognizing that the finite has no veritable being," and that by virtue of recognizing this "[e]very philosophy is essentially an idealism."[16] Similar examples can be multiplied, so James's misgivings would seem to have more than adequate textual support.

And yet, in a way that critics find so frustrating, it is not clearly the case that Hegel's position is as simple as these various passages suggest, for they arguably represent but one side of a more nuanced view, which must at least be taken into account before pronouncing on the effectiveness of James's critique. Perhaps the most important point to make on Hegel's behalf is that these sort of passages come in a context in which Hegel is himself trying to administer a corrective to those who themselves one-sidedly decry the significance of concepts and thought to our metaphysics and epistemology, as if "mere experience" of things in purely sensory terms might be enough to give us an adequate grasp of the world around us, and as if any process of thinking and conceptualization must involve a distorting abstraction away from what is fundamentally real in this respect. Against such positions (which had defenders in Hegel's time, as well as in James's and our own), Hegel is keen to stress the positive role thought and concepts can play in giving us knowledge of the world, and the metaphysics required to make sense of this—namely, a form of conceptual realism which treats substance-kinds and laws, for example, as fundamentally real. Thus, while Hegel's rhetoric in this context may sound a Platonic note at times, many other passages make clear he would be closer to a more Aristotelian view that treats these conceptual structures as embodied in the world, rather than subsisting in some ideal and transcendent realm of pure abstractions.[17]

Turning now to point (b), concerning James's criticisms of Hegel's treatment of concepts as related through negation, James's points seem to apply best to Hegel's account of concepts at the level of Being, where the "determination by negation" principle is used most and where he characterizes the relation between categories or "thought-determinations" as one of "transition" or "going over" (*Übergehen*): but later levels in the *Logic* of Essence and Concept treat concepts as inherently more interrelated, without any "atomistic" moment to be overcome, characterized in terms of "reflection in the other" (*Scheinen in Anderes*) and "development" (*Entwicklung*), respectively, such that the categories of the "concept" (*Begriff*) are understood as each requiring the others in a holistic manner. James would therefore seem to have mischaracterized the way that Hegel's dialectic works and the way he conceives of the relation between the higher categories.[18]

However, even if these points in Hegel's defense are successful, we might think that James could nonetheless concede these replies without damaging his overall case: for, in effect, they mean that Hegel does not subscribe to the premises that the a priori argument for the absolute was said to require. He must therefore argue for the absolute not on a priori grounds after all, but on other grounds, namely, that it is most likely to allow us to feel at home in the world. For James, this is to offer the absolute as a kind of hypothesis, and for its validity to be assessed by how well it fulfils this role of allowing us to feel "at home." It is to this way of deciding the issue between James and Hegel that we now turn.

Rationalism and Monism

Having dealt to his satisfaction with what he takes to be a priori proofs for absolute idealism, James is now free to treat his own position and absolute idealism as co-ordinate metaphysical hypotheses, to be assessed in part by how rational they allow us to find the world, or how "at home" they allow us to feel:

> The great claim made for the absolute is that by supposing it we make the world appear more rational. Any hypothesis that does that will always be accepted as more probably true than an hypothesis that makes the world appear irrational. Men are once and for all so made that they prefer a rational world to believe in and to live in. (PU 1909, 54–55)

James's central claim, when the problem is understood in this way, is that a monistic and rationalistic system of the sort James takes Hegel to be committed to *cannot* provide a sufficiently intimate philosophy, and will leave us alienated from the world in which we are attempting to feel at home. We can treat the accusation of monism and the accusation of rationalism separately, though James saw them as clearly linked. The monistic claim is commonly expressed by James as the view that there is a total form, or an "all-form" to the universe, contrasted to James's own pluralistic standpoint in which "no single point of view can ever take in the whole scene" (WB 1897, 136). The rationalistic claim is that the real nature of the universe can be exhaustively described conceptually, with nothing relevant being lost.

The difference between monism and pluralism is one of form. In *A Pluralistic Universe*, James suggests that the major difference between his own philosophy and any monistic idealism is that the latter privileges unity and totality, holding that the "all-form" is the real form of reality, whereas his own account holds that "a distributive form of reality, the *each*-form, is logically as acceptable and empirically as possible as the all-form" (PU 1909, 20). We should understand the "all-form" to be essentially what James means by "the absolute." It is for this reason that "monistic idealism" and "absolute idealism" are used interchangeably in these lectures. James's suggestion, contra the absolutist, is that the "each-form" is sufficient for our empirical needs, and for finding the world to be a rational place.

First, what precisely does James mean by "the absolute"? James spends a good deal of time describing the properties he takes the absolute to have, but because he rarely distinguishes between different versions of absolute idealism, it is hard to tell which properties he takes to be applicable to which accounts. For an idealist like Royce, the absolute is a kind of mind active in unifying the universe. For Hegel, the absolute is some kind of final or total fact, the universe seen as an organic whole. Though we can find upward of sixteen different properties attributed to the hypothesis of the absolute in these lectures, the properties most relevant to James's conception, and definitely attributed to Hegel, are the following: that the universe can be successfully understood as one total fact, or as having an "all-form" (PU 1909, 21); that this one fact has no environment, that there is nothing outside of itself (ibid.); that we are to understand the absolute as being mind, minded, or mind-like (PU 1909, 22); that the universe *qua* absolute is complete, perfect, and timeless (PU 1909, 22); that the absolute denies chance or contingency any real role in the universe (PU 1909, 39); and that the universe *qua* absolute has no "history" (PU 1909, 22). Finite beings have history insofar as they impact on one another, help or hinder each other, whereas the absolute "neither acts nor suffers, nor loves nor hates; it has no needs, desires, or aspirations, no failures or successes, friends or enemies, victories or defeats" (PU 1909, 27). As such, it "stands outside of history" (PU 1909, 28).

Monists will claim that it is only by comprehending the universe in its "all-form" that we can come to see it as rational. As James puts it, understanding the world as an absolute in this way produces a "spherical system," a world with no outside, and "with no loose ends hanging out for foreignness to get a hold upon" (PU 1909, 51). As James contrasts "foreignness" with "intimacy," we might think that James here is conceding that conceiving the world under the absolute hypothesis allows us to feel most at home within it. But, in fact, James finds such an interpretation of the world wanting on grounds of intimacy, for reasons continuous with his earlier concerns.

To demonstrate this, we can return to James's multifarious notion of rationality. Toward the end of his lecture on Hegel, once he takes himself to have refuted the logical necessity of absolute idealism, and before he supersedes the notion of rationality with intimacy, James introduces the following distinction:

> [R]ationality has at least four dimensions, intellectual, aesthetical, moral, and practical; and to find a world rational to the maximal degree *in all these respects simultaneously* is no easy matter. (PU 1909, 55)

Once again, we find the assertion that different philosophies attempt to meet these differing demands for rationality in different ways, but that the aim should be to provide an account which "will yield the largest *balance* of rationality" (PU 1909, 55). James's more subtle evolution of his earlier accusation that Hegel privileges only one of the competing demands of rationality is that Hegel does not succeed in balancing these competing dimensions.

Firstly, James concedes that the absolute idealist hypothesis is aesthetically rational, in the sense that the human mind tends to find unity more aesthetically pleasing than disunity. Secondly, although it is an intellectualist thesis, James claims that the absolute is intellectually obscure, once we deny (as James takes himself to have done) its logical necessity (PU 1909, 55–57). Finally, practically and morally, the thesis of the absolute fares worse. Practically, the hypothesis of the absolute is "useless," in the sense that it cannot offer any predictions about experiential events, though it will subsequently "adopt" these events into its theory. It is, James tells us, a "hypothesis that functions retrospectively only, not prospectively" (PU 1909, 61). Morally, the thesis of absolutism brings with it a speculative problem of evil, and a license to take "moral holidays." Let us consider each of these objections regarding practicality and morality in more detail.

Though we might suspect such a speculative problem of evil will bother only those theorists who understand the absolute as a kind of active mind, there is a broader way of articulating this concern. James is struck by the fact that the universe *qua* absolute and the universe *qua* finite beings have wildly different properties. Whereas the finite beings suffer, strive, and value the world, the universe as a whole does not. "The absolute" is final, complete, and finished, and has no environment in which to strive. As such, James thinks the monistic hypothesis often engenders a feeling of alienation from the universe as a whole. *Qua* absolute, the universe is perfect and complete, and has overcome all evil and error. "On the ground," though, in our own experiences, we find evil and error in abundance, and so find ourselves alienated from the universe as a whole. This discordance or "lack of fit" between ourselves as finite entities, and the universe understood as absolute, is what constitutes this sense of alienation or foreignness. We cannot feel intimate with, or at home in, a reality which is so removed from our own concerns. In a pluralistic conception, on the contrary, the "problems that evil presents are practical, not speculative" (PU 1909, 60).

Turning now to the second objection, by "moral holidays" James means the capacity to take a kind of rest from the problems of our moral lives. This issue once again stems from the idea of the all-form as complete, and as having no history, in the sense of interactions with finite beings such as ourselves. If the absolute is already complete and perfect, we can relax our concerns about making the world a better place. At its best, this license to take moral holidays may satisfy the need in us to rest once in a while, to put the success of our moral interests in hands other than our own. In this sense, it could be seen as a strength of the absolutist position (see P 1907, 42–44; MT 1909, 123 ff.). At worst, however, such an approach negates *any* need to adopt the "strenuous" attitude in our moral lives. Under the absolutist hypothesis, seeing as the universe is already perfect and complete, and our actions can make no real difference to it, we have no reason to act morally.[19] We will return to this idea in the next section.

Now let us look at James's criticisms of rationalism, insofar as they differ from his criticisms of monism. In James's sense, rationalism either means prioritizing the whole above the part, in which case it is very close to monism, or the belief that reality can and should always be understood conceptually. This latter line of thought is often found in Hegel, for instance in his introduction to the *Encyclopedia Logic*, in which he claims that "the true *content* of our consciousness is *preserved* in its translation into the form of thought and the concept, and indeed only then placed in its proper light."[20]

In James's earlier papers, James attributes a kind of arrogance or hubris to this rationalistic side of Hegel. Hegel's solely intellectualistic and rationalistic way of approaching reality demands its "unconditional surrender" to the intellect, the demand that "all of existence must bend the knee to its requirements." In comparison to this "intellectual despotism," James presents pluralism as a more democratic view, in which the reasoning agent "gives to other powers [in the universe] the same freedom it would have itself," rather than demanding that everything be part of one intellectual system (WB 1897, 201–202). This presentation of his own metaphysical position as somehow more democratic, and the rationalist's as more despotic, recurs throughout his assessment of idealism (e.g., PU 1909, 145). James's un-argued assumption seems to be that the democratic attitude is preferable because it encourages more intimacy with the world than does the despotic attitude.

What is missed, according to James, if we treat the world solely by conceptual means? The answer is: the non-conceptual elements of reality which cannot be generalized, which cannot, without violence, be described exhaustively in general terms. Consider James's example of lovers from "What Makes Life Significant" (1898):

> Every Jack sees in his own particular Jill charms and perfections to the enchantment of which we stolid onlookers are stone-cold. And which has the superior view of the absolute truth, he or we? Which has the more vital insight into the nature of Jill's existence, as a fact? [. . .][S]urely to Jack are the profounder truths revealed [. . .] For Jack realizes Jill concretely, and we do not. (TT 1899, 150–151)

In such examples, James focuses on those elements of reality which we can only access via sympathy with the concrete feeling of those elements. Treating the sensational, concrete, particular, and personal aspects of the world as somehow less real or less important than the universal and the general, again, renders the universe alien to us, seeing as these former elements are those with which we are most intimately acquainted.

These thoughts support James's assertion that the pluralistic and empiricist hypothesis which he proposes meets more of the requirements of rationality—namely the practical and the moral aspects—than the rationalist model of the idealist. In offering these criticisms of Hegel, James's position may be compared to a long line of critics, from the late Schelling onward, who have found Hegel's idealism problematically conceptualist and "totalizing," submerging within it all particularity, difference, and finitude. What makes James's criticism interestingly distinctive, however, is that this is offered as a form of internal critique, in arguing that Hegel's outlook must in the end fail to achieve its own goal, of enabling us to feel "at home," for it ultimately leaves us unable to feel "intimate" with the universe in the way that James's thinks their shared project requires.

Nonetheless, the Hegelian may make several replies to James's criticisms. Firstly, the Hegelian might suggest that James provides an interpretation of Hegel's absolute which is too transcendent. James's presentation of the absolute as outside of time and history seems to run counter to Hegel's, who treats spirit as immanent within the world and so—in a more processual and concrete manner—as embodied within history. It is less clear that a non-transcendent notion of the absolute would lead to the same problems that James identifies for the more transcendent interpretation he criticizes, which is said to reduce the absolute to a bare "one" in a monistic manner. Indeed, Hegel himself criticizes such monistic conceptions, which he identifies with Spinoza in particular, on grounds that James might well share.[21]

As for the accusation of rationalism, contemporary Hegelians may well argue that James's approach assumes that conceptualization involves a process of abstraction, which removes us from the concrete world. However, in developing his account of the "concrete universal," Hegel aims to create room within universal concepts for precisely the kind of particularity which concerns James, while avoiding cutting such particularity off from conceptualization in a way that itself might look dubiously antirationalistic and dualistic, as if the world of particulars remained fundamentally alien to the mind.[22] The problem James's approach might encounter is that placing particular aspects of the world outside of conceptual understanding would itself be alienating. James's more extreme anti-rationalist statements would seem to leave the world opaque and mysterious in a manner that would leave us rationally dissatisfied and without a proper home.[23] This was precisely Hegel's concern about Kant, for whom "what [things] are in *themselves* remain for us an inaccessible world beyond this one [*Jenseits*]."[24]

Practicality and Contingency

Thus, in response to James's anti-rationalist assertion that certain elements of reality cannot be fully captured by conceptual thought, the Hegelian could argue that any such reality would in fact be one in which we could not experience the "intimacy" that James seeks. However, it is precisely at this point that the force of James's claim that philosophical systems must satisfy the practical as well as the intellectual aspects of our natures is felt. Strange though it might seem to the Hegelian or the rationalist, James's claim is that a reality which was perfectly rational and complete would in fact be profoundly alienating to beings like us, because our practical natures could find no function within it.

We can find this line of thought expressed in *A Pluralistic Universe*, especially in James's exploration of Henri Bergson (e.g., PU 1909, 144). But it is perhaps best expressed in James's earlier work. There James emphasizes that finding the world rational in a practical sense involves us finding it a place in which we have both the power and the motive to act, with one vital motivation being the awareness that our actions matter to the wider world. According to James, it is precisely this which is lacking in Hegel's picture. The aim of our philosophy, James argues, cannot be to conceive of reality as a conceptually rational whole, or to bring the already rational structure of the universe to consciousness. Such aims would ignore the need of our practical natures to *contribute* to the world. According to James, the idea that we have nothing to contribute to reality can only lead us to a sense of alienation, or a "nameless *unheimlichkeit*" (WB 1897, 71).

An example of this thought can be found in James's assessment of moral action. A vital part of our moral lives, for James, is acting under our ideals and faiths. So, finding the world to be rational in a moral sense involves our ideals and faiths having the requisite power and motivation. But it is only when the outcome of the universe remains undecided, when there remains some contingency to be overcome, that our moral action has the power to contribute something real to the outcome of the universe. It is only with the admission of "real, genuine possibilities"—for both good or bad outcomes—that we gain the "willingness to act, no matter how we feel" (WB 1897, 135). As such, if our moral and practical natures are involved in feeling at home in the world, rather than just our intellectual natures, then we must provide an account of reality in which they truly matter to its makeup.

The practical difference, according to James, is between seeing the universe as something like a fight and seeing it as something like a game:

> If this be not a real fight, in which something is eternally gained for the universe by success, it is no better than a game of private theatricals from which one may withdraw at will. But it *feels* like a real fight – as if there were something really wild in the universe which we, with all our idealities and faithfulnesses, are needed to redeem [. . .] For such a half-wild, half-saved universe our nature is adapted [. . .] [H]ere possibilities, not finished facts, are the realities with which we have actively to deal. (WB 1897, 55)

Ideals and faiths are motivations to act on realities which are not yet decided, and to which our action will make some difference. It is this idea which can be taken as the vital difference between the monistic and pluralistic theses. The pluralistic hypothesis holds that reality is still in the making, that it will always be so, and that the direction of its growth depends in part on our actions. The monistic world, on the other hand, is already complete and rational, either already or eventually, and its growth proceeds via a logical and necessary order of which we are at best the instantiators.

The clash presented by James between himself and Hegel, then, is between two very different approaches to feeling at home in the world. Hegel presents our project of feeling at home in the world as one in which we can comprehend and understand everything as part of the rational whole, and so rest in peace and intellectual satisfaction. For James, this is akin to the "tranquillity of the boor" (WB 1897, 62). Though there will always be those who find such a merely intellectual picture satisfying, James aims to present an alternative and more encompassing picture of feeling at home in the world.[25] We can think of James's criticism as having two levels. The first is that any philosophy which aims to provide an account of reality which will allow us to feel "at home" within it must not merely provide a description which satisfies our intellectual natures, but must also leave room for our practical natures to have power and motive to act. The second level of this criticism is that in order for our practical natures to have a meaningful motive to act in the world, that world must be indeterminate, incomplete, or have elements of contingency. According to James, Hegel underestimates the richness of human rationality, and so what it takes for creatures like us to feel at home in the world.

Now, again, there are Hegelian responses to be considered. One might be that James once more underestimates the place for contingency and openness in Hegel's rationalism, where such contingency is even said to be itself necessary.[26] But a more radical response might be to allow that James is right, and that in the end the Hegelian picture does aim to overcome the need for our practical natures to be exercised, instead encouraging us to become purely contemplative and reach a kind of rational satisfaction to be found at the "end of history" when the work of reason has been fully realized and achieved. What would be so bad about that, the Hegelian might ask—why would it not rather be the attainment of the highest good, taking us beyond the toils of the world?[27]

It is clear, however, that for James such a vision of humanity would be profoundly lacking. Offering an example of such a purely contemplative life which he found in the Chautauqua Lake Institution, James complains of the "absence of human nature *in extremis*" which resulted in a "flatness and lack of zest." And even if we were somehow able to change our natures so as to find such "atrocious harmlessness" satisfying to us (TT 1899, 152–154), our natures would thereby be made less rich, less diverse, less strenuous and less emotional. And this, James would argue, is precisely the difference between the pluralistic and monistic theses.

Here, again, James touches on deep concerns that can be raised against Hegel's position from an internal perspective. In particular: does Hegel offer a final and complete vision of a rationally ordered world, from which all agency and further progress is ultimately removed at the "end of history" or from the "absolute standpoint"? Or does Hegel allow that the world remains open-ended, and that human agents are always required to contribute in a significant manner? And, if he does not allow for this practical element, is it correct to say that the ideal of contemplation only satisfies part of our natures, albeit a significant part? It is certainly the case that Hegel's rationalism is far from one-sided, that his picture of the human good is much broader than many philosophers, and that it aims to bring in several of the pluralistic elements which can also be found in James. It is also clear that there are dangers for James if he embraces a more extreme pluralism, in which dualisms and incommensurable clashes might put pressure on his claim to have shared with the idealist the pursuit of a coherent view of the universe. If such issues are not to be fully settled here, the hope is that at the very least, this discussion has shown that James's contribution to debates concerning Hegelianism are both more insightful and also more closely connected to Hegel's own project than has been previously appreciated.

Conclusion

We have argued that despite James's own frequent presentation of his and Hegel's positions as diametrically opposed, James in actual fact argues from what he understands as a project which he and the idealists share: that of finding the world to be a rational place, or of finding ourselves "at home" in the world. We have shown that James appreciates much of the empirical and dynamic side of Hegel's philosophy, and sees it as similar to his own in many respects. But through his career-long engagement with Hegel, James examines what it *is* to find the world rational, and finds Hegel's account lacking. Whereas Hegel sees our aim as comprehending the universe as a rational whole,

James argues that for creatures like us, such a world would be profoundly alienating. James's contrary vision is of a world which is, in part, still in the making, and in which there is room for our practical needs to be exercised. As such, James offers a unique and internal criticism of the Hegelian position which, at the very least, deserves more serious engagement than it has often received.[28]

Notes

1. This "new" Hegel is to be found in the work of Robert Pippin, Terry Pinkard, Robert Brandom, and many others, and may be said to constitute the current orthodoxy—which, of course, does not mean it is without critics.
2. This sense of dissatisfaction might explain the relatively small number of published studies on the Hegel–James relationship. Of this small number, the following are the most notable: Wilkins (1956), Reeve (1970), Cook (1977), Morse (2005), and Schultz (2015). There is also a brief but useful discussion of James's response to Hegel in Kaag and Jensen (2017).
3. In one letter to George W. Howison in 1893, James complains that—though he agrees with some aspects of Hegel's vision—he "can't follow Hegel in any of his applications of detail" and that "his *manner* is pure literary deformity" (quoted in Perry 1935 I, 774; CWJ 7.466). And as late as 1909, James is still complaining about the "intolerable ambiguity, verbosity, and unscrupulousness of [Hegel's] way of deducing things" (PU 1909, 52).
4. In *A Pluralistic Universe*, James goes so far as to claim that "I do not [. . .] take Hegel's technical apparatus seriously at all," aiming instead to focus on "the generalized vision, and feel the authority of the abstract scheme" (PU 1909, 51–53).
5. In a letter to Josiah Royce in 1880, for instance, James claims that he has a growing "prejudice against all Hegelians, except Hegel himself" (quoted in Perry 1935 I, 787; CWJ 5.85).
6. This translation is taken from William Wallace's 1873 Oxford University Press edition, a copy of which James owned and annotated (Hegel 1873/1975: §194 Addition 1, 261; cf. PU 1909, 166, editors' notes, where the date of the edition is wrongly given as 1874). The translation is not quite accurate, however, and the "home" metaphor is not there in German; but Hegel expresses himself this way elsewhere, for example: "'I' is at home in the world when it knows it, and even more so when it has comprehended it" (Hegel 1991, §4 Addition, 36).
7. Henry Norman Gardiner to James, 1909 (CWJ 12.322).
8. As Burleigh Taylor Wilkins puts it, "in time James came to treat Hegel more as a philosopher than as a protagonist in a street brawl" (Wilkins 1956, 339).
9. David C. Lamberth is one interpreter who places James's notion of "intimacy" as central to his philosophical project. See Lamberth (1997) and (1999), especially Chapter 4.
10. James O. Pawelski, in contrast to this interpretation, contends that James argues against "every step" of this argument for the necessity of the absolute, including this first one (2007, 85).
11. Morse points out that James was actually quite prescient in this interpretation: "in light of more recent Hegel research that has managed to be quite fair to Hegel's position, James himself initially exhibits a remarkably accurate sense of Hegel's basic standpoint" (Morse 2005, 200).
12. James calls this the difference between a "concatenated" unity and a total, or "through-and-through," type of unity (ERE 1905, 52).

13. A more accurate translation is given in Hegel (2010, 179): "To be sure, the concept and, further, the idea are self-identical, but only insofar as they contain the difference in themselves at the same time."
14. See Slater (2014) for a more detailed analysis of James's criticism of Royce and the other Anglophone idealists.
15. Cf. Hegel (1873/1975 §51, 85).
16. Hegel (1969, 154–155). For an equivalent passage in Hegel (2010, see §95, 152): "Thus, too, finitude is at first determined in terms of reality. But the truth of the finite is rather its *ideality*... This ideality of the finite is the chief proposition of philosophy, and every true philosophy is for that reason *idealism*."
17. For more on this reading of Hegel's Idealism, see Stern (2009, 45–76).
18. Cf. Hegel (2010, §161, 234).
19. See, for instance, James's discussion of the problems of Gnosticism and Romanticism in "Dilemma of Determinism" (WB 1897, 128–132).
20. Hegel (2010, §5, 32).
21. Cf. Hegel (2009, 122).
22. For more on these issues in Hegel, see Stern (2009), particularly the chapters on "Hegel, British Idealism, and the Curious Case of the Concrete Universal" and "Individual Existence and the Philosophy of Difference."
23. E.g. James (PU 1909, 96–97): "Reality, life, experience, concreteness, immediacy, use what word you will, exceeds our logic, overflows and surrounds it ... I prefer bluntly to call reality if not irrational then at least non-rational in its constitution."
24. Hegel (2010, §45 Addition, 90).
25. Though monistic idealism might satisfy a select few philosophers, it is because of the narrowness of idealism's vision that it will at best be "the creed of some partial sect," as we have seen earlier. Ignoring as it does several important aspects of our collective human experience, monistic idealism is unstable, and will always be challenged by someone with a richer perspective. As James puts it, "[s]omeone," eventually, "will be sure to discover the flaw" (WB 1897, 100).
26. For classic discussions of this issue, see Henrich (1959) and Burbidge (1980).
27. Cf. Hegel's quotation from Aristotle's *Metaphysics* XII, 7, with which the entire *Encyclopedia* system concludes, where central to the passage Hegel quotes is Aristotle's suggestion that "contemplation is what is most pleasant and best" and that "God is always in that good state which we sometimes are" (1072b, 24–26).
28. Previous drafts of this chapter were given at conferences on "Rethinking Modern Philosophy" (Sheffield), "Idealism and Pragmatism" (Paris), and at the Second European Pragmatism Conference (Paris); we are grateful to members of the audiences who responded on those occasions. We are particularly grateful to Alexander Klein for his very helpful comments as editor of this collection.

Bibliography

Burbidge, John. 1980. "The Necessity of Contingency." In *Art and Logic in Hegel's Philosophy*, edited by Warren E. Steinkraus and Kenneth I. Schmidtz, 201–218. Atlantic Highlands, NJ: Humanities Press.

Cook, David J. 1977. "James's 'Ether Mysticism' and Hegel." *Journal of the History of Philosophy* 15: 309–319.

Hegel, G. W. F. 1873/1975. *Hegel's Logic: Part One of the "Encyclopaedia of the Philosophical Sciences" (1830)*, translated by William Wallace. Oxford: Oxford University Press; 1st ed. 1873, 3rd ed., 1975, page references are given to the 3rd ed.

Hegel, G. W. F. 1969. *Science of Logic*, translated by A. V. Miller. London: George Allen & Unwin.

Hegel, G. W. F. 1991. *Elements of the Philosophy of Right*, translated by H. B. Nisbet. Cambridge: Cambridge University Press.

Hegel, G. W. F. 2009. *Lectures on the History of Modern Philosophy 1825–6, Volume III: Medieval and Modern Philosophy*, edited by Robert F. Brown, translated by R. F. Brown and J. M. Stewart. Oxford: Oxford University Press.

Hegel, G. W. F. 2010. *Encyclopedia of the Philosophical Sciences in Basic Outline: Part 1: Science of Logic*, translated by Klaus Brinkmann and Daniel O. Dahlstrom. Cambridge: Cambridge University Press.

Henrich, Dieter. 1959. "Hegels Theorie über den Zufall," *Kant-Studien* 50: 131–148; reprinted in his 1971 *Hegel im Kontext* (Frankfurt: Suhrkamp, 1975), 157–186.

Kaag, John, and Kipton E. Jensen. 2017. "The American Reception of Hegel (1830–1930)." In *The Oxford Handbook to Hegel*, edited by Dean Moyar, 670–696. Oxford: Oxford University Press.

Lamberth, David C. 1997. "Interpreting the Universe after a Social Analogy: Intimacy, Panpsychism, and a Finite God in a Pluralistic Universe." In *The Cambridge Companion to William James*, edited by Ruth Anna Putnam, 237–259. Cambridge: Cambridge University Press.

Lamberth, David C. 1999. *William James and the Metaphysics of Experience*. New York: Cambridge University Press.

Morse, Don. 2005. "William James's Neglected Critique of Hegel." *Idealistic Studies* 35: 199–214.

Pawelski, James O. 2007. *The Dynamic Individualism of William James*. Albany: State University of New York Press.

Perry, Ralph Barton, and William James. 1935. *The Thought and Character of William James, Volume I: Inheritance and Vocation*. 2 vols. London: Oxford University Press.

Reeve, G. E. 1970. "William James on Pure Being and Pure Nothing." *Philosophy* 45: 59–60.

Schultz, Lucy Christine. 2015. "Pluralism and Dialectic: On James's Relation to Hegel." *Hegel Bulletin* 36: 202–224.

Slater, Michael R. 2014. "James's Critique of Absolute Idealism in *A Pluralistic Universe*." In *William James and the Transatlantic Conversation: Pragmatism, Pluralism and Philosophy of Religion*, edited by Martin Halliwell and Joel D. S. Rasmussen, 167–182. Oxford: Oxford University Press.

Stern, Robert. 2009. *Hegelian Metaphysics*. Oxford: Oxford University Press.

Wilkins, Burleigh Taylor. 1956. "James, Dewey, and Hegelian Idealism." *Journal of the History of Ideas* 17: 332–346.

CHAPTER 23

JAMES AND EMERSON

On the Pragmatic Use of Terms

RUSSELL B. GOODMAN

Introduction

In the second chapter of *Pragmatism*, "What Pragmatism Means," William James writes that such traditional metaphysical terms as 'God, Matter, Reason, Energy, and the Absolute' are not—as those who wield them often contend—the final answer to some metaphysical, physical, moral, or religious question. "[I]f you follow the pragmatic method," James writes, "you cannot look on any such word as closing your quest. You must bring out of each word its practical cash-value, set it at work within the stream of your experience. It appears less as a solution, then, than as a program for more work, and more particularly as an indication of the ways in which existing realities may be *changed*" (P 1907, 31–32). James applies the pragmatic method in this sense to his own terms, setting them to work, seeing what can be done with them, in the course of his (and our) philosophical experience. The term *pragmatism* itself, and terms such as *tough* and *tender minded*, the *once* and *twice born*, *pluralism*, *radical empiricism*, and so on, are best understood as programs for work rather than as lasting answers to some philosophical issue or as elements in a final system. These terms cohere with one another to some degree—after all, they are products of that unique philosopher William James—but their work is often local or regional, in that James is more interested in what they can do in confronting a certain problem, conceptualizing a certain subject, than in how they all fit together.

Consider the history of two of James's most important terms, *pragmatism* and *radical empiricism*. In *Pragmatism*, James states that "there is no logical connection between pragmatism, as I understand it, and a doctrine which I have recently set forth as 'radical empiricism.' The latter stands on its own feet. One may entirely reject it and still be a pragmatist" (P 1907, 6). Two years later, in the Preface to *The Meaning of Truth* (1909), he finds that "the establishment of the pragmatist theory of truth is a step of first-rate importance in making radical empiricism prevail" (MT 6). Radical empiricism, he now explains, is based on the "fact" that relations, including the truth relation, are matters of "direct particular experience." The pragmatic theory of truth supports this claim by offering experiential accounts of the truth relation (see Gale 1999, 155). James's work with his own terms takes on a life of its own, leading sometimes to connections that he had not foreseen, at other times taking him to areas of investigation that "have nothing to do with one another" (ERE 1904, 24).

James's pragmatist understanding of terminology is entwined with his pluralist understanding of terms, philosophies, and the universe itself. The universe is "largely chaotic," James writes in "A World of Pure Experience" (1904), and "[n]o one single type of connection runs through all the experiences that compose it." It is, he continues,

> like one of those dried human heads with which the Dyaks of Borneo deck their lodges. The skull forms a solid nucleus; but innumerable feathers, leaves, strings, beads, and loose appendices of every description float and dangle from it, and save that they terminate in it, seem to have nothing to do with one another. Even so my experiences and yours float and dangle, terminating, it is true, in a nucleus of common perception, but for the most part out of sight and irrelevant and unimaginable to one another. (ERE 1904, 24)

So it sometimes seems with James's philosophy. There is no one common thread, but it does hang together in various ways.[1]

In *Pragmatism*, James explains the unity of a philosopher's thought by its grounding in an individual personality. We labor to master the details of philosophical systems, he points out, but:

> when the labor is accomplished, the mind always performs its big summarizing act, and the system forthwith stands over against one like a living thing, with that strange simple note of individuality which haunts our memory, like the wraith of the man, when a friend or enemy is dead.... Our sense of an essential personal flavor in each one of them, typical but indescribable, is the finest fruit of our own accomplished philosophic education. (P 1907, 24)

This passage and the previous one about the Dyak heads are about coherence, how things fit together, but the Dyak metaphor is also about how things fit only partially, imperfectly, or not at all; how they are foreign to one another, separate, unknown, uninvolved. James thinks of his radical empiricism as "fair to both the unity and the disconnection" of the universe. In this chapter, I want to consider James's pragmatic use of language from some perspectives offered by a writer who also tried to be fair to the unity and the disconnection of the universe, who anticipates James's pragmatism, and whose thought is part of James's intellectual formation. This is Ralph Waldo Emerson, a friend of James's father, Henry James Sr., who was introduced to the infant William James in his first year, 1842, when Emerson was thirty-nine.

James and Emerson

I have written about James and Emerson elsewhere (Goodman 2008; Goodman 2015, 234–243), so will say only a few words here about the deep connections between them. The special place Emerson had in the James household is indicated by a letter the elder James sent Emerson in 1870, when William was twenty-eight, a recent graduate of the Harvard Medical School who suffered from depression and was studying the works of the philosopher Charles Renouvier (Kuklick 1987, 1328). The senior James wrote:

> My dear Emerson,—
> Many thanks for *Society and Solitude*, of which I have read several chapters with hearty liking. But unfortunately just before the new volume arrived we had got a handsomely bound copy of the new edition of the old essays, and I had been reading them aloud in the evening to Mama and Willy and Alice with such delectation on all sides, that it was vain to attempt renewing the experience.

Later in life, "Willy" owned multiple editions of Emerson's writings, the first two volumes of which (including *Nature*, the early addresses, and *Essays, First Series*) are dated 1871 in his hand. He eventually underlined these and the other volumes in the series in pencil, pen, and blue pencil, and constructed indices of topics, notes, and quotations in the volumes (Carpenter 1939, 42; Kovalainen 2010, 118–123).

Emerson shows up from time to time in James's published works, including *The Principles of Psychology* (1890), where in his chapter on "The Perception of Reality" James considers the way moral and religious truths:

> come "home" to us far more on some occasions than on others. As Emerson says, "There is a difference between one and another hour of life, in their authority and subsequent effect. Our faith comes in moments. . . . Yet there is a depth in those brief moments which constrains us to ascribe more reality to them than to all other experiences." (PP 1890, 935)

James is quoting from "The Over-Soul" (CW 2:159). The experiences Emerson has in mind, the authority which they seem to have, and the effects which they clearly do have are the subjects of James's second great psychology book, *The Varieties of Religious Experience: A Study of Human Nature* (1902). Emerson's "depth in those brief moments" becomes, in *Varieties*, the "noetic quality" and "transiency" of mystical experience.

Many commentators have found a "pragmatic," "humanist," or "Promethean" streak in Emerson.[2] James was the first of these, as is evident from the index he constructed under the term *pragmatism* in his copy of Emerson's works. He included such statements as: "An action is the perfection and publication of thought" (from the "Discipline" chapter of *Nature*; CW 1:28); and "Colleges and books only copy the language which the field and work-yard made" (from "The American Scholar"; CW 1:61). In the following sections, we shall explore some other ways in which Emerson anticipates James's conception of pragmatism, emphasizing his idea of pragmatism as a kind of temperament.

James read Emerson intensively in the years before he published *Pragmatism*, as he prepared for the address he gave at the Emerson centenary celebrations in 1903. We know from his index entries on pragmatism and other topics (e.g., "idealism," "against my philosophy") that he was using Emerson as a sounding board for his own ideas. In his address, he praises Emerson's ability to register not only the higher domains of existence but "the full squalor of the individual fact," something he was to attempt four years later in *Pragmatism*. Moreover, he was inspired by Emerson, as he wrote to his brother Henry James Jr. some weeks before delivering the address:

> The reading of the divine Emerson, volume after volume, has done me a lot of good, and, strange to say has thrown a strong practical light on my own path. The incorruptible way in which he followed his own vocation, of seeing such truths as the Universal Soul vouchsafed to him from day to day and month to month . . . seems to me a moral lesson to all men who have any genius, however small, to foster. I see now with absolute clearness, that greatly as I have been helped & enlarged by my University business hitherto, the time has come when the remnant of my life must be passed in a different manner, contemplatively namely, and with leisure and simplification for the one main thing, which is to report in one book, at least, such impression as my own intellect has received from the Universe. (CWJ 1903, 3: 234)

Four years later, James published *Pragmatism*, a reasonable candidate for such a book (see Girel 2004).

The Pragmatic Temperament

A year after *Pragmatism* appeared, Arthur Lovejoy published a critique in which he distinguished thirteen pragmatisms (Lovejoy 1908a, b), and one finds at least six of them in James's book: pragmatism as (1) a temperament, (2) a method for resolving philosophical disputes, (3) a theory of meaning or significance, (4) a theory of truth, (5) a theory of knowledge ("humanism"), and (6) a metaphysics (a universe "still in the making"). Contemporary treatments of pragmatism focus on (3), (4), and (5), but I will be concentrating on the first of these, the pragmatic temperament, a main subject of *Pragmatism*'s first chapter, "The Present Dilemma in Philosophy."[3]

James was always a psychologist as he was always a philosopher. His first great book, *The Principles of Psychology*, announces that it is a scientific work of physiology and introspection, yet currents of philosophy penetrate its discussions. *The Varieties of Religious Experience* announces that it is a book of psychology ("A Study in Human Nature" is its subtitle), but contains a chapter called "Philosophy" that discusses pragmatism near the end and has bursts of philosophical speculation throughout. It sometimes seems that James's subjects are like the pails and buckets of his chapter on "The Stream of Thought," which capture only part of the stream, missing the free-flowing waters between. James's philosophy operates as much in the buckets of his concepts as in the less-articulated waters of his thought and life.

In the first chapter of *Pragmatism*, officially a book of philosophy, James writes:

> Not only Walt Whitman could write "who touches this book touches a man." The books of all the great philosophers are like so many men. Our sense of an essential personal flavor in each one of them, typical but indescribable, is the finest fruit of our own accomplished philosophic education. What the system pretends to be is a picture of the great universe of God. What it is—and oh so flagrantly!—is the revelation of how intensely odd the personal flavor of some fellow creature is. (P 1907, 24)

The personal flavor of a great philosopher may be indescribable, but James presents his scheme of the *tough-* and *tender-minded* in this first chapter as a way of placing himself—the mediating, "happy-go-lucky" (P 1907, 124) pragmatist—within the broad range of philosophical possibilities. In this way, the book records "such impression as my own intellect has received from the Universe."

James introduces the terms *tough-* and *tender-minded* at the head of two lists:

THE TENDER-MINDED
Rationalistic (going by 'principles'),
Intellectualistic,
Idealistic,
Optimistic,
Religious,
Free-willist,
Monistic,
Dogmatical
THE TOUGH-MINDED
Empiricistic (going by 'facts'),
Sensationalistic,
Materialistic,
Pessimistic,
Irreligious,
Fatalistic,Pluralistic,
Sceptical (P 1907, 13).

These lists, versions of what philosophers call rationalism and empiricism, are a guide to tendencies within James himself as well as in philosophy more broadly. James is generally optimistic, for example, although he is critical of those who acknowledge no suffering or evil in the universe. He is religious, but with a strong empirical and non-dogmatical approach, and he is "free-willist" in ways that we shall explore later. As for his tough-minded side, James likes to go by facts (his university training was in chemistry and medicine), he is sensationalistic (but revises our notion of what experience is), pluralistic (see Goodman 2012), and skeptical (e.g., about the claims of religion, philosophy, and even science).

James proposes pragmatism as a philosophical resolution of the dilemma these lists present, but he gives that resolution a distinctly psychological and temperamental cast:

"Most of us," he writes, "have a hankering for the good things on both sides of the line" (P 1907, 14), but we do not know how to combine them more or less harmoniously and prosperously. Pragmatism, he maintains, will "combine . . . the scientific loyalty to facts and willingness to take account of them, the spirit of adaptation and accommodation, in short, but also the old confidence in human values and the resultant spontaneity, whether of the religious or of the romantic type" (P 1907, 17). It is not evident at this point what James means by "human values," nor by "the resultant spontaneity," but he amplifies his account in the concluding chapter of his book, "Pragmatism and Religion," to which we shall turn in the final section of this chapter.

For some types of thinkers, lists like those James presents would be the foundation of a general system, or a device for placing historical figures like Plato and Aristotle, Hobbes and Kant, within one general scheme. Not for James. He never uses these lists again, and rarely employs the terms *tough-* and *tender- minded* later in the book, and hardly again in any other work. They do their work in the first chapter of *Pragmatism* by introducing pragmatism and philosophy more generally as a temperamental matter,[4] and especially in the book's final chapter by conceiving of the pragmatist as responding to a "present dilemma in philosophy" in which empirical philosophy "is not religious enough," and "religious philosophy . . . is not empirical enough" (P 1907, 15).

Emersonian Schemes

I turn now to some anticipations of James's scheme of the tough- and tender-minded in two of Emerson's essays, "Nominalist and Realist" and "Montaigne, or the Skeptic." An essay is literally a trial, and Emerson tries things out in short pieces, many of which have their own set of key terms: *scholar* (in "The American Scholar,") *self-reliance, circles, the poet, East and West*, and *Unity and Variety* (in "Plato"), and so on. His terms do their work in an essay, sometimes reappear briefly or in another guise in another essay, but are often left behind as Emerson passes to another topic. One of Emerson's most ambitious and effective schemes is that of "the Lords of Life" in "Experience" (including *Temperament, Succession, Surprise, Use, Reality* and *Illusion*), but they never appear again. They do their work in the multi-perspectival account of human life that Emerson develops in the essay, but he renounces any claim for their finality or completeness. Indeed, he provides a different list of these fundamental categories at the beginning and end of the essay and proclaims: "I name them as I find them in my way. I know better than to claim any completeness for my picture. I am a fragment, and this is a fragment of me. . . . I am too young yet by some ages to compile a code. I gossip for my hour concerning the eternal politics" (CW 3:47).

"Nominalist and Realist" is the final essay in the *Essays, Second Series* (1844), and it presents another of Emerson's provisional schemes, this time, like James's tough- and tender- minded, as the opposition between temperaments. Emerson begins with the case for the realist, and assumes an attitude of careful assessment toward the essay's center: "In the famous dispute with the Nominalists, the Realists had a good deal of reason. General ideas are essences. They are our gods: they round and ennoble the most partial and sordid way of living. Our proclivity to details cannot quite degrade our life, and divest it of poetry" (CW 3:136). But there is a skeptical note here (and throughout the essay). The image of enobling and rounding out the sordid details suggests that the details, not the rounding, are real. If the realists "had a good deal of reason," they are not fully convincing.

As the essay continues, Emerson—a writer of various moods—warms to the realist idea of unity, in this case the idea of one central person. He writes:

> I am very much struck in literature by the appearance, that one person wrote all the books; as if the editor of a journal planted his body of reporters in different parts of the field of action, and relieved some by others from time to time; but there is such equality and identity both of judgment and point of view in the narrative, that it is plainly the work of one all-seeing, all-hearing gentleman. I looked into Pope's Odyssey yesterday: it is as correct and elegant after our canon of today, as if it were newly written. The modernness of all good books seems to give me an existence as wide as man. What is well done, I feel as if I did; what is ill-done, I reck not of. (CW 3:137)

Applying James's terminology to this statement, we can say that it is "tender-minded" in its monism ("one person,"), optimism (the possibility of "an existence as wide as man"), and rationalism ("equality and identity . . . of judgment").

But now comes the second part of "Nominalist and Realist." Departing from the buoyant monism of the realist, Emerson leaves a break in the printed text and begins a new, nominalist section:

> Thus we settle it in our cool libraries that . . . life will be simpler when we live at the centre, and flout the surfaces. . . . But . . . [n]ature will not be Buddhist: she resents generalizing, and insults the philosopher in every moment with a million of fresh particulars. It is all idle talking: as much as a man is a whole, so is he also a part; and it were partial not to see it. . . . You have not got rid of parts by denying them, but are the more partial. You are one thing, but nature is *one thing and the other thing*, in the same moment. (CW 3: 138–139)

Emerson didn't know much about Buddhism (though he read and used many Hindu texts),[5] but what he means in saying that nature will not be Buddhist is clear enough: the general principles, laws, and unity that the realist discerns are only part of the story about nature.

We do not "live by general views," Emerson's nominalist observes, and nature "loves better a wheelwright who dreams all night of wheels, and a groom who is part of his horse" than "universal geniuses" who get nothing done (CW 3:139). Like James's pragmatist, the Emersonian nominalist is a person of work, power, and originality:

> Why have only two or three ways of life, and not thousands? We want the great genius only for joy; for one star more in our constellation, for one tree more in our grove. . . . I think I have done well, if I have acquired a new word from a good author; and my business with him is to find my own, though it were only to melt him down into an epithet or an image for daily use. (CW 3:141)

The wise nominalist does not disparage the universal genius, but puts the genius to "daily use"; not only as an inspiration or guide, but as a check on the tyranny of other geniuses: "Each man, too, is a tyrant in tendency, because he would impose his idea on others.... Jesus would absorb the race; but Tom Paine or the coarsest blasphemer helps humanity by resisting this exuberance of power" (CW 3:140–141). One genius helps us to be skeptical of others, and none of them replaces our own original actions.

Emerson is attracted to both nominalism and realism, but neither satisfies him, and he can't seem to find a stable, acceptable middle ground. Rather, his essay dramatizes what he calls (in "Experience") "contrary tendencies" (CW 3:36) that cannot be blended or accommodated one to the other. Each position, he laments, "denies and tends to abolish the other. We must reconcile the contradictions as we can, but their discord and their concord introduce wild absurdities into our thinking and speech. No sentence will hold the whole truth, and the only way in which we can be just, is by giving ourselves the lie.... I am always insincere, as always knowing there are other moods" (CW 3:143–145).

Emerson's essay ends (and thus the *Essays, Second Series* concludes) with a departure from the dialectic of the essay:

> I talked yesterday with a pair of philosophers: I endeavored to show my good men that I love everything by turns.... Could they but once understand, that I loved to know that they existed... yet, out of my poverty of life and thought, had no word or welcome for them when they came to see me, and could well consent to their living in Oregon, for any claim I felt on them, it would be a great satisfaction. (CW 3:145)

There are many ways to take this final paragraph. Perhaps yesterday the writer spoke with the philosophers, but today he is off doing something else. Or perhaps it is a philosophical statement or speech act, about the impossibility of resolving the dispute. Or again, Emerson may find two particular philosophers or philosophical types, perhaps the nominalist and realist portrayed in the essay, to be uninstructive at this time, although there might be other philosophers or other times for philosophy.

Although Emerson walks away from the two philosophers, he does so at the end of an essay that is for the most part devoted to philosophy, in which he maintains—much as his reader William James does about the tough- and tender-minded—that we are a mixture of both sets of characteristics. "We are amphibious creatures," Emerson states, "weaponed for two elements, having two sets of faculties, the particular and the catholic" (CW 3:135).

Emerson's nominalist, like James's tough-minded philosopher, embraces facts, experience, the material world (where the wheelwright works), and the pluralism of millions of particulars. The nominalist is skeptical in various registers, from the genial assessment of the best that life has to offer ("let us see the parts wisely"), to the disoriented buffeting by moods and shifting points of view that characterizes the essay's ending. But the nominalist lacks the appreciation of connections or unity and, if not irreligious, is not explicitly religious. Yet in the idea that "we want the genius only for joy; for one star more in our constellation," we find something James might have called "romantic spontaneity" (P 1907, 15), something that, as we will see in the final section, has a place in what James calls "pluralistic religion."

"Montaigne, or the Skeptic" was published six years after "Nominalist and Realist" in *Representative Men* (1850), along with essays on Plato, Shakespeare, Swedenborg, Goethe, and Napoleon. The essay's two-sided scheme of philosophical personalities, which Emerson at times calls the "abstractionist" and the "materialist," resembles the earlier scheme of realist and nominalist, but there is now a hero of the essay, in the person of Montaigne, and the essay's dialectical scheme is used to place him in the history of philosophy, specifically the history of skepticism. Although the skeptic achieves a more or less stable blend of the two sides, Emerson abandons the skeptic at the end of his essay—just as he had abandoned the two philosophers of "Nominalist and Realist." This time, he states his reasons, which are basically mystical, religious, or—in James's terms—tender-minded.

"Montaigne" begins by describing the "two faces" or "two sides" of nature. One face consists of "facts," "sensation," the "relative," and the "finite"; the other of "design," "morals," the "infinite," the "absolute," and "abstractions." The first list is more nominalist and tough minded, the second more realist and tender-minded. Emerson emphasizes that his list of characteristics is initial and open ended: it includes the terms he mentions, he maintains, "and many fine names beside" (CW 4:85).

Passing to psychology and epistemology, Emerson holds that each of us has "a predisposition to one or the other" of these faces. One class of people "has the perception of Difference, and is conversant with facts and surfaces, cities and persons, and the bringing certain things to pass;—the men of talent and action. Another class have the perception of Identity, and are men of faith and philosophy, men of genius" (CW 4:85).

Emerson is dissatisfied with both. The genius, he writes, will "undervalue the actual object" (CW 4:86) even as she beholds a grand design. And there are degraded forms of genius, found especially in the "studious class." These "abstractionists . . . spend their days and nights in dreaming some dream; in expecting the homage of society to some precious scheme, built on a truth, but destitute of proportion in its presentment, of justness in its application, and of all energy of will in the schemer to embody and vitalize it" (CW 4:88–89). The abstractionists are ineffective. They lack will, power, engagement with the world.

While the abstractionists are lost in creative thought about the universal, the other face of nature appears to "the men of practical power," the materialists. Each has contempt for, and little understanding of, the other:

> The trade in our streets believes in no metaphysical causes, thinks nothing of the force which necessitated traders and a trading planet to exist; no, but sticks to cotton, sugar, wool, and salt. . . . To the men of this world, to the animal strength and spirits, to the men of practical power, whilst immersed in it, the man of ideas appears out of his reason. They alone have reason. (CW 4:86)

Yet when not consumed by the allure of practical power, these "men of the world" find there is nothing to sustain them. "The inconvenience of this way of thinking," as Emerson drily puts it, "is that it runs into indifferentism, and then into disgust" (CW 4:87).

The stage is thus set for the entrance of the skeptic, who stills the conflict and satisfies the legitimate demands of both parties: "The abstractionist and the materialist thus mutually exasperating each other, and the scoffer expressing the worst of materialism, there arises a third party to occupy the middle ground between these two, the skeptic, namely. He finds both wrong by being in extremes" (CW 4:88).

The "wise skepticism" Emerson endorses and finds in Montaigne is not that of "universal denying or universal doubt" but of finding that "there is much to say on all sides." Like ancient skepticism, it is a way of life. Emerson's skeptic is cautious and pragmatic: "we ought to secure those advantages which we can command, and not risk them by clutching after the airy and unattainable" (CW 4:90). The skeptic is "the Considerer, the prudent, taking in sail, counting stock, husbanding his means, believing . . . that we cannot give ourselves too many advantages in this unequal conflict, with powers so vast and unweariable ranged on one side, and this little conceited vulnerable popinjay that a man is, bobbing up and down into every danger, on the other (CW 4:91).

Emerson praises Montaigne's rootedness and earthiness, though even as he does so he suggests some criticism. Montaigne "keeps the plain; he rarely mounts or sinks; likes to feel solid ground, and the stones underneath. His writing has no enthusiasms, no aspiration; contented, self-respecting, and keeping the middle of the road" (CW 4:95-96). Emerson himself, in contrast, is a philosopher of aspiration and enthusiasm who writes in "Circles" that "nothing great is achieved without enthusiasm," and states: "The simplest words,—we do not know what they mean except when we love and aspire" (CW 2:189). To say that the skeptic has no enthusiasms or aspiration is to say that he lacks something that is central to Emerson's philosophical project.

Emerson turns from Montaigne for a reason that would also have weight with James: the absence of the religious in Montaigne's synthesis.[6] The skepticism of Montaigne, Emerson holds, is "a domain of equilibration" that every "superior mind" must pass through and avail itself of, but it is not a "permanent expression of the human mind." There is, he now writes, a "final solution in which Skepticism is lost," and which escapes the play of moods. His term for this solution, "the moral sentiment," is one he had used thirteen years earlier in "The Divinity School Address" (1837) to describe the origins of the world's religions in religious experience. In deploying this term at the end of "Montaigne," Emerson jumps out of his own dialectic, however satisfactorily he might have seemed to control or work within it. He writes:

> The final solution in which Skepticism is lost, is in the moral sentiment, which never forfeits its supremacy. All moods may be safely tried, and their weight allowed to all objections: the moral sentiment as easily outweighs them all, as any one. This is the drop which balances the sea. I play with the miscellany of facts, and take those superficial views which we call Skepticism; but I know that they will presently appear to me in that order which makes Skepticism impossible. A man of thought must feel the thought that is parent of the universe; that the masses of nature do undulate and flow. (CW 4:103)

Emerson here leaps to the side of what he had called the "realist" in "Nominalist and Realist," to something absolute, perhaps eternal, a concentrated drop that stands outside the play of sensation and mood.

Emerson's "thought that is parent of the universe" is tender-minded. As thought, it is "intellectualistic," and it is monistic (it's not one of *several* parents of the universe). But it is not "abstract," since it is a matter of feeling and experience. And it is not static, like the monist "One" that James rejects, but rather flowing, undulating. We are in the realm here of what James calls mysticism in *The Varieties of Religious Experience*, more than in that of any religious creed or dogma. Although Emerson does not see it this way, there is material here for a religious element in a pragmatist synthesis.

Pragmatism and Religion

Although the epistemological and semantic aspects of *Pragmatism* have provoked much of the contemporary interest in the book, James's concern in the first and the last chapters is at least as strongly with religion, though not with any set of religious doctrines or texts. Reading James with Emerson in mind highlights these concerns, and raises the question of how James manages to include something one might want to call religion in his pragmatist picture. Does James reconcile the religious with the empirical, developing a version of pragmatism that will "remain religious like the rationalisms, but at the same time, like the empiricisms, . . . preserve the richest intimacy with facts" (P 1907, 23)? Or does he abandon the project as impossible or inadvisable? And what does he mean by, or include within, religion? A close look at *Pragmatism*'s last chapter, "Pragmatism and Religion," will shed light on these questions.

James opens the chapter with his characteristic accommodating, inclusive attitude. He is open to the reality of what he calls "universal conceptions," which "as things to take account of, may be as real for pragmatism as particular sensations are" (P 1907, 131). He also tries to be fair to "monism." It plays a positive role in the lives of many people, he points out, who believe that you are "safe" no matter what happens to you and that you can learn to "*lie* back, on your true principle of being." James's acceptance of this way of life is tinged with his report of some harsh criticisms. He writes of tender-minded monism: "This is the famous way of quietism, of indifferentism. Its enemies compare it to a spiritual opium. Yet pragmatism must respect this way, for it has massive historical vindication" (P 1907, 133). The vindication is historical, but perhaps not metaphysical.

Later in the chapter, James's critique is more direct, as he accuses the monist of lacking the appetite and courage for the challenges of life: "Nirvana means safety from this everlasting round of adventures of which the world of sense consists. The hindoo and the buddhist, for this is essentially their attitude, are simply afraid, afraid of more experience, afraid of life" (P 1907, 140).[7] James concedes that we all have moments or periods in which "our own life breaks down, and we . . . want a universe where we can just give up, fall on our father's neck, and be absorbed into the absolute life as a drop of water melts into the river or the sea" (P 1907, 140). But the monists believe these moments constitute our essential relation to the universe.

James defends a pluralistic form of religion that finds "salvation" not in the static One of the monists,[8] but in "your better possibilities phenomenally taken, or the specific redemptive effects even of your failures, upon yourself or others." This "pluralistic way" of understanding religion, James writes, "agrees with the pragmatic temper best, for it immediately suggests an infinitely larger number of the details of future experience to our mind. It sets definite activities in us at work" (P 1907, 133).

Pluralism suggests a larger number of details to us because possibility is greater than actuality or necessity. For monism, James states, *must* and *shall be* are the key terms, whereas for pluralism, what *may be* is essential. "The world," James writes, "*may be saved*" (P 1907, 135), and "some of the conditions" of that salvation "actually are here" (P 1907, 136). Every ideal realized, he continues, will be "one moment in the world's salvation" (P 1907, 137). Here we have a portrayal of James's open universe, an example of pragmatism as a metaphysical position.

James finds monism respectable because of the important role it plays in human life, but pluralistic religion is grounded in the nature of the universe in a deeper way, James thinks, because of the creative role it allots to our actions in the face of the universe's possibilities. Our ideals, James holds, are more than "bare abstract possibilities." They are

> grounded, they are *live* possibilities, for we are their live champions and pledges, and if the complementary conditions come and add themselves, our ideals will become actual things. What now are the complementary conditions? They are first such a mixture of things as will in the fulness of time give us a chance, a gap that we can spring into, and, finally, *our act*. (P 1907, 137–138)

James insists that what he calls "*our act*" creates something not merely within human life, but within the world. Our acts, he asserts, are "growing-places . . . of the world" and they achieve a pluralistic, humanistic, romantic, form of salvation. James writes:

> Does our act then *create* the world's salvation so far as it makes room for itself, so far as it leaps into the gap? Does it create, not the whole world's salvation of course, but just so much of this as itself covers of the world's extent?
> Here I take the bull by the horns, and in spite of the whole crew of rationalists and monists, of whatever brand they be, I ask *why not?* Our acts, our turning-places, where we seem to ourselves to make ourselves and grow, are the parts of the world to which we are closest, the parts of which our knowledge is the most intimate and complete. Why should we not take them at their face-value? Why may they not be the actual turning-places and growing-places which they seem to be, of the world— why not the workshop of being, where we catch fact in the making, so that nowhere may the world grow in any other kind of way than this? (P 1907, 138)

This passage is as difficult as it is fascinating, but it seems to me one of the clear places in *Pragmatism* where James presents the "impression" that the universe makes on him, as he wrote to his brother Henry of wanting to do. James grants that monist religions make people feel good and make some lives better, while denying that they operate at the level of the "workshop of being" described by pluralistic pragmatic religion.

James sets forth a second feature of pluralist religion, though he doesn't quite realize it. We have so far discussed his conception of religion as a series of human *acts*, but at the very end of "Pragmatism and Religion" James conceives his pluralist religion as involving *levels of being* or *levels of consciousness*. Those forces that the pragmatist "trusts to cooperate with him" (P 1907, 143) include other people, James holds, but also "superhuman forces." James is thinking not about a unitary god, but of something in accord with what he calls "the original polytheism of mankind." He refers to his *Varieties of Religious Experience*,[9] describing it as "a book on men's religious experience, which on the whole has been regarded as making for the reality of God." Without going into any further detail about *Varieties*, James explains his own idea about the "superhuman" by an analogy with our relation to dogs and cats:

> I firmly disbelieve, myself, that our human experience is the highest form of experience extant in the universe. I believe rather that we stand in much the same relation to the whole of the universe as our canine and feline pets do to the whole of human life. They inhabit our drawing rooms and libraries. They take part in scenes of whose significance they have no inkling. They are merely tangent to curves of history the beginnings and ends and forms of which pass wholly beyond their ken. But, just as many of the dog's and cat's ideals coincide with our ideals, and the dogs and cats have daily living proof of the fact, so we may well believe, on the proofs that religious experience affords, that higher powers exist and are at work to save the world on ideal lines similar to our own. (P 1907, 143–144)

We taste here again the "peculiar flavor" of William James, and see another of the places in *Pragmatism* where he reports "such impression as my own intellect has received from the Universe."[10]

If we do not seem close to Emerson in James's idea of external, higher powers that assist us in our most authentic and creative acts, we are closer in James's idea that there *are* such acts, in particular times and places and for particular, ordinary people. In "Self-Reliance," Emerson advises us to accept "the place the divine Providence has found for you; the society of your contemporaries, the connexion of events." He gives this advice a proto-pragmatist flavor when he emphasizes not just the place but the "toil" each of us has as his or her portion in life: "though the wide universe is full of good, no kernel of nourishing corn can come to him but through his toil bestowed on that plot of ground which is given to him to till" (CW 2:28). James and Emerson both think we have work to do, and both seek a mediating position between tough and tender-minded philosophical temperaments. Emerson, a philosopher of moods and "contrary tendencies" (CW 3:36), finds a domain of equilibration in the skepticism of Montaigne, but no stable synthesis there, or anywhere else. James, also a writer of contrary tendencies and even a "divided self,"[11] conceives himself in *Pragmatism* as a philosopher who by deploying his scheme of the tough- and tender-minded shows the way to mediate their conflicts.

Notes

1. Compare his metaphor when describing religion and government in *The Varieties of Religious Experience*: "[T]he word 'religion' cannot stand for any single principle or essence, but is rather a collective name. The theorizing mind tends always to the over-simplification of its materials" (VRE 1902, 30). For the similarities to Wittgenstein's notion of family resemblance, see my Goodman (2002) and Boncompagni (this volume). Compare Cooper (2002).
2. See for example West (1989), Poirier (1992), and Robinson (1993).
3. The germ for the first chapter may be found in the notes for James's third Wellesley lecture of 1905, which, under the heading *Empiricism & Rationalism*, contain the idea that James will offer "My solution of dilemma" (*Pragmatism*, Cambridge, MA: Harvard University Press, 1977, 282). He does not formulate two opposing lists in his outline, nor stress temperament. That comes into public view in March 1907, in a paper probably written in late 1906 (P 186). In January 1907, when the first lecture was delivered at Columbia, its title was "Philosophy and Life" (186). When published in *The Popular Science Monthly* in March 1907, its title was "A Defence of Pragmatism I: Its Mediating Office" (188).
4. This is not to attribute to James the reductionist view that philosophy is nothing but a matter of temperament. What satisfies my temperament does so in part because I think it is true. I don't think it's true just because it satisfies my temperament (whatever that might mean). Notice that James articulates his temperaments according to beliefs—in monism, free will, materialism, and so on, providing a way in which temperaments can clash or cohere with the rest of our beliefs. In his chapter on "What Pragmatism Means," James maintains that while established, "older truths" have a "controlling," if not final, influence on our view of the world, temperament is also part of the mix: in grafting new beliefs onto the mass of old opinions, he writes, "individuals will emphasize their points of satisfaction differently" (P 1907, 35).
5. See Goodman (2015).
6. This does not quite fit the historical Montaigne, who was a skeptic but also a Catholic whose bedroom in his famous tower was above his private chapel and below his library, and who ends his "Apology for Raymond Sebond" by speaking of "our Christian faith" and its aspiration to a "holy and miraculous metamorphosis" (Montaigne 2003, 683).
7. Just for the record, I don't think this is a fair criticism. Note that James is more favorably disposed to Indian philosophy and religion in *Varieties*, where, for example, he links Buddhism with Christianity among the twice-born and, he thinks, more profound religions.
8. James does not distinguish the variety of monistic views, many of which assert the reality of living, rather than dead or static ideas (as in Emerson's ebbing and flowing "thought that is parent of the universe"). See, for example, Bussanich (1987).
9. Here is a place where some feathers of James's philosophy have more to do with one another than simply terminating in or dangling from a single dried head, as in James's Dyak metaphor discussed earlier.
10. There are antecedents of these two aspects of James's pluralistic pragmatism in his lectures on *Human Immortality* and in the "Conclusion" to *Varieties*. He notes a contrast between scientific impersonality and "the personal point of view" (VRE, 387) and writes: "so long as we deal with the cosmic and the general, we deal only with the symbols of reality, but *as soon as we deal with private and personal phenomena as such, we deal with realities in the completest sense of the term*" (VRE, 393). He also writes: "Individuality is founded

in feeling; and the recesses of feeling, the darker, blinder strata of character are the only places in the world in which we catch real fact in the making, and directly perceive how events happen, and how work is actually done" (VRE, 395). (In corresponding passages in *Pragmatism*, the concept of action infiltrates James's formulations more clearly.)

11. This is James's term in *Varieties*, applied to James's philosophy as a whole by Gale (1999).

Bibliography

Bussanich, John. 1987. "Plotinus on the Inner Life of the One." *Ancient Philosophy* 7: 163–189.
Carpenter, Frederic I. 1939. "William James and Emerson." *American Literature* 11(1): 39–57.
Cooper, Wesley E. 2002. *The Unity of William James's Thought*. Nashville, TN: Vanderbilt University Press.
Emerson, Ralph Waldo, *Collected Works of Ralph Waldo Emerson*, ed. Robert E. Spiller, Alfred R. Ferguson, et al. 10 vols. Cambridge, MA: Harvard University Press, 1971–2013.
Gale, Richard M. 1999. *The Divided Self of William James*. Cambridge: Cambridge University Press.
Girel, Mathias. 2004. "Les Angles De L'acte, Usages D'emerson Dans La Philosophie De William James." *Cahier Charles* 5(37): 207–245.
Goodman, Russell B. 2002. *Wittgenstein and William James*. Cambridge: Cambridge University Press.
Goodman, Russell B. 2008. "Emerson, Romanticism, and Classical American Pragmatism." In *The Oxford Handbook of American Philosophy*, edited by Cheryl J. Misak, 19–37. Oxford: Oxford University Press.
Goodman, Russell B. 2012. "William James's Pluralisms." *Revue Internationale de Philosophie* 66 (260 (2)):155–176.
Goodman, Russell B. 2015. *American Philosophy before Pragmatism*. Oxford: Oxford University Press.
Kovalainen, Heikki A. 2010. *Self as World: The New Emerson*. Tampere: University of Tampere Press.
Kuklick, Bruce 1987. "Chronology," in William James, *Writings 1902–1910*. New York: Library of America, 1315–1349.
Lovejoy, Arthur O. 1908a. "The Thirteen Pragmatisms, I." *The Journal of Philosophy, Psychology and Scientific Methods* 5(1): 5–12.
Lovejoy, Arthur O. 1908b. "The Thirteen Pragmatisms, Ii." *The Journal of Philosophy, Psychology and Scientific Methods* 5(2): 29–39.
Montaigne, Michel de. 2003. *The Complete Essays*. Translated by M. A. Screech. London: Penguin Books.
Poirier, Richard. 1992. *Poetry and Pragmatism*. Cambridge: Harvard University Press.
Robinson, David. 1993. *Emerson and the Conduct of Life: Pragmatism and Ethical Purpose in the Later Work*. Cambridge: Cambridge University Press.
West, Cornel. 1989. *The American Evasion of Philosophy: A Genealogy of Pragmatism*. Madison, WI: University of Wisconsin Press.

PART VII

CONVERSATIONS, PRESENT

CHAPTER 24

WILLIAM JAMES AND RENOUVIER'S NEO-KANTIANISM

Belief, Experience and Consciousness

MATHIAS GIREL

Introduction

THE two-way relationship between James and Renouvier is a well-known landmark in the history of philosophy.[1] Any reader of James will know the entry from his diary, in 1870, where he recorded the revelation inspired by Renouvier's philosophy of free will: having read the French philosopher in the midst of a philosophical crisis,[2] James claimed that he had chosen to follow Renouvier's lead, and to believe "freely in free will." We also know that Renouvier's philosophical journal, *La Critique Philosophique*, published and translated James's earliest articles, starting with "Quelques considérations sur la méthode subjective" (EPh 1878, 23–31) in 1878, contributing significantly to James's international fame and even to his career in America. There are several ways to address this relationship: some have stressed one aspect—the will to believe doctrine, or pluralism more generally—while others have been more concerned with the role of idealism in their thought and with the general neo-Kantian influence on James.[3] All these studies contain precious insights and provide a better understanding of James's philosophy, but I will focus here on the complexity of their relationship, which involves agreements as well as major disagreements.

My concern here is not to document the trivial fact that a major philosophy is not confined to a single claim and that philosophers can agree on one point and disagree on others. My goal is rather to show that, in the exchanges between Renouvier and James, a major threefold disagreement over philosophical method, mind, and perception soon emerged, and that this disagreement was by no means a peripheral matter, if we have James's development as an original philosopher in the 1880s in view. This should not lead us to downplay Renouvier's influences, but rather to articulate this uncontroversial influence with other claims James was endorsing. With rare exceptions, a major philosophy is not built at the outset and is not only the synthesis of "influences." This is true of James: the problem of determinism was at the core of his first philosophy, but the philosophy of psychology and of mind were crucial in the 1880s, as well as the three problems of "exceptional mental states," radical empiricism, and ethics in the 1890s, not to mention pragmatism after 1898 and the sundry attempts at reconciling radical empiricism and the holistic view of consciousness after 1900. Some of these concerns led him to reassess his debt toward Renouvier.

In order to show this, we have to dig deeper than the standard narrative, not because it is wrong—it is correct in its general features—but because it does not get to the essence of the relationship between James and Renouvier. What do Renouvier and his magazine represent for James? Why was the author who was to found an "American philosophy," in the eyes of the editors, published in the columns of a neo-Kantian publication? Indeed, there are surprisingly few detailed studies on this,[4] and those that are detailed generally address one aspect only—the will to believe, idealism, or the question of what philosophy is and what it does.

After having presented the core of Renouvier's main influence in the section "Free Will's Champion, Kantian Style," I shall give a brief survey of James's presence in the *Critique Philosophique* in the section "James's Contributions," and shall deal, in the following sections, with James's early criticisms of Renouvier on philosophical method (the section "Methods and Categories"), on the perception of space and time (the section "Unbounded Spaces") and on consciousness (the section "The Stream of Thought"). In order to accomplish this, I shall give myself here a somewhat more limited period than James's career as a whole: I shall follow him from the early writings to the series of articles of 1884–1885 that would be so important both for psychology and for philosophy—that is, precisely to the point where James and Renouvier's philosophical itineraries begin to diverge.[5] I shall illustrate how the *Critique philosophique* was at first a hospitable publication for the young James, but also how, from the end of this period on, important disputes emerged, in particular over consciousness, which gave rise to a paradoxical situation: the very organ that contributed to make James known turned out to be at odds with several of his most important theses, before the publication of the *Principles*, and even more before *Pragmatism*.

FREE WILL'S CHAMPION, KANTIAN STYLE

Two Sides of the Relationship

On James's side, the relationship entails an admiration for Renouvier, from the first texts to the last ones. I have mentioned James's diary, for April 30th, 1870, where he writes, about the *Essais de Critique générale*:

> I finished the first part of Renouvier's Second *Essais* and see no reason why his definition of free will—"the sustaining of a thought *because I choose to* when I might have other thoughts"—need be the definition of an illusion. . . . My first act of free will shall be to believe in free will.[6]

Renouvier stands first as a philosopher of freedom, but he is also, for James, more and more a "pluralist" philosopher, insofar as he criticizes the claims of neo-Hegelian monism. Nearly forty years later, James would dedicate his unfinished work, *Some Problems of Philosophy*, to Renouvier's pluralism, stressing that without him, he would "never have got free from the monistic superstition under which [he] had grown up" (SPP 1911, 85).

This is an important acknowledgment indeed, even if it implies that this influence was at its strongest in his very early texts. The *Principles of Psychology*, just in between, was dedicated to François Pillon, one of Renouvier's disciples, editor both for the *Critique Philosophique* and for the *Année Philosophique*. The dedication underlines the role this periodical played in the diffusion of James's ideas (PP 1890, front matter).

Renouvier's influence on James was not missed by his contemporaries. Horace Kallen, just after James' death, wrote, in reference to Renouvier, that "it was from France that William James received his first philosophical inspiration, from France that he received his first recognition and his greatest honor" (Kallen 1911, 583). This was a quite clear reference to the complex role of the latter in the formation and subsequent dissemination of James' ideas.

For Renouvier's part, James seems to be at first a European ally, and sometimes the prototype of an emerging character, the "American" philosopher. An ally, since Renouvier interprets James's texts as a local version of his own criticism: "your version of *criticisme*"—he would say after one of James's publications—"is presented with a startling originality, or happiness of expression, with an accent of your own."[7] James's philosophy is a "version," the originality is "of expression," and this is certainly what prompts Renouvier to translate, to comment upon James, and finally to introduce him to his French readers. Renouvier also holds that James is to found an "American philosophy," but in one letter the phrase is underlined, which suggests that this category is still unstable: "Your originality, your direct view of that which is really *to be seen*, will lose rather than gain by much reading, and especially by the reading of German philosophical books. It seems to me when I read you that you are called to found an *American philosophy*. So it would not do for you to make sacrifices to alien gods (*dieux étrangers*)."[8] This sounds like a paradoxical prophecy, since James was then quoting at length a French philosopher, another "alien god", but this should not obscure the first part of the letter, which portrays James as an original philosopher and as a key character of an "emerging" American philosophy.[9]

From James's perspective, there are many reasons why he could be interested in Renouvier. First, he persistently looked for alternative "champions." His acknowledgments of Renouvier, Hodgson, Peirce, Blood, and even Royce at first, have all the same structure: they seem to endorse a "way out" of the extant alternatives in favor of a minor voice or of an unorthodox philosophic position. Renouvier was in no way a representative of the main, dominant philosophical schools, whether empiricist, neo-Hegelian, naturalist, or even positivist. Still, in the late 1860s and the 1870s, Renouvier was, for James, *the* French philosopher and his *Essais de Critique Générale* "the ablest philosophical speculation to which France has given birth during this century" (ECR 1873, 266).[10] "Playing," so to speak, Renouvier against other major philosophers was similar to a wager, as appears clearly in later correspondence with Alice: on James's telling, Hodgson calls Renouvier "the most important philosophical writer of our time—You can't think how it pleaseth me to have this evidence that I have not been a fool in sticking so to R" (CWJ 1880, 5.109). But obviously, Renouvier's alternative status was not the main reason why James was interested in him. It would have been more important that Renouvier was, at that time, fighting hard against monists, absolutists, and, most of all, determinists.

James had noticed Renouvier as early as 1868, when the latter had published a long "note" on the state of philosophy in France (Renouvier 1868). Writing to his father, James claimed that it differed from the "namby pamby diffusiveness" (*sic*) of most French philosophers (CWJ 1868, 4.342). In this note by Renouvier, two major Jamesian concerns and a philosophical problem already stand out.

Firstly, Renouvier criticized extant positions (Cousin, Royer-Collard, and Comte among others) and the general determinist atmosphere of the nineteenth century. Bringing together Hegel, the positivists, and the eclectics, he showed that they were all, in fact, subscribing to common principles:

> A cosmic progress, which is both God and the World, a human progress inherent in the substance, so to speak, of humanity, and which leads it to its goal, necessarily, by all paths; an action of the environment which everywhere, in the universe, in society, generates the individual, shapes him in his states and induces him to his actions: these are the principles. Then there is a marked weakening of the notions of responsibility and duty, a marked tendency to legitimize the fact and the force, to sanction either the march of things as it is and as the best, by losing interest in the events that always go best without us, with us, against us, sometimes, or, if we think we can foresee it, to justify the injustice of the Prince by the Reason of State and that of the citizen by the Sovereignty of the Goal; a certain obliteration, not, for sure, of the feeling of good and noble passions, but of the notion of strict justice and belief in the freedom of the moral agent. (Renouvier 1868, 99–100, my translation)

In a few lines, all the moral and political consequences of determinism were traced.

Secondly, against this "philosophy of the Nineteenth century," Renouvier advocated a philosophy "which brings back and subordinates everything to the recognition of human freedom. This recognition is itself a free act, and this act, critical philosophy requires each of us to do it, then to pursue its results in all orders of intelligence and life" (Renouvier 1868, 107). This summed up, in a few words, exactly what appealed to James in the midst of his philosophical and existential crisis, and a good part of what he would develop in his early essays.

Thirdly, there is a problem. There is an underlying Kantian spirit to Renouvier's philosophy. The last section of the "Note" recommends a kind of "back to Kant" strategy, and a good part of the ambiguity in the James-Renouvier relationship starts just here. The problem is not that a good deal of pragmatism can be read as a revision of the transcendental in a naturalistic (and social) setting. Such a reading has been offered, for example, by Sami Pihlström (2011, 7).[11] Nor is it that, as Carlson (1997) has suggested, one can find an equivalent of the four main Kantian questions in James.[12] The concern is rather that James is generally very attentive to the presuppositions of major empiricists and evolutionists of his time—he even has a special flair for excavating them— and it is startling that he would not devote the same critical attention to the Kantian presuppositions of Renouvier's philosophy at that time. Again, this is not a peripheral question: Renouvier explicitly emphasizes his debt to Kant, as well as key points of divergence *from* Kant.[13] These criticisms are defining features of his own philosophy, so much so that *to understand Renouvier is also to understand his particular, critical way of reading Kant*.[14]

Four Renouvieran Claims

An important feature of Kantianism is its systematicity, and Renouvier is also a systematic philosopher. When their exchanges really began in 1872, James wrote to Renouvier to ask him for a copy of Jules Lequier's *Recherche d'une première vérité*,[15] which Renouvier had cited,[16] and the young James congratulated Renouvier for having proposed an "intelligible and reasonable conception of freedom" (CWJ 1872, 4.430). Giving a complete account of Renouvier's system—of this "reasonable conception"—is beyond the scope of this chapter, but one can borrow a description from Pillon's summary of Renouvier's philosophy, just after his death:

> The essential principles by which reformed criticism or neocriticism [= Renouvier] is opposed to Kant's criticism consist in the triple negation of noumena, of the infinity of quantity and of the universal determinism of phenomena. On the other hand, by the important role he gives to the categories or laws of reason, he opposes David Hume's empirical phenomenalism. It is very precisely characterized by the terms rational phenomenalism, finitism and libertarism. (Pillon 1904, 310; my translation)

Let's stress four points, which correspond roughly to four claims by Renouvier:

(1) The first, already mentioned, is obvious and endorsed repeatedly by Renouvier:[17] the main touchstone for him is Kant. The goal is not to circumvent Kant, as James will recommend later in his "Philosophical Conceptions and Practical Results," but to *refine* his position, by purging it in particular of the last remains of substantialist metaphysics.
(2) "Phenomenism"[18] consists here mainly in the dismissal of the "thing in itself" and the "noumena": "Things are given to knowledge as representations. Things as representations are phenomena. . . . There is no knowledge of a thing in itself;

but everything stands as complex, and relative to other things, in the relationship in which it stands" (Renouvier 1859, i–ii, my translation; for more on Renouvier's phenomenism, see Dunham, this volume). We never know anything but phenomena. They are not appearances of something other than themselves. Still, Renouvier claims, against Hume and his more recent followers, that it is necessary to allow for categories and a priori forms. He does not deduce them from the forms of judgment, as in Kant. But he offers several tentative lists in the course of his life. He describes them in the *First Essays* as "laws of representation," the category of relation being the most universal.[19] There are phenomena and relationships between them: "to be" is to be, or to be in, a relationship. As Renouvier clearly summarizes in the preface to the *Second Essays*, "the word *being* expresses the relationship, both in general acceptance and in all particular meanings" (Renouvier 1859, ii). His way of explaining this should ring a bell for contemporary readers: "A being is a function. The definition of beings in the different spheres of knowledge is that of the functions that constitute them, and outside of which nothing real is known or knowable" (Renouvier 1859, iii). In other words, well before Cassirer (another neo-Kantian),[20] Renouvier clearly tells us that substance is function: it's all about relationships. This is also one overlooked source of Renouvier's pluralism: one can perfectly imagine encompassing systems of relationships widely independent from each other. "Two worlds entirely different from and alien to each other could ... coexist in the same places" (Renouvier 1864a, 24).

(3) This philosophy defends *finitism*, which is characterized by the negation of all "actual infinity." Renouvier's conversion to "finitism" and what he later called the *principe du nombre* dates back to the 1850s: the idea of an infinite number seems to him to be deeply contradictory (for more on Renouvier's *principe du nombre*, see Bordogna, this volume). Any notion of an infinite number is a misleading way of actualizing an indefinite enumeration, which is again a Kantian move: the actual infinite is an erroneous reification of a never-ending process of synthesis. Renouvier would draw the consequences of his "finitism" in many regions of philosophy, including cosmology and creation. His world is finite; it has and includes absolute beginnings.

(4) Renouvier finds freedom behind all certitude (even behind determinist claims). The doctrine does not presuppose any "noumenal" freedom, and there are at least three steps involved:

 (a) A claim about the will. The will is not, for Renouvier, a mysterious and "mythological" entity, but, in phenomenal terms, is the power to sustain an idea, the idea itself giving rise to movements and actions. There is no need of an intermediary act between the representation and the movement, as the classical account of the will would have it: representations themselves are followed by movements, whether voluntary or not. For Renouvier, the action of the will is psychical through and through: it is only a name for a certain relationship our attention has with a representation.

(b) A claim about assent and certitude. One can refer to Lequier, but the idea that the primacy of practical reason plays an important role even in epistemology and metaphysics can be traced to Fichte too. In *The Destination of Man*, Fichte argued that "the organ by which to apprehend" reality is "not knowledge, for knowledge can only demonstrate and establish itself."[21] Renouvier found freedom even in theoretical assertions:

> We can affirm nothing systematically without any representation of a group of relationships as true, nor without an attraction of any kind that leads us to commit ourselves in this way to the perceived truth, nor without a determination of the will that is fixed, whereas it would seem possible to suspend judgment and seek new motives and new reasons, or simply to abandon ourselves to everything that presents itself. (Renouvier 1859, 377)

This belief requirement holds not only for morals, but for all kinds of knowledge.

(c) A claim about free will, which is a direct consequence of the two other claims. Freedom, freedom of the will, free acts, belief, and certainty are just different aspects of the more fundamental process of holding fast to an idea. The previous argument about certitude applies to all statements, and in particular to the alternative between determinism and free will: we can choose to endorse either side, but if we choose determinism, we should be aware that we are freely endorsing the very negation of freedom.

Most of Renouvier's influences on James, early on, can be traced to the "destructive" virtues of phenomenism or to variants of the fourth claim about free will.

In addition to reading Renouvier, James also introduced him to American readers, through reviews, in 1873, and again in 1876. Renouvier endorsed James's reading, in particular the comparisons between his own philosophy and the British empiricist, associationist, and determinist doctrines (Perry 1929, 6). The 1873 and 1876 reviews do not deal with criticism in its technical, Kantian sense, but each one clearly articulates the second and the fourth claims mentioned.

In the 1873 piece, a review of *La Critique Philosophique*,[22] James clearly underlines the originality of Renouvier, compared to absolutists as well as to determinist phenomenists: "he finds the *possibility*, which British empiricism denies, of absolute beginnings, or, in other words, of free will" (ECR 1873, 266). Novelty is not only an appearance but an indefeasible dimension of action. James also gives his version of the fourth claim:

> Since we *may* affirm free-will, what more fitting than that its first act should be that of its own self-affirmation? So that we have an *act* enthroned at the heart of philosophic thought. Liberty is the centre of gravity of the system, which henceforth becomes a moral philosophy. (ECR 1873, 266)

In the second, more complete review (ECR 1876, 321–327), James gives a more detailed account of the last claim. The core of his version of 4(a) is the "stable survival of one representation," which is called a "volition" (ECR 1876, 324). Then the question is to assess whether this "survival" is predetermined *or* involves some free act. For James, the choice in favor of one of the options in the dilemma of determinism is not a mere intellectual affair; it involves the entire human nature: "the entire nature of man, intellectual, affective, and volitional is (whether avowedly or not) exhibited in the theoretical attitude he takes in such a question as [determinism vs. indeterminism]" (ECR 1876, 325). Secondly, Renouvier's account of belief, as belonging to the "active" dimension of our intellectual life, contains most of the elements of the conception that James would develop for the next two decades: "the act of belief and the object of belief coalesce, and the very essential logic of the situation demands that we wait not for any outward sign, but, with the possibility of doubting open to us, voluntarily take the alternative of faith" (ECR 1876, 326). James would be permanently struck by the fact that, if there is no theoretical solution to the dilemma between determinism and freedom, the solution can only be practical.

Of course, it is possible to locate elsewhere Renouvier's main influence. Renouvier's role, if one follows Jean Wahl, is then that of a philosophical "catalyst" that enabled James to sharpen his ideas, particularly in the critique of the "triple illusion of infinity, substance and necessity" (Wahl 2004, 103). More importantly, the recognition of the irreducibility of time would have made Renouvier, and James later, conceive of a universe made up of "pulsations of time, discontinuous surges in duration" (Wahl 2004, 103). Indeed, James himself had noted this point in his review of the *New Monadology*, insisting on Renouvier's cosmology, where "the world, so far as real, is like an immense pulsation composed of a number (unassignable though at all times determinate) of concerted elementary pulsations of different grades" (ECR 1893, 443). To this is added the recognition of the radical evil that alone gives meaning to the meliorist attitude, and we thus have, with pluralism and the possibility of evil, two dimensions common to both authors, which were to interest James until the end. But the pluralist strain is not prominent in the 1870s papers, even though it would become a major concern later, in particular when James developed his radical empiricism and his moral philosophy, for example in "The Moral Philosopher and the Moral Life."

We have two different perspectives here: in the 1870s, Renouvier sees James as developing in an original way his own neo-criticism,[23] that is to say a refined form of Kantianism, while James reads Renouvier as belonging to a "trend launched by Hume."[24] The term *phenomenism* certainly allowed such a misunderstanding, and was at the very least ambiguous. In the 1870s, though, James remains unconvinced, even if he does not voice his criticisms, when it comes to Renouvier's Kantianism about categories. Renouvier's indeterminism was undoubtedly welcome for James' empirical and indeterminist temperament, but Renouvier's claims about pluralism[25] and infinity were to remain an open question. In any case, for a time at least, the two men could feel they were on a common path: Renouvier reading James's texts as an original and striking formulation of the practical postulates of theoretical activity; James reading Renouvier as an inspiration regarding free will and as offering a radical critique of philosophical superstitions then dominant (what Renouvier calls "idolology").

James's Contributions

Soon after he began corresponding with Renouvier, James became a contributor for the *Critique Philosophique* but, interestingly, his contributions mostly involve variants of the fourth claim. There is an influence, an agreement, and perhaps a philosophical program shared by both philosophers, but one should keep in mind that it involves only one part of what constitutes for Renouvier a system, and, conversely, only one part of the philosophy James is developing.

Indeed, 1877–1878 is a turning point in James's development. That year he wrote his first paper, "*Quelques considérations sur la méthode subjective*," (EPh 1878, 23–31) in which he argued in favor of indeterminism and of the efficacy of free will. Renouvier added an introduction. James, relying on "the principles of the philosophy to which [Renouvier's] review is dedicated" asked whether "one [can] be justified in rejecting a theory which many objective facts apparently confirm, solely because it does not in any way respond to our inward preferences" (EPh 1878, 331).

This did not mean, of course, defending a right to believe in a thesis that has been positively refuted. Instead, James was reflecting on what guides the adoption of a philosophy, when several positions are in competition and when nothing makes it possible to decide definitively in favor of one or the other. James' argument was both critical and constructive. It was critical in showing that in some scientific versions of philosophy, choices were expressed that were not necessarily argued for. He contended, in short, that a philosophical temperament was at play. The argument was constructive because it linked the adoption of a philosophy, concerning for example "pessimism" or "optimism," to underlying temperamental preferences, affects, and postulates. For James, this choice was not determined univocally by the "facts" or by the "data," but by the whole nature of man.

James presented his paper as compatible with Renouvier's views,[26] and Renouvier concurred.[27] A line of thinking, prominent in Chapters 2 to 5 of the *Will to Believe*, appears thus for the first time in the late 1870s, in Renouvier's *Critique*. These chapters, in *The Will to Believe*, often pay due compliments to Renouvier[28] and develop the insights we have discerned in the last section "Free Will's Champion, Kantian Style."

This first paper in French is the only text written solely for the *Critique*. Later French papers are usually summaries and translations.[29] James, then, is a frequent contributor between 1878 and 1884, as well as the only non-French regular author for this journal.

In addition to Renouvier's short introductions to his translations, some of James's views are discussed in detail in Renouvier's books. For example, Renouvier's *Esquisse d'une Classification* (1885–1886) provides an account of James's analysis of the teleological nature of mind and of faith.[30] Renouvier reproduces large portions of James's articles that had been translated in the *Critique*, emphasizing and agreeing with passages where James showed that in all mentality, sensation, representation, and action are indissolubly linked, as he had shown in "Reflex Action and Theism" and, before, in his 1878 article on Spencer's definition of the mind as correspondence (EPh 1878, 7–22). Renouvier put the following description of misleading philosophical claims, criticized both by himself and by James, at the end of his summary:

> 1st Pretention to make all philosophical questions subjects of scientific decision; particularly, to impose from now on, in the name of Science, the negation of the most ordinary objects of philosophical or religious "faith," as irreconcilable with scientific theories that we imagine are free from hypothesis and unshakeable.
>
> 2nd Pretending to banish from the human mind any belief in philosophical matters, and to give philosophy the same limit as the sciences, which is correct generalizations, so that one recognizes never being able to reach the ancient objects of philosophy and religion.
>
> 3rd The claim to arrive, through the natural progress of humanity, at the establishment of a definitive philosophical and religious authority, prohibiting any critical examination [of that authority], and decreeing forever what is and remains, in all things, or [decreeing] the truth or the equivalent of truth, in relation to the social organism and universal happiness.
>
> 4th Philosophy's own claim to reach, through its own method, either a priori or a posteriori, a solution to questions with such evidence that, since doubt is no longer possible for those who examine it, an area of faith no longer exists except for the ignorant. (Renouvier 1885–1886, 326; my translation)

Renouvier gave James new readers, like a certain Charles Jeanmaire, who in his *Idée de la personnalité humaine dans la psychologie moderne* (1882) noted the close link between belief and will in both Renouvier and James: "If volition, considered in itself, consists only in acting on ideas, in order to maintain them, suspend them, discard them, in what does it differ from belief, which is also an act by which we accept or reject ideas? Mr James, again following Mr Renouvier's example, thinks that the difference is not great" (Jeanmaire 1882, 315). In other words, in France, in the 1880s, there were readers who understood very well that the two terms that James was going to unite in *The Will to Believe* (volition and belief) designated two aspects of the same process.

There were more famous readers, for example Joseph Delboeuf, who devoted some fifteen pages in the *Revue Philosophique* to James's paper on "the Feeling of Effort," just published in the *Critique* (Delboeuf 1881), or again Bergson who, in the opening pages of his *Essais sur les données immédiates de la conscience*, quotes the same paper (Bergson 1889, 16–17). James's papers in the *Critique* give his philosophy a distinctive footprint in France, and this first reception had enduring consequences: his French readers were acquainted with the core of his Will-to-Believe papers, and these discussions provided the background when the controversy over pragmatism and radical empiricism started around 1900. His later views, most of them not translated into French until the end of the decade, were thus read from the perspective of *The Will to Believe*.

Still, when James and Renouvier finally met in 1880 (CWJ 1880, 5.135), serious doubts were beginning to temper James' admiration.

Method and Categories

From both perspectives, a gap began opening. In James's eyes, the differences between Renouvier and the narrow rationalism he was allegedly fighting were becoming less and less evident. As for Renouvier (and his lieutenants), James seemed to reach conclusions that were in tension with his earlier commitments. After the reception of "What Is an Emotionn" and of "On Some Omissions of Introspective Psychology," as new trends emerged in James's psychology, important differences would surface, even if in his very last letter to Renouvier, James still insisted that he was one of his disciples.[31]

One reason a gap was opening was related to the naturalistic context of James's thought. It might be claimed, and has been claimed, that Darwin's ideas were another important influence on James. Still, despite James's later efforts to find points of agreement between Renouvier's system and evolution (ECR 1893, 444), Renouvier had strong concerns over Darwin:

> Evolution is a craze (*une toquade*). It will last fifteen or twenty years, and then we shall again speak of it as one spoke of the system of Lamarck at the time of Cuvier. So the world goes. It will be found strange to have, on behalf of gratuitous inductions and in the name of experimental method, denied such a fact as the existence of species, which *crève les yeux* [stares you in the face], as we say in French.[32] (CWJ 1878, 5.7–8)

Renouvier was also extremely dubious about the role psycho-physiological schemes were beginning to play in James's thought. This is true of the 1884 text on emotions, but the most interesting documents are provided by the papers on the will. In 1888, Renouvier translated James's paper on "What the Will Effects" (EPs 1888, 216–234) and added some remarks (Renouvier 1888), which were soon followed by a reply from James (EPs 1888, 235–238). These remarks expressed both admiration for James—insofar as his views converged with Renouvier's own utterances, thirty years before, in the *Second Essay* (1859)[33]—and criticisms.

James explicitly used Renouvier's own example of the person who thinks of getting out of bed, and then instantly gets out of bed, without any intermediary representation or act, and offered the general law: "anywhere and everywhere the sole known cause for the execution of a movement is the bare idea of the movement's execution" (EPs 1888, 221). So far, both men clearly agreed: most of the representations of the Will were mythological and misleading. Still, James, in Renouvier's eyes, conceded too much to the "new psychology" and to the psycho-physiological scheme, threatening the distinction between mere reactive movements and original "acts" of consciousness. Renouvier suspected that, once the reflex act scheme was generalized, James could be read as denying consciousness a real initiative power. James resisted the charge: the will chooses between equipossible reactions that would lead to different results. This called for a new account of consciousness, perhaps less likely to be shared by Renouvier:

> We only have to admit that the consciousness which accompanies material processes can react in such a way that it adds at leisure to the intensity or the duration of some particular processes; a field of *selection* opens at once, which leads us far away from mere mechanical determination. (James, in EPs 1888, 238; my translation)

For Renouvier, this would mean both maintaining the reflex act scheme and reintroducing an unspecified entity able to "act" on these processes. Still, this left room for a variety of conceptions of consciousness.[34] James, in later texts, would maintain a phenomenist reading of it in his *Essays in Radical Empiricism*, in connection with the problem of novelty (ERE 1912, 93, n.). If the dispute over the will was perhaps a temporary misunderstanding, Renouvier's doubts about physiological arguments were clear, and James's own doubts about Renouvier's treatment of perception, the categories, and consciousness would be still clearer.

Unbounded Spaces

Even in the early 1880s, James and Renouvier were not in a master/disciple relation anymore. The year before they met, James had lectured on Renouvier's *Essays* at Harvard (1879–1880), and this experience certainly led him to reassess their relationship. He then realized that Renouvier's "exposition offer[ed] too many difficulties" (CWJ 1880, 5.84), a diagnosis confirmed by a letter to Renouvier confessing that this course had left him "more unsettled than [he had been] for years" (CWJ 1880, 5.98). One of the main reasons for this statement was his difficulty explaining to his students Renouvier's denial of the infinite, that is, his finitism concerning time and space, as is witnessed by an eighteen-point letter to Renouvier on that topic (CWJ 1880, 5.75–79). The questions were soon followed by a lengthy answer (Perry 1935b, 310–318), which, according to James's confession, "fail[ed] to awaken conviction" (CWJ 1880, 5.98). One might easily miss the importance of this exchange because fundamental arguments are mixed with more parochial discussions. The exchange is crucial though, since it involves the nature of the second claim regarding phenomenism.

On the surface, the discussion seems to be a long misunderstanding on the very principle of neocriticism: James seems to oppose time and space "in themselves," or *in se*, to the infinity of the forms of time and space. He allows that an actual infinity of composition or division is contradictory, as far as our representations are considered (thus granting Renouvier's third claim about the *principe du nombre*), but holds that this does not imply that times and spaces are "unreal": "to me the forms seem as real, as actual, as 'given,' as the phenomena" (CWJ 1880, 5.75).

This opened an easy line for Renouvier to answer that they were "real" *as* intuitions, but that since we could not make sense of an actual infinite, whether spatial or temporal, and since these forms implied an infinite divisibility as well as infinite additions, they could not be "real," *except as* representations (or "as reality of the law of intuition and as reality of the application of this law to all sentient beings", Perry 1935b, 312). The reasoning seems to be the following: we can only perceive parts of time and space; as "given" parts they imply a whole (if they are given, the whole is given and conversely), and this whole cannot be actually infinite; ergo time and space are unreal *in se*, they are only "represented" or a "process of the imagination." The principle of number and the principle of totality are just two names for the same thing here:

> Number is the essence of space and time, in the sense that the spaces and durations determined by the setting of limits form numbers (the whole body of mathematical sciences is proof of this) and that the assumption of these circumscribed and numerable parts is indissolubly linked to any empirical use of representations of phenomena in space and time. Without the thought of such numbers (an hour, a sidereal day, a cubic meter, the terrestrial sphere, etc.), we cannot say that we actually perceive phenomena in space and time, nor consequently space and time themselves. That said, I would add: if the subject-matter (*material*) of space and time considered in itself does not have parts in itself that correspond to these measurable constituencies and their indefinite multiplication, I no longer understand what is called being in itself; because the existence that intuition lends to space and time seems to me to be the very existence of such parts; so that if I want space and time to exist in themselves, I must want these parts to exist as well. Otherwise, please tell me what this *in itself* means. This *in itself* is in my opinion only the obscure and useless personification of my intuition considered in a vague state. (Perry 1935b, 313–314; my translation)

James's reply, if clumsy since he still uses the "in themselves" talk, is a criticism of Renouvier's assumptions. First, he sides with Hodgson's *Time and Space*. Number applies only to the adventitious marks our attention applies to times and spaces: "Number, depending thus on limits, is not of the essence of Time or Space" (CWJ 1880, 5.76). Second, James holds that there's no reason why given spaces might not be "continuous," this continuity being a "condition," or a "ground," for the actual divisions we draw, which will always be finite in number: "These parts of course so far as they are determined by limits actually set, are always in finite number" (CWJ 1880, 5.76). But the most strategic move is the third: he also draws a distinction between *unboundedness*, which he considers as a property of given times and spaces, and infinity. In other words, we can perfectly well consider spaces and times as unbounded without considering them as infinite, as implying the notion of an impossible infinite actual totality.

Regarding these times and spaces, the very problem of *givenness* seems to be the bone of contention between the two men. James remarks that the ambiguity lies in the phrase, times and spaces "don't exist as wholes": "'they don't exist as wholes' sounds equivalent to 'they don't wholly exist' or 'are not wholly given'" (CWJ 1880, 5.77). He would allow the first statement (they are not wholes understood as a complete collection of parts) without allowing the conclusion: "The *not* may negate the *given* or it may negate the *wholly*. In the former case we mean: They are wholes, but not given. In the latter they are given, but not wholes" (CWJ 1880, 5.77). James clearly attributes the first meaning to Renouvier, and endorses the second.[35]

The importance of this discussion might be obscured by the apparent subject matter of the discussion, the unbounded past, or the unbounded universe, but there are reasons to think that James has a more general agenda in mind. In 1879, James had published "The Spatial Quale" (EPs 1879, 62–82) [36] (a text he does not mention in his correspondence to Renouvier), and if his explicit targets were Cabot and Spencer as well as Helmholtz, his claims would equally apply to Renouvier. In a line that would be amplified in the *Principles*, James criticizes the idea that space "forms a system of relations, ... [and so] cannot be given in any one sensation," and "that it is a symbol of the general relatedness of objects constructed by thought from data which lie below consciousness." His own claim, in that paper, was exactly to argue that we *perceive* continua, or, in other terms, that "this quality of extension or spatial quale" exists "at the outset [of perception] in a simple and unitary form." Of course, there will be parts, relations, syntheses of positions, but they belong to a later stage: "The *positions* which ultimately come to be determined within it, in mutual relation to each other, are later developments of experience, guided by attention." Spaces and times are thus given, and they are given in the same way other phenomena are given: "this vague original consciousness of a space in which separate positions and directions have not, as yet, been mentally discriminated, deserves, if it exists at all, the name of sensation quite as much as does the color, 'blue,' or the feeling, 'warm.'" (For more on James's account of spatial perception, see Hatfield, this volume).[37]

The broader question of whether the *principe du nombre* was sound at all remained an open question in James's thought, and for a long time indeed. James seemed later to entertain serious doubts over Renouvier's account of the infinite, especially after he became aware of the new mathematical theories on that topic.[38] But the main lesson should be that in this correspondence emerges a major source of disagreement, and that the disagreement involves the neocriticist position concerning time and space. Renouvier objected thus to an important psychological and philosophical Jamesian thesis, and this sentence about James's papers on space, amplifying the lessons of the "Spatial Quale", in a letter of 1887, summarizes his general attitude during the last years of their correspondence: "My Kantian habits of mind make this reading and the understanding of your processes of thought and your language more difficult than I should like."[39]

Another bone of contention involved the role of *conceptual categories*. The major event is the controversy between Hodgson and Renouvier. Its episodes are (1) Hodgson's criticisms of Renouvier's *Essais* in the columns of *Mind* (Hodgson 1881a), (2) the translation of these criticisms in the *Critique*, with comments by Renouvier (Hodgson 1881b),

(3) Renouvier's analysis of Hodgson's *Philosophy of Reflection* (Renouvier 1882–1883), and (4) Hodgson's replies (Hodgson 1882). This discussion would deserve further research, as it certainly recapitulates some major controversies of the time. Both men were phenomenists and shared an interest in epistemology, metaphysics, and ethics,[40] but confronted each other on major issues: Renouvier defended free will and the role of conceptual categories against Hodgson; Hodgson defended universal determinism and the infinite against Renouvier.

James paid acute attention to this dispute and its overall effect upon him is interesting. On the one hand, he seems to have been confirmed in his high opinion of Renouvier as a major philosopher, worthy of such a charge by Hodgson.[41] He also still seemed to share Renouvier's arguments in favor of free will.[42] On the other hand, Renouvier's Kantianism as regards categories came under Hodgson's attack, both in *Mind* and in his "Replies" in the *Critique*. Since James was then arguing against Kantian approaches to perception,[43] he would likely have agreed with Hodgson's criticisms here. Hodgson, in his long comments on Renouvier in *Mind*, remarked that Renouvier seemed to obliterate the distinction between perception and thought, and Kant's distinction between transcendental aesthetics and transcendental logic:

> Time and Space too, it will be observed, which are Kant's forms of perception or intuition as opposed to thought, are here made moments of the two categories, position and succession. The effect of this is, first, to obliterate the distinction between perception and thought, at least as a cardinal distinction of the analysis, by sinking them in one single class of phenomena, representation; and secondly, to subordinate the forms of perception to those of thought (and not vice versa), by making the forms of that single class of phenomena, in which the distinction is obliterated, the ultimate laws of consciousness, in which the forms of perception as such are comparatively insignificant moment. (Hodgson 1881a, 38)

That was the published version. In correspondence with James, Hodgson even claimed that Renouvier had retained the worst part of Kant's philosophy:

> He makes just the same mistake that Kant made, namely, to assume a spiritual agent working in certain indispensable forms of thought ... I class him with the German Cognition-theorists; his system is a French *Erkenntnistheorie*; neither psychology nor philosophy but a *Mittelding*, half science half philosophy.[44]

This was precisely the position of the "psycho-mythologists" James was trying to undermine in the field of psychology (see PP 1890, 520). James felt that there was no need for any "Kantian machine-shop" to explain the articulation of experience, and Hodgson's warnings about Renouvier, "who *starts* with a list of conceptual categories as his ultimates and basis [sic] of experience,"[45] certainly reinforced the doubts he had started raising in the correspondence over the *principe du nombre*.

If that is true, the consequence is that, already in 1881, James had reason to think that Renouvier's second claim, about phenomenism, had to be revised. It had to be revised precisely because he was not ready to accept all the aspects of the first, methodological and Kantian, claim.[46] Later comments by James upon Renouvier[47] confirm that point. Reading the *Principles of Nature*, James would now regret the "strenuous abstractness of Renouvier's terms" (ECR 1893: 440). He would still portray Renouvier as the main opponent of the neo-Hegelian monists, as he had done in the late 1870s,[48] sometimes venturing into prophecy: "the present reviewer feels like saying that the philosophy of the future will have to be that either of Renouvier or of Hegel" (ECR 1893, 441). Still, the same James would confess to Royce that "Renouvier cannot be true – his world is so much dust,"[49] and to Peirce that his "form" was "atrocious."[50] In a letter to Flournoy, James gave a more balanced reading of Renouvier as a "classical" philosopher: "I entirely agree that Renouvier's system fails to satisfy, but it seems to me the classical and consistent expression of *one* of the great attitudes, that of insisting on logically intelligible formulas. If one goes beyond, one must abandon the hope of formulas altogether" (CWJ 1892, 7.317–318). One might wonder, though, if that was still a compliment.

The Stream of Thought

The last major difference between James and Renouvier concerns the *continuity of consciousness*. It provides the substance of Chapter 9 of the 1890 *Principles*, but it had already been developed in "On Some Omissions of Introspective Psychology" (James 1884), where James famously claimed that the stream of thought is continuous. This is crucial for James's account of mind as well as for his methods in psychology, since the confusion between the clear-cut concepts the analyst introduces in the context of a theory and the actual "vague" mental states analyzed is what James dubs the "Psychologist's Fallacy" (see PP, 911). Renouvier, commenting on "On Some Omissions," made it clear that he could not accept James's statements about the "stream" and about its continuity. His objection was a Kantian one, insofar as to him a rational approach to the human psychical life was possible only after we have "grouped" them under categories:

> The human, psychical function, is rational only by virtue of groupings of phenomena under different categorical functions, which bring order and classification into the manifold of these impressions and ideas – forming, as they do, an apparent infinity. There, it seems to me, are the file-leaders which guide the sensible phenomena, as they are the stakes and surveyor's marks for the understanding. How can we classify and create science in psychology, without recognizing an intellectual basis for such general terms as *where, who, when, what, for what, by what, etc.*?[51]

Basically, Renouvier's objection was to challenge James's own point of departure, which claimed to make the stream of thought, or consciousness, itself carry these accents: the *who*, the *what*, the *where*. For Renouvier, this amounts to saying that consciousness is what we can *know* about it, and that what we can know about it is already structured, like all phenomena, by categories. In contrast, James wished to defend the primacy and the continuity of the stream of consciousness:

> You accuse me of bringing *To apeiron* into the mind, whose functions are essentially discrete. The categoric concepts you speak of are concepts of objects.... But before it is reflected on, consciousness is *felt*, and as such is continuous, that is, potentially allows us to make sections anywhere in it, and treat the included portion as a unit.... But as we divide *them* arbitrarily, so I say our divisions of consciousness are arbitrary results of conceptual handling of it on our part. The ordinary psychology, on the contrary, insists that it is naturally discrete and that the divisions *belong* in certain places. This seems to me like saying that space exists in cubes or pyramids, apart from our construction.[52]

This time, the disagreement was not local anymore. It involved a major Jamesian thesis, and certainly not one he was ready to disown.

Conclusions

Like all relationships, the one between James and Renouvier is not univocal. It had different effects on each person, and it cannot be limited to moments of reciprocal welcome and inspiration. There is a naturalistic, evolutionist dimension in James. There is also a fundamental thesis concerning the primacy of the continuous and even of the vague—the analysis being, so to speak, always second. Both go against the fundamental presuppositions of Renouvier.

From a Renouvieran standpoint, *The Will to Believe* papers seemed compatible with the philosophical programme of *La Critique Philosophique*, and this also holds for some parts of the papers on the will. But major Jamesian arguments, involving his methodology, his views on the stream of consciousness, and on the import of physiological processes in psychology, would have to be dismissed or revised. There is a massive influence on the will to believe doctrine, but to attribute such an influence, whether we call it *idealist* or *neo-Kantian*, on James's empiricism in general, and even on his pragmatism, would be to seriously disregard his sharp criticisms of Renouvier's first and second claims.

In other words, if we were to limit James to what appears in the columns of the *Critique*, or to what he borrows from Renouvier, we would have a James before he became himself, before he became the distinctive empiricist he was. My argument, here, has been that he perceived this danger very early in his exchanges with Renouvier and that by around 1880 he had taken all he needed from Renouvier: the core of *The Will to Believe*. If James—although less and less frequently—still read Renouvier's volumes, most of what he could use of Renouvier's insights had already been captured. It is no accident if, mentioning a possible summer stay with Renouvier and the Pillons, as early as 1883, he was prone to affirm his own philosophical independence:

Philosophers must part, as soon as they have extracted each other's juice; that is, if they are each working on his own line there inevitably comes a day when they have gone as far together as they can ever go, & after that it is nothing but the accentuation & rubbing in differences, without change.[53] (CWJ 1882, 5.276)

That certainly is a striking description of what we might call "philosophical vampirism." It is also definitely an accurate account of the James-Renouvier relationship.

Notes

1. The present chapter builds on historical research and reconstructions in Girel (2007), to which the reader is referred. There I tried to give a fine-grained, extensive, and historical assessment of James's relationship not only to Renouvier but also to his disciples, Pillon and Dauriac. The present chapter covers new ground by focusing on Renouvier's neo-Kantianism.
2. See Richardson (2006, 120–121) and Gunnarsson (2010).
3. See, already in 1879, Hall's claim: "the philosophical stand-point of Dr. James is essentially that of the modified neo-Kantianism of Renouvier" (Hall 1879, 97).
4. See O'Connell (1997), Viney (1997), and Dunham (2015). Fedi (1998) is an outstanding monograph on Renouvier's epistemology and has many mentions of James. See also Carrette (2013, 173–174 and esp. p. 120 on James, Renouvier, and individuality); Croce (2017, 308n.). On Renouvier's philosophy of science, see Amet (2015), Schmaus (2007; 2018; 2020).
5. I am thus bracketing two dimensions here: (1) the building of radical empiricism, of pragmatism as a method and James's mature view on pluralism, on the one hand, and (2) Renouvier's own evolution, including his late views on monadology and personalism, on the other hand.
6. As quoted in Perry (1948, 121). The reference goes to Renouvier 1859. This second essay would be later retitled *Psychologie rationnelle* in the 1875 edition.
7. Charles Renouvier to William James, Aug 21, 1879 (Perry 1929, 2); translated in Perry 1935a (1, 669). When a letter is calendared in CWJ, I am using the edition of the James-Renouvier correspondence provided by Perry in Perry (1929), completed with Perry (1935b). When a translation from the French is available either in CWJ or in Perry (1935a), I use it. All other translations (from Perry 1935b) are mine.
8. Charles Renouvier to William James, Sept. 5, 1882 (Perry 1929, 24); translated in Perry (1935a, 1, 679, slightly edited). Italics are Renouvier's.
9. On this, Kuklick (1977) is still a precious resource.
10. See a later description at CWJ (1884, 5.503): "A philosopher armed from head to foot with all the implements of his profession."
11. These ideas are currently an interesting subject of controversy among pragmatists. See, for another view, highly critical of the "Kantian Pragmatism" thesis, Maddalena (2015).
12. Carlson identifies, as the core of this revised Kantianism, "the search to establish what are the most reasonable philosophical views for us to hold through examination of our nature as autonomous rational individuals" (Carlson 1997, 382). See also Ferrari (2014).
13. See Renouvier (1869, 94–102) in particular.
14. Fedi has an interesting list of some of the most important differences, as seen by Renouvier (Fedi 1998, 14). Renouvier left an unpublished manuscript, on the "Critique of Kant's doctrine", which summarized his late views; see Renouvier (1906).

15. On this, see Viney (1997). Lequier is sometimes spelled "Lequyer."
16. Renouvier (1859, 371). Renouvier disapproved of Lequier's Catholicism, and is more explicit still in the second edition of this Essay.
17. See Renouvier (1875, I, 1, xv). In October 1868 James had already clearly perceived that Renouvier took "his stand on Kant." In the same letter, James's first on Renouvier, he also noted that he had just "begun" reading the first *Critique* (CWJ 1868, 4.342). By then James had already read the *Prolegomena* and the *Anthropology*, as well as Cousin on Kant (CWJ 1868, 4.298-299).
18. For a short presentation, including a comparison with phenomenology, see Dupont (2014, 20). On Renouvier's phenomenism and his criticism of the notion of "substance," see the detailed analysis of Fedi (1998, 338-380).
19. In the *Essais*, the list is the following (in order): "Relation, Number, Position, Succession, Quality, Change (*devenir*), Causality, Finality/Purpose (*finalité*), Personality" (Fedi 1998, 104). See also Renouvier (1859, iv-v).
20. On Renouvier and neo-Kantianism, see Ferrari (2003).
21. "It is Faith, that voluntary reposing on the views naturally presenting themselves to us, because through these views only we can fulfil our destiny; which approves of knowledge and raises to certainty and conviction that which without it might be mere delusion. It is no knowledge, but a resolution of the will to admit this knowledge" (Fichte 1846, 73).
22. "Renouvier's Contribution to *La Critique Philosophique*," in ECR (1873, 265-267).
23. See Perry (1929, 6), July 17, 1876.
24. See Perry (1929, 7), July 29, 1876.
25. William James to Renouvier (CWJ 1876, 4.541).
26. "To talk of freedom in the *Critique Philosophique* is to carry gold to California" (EPh 1878, 338).
27. James's thoughts are deemed to "conform to the criticist method and we would be glad to sign them" [*nous nous estimerions heureux de pouvoir les signer*], quoted at (EPh 1878, 31).
28. For example, in the original text of the essay "Dilemma of Determinism" James wrote: "I am in duty bound to say that my own reasonings are almost entirely those of Renouvier, and may be found in his *Psychologie Rationnelle*, as well as in the periodical *Critique Philosophique, passim*" (WB, 268 n.).
29. I give a more detailed list in Girel (2007).
30. See in particular Renouvier (1885-1886, 176-185, 280-283, 320-324).
31. William James to Renouvier (CWJ 1896, 8.179). See also James's attempts, in 1900, to have Renouvier elected as a foreign correspondent for the Berlin Academy of Science (CWJ 1900, 9.224).
32. Charles Renouvier to William James (CWJ 1878, 5.7-8); my translation for the lines not translated by Perry, who gives only part of the letter in Perry (1935a, vol. 1, 667).
33. As early as "The Feeling of Effort" (1880), translated in the *Critique Philosophique* the same year as "Le Sentiment de l'effort," James claimed that Renouvier's "account of the psychology of volition was the firmest, and in [his] opinion, the truest connected treatment yet given to the subject" (EPs 1880, 109).
34. See Klein (forthcoming).
35. The same line of argument surfaces, much later, in SPP (1911, 84).
36. All quotes in this paragraph are from EPs (1888, 62-65).

37. See also Klein (2009).
38. "The new infinitists have disproved the contention of Renouvier *et al.* that the realization of a cardinal infinite is *impossible*. They may have proved it possible. They haven't yet proved it actual" (Fragment on the Infinite, 1902–1910; MEN 217).
39. Charles Renouvier to William James, March 27, 1887; Perry (1929, 211–212); translated in Perry (1935a, 1, 701).
40. See CWJ (1879, 5.43–44). Hodgson, contrariwise to Renouvier, did not admit that the denial of free will involved the denial of moral distinctions between right or wrong.
41. CWJ (1880, 5.109), to Alice Howe Gibbens James.
42. CWJ (1883, 5.396). See also an interesting letter by Hodgson (CWJ 1882, 5.199).
43. See Girel (2003, §1).
44. Shadworth Hodgson to William James (CWJ 1882, 5.276).
45. Shadworth Hodgson to William James (CWJ 1886, 6.120).
46. That is the main reason why I have doubts about the label "idealist" when applied globally to James. Dunham, in his fine piece on Renouvier and James, has the following characterization as applied to Renouvier: "he was an idealist insofar as he believed that: (i) our mental ideas are the exemplars of the 'really real'; (ii) reality is exclusively experiential in nature; and (iii) our experience is shaped or organized by the intellect" (Dunham 2015, 4). Item (ii) is of course shared by James, but regarding (i), which Dunham later describes as "the point of view of knowledge", the whole point of most of James's *Principles* period is to criticize the vocabulary of ideas, and it includes a sharp criticism of (iii) as well (which is not addressed in Dunham's paper).
47. James's review of *Les Principes de la nature*, 2nd ed., by Charles Renouvier, can be found at ECR (1893, 440–446). See also James's 1892 review of *L'Année Philosophique*, 2e année, ed. by François Pillon, at ECR (1892, 426–432).
48. See CWJ (1879, 5.48): "This [Hegelian] school and that of Renouvier are the only serious alternatives today."
49. William James to J. Royce (CWJ 1892, 7.351).
50. William James to C. S. Peirce (CWJ 1897, 8.324).
51. Charles Renouvier to William James (Perry 1929, 204); translated in Perry 1935a, 1.697.
52. William James to Charles Renouvier, Sept 30, 1884 (Perry 1929, 206); translation in EPs, 403.
53. William James to Alice Howe Gibbens James (CWJ 1883, 5.410).

References

Amet, Samuel-Gaston. 2015. *Le néocriticisme de Renouvier: fondations des sciences*. Paris: L'Harmattan.
Bergson, Henri. 1889. *Essais sur les données immédiates de la conscience*. Alcan, Paris. Reprint P.U.F., Paris, 1993.
Carlson, Thomas. 1997. "James and the Kantian Tradition." In *The Cambridge Companion to William James*, edited by Ruth Anna Putnam, 363-383. New York: Cambridge University Press.
Carrette, Jeremy. 2013. *William James's Hidden Religious Imagination: A Universe of Relations*. London: Routledge.
Croce, Paul Jerome. 2017. *Young William James Thinking*. Baltimore: JHU Press.

Delboeuf, Joseph. 1881. "Le sentiment de l'effort." *Revue Philosophique de La France et de l'Étranger* 12: 513–27.

Dunham, Jeremy. 2015. "Idealism, Pragmatism, and the Will to Believe: Charles Renouvier and William James." *British Journal for the History of Philosophy* 23 (4): 1–23. doi: 10.1080/09608788.2014.1002074.

Dupont, Christian Yves. 2014. *Phenomenology in French Philosophy: Early Encounters*. Dordrecht: Springer.

Fedi, Laurent. 1998. *Le problème de la connaissance dans la philosophie de Charles Renouvier*. Paris: L'Harmattan.

Ferrari, Massimo. 2003. "Renouvier à Marbourg. La réception de Renouvier dans le néo-kantisme allemand." In *Renouvier: philosophie politique*, edited by Marie-Claude Blais, 207–224. Paris: Fayard.

Ferrari, Massimo. 2014. "Pragmatism and European Philosophy: William James and the French-Italian Connection." In *New Directions in the Philosophy of Science*, edited by Maria Carla Galavotti, Dennis Dieks, Wenceslao J. Gonzalez, Stephan Hartmann, Thomas Uebel and Marcel Weber, 609–625. Cham: Springer International Publishing.

Fichte, Johann Gottlieb. 1846. *The Destination of Man*. Translated by Percy Sinnett. London: Chapman.

Girel, Mathias. 2003. "The Metaphysics and Logic of Psychology: Peirce's Reading of James's Principles." *Transactions of the Charles S. Peirce Society* 34 (2): 163–203.

Girel, Mathias. 2007. "A Chronicle of Pragmatism in France before 1907. William James in Renouvier's Critique Philosophique." In *Fringes of Religious Experience, Cross-Perspectives on James's The Varieties of Religious Experience*, edited by Sergio Franzese and Felicitas Kraemer, 169–200. Frankfurt: Ontos Verlag.

Gunnarsson, Logi. 2010. "The Philosopher as Pathogenic Agent, Patient, and Therapist: The Case of William James." *Royal Institute of Philosophy Supplements* 66:165–186.

Hall, G. Stanley. 1879. "Philosophy in the United States." *Mind* 4 (13): 89–105.

Hodgson, Shadworth H. 1881a. "M. Renouvier's Philosophy." *Mind* 6 (21): 31–61, 173–211.

Hodgson, Shadworth H. 1881b. "Examen *des Essais de critique générale*", *Critique Philosophique* (t. 1, 161–172, 177–186, 193–198, 209–2014, 241–245, 258–264; t. 2, 188–192, 209–216, 225–234, 305–312, 342–351, 353–364, 369–374).

Hodgson, Shadworth, 1882. "Réponse aux notes de Renouvier sur mon examen des essais de critique générale." *Critique philosophique*, t. 1, 241–253, 373–379, 391–408.

James, William. 1884. "On Some Omissions of Introspective Psychology." *Mind* 9 (33): 1–26.

Jeanmaire, Charles. 1882. *L'Idée de la personnalité humaine dans la psychologie moderne*, Toulouse: Douladoure-Privat.

Kallen, Horace M. 1911. "Review of Boutroux's William James." *Journal of Philosophy* 8 (21): 583–584.

Klein, Alexander. Forthcoming. *Consciousness Is Motor: William James on Mind and Action*. New York: Oxford University Press.

Klein, Alexander. 2009. "On Hume on Space: Green's Attack, James' Empirical Response." *Journal of the History of Philosophy* 47 (3): 415–449.

Kuklick, Bruce. 1977. *The Rise of American Philosophy, Cambridge, Massachusetts, 1860–1930*. New Haven: Yale University Press.

Maddalena, Giovanni. 2015. *The Philosophy of Gesture. Completing Pragmatists' Incomplete Revolution*. Montreal: University of McGill-Queen's Press.

O'Connell, Robert J. 1997. *William James on The Courage to Believe*. New York: Fordham University Press.
Perry, Ralph Barton. 1929. "Correspondance de Charles Renouvier et de William James." *Revue de Métaphysique et de Morale* (1): 1–35, 193–222.
Perry, Ralph Barton. 1935a. *The Thought and Character of William James: As Revealed in Unpublished Correspondence and Notes, Together with His Published Writings*. Boston: Little, Brown and Company.
Perry, Ralph Barton. 1935b. "Un échange de lettres entre Renouvier et William James." *Revue de Métaphysique et de Morale* 42 (3): 303–318.
Perry, Ralph Barton. 1948. *The Thought and Character of William James, Briefer Version*. Cambridge, MA: Harvard University Press.
Pihlström, Sami, ed. 2011. *The Continuum Companion to Pragmatism*. New York: Continuum.
Pillon, François. 1904. "Nécrologie. Charles Renouvier." *L'année philosophique (1903)*: 309–311.
Renouvier, Charles. 1854. *Premier essai. Analyse générale de la connaissance, Essais de critique générale*. Paris: Ladrange.
Renouvier, Charles. 1859. *Deuxième essai. L'Homme: la raison, la passion, la liberté, la certitude, la probabilité morale. Essais de critique générale*. Paris: Ladrange.
Renouvier, Charles. 1864a. *Troisième essai. Les Principes de la nature. Essais de critique générale*. Paris: Ladrange.
Renouvier, Charles. 1864b. *Quatrième essai. Introduction à la philosophie analytique de l'histoire. Essais de critique générale*. Paris: Ladrange.
Renouvier, Charles. 1868. "Introduction: De la philosophie en France au XIXe siècle." *L'Année philosophique (1867)*: 1–108.
Renouvier, Charles. 1869. "L'infini, la substance et la liberté." *L'Année philosophique (1868)*: 2–180.
Renouvier, Charles, 1875. *Essais de Critique générale*, second edition. (I. *Traité de logique générale et de logique formelle* (3 volumes); II. *Traité de psychologie rationelle d'après les principes du criticisme* (3 volumes)). Paris: Bureau de la Critique Philosophique.
Renouvier, Charles. 1882–1883. "La philosophie de la réflexion." *Critique Philosophique* 1882, t. 1, 17–27, 55–63, 170–176; t. 2, 209–219, 241–246; 1883, t. 1, 36–48, 65–75, 97–104, 113–123, 134–143.
Renouvier, Charles. 1885–1886. *Esquisse d'une classification systématique des doctrines philosophiques*, vol. 2. Paris: Bureau de la critique philosophique.
Renouvier, Charles. 1888. "Quelques remarques sur la théorie de la volonté de M.W. James." *Critique Philosophique* t. 2, 117–126.
Renouvier, Charles. 1906. *Critique de la doctrine de Kant*. Paris: Félix Alcan.
Richardson, Robert D. 2006. *William James: In the Maelstrom of American Modernism*. Boston: Houghton Mifflin.
Schmaus, Warren. 2007. "Renouvier and the Method of Hypothesis." *Studies in History and Philosophy of Science* 38 (1): 132–148.
Schmaus, Warren. 2018. *Liberty and the Pursuit of Knowledge: Charles Renouvier's Political Philosophy of Science*. Pittsburgh: University of Pittsburgh Press.
Schmaus, Warren. 2020. "From Positivism to Conventionalism: Comte, Renouvier, and Poincaré." *Studies in History and Philosophy of Science Part A* 80:102–109.

Viney, Donald Wayne. 1997. "William James on Free Will: The French Connection." *History of Philosophy Quarterly* 14 (1): 29–52.

Wahl, Jean. 2004. *Les philosophies pluralistes d'Angleterre et d'Amérique*. Original edition 1920. Paris: Les empêcheurs de penser en rond.

CHAPTER 25

JAMES AND PEIRCE

CLAUDINE TIERCELIN

DESPITE the wide range of writers enrolled under the banner of "pragmatism," it is still "commonplace to think of it in terms of its two main varieties, one of which stems from Peirce and the other from James,"[1] and to stress some deep differences between them: in particular, James chose nominalism and Peirce, realism. Owing to Peirce's maxim (5.402), the meaning of a concept seems to depend on the whole of its practical effects, which *suggests* nominalism. Indeed for James, Pragmatism "agrees with nominalism... in always appealing to particulars."[2] But Peirce defined himself as a "scholastic realist of a somewhat extreme stripe" (5.470), adapting Duns Scotus's theory to modern science, finding the latter's reasons for realism compelling (4.1). While at first "blinded by nominalistic preconceptions" (6.103), Peirce claimed to have "never been able to think differently on that question of realism" (1.20). Contrary to James, then, Peirce found a logical affinity (2.58) between pragmatism and realism.

Commentators often point out irreducible differences of "temperament" between the tender "popular philosopher" or humane "psychologist" James and the cold, abstruse logician of Milford—which the two close friends were themselves ready to admit.[3] It is also common to emphasize different trends in the pragmatism each man developed. Peirce invented a new word, "pragmaticism" (5.143–144), in opposition to the "philistine, humanistic and materialistic" reading of pragmatism, especially by F. C. S. Schiller. But he also lamented that the "philosophers of today" "should allow a philosophy so instinct with life to become infected with seeds of death in such notions as that of 'the mutability of truth'" (6.485), an expression clearly directed at James.

However, even if a gap between radical forms of pragmatism makes sense, for example, between Peirce and Rorty (Haack 1997a, 31–47), Peirce and James are much closer than is often claimed, on psychology, truth, ethics, and even realism. Peirce stressed his "theoretical divergences" with James, who pushed pragmatism "to such extremes as must tend to give us pause" (5.2), while noting that the divergences "for the most part, became evanescent in practice" (5.466).[4] Many fine studies of their correspondence have revealed that "Willie" and "Chas" were dedicated friends (Houser 2011), who did not care who had first "coined" the term "pragmatism," or who was the "leader" of the movement (Hookway 1997, 145–165), perhaps because neither the determination of "pragmatism" nor its advocacy (clearly a "means," not an "end") was viewed by them as of primary importance.[5] Even if James's pragmatism is supposed to focus on *truth*, Peirce's on *meaning* (and Dewey's on *inquiry*), for the three of them, pragmatism was less a doctrine than a weapon against false abstractions. For Peirce, it was explicitly a therapeutic *method* aimed at elucidating the meaning of our concepts and distinctions, so as to eliminate pseudo-problems encumbering metaphysics (5.2).[6]

This is not to say that there are no important differences, even oppositions, between them, but these may have more to do with what they took as decisive in philosophy and, more generally, with their respective conceptions of our ethical priorities.

So Many Things in Common

The common elements concern, first, Peirce's and James's relations to psychology.[7] Even if James is rightly praised as a first-rate psychologist for his pioneering work, to view him as the "mathematically imbecile" "psychologist," and Peirce as the "antipsychologist" "logician" of pragmatism, is hard to defend. Peirce did not achieve such complete books as *The Principles of Psychology*, but his "interest in philosophy grew out of his intense curiosity about cosmology and psychology" (4.2), and he was as early as James, involved in the revolution occurring in their time.[8]

Several disagreements are famous. So are Peirce's criticisms of James's method and reasoning in the *Principles*, judged circular and virtually self-refuting (W8, 239), "materialistic to the core" (W8, xlix), and failing to understand the concept of "unconscious inference." But Peirce also granted that the "directness and sharpness" of his objections should be "understood as a tribute of respect" and that James's *Principles* was "the most important contribution [. . .] made to the subject for many years" (Houser 2011, 48–49, passim). Now, without minimizing James's impact on some of Peirce's views (Girel 2003; Houser 2011), several aspects of Peirce's independent position should also be considered.

First, Peirce was against *psychologism*, if this meant that logic should be *based on* or *derived from* psychology in the (mainly Anglo-Scottish or German[9]) sense of introspection, association, intuition, sense data, consciousness, *Schwärmerei*, faculties, etc.[10] He was an acute critic of the "Old School," eager to forget the disasters generated by the *Gefühlpsychologie* in logic, science and metaphysics,[11] which held that general ideas, truth, or the classifications of reality are reducible to our creations or practices, and depend on or emerge from mere human action, and not from reality itself. The gist of the 1868 *Journal of Speculative Philosophy* Series (W2, 193–272) was to ruin the Cartesian and Lockean myths of intuition, introspection and "inwardness," the foundationalist value of first principles, to show the irrelevance of a distinction between internal and external views of the mind, and to endorse an externalist (inferential) conception of sensations, emotions and cognition in general, close to what Wittgenstein was to develop,[12] and enhanced by Peirce through a *social* conception of logic and a *dispositional* account of mental properties. By contrast with the "German theory of logic," Peirce claimed his linkage with the "English" or "objective conception of logic" (2.185), which made the criterion of good reasoning depend on the logical structure of the reasoning itself, not on what the reasoner might subjectively think of it (2.153; see Tiercelin 1993a, ch. 2, 56–118).

However, this should not be viewed as an opposition between Peirce and James. First, to present James as the paradigmatic advocate of "psychologism" (as the logical positivists did, and as Peirce, at times, also does) minimizes several aspects of James's approach to psychology, such as his attempt at developing "a form of conventionalism that anticipated the so-called 'relativized' *a priori* positivists themselves would independently develop," "an account of the *a priori* which grew from his reflections on the biological evolution of cognition, particularly in the context of his Darwin-inspired critique of Herbert Spencer" (Klein 2016).[13] Secondly, presenting Peirce as a radical "antipsychologist," even in logic, would also be unfair, for the main following reasons, at least:

a. He had nothing against *experimental* psychology (in the sense of Wundt or Fechner);[14] he was himself, even before James,[15] publishing in this area (Cadwallader 1975, 173), and never gave it up (Fisch and Cope 1952, 292).[16]

b. He rejected the "untrustworthy" psychology of introspection (contrary to James, indeed, in that respect) and insisted on verifying that the deduction of categories was in keeping with "facts" coming from "empirical psychology" (1.545–559; see Cadwallader 1975, 169–170). If "all attempts to ground the fundamentals of logic on psychology are seen to be essentially shallow" (5.28), psychological information can still be useful in other ways (2.710). Peirce's "antipsychologism" never went so far as to deny *all* facts of psychology (5.110). On the contrary, since logic is a *positive* science—unlike mathematics, it is a science of pure *hypotheses*—logic must appeal to facts (doubts, beliefs, etc.) or indubitable observations concerning mind, "or else it is in danger of degenerating into a mathematical recreation" (2.710) and would only concern "irrational" or "abnormal" men (5.438–463; 5.502-37; see Tiercelin 1991,191). Hence such observations are not to be made *only* by empirical or experimental psychology. They pertain to our everyday phenomenology or "phaneroscopy"(1.24; 4.116).[17] Now, James, too, "relied on some delightfully homespun psychological observations,"[18] for example in *The Principles of Psychology* (PP 1890, esp. ch. 13, 14, 22), offering associationistic accounts of reasoning as early as 1878 ("Brute and Human Intellect," EPs, 1-37). As Klein puts it, "James clearly held that we stand to learn something about logic by studying how people (and non-human animals) actually reason" (Klein 2016, 6–7), and here James and Peirce agree.

c. Peirce thought that a sharp distinction between logic and psychology, as drawn by Kant and most writers of the classical age, was not viable: logic, "the science of the forms of thought in general," was hardly different from "a logical analysis of the products of thought" (W1, 306). Peirce insisted on relying on what is classically referred to (e.g., by Kant) as either "psychology proper" or the "physiology of the mind" (1.579; 8.303) to throw light on doubt, habit or belief, and even calls the general science of signs a "physiology of forms" (Ms 478, 1903). "How to Make our Ideas Clear" (1878; 5.388–410) shows, through a physiological analysis, how habit is a "general rule operating in the organism" (5.594, W4, 39), and why habit is "the very market place of psychology" (7.367). But psychology also covers doubt, belief, sensation, emotion, the various kinds of (abductive, inductive, deductive) inferences, and the psychology of learning: all are fully integrated into pragmatism throughout Peirce's life (Cadwallader 1975, 170), as is clear from the 1891–1893 *Monist* series (6.102–163; 6.238–271), the unpublished *Grand Logic* (1893) and the 1898 *Cambridge Lectures* (7.468–517).

d. Peirce's complex position toward psychology and the somewhat strange mixture of transcendental, idealistic, normative, *and* naturalistic elements,[19] are also made clearer by his original conception of normativity (partly inherited from his interpretation of the theories of evolution) and his views on the relations between norms and nature: logical laws and norms are more *emerging* from nature than radically distinct from it. The rationality of a system of beliefs obeying logical norms is neither a transcendent *fact*, in a Fregean sense, nor a natural *fact*, as psychologists think, when they try (cf. Mill or Bain) to reduce the laws of thought to the laws of human psychology and the latter to natural laws. Hence, Peirce's *natural* logic avoids both subjective idealism and reductive naturalism (Tiercelin 1997). There is indeed but a gradation between a "cerebral" habit, a belief, and a full-fledged judgement, and our logical beliefs are the product of evolution and come from "irresistible" or "self-evident" feelings of approval or disapproval reached after a long history of relationships with our cultural peers (1.56; 3.160–361). But even if such a capacity has grown ("we outgrow the applicability of instinct"), one may not derive the *content* of the inferential rules from history. Since such rules state ideals of thought and action, their origin becomes opaque, an opacity which constitutes their normativity.

James was as much as Peirce hostile to the *reductionist* account of such authors as Spencer, who were guilty of confusing "a descriptive for a regulative account of cognition" and of believing that "appealing merely to descriptive facts" could "vindicate normative judgments." For James, "[b]iological description is based on perceptual 'experience,'" and hence cannot be normative, i.e., "an expression of values," since "values are not things we perceive" (Klein 2016, 4–5, citing EP 1878, 11, 11n, 15, 21). Even if Peirce formulates this more clearly, for both, logic is neither a science which can describe *directly* the processes of natural reasoning, nor a science able to codify anything which is totally distinct from the steps of reasoning. One can neither derive logical contents from any acts of the mind (both reject a naturalistic or evolutionary account of rationality or logic), nor follow a Fregean-type position, whose major difficulty is to leave unexplained how logic can simply be *applied*.

e. Last, not to call Peirce a "psychologist" would be all the more misleading as one of his achievements consisted in *redefining psychology itself* so as to widen its domain (the same being true of *logic*), by inventing, with the tools provided by his *semiotic* conception of logic, an original, broad, and new model of the *mind*, in no way limited to the *human* mind, but wide enough to extend to machines and even crystals,[20] which explains why Peirce's views are still relevant in so many research areas (cognitive psychology, metacognition, artificial intelligence, etc.).

Hence, neither was James the radical "psychologist" nor Peirce the radical "antipsychologist" they are often taken to be. Peirce was, from the start, just like James, a participant in all the liveliest discussions related to psychology (on consciousness, the association of ideas, the nature of inference, introspection, sensation, emotion, perception, belief and habit, doubt, abduction, the mind-matter distinction, free will, etc.).

Second, when it comes to Peirce's and James's respective views on truth, again they have some proximity.[21] Indeed, it is hard to identify "the one 'theory of truth'" either of James or of Peirce.[22] Attacks against the various pragmatists' views are famous.[23] So are the criticisms of James's views in his own time and later on (by Moore, Russell, and Ramsey, in particular): on his equation of truth with utility (P 1907, 106; MT 1909, 4),[24] with cash value or satisfaction, on his confusion between criteria and definitions,[25] and on his relativistic "subjectivism" and "verificationism."[26] So are the sarcastic comments on Peirce's sociological prophetism (Russell) or "tropism" concerning how to interpret his conception of truth as an "ideal limit" (Quine 1960, 23)[27] or as "the opinion which is *fated* to be ultimately agreed to by all who investigate" (W3, 273; W2, 254).[28] Also familiar are criticisms of how his "optimism" about reaching truth is compatible with a strong fallibilism,[29] so that he seems at times "to be separated from skepticism by a hair's breadth" (Hookway 1985, 73). More generally, his *conditional* conception of truth (2.661; 5.457; 2.664; 6.610),[30] and also his supposed incapacity—ruinous for a realist—to explain the reality of past events have been subject to criticism as well.[31]

However, not only are there many fruitful themes common to most pragmatists on truth,[32] but James and Peirce, themselves, were not so far from each other. For both of them:

a. Truth must be submitted to an examination of its *meaning* and to be given a real definition, not a nominal or abstract one (P 1907, 31; MT 1909, 6; W2, 356).[33] In many respects, they side with deflationist or minimalist theories of truth:[34] it is pure "tautology" or bad "metaphysics" to keep seeking truth when one has reached "a state of belief unassailable by doubt" (5.416; 5.525; 5.572). To clarify truth, then, is to link it with beliefs and assertions, i.e., dispositions to act which have effects and are normative for our conduct. "The whole function of thought is to produce habits of action" (5.398–400).

For James, the pragmatic *method* interprets each conception according to its *practical* consequences: "There can *be* no difference anywhere that doesn't *make* a difference elsewhere . . . . . ." (P 1907, 30).[35] "Real pragmatic truth is truth as can and ought to be used as a guide for conduct" (Ms 684, p. 11, 1913).[36] Both try to "humanize the notion of truth," to view it as a human instrument, not an idea dropped from the sky (Putnam 1995, 21).

b. Deflationists have criticized classical theories of coherence and correspondence as superfluous, "truistic" (Ramsey 1991, 12) platitudes (Hookway 2000, 82, 90)[37] providing no interesting information on the pragmatic meaning of the concept (5.578), and hence, having no consequences for our practices (Misak 2004, 6–7). But what Peirce and James share is more on par with a deflationist criticism of a *metaphysical realism* that harbors the illusion of a possible agreement with a real that is independent from or transcendent to what we might know of it,[38] which tends to mask the real problems at stake in the concept of truth, to mistake a "nominal" for a "real" definition, to favor a "transcendental" approach to truth (5.572), and to introduce even more obscure elements than the word "truth"(1.578). Peirce and James regard this metaphysical realism as distracting from what happens with our assertions and commitments, from our links with the community, from our "acts of thought," and finally, from knowledge, inquiry, and the role played by induction and probability in our approach to the true (Misak 1991, 38).

James, too, is convinced that truth is not an "inert static" *property* of our ideas (P 1907, 96), or a "duplication" of the corresponding reality. However, he insists—like Peirce who stresses the constraints both of existential resistance (or *Secondness*) and of the capacity of resistance of our hypotheses to experience—on the constraining power of reality with which our ideas must not, strictly speaking "correspond," but assuredly "*agree*" (P 1907, 96; MT 1909, 3). Such an agreement by a "direct acquaintance" with the external realities is shaped in radical empiricism (MT 1909, 104–106), so that an idea that is not directly verified can also "agree with reality" by "substituting" for it (ERE, 31–33; P 1907, 102; MT 1909, 4). Thus, even if there is something right in the idea of coherence, as Ramsey was later to insist on (1991, 39–40, 64), we must resist any coherentist temptation, for it creates an "entirely illusory difficulty" (1991, 39–40) "Realities are not *true*, they *are*; and beliefs are true *of* them" (MT 1909, 106; MT 1909, 9–10). This is why Putnam rightly sees in the "nominalist" James a strong Peircian strain, a constant "realist insistency," leading him to conceive truth as "the opinion which is fated to be ultimately agreed to by all who investigate" (5.407, W3, 273) (Putnam 1997, 166–170). While both are empiricists, urging that our knowledge is based on experience, they reject the passive, atomistic conception of experience consisting in scattered individual sensations assumed in much of the empiricist tradition (Hookway 2000, 292; Pihlström 2004, 36).

c. Again, both view truth as a serious business, as an *ideal* which guides—James (MT 1909, 142) as much as Peirce. James sticks to a distinction between what is *relatively* and *absolutely* true (MT 1909, 143; see Putnam 1997, 181). Truth is but a platitude, but it is a serious one and a norm. It is not a proposition written in a Fregean or Platonic world of ideas (Misak 1998; Hookway 2000, 62–63). It is *metaphysically* neutral (Hookway 2000, 53, 77, 80–81), but as it is connected with assertion, one should focus on the consequences such an *assertion* has for our beliefs, judgments, and actions (Haack 1976, 247–248; Hookway 2000, 97; Misak 2004, 6). In defining truth by the utility, not of what we do believe in fact, but of what an ideal agent would believe, placed in ideal conditions, or "at the limit of inquiry," the pragmatists indicate that the criteria of utility they are aiming at are first of all *cognitive* or epistemic (although not intellectualist) criteria;[39] the true is what pays *cognitively*, in a domain where the supreme value (even if more clearly for Peirce and Dewey than James) is understood as a value of *knowledge* and *inquiry*. Truth cannot be conceived within "moral solitude" (James): it works with the ideas of *inquiry* and *reality*, and also of *community*—which is in no way ethereal. Even if it is close to a "transcendental" (5.357), it must at any rate be "wider than man" (W2, 469), since "to make single individuals absolute judges of truth is most pernicious" (W2, 212). If the concept of truth is linked with the idea of community as to a "social logical principle" (W2, 242, 270–272; 5. 353), it is because the true is necessarily inter-subjective.

As Putnam noted, what James and Peirce want to deny is that truth might go faster than what humans could verify or discover. If "practical" has a more individualistic, vital, and emotional sense for James,[40] whereas Peirce, refusing such a "nominalistic" reading, gives it the meaning of a rational end (in Kant's sense; see 5.412), James does not yet go so far as is often said in that direction: indeed, beliefs have a vital importance, and would never have acquired the status of true beliefs if they had not been advantageous and useful, did not run the risk of being contradicted by experience, thus protecting us from later failures. For James, true beliefs are also those that allow us to maximize the conservation of our old beliefs while preserving consistency (MT 1909, 105). This is why, after observing that a belief in the Absolute would provide him with a sort of moral holiday, and would be good, i.e., "agreeable to believe," James rejects it, for it is inconsistent with other beliefs. James holds, like Peirce—who finds himself close to James (5.494)—that it would amount to a reduction of the meaning of "practice," to oppose it to "theoretical," when he essentially meant to oppose "practice" to "vague and abstract" (MT 1909, 112–113). If truth is in direct contact with reality through our beliefs or dispositions to action, then it is an instrument of inquiry, which occasionally allows us to get "an indication of the ways in which existing realities may be *changed*" (P 1907, 31–32). Hence, truth cannot be *dissociated from* verification, justification or confirmation of our beliefs (P 1907, 97).

Third, as far as ethics is concerned, James and Peirce are also very close. Both reject strict dualisms, between logic or epistemology and ethics, between fact and value, or between reason and sentiment. Ethics is *primary*.[41] Their common worry is the risk of neutralization, by indifference, of our ethical choices, "the anesthesia of the moral sceptic brought to bay and put to his trumps" (WB 1897, 87), the acuteness of the skeptical challenge in ethics (Tiercelin 2007).

More precisely: both reject moral rationalism and have an anti-theoretical reaction. There cannot be an ethical philosophy "made up in advance" (WB 1897, 141). Both favor conservative sentimentalism. There is no possible confusion between vital questions in which instinct or the feeling of some "primitive obligation" should operate, and scientific questions[42] in which *belief*—as a disposition to act—has no place (1.635).[43] But we have moral *obligations*. The condemnation of moral rationalism calls for a strict conception of rationality as a norm, a "system of ethics" (James), a "doctrine of the normative sciences" (Peirce), transcending the laws of "association" and utility, guided by *ends* and *ideals*. An "ideal of *conduct* is not a motive to *action*," but they cannot be viewed as utterly separated.

Hence, a subtle analysis of how both Sentiment *and* Rationality combine in shaping moral conduct so as to educate not so much a moral sense as a delicate balance between our ideals and motives, contributes to a "directly felt fitness with things" (WB 1897, 187). Unless ethical norms (neither "transcendent" prescriptions nor pure cultural products) were "inhabited" by motives, i.e., not so much moved by emotions as shaped by feelings—dispositions, involving evaluations[44]—they could not really lead us to action, function as genuine regulative principles, as "living hopes" (7.506; this is Peirce's equivalent to James's "living options").[45] Even if the "cool-hearted," "scholastic absolutist" Peirce stresses more the emergence of ethical norms from nature on the model of logical norms, and the controlled and deliberate character of conduct, while the "human" James emphasizes our perception of our underived or primitive *obligations* toward the "cries of the wounded," our "moral impulse," and the links between our obligations and *concrete* persons (WB 1897, 141, 147–148),[46] both call for an *ethical community* (or "moral republic") in which it is less crucial to aim at a "system" than to refine one's ethical *dispositions* or virtues by deepening one's skills, regarding both the "specific emotions" and "moral perceptions" required for the determination of the ideals to follow, and the capacities for deliberation and decision needed to meet the complexity of ethical situations.

In that sense, there is for both, a perfect (Aristotelian[47]) awareness of the links to be drawn between our cognitive or epistemic *and* practical or ethical reasons and virtues. Although Peirce is not what we would call today a "virtue epistemologist," he stresses the qualities of character one needs in order to lead inquiry properly, and finds it hard to conceive that "a rogue might be as good a reasoner as a man of honor" (1.576). Now, even if James's approach does not concern *inquiry* proper, the much discussed debate between him and Clifford in "The Will to Believe" may be seen as James's conviction that in order to act ethically (hence, for him, rationally and logically) one should take the "risk" of considering that, in some cases, *practical reasons should outweigh epistemic reasons*. If we have not only the will but the *obligation* to believe, it is because the only way to overthrow the moral sceptic, this "active ally of immorality," is by refusing the *illusion* of a possible neutrality. To that extent, as Putnam rightly saw, the main contribution of the pragmatists to the ethical debate laid in rejecting the positivist distinction between fact and value, in refusing to reduce rationality to mere scientific or instrumental rationality,[48] but also in refusing ethical relativism and adopting a cognitive approach to ethics.[49] Indeed, Peirce is closer to Dewey, insisting as he does on the ethical and social principle of logic, on the collective nature of science, a place of cooperation and interaction where ideas must be put to the test in order to be valued or rejected, whenever they encounter the resistance, the shock of reality, which is the creator of genuine (and not mere paper) doubt,[50] which obliges us to revise our beliefs and which can alone "fix" them. However, just as, for Peirce, science would only grow if we stuck to the spirit of fallibilism and continued to experience abduction and ethics, James was no less convinced that social progress would result from the same spirit and from our ongoing efforts in the elaboration and passionate defense of "ideals" (Putnam 1990, 411).[51]

From these brief remarks, we might be tempted to conclude that there were no major differences between James and Peirce: we have noted the "Peircean strain" in James's account of truth as "agreement"; now, even the so-called standard opposition between the "nominalist" pragmatism of James *versus* Peirce's "realist" version seems farfetched. For Haack (1977, 392–393), the difference is not that Peirce accepted and James denied the reality of universals, but that Peirce denied that real universals can be reduced to particulars, while James thought they can. James, recognizing the significance of "general ideas," "was never [in spite of Peirce's strictures] a thoroughgoing nominalist" (Perry 1935/1936, I, 547; II, 407), nor even a straightforward "verificationist" in logic (Klein 2016, 17ff.), and even approached the realistic position in his mature writings, especially in the *Pluralistic Universe*.[52]

However, such conclusions would overlook several important differences.

The Main Differences

First, Peirce pays more attention to the *methods* of inquiry. Both underline the dynamical (genetic, James says) character of truth (a possible influence of Darwin), but Peirce cares more than James (and much like Dewey who stresses the "biological" and "cultural" matrices of inquiry) about the *modalities* and *methods* governing the process of inquiry in its naturalistic and normative aspects. Finally, the definition or real *meaning* of truth lies in its capacity to determine which beliefs resist doubt and are stable (5. 416; 5.375). In defining the true as that which inquiry aims at, Peirce also chooses the method which, contrary to the methods of authority, tenacity or a priori, can fix belief, i.e. the scientific method, which gets its strength from the constraint exerted by reality and realizes, by its *independence* from individual minds, the consensus of the *community* (Haack 1976, 234–235). Truth is not an "honorific" term which we put on warranted beliefs (James, Rorty); it is "the best that inquiry would do, given as much time and evidence as it takes to reach beliefs which would not be overturned "(Misak 1991, 154).

A second important difference concerns James's notion of "verifiability," which Peirce, like most—even generous—critics finally find untenable. His nominalism forced him to replace "verifiable" by "true" and to view Truth as a "growing corpus" which individual truths join as they are verified. James can hardly face the objection according to which "if a belief is true just in case it is *verifiable*, all these individual truths are true *before* they are verified (which is what James plainly says in his [MT 1909, 121]); so the Truth consists always of the same truths, and does not, after all grow" (Haack 1976, 239). Hence a tension (or rather "inconsistency," Haack 1984; Putnam 1997, 177ff.), denounced by Peirce as James's " 'mutability of truth' conception" (6. 485).[53]

A third important difference, granting the *primacy of* ethics, concerns what they take as *primary in* ethics and as *the best way to resist the sceptic*. If truth is metaphysically neutral, we avoid formalism and deflationism by focusing on *what* counts *in truth* and on our practices (Misak 2004, 5; 150ff.). Epistemology is never divorced from ethics. However, if both have a sentimental *and* normative conception of rationality (see Peirce's "normative sciences"[54] and James's "Sentiment of Rationality"), for Peirce, ethical justifications cannot be merely instrumental: they rest on special *norms of rationality*. What a rational person pursues in any action is not his own benefit, but what might benefit mankind (or the community of rational investigators) in the *infinitely long run*, as is shown in the *Doctrine of Chances* (W3, 276–289), where Peirce defends "altruistic" and even "Buddhistic" virtues of self-abnegation:[55] to act otherwise would mean to be "illogical in all one's inferences." In that sense, there are "crucial differences" between Peirce and James.[56] Belief is a rule of conduct or a habit, tied to an end or a purpose. But for James, all purposes, "mundane and not-so mundane," are relevant, according to Putnam. For Peirce:

> Whenever we speak of a rule of conduct, whether in ethics (... the science of the admirable in the way of conduct, and hence ... presupposing aesthetics, or the science of the admirable in general), or in logic (... the science of the admirable by way of *scientific* conduct, and hence ... presupposing ethics) we "speak with a universal voice," as Hookway puts it [Hookway 1985, 62], deliberately using language from Kant's third critique.... With one stroke, Peirce thus advances a conception of inquiry according to which "practice" in precisely the sense that interests James—what we do about our weal and woe in our day-to-day and year-to-year struggles and adventures in living—is *irrelevant* both to the meaning of our concepts and to the rules for the conduct of inquiry. (Putnam 2002, 222–223; introduction)

And although "Peirce expresses enthusiastic agreement with James's 'splendid argumentation on the conterminousness of minds' (January 23, 1903, p. 181) ... [Peirce is referencing] the heading of section 6 of James's 'A World of Pure Experience' [ERE, 37]," (Putnam 2002, 224, n.67) he

> accuses James of "nominalism" ... [for insisting] that relations are real because they are *given in experience*. But what we directly experience, according to Peirce, is feelings or firstness, ... and reactions, or secondness. But the reality of a relation is the reality of a *general*. If you are not a realist about *counterfactuals*—and I believe with Peirce that James was not—then in Peirce's view, you cannot understand the *way* in which universals are real. (Putnam 2002, 224; see CWJ 10.xlvi–xlvii)

Hence, even if Putnam takes James as "the greatest exponent" of pragmatism (Putnam 1995, 6; 1987, 84–85), he praises Peirce for understanding the "depth" of the problem of objectivity in ethics (Putnam 1987, 8ff.; 1994a, 160–169) and the deeply ethical side of epistemology. "It is impossible to be completely and rationally logical except on an ethical basis" (2.198)[57] since "one can *only* be rational if one *identifies himself* psychologically with a whole ongoing—in fact a potentially infinite—community of investigators" (Putnam 1987, 83; 1994a, 160),[58] something which appears as "immediately" rational (Hookway 2000, 239), as a "primitive conception of rationality," a sentiment imperatively required by logic, something which has more to do with a kind of "revelation" of our duties as "mere cells of the social organism" merging into "the universal continuum" than with any prescription (1.673).

Now, such a difference in what primarily counts in ethics appears in the way James and Peirce address the sceptic, or even deem it decisive (or not) to address him. Peirce (and later on, Dewey and Ramsey too) takes the epistemological and metaphysical challenges raised by scepticism seriously, much more, at least, than James (or, for that matter, the *latest* Putnam). This can be shown through another possible reading of the dialogue of the deaf (Haack 1997b) between James and Clifford,[59] the latter being finally too demanding, morally speaking, while James sounds too permissive, epistemically speaking (WB 1897, 20–21, or 79–81), both failing to make a clear enough distinction between an *epistemological* and an *ethical justification*.[60] Although Peirce would ethically agree with James and, notwistanding his evidentialist tendencies, would qualify Clifford's position, he would probably favor some *overlap* (rather than strict *correlation* or much less *reduction*) between epistemic and ethical norms, and be against a pure reduction of epistemic norms to ethical ones.[61]

This already makes a difference of approach between James and Peirce to the sceptical challenge as such. The condemnation by the doxastic voluntarist James of *moral* scepticism, presented as a sick obsession with the risk of error (WB 1897, 24, 81), is all the more offensive given that the threat of epistemological scepticism and of an inaccessible objective certainty is strong. In other words, James's rejection of moral scepticism is all the more "justified" as James has, at the outset, conceded a lot to the sceptic, in the end claiming that there is no way to "refute" the sceptic with logic, which remains "speechless" in front of it (WB, 19; also see 22, 26, 32–33, 50).

Now, if James the empiricist is never far from Sextus or Montaigne, neither is Peirce, the experimentalist, the sentimental conservative, far from the Reidian Commonsensist. But Peirce also resembles more a Carneades in viewing probability as the guide in life (like Ramsey).[62] This situation is even worse for Peirce, since his scepticism is not as peaceful as academic scepticism. Fallilism is not merely *epistemological* but *ontological*—due to a strong metaphysical commitment to a realism of vagueness (Tiercelin 1992)—thus it is closer, at times, to mere dogmatic scepticism (Hookway 1985, 73). If our knowledge is basically conjectural and provisional, if nothing may even correspond to our idea of what reality is (4. 61) then we are not far indeed from falling into the sceptic's well.

However, we face a real difference here: while Peirce condemns *radical* or *dogmatic* forms of scepticism (see his rejection of radical—or paper—doubt and of the whole of Cartesianism),[63] he never gives up the basically *evidentialist* ideal (what he names "the logic of pragmatism") of relying on logic or knowledge in order to justify our beliefs. This is strictly required by the Scientific Method, whose aim is to help the "Scientific Intelligence" to reach the truth, a method not only subjected to observation and experience, but also to our normative capacity of reasoning, inference, deliberation,[64] self control, criticism, criticism *of* criticism included.[65] He provides a detailed analysis of the *nature* of belief (3.160–161), self control (5.440–441), reasoning "viewed as thinking in a controlled and deliberate way" (1.573); he explains *how* norms *emerge* from nature,[66] why "the phenomena of reasoning are in their general features, parallel to those of moral conduct" (1.606), why logical norms are so close to ethical norms *and vice versa*, and defines the *role and aims* of the Normative sciences.[67] He also describes the (both natural and normative) mechanisms governing beliefs and doubts in inquiry, underlining *both* the necessity of *genuine* doubts prompted by real external causes, which stimulate our inquiry and finally contribute, thanks to the method of *scientific* inquiry ruled by *reality*, to fix our beliefs, *and* the necessity of applying fallibilism to *all* domains whatsoever. This explains why, while rejecting the Cartesian sceptical scenario, Peirce admires the Cartesian method and claims that one should be a fallibilist regarding fallibilism, too.[68] Radical *fallibilism* and *Critical* Commensism[69] are two sides of the same coin.

This takes us to the fourth important difference (maybe the most important one), between James and Peirce, namely, an issue concerning metaphysics.

Most pragmatists think that questions of metaphysics or ontology should be treated only to the extent that one quickly gets rid of them. "Ethics *without* ontology" (Putnam 2004) should be the *motto*. This is also, in part, Peirce's reaction toward metaphysics and its pseudo-problems. However, once philosophy has been purified (thanks to the pragmatic maxim), it becomes possible to erect a *scientific* and *realistic* metaphysics (Tiercelin 2003a).

We may take James's *radical empiricism* or Putnam's *natural realism* as ways of calming most metaphysical worries, and as answering the Cartesian sceptical challenge in explaining how our perceptions relate us to the real world.[70] However, Peirce's subtle account of perception, his sophisticated categorial and semiotic framework, and his original account of abduction,[71] provide a more convincing response to the most enduring challenge posed by scepticism, namely, its metaphysical part: how to prove the reality of the external world. This is crucial since, for a pragmatist, ethics deals less with universal norms, categorical imperatives or prescriptions than with a *perception of moral values* and an *education of our ethical dispositions*, thus implying a careful analysis of *perception* and of the *nature* of such dispositions: are these categorial, higher order, or merely functional *properties*? Peirce offers such a discussion and a fruitful and original approach to the still lively debate about the real nature and importance of dispositions as irreducible ontological properties (Tiercelin 2007).

Such a metaphysical approach is decisive for a second reason: the objectionable psychologization of pragmatism and the individualism it induces, for which, incidentally, Peirce finds Schiller more guilty than James, exposing us to the clutches of the literary circles and to "sham" reasoning. Both James and Peirce agree: there is no difference in thinking that should not imply a difference in action. So there is always a link between epistemology and ethics which is, in the end, primary. Peirce took pragmatism to be the spiritual heir of Kantianism, and his own lineage as that of "a pure Kantian" who was simply forced "by successive steps" into Pragmaticism. Peirce saw Kant as a "somewhat confused pragmatist" (5.412) because he could see "the inseparable link which exists between rational knowledge and rational finality" (5. 412). But, as is notorious, "What should I do?" can *either* mean, as Kant does, the primacy of practical reason, *or* the primacy of the question of "life" over the question of knowledge. More than James, Peirce was suspicious of what might turn into any idolatry of *life*. For him, progress could only be achieved through the *scientific* method, all the others (tenacity, authority, a priori) being doomed to fail. He depicted his philosophical enterprise as growing "out of a contrite fallibilism, combined with a high faith in the reality of knowledge, and an intense desire to find things out" (1.14). Hence a conception of philosophy favoring such epistemic virtues as rationality, humility, professionalism, discussion, argumentation, intellectual exchange, rather than visionary outbursts, cults of individuality, romantic unbound subjectivity, or literary conversation: philosophy should always stay close to the laboratory, which, contrary to scientism and dogmatism, promotes the hypothetical, the fallible, the experimental, and the irreducible indeterminacy involved in all thinking.

Being both fallibilists *and* anti-sceptics is "*the* unique insight of American pragmatism," Putnam rightly noted (1994a, 152). But how can one maintain the truth there is in fallibilism without giving everything to the sceptic or to the irrationalist relativist? Both James and Peirce were eager to "value tolerance and pluralism" and to avoid "the epistemological scepticism that came with that tolerance and pluralism" "without tumbling back into moral authoritarianism" (Putnam 1995, 2). Both showed that pragmatism is "a way of thinking ... of lasting importance and an option (or at least an 'open question') that should figure in present-day philosophical thought" (Putnam 1995, xi). However, James was no doubt closer to a romantic and existentialist version (Putnam 1990, 229), and Peirce to a rationalist version of the values praised by the Enlightenment. For Peirce, it is no doubt through *knowledge* that philosophy contributes to the "melioration" of the human condition, which he proved, by offering a new definition of the territory of epistemology itself (Tiercelin 2005a, 259 ff.), and by suggesting several parries to the epistemological, ethical, but also importantly metaphysical aspects of the sceptical challenge.

Indeed, if ethics is, as both Peirce *and* James claim, an *education* of our moral capacities and dispositions having more to do with moral *perceptions* than with some a priori faculty, moral sense, or normative prescriptions to follow, then, we face the obligation to find a solid basis for a correct account of how our perceptions relate us to the real world and to make our ideas clear about the nature of *reality* itself. Notwithstanding Putnam's latest claims, this is not a pseudo-problem (Putnam 1994b, 509). Peirce was rightly convinced of the seriousness of the problem of universals and, contrary to James, he thought nominalism was the wrong answer to it. He saw a necessary link between pragmatism and realism, so that "pragmaticism could hardly have entered a head that was not already convinced that there are real generals" (5.503). In the end, even if this is not the major option chosen by most pragmatists today (Tiercelin 2013), Peirce may have been more on the right track than James, when in a very Jamesian spirit, he revealed his realistic "temperament," in the following way:

So long as there is a dispute between nominalism and realism, so long as the position we hold on the question is not determined by any proof *indisputable*, but is more or less a matter of inclination, a man as he gradually comes to feel the profound hostility of the two tendencies will, if he is not less than man, become engaged with one or other and can no more obey both than he can serve God and Mammon. If the two impulses are neutralized within him, the result simply is that he is left without any great intellectual motive. . . . [T]hough the question of realism and nominalism has its roots in the technicalities of logic, its branches reach about our life. The question whether the *genus homo* has any existence except as individuals, is the question whether there is anything of any more dignity, worth, and importance than individual happiness, individual aspirations, and individual life. Whether men really have anything in common, so that the community is to be considered as an end in itself, and if so, what the relative value of the two factors is, is the most fundamental practical question in regard to every public institution the constitution of which we have it in our power to influence. (1871; Peirce W2, 486–487)

Such a position may explain why, paradoxically enough, the logician of Milford's views (more than James's, but more than Dewey's, too) are increasingly taken today as a fruitful source of inspiration for a convincing defense of democracy (see Misak 2000 or Talisse 2007).

Notes

1. Haack (1977); Robin (1997, 139).
2. Quoted by Haack (1977, 378).
3. Without denying James's generosity toward "Chas" (or "Charley"), one is somewhat disappointed that such a great philosopher (see Putnam 2002, introduction to CWJ 10.xlii–xliii) did not try hard, as all his (most often very short) letters testify, to understand (or even read?) someone who, "quite accurately" is taken by "many people" to be "a philosophical giant, perhaps the most important philosopher to have emerged in the United States" (Hookway 1985, ix). See, e.g., CWJ (1910, 12.457).
4. For other parallels, see Hookway (1997, 145–165).
5. 5. 466; 5. 494. On Peirce's "ambivalence" toward James, see Hookway (1997, 146).
6. Gallie (1966, 11–21); Tiercelin (1993a, ch. 1).
7. Fisch and Cope (1952); Cadwallader (1975); Tiercelin (1985, 1993a, 1993b, 2017); Girel (2003); Houser (2011); Klein (2016).
8. Cadwallader was one of the first scholars to show this (1975, 166–170); Tiercelin (1993a, 29–41, 2005b, 2006). W3, 114–160 (1873); W3, 211–216; W3, 382–493 (*Photometric Researches*, 1878); 7.21-35; W4, 122–135, 1884, with Jastrow. See Cadwallader (1975, 175–176). Beside Jastrow, Peirce had others as students and/or members of his *Metaphysical Club*, who became prominent as psychologists: J. Dewey, J. McKeen Cattell, and Ch. Ladd-Franklin (Cadwallader and Cadwallader 1974).
9. On Sigwart's "*Gefühl-criterion*" (5.85; 2.232; 2.210; 5.329), on Schröder (5.85; 3.432), on Stuart Mill (2.52; 3.432; 8.144). Peirce wrote that knowing how the mind works has no place in logic (2.63); see Cadwallader (1975, 184–185).

10. See W1, 63; W1, 164–167; 1.310; 2.40–43; 2.47; 5.85; 5.157; 5.244–249; 5.265; 7.376; 7.419–425; 8.144; Ms 633; Ms 645. The dominant psychology in America was a blend of theology and philosophy, mostly in the hands of such minister-college presidents as L. P. Hickok: *Rational Psychology* (1849) and *Empirical Psychology* (1854), or F. Wayland: *The Elements of Intellectual Philosophy* (1854); see (Cadwallader 1975, 170–171), and Peirce's Reviews in *The Nation* of Porter's *The Human Intellect* (W2, 273–281) and of James Mill's *Analysis of the Phenomena of the Human Mind* (W2, 302–307).
11. On Peirce's relation to psychology, and the various meanings he gave to it, Tiercelin (1993a, 32ff, 2006, 2017).
12. Tiercelin (1993a, 1993b, 2000. 2005a, 2012). Calcaterra (2006, 36–37).
13. See James's response to anti-psychologistic criticism (MT, 86; Klein 2016, 6).
14. Peirce started reading Wundt as early as 1862 (Ms 326, 1; 8.196; 7.597).
15. "Peirce, rather than James, should be considered 'America's first modern psychologist'" (Cadwallader 1975, 173–174). In particular, James "published nothing in the nature of a psychological experiment until 1881." See also Cadwallader (1974, 10, 291–298).
16. See the 1868 papers, the 1878–1879 papers: "How to Make Our Ideas Clear" and "The Fixation of Belief"; and 8.196; 7.597; Ms 891; Ms 919-930; W3, 111-137; W3, 382-493.
17. On the implications of phaneroscopy for psychology, Cadwallader (1975, 185–186); Calcaterra (2006, 42–43).
18. See PP, 438n, quoted by Klein (2016, 11).
19. So, I partly disagree with Hookway: "Perhaps the most distinctive feature of his philosophical system . . . is, from his earliest work, a total repudiation of naturalism, and a defence of epistemology (Grammar and Logic) as a prior philosophy" (1984, 2).
20. Tiercelin (1984, 1991, 1994a, 1995, 1997, 2017).
21. I have elaborated this at length in Tiercelin (2005a/2016, ch. 4, 109–145), and Tiercelin (2014).
22. Assertions are found in favor of extreme subjectivism (MT 1909, 129), objectivism (MT, 105), relativism—albeit not implying a refusal of absolutism (MT, 142–143), correspondentism (P 1907, 96), coherentism (P, 34–37; MT, 104–105), and a consensus-theory *à la* Peirce (MT, 142–143); see Kirkham (1992, 88).
23. Putnam (1997, 166); H. Thayer (1981, 322); Haack (1998); Tiercelin (1994a); Dokic and Engel (2002), conclusion.
24. Many objections have been met by James (*contra* Russell see MT, 146–149); see Haack (1976, 237); Putnam (1997, 180). For F. P. Ramsey on James, see Ramsey (1991, 91–92), and for discussions see Dokic and Engel (2002, 43) and Tiercelin (2004b, 2015).
25. This is an ill-founded criticism, as noted by Haack (1976, 237). On the main differences between James and Peirce, see Thayer (1981, 140); Misak (2004, 4).
26. Although Peirce was also associated with "verificationism" (see Quine or the early Putnam), it is James who has mostly defended truth in terms of *verification* and been criticized on such (partly unfair) grounds (Haack 1976, 234; Haack 1984; Thayer, introd. to MT and to P, 1975, xxii).
27. Although Quine (1981, 31) is partly right (see Ms 473, Ms 333, Ms 289; 5.494; 5.608; 5.416; Ms 374; 7.119, 8.226; 7.78), this is a reductive view of Peirce's concept of inquiry. Reaching theories means coming closer to the truth at least as much by *consensus* (i.e., agreement) as by *convergence*. See Misak (1991, 121–122).
28. Although Peirce seems to waver between a *future* and a *conditional* interpretation, the second one is the right one (2.654; 8.43; 5. 409; 5.587; 8. 43). See Hookway (2000, 50ff).

29. Knowledge is *conjectural* and *provisional* (1.137–140; 1.141; 1.171; 1.403; 5.541; 5.168; 5.569; 5.2; 6.526). The "intellectual hope" that our hypotheses get closer and closer to the truth if we pursue our inquiries long enough is "a rational requirement" (NEM.IV, xiii), although we are "so far from ever being authorized to conclude that a theory is the very truth itself, that we can never so much as understand what that means" (7.119).
30. Such a fate to come to agreement does not obey a blind mechanism. Adopting a *propensity* view of probabilities, Peirce compares this rather to the throwing of a pair of dice: when you throw a pair of dice, you can be sure it will not fail to obey its *would-be*, or propensity to fall on a double six, but this outcome has no *logical* necessity (4.547n1; 7.35).
31. W3, 274, 1878; 5.589. Even then, we must *hope* for the possible application of the principle of bivalence, for "the only assumption upon which [we] can act rationally is the hope of success" (W2, 272). We must have the regulative (though living) hope that for any hypothesis "a prolonged inquiry would declare it to be either true or false" (Misak 1991, 139–140).
32. I have shown this in detail, not only with regard to Peirce and James, but also to Dewey, Ramsey, Putnam, and, to some extent, Wittgenstein (Tiercelin 2005a, 2014).
33. About the "linguistic muddle" surrounding the concept of truth, see also F. Ramsey PP, 39.
34. On Peirce, see Misak (1991, 1998, 412–415); Tiercelin (1993a, 106 ff., 2005a); Hookway (2000, chs. 2, 3, and 4). On Ramsey, see Dokic and Engel (2002, 31–37).
35. This goes for Ramsey, too (1990, 51; 1991, 44).
36. Hookway (2000, 239); Tiercelin (2005a, 172ff).
37. 1.427; 8.126; 5.549; 5.553; 6.67; 8.26. See Hookway (2000, 86).
38. What is condemned in correspondence is an illusory relation between our ideas and the world. Putnam's most constant adversary, from 1981 on, is, just like Peirce, metaphysical realism or "externalism" (1981, 49).
39. In that respect, it is wrong to underestimate Peirce's emphasis on the role of instinct, but also of sentiments, feelings and affects in knowledge (Tiercelin 1993a, 377ff.; Hookway 2000), as well as to oppose "pragmatic" and "cognitive" in James.
40. This is why he is (while Peirce is not) ready to say that if we have no evidence for deciding between two rival conceptions, our choice can be made on subjective or aesthetic reasons, in terms of taste, "elegance," or economy (P 1907, 104).
41. I have analyzed this in detail in chapter 5 of Tiercelin (2005a, 146ff and 173ff).
42. See RLT, 107–117; 1.50–58; 1.76; 2.82; 1.13; 1.236; 5.582–589. Tiercelin (2002b and 2005a, 149–160).
43. Peirce, 1.655, 5.60; RTL, 110–112; WB 1897, 161–162.
44. Hookway (2000, 239); Tiercelin (2005a, 172ff).
45. For Peirce, norms are never separated from values, since norms are "emerging" from (and not irreducible to) nature. Tiercelin (1997 and 2005a, 170ff).
46. James's individualistic nominalism, stressing more the *accessibility* than the *independance* (Peirce) of truth is, in that respect, more "palatable" to Putnam in its "modesty" and "humanity" (1990, 217–218).
47. On the importance of Aristotle for Peirce, see Tiercelin (2004a).
48. Putnam (1994a, 154–156, 156–160, 170–171, 201; 1995, 22). On Putnam's views, see Tiercelin (2002a, 85ff).
49. Tiercelin (2002a, 24ff; 2003b; 2005a, 184 ff). These are themes Putnam has been stressing (e.g., Putnam 1981, 137, 211–216; 1995, 15).
50. On this and the closeness of views of Peirce and Wittgenstein, see Tiercelin (2005a, ch. 3).

51. Our principles can be corrected according to the new experiences we make (WB, 115–116). Such "a deep link between truth, reality and community, is expressed in his meliorist religion" (Putnam 1990, 231).
52. Seigfried (1990, 267, 399n5); Rosenthal (2000, 94).
53. See CWJ 10.511–513 for the exchange between Peirce and James (letters from Dec. 6–7, 1904).
54. The *Normative Sciences* (logic, ethics, and aesthetics) are "the purely theoretical sciences of purpose" (1.282). See 2.197–2.198; 1.573; 1.574; 5.27; 5.35; 5.429.
55. On Peirce's Parfitian emphasis on "survival" rather than "personal identity" (5.313; 4.448; 1.349), in keeping with his semiotic realism and the view that not only thought, but man itself is a sign, so that one should favor a third person stance—or unity of symbolization (7.592–594)—rather than a first person individual or private standpoint (substance, consciousness, or physiological unity), i.e., "a special determination of the generic soul of the family, the class, the nation, the race to which he belongs..." (7.592), see Tiercelin (1993a, 254ff).
56. Putnam 2002, introduction to CWJ 10.xlv; on this, see Tiercelin (2005a, 146ff and 173ff).
57. Compare here W3, 281–284, and WB 1897, 79 n.
58. On this, see Tiercelin (2005a, 146ff and 173ff).
59. Cf. Clifford: "It is wrong always, everywhere, and for everyone, to believe anything upon insufficient evidence" ("The Ethics of Belief," 1879, 77).
60. See my analysis in Tiercelin (2005a, ch. 5, 195–201).
61. Haack (1993, ch. 10). Hence the reservations of the "good old friend" Peirce to whom the *Will to Believe* had been dedicated (8.251; 1897).
62. See in particular Ramsey (1991, 58 and 63), where he combines this position with an attitude close to the Peirce's Critical Commonsensism. Tiercelin (2005a, 254; 2015; 2016).
63. He is close to Wittgenstein's views in *On Certainty*, in particular. See Tiercelin (2000 and 2005a, ch. 3).
64. 7.326, W3, 40ff.; 8.41; W2, 8 and 16; Ms 749; Ms 596.
65. 5.108; 2.182; 2.204; 5.55; 7. 444; 7.457; Ms 692; Ms 453; 8.191, etc.
66. See Tiercelin 1997 for an analysis of this "emergentism," inspired by the "middle-way" suggested by Kant in (*Kritik der reinen Vernunft*, B 166–167).
67. On Peirce's stress on norms and values so as to elaborate such a doctrine, see Robin (1964, 271–288) and the classical Potter (1967). See also Tiercelin (1993a, 335–384; 1994, 642–660; 1997, 35–58).
68. This is why, despite links between Peirce and Wittgenstein and their common criticism of radical doubt, Peirce's analysis is more elaborate than Wittgenstein's, and his *critical commonsensism* more efficient too, as a parry to the epistemological side of the sceptical challenge (Tiercelin 2005a and 2016).
69. On Peirce's Critical Commonsensism, inspired both by Th. Reid and by Kant, see in particular: 5.416; 5.442; 5.498; 5.517; 5. 522.
70. For a comparison and evaluation of the three approaches, see Tiercelin (2005a, ch. 6).
71. See Tiercelin (2005b and 2005a, ch. 6).

Bibliography

Cadwallader, T. C. 1974. "Charles S. Peirce (1839–1914): The First American Experimental Psychologist." *Journal of the History of the Behavioral Sciences* 10: 291–298.

Cadwallader, T. C. 1975. "Peirce as an Experimental Psychologist." *Transactions of the Charles S. Peirce Society* 11 (3): 167–186.
Cadwallader, T. C., and J. W. Cadwallader. 1972. "America's First Modern Psychologist: William James or Charles S. Peirce?" *Proceedings of the 80th Annual Convention of the American Psychological Association* 7 (Pt.2): 773–774.
Calcaterra, R. M. 2006. "Psychology and Anti-psychologism in Peirce." In *Semiotics and Philosophy in Charles Sanders Peirce*, edited by Leo R. Fabbrichesi Leo and S. Marietti, chap. 4: 35–50. Cambridge, UK: Cambridge Scholars Press.
Clifford, W. K. 1879/1947. "The Ethics of Belief." In *The Ethics of Belief and Other Essays*, 70–96. London: Watts and Co.
Dokic, J., and P. Engel. 2002. *Ramsey, Truth and Success*. London: Routledge.
Fisch, M., and J. I. Cope. 1952. "Peirce at the Johns Hopkins University." In *Studies in the Philosophy of C. S. Peirce*, edited by P. Wiener and F. H. Young, 277–311, 355–360. Cambridge: Harvard University Press.
Gallie, W. B. 1966. *Peirce and Pragmatism*. New York: Dover.
Girel, M. 2003. "The Metaphysics and Logic of Psychology: Peirce's Reading of James's *Principles*." *Transactions of the Charles S. Peirce Society* 39 (2): 163–203.
Haack, S. 1976. "The Pragmatist Theory of Truth." *British Journal for the Philosophy of Science* 27 (3): 231–249.
Haack, S. 1977. "Pragmatism and Ontology: Peirce and James." *Revue Internationale de Philosophie* 31 (12): 377–400.
Haack, S. 1984. "Can James's Theory of Truth Be Made More Satisfactory?" *Transactions of the C.S. Peirce Society* XX (3): 270–278.
Haack, S. 1993. *Evidence and Inquiry. Towards Reconstruction in Epistemology*. Oxford: Blackwell.
Haack, S. 1997a. "We, Pragmatists ... Peirce and Rorty in Conversation." *The Partisan Review* LXIV (1): 91–107.
Haack, S. 1997b. "The Ethics of Belief" Reconsidered." In *The Philosophy of Roderick Chisholm*, edited by L. E. Hahn, 129–144. La Salle, IL: Open Court.
Haack, S. 1998. *Manifesto of a Passionate Moderate: Unfashionable Essays*. Chicago and London: Chicago University Press.
Hookway, C. 1985. *Peirce*. London: Routledge and Kegan Paul.
Hookway, C. 1997. "Logical Principles and Philosophical Attitudes: Peirce's Response to James's Pragmatism." In *The Cambridge Companion to William James*, edited by R. A. Putnam, 145–165. Cambridge, UK: Cambridge University Press.
Hookway, C. 2000. *Truth, Rationality and Pragmatism: Themes from Peirce*. Oxford, UK: Clarendon Press.
Houser, N. 2011. "Peirce's Post-Jamesian Pragmatism." *European Journal of Pragmatism and American Philosophy* III (I): 39–60.
Kirkham, R. 1992. *Theories of Truth*. Cambridge, MA: MIT Press.
Klein, A. 2016. "Was James Psychologistic ?" *Journal for the History of Analytical Philosophy* 4 (5): 1–21.
Misak, C. 1991. *Truth and the End of Inquiry a Peircean Account of Truth*. Oxford, UK: Clarendon Press.
Misak, C. 1998. "Deflating Truth: Pragmatism *vs* Minimalism." *The Monist* 81: 407–425.
Misak, C. 2000. *Truth, Politics, Morality*. New York: Routledge.

Misak, C., ed. 2004. *The Cambridge Companion to C.S. Peirce*. Cambridge, UK: Cambridge University Press.

Peirce, C. S. 1931–1958. *Collected Papers of Charles Sanders Peirce* (1931–1958), Vols. 1–6, edited by C. Hartshorne and P. Weiss (1931–1935); Vols. 7–8, edited by A. Burks (1958). Cambridge, MA: Belknap Press of Harvard University Press. Abbrev: Volume number, paragraph number (e.g: 5.348).

Peirce, C. S. 1967. *The Papers of Charles S. Peirce* (1857–1914), Abbrev. MS or L = number, or L + number. The numbering is that of R. Robin, ed., *Annotated Catalogue of the Papers of Charles S. Peirce*. Amherst: University of Massachusetts Press.

Peirce, C. S. 1976. *The New Elements of Mathematics* (NEM), edited by C. Eisele, 4 vols. The Hague: Mouton.

Peirce, C. S. 1982–2000. *Writings of Charles S. Peirce: A Chronological Edition* (1982–2000), 6 vols. Peirce Edition Project (Ed.), Bloomington: Indiana University Press, 1982–2000. (W+ Volume Number + Page number; e.g: W2: 234).

Peirce, C. S. 1992. *Reasoning and the Logic of Things: The Cambridge Conferences Lectures of 1898*, (RLT), edited by K. Ketner. Cambridge, MA: Harvard University Press.

Perry, R. B. 1935. *The Thought and Character of William James* (2 vols.). Atlantic, Little, Brown.

Pihlström, S. 2004. "Peirce's Place in the Pragmatist Tradition." In *The Cambridge Companion to C.S. Peirce*, edited by Misak, 27–57. Cambridge, UK: Cambridge University Press.

Potter, V. G. 1967. *Charles S. Peirce On Norms and Ideals*. Amherst: University of Massachusetts Press.

Putnam, H. 1981. *Reason, Truth and History*. Cambridge/New York: Cambridge University Press.

Putnam, H. 1987. *The Many Faces of Realism*. La Salle, IL: Open Court.

Putnam, H. 1990. *Realism with a Human Face*, edited by J. Conant. Cambridge, MA: Harvard University Press.

Putnam, H. 1994a. *Words and Life*, edited by J. Conant. Cambridge, MA: Harvard University Press.

Putnam, H. 1994b. "The Dewey Lectures." *Journal of Philosophy* XCI (9): 445–517, reprinted in Putnam (2000): 3–70.

Putnam, H. 1995. *Pragmatism, an Open Question*. Oxford, UK: Blackwell.

Putnam, H. 1997. "William James's Theory of Truth." In *The Cambridge Companion to William James*. edited by R. A. Putnam, 166–185. Cambridge, UK: Cambridge University Press.

Putnam, H. 2002. *Introduction to The Correspondence of William James*, edited by Ignas K. Skrupskelis and Elizabeth M. Berkely, with the assistance of Wilma Bradbeer. Charlottesville and London: University Press of Virginia.

Putnam, H. 2004. *Ethics without Ontology*. Cambridge, MA, Harvard University Press.

Quine, W. V. O. 1960. *Word and Object*. Cambridge, MA: M.I.T. Press.

Quine, W. V. O. 1981. "The Pragmatist's Place in Empiricism." In *Pragmatism, its Sources and Prospects*, edited by R. Mulvaney and P. Zelner, 21–39, Columbia: University of South Carolina Press.

Ramsey, F. P. 1990. *Philosophical Papers* (PP), edited by D. H Mellor. Cambridge, UK: Cambridge University Press.

Ramsey, F. P. 1991. *On Truth*, edited by N. Rescher and U Maier. Episteme 16. Netherlands: Kluwer.

Robin, R. S. 1964. "Peirce's Doctrine of the Normative Sciences." In *Studies in the Philosophy of C. S. Peirce*, edited by R. S. Robin and E. C. Moore, 271–288. Second Series. Amherst: University of Massachusetts Press.

Robin, R. S. 1997. "Classical Pragmatism and Pragmatism's Proof." In *The Rule of Reason*, edited by J. Brunning and P. Forster, 139–152. Toronto/Buffalo/London: University of Toronto Press.

Rosenthal, S. B. 2000. "William James on the One and the Many." In *William James, Pragmatismus*, edited by K. Oehler, 93–108. Berlin: Akademie Verlag.

Seigfried, C. H. 1990. *William James's Radical Reconstruction of Philosophy*. Albany, NY: SUNY Press.

Talisse, R. B. 2007. *A Pragmatist Philosophy of Democracy*. New York: Routledge.

Thayer, H. S. 1981. *Meaning and Action: A Critical History of Pragmatism*. (2nd edition) New York: Bobbs-Merrill Company.

Tiercelin, C. 1984. "Peirce on Machines, Self-control and Intentionality." In *The Mind and The Machine: Philosophical Aspects of Artificial Intelligence*, edited by S. Torrance, 99–113. Chichester, Sussex.

Tiercelin, C. 1985. "Logique, psychologie et métaphysique: les fondements du pragmatisme selon C.S. Peirce." *Zeitschrift für allgemeine Wissenschaftstheorie* XV (1/2): 229–250.

Tiercelin, C. 1991. "Peirce's Semiotic Version of the Semantic Tradition in Formal Logic." In *New Inquiries into Meaning and Truth*, edited by N. Cooper P. Engel, 187–213. Harvester Press.

Tiercelin, C. 1992. "Vagueness and the Unity of Peirce's Realism." *Transactions of the C.S. Peirce Society* XXVIII (1): 51–82.

Tiercelin, C. 1993a. *La pensée-signe: études sur Peirce*. Nîmes, Editions Jacqueline Chambon, 1993; online version: http://books.openedition.org/cdf/2209.

Tiercelin, C. 1993b. *C. S. Peirce et le pragmatisme*. Paris: Presses Universitaires de France, 1993; online version http://books.openedition.org/cdf/1985.

Tiercelin, C. 1994a. "Entre grammaire spéculative et logique terministe: la recherche peircienne d'un nouveau modèle de la signification et du mental." *Histoire, Epistémologie, Langage* 16 (I): 89–121.

Tiercelin, C. 1995. "Peirce's Relevance for Contemporary Issues in Cognitive Science." *Acta Philosophica Fennica* (58): 37–74.

Tiercelin, C. 1997. "Peirce on Norms, Evolution and Knowledge." *Transactions of the Peirce Society* XXXIII (1): 35–58.

Tiercelin, C. 2000. "Wittgenstein et Peirce," *La philosophie autrichienne: spécificités et infuences*, edited by M. Ouelbani, Publications de l'université de Tunis, Tunis, 46–74.

Tiercelin, C. 2002a. *Hilary Putnam, l'héritage pragmatiste*. Paris: Presses Universitaires de France, 2002; online version: http://books.openedition.org/cdf/2010.

Tiercelin, C. 2002b. "Philosophers and the Moral Life." *Transactions of the C.S. Peirce Society*, Essays in Honor of Richard S. Robin, XXXVIII (½): 307–326.

Tiercelin, C. 2003a. "Le projet peircien d'une métaphysique scientifique." In *Cent ans de philosophie américaine*, edited by J.-P. Cometti and C. Tiercelin, 157–182. Presses de l'Université de Pau.

Tiercelin, C. 2003b. "Expliquer et comprendre: l'approche pragmatiste de Putnam." In *Explication et Compréhension: regards sur les sources et l'actualité d'une controverse épistémologique*, edited by N. Zaccaï-Reyners, 129–147. Editions de l'université de Bruxelles.

Tiercelin, C. 2004a. "Peirce, lecteur d'Aristote." In *Aristote au XIXe siècle*, edited by D. Thouard, 353–376. Villeneuve d'Ascq: Presses Universitaires du Septentrion.

Tiercelin, C. 2004b. "Ramsey's Pragmatism." *Dialectica*, numéro spécial sur, edited by F. P. Ramsey, P. Engel, and J. Dokic, 58 (4): 529–547.

Tiercelin, C. 2005a. *Le doute en question: parades pragmatistes au défi sceptique*. Paris: Editions de l'éclat, 2005. Re-edit. 2016 with a new postface.

Tiercelin, C. 2005b. "Abduction and the Semiotics of Perception." *Semiotica* edited by F. Merrell and J. Queiroz, 153–1/4, 389–412. Berlin, Germany: Walter de Gruyter.

Tiercelin, C. 2006. "The Importance of the Medievals in the Constitution of Peirce's Semeiotic and Thought-sign Theory." In *Semiotics and Philosophy in Charles Sanders Peirce*, edited by Leo R. Fabbrichesi and S. Marietti, 158–183. Cambridge, UK: Cambridge Scholars Press.

Tiercelin, C. 2007. "Ethics and the Sceptical Challenge: A Pragmaticist Approach." *Cognitio* 8 (2): 315–340.

Tiercelin, C. 2010. "Peirce et Wittgnstein face au défi sceptique," *Paradigmi*, 3: 13–28. Franco Angeli publisher.

Tiercelin, C. 2013. "No Pragmatism without Realism." Review of Huw Price's *Naturalism without Mirrors*. Oxford, UK: Oxford University Press, 2011, *Metascience* 11, 22 (3): 659–665.

Tiercelin, C. 2014. *The Pragmatists and the Human Logic of Truth*. Paris, online edition series, "La Philosophie de la connaissance au Collège de France." http://books.openedition.org/cdf/3652.

Tiercelin, C. 2015. "Chance, Love and Logic: Ramsey and Peirce on Norms, Rationality and the Conduct of Life." In *Against boredom. 17 essays on ignorance, values, creativity, metaphysics, decision-making, truth, preference, art, processes, Ramsey, ethics, rationality, validity, human ills, science, and eternal life to Nils-Eric Sahlin on the occasion of his 60th birthday*, edited by J. Persson, G. Hermerén, and Sjöstrand, 221–256. Stockholm: Fri Tanke.

Tiercelin, C. 2016. "In Defense of a Critical Commonsensist Conception of Knowledge." *International Journal for the Study of Scepticism* 6: 182–202.

Tiercelin, C. 2017. "Was Peirce a Genuine Antipsychologist?" In *European Journal of Pragmatism and American Philosophy*, edited by R. Calcaterra and R. Dreon, IX–1. Symposia: Pragmatism and Psychologism, https://journals.openedition.org/ejpap/1003.

CHAPTER 26

JAMES'S AND DEWEY'S RADICAL RATIONALISM

F. THOMAS BURKE

WILLIAM James and John Dewey are often compared and contrasted as original American *pragmatists*. It is likewise interesting to compare ways in which they each endorsed a form of *radical empiricism*. James considered radical empiricism to be something other than pragmatism as such. He was quite explicit about what he thought radical empiricism is. Here we investigate the extent to which Dewey took this baton and ran with it in directions that James would have supported if he had lived long enough to see it. In particular, Dewey also promoted a parallel kind of *radical rationalism*, so to speak, in support of James's insights regarding the shortcomings of modern epistemology. James's radical empiricism is encapsulated in a Postulate-Fact-Conclusion formula. Here we present and discuss a corresponding Postulate-Fact-Conclusion encapsulation of radical rationalism.

BACKGROUND

The publication of James's two-volume *Principles of Psychology* in 1890 influenced Dewey's transition away from Hegelian idealism toward a localized Darwinesque functionalism. This influence continued in conjunction with James's later radical empiricism to shape the subsequent development of Dewey's thinking, particularly in regard to his emerging unease with the "new psychology" of Wundt and Wundt's students (Schilpp 1939, 32). "The impact of James's *Principles* [on Dewey] was revolutionary in showing that the idealist's proffered solution of a 'synthetic power' as a unifying condition of experience was simply not needed because experience didn't require 'synthesis' to begin with" (Alexander 2008, 565).

Dewey's publications and correspondence in the early 1890s display the changing character of his thought at that time. For instance, G. H. Mead's (1934, 1956) influence on Dewey during this period is clearly evident. Dewey was apparently coming around to the view that "the self as *activity*" (rather than as a "thing" or a "substance" or an "event") is a dynamic integration of social, psychological, biological, and ecological transactions and, while just as real, is not reducible to any one structural or functional component of the process. This reflects James's characterizations of the dynamic "self" in *Principles* (PP 1890, ch. X; PBC 1892, chap. XII), some of which were reiterated a decade later in "Does Consciousness Exist" (1904a) where he argued that consciousness (and thus mind? self?) exists not as a thing or substance but as an integral dynamic feature nonetheless of experience.

Jane Addams's effect on Dewey in the early 1890s also seems to have been pivotally epiphanous. In a letter to his wife Alice (Dewey 1999–2002, 00206) after contemplating "an argument" with Addams concerning the strikers' use of force during the 1894 Pullman strike in Chicago, Dewey wrote: "I can sense that I have always been interpreting the dialectic wrong end up—the unity as the reconciliation of opposites, instead of the opposites as the unity in its growth" (quoted in Hickman 2008, 574). Dewey was developing an ambivalence regarding Hegelians if not Hegel directly. As of 1894, the cumulative result was that Dewey had turned Hegel's dialectic inside out and revised it in such radical ways that it became unrecognizable as such. In place of a *grand sweep of history* at the core of an account of the dialectical self-realization of universal and/or absolute Spirit, Dewey put a *comparatively mundane sweep of growth* at the core of a generic account of singular everyday experiences typical of any individual sentient creature. This yielded a miniaturized synthesis of Hegel and Darwin resulting in a version of what we now label as *Chicago functionalism* (Backe 2001; Burke 2018).

Dewey's miniaturization of Hegel's dialectic resulted in a characterization of thinking as *conversing*. One's thinking functions (works, takes place) only as a matter of facilitating conceptual readjustments when existing ideas or rules cannot be routinely maintained. In such cases, old ideas are modified in the face of "the friction of circumstance" that "melts away their congealed fixity" (Dewey 1976–1980, vol. 1, 158). Such episodes of reconstructive readjustment may proceed in numerous ways, but the process exhibits a common pattern in every case, namely, that of a *sweep of growth* that moves from the relative breakdown of existing ideas and rules and routines to some new workable form of relative stability (fixity). This reconstructive process is discursive, dialogical, conversational (dialectical), even if only as carried on by a sole individual as "a miniature social assemblage" (cf. James 1890 and Mead 1934 on "I" and "me").

This transformation of Hegel's pattern of the sweep of history more broadly became Dewey's common pattern of an individual's singular everyday experiences, whether contemplative (discursive) or otherwise. It was presented as the overall pattern of inquiry in his 1938 *Logic*.

Dewey's later writings about James confirm that he counted *Principles of Psychology* as the one greatest influence on his own thinking in the 1890s and thereafter. Dewey reviewed James's *Essays in Radical Empiricism* in 1912 in positive and insightful terms. In 1916 and again in 1925 he objectively compared and contrasted Peirce's and James's respective views of pragmatism. The two lectures devoted to James in Dewey's 1920 lectures in Peking on "three contemporary philosophers" pivoted around an account of James's 1890 *Psychology*.

Throughout the 1930s and thereafter Dewey often wrote about James largely in historical and biographical rather than technical philosophical terms. But Dewey clearly regarded James's *Psychology* and his radical empiricism as being more significant than his (James's) pragmatism. In 1940, 1942a, and 1942b, Dewey took it to the mat to defend James's non-dualistic, post-"empiricism-versus-rationalism" radical empiricism:

> I take it for granted that the *Principles of Psychology* is the greatest among the great works of James. . . . [T]he *Principles* contain an exposition of the nature of experience which renders both sensationalistic empiricism and rationalistic criticisms of empiricism wholly out of date. . . . Fundamentally, he has accomplished this task by showing that experience is intimately connected with nature instead of existing in a separate world. (Dewey 1981–1990, vol. 15, 11)

In the decade spanning roughly 1893 to 1903, Dewey's transformation of Hegelian logic resulted in the publication of *Studies in Logical Theory* (1903). James applauded this collection of essays. Between 1903 and 1907, Dewey focused on articulating the new conception of experience he had proposed in *Studies in Logical Theory*, such as in his 1905 "Postulate of Immediate Empiricism." While James became increasingly distracted by attacks on his pragmatism from several fronts after 1907 (Russell 1909; Moore 1907; Lovejoy 1908a, 1908b), Dewey worked in relative obscurity as a quasi-proponent of pragmatism. Dewey meanwhile was focused on integrating James's radical empiricism and Peirce's pragmatism (or James's initial version of it) into his own Chicago-functionalist theory of experience as it had emerged in the 1890s.

Up through 1907, James focused largely on articulating his own so-called radical empiricism more than on explaining and defending Peirce's so-called pragmatism as advertised in James 1898 (see also 1881, 400; 1885, 43). But after 1907 or so, James was looking for support for his rendition of Peirce's "pragmatism." Dewey's support at that time was insufficiently enthusiastic, though the fact that James valued such support is evidence of Dewey's impact on his thought in this time period (see P 1907, 33–36, 95; 1904c).

JAMES'S AND DEWEY'S RADICAL EMPIRICISM

Pragmatism aside, the connection between James and Dewey that we want to explore here revolves around James's so-called radical empiricism.

James's Radical Empiricism

In the course of characterizing what he meant by radical empiricism, James ran together discussions of at least three distinctions: particulars versus universals, parts versus wholes, and the epistemic priority of experience versus that of reason. James's discussions of any one of these distinctions might slide from one to another as if ontology, mereology, and epistemology were all one thing. That unity may well be the case, but it is not so obvious as James's nonchalance makes it seem.

In section I of "A World of Pure Experience" (1904b), James begins with the following thumbnail sketch of his radical empiricism:

> To be radical, an empiricism must neither admit into its constructions any element that is not directly experienced, nor exclude from them any element that is directly experienced. For such a philosophy, *the relations that connect experiences must themselves be experienced relations, and any kind of relation experienced must be accounted as "real" as anything else in the system*. Elements may indeed be redistributed, the original placing of things getting corrected, but a real place must be found for every kind of thing experienced, whether term or relation, in the final philosophic arrangement.... *Radical empiricism*, as I understand it, *does full justice to conjunctive relations*, without however, treating them as rationalism always tends to treat them, as being true in some supernal way, as if the unity of things and their variety belonged to different orders of truth and vitality altogether. (ERE, 23–24)

In the preface of MT (1909, 6–7) James more succinctly states that his radical empiricism is an epistemological stance (perspective, attitude) that can be characterized by a postulate, a statement of fact, and a generalized conclusion:

- *Postulate*: The only things debatable among philosophers should be things definable in terms drawn from experience.
- *Fact*: Relations among things, conjunctive as well as disjunctive, are matters of direct experience no more and no less than are the things themselves.
- *Conclusion*: It must be assumed that parts of experience hang together by relations that are themselves parts of experience.

These three claims allegedly characterize an anti-rationalist, pro-empiricist stance that undermines the metaphysical substance and methodological ground rules of modern epistemology. James is talking here about relations (among things) as a generic way of talking about universals (versus particulars) (cf. 1904b; P 1907, lect. 6; but especially SPP 1911, ch. 4). Even now we might be disposed to think of relations as a separate matter from universals; but the parochial notion of universals as strictly unary is based historically in Greek realism (reflecting metaphysical issues inspired by Platonism and Aristotelean logic). This was debated in medieval times at least to the point that realism with regard to *n*-ary relations as such was seriously considered (Brower 2018). By the latter half of the nineteenth century, logicians like DeMorgan and Peirce had developed a full-blown logic of relations qua "non-monadic predicates" (cf. Shin and Hammer 2016; Russell 1911; Ramsey 1925) rendering *n*-ary relations (for $n > 1$) as "predicables" with the same ontic status as unary properties. By 1900 or so, James apparently took such results for granted.

But here is the point. These three statements encapsulate an attitude not about realism versus nominalism, nor about innate ideas versus blank slates, but about the *empirical* character of universals. Centuries of debate notwithstanding, we need neither ask nor decide which is more basic or real, particulars versus universals. If so-called particulars and universals are each directly discernible in our experience, that means that we experience properties of things or relations among things as directly as we experience things so propertied and/or related. We may experience a leaf here and a limb there, but also an "attached-ness" of a leaf to a limb if not the very *fact* that a leaf is attached to a limb. We may routinely see the redness of an apple, or the fact that the apple is red, as readily as we may routinely see the apple itself. Neither things nor relations nor facts comprised by things and their relations are disposed to be more or less present (existent) in our experience. This in essence is radical empiricism.

What is "radical" here is the claim that *relations* among things and *facts* comprised by things being so related are just as much experienced as are the things so related. Universals and facts are as much in our immediate experience as are particular things. This is not just realism regarding universals. It is *empiricism* regarding universals—and thus empiricism of a rather radical sort (circa 1900).

This states in summary form what radical empiricism is. One of James's better arguments in favor of this view of relations qua universals is found in SPP 1911, chapters 4 and 5. There the discussion is in terms of percepts (qua particulars) versus concepts (qua universals) where the latter are treated as *regularities* (n-ary generalities for $n = 1, 2, 3, \ldots$) directly discernable as such in fluxes of percepts. Namely, we epistemic agents rightly tend to become habituated to such regularities in light of any functional utility of such evolutionary adaptations. Philosophers of a rationalist bent unfortunately tend to hypostatize such regularities inappropriately, the latter being posited as entities in some "intellectual" realm that transcends concrete experience, as opposed to simply acknowledging their presence (their reality) in and as part of our concrete experience. James is essentially advising against this latter intellectualist move without denying the discernible functional (logical, rational) presence and significance of such regularities in our experience.

Dewey's Immediate Empiricism

Dewey's presentations of his "immediate empiricism" after 1900 comport with James's radical empiricism. Dewey aimed not simply to justify James's radical empiricism but to appropriate it as part of promoting his own "Chicago functionalism."

Dewey's 1912 review of James's *Essays in Radical Empiricism* centered around the summary postulate/fact/conclusion characterization of radical empiricism. Dewey (1903; 1905) had already explored and developed similar ideas presented in this 1912 review. In

"The Postulate of Immediate Empiricism" (1905), Dewey argued that *things*—whether they be particulars or universals, particulars or *sorts* of particulars—are what they are experienced as. For example, neither a horse-trader nor a zoologist may claim ontological priority in their accounts of "horeseness." This entails a kind of noetic point-of-view *pluralism* that James would happily endorse.

But there are some subtler issues here. For example, let us agree that Triple Crown winner Secretariat in particular and racehorseness in general are equally *real* in that they are equally potentially existent as such in an experience of the 1973 Belmont Stakes.

But more than that, "racehorseness" may name a property of things in one context and a particular thing in another context—for instance, in the latter case, where this property is a mere element of a *set* of properties serving as a universe of discourse (a domain of quantification) for a first-order language being used to talk about particular "abstract entities" (not unlike, e.g., first-order axiomatic treatments of sets or of natural numbers, or biologists' discussions of properties of and relations among species, breeds, etc.). This is just an illustration of Quine's principle of so-called ontological relativity. Dewey's point is that neither racehorseness as a general property nor racehorseness as a particular thing is more or less experienceable than the other (in the post-Hegelian sense of the term "experience" that he had been proposing since the early 1890s).

Conversely, the name "Secretariat" will name a particular horse in one context and a kind or property (or meme) in another context ("Believe me, Secretariat was my horse, and your horse, sir, is no Secretariat"). In this way, the word "Secretariat" will in some contexts denote an immediate particular, while in other contexts it will denote a mediating universal (and the context might change very quickly even within the bounds of a single sentence)—or so it goes according to immediate (radical) empiricism. It depends on what "Secretariat" is experienced as (namely, employing the word "Secretariat" as I watch my horse win the 1973 Belmont Stakes, or later as I watch your horse win the 1983 Belmont Stakes but deny your claims of its greatness relative to my Secretariat).

More broadly, Dewey's immediate empiricism reflects his post-Hegelian characterization of "experiences" as dynamic and directed episodes of, what, life?—directed toward resolving potential difficulties that respectively command attention, much like Peirce's doubt-belief conception of inquiry (1877-1878) as a process of establishing and stabilizing a *belief* in response to a respective destabilizing *doubt* (where scientific methodologies supply the best way to find such solutions). Dewey's notion of "an experience" or of "experiences" (versus a modern reflex-arc template) presents a radical reconstruction of what is meant by "empiricism." If "stimuli" are not just sensations but are instead situations (instances) of discordance (perplexity, excitement, etc.), then we need to reconstruct the usual empiricism/rationalism debate altogether.

Dewey's notion of the qualitative nature of a *situation*—as a qualitative whole that is functionally "immediate"—was just one of many results of his supplanting Hegel's account of the grand dialectical sweep of history with a generic account of the mundane reconstructive sweep of an individual creature's "unit of behavior." Dewey's 1903 *Studies in Logical Theory* characterizes a situation as a conflict or tension (a potentially complex set of relations among particulars) that nevertheless, as such, is an irreducible qualitative datum. This characterization of situations comports with the alleged Fact and Conclusion of James's radical empiricism at least with regard to "conflicts or tensions" which, by their nature as relations, are thus "parts of experience."

In "The Postulate of Immediate Empiricism" (1905), Dewey states that an experience of Zoellner's lines as being convergent (seeing a complex relation among the particular streaks of ink) from one point of view (above and perpendicular to the surface on which the lines are drawn) is just such an immediate, whole, gestalt-like "quale." *But* the same may be said for an experience of these same lines as being parallel from a different point of view (e.g., as a result of tilting the surface relative to the line of sight by roughly 85 degrees). As such, the "immediacy" of either of these qualia is a functional designation, neither finally ontic nor once-and-for-all epistemic. Any thing or relation or fact or complex of facts that (functionally) has such immediacy in one context may be a variegated subject-matter of extended attention in another context, and vice versa.

The functional relativity of qualitative immediacy regarding such relations among particulars reflects a radical kind of empiricism in James's sense. It is also a non-arbitrary yet flexible empiricism in Quine's ontological-relativist sense in that such designations of immediacy (or not) are optional, provisional, negotiable, supporting at best only a *methodological* nominalism, driven by contingent *needs* to focus attention wherever or however called for.

Dewey reiterated similar points in his 1930 "Qualitative Thought" and again in his 1938 *Logic: The Theory of Inquiry*, the latter being one of his last great efforts to spell out a theory of inquiry as an integral part of his more general Chicago-functionalist theory of experience. The latter book addresses, for instance, how his immediate empiricism handles Locke's 1689 distinction between primary and secondary qualities. It quickly runs past this distinction (with a respectful salute) to focus as much or more on tertiary qualities (see Sinico 2015). Speaking from within the newer framework of a Chicago-functionalist theory of experience, versus Locke's outdated paradigm, and citing Santayana (1905) specifically, Dewey grounds rational sense-making in overall qualitative aspects of respective unfolding experiences (Dewey 1981–1990, vol. 12, 75). Dewey's claim, namely, is that rational sense-making is grounded not in atomistic sense data but in qualities pervading respective situations (not in sense data *de re* but in qualities *de situ*):

> Probably the meaning of *quality*, in the sense in which quality is said to pervade all elements and relations that are or can be instituted in discourse and thereby to constitute them an individual whole, can be most readily apprehended by referring to the esthetic use of the word. A painting is said to have quality, or a particular painting to have a Titian or Rembrandt quality. The word thus used most certainly does not refer to any particular line, color or part of the painting. It is something that affects and modifies all the constituents of the picture and all of their relations. It is not anything that can be expressed in words for it is something that must be *had*. Discourse may, however, point out the qualities, lines and relations by means of which pervasive and unifying quality is achieved. But so far as this discourse is separated from *having*

the immediate total experience, a reflective object takes the place of an esthetic one. Esthetic experience, in its emphatic sense, is mentioned as a way of calling attention to situations and universes of experience. The intended force of the illustration would be lost if esthetic experience as such were supposed to exhaust the scope and significance of a "situation." As has been said, a qualitative and qualifying situation is present as the background and the control of *every* experience. It was for a similar reason that it was earlier stated that reference to tertiary qualities was not adequately exemplary. For such qualities as are designated by "distressing," "cheerful," etc., are *general*, while the quality of distress and cheer that marks an existent situation is not general but is unique and inexpressible in words. (Dewey 1981–1990, vol. 12, 75–76)

[A situation] is a qualitative existential whole which is unique. "Individual" as here used has nothing to do with simplicity of constituents. On the contrary, every situation, when it is analyzed, is extensive containing within itself diverse distinctions and relations which, in spite of their diversity, form a unified qualitative whole. (Dewey 1981–1990, vol. 12, 125)

Enough said. These passages show how Dewey's immediate empiricism is most clearly illustrated by his innovative conception of *a situation* as a unified qualified (immediately (radically?) empirical) whole.

James's and Dewey's Radical Rationalism

We have addressed how Dewey's immediate empiricism aligns with James's radical empiricism. But here now is an even more interesting point. Whether they acknowledge it or not, James and Dewey are as much rationalists as they are empiricists—in a respectively radical way, of course.

This appears at first to be inconsistent with James's "*Weltanschauung*." For various reasons James was impelled toward empiricism and away from rationalism. Yet, as shown above, his radical empiricism insists upon the non-transcendent nature of universals as directly discernible regularities in concrete experience. This cuts to the heart of rationalist epistemology and suggests not necessarily a rejection but actually a new version of rationalism. James did not see it that way, but we may chalk that up to a missed opportunity on his part.

With the benefit of longer hindsight, Dewey was more measured in his reactions against the alleged dualities of empiricism versus rationalism, nominalism versus realism, etc. Working within a Chicago-functionalist framework, Dewey was never more nor less rationalist than he was empiricist, and vice versa—thus always being as much the one as he was the other? Following James, his concern rather was to reconstruct outdated presuppositions and ground rules of eighteenth-century metaphysics and epistemology in ways that opened up avenues for progress in philosophical thought. Most of what follows regarding radical rationalism is derived from Dewey's writings, though, despite James's occasional derogations of rationalism, one will find a *radical* kind of rationalism coursing through his writings as well.

To cut to the chase, like James's radical empiricism, a corresponding radical rationalism can be characterized by a postulate, a statement of fact, and a generalized conclusion, as follows:

- *Postulate*: The only things debatable among philosophers should be things definable in terms drawn from rational reflection.
- *Fact*: Particular things, singularly or as multiplicities, are matters of direct rational reflection no more and no less than are properties of and relations among things.
- *Conclusion*: It must be assumed that rational thought is anchored in particular things that together are parts of rational reflection.

These three statements are presumed to encapsulate an epistemological stance regarding the "rational" character of particulars—just as radical empiricism encapsulates an epistemological stance regarding the "empirical" character of universals. This reciprocity reflects the Chicago-functionalist view that rational reflection is a component of experience just as experience "is intimately connected with nature instead of existing in a separate world" (Dewey 1981–1990, vol. 15, 11).

Consider each of the three components of radical empiricism (RE) and radical rationalism (RR) in turn.

The Two Postulates

- *RE Postulate*: The only things debatable among philosophers should be things definable in terms drawn from *experience*.
- *RR Postulate*: The only things debatable among philosophers should be things definable in terms drawn from *rational reflection*.

These two postulates are complementary, not incompatible. The least we can say is that each specifies a range of things worthy of philosophical debate so that proponents of radical empiricism and radical rationalism should be particularly interested in the overlap of those two respective ranges (hoping, if not assuming, that the overlap is nonempty). These two postulates cannot be incompatible if, as in Dewey's view, particular instances of *rational reflection* are just potential components of *experience* more broadly.

Dewey indeed argued at length that rational reflection is necessarily a constituent aspect of experience *and* that only such experience that is thus imbued with rational reflection is suited for "philosophical debate." We just need to get beyond old ways of thinking that stand in the way of seeing that experience and reason do not exclude one another as ultimate sources of knowledge but together, when properly orchestrated, constitute a single variegated source of knowledge.

Relative to the general Chicago-functionalist framework, an explanation of the RR postulate is given in Dewey's 1922 "Syllabus: Types of Philosophic Thought" where he steps back and critiques his own theory of experience:

> Hence the methodological use of experience which has been indicated [namely, "taken non-technically ... [its] nearest equivalents [being] such words as 'life,' 'history,' 'culture' (in its anthropological use)"] makes possible a truly critical philosophy, types of philosophy being interpreted on the basis of their special origin and context within history-experience. Philosophy is seen to be a philosophy of history, not in the sense of explaining why history is or must be as it is, but in the sense that philosophies spring from and embody characteristic conditions and crises of human history. They are akin to religious, artistic or economic institutions and problems, to other forms of *culture* in short, and to a science as a historic mode of culture rather than to science in its abstract, non-historic sense.
>
> The resulting philosophy may be labelled critical radical empiricism: radical, in the sense that it recognizes the claims and traits of all the qualitative modes and organizations of experience, instead of setting up some one form as ultimate and "real"; critical, in that each philosophy is interpreted not in terms of abstract criteria of truth and value (a method which of necessity begs the question), but of concrete historic origin, context and operation. (Dewey 1976–1980, vol. 13, 353)

Dewey explains here what he means by the words "radical" and "critical." He also states in a footnote that what he means by "critical radical empiricism" (as a *truly* critical philosophy) is not what is meant by Critical Philosophy in a Kantian sense, referring the reader to the first chapter of Caird's two-volume 1889 *The Critical Philosophy of Immanuel Kant* for clarification.

We note two things regarding Caird's first chapter. First, the RE and RR postulates here are complimentary *normative* statements about what is worthy of philosophical debate. Second, the first chapter of Caird 1889 is strikingly harmonious with Peirce's "The Fixation of Belief" (1877–1878) in that both are concerned with discerning *better and worse* ways of coming to believe what we believe. Peirce's familiar argument for the superiority of scientific method over tenacity, authority, or a priori reasoning need not be recounted here. The point is that Caird proceeds in similar fashion, beginning with a discussion of ways of coming to believe what we believe that are clearly inferior if at all workable and progressing to ways that are inevitably superior and therefore preferable.

Caird's thesis, namely, is that *criticism* (using critical methods; "critique-ism"?) is superior to *skepticism* (using uncritical skeptical methods; wholesale rejection of all dogma) which is (only slightly) superior to *dogmatism* (using uncritical dogmatic methods). Where Peirce moves from tenacity through authority and a-priorism to science, Caird moves from dogmatism through skepticism to criticism.

Caird's aim is to characterize Critical Philosophy in Kant's sense, which is critique-ism not with regard to just any beliefs but with regard to beliefs about beliefs and in particular with regard to epistemology at large. That is, Kant takes perilous steps beyond everyday practical critique-ism to pursue a broader and deeper Critique-ism. This is the intellectualist move that James repeatedly advised against. Dewey's (and James's) critical radical empiricism stops short of taking these latter steps, and therein lies the alleged difference between their "truly critical philosophy" and a Kantian (faux) Critical Philosophy. Whether as ordinary epistemic agents or as philosophers of various persuasions, we may well come to believe various things about the nature of beliefs (our own particular beliefs or beliefs in general); but it is a fallacy—the philosopher's fallacy—to regard ultimately transcendent Critical pronouncements as providing a final one-size-fits-all template for assessing what we should finally believe. The latter should instead be left, case-by-case, to the fallible, yet-to-be-perfected techniques of science à la Peirce 1877–1878, or what Dewey referred to more broadly as methods of intelligence.

The point is that critique-ism, as encapsulated in the two postulates of radical empiricism and radical rationalism, can afford to be less ambitious and are more practicable than Critique-ism. Dewey (1938) argues that inquiry (including philosophical inquiry) is a process of dealing with disputes, controversies, or similar challenges and predicaments. Dewey (1922, esp. Part III) tells us moreover that anything debatable among philosophers *should* be approached critically (and otherwise intelligently) rather than dogmatically or skeptically. Thus what is meant by "rational reflection" in the RR postulate is what Caird means by critical examination of our ideas, in given cases, whenever they emerge as contentious. Without following Kant's a priori methodology over a transcendental cliff, we may instead reasonably assume, from case to case, that we should be cognizant if not respectful of normative standards for what counts on independent grounds as common footing that all disputants in conflicts among opposing ideas might "tacitly acknowledge." The search for such standards leads inevitably into a realm of general principles that we might say are tentative marks of objective (disinterested, impartial, honest, transparent, etc.) rationality.

Small-"c" critique-ism is thus concerned to discover and apply general principles that characterize and distinguish better and worse kinds of inquiry. Rather than psychology or metaphysics, this falls to what Dewey thought of as *logic* (a normative theory of inquiry; a scientific inquiry into inquiry itself, echoing Peirce 1877–1878). This will sound odd if one thinks of logic as some kind of formal mathematical linguistics. Nevertheless, within the general Chicago-functionalist framework of Dewey's theory of experience, an integral component of which is his theory of inquiry, we instead move beyond any such merely formal exercise into an open-ended study of the nature and use of the full range of abductive, deductive, and inductive methods of inference as typically orchestrated in rational inquiry. Norms that distinguish proper rational reflection (general principles that are marks of objective rationality), as the source of anything worth debating, are norms of logic in this broader sense that was originally introduced by Peirce, a fact that Dewey (and James) would not hesitate to acknowledge. In short, our RE and RR postulates together essentially entail that philosophical debate should proceed in accordance with logical norms, properly understood.

The Two Facts

- *RE Fact*: Relations among things, conjunctive as well as disjunctive, are matters of direct experience no more and no less than are the things themselves.
- *RR Fact*: Particular things, singularly or as multiplicities, are matters of direct rational reflection no more and no less than are properties of and relations among things.

In the general Chicago-functionalist framework of Dewey's theory of experience, the distinction between particulars and universals is only a *functional* distinction that may be employed in *various* ways relative to respective situations and thus relative to various points of view, not as a once-and-for-all categorical distinction independent of (yet somehow to be imposed from on high upon) such situations or points of view.

In that light, our two facts are grounded in the notion that situations are concrete occurrences in some one or more rational creatures' experience. In any such context, what works as a particular (just as what works as a universal) is not arbitrary. Rather it depends on the concrete situation, which affects what the particular (or universal) is experienced as. Yet *nothing* within such a context falls outside the scope of possible rational reflection (RR) just as nothing there falls outside the scope of possible immediate experience more broadly (RE). Interestingly, this is not just an issue regarding what rational reflection may be about (its referents) but rather regards what rational reflection is (its constitution).

For some context, our RR fact can be found in various forms throughout Peirce's writings, for example, in "The Fixation of Belief" (1877–1878) where he claims that Lavoisier's "way was to carry his mind into his laboratory, and to make of his alembics and cucurbits instruments of thought, giving a new conception of reasoning, as something which was to be done with one's eyes open, by manipulating real things instead of words and fancies." In the context of trying to answer some alchemical question, heating a cucurbit while expecting production of a respective distillate is itself an operation of thought—that is, the heating, not just the expecting.

Recall that Dewey (e.g., 1903) emphasized the "immediately given quality" of any given situation as "an irreducible datum" (for a respective rational creature). Such remarks throughout Dewey's work are invariably accompanied by passages that also emphasize the concreteness of rational thought insofar as the latter may extend into the most particular of particulars (functionally speaking) in light of what they are "experienced as." Couched within Dewey's Chicago-functionalist picture of the reconstructive sweep of an experience, this says that the "antecedents of thought" in any specific instance are not "innate ideas" or any such abstractions purported to lie once-and-for-all outside of concrete situations but instead are concrete features (particular or universal) of the concrete situation itself.

This already applies of course to the simplest kinds of "irreducible" sensory data. In critical but sympathetic reference specifically to Lotze's *Logic* (1884, 28–34), Dewey states that "even the universal, the common color which runs through the various qualities of blue, green, white, etc., is not a product of thought, but something which thought finds already in existence" (Dewey 1976–1980, vol. 2, 342). For instance, a simple yellow patch given/taken as a datum is in fact characterized by a visual *regularity* (constancy, invariance) across the spatiotemporal extension of the respective "patch" if not otherwise. This simplest kind of regularity is a distinctive "peculiarity of the datum" that is directly "given, presented, to our ideational activities," not imposed upon it (cf. Burke 2013, ch. 7). This nicely expresses and integrates our two RE and RR facts.

The Two Conclusions

- *RE Conclusion*: It must be assumed that parts of experience hang together by relations that are themselves parts of experience.
- *RR Conclusion*: It must be assumed that rational thought is anchored in particular things that together are parts of rational reflection.

What kind of world might anchor rational thought in particular things that together are parts of rational reflection? By Dewey's lights, the many particulars that are supposed to be available as matters of direct rational reflection and that anchor rational thought belong to a broad, varied, and changing range of subject matters ("in art, industry, religion, science, politics, morals," etc.), all from different perspectives ("societal, historical, biographical," etc.) (Dewey 1976–1980, vol. 13, 353–354).

These many sorts of subject matters of thought are anchored in their respective ways (and thus anchor rational thought) by characteristic concrete particulars. Any one of these subject matters may be resolved into various less general sorts of subject matters of thought (sub-fields, sub-disciplines), and each of those again, etcetera, virtually ad infinitum, and in ways that may at any stage cross boundaries among any original list of such subject matters.

For all practical purposes, inquirers will continue to uncover general subject matters no matter how they might resolve these things into their constituent (e.g., particular) subject matters. Such elaborate resolutions will never bottom out with honest-to-God atomic particulars. Such resolutions will instead be exploratory exercises in logic—in the sense that logic is a theory of inquiry, and assuming that inquiry is an integral component of experience (at least within a Chicago-functionalist framework). Any such resolution at any point in time will only be a current retrospective survey of various fields of experience in which disputes, controversies, and/or conflicts may arise. Such a list may look quite different a hundred years from now.

The point is that, at any given level or stage of any such honest state-of-the-art survey of subject matters that harbor potential disputes, controversies, and/or conflicts worthy of rational debate, the *functional* distinction between generals and particulars will make logical sense. In other words, we may have general subject matters all the way up or down in our current ordering of potential subject matters of inquiry, but so will we have concrete particulars all the way up or down in *each* and *every one* of those subject matters (depending on the nature of the respective disputes, etc.). That is the surely uncontentious conclusion of radical rationalism.

Pragmatism and Radical Rationalism

To nail down this presentation of radical rationalism more securely, if the foregoing is not conclusive, it will help to address James's and Dewey's common orientation to pragmatism.

In particular, for the sake of clarification and as a kind of self-critical challenge, we may ask what the foregoing account of radical rationalism as a kind of realism says about the nature of the subsistence of universals. This is a meaningful question that has not yet been clearly answered.

An answer to this query is forthcoming by considering the pragmatist conception of meanings qua contents of our ideas that James and Dewey more or less held in common. This common pragmatist conception of meaning is of course drawn from Peirce's "How to Make Our Ideas Clear" (1877–1878) where, in talking about how better to clarify one's ideas, Peirce musters and develops some substantive claims about what ideas are in the first place.

We need not recount in detail James's original characterization of *pragmatism* both as a *method* of clarifying *meanings* and as a *doctrine* regarding the nature of *truth* (but see below; also Kitcher in this volume). Briefly, in the first half-dozen pages of "What Pragmatism Means" (P 1907, 27–32) James presents and interprets Peirce's "principle of pragmatism" (the so-called pragmatic maxim) as a principle that specifies (vaguely) a *methodology if not a method* of defining one's terms with a degree of clarity that is available only by reference to concrete activities and their consequences—for example, including but not limited to operational definitions, to use some more recent terminology, as opposed to purely formal axiomatic methods used in pure mathematics (Burke 2013, chs. 1–4; 2018). Peirce probably found this initial part of James's lecture to be not unacceptable so far as it goes. Where James diverges from Peirce's pragmatism is in the doctrine of truth that he (James) attributes to proponents of pragmatism generally. Extended pursuit of that topic could take us too far afield, but one way to read James's doctrine of truth that is more compatible with Peirce's views is to regard that doctrine as a loose way of talking about what Peirce meant by belief. For instance, James could just as well have said that we tend to believe that P depending on how the hypothesis that P proves itself by way of how it "works" in our ongoing experience. James's discussion of truth becomes quite uncontentious if we make this one simple terminological substitution.

The point here is that this shift would more obviously connect James's summary of pragmatism directly with Peirce's discussion of belief, ideas, thinking, inquiry, action, habits, etcetera—especially in the second section of "How to Make Our Ideas Clear"

(1877–1878)—that serve as his (Peirce's) argument in support of the purely methodological principle of pragmatism. Various pragmatists may ignore or even reject that argument while endorsing the pragmatic maxim to some degree, in some sense; but pragmatism in general should be understood to be a school of thought that originated as a *method* of clarifying *meanings* with a supporting *doctrine* regarding the nature of *belief*. This is relevant to us here in that the latter doctrine easily provides a cogent answer to the question of what radical rationalism as a kind of realism says about the nature of the subsistence of universals. The answer is that universals subsist in whatever way "habits of action" subsist.

Dewey's critique of Peirce's pragmatism helps to clarify this simple answer.

Dewey (1916) summarizes Peirce's 1905 account of the origins and nature of *pragmatism* as follows. Peirce framed the theory that the "rational purport" of an expression lies exclusively in its bearing upon the conduct of life, consisting of some array of conceivable experiential phenomena that might be implied respectively by affirmative or negative uses of that expression. That conception of rational purport allegedly identifies a method for clarifying meanings in specific cases. For instance, the meanings of various expressions in a given language may be anchored by means of possible experimental actions (e.g., in the case of Euclidean geometry, drawing particular dots and streaks in controlled ways on specific flat sheets of paper; in the case of Newtonian physics, tracking relative motions and positions of planets or ballistic missiles; etc.).

But Dewey (1916) burrows further into Peirce's conception of meaning by considering the latter's realism regarding universals and in that context focuses on what such meaning amounts to, namely, on how such meaning is constituted. Dewey first reminds us of Peirce's (1905) reference to an inseparable connection between rational cognition and human purpose. This comports with the general Chicago-functionalist framework of Dewey's theory of experience as a theory in general of how such purposes arise and are fulfilled. Dewey then underlines Peirce's emphasis on *the process* (the proto-dialectic) of establishing habits where such habits (as ongoing achievements, "generalized as widely as possible") constitute generic contents (rational purports) of respective beliefs. Dewey in effect is acknowledging (again) that Peirce's pragmaticist conception of meaning fits within the framework of a Chicago-functionalist theory of experience particularly when the formation (evolution) of habits is understood as applying in particular to individuals' everyday experiences.

So, reconsider James's 1898 statement that the "effective meaning of any philosophic proposition" cashes out as "some particular consequence, in our future practical experience," where emphasis is placed on this experience being *particular*, contrasting, as Dewey points out, with Peirce's emphasizing the generality of habits as rational purports of any given "proposition." This contrast is not an inconsistency but is just a difference of emphasis between two complementary ways to get at what *meaning* is. James's point is nothing more nor less than our RR conclusion. Peirce's counterbalancing point is that such particular *things* are integral parts of rational reflection insofar as they are in part or in whole constitutive of our habits and thus of our beliefs and thus of our rational cognition. Peirce's emphasis on habituation and habits as ways of acting (and as constituents if not contents of *beliefs*) thus complements James's radical empiricism by explaining (not just stating) the radical rationalism that is implicit in James's position.

Thus, following Peirce, a radical rationalist position regarding the nature of the subsistence of universals is fleshed out in terms of the nature of the subsistence of habits. For example, the particular activity of your tying your shoe here and now may exist (i.e., play out) here and now, as it were, but where and in what sense does your shoe-tying habit exist (whether or not you are here and now tying you shoe)? Where and how and in what sense do habits exist? In what sense are habits real? Answer those questions, and you will have explained the nature of the subsistence of universals so far as James's and Dewey's radical rationalism is concerned. That explanation is at least as good as any other realist explanation, or so the claim goes.

This pragmatist's answer, and the point to highlight here, is that the generic meanings of our terms (of our words, sentences, diagrams, gestures, etc.) function as universals that are realized in or as specific habits that are themselves anchored in particulars by virtue of uncertain but robust long-term evolutionary stabilities that characterize our species as a whole and/or that are variously embodied in individual members of our species. A radical-rationalist version of realism regarding universals no doubt requires something like this.

Conclusions

We have argued that James's radical empiricism implicates a respective radical rationalism. James's emphasis on particulars as cashing out the "effective meanings" of any given proposition is complemented by Peirce's point that such particulars are integral parts of rational reflection insofar as they are constitutive of our general habits and thus of our beliefs and thus of our rational cognition.

This synthesis of James's and Peirce's views on the nature of meaning has been presented in the context of Dewey's Chicago-functionalist theory of experience—a theory that emphasizes the functional complementarity of facts and ideas, data and theory, in the unfolding and furtherance of this or that inquiry (qua experience). Chicago functionalism in this way helps to explain James's radical empiricism in conjunction with Peirce's original version of pragmatism. The three principles of radical rationalism joined together with James's three principles of radical empiricism thus provide a useful guide to understanding Dewey's innovative conception of experience.

References

Alexander, Thomas M. 2008. "Comments on James Good, *A Search for Unity in Diversity.*" *Transactions of the Charles S. Peirce Society* 44 (4): 563–568.

Backe, Andrew. 2001. "John Dewey and Early Chicago Functionalism." *History of Psychology* 4 (4): 323–340.

Brower, Jeffrey. 2018. "Medieval Theories of Relations." In *The Stanford Encyclopedia of Philosophy*, edited by Edward N. Zalta, Winter 2018 edition. https://plato.stanford.edu/archives/win2018/entries/relations-medieval/.

Burke, F. Thomas. 2013. *What Pragmatism Was*. American Philosophy Series. Indianapolis: Indiana University Press.

Burke, F. Thomas. 2018. "Dewey's Chicago-Functionalist Conception of Logic." In *The Oxford Handbook of Dewey*, edited by Steven A. Fesmire, 507–536. Oxford: Oxford University Press.

Caird, Edward. 1889. *The Critical Philosophy of Immanuel Kant*. In two volumes. New York: Macmillan and Company.

Dewey, John, ed. 1903. *Studies in Logical Theory*. Chicago: University of Chicago Press. University of Chicago Decennial Publications, Second Series, vol. 11.

Dewey, John. 1905. "The Postulate of Immediate Empiricism." *Journal of Philosophy, Psychology, and Scientific Methods* 2: 393–399.

Dewey, John. 1912. "Review of *Essays in Radical Empiricism* by William James." *New York Times*, June 9, 1912, Review of Books, 357.

Dewey, John. 1916. "The Pragmatism of Peirce." *Journal of Philosophy, Psychology, and Scientific Methods* 13: 709–715.

Dewey, John. 1920. "Three Contemporary Philosophers: A Series of Six Lectures Delivered in Peking." First published as "Five Major Lecture Series of John Dewey in Peking," *Peking Morning Post*, translated into English by Robert W. Clopton and Tsuin-chen Ou.

Dewey, John. 1922. "Syllabus: Types of Philosophic Thought." For a course at Columbia University, 1922–1923. Included in 1976–1980, vol. 13, 349–395.

Dewey, John. 1925. "The Development of American Pragmatism." *Studies in the History of Ideas* 2: 353–377.

Dewey, John. 1930. "Qualitative Thought." *The Symposium* 1: 5–32.

Dewey, John. 1938. *Logic: The Theory of Inquiry*. New York: Henry Holt.

Dewey, John. 1940. "The Vanishing Subject in the Psychology of James." *Journal of Philosophy* 37: 589–599.

Dewey, John. 1942a. "William James and the World Today." In *William James, the Man and the Thinker: Addresses Delivered at the University of Wisconsin in Celebration of the Centenary of his Birth*. Madison: University of Wisconsin Press.

Dewey, John. 1942b. "William James as Empiricist." In *In Commemoration of William James 1842–1942*. New York: Columbia University Press.

Dewey, John. 1976–1980. *The Middle Works*, vol. 1–15 (1899–1924). Edited by Jo Ann Boydston. Carbondale: Southern Illinois University Press.

Dewey, John. 1981–1990. *The Later Works*, vol. 1–17 (1925–1953). Edited by Jo Ann Boydston. Carbondale: Southern Illinois University Press.

Dewey, John. 1999–2002. *The Correspondence of John Dewey*, vol. 1. Edited by Larry Hickman. Charlottesville: InteLex Corporation.

Hickman, Larry A. 2008. "Dewey's Hegel: A Search for Unity in Diversity, or Diversity as the Growth of Unity?" *Transactions of the Charles S. Peirce Society* 44 (4): 569–576.

James, William. 1881. "Reflex Action and Theism." *Unitarian Review* 16 (5): 389–416.
James, William. 1885. "On the Function of Cognition." *Mind* 10 (37): 27–44.
James, William. 1890. *The Principles of Psychology*. New York: Henry Holt.
James, William. 1898. "Philosophical Conceptions and Practical Results." University of California *Chronicle* 1 (4): 287–310.
James, William. 1904a. "Does "Consciousness" Exist?" *Journal of Philosophy, Psychology, and Scientific Methods* 1 (18): 477–491.
James, William. 1904b. "A World of Pure Experience." *Journal of Philosophy, Psychology, and Scientific Methods* 1 (20/21): 533–543, 561–570.
James, William. 1904c. "The Chicago School." *Psychological Bulletin* 1: 1–5.
Locke, John. 1689. *An Essay Concerning Human Understanding*. London: Thomas Bassett. First volume in *The Clarendon Edition of the Works of John Locke*, edited by Peter H. Nidditch (Oxford: Oxford University Press, 1975).
Lotze, Rudolf Hermann. 1884. *Logic*. English translation of Volume 1 of *System der Philosophie* (Leipzig, 1874). Oxford: Oxford University Press.
Lovejoy, Arthur Oncken. 1908a. "The Thirteen Pragmatisms, I." *Journal of Philosophy, Psychology and Scientific Methods* 5 (1): 5–12.
Lovejoy, Arthur Oncken. 1908b. "The Thirteen Pragmatisms, II." *Journal of Philosophy, Psychology and Scientific Methods* 5 (2): 29–39.
Mead, George Herbert. 1934. *Mind, Self, and Society*, edited by Charles W. Morris. Chicago: University of Chicago Press.
Mead, George Herbert. 1956. *On Social Psychology*, edited by Anselm Strauss. Chicago: University of Chicago Press.
Moore, George Edward. 1907. " 'Professor James' 'Pragmatism.'" *Proceedings of the Aristotelean Society* 8: 33–77.
Peirce, Charles Sanders. 1877–1878. "Illustrations of the Logic of Science." *Popular Science Monthly* 12–13.
Peirce, Charles Sanders. 1905. "What Pragmatism Is." *The Monist* 15: 161–181.
Ramsey, Frank P. 1925. "Universals." *Mind* 34 (136): 401–417.
Russell, Bertrand. 1909. "Pragmatism." *Edinburgh Review* 209 (428): 363–388.
Russell, Bertrand. 1911. "On the Relations of Universals and Particulars." *Proceedings of the Aristotelean Society* 12: 1–24.
Santayana, George. 1905. *Reason in Common Sense. The Life of Reason*, vol. 1. New York: Charles Scribner's Sons.
Schilpp, Paul Arthur, ed. 1939. *The Philosophy of John Dewey*, The Library of Living Philosophers, vol. 1. New York: Tudor Press.
Shin, Sun-Joo, and Eric Hammer. 2016. "Peirce's Deductive Logic." In *The Stanford Encyclopedia of Philosophy*, edited by Edward N. Zalta, Winter 2016 edition. http://plato.stanford.edu/archives/win2016/entries/peirce-logic/.
Sinico, Michele. 2015. "Tertiary Qualities, from Galileo to Gestalt Psychology." *History of the Human Sciences* 28 (3): 68–79.

PART VIII

CONVERSATIONS, FUTURE

CHAPTER 27

JAMES AND BRITISH PHILOSOPHY

CHERYL MISAK

Two Apparently Opposing Traditions

It may seem as if American pragmatism and British philosophy have been at war for the whole of the twentieth century.[1] The modern British tradition was initiated by Russell and Moore in the late 1800s, as they turned their backs on the absolute idealism of their teachers. The early Wittgenstein's *Tractatus*, published in 1922 after a gestation slowed by the Great War, continued in this logical analyst framework. Indeed, the whole of the 1920s was dominated by this logical mindset. Russell, Moore, and Wittgenstein, in slightly different ways, saw the mind's fundamental relation to the world as an unmediated isomorphism between elementary propositions and objects, and they saw truth as a matter of these elementary propositions corresponding to objects in the world.

The pragmatist tradition, on the other hand, insisted that there is no unmediated perception and saw truth as the best we could do by way of belief. Hence the clash of viewpoints, which we shall see played out in print and in person. But I will argue that the story is more complicated and more interesting than it first appears. Despite enduring hostility to James's theory of truth, other kinds of deep pragmatist commitments came to infuse British philosophy and remain in place. James and his disciple in Oxford, F. C. S. Schiller, are present at all the twists and turns, but we need also to see how two other pillars of American Pragmatism, C. S. Peirce and John Dewey came to influence British philosophy in order to get a full and accurate picture of the intertwining of these apparently opposite traditions during the first decades of the twentieth century.

The Pragmatism of James and Schiller

James's Gifford Lectures were delivered in Edinburgh in 1901 and published as *The Varieties of Religious Experience*. His "The Will to Believe" was already well known. There James argued that it is sometimes reasonable to believe a hypothesis before one has conclusive evidence in its favor. If the evidence underdetermines the competing hypotheses or if the evidence is not yet available for a hypothesis, it can be reasonable to take a position if there is something to gain by so doing. This is especially true, James argued, of religious beliefs, on which one is forced to take a stand. Agnosticism, he argued, entails acting as if God does not exist. Since action and belief walk hand in hand for the pragmatist, if you act as if God does not exist, you believe that God does not exist. When we are in this way forced to make a decision pro or con in advance of the evidence, a hypothesis may be embraced for the role it plays in our lives. That is, on the most charitable reading of "The Will to Believe," the paper is about cognitive strategies for discovery (i.e., when you don't yet have evidence), not strategies for justification (Klein 2015; Misak 2015).

In *The Varieties of Religious Experience*, James follows this line further, exploring in detail the significance of religious ideas in personal life. He cites the following, for instance, as a reason to believe in God: the experience of "the phenomenon of 'prayerful communion,'" in which "something ideal, which in one sense is part of ourselves and in another sense is not ourselves, actually exerts an influence, raises our centre of personal energy, and produces regenerative effects unattainable in other ways." James attests that he is "so impressed by the importance of these phenomena" that he adopts "the hypothesis which they so naturally suggest" (VRE 1902, 411–412).

But while *Varieties* was a publication sensation in the United Kingdom, it and "The Will to Believe" were shaky primers for pragmatism. In *Varieties*, James also argued that experiences such as déjà-vu, trances, dreams, and the meditative and heightened states of consciousness cultivated by adherents to various religions give us a window into both our subconscious and also into reality. Even experiences had under the influence of alcohol and nitrous oxide "stimulate the mystical consciousness in an extraordinary degree" (VRE 1902, 307). And "The Will to Believe," fairly or not, was taken to promote the view that if a belief would be good for an individual's life, he has the right to believe it to be true. More specifically, it was taken to promote the view that if the hypothesis of God's existence makes one's life more bearable, then that is a kind of evidence that God exists.

Russell and Moore were up in arms about this position, and James's 1907 *Pragmatism* made matters worse by seeming to be about *all* beliefs, not merely religious ones. In that book he argued that "Any idea upon which we can ride ... any idea that will carry us prosperously from any one part of our experience to any other part, linking things satisfactorily, working securely, simplifying, saving labor; is ... true *instrumentally*" (P 1907, 34). "Satisfactorily," he says, "means more satisfactorily to ourselves, and individuals will emphasize their points of satisfaction differently. To a certain degree, therefore, everything here is plastic" (P 1907, 35).

James then gave the Hibbert Lectures in Oxford in 1908, where his ally Schiller was a well-known don in a state of rebellion against the British philosophical establishment. His 1901 spoof *Mind! A Unique Review of Ancient and Modern Philosophy. Edited by A. Troglodyte, with the Co-operation of the Absolute and Others* was a parody of the eminent journal *Mind*. While it explicitly took aim at absolute idealism, Schiller was as unimpressed with the new atomist philosophy of Russell and Moore. He called his alternative at various points "personal idealism" "anthropomorphism," "voluntarism," "humanism," and "pragmatism." His aim was one of "*humanising* Truth" (Schiller 1907/1969, viii). James publicly supported Schiller's view and together they seemed set against the British establishment position. Schiller contended that "it is a *methodological necessity*" to hold that both truth and reality are "*wholly plastic*" (Schiller 1902, 61).

James's Hibbert Lectures were published as *A Pluralistic Universe*, which, as the title suggests, is in step with Schiller. They were happy to see themselves as engaged in a revolution against both the old British idealists Bradley and McTaggart and the new realists Russell and Moore. Both kinds of "intellectualist philosopher" yearn for a truth "that shall be absolutely true, self-testing, and self-dependent, icily exercising an unrestricted sway over a submissive world, whose adoration it requites with no services, and scouting as blasphemy all allusion to use or application" (Schiller 1907/1969, 9). They argued, against those intellectualist views, that meaning and truth cannot be pulled apart from use and application.

James often put forward less plastic, less pluralistic, views of truth and reality. Some of the essays in *The Will to Believe*, especially "The Moral Philosopher and the Moral Life," show a James who is closer to C. S. Peirce, the other founder of pragmatism. In these better moods, James is concerned to characterize truth as something that is of human value, without suggesting that true belief might be what this or that human finds valuable at this or that time. He often expressed regret that he did not always make this clear and he tried to correct the resulting misunderstanding by arguing that, contrary to his critics' understanding of him, his claim in *Pragmatism* was that the true is "the expedient," but the expedient "in the long run and on the whole, of course" (P 1907, 106; cf. MT 1909, 4). True beliefs are beliefs that survive because they deserve to survive.[2]

Schiller was also at times more careful. In "Axioms and Postulates," for instance, he argues that knowledge is a matter of accepting "postulates which had suggested themselves as desirable if true, and had succeeded and survived, for transparent reasons." We assume that something is true because we desire it to be true—it serves an interest of ours. Then we test it to see if it fits with our experience. If it survives, it is indeed true. That is the moderate and better pragmatist view, on which the human organism "needs assumptions it can act on and live by, which will serve as means to the attainment of its ends" (Schiller 1902, 91).

The British philosophical establishment was unwilling to take such disclaimers seriously. They were resolute in taking James and Schiller to argue that truth is what "works" or "pays," and what works or pays varies from context to context. Russell wrote something substantial and critical on pragmatism every year from 1908 until 1912. Moore joined in the attack, which is not misdescribed as savage.

THE TEN YEARS WAR

Russell, from his very beginnings as a philosopher, had considerable exposure to and engagement with pragmatist ideas. As a young man, he met both Santayana and James at the family home of his future wife, the American Alys Smith. He read both volumes of James's *Principles of Psychology* shortly after he completed his undergraduate degree. He paid special attention to, and had special respect for, James on spatial perception. In 1896, before he secured his Cambridge fellowship, he spent three months in America and wrote to James, asking if he might come and see him. He did more than that— he stayed with James during this trip (Russell 1967/2000, 220). That very year, James published "The Will to Believe," which contained the early percolations of his pragmatist account of truth. It was that view of truth that Russell loathed (Russell 1909/1992, 260–261). But the personal feelings between the two men were warm, and James felt betrayed when what I shall call the Ten Years War began.

It started in earnest after James's Gifford Lectures. By 1902 Schiller was writing to James, noting that Russell and others were discussing and criticizing pragmatism and that Russell was reading James's *The Varieties of Religious Experience* and rereading *The Principles of Psychology*.[3] In 1904 James wrote to Schiller to try to guess the identity of a reviewer of Schiller's *Humanism*. The reviewer, James says, let loose "a long smothered volcano of irritation at your general tone of belligerency and flippancy." In the margins of James's letter, Schiller scribbled "Mind! &c &c," suggesting that the reviewer's irritation was due to Schiller's spoofing the establishment's journal (CWJ 1904, 10.369). James also reported on further reactions Schiller had provoked: "One man recently said to me 'I *hate* him'—another: 'he is intolerable and odious.'" James gently advised that perhaps Schiller might "assume a solemn dignity commensurate with the importance of your function" as the champion of pragmatism in England. He said: "I confess that as I grow older I find myself believing more and more in the excellence of colorless *objectivity* of statement, keeping any personal oddity out, and letting brevity and pellucidity do the work" (CWJ 1904, 10.370). He ended the letter by repeating the entreaty: "Good bye! buckle down now to s'thing very solemn and systematic! Write your jokes by all means, but expunge them in proof, and save them for a posthumous no. of Mind!" (CWJ 1904, 10.371).

Six months later, we find James again trying to rein in Schiller, begging him to tone down his rhetoric in a piece actually submitted to *Mind*: "What I *earnestly beseech you to do therefore is* (no matter what *literary* cost) *to suppress those pages*.... Your paper's *total forensic effectiveness* will be 4 times greater without than with it" (CWJ 1904, 10.446–448). He then wrote to the Stout, the editor of *Mind*, asking him not to typeset Schiller's paper until Schiller had a chance to receive and consider his letter. Schiller refused James's request, asking, "why [should] we *both* speak honied words?" He was content to have James "present the peaceable face of Janus," while he would present the "warlike." In the end, he asked: "will you pardon me if I'm neither willing nor able to take your advice?" (CWJ 1904, 10.455).

Schiller's paper was published as "In Defense of Humanism" in the October 1904 issue of *Mind*. His refusal to use honied words had a deleterious effect on pragmatism's reputation in England, as James predicted and tried to prevent. James complained that Schiller was forever delivering a "butt-end-foremost statement of the humanist position" (P 1907, 117), although he remained clear that he and Schiller were on the main philosophical points in perfect agreement. Indeed, some of Schiller's essays in *Studies in Humanism* "seem to be written with my own heart's blood—it's startling that two people should be found to think so exactly alike" (CWJ 1907, 11.345). But he seemed well aware that when Schiller was in pragmatism's corner, fighting its battles, both James and Schiller were in danger of getting knocked out.

Russell and Moore took aim at this butt-end first presentation of pragmatism. James and Schiller wrote to each other that Russell's objection to pragmatism and especially to the will-to-believe idea "is at bottom emotional & the result of a revolt against his religious education" (CWJ 1909, 12.393). But while Russell was certainly capable of being emotional and careless in his writing on pragmatism, his objections often had the cold steel of excellent reasoning behind them.

Russell reviewed James's *Pragmatism* hot off the press, under the title "Transatlantic 'Truth'" (subsequent reprintings are under the title "William James's Conception of Truth"). He begins by noting that he and James are both empiricists and hence are in broad agreement. But the book "is like a bath with hot water running in so slowly that you don't know when to scream" (Russell 1908/1992, 472). Russell takes James to argue that "a belief is to be judged true in so far as the practical consequences of its adoption are good" (Russell 1908/1992, 475). Russell thinks that "usefulness" is too woolly a concept to be identified with truth, and even when it can be made precise, truth and usefulness come apart.

He says, regarding the difficulty of determining whether a belief "pays" or has useful consequences:

> We must suppose that this means that the consequences of entertaining the belief are better than those of rejecting it. In order to know this, we must know what are the consequences of entertaining it, and what are the consequences of rejecting it; we must know also what consequences are good, what bad, what consequences are better, and what worse. (Russell 1908/1992, 476–477)

This is a very tall order, which Russell immediately illustrates with two examples. First, the consequences of believing the doctrine of the Catholic faith might be that the belief makes a person happy "at the expense of a certain amount of stupidity and priestly domination" (Russell 1908/1992, 477). It is unclear how we are to weigh these benefits and burdens against each other. Second, the effects of Rousseau's doctrines were far reaching—Europe is a different place from what it would have been without them, not least because of the role of those doctrines in leading to the French Revolution. But how can we isolate from the whole history of Europe after Rousseau all and only those events that are effects of his views? And even if we could do that, whether we take these effects to be good or bad will itself depend on our political views. The question of whether the consequences of believing something are good or bad is an extraordinarily difficult one: often much more difficult to settle, Russell suggests, than the simple question of whether it is true.

In a related objection, Russell challenges James's use of the words "works" and "pays." Pragmatism is an extension of the method of the inductive sciences, and Russell commends it for being such. But pragmatism, he says, misapplies this method in its understanding of what "works":

> When *science* says that a hypothesis works, it means that from this hypothesis we can deduce a number of propositions which are verifiable.... But when *pragmatism* says that a hypothesis works, it means that the effects of believing it are good, including among the effects ... the emotions entailed by it or its perceived consequences, and the actions to which we are prompted by it or its perceived consequences. This is a totally different conception of "working," and one for which the authority of scientific procedure cannot be invoked. (Russell 1908/1992, 484)

Russell finds this conception of "working" in "The Will to Believe", but if he had focused on James's other work, he would have seen that James was considering the consequences of *p* obtaining, rather than the consequences of believing that *p* obtains.[4] But fair or not, his accusation stuck to James like glue.

Finally, Russell accuses the pragmatist of conflating the criterion of truth with the meaning of truth. He illustrates: if you wish to consult a certain book in the library, you check the catalogue—but a book's being in the catalogue is not the same thing as its being in the library. In a similar way, utility is a mark or a criterion of truth, but it is not identical to truth. Just as what we want is for the book to be in the library and not merely in the catalogue, what we want is for beliefs to be actually true, not merely to work for us. Russell considers, for example, the belief in the existence of other minds:

> if I am troubled by solipsism, the discovery that a belief in the existence of others is "true" in the pragmatist's sense is not enough to allay my sense of loneliness: the perception that I should profit by rejecting solipsism is not alone sufficient to make me reject it. For what I desire is not that the belief in solipsism should be false in the pragmatic sense, but that other people should in fact exist. (Russell 1908/1992, 479)

James, Russell argues, "ignores" the meaning commonly given to the word "true" (Russell 1908/1992, 478). When we search for the truth about some phenomenon, we do not desire to hold onto a belief simply because it works for us. We desire to hold onto a belief that works for us because its working for us is a sign that that belief is connected to the facts.

While James was preparing a reply to Russell's first piece (the reply would be published as "Two English Critics" in the 1909 *The Meaning of Truth*), Russell published "Pragmatism". James and Schiller were at the time writing frequent letters to each other about Russell and his new formal, logic-heavy way of doing philosophy. This is James to Schiller in 1909:

> *I*, as you know, despise logic ... and I think that if one wants to see what sorry tricks it will play with a man of genius one need only read over again, as I have recently done, the epistemological contributions of Bertrand Russell. Really pathological stuff, in my opinion. (CWJ 1909, 12.175)

Many of Russell's objections in "Pragmatism" mirror the ones he had already articulated. But he adds another argument—that "a confusion which runs through the whole pragmatist account of knowledge, namely the confusion between acting on an hypothesis and believing it" (Russell 1909/1992, 263–264). The idea that belief is forced whenever a practical decision is forced stands "contrary to many of the plainest facts of daily life":

> If, in walking along a country road, I come to a fork where there is no signpost and no passer-by, I have, from the point of view of action, a "forced" option. I must take one road or other if I am to have any chance of reaching my destination; and I may have no evidence whatever as to which is the right road. I then *act* on one or other of the two possible hypotheses, until I find some one of whom I can ask the way. But I do not *believe* either hypothesis. My action is either right or wrong, but my belief is neither, since I do not entertain either of the two possible beliefs. The pragmatist assumption that I believe the road I have chosen to be the right one is erroneous. (Russell 1909/1992, 264)

Russell thinks that to "infer belief from action, in the crude way involved in the assumption that we must 'either accept this truth or go without it', is to ignore the plain fact that our actions are constantly based on probabilities" (Russell 1909/1992, 264). While James (and, especially, Peirce) could well have accepted that belief comes in degrees, they tended to think of it as all or nothing. We have a belief, or we are in an unsettled state of doubt. Russell's objection holds especially for our actions in scientific practice, when we test working hypotheses without believing them. Rather, we entertain them or think there is at least some small chance that they are true:

> Pragmatists tell us that, in such cases, the initial unverified *belief* is a necessary condition for the subsequent established theory, and by so doing they make out a case for the usefulness of believing before we have evidence. This is, however, a mistaken analysis of the state of mind of a man who is testing an hypothesis. All that is required, and all that occurs among careful investigators, is the belief that the hypothesis has a

greater or smaller chance of being true, and for this belief there is probably sufficient evidence. (Russell 1909/1992, 264)

James's distinction between full belief and no belief at all is "far too crude" (Russell 1909/1992, 265). There is also partial belief, based on probabilities. It is here and only here that we are permitted to hope that a belief is true and be comforted by it, to the extent that it is probable. Russell adds that we will be less prone to persecuting others if we take our religious beliefs to be probable, as opposed to certainly true.

Russell's tone in "Pragmatism" swings between taking his target seriously, as in the above passage, and caricaturing it. In one of the least charitable descriptions of pragmatism we will ever find, he says: "The scepticism embodied in pragmatism is that which says 'Since all beliefs are absurd, we may as well believe what is most convenient'" (Russell 1909/1992, 280). And he chalks up pragmatism's popularity to recent trends regarding democracy, which he sees "in almost every page of William James's writing"—"an impatience of authority, an unwillingness to condemn wide-spread prejudices, a tendency to decide philosophical questions by putting them to the vote" (Russell 1909/1992, 281). James is under full attack:

> A thing which simply *is* true, whether you like it or not, is to him as hateful as a Russian autocracy; he feels that he is escaping from a prison, made not by stone walls but by "hard facts," when he has humanized truth, and made it, like the police force in a democracy, the servant of the people instead of their master. (Russell 1909/1992, 281)

Russell links this tendency to think of human beings as all-powerful to an American focus on optimism, virility, energy, and hope that all obstacles can be overcome, with the correlative conviction that failure to overcome them is a mark of "laziness or pusillanimity" (Russell 1909/1992, 282). On those views on which there really is no standard of truth apart from a Jamesian kind of success, "Maxim guns must be the ultimate arbiters of . . . truth" (Russell 1909/1992, 282). If truth is not grounded in objective reality, but only in what works for particular individuals or cultures in the short term, then might will turn out to be right.

James's response, in "Two English Critics," did not allay Russell's worries:

> Mr. Russell . . . joins the army of those who inform their readers that according to the pragmatist definition of the word "truth" the belief that A exists may be "true," even when A does *not* exist. This is the usual slander, repeated to satiety by our critics. They forget that in any concrete account of what is denoted by "truth" in human life, the word can only be used relatively to some particular trower. Thus, I may hold it true that Shakespere wrote the plays that bear his name, and may express my opinion to a critic. If the critic be both a pragmatist and a baconian, he will in his capacity of pragmatist see plainly that the workings of my opinion, I being what I am,

make it perfectly true for me, while in his capacity of baconian he still believes that Shakespere never wrote the plays in question. But most anti-pragmatist critics take the word "truth" as something absolute, and easily play on their reader's readiness to treat his own truths as the absolute ones. (MT 1909, 147)

At other times, James provides a much better response. In a letter to Russell, railing against "Transatlantic 'Truth,'" he says: "no pragmatist forgets that *concretely* our wish to square ourselves with hard *fact* may be irreconcilable with our other wishes" (CWJ 1909, 12.220).

After the death of James in 1910, Russell's polemic lost some of its edge. He makes clear his sorrow at losing a personal friend, a loss felt more keenly because of the distance imposed by the "acute controversy" of the final years (Russell 1983, 6.286, 1910). Russell considered revising "William James's Conception of Truth," as it was about to be reprinted in his *Philosophical Essays*, in order to tone down some of those polemical remarks. Instead, he added a postscript (in the preface to the volume) in which he said:

> The death of William James, which occurred when the printing of this book was already far advanced, makes me wish to express, what in the course of controversial writings does not adequately appear, the profound respect and personal esteem which I felt for him.... For readers trained in philosophy, no such assurance was required; but for those unaccustomed to the tone of a subject in which agreement is necessarily rarer than esteem, it seemed desirable to record what to others would be a matter of course. (Russell 1983, 6.257–258, 1910)

Moore seems not to have shared any of these warm feelings. He reviewed James's *Pragmatism* in the 1907 *Proceedings of the Aristotelian Society*. The review is long, harsh, and labored, with Moore repeatedly identifying James's main assertions as things that he is "anxious" to say, picking them apart in a repetitive way, finding "obvious objections" to them (Moore 1907, 33). He takes James to be "particularly anxious to assert" three things about truth: that true ideas are those that are verifiable or work; that truth is not static and immutable; and that truth is in some measure human-made (Moore 1907, 33). He cannot see how James could be offering anything but a definition of truth, on which all our true beliefs are verifiable and useful in the short term, and all our ideas that are verifiable and useful in the short term are true.

Despite Moore's unbecoming tone, he too lands some real blows. First, he deals with verifiability. He agrees that all completely verified statements are true, but he objects to the claim that all true statements are verifiable. For there are plenty of statements for which the evidence has been destroyed, or was never recorded, or lies buried deep in the past. That a particular whist player had the seven of diamonds in his third hand last night is either true or false, despite there now being no way of telling (Moore 1907, 36–38). Peirce put much effort into dealing with this problem. He argued that the principle of bivalence is nothing more than a regulative assumption of any inquiry in which we are engaged. Peirce, however, was hardly known during the early 1900s and James's own solution is to fall back, in a very unpragmatist way, on the correspondence theory of truth.[5]

Moore also adds to Russell's interrogation of the linkage between the true and the useful. He argues that sometimes a true belief will not be useful—it will positively be "in the way" (Moore 1907, 44). And sometimes a useful belief will not be true. Moreover, usefulness is a property that may come and go, and hence James's view entails, Moore says, that a belief that occurs at several different times may be true at some of the times at which it occurs, and yet untrue at others (1907, 61). The truth of a belief, that is, will vary from time to time. Truth is not a stable property of beliefs but is mutable. This is an anathema, as far as Moore is concerned:

> Does he hold that the idea that Julius Caesar was murdered in the Senate-House, though true now, may, at some future time cease to be true, if it should be more profitable to the lives of future generations to believe that he died in his bed? (Moore 1907, 70)

In a related objection, Moore attacks James's claim that we make the truth: "I think he certainly means to suggest that we not only make our true beliefs, but also that we *make them true*" (Moore 1907, 71–72). Moore thinks that it is crazy to suggest that my belief that *p* makes it true that *p*. My (correct) belief that it rained today did not make it rain today.

Moore provides a number of illustrations that pull apart truth from usefulness, including the following, which picks up on James's will-to-believe argument:

> It seems to me very difficult to be sure that the belief in an external hell has not been often useful to many men, and yet it may be doubted whether this idea is true. And so, too, with the belief in a happy life after death, or the belief in the existence of a God; it is, I think, very difficult to be sure that these beliefs have not been, and are not still, often useful, and yet it may be doubted whether they are true. (Moore 1907, 48)

He goes on to say that he is not at all sure that James wants to assert the misguided idea that all our true beliefs are useful and all our useful beliefs are true (Moore 1907, 49). But this is not a sudden charitable impulse toward James. For it is now that he gets nasty:

> I think it is quite possible he would admit that they are [false], and would say that he never meant either to assert or to imply the contrary. He complains that some of the critics of Pragmatism are unwilling to read any but the silliest of possible meanings into the statements of Pragmatists; and, perhaps, he would say that this is the case here. I certainly hope that he would. I certainly hope he would say that these statements, to which I have objected, are silly. For it does seem to me intensely silly to say that we can verify all our true ideas; intensely silly to say that every one of our true ideas is at some time useful; intensely silly to say that every idea which is ever useful is true. I hope Professor James would admit all these things to be silly, for if he

and other Pragmatists would admit even as much as this, I think a good deal would be gained. (Moore 1907, 49)

Moore goes on and on in this vein, concluding that James

> may protest, quite angrily, when a view is put before him in other words than his own, that he never either meant or implied any such thing, and yet it may be possible to judge, from what he says, that this very view, wrapped up in other words, was not only held by him but was precisely what made his thoughts seem to him to be interesting and important. (Moore 1907, 50)

He then assesses what James has insisted is his considered view—that truth is expedient, but expedient in the long run. Moore hopes that James is right, but thinks that such prophecies are too difficult to make. In any event, Moore is simply unwilling to conclude that James meant to assert this more plausible position and sticks the implausible position back onto him, providing textual evidence from James.

James returns the snarky tone in letters to friends: "I wonder what makes every word that man writes fill me so with a feeling of offense on behalf of human nature, insulted so to the full by his insufferable arrogance of manner" (CWJ 1908, 11.526). And:

> Poor childish Moore! . . . He is too weak & silly for any comment at all, so I won't waste a minute on him. A monument to the folly of pretending to have no *vision* of things, but to admit anything as possible and then select by "logic" which is most probable! He crawls over the outside of my lecture like a myopic ant over a building, seeing only the spot he touches, tumbling into every microscopic crack, and not suspecting even that there *is* a centre or a whole at all. Bah! (CWJ 1908, 11.538–589)

Thus was the hostile state of the relationship between pragmatism and British philosophy in the mid-1920s. It was soon to change dramatically.

Russell's Turn to Pragmatism

The title of this section will surprise many. But despite Russell's scorn for pragmatism, by 1921, while Russell himself may not have admitted it, he was considered by others to have been largely converted. I say "largely" because the pragmatist account of *truth* was never to appeal to him. But he was to adopt other essential elements of pragmatism. By 1914, he already knew something about James's psychology and a little about Peirce. His knowledge of pragmatism as a whole was enlarged in the spring term of 1914 when he delivered the Lowell Lectures in Boston. James had died in 1910 and Peirce would die during Russell's stay. So, obviously, they had no direct contact with Russell during his semester at Harvard. Russell was to give two courses, but he arrived a couple of months late, and Josiah Royce and a young instructor named Harry Costello stepped up to start his lectures. The pragmatist positions of Peirce, James, Dewey, and Schiller were a frequent topic of discussion and continued to be so after Russell's arrival. For instance, Royce was at pains to distinguish pragmatism from the "wider" humanism of Schiller and James.

When Russell finally arrived, his own lectures were well attended by students and faculty. Royce had critical interactions with him, and Costello says that both "Royce and Russell were big enough to take it and like it" (Costello 1963, 194). The physicist Victor Lenzen, then a PhD student in philosophy, tells us that "On one occasion when Mr. Russell was expounding his dualism between mind and matter," Ralph Barton Perry was "drawn into defense of his behavioristic theory of mind" (Lenzen 1971, 5). By this Lenzen meant the pragmatist alternative to extreme behaviorism. That alternative linked belief to action without reducing it to action. Thus, we have Russell being exposed to the pragmatist link between belief and behavior in 1914, a link that we have seen him try to dismantle in "Pragmatism."

The exposure to pragmatist ideas, divorced from rhetoric and fisticuffs, would prove effective. By the 1921 *The Analysis of Mind*, Russell was putting forward what many of his colleagues saw as a pragmatist position. For they saw the heart and soul of pragmatism lying first in its account of belief as a disposition to behave. The star of the up-and-coming generation, Frank Ramsey, who was a card-carrying pragmatist, said the following:

> My pragmatism is derived from Mr. Russell ... The essence of pragmatism I take to be this, that the meaning of a sentence is to be defined by reference to the actions to which asserting it would lead, or, more vaguely still, by its possible causes and effects. Of this I feel certain, but of nothing more definite. (Ramsey 1927/1990, 51)

Richard Braithwaite repeated the claim in his obituary of Ramsey: "Recently (in company with Bertrand Russell) he had been descending the slippery path to a sort of pragmatism" (Braithwaite 1930, 216). Keynes too made the assertion that Russell was friendly to pragmatism. Ramsey was moving toward "what he himself described as a sort of pragmatism, not unsympathetic to Russell, but repugnant to Wittgenstein" (Keynes 1931/1972, 338). It is astounding that Russell, in 1927, would so casually be described as a pragmatist. It seems that not only had peace been made, but that there was almost a surrender.

But while Russell had indeed adopted some key pragmatist claims about perception and about the link between belief and behavior, he could not enroll fully in the pragmatist project, since he took this to require endorsement of the pragmatist theory of truth that James was inclined to articulate. Nevertheless, Russell's new account of *belief* in *The Analysis of Mind* was pragmatist in spirit. In that book, Russell made another attempt at analyzing the relationship between thought and the world. This time, the dualism of his earlier tries was tempered by an appeal to James's rich account of experience, what

Russell termed James's neutral monism, as well as to Dewey's behaviorism.[6] He said in *My Philosophical Development* that by 1918 he had become convinced "that William James had been right in denying the relational character of sensations" (Russell 1959, 134). Russell, in "Transatlantic Truth," had denied James's distinction between seeing and having knowledge. But now, in admitting that "it is a mistake to regard . . . mere seeing itself as knowledge" (Russell 1921/2005, 83; cf. Russell 1959, 135), Russell had come to recognize the insight in this Jamesian point: that cognitive states always involve the activity of the mind, and not its merely passively receiving the world as it is in itself.

Russell and his generation of British philosophers continued to identify the pragmatist theory of truth with what they took to be James's idea that truth is what works or pays. Had Ramsey, who was putting forward a sophisticated version of the pragmatist theory of truth, not died at the age of twenty-six in 1930, perhaps British philosophy would have been thought of as having a strong pragmatism at its core. For as we shall see in what follows, the later Wittgenstein, like Russell, was also moving toward pragmatism.

Wittgenstein and James

Wittgenstein's later work seems very pragmatist, with his interest in philosophy as method rather than as a body of truths; his focus on the primacy of practice and meaning as use; his special regard for those propositions that we do not doubt; and his concern to describe the complex detail of human language and life. And while he was dead set against any kind of theory, such as a general theory of truth, he was happy to have James's pragmatist criterion of truth stand as what counts for truth in science and other practical endeavors:

> Whether an application has a use in practice depends on the kind of life we lead. The pragmatic criterion of the truth of a proposition is its usefulness in practice. But the person who says this has in mind one particular use of "useful": its use in the lab, say, to predict the future. (Wittgenstein 1979, 142)

Wittgenstein was not terribly interested in the history of philosophy and was remarkable for not talking much about the work of others. James was one of the few philosophers he would admit to having read. A. C. Jackson reported that for a time James's *Principles of Psychology* was the only book on Wittgenstein's shelf and that in the 1940s he "very frequently referred to James in his lectures, even making on one occasion—to everybody's astonishment—a precise reference to a page-number!"[7] As Russell Goodman has argued, Wittgenstein admired James as a deep thinker, one who did not suffer from the "loss of problems" syndrome that diminished so many philosophers (Goodman 2002, 62–63). Wittgenstein, as always, pulled no punches:

> Some philosophers (or whatever you like to call them) suffer from what may be called "loss of problems." Then everything seems quite simple to them, no deep problems seem to exist any more, the world becomes broad and flat and loses all depth, and what they write becomes immeasurably shallow and trivial. Russell and H. G. Wells suffer from this. (Wittgenstein 1967/1981, §456)

What impressed Wittgenstein most about James were his thoughts on religious experience and the meaning of life. He was a spiritual man, and James's idea that religious experience could give us flashes of insight attracted him. In 1912, Wittgenstein wrote to Russell:

> Whenever I have time I now read James's "Varieties of religious exp." This book does me a *lot* of good. I don't mean to say that I will be a saint soon, but I am not sure that it does not improve me a little in a way in which I would like to improve *very much*: namely I think that it helps me to get rid of the *Sorge* (in the sense in which Goethe used the word in the 2nd part of Faust). (McGuinness 2012, 30)

Wittgenstein thought that James's writing on religious experience was good for his soul—good for helping to humanize him and for dealing with his despair.[8] Many years later Wittgenstein commended *Varieties* to his friend Maurice Drury as "a book that helped me a lot at one time" (Drury 1981, 121). He told Drury that one must not try to "give some sort of philosophical justification of Christian beliefs, as if some sort of proof was needed" (Drury 1981, 117). The beauty of religions is grounded not in their accurately describing reality, but in their role as "the ways in which people express their religious feelings."

In 1929, Wittgenstein presented a short paper to the Heretics Society titled "A Lecture on Ethics." By "ethics," Wittgenstein mostly meant religion. In the lectures, he reiterated the idea, already present in the *Tractatus*, that ethical and religious matters cannot be stated in words, as they go beyond the facts: "Ethics, if it is anything, is supernatural and our words will only express facts" (Wittgenstein 1965, 7). On Wittgenstein's view, "What is ethical cannot be taught. . . . Here there is nothing to be stated any more; all I can do is to step forth as an individual and speak in the first person" (Waismann and McGuinness 1979, 117).

In 1939–1940, he gave a course of lectures on these topics, the student notes of which were later published as *Lectures and Conversations on Aesthetics, Psychology, and Religion*. In them, Wittgenstein argues that our religious and ethical statements are unlike those of science (Wittgenstein 1966, 57). We can be certain about religious matters, quite apart from questions of evidence. For, in religious controversies:

> Reasons look entirely different from normal reasons. They are, in a way, quite inconclusive. The point is that if there were evidence, this would in fact destroy the whole business. Anything that I normally call evidence wouldn't in the slightest influence me. (Wittgenstein 1966, 56)

Religious doctrines "are not treated as historical, empirical, propositions" (Wittgenstein 1966, 57). The attitude that licenses us in accepting them is "faith" or taking them as "dogma" (Wittgenstein 1966, 57). For the meaning of religious and ethical expressions, and the significance of our religious and ethical practices, are grounded in their role in our lives. Contrary to appearances, they are not descriptions of reality. Religious terms do not refer to entities, and religious explanations of events are not causal. Neither are religious stories historical narratives. Rather, religious beliefs are "pictures" that we can make use of in our lives. Since "[p]*ractice* gives the words their sense" (Wittgenstein 1980, 97), to embrace religious belief is

> (something like) passionately committing oneself to a system of coordinates. Hence although it's belief, it is really a way of living, or a way of judging life. (Wittgenstein 1980, 73)

An ethical stance is an individual, personal response to the world.

All this shows James's strong influence, despite the fact that the epistemological cast of James's arguments is abandoned by Wittgenstein. Part of the argument of "The Will to Believe" is all about whether we are *justified* in believing in God, given the dearth of evidence. And in *Varieties* James takes religious belief to be subject to revision in light of a certain kind of perceptual experience. What Wittgenstein found important in James is not his thoughts about justification, but the exploration of "the feelings, acts, and experiences of individual men in their solitude" (VRE 1902/1985, 34; italics removed).

Wittgenstein places himself in the Jamesian context (not addressing James specifically):

> Life can educate you to "believing in God." And *experiences* too are what do this but not visions, or other sense experiences, which show us the "existence of this being", but e.g. sufferings of various sorts. And they do not show us God as a sense experience does an object, nor do they give rise to *conjectures* about him. Experiences, thoughts,—life can force this concept on us. (Wittgenstein 1980, 97)

Experience has a role in religious commitment, but Wittgenstein construes this role as merely causal, not epistemic. In committing to a religion, we adopt a way of living without basing its adoption on evidence. Hence, he thinks it is wrongheaded to inquire, as James inquires in *Varieties*, into the merits of the evidence that supports belief in God's existence. Accepting God's existence is a matter of "shaping" one's life a certain way (Wittgenstein 1980, 97), but the decision to do so is not based on reasons, practical or evidential.

But this difference is easily enough bridged, in that James too was set against evidentialism—at least as it manifested itself in the work of W. K. Clifford. He too thought that empirical and logical evidence was not all that was relevant to religious and other kinds of forced beliefs. The upshot is that Wittgenstein, along with the late 1920s Russell, can also be seen as having been heavily influenced by pragmatism. Despite Wittgenstein's wariness about aligning his view with any kind of theory, and despite Russell's continued hostility to the pragmatist theory of truth, the war against American pragmatism waged by the British at the beginning of the 1900s settled down to something like a peaceful coexistence. It is no accident that pragmatism, as Huw Price and I have argued,[9] continues to thrive in Britain.

Notes

1. This article is partly drawn from Misak (2016), piecing together and expanding upon an argument contained over a number of chapters. I thank Alex Klein for helpful comments.
2. See Suckiel (1982, 105–115) for this way of putting the point.
3. See CWJ (1904, 10.165), Griffin (1992, 250), and Proops (2011, 2014).
4. See Jackman (2016).
5. For more on James and the correspondence theory of truth, see contributions to this volume by Tom Donaldson and Ignas Skrupskelis.
6. Alex Klein (2017) argues that even Russell's construction of the external world in his 1914 Lowell Lectures owes much to James's view of spatial relations.
7. See Passmore (1966, 434).
8. It also did him some philosophical good. As Arif Ahmed pointed out to me, James anticipated the Wittgensteinian idea of family resemblance. See VRE (1902/1985, 30–31). For more on the relationship between Wittgenstein and James, see Boncompagni, this volume.
9. See Misak and Price (2017).

Bibliography

Braithwaite, Richard. 1930. "Frank Plumpton Ramsey." *Cambridge Review* (January 31): 216.
Brennan, Frances, and Nicolas Griffin. 1997. "Russell's Marginalia in HHHis Copy of William James's *Principles of Psychology*." *Russell: The Journal of the Bertrand Russell Archives* 17: 123–170.
Costello, Harry T. 1963. *Josiah Royce's Seminar, 1913–14: As Recorded in the Notebooks of Harry T. Costello*. Edited by G. Smith. Brunswick, NJ: Rutgers University Press.
Drury, M. O. 1981. "Conversations with Wittgenstein." Reprint. Edited by R. Rhees, 112–189. Oxford: Basil Blackwell.
Goodman, Russell. 2002. *Wittgenstein and William James*. Cambridge: Cambridge University Press.
Griffin, Nicholas, ed. 1992. *The Selected Letters of Bertrand Russell*, vol. 1. London: Penguin.
Jackman, Henry. 2016. "The Pragmatic Method," *Oxford Handbook of Philosophical Methodology*. New York: Oxford University Press, 193–208.
Kappy Suckiel, Ellen. 1982. *The Pragmatic Philosophy of William James*. Notre Dame, IN: Notre Dame University Press.
Keynes, John Maynard. 1931/1972. Review of *The Foundations of Mathematics*, by F. P. Ramsey. Originally appeared in *The New Statesman and Nation*, October 3. Reprinted in *The Collected Writings of John Maynard Keynes*, vol. X. Edited by D. E. Moggridge. London: Macmillan.
Klein, Alexander. 2015. "Science, Religion, and 'the Will to Believe.'" *HOPOS: The Journal for the International Society for the History of Philosophy of Science* 5(1): 72–117.

Klein, Alexander. 2017. "Russell on Acquaintance with Spatial Properties: The Significance of James." In *Innovations in the History of Analytic Philosophy*, edited by C. Pincock and S. Lapointe, 229–263. London: Palgrave Macmillan.
Lenzen, Victor F. 1971. "Bertrand Russell at Harvard." *Russell: The Journal of Bertrand Russell Studies* 3: 4–6.
McGuinness, Brian, ed. 2012. *Wittgenstein in Cambridge: Letters and Documents 1911–1951*. Oxford: Blackwell.
Misak, Cheryl. 2015. "Klein on James on the Will to Believe." *HOPOS: The Journal of the International Society for the History of Philosophy of Science* 5(1): 118–128.
Misak, Cheryl. 2016. *Cambridge Pragmatism: From Peirce and James to Ramsey and Wittgenstein*. Oxford: Oxford University Press.
Misak, Cheryl, and Huw Price 2017. *The Practical Turn: Pragmatism in Britain in the Long 20th Century*. Edited by C. Misak and H. Price. Oxford: Oxford University Press.
Moore, G. E. 1907. "Professor James's 'Pragmatism.'" *Proceedings of the Aristotelian Society* 8: 33–77.
Passmore, John. 1966. *A Hundred Years of Philosophy*. 2nd ed. London: Gerald Duckworth & Co. Ltd.
Peirce, Charles Sanders. 1931–1958. *Collected Papers of Charles Sanders Peirce*. 8 vols. Edited by C. Hartshorne and P. Weiss (vols. I–vi), A. Burks (vols. vii and viii). Cambridge, MA: Belknap Press.
Proops, Ian. 2011. "Logical Atomism in Russell and Wittgenstein." In *The Oxford Handbook of Wittgenstein*, edited by O. Kuusela and M. McGinn, 214–239. Oxford: Oxford University Press.
Proops, Ian. 2014. "Russellian Acquaintance Revisited." *Journal of the History of Philosophy* 52(4): 779–811.
Ramsey, F. P. 1927/1990. "Facts and Propositions." Reprint. 34–51. Edited by D.H. Mellor. Cambridge: Cambridge University Press.
Ramsey, F. P. 1990. *F.P. Ramsey: Philosophical Papers*. Edited by D.H. Mellor. Cambridge: Cambridge University Press.
Rhees, Rush, ed. 1981. *Ludwig Wittgenstein: Personal Recollections*. Oxford: Basil Blackwell.
Russell, Bertrand. 1908/1992. "William James's Conception of Truth." Reprint. *The Collected Papers of Bertrand Russell*, vol. 5, 465–485. London: Routledge
Russell, Bertrand. 1909/1992. "Pragmatism." Reprint. *The Collected Papers of Bertrand Russell*, vol. 6, 257–284. London: Routledge
Russell, Bertrand. 1921/2005. *The Analysis of Mind*. Reprint. London: G. Allen & Unwin.
Russell, Bertrand. 1959. *My Philosophical Development*. London: George Allen and Unwin.
Russell, Bertrand. 1967/2000. *Autobiography*. Repr. London: Routledge.
Russell, Bertrand. (1983–). *The Collected Papers of Bertrand Russell*. 36 vols. London: Routledge.
Schiller, F. C. S. 1902. "Axioms and Postulates." In *Personal Idealism: Philosophical Essays*, edited by H. Sturt, 47–133. London: Macmillan.
Schiller, F. C. S. 1903/1912. *Humanism: Philosophical Essays*. 2nd ed. London: Macmillan.
Schiller, F. C. S. 1907/1969. *Studies in Humanism*. Reprint. Freeport, NY: Books for Libraries Press.
Waismann, Friedrich, and Brian McGuinness (eds.) 1979. *Ludwig Wittgenstein and the Vienna Circle: Conversations Recorded by Friedrich Waismann*. Oxford: Basil Blackwell.

Wittgenstein, Ludwig. 1922. *Tractatus Logico-Philosophicus*. Translated by C. K. Ogden and F. P. Ramsey. London: Routledge and Kegan Paul.
Wittgenstein, Ludwig. 1965. "A Lecture on Ethics." *The Philosophical Review* 74(1): 3–12.
Wittgenstein, Ludwig. 1966. *Lectures and Conversations on Aesthetics, Psychology, and Religion*. Edited by C. Barrett. Berkeley: University of California Press.
Wittgenstein, Ludwig. 1967/1981. *Zettel*. Edited by G. E. M. Anscombe and G. H. von Wright. Translated by G. E. M. Anscombe. Oxford: Basil Blackwell.
Wittgenstein, Ludwig. 1979. *Wittgenstein's Lectures: Cambridge 1932–1935*. Edited by A. Ambrose. Chicago: University of Chicago Press.
Wittgenstein, Ludwig. 1980. *Culture and Value*. Edited by G. H. von Wright in collaboration with H. Nyman. Translated by P. Winch. Oxford: Basil Blackwell.

CHAPTER 28

JAMES AND WITTGENSTEIN

ANNA BONCOMPAGNI

Introduction: "A Real Human Being"

According to a common reading in the Wittgensteinian literature, William James was, for the Viennese philosopher, a perfect case study, which he used in order to show his students the typical symptoms of a disease in need of urgent therapy: the disease of a philosopher introspecting with the aim of observing and explaining mental phenomena, broadly imitating a scientist who observes and explains physical phenomena in the "outer" world. From a Wittgensteinian standpoint, such an attitude could only lead to conceptual mistakes. In this reading, James was the later Wittgenstein's "major whipping boy" (Gale 1999, 165); Wittgenstein used *The Principles of Psychology* mainly "to provide examples of confusion in the philosophy of psychology" (Monk 1991, 478);[1] and James's conception of the stream of thought was for him "largely a meaningless babble" (Hacker 1990, 305). To be sure, Wittgenstein himself was often not particularly kind in describing James:

> How needed is the work of philosophy is shown by James' psychology. Psychology, he says, is a science, but he discusses almost no scientific questions. His movements, are merely (so many) attempts to extricate himself from the cobwebs of metaphysics in which he is caught. *He cannot yet walk, or fly at all, he only wiggles* [in English in the original text]. Not that that isn't interesting. Only, it is not a scientific activity. (MS 165, 150–151)[2]

> James is a goldmine for the psychology *of philosophers*. (MS 124, 292)

Yet, James is one of the thinkers whose name appears most often in Wittgenstein's work. Indeed, he read James's *The Varieties of Religious Experience* (1902) as early as 1912.[3] In the same year, he probably came into contact also with James's psychology, by attending G. E. Moore's lectures in Cambridge.[4] PP (1890) appeared in Wittgenstein's writings at the beginning of the 1930s and, together with *Psychology: Briefer Course* (1892), would accompany Wittgenstein through the years, sometimes being used during his classes in Cambridge.[5] It may also be that Wittgenstein read other texts by James, like *Essays in Radical Empiricism* (1912) and *Pragmatism* (1907).[6]

In what follows, largely in the spirit of Goodman (2002), I will argue that it was *not only* as a paradigmatic example of confusion that Wittgenstein continued to be interested in James's thought, and that a good key for understanding why is what he said to his friend Maurice Drury in 1931:

> *Wittgenstein*: . . . A book you should read is William James' *Varieties of Religious Experience*; that was a book that helped me a lot at one time.
> *Drury*: Oh yes, I have read that. I always enjoy reading anything of William James. He is such a human person.
> *Wittgenstein*: That is what makes him a good philosopher; he was a real human being. (Rhees 1984, 106)

It will not by my aim to attempt to judge whether Wittgenstein was right or wrong in interpreting James; rather, I will limit myself to figuring out what picture of James Wittgenstein offers, and if and in what terms anything specifically Jamesian remains in Wittgenstein's work. Since it was through VRE that Wittgenstein first came into contact with James, religion will offer the starting point for this reflection. In the third section, I will dwell on the pragmatic maxim and Wittgenstein's comments about the Jamesian conception of truth. The following sections will focus on psychology. I will then broaden the discussion to the theme of aspect-seeing, and finally, in the last section, examine Wittgenstein's observations about the "good" in pragmatism in order to draw some concluding remarks.

A Religious Point of View

In June 1912, Wittgenstein wrote to Bertrand Russell:

> Whenever I have time I now read James's "Varieties of religious exp[erience]". This book does me *a lot* of good. I don't mean to say that I will be saint soon, but I am not sure that it does not improve me a little in a way in which I would like to improve *very much*: namely I think that it helps me to get rid of the *Sorge* (in the sense in which Goethe used the word in the 2nd part of Faust). (McGuinness 2012, 30)

Other religious readings accompanied Wittgenstein during the time spent in almost complete solitude in Norway and then as a volunteer, often at the front, in World War I; but it seems that the role of James's book was pivotal in this troubled phase of Wittgenstein's life. After meeting Wittgenstein in December 1919, Russell wrote to Lady

Ottoline that he was "astonished" to discover that Wittgenstein had become "a complete mystic" and "seriously contemplate[ed] becoming a monk," adding that "it all started from William James' Varieties of Religious Experience" (McGuinness 2012, 112).

What was so valuable in this book if it led Wittgenstein to think seriously about monasticism and remained so important for him that he still recommended it to friends almost twenty years later? Two sets of reasons can be given. On the one hand, in VRE (1902), Wittgenstein, the man, found a book that talked to him, a collection of experiences resonating with his own personality. On the other hand, thanks to VRE, Wittgenstein, the philosopher, came across themes and views that were congenial to his outlook, and that would then emerge in his own work.

A few words on these two points.

Regarding the former, one must remember that the young Wittgenstein had a troubled and complex personality, oppressed and exalted at the same time by the "duty of genius" (Monk 1991) which commanded him to do something worthy with his life. He went to war as a volunteer, because he felt that only by being near death could he try to be a better person. Son of an incredibly rich and powerful family, he would renounce all his goods and money in favor of his brothers and sisters, and live, at times, only thanks to the generosity of his friends. It was this man that found in VRE the existential help he told Russell about. Wittgenstein's 1914–1916 notebooks, particularly the coded pages, bear signs of a deep attunement with many of the testimonies recollected in VRE (1902) and with many views expressed by its author.[7] As McGuinness (1988, 156) and Goodman (2002, 8, 41) note, Wittgenstein may have found in James's description of the "sick soul" a portrait of his own condition, a man in need of a definitive existential experience that could lead him toward a rebirth and a reconciliation with the world. A further testimony can be found in two letters written to Wittgenstein by his sister Hermine in 1916 and 1917 (CF, 27, 34): she expressed, tactfully and ironically, her worries about his wish to become a "James-Mensch" (James-man; what James described as "the saint," according to the editors of CF), telling him that there would be time after the war to try to accomplish that end.

Regarding the latter set of reasons, it is clear that many themes in *Tractatus Logico-Philosophicus* (TLP) and "A Lecture on Ethics" (LE) were inspired, in part at least, by James's book.[8] One of them is the connection between surrendering to the will of God and happiness, a state in which the whole world, although unchanged, is perceived and experienced in a completely different manner. James describes what happens after a rebirth, saying that "a new heaven seems to shine on a new earth" (VRE 1902, 127), that the world seems to undergo "an objective change" with a sense of beauty and newness surrounding everything (VRE 1902, 201–202). The opposite characterizes the melancholic state, in which "the world . . . looks remote, strange, sinister, uncanny[, i]ts color is gone, its breath is cold" (VRE 1902, 127). Wittgenstein appears to work on the same themes when he writes that to be happy one must be in harmony with the will of God and that "the world of the happy is quite another than that of the unhappy" (NB, 74–75, 78; TLP, 6.43).

The presence of James is also detectable in Wittgenstein's words about 'the Mystical' and about ineffability. Ineffability is indeed, in James's description, "the handiest of the marks" of the mystical state of mind: the subject of such a state of mind, he wrote, "immediately says that it defies expression, that no adequate report of its contents can be given in words" (VRE 1902, 302). When reporting a quote from Saint John of the Cross, he added that in this state one "finds no terms, no means, no comparison whereby to render the sublimity of the wisdom" (VRE 1902, 323; see also 312, 317, 333). Wittgenstein would use similar words: "There is indeed the inexpressible. This *shows* itself; it is the Mystical" (TLP, 6.522), and "What *can* be shown *cannot* be said" (TLP, 4.1212), concluding, famously, that "Whereof one cannot speak, thereof one must be silent" (TLP, 7).

VRE, more generally, offered Wittgenstein a view focusing on religion and the mystical as an experience, as an intimate and personal way of feeling existence on the whole. This is also dealt with by Wittgenstein in LE, in which the ethical, the religious, and the aesthetical dimensions appear to be intertwined and cannot be properly explained but through examples of personal experiences. "This is an entirely personal matter" Wittgenstein remarked, speaking of the meaning of "absolute or ethical value" (LE, 41). Just like James, who wrote that the basis of religion is a "sense of the world's presence" (VRE 1902, 37) and that one of the characteristics of faith is the non-intellectual but immediate and intuitive "assurance that I . . . am saved now and forever" (VRE 1902, 200), or "the loss of all the worry" (VRE 1902, 201), Wittgenstein wrote of the experience of "wondering for the existence of the world" and of "feeling absolutely safe" (LE, 41) as examples of how he himself felt when tempted to say something about the absolute good.

Again, just like James, who underlined that it is impossible to give a rational foundation to faith, to prove the truth of religious revelations, as well as to argue against religion (VRE 1902, 67, 345–346, 359), Wittgenstein, in a lecture on religious belief given in 1938, observed that in controversies between a religious person and an atheist, "reasons look entirely different from normal reasons"; they are "inconclusive," because "anything that I normally call evidence wouldn't in the slightest influence me" (LA, 56), and repeated that "religious matters are not matters of historical evidence nor of science" (LA, 57). In short, as Hilary Putnam (1991, 66) has suggested, for Wittgenstein—and this is something that is clear in James's case too—"understanding the words of the religious person . . . is not a matter of 'semantic theory' [nor of any other theory at all, one might add], but a matter of understanding a human being."[9]

There are also other topics and hints in VRE, not strictly connected to religion, which would resurface in Wittgenstein's work. One of them is the Wittgensteinian concept, or methodological tool, of 'family resemblances', which according to many commentators has in James one of its main sources.[10] Another one, also present in other writings by James, is the principle of pragmatism or the pragmatic maxim, to which we now turn.

Pragmatism and Truth as Usefulness

In order to judge the value and the meaning of religion for life, James introduces the Peircean pragmatic maxim in these terms:

> To develop a thought's meaning we need ... only determine what conduct it is fitted to produce; that conduct is for us its sole significance. ... To attain perfect clearness in our thoughts of an object, we need then only consider what sensations, immediate or remote, we are conceivably to expect from it, and what conduct we must prepare in case the object should be true. Our conception of these practical consequences is for us the whole of our conception of the object, so far as that conception has positive significance at all. (VRE 1902, 351)

The later Wittgenstein's way of looking at the contexts and modes of the use of words when investigating meaning clearly shares something of the spirit of the maxim (Hutchinson and Read 2013, 164), particularly in the notes of *On Certainty* (OC), in which Wittgenstein is interested in exploring the connections between certainty, claims to knowledge, predicting consequences, action, and conduct.[11]

Did Wittgenstein get all he knew about James's pragmatism from VRE (1902)? Most likely no. *Pragmatism* (1907), although as far as I know never cited directly in Wittgenstein's writings (a reference to it only appears in a conversation recorded in PPO, 388–389), was widely debated in Cambridge when Wittgenstein lived there. He probably knew at least some parts of that book through the very critical reviews and commentaries that his friends Bertrand Russell and G. E. Moore published,[12] or thanks to the "innumerable conversations" (PI, 4) he shared with Frank Ramsey—who also was familiar with *The Meaning of Truth* (MT) (1909)[13]—in 1929. Yet, the main topic of the philosophical discussions around pragmatism was not the pragmatic maxim, but the pragmatist conception of truth. Not surprisingly, the first reference to pragmatism in Wittgenstein's manuscripts is precisely about truth. This remark dates back to January 20, 1930.

> When I say "There is a chair over there," this sentence refers to a series of expectations. I believe I could go there, perceive the chair and sit on it, I believe it is made of wood and I expect it to have a certain hardness, inflammability, etc. If some of these expectations are mistaken, I will see it as proof for retaining that there was no chair there.
>
> Here one sees the access to the pragmatist conception of true and false. A sentence is true as long as it proves to be useful.
>
> Every sentence we utter in everyday life appears to have the character of a hypothesis. (MS 107, 248–249)[14]

Among the classical pragmatists, as is well known, it was mainly James who emphasized the connection between truth and usefulness, and it was certainly his conception of truth, as proposed in P, that both Russell and Moore attacked in their reviews. Therefore, it is quite straightforward to conclude that Wittgenstein's reference to the pragmatist conception of truth is a reference to James's conception.

What is interesting in the quoted remark is that Wittgenstein did *not* give judgments about the pragmatist conception of truth, whether positive or negative.[15] Indeed, he simply pointed out that this conception is a possible outcome of a reflection concerning expectation and fulfilment, or the hypothetical nature of the sentences of everyday life. As long as the expectations are not contradicted by experience, the sentence expressing them works; as long as it proves to be useful, it is true: this seems to be the core of his line of reasoning here.

Although some echoes of this attitude resonate in the "middle" Wittgenstein's reflections on language and meaning,[16] in later years, he *did* criticize pragmatism, and explicitly distanced himself from it.[17] In fact, the concept of usefulness in connection to truth, so relevant in pragmatism, and the concept of use in connection to meaning, a key notion for the later Wittgenstein, though presenting similarities, do not overlap at all.[18] Yet, as we shall see, Wittgenstein also found something "good" in pragmatism.[19] Before turning to this, it is time to devote some attention to the main field in which Wittgenstein engages with James, namely, psychology.

Mind and Meaning

The first time the name "James" appears in Wittgenstein's notebooks is on February 14, 1931, in a remark concerning his theory of emotion (MS 110, 73).[20] From then on, James would be a constant presence in Wittgenstein's writings on psychology and related subjects. I will deal with psychological themes in this and the next two sections.

In general terms, Wittgenstein criticized James for his emphasis on the *feelings* connected with meaning, belief, thoughts, and understanding, and on introspection as a reliable way of knowing what the "self" is and what goes on in one's mind. His move is to underline that feelings and introspection are insufficient and misleading if taken as the only means by which to investigate psychological concepts, and that the temptation to rely exclusively on them may derive from a scientific and empirical attitude inappropriately applied to this context. Nevertheless, Wittgenstein shows his appreciation of James's detailed and nuanced "phenomenology" (Goodman 2002, 85) of psychology and his frequent use of examples and stories.

One paradigmatic example of the Jamesian attitude criticized by Wittgenstein is the former's insistence on the feelings connected to what he called the transitive parts of thoughts, as opposed to the substantive parts:

> There is not a conjunction or a preposition, and hardly an adverbial phrase, syntactic form, or inflection of voice, in human speech, that does not express some shading or

other of relation which we at some moment actually feel to exist between the larger objects of our thought....

We ought to say a feeling of *and*, a feeling of *if*, a feeling of *but*, and a feeling of *by*, quite as readily as we say a feeling of *blue* or a feeling of *cold*. (PP 1890, 238)

A closely related issue is the *feeling of tendency*, by which James means "a sense of the direction from which an impression is about to come" (PP 1890, 343), offering as examples the way one feels when hearing an expression like "Look!" or "Wait!," or when trying to recall a forgotten name. Other similarly peculiar feelings are linked, according to James, to the sense of familiarity (PP 1890, 344) and to the intention to say something (PP 1890, 345). He used these examples to object to the traditional empiricist idea that thought has to do exclusively with definite images, affirming that the stream of consciousness is actually mainly constituted by vague feelings (PP 1890, 346).

In opposing James, Wittgenstein did not mean to defend the empiricist assumptions, nor had he anything to say against the relevance of vagueness. What somehow disturbed him is that James's account risked suggesting that, in general, *understanding* and *meaning* are reducible to the *feelings* connected with hearing or uttering the word. One *can* account for meaning in these terms; yet, it is not the only way.

> What do we want to understand by the "meaning" of a word? A characteristic feeling that accompanies the uttering (hearing) of the word? (James's and-feeling, if-feeling). Or do we want to use the word "meaning" completely differently; and say, for instance, that two words have the same meaning if the same grammatical rules apply to both? We can do as we like, but we must be aware that these are two completely different uses (meanings) of the word "meaning." (Perhaps one can also speak of a specific feeling felt by a chess player when he moves his king).[21] (BT, 29)

Moreover, as Wittgenstein progressively realized, even once it has been admitted that words like *if* or *and* are accompanied by a feeling, it is not the same feeling on all occasions, and there need not *always* be a feeling.[22]

Nevertheless, according to the later Wittgenstein, the phenomenon of the if-feeling *does* bear a psychological interest:

> One misjudges the psychological interest of the if-feeling if one regards it as the obvious correlate of a meaning; it needs, rather, to be seen in a different context, in that of the special circumstances in which it occurs.[23] (PPF, §41)

This is not a behavioristic move *sic et simpliciter*: it is a move from the inner to the outer but it does not negate the inner, rather, it shows that "an 'inner' process stands in need of outward criteria" (PI, §580), and that we *do*, normally, use outward criteria. So, for some aspects—in its pointing to inner and private experiences—James's attitude is neutralized, but at the same time it is valorized in its suggesting more attentive descriptions of what happens.[24]

An approach focused on feeling what is happening "inside" presupposes that the stream of thought is somehow graspable through attention and introspection. This approach, according to Wittgenstein, is prone to fall victim to an empiricist picture: the idea that "inside" the person processes take place which are liable to observation, examination, perhaps experimentation, and measurement. What actually happens when people introspectively look at their stream of thought, is that they look *at their own looking* at the stream of thought. This is Wittgenstein's criticism of introspection, which he particularly addresses against James's account of the "self"[25]:

> The feeling of an unbridgeable gulf between consciousness and brain-process: how come that this plays no role in reflections of ordinary life? . . . It is when I, for example, turn my attention in a particular way on to my own consciousness and, astonished, say to myself: "THIS is supposed to be produced by a process in the brain!"—as it were clutching my forehead. . . .
> Here we have a case of introspection, not unlike that which gave William James the idea that the "self" consisted mainly of "peculiar motions in the head and between the head and throat." And James' introspection showed, not the meaning of the word "self" (so far as it means something like "person," "human being," "he himself," "I myself"), or any analysis of such a being, but the state of a philosopher's attention when he says the word "self" to himself and tries to analyse its meaning. (And much could be learned from this).[26] (PI, §§412–413)

As Goodman (2002, 96) and Steiner (2012, 272 ff.) suggest, James's mistake, according to Wittgenstein, is not dissimilar to what James himself called "the psychologist fallacy", that is, "the *confusion of [the psychologist's] own standpoint with that of the mental fact* about which he is making his report" (PP 1890, 195). In order to free the philosopher from this tendency, Wittgenstein's strategy is to point at the possible ordinary circumstances in which a word like *consciousness* is effectively used, so that its meaning can come to the fore with no strangeness or mystery.[27] And yet, in the case of meaning, again, Wittgenstein also learns something from James, and not only from James's mistakes. Indeed, as Hilmy (1987, 306 n.477) notices, it is likely that Wittgenstein's discussion of what he calls "meaning blindness," although embedded within a different framework and having a different scope, owes something to James's examples of "mental blindness" and "word deafness."[28]

PRIVATENESS AND THE STREAM OF THOUGHT

One of the misleading effects of the Jamesian way of considering things, according to Wittgenstein, is that experiencing meaning is easily considered "what distinguishes speech with thought from talking without thought" (PI, §330). If this is the case, then it would seem that thinking is "a process which may accompany something else or go on by itself" (PI, §330). This is the interpretation one could give of James's famous example of the deaf-mute Mr. Ballard (PP 1890, 256 ff.), which Wittgenstein quotes too:

> William James, in order to show that thought is possible without speech, quotes the reminiscence of a deaf-mute, Mr. Ballard, who wrote that in his early youth, even before he could speak, he had had thoughts about God and the world.—What could that mean!?—Ballard writes: "It was during those delightful rides, some two or three years before my initiations into the rudiments of written language, that I began to ask myself the question: how came the world into being?"—Are you sure—one would like to ask—that this is the correct translation of your wordless thoughts into words? And why does this question—which otherwise seems not to exist—arise here? . . .[29] (PI, §342)

The question as to how a wordless thought can be translated into words arises here, Wittgenstein seems to suggest, because we are tempted to think about thought and speech as two separate entities (Goodman 2002, 126). This temptation is an instance of the more general tendency to maintain that a thought is already there, in the head, before one puts it into words by pronouncing a sentence. James seems to think this way when he affirms that "whatever things are thought in relation are thought from the outset in a unity, in a single pulse of subjectivity, a single psychosis, feeling, or state of mind" (PP 1890, 268),[30] and that "immediately after or even before we have opened our mouths to speak, the entire thought is present to our mind in the form of an intention to utter the sentence" (PP 1890, 269). But Wittgenstein does not subscribe to this "separate" notion. Wittgenstein's further point is that "here again, we are forming a misleading picture of 'intending': that is, of the use of this word. An intention is embedded in a setting, in human customs and institutions" (PI, §337).[31]

It is, ultimately, the *privateness* of thought that Wittgenstein aimed to contest. Mr. Ballard as a young boy learning to think before speaking is like a solitary person on an island inventing their own private language: this image is inconsistent and unintelligible, because thought itself is conceptually related to (public) language.[32] What is generally known as Wittgenstein's 'Private Language Argument'[33] is specifically set against the idea that a private thought or a private language is possible, an idea he opposes on the grounds that in order to have a language one already has to have rules which are understandable only in terms of shared forms of life. According to Gale (1999, 29, 165), it is "James' Robinson Crusoe approach to philosophical topics," that is, James's implicit commitment to the idea that a private language is possible, together with his privileging a first-person perspective, that Wittgenstein set out to combat, through his usual technique of recalling the concrete contexts in which words are used.[34]

In a sense, by looking for the outward criteria, Wittgenstein externalized the *stream of thought* into a *stream of life*, in which not only thoughts and feelings are involved, but also ways of living, practices, customs, actions, gestures, and contexts. "Stream of life," or "'flux of life," are, indeed, expressions Wittgenstein used, especially in his later writings, with the aim of suggesting that words and even experiences only have meaning in the context of surroundings which are not confined to consciousness.[35] Wittgenstein's choice of words suggests that he had James's stream of thought in mind when writing, for instance, that "only in the stream of thought and life [*in dem fluß der Gedanken & des Lebens*] do words have meaning" (RPP II, §504),[36] or that "what goes on within [*was im Inneren vorgeht*] also has meaning only in the stream of life" (LW II, 30).[37]

Similarly, it can be argued that Wittgenstein's image of the "riverbed of thoughts," in OC, was also elaborated with James's image of the stream of thought in mind, and constitutes a part appraisal, part critique of that image. Indeed, Wittgenstein's metaphor was meant to suggest that there is a difference, though not a sharp one, between that which flows and that which is part of the bed and the banks of the river, that is, between *empirical* and *grammatical* propositions:

> It might be imagined that some propositions, of the form of empirical propositions, were hardened and functioned as channels for such empirical propositions as were not hardened but fluid; and that this relation altered with time, in that fluid propositions hardened, and hard ones became fluid.
>
> The mythology may change back into a state of flux, the river-bed of thoughts may shift. But I distinguish between the movement of the waters on the river-bed and the shift of the bed itself; though there is not a sharp division of the one from the other. (OC, §§96–97)

That the *lack* of this distinction was the problem in James's image of the stream, in Wittgenstein's reading, is clear in these manuscript notes:

> I'm waiting for two people A and B. I say: "When will he come!" Someone asks me: "Who do you mean?" I say, "I thought about A." And these very words have built a bridge. Or he asks "Who do you mean?" I say, "I thought about . . .," [for instance] a poem in which there is this sentence. I make these connections among what I say in the course of my thoughts and actions. (This remark is in relation with what W. James calls "the stream of thought." The mistake in his picture is that a priori and a posteriori[,] grammatical and experiential are not distinguished. So he speaks about the continuity of the stream of thought and he compares it with that of spaces, not with that of a sort of jet of water).[38] (MS 165, 24–25)

It must be noted that, perhaps not in the *Principles of Psychology* chapter on the stream of thought, but elsewhere, James does distinguish between different layers or types of thinking (see for instance chapter 5 of *Pragmatism*, on common sense, or chapter 28 of *Principles of Psychology*, on necessary truths and the effects of experience); yet, Wittgenstein either did not consider these other sources, or maybe thought that James's distinctions remained nevertheless within too empiricist a framework.[39]

To conclude these themes, Wittgenstein's appreciation of James's approach emerges in relation to the latter's rich phenomenology of psychological experiences, as well as to his pointing out some peculiar phenomena which give impulse to philosophical reflection;[40] Wittgenstein's criticism of James emerges with reference to the latter's persistent empirical, sometimes empiricist, and in a broad sense scientific perspective, which leads him to lose sight of the conceptual confusions caused by an alleged scientific attitude imported into philosophy.[41] Needless to say, James's own ideas on the relationship between philosophy and science were deeply different, and against Wittgenstein he would have claimed the right and the capacity to work precisely in the middle ground between science and philosophy.

Emotions and Will

One of Wittgenstein's typical (but perhaps not so accurate) reproaches was that James attempted to find the "ultimate components or constituents" (Citron 2015, 33) of phenomena and to put forth theories on that basis. The so-called James-Lange theory of emotion is an example. Wittgenstein illustrated James's approach by saying that according to it "a man doesn't cry because he is sad, but he is sad because he cries":

> ...... [T]he personal experiences of an emotion must in part be strictly localized experiences. . . . This is, I think, what William James meant when he said that a man doesn't cry because he is sad but that he is sad because he cries. The reason why this point is often not understood is that we think of the utterance of an emotion as though it were some artificial device to let others know that we have it.[42] (BBB, 103)

At the beginning of the 1930s, Wittgenstein seemed to accept at least in part the idea that some personal experiences of emotion are localized sensations: this helped him contrast the opposite idea that particular artificial devices need to be adopted in order to express an emotion. In later years, Wittgenstein became more hostile toward the assumption of localized sensations.[43] "If one understands this to mean that part of sadness is the *feeling of* crying, it is wrong—he explained—. But if one means that part of sadness is *crying*, this may be allowed" (PGL, 161, my emphasis). James's position bore the danger of suggesting that we know about our emotions *thanks to* our localized sensations. But for Wittgenstein, this is not how things work, as the simple consideration of how we talk about emotion shows.

> You cannot discover *now* that depression is a queer set of bodily feelings. If human beings *don't know* that depression is bodily feelings, this is important. (PGL, 46)

> James's theory of emotion as a vaguely located bodily feeling can be answered by asking, "How are the words for emotions learnt?" (PGL, 68)

The language and the behavior in which emotions are embedded show that, to understand them, other elements, besides bodily sensations, are relevant—for instance, the *tone* in which one expresses emotions, the *pattern* within which this happens, and, why not, the very *words or phrases* a person uses—and that emotions, sensations and impressions differ in many respects—not only in bodily localization, but also in length, directedness toward an object, informative content, connection to facial expression, and action[44].

Why was James so interested in the connection between emotion and bodily sensation that he made a theory of it? According to Wittgenstein, the first step—the opening question—was the problem. "*You ask a question as though a theory were its answer*" (PGL, 5), Wittgenstein remarked, after citing the James-Lange theory of emotions. The appropriate question, in his perspective, is a different one, and it does not lead to any scientific hypothesis:

> ...... [P]hilosophy could be taught (cf. Plato) just by asking the right questions so as to remind you—to remind you of what? In this case, that a man does not say "I'm depressed" on the basis of observed bodily feelings. (PGL, 45)

By appealing to bodily sensations, in Wittgenstein's view, one is misled by a picture of experience, according to which "the paradigm of experience is sense-experience eked out by kinaesthetic and somatic feelings" (PGL, 39–40).[45] This is especially deceptive if one thinks that it is kinaesthetic sensations which inform us of the position of our limbs. We normally know where our limbs are, without the need for anything to tell us.[46]

Wittgenstein made the same charge against the attempt to describe volition in terms of experiences, like the "feeling of innervation." Of course, James cannot be accused of endorsing a theory of volition based on the feeling of innervation: this is indeed something he explicitly fought against in the chapter on the will in PP (1890). In his pages on volition, Wittgenstein was not very careful to distinguish subtly different positions, and although he never explicitly associated James's name with the innervation theory, neither did he acknowledge that James denied it. The fact is that probably in Wittgenstein's view the same *kind* of theoretical temptation was at work both in the case of the theory of innervation and in the case of many of James's claims about psychology, emotion, and the will.

> The association of voluntary movement with a feeling of innervation is an important view. It is important because there is no good reason for holding it. But that it is held is not without a reason.
>
> ...
>
> The most absurd things are said because one feels one ought to say them, for example, James' statement that thought precedes speech. (PGL, 202)

In order to contrast the psychologists' theories and tendencies to postulate feelings, impulses, or other entities for explaining, for instance, the will or voluntary actions, Wittgenstein's strategy is to look instead at how we learn words connected to volition and at the circumstances within which we use them. Hence:

> What do we mean by voluntary acts? The best thing to do is to ask! Under what circumstances do we say "he acts voluntarily" or I say "I act voluntarily"? Is it a feeling, or do I observe anything? Has it anything to do with feeling? And if so, what? (PGL, 157)

Voluntarily and involuntarily are not differentiated by feelings but by surprise, observing, relaxing, etc. (PGL 204)

"It is voluntary" is an utterance, but not an utterance of feeling.[47] (PGL 206)

In spite of his antipathy to the category of feeling associated with willing, it must be acknowledged that on the topic of the will Wittgenstein in many respects also worked along with James, using very similar examples, and contrasting, together with him, more traditional views (Goodman 2002, 78 ff.). The interest in James is absolutely clear in Wittgenstein's discussion of the will in *The Blue and Brown Books* (BBB). With James, who wrote about how in everyday life we act voluntarily but naturally, without the need for any explicit act of volition (PP 1890, 1131), Wittgenstein underlined that in ordinary life no explicit deliberation is needed when, for example, we spontaneously offer to light someone else's cigarette, or just move our hand when writing and our larynx when talking (BBB, 150). With James, who asserted that "the popular notion that (. . .) activity must result from some superadded 'will-force' is a very natural inference from (. . .) special cases" (PP 1890, 1134), Wittgenstein remarked that the way we usually think about volition derives from "very special applications of the words 'willing', 'thinking', 'meaning', 'reading' etc etc."(BBB, 151).[48] The latter also openly used James's example of getting up in the morning "finding that we *have* got up" once the contrasting ideas have disappeared in the mind (PP 1890, 1132; BBB, 151, WWCL, 267),[49] although he also added complications and other cases in order to test the appropriateness of James's description.

James, then, offered Wittgenstein plenty of examples and fruitful ideas for a nontraditional account of the will, which Wittgenstein transposed within a linguistic terrain. What Wittgenstein could not accept of James's approach, both on emotions and the will, was, once again, his empiricism, which piloted him toward the search for causal connections with somatic feelings, instead of maintaining the investigation at a logical, grammatical, or criterial level.[50] It is this empiricist and scientific aspiration which constitutes the problem of James's psychology, and probably of psychology in general, according to Wittgenstein. Thus, as he states in the concluding section of PPF, "the confusion and barrenness of psychology is not to be explained by its being a 'young science'; its state is not comparable to that of physics, for instance in its beginnings"—as both James and Köhler maintained—but by the coexistence, within it, of "experimental methods and *conceptual confusion*" (PPF, §371).[51]

Aspect-Seeing

According to James, the will depends essentially on attention, which in turn is activated by the person's interest. Interest is a key notion in James's psychology. One of the features of the stream of thought is that "it is always interested more in one part of its object than in another, and welcomes and rejects, or chooses, all the while it thinks" (PP 1890, 273). In introducing the chapter on attention, James states:

> Millions of items of the outward order are present to my senses which never properly enter into my experience. Why? Because they have no *interest* for me. *My experience is what I agree to attend to.* Only those items which I notice shape my mind—without selective interest, experience is an utter chaos. Interest alone gives accent and emphasis, light and shade, background and foreground—intelligible perspective, in a word. (PP 1890, 380–381)

A part of this chapter is focused on what James calls "preperception," namely, having the mind predisposed (because of education, habit, or other influences), or preparing it deliberately, to the perception of a particular aspect of a picture. James's examples of ambiguous images which can be perceived in more than one way anticipates both the Gestalt theorists' and Wittgenstein's reflection on aspect-seeing. James and Wittgenstein's views on these phenomena do not coincide,[52] yet this theme emerges in some writings by Wittgenstein which were particularly influenced by the reading of *James's Principles of Psychology*, such as BBB[53] and the writings and lectures of the second half of the 1940s.[54] For instance, here we can read:

> The concepts we have show what selection of phenomena we make—what *interests* us. (N.b. that word "interest" does not mean that things are practically useful). (PGL, 52)

> Aspects may change automatically; but one always *can* change an aspect voluntarily. This distinguishes "seeing as" from seeing red, say. (PGL, 113)

> I am occupied with what I am now noticing, with what strikes me. In that respect, experiencing a change of aspect is similar to an action.
>
> It is a paying of attention.[55] (LW II, 14–15)

Curiously, in the first quote, Wittgenstein makes it clear that he is not referring to usefulness, thus distancing himself from something that could sound too much like a pragmatist move. Similarly, in another remark concerning aspect-seeing and the voluntariness of the change of aspect, he states:

> Is it important that an imagined figure can in one's imagination be seen both in this way and in a different way—that one can make the transition from one aspect to another one[?]
> The question "What's the advantage?" ["Was habe ich davon?"] sounds quite pragmatist [*pragmatistisch*]. Though of course it is not.[56] (MS 136, 119a–119b)

Although he did not like James's pragmatist appeals to usefulness, Wittgenstein agreed with him in highlighting the relevance of interest and of the connected theme of aspect-seeing (Goodman 2002, 149). In my view, this is a sign of a deeper attunement regarding a way of doing philosophy that primarily acknowledges the centrality of the individual's needs and aspirations.

For both James and Wittgenstein, philosophy was a way of working on oneself, of trying to face disquiet and put an end to it, to free the mind from useless if not harmful puzzles, to transform and deepen one's own sensibility—a way of practicing the change of aspect which is sometimes required to see the solution, or the dissolution, of problems. As James put it,

> ... philosophic study means the habit of *always seeing an alternative*, of not taking the usual for granted, of making conventionalities fluid again, of imagining foreign states of mind. (EPh 1876, 4, my emphasis)

And, as Wittgenstein said of his own method,

> I have being trying to change the point of view. Everything is of the form "Look at it this way"; "Compare it to this and not to that." (PGL, 285)

> For me to write or teach philosophy is futile unless it brings in those who read or hear and discuss with me a <u>deep</u> change in their way of thinking.... It is hard to change one's way of thinking where this goes deep—one's whole way of thinking about "intelligibility," for instance.[57] (Citron 2015, 60–61)

This view has obvious ethical aspects, because it leads one to think of ethics itself as something totally different from theories and general systems. In this sense, ethics is a personal attitude, a way of seeing things, not a theory. It is impossible to dwell on this wide topic now, but let me just add that, as Pihlström (2005, 41) sums up, "Wittgensteinian ethical thought, precisely like pragmatism, highlights the idea that personally relevant moral conclusions cannot be dictated by general (reductive) ethical theories." What matters for both is an ethics of personal responsibility which, for a philosopher, means being able to bring words and concepts back from metaphysics to ordinary language and life, and to stick to a form of realism which has nothing to do with traditional ontology and everything to do with what life "really" is.[58] This is the reason why, as we saw, Wittgenstein regarded James a good philosopher in virtue of his being a "real human being": through his philosophical activity, the whole person found expression (Nubiola 2000, 3; Goodman 2002, 38). As James himself stated: "Pretend what we may, the whole man within us is at work when we form our philosophical opinions" (WB 1897, 77).

Concluding Remarks: "The Good in Pragmatism"

Wittgenstein both criticized and admired James. In his early years, he found solace as well as a source of reflection in James's writings on religion; he found in James's pragmatic theory of truth, despite the negative reception it had in Cambridge, some elements which were worth considering; he found in James's psychology both examples of a fundamentally mistaken approach, and detailed narratives of cases and episodes which deserved attention; he found in James's ethical and personal attitude toward life an important affinity of temperament.

Of course, divergences remain. Wittgenstein could not share the empiricist approach which James always kept at the core of his perspective.[59] Moreover, James was a representative of pragmatism, with respect to which Wittgenstein often expressed doubts, particularly when his own view risked being confused with it (OC, §422). Yet, according to what Wittgenstein said during a lecture in 1946, there was also something "good" in pragmatism, and this "good," I submit, was fairly evident in the Jamesian side of pragmatism. Let me conclude with this not very well-known remark.

> *X [a student]*: If the child has counted 100, the problem still arises whether it can count to 100.
> *Wittgenstein*: This is quite true. Well, is saying what a child can do a description?
> *Kreisel*: One might ask what you want the description for.
> *Wittgenstein*: Yes; this is the good in pragmatism. What is the description for?[60] (PGL, 26–27)

The good side of pragmatism lies in its typical methodological "what is this for?" question, an approach always privileging the practical, concrete, contextualized application of descriptions and, more generally, of philosophical reasoning and activity. To be sure, according to Wittgenstein, this very approach has its shortcomings, as not everything necessarily and always needs to be understood in terms of purposes and practical application.[61] When this way of seeing becomes a *Weltanschauung*, too many other aspects of life risk being unjustifiably excluded from consideration.[62] But James's interpretation of the pragmatic maxim as an attitude which "turn[s] [its] back resolutely and once for all upon a lot of inveterate habits dear to professional philosophers, ... from abstractions and insufficiency, from verbal solutions, from bad *a priori* reasons, from fixed principles, closed systems, and pretended absolutes and origins," toward "concreteness and adequacy," "facts", and "action" (P 1907, 31), squares quite well with what Wittgenstein probably thought was "the good" in pragmatism. Surprising as it may sound, it seems that Wittgenstein used to say: "My father was a business man, and I am a business man too. I want my philosophy to be business like, to get something settled, to get something done" (Drury 1996, 1).[63]

Notes

1. Monk (1991, 478) also acknowledges that this "implies no lack of respect."
2. Translation from Hilmy (1987, 196–197). Wittgenstein's manuscripts (MS) and typescripts (TS) are quoted from the *Bergen Electronic Edition* of the *Nachlass* (BEE). Translations are mine, unless differently specified and except for the passages which also appear in published works.

3. McGuinness (2012, 30).
4. According to Moore's autobiography, James's PP was among the books that were commonly recommended in Cambridge for courses on psychology, and Moore lectured on psychology from 1911 to 1918 (Moore 1952, 29); Wittgenstein attended his classes during his first year in Cambridge, namely, 1912 (Moore 1952, 33). I owe this information and the bibliographic reference to Balbina Ferrando Bagán. See also McGuinness (1988, 116) and Monk (1991, 42).
5. Goodman (2002, 60), Haack (1982, 163), PPO, 353, and WWCL, 252.
6. According to Biesenach (2014, 282), it is to ERE (1912) that Wittgenstein referred in MS 179, 19v–20r, when he examined the sentence: "'Change taking place' is a unique content of experience," adding the name of James in parentheses. That Wittgenstein read ERE (1912), or at least the article "Does 'consciousness' exist?", seems confirmed by a reference in Moore's notes on Wittgenstein's lectures 1930–1933 (M, 319, n.13). Bertrand Russell heavily quoted from ERE (1912) in his *Analysis of Mind* (Russell 1921), which Wittgenstein read extensively. As for P (1907), although there are no direct references to it in Wittgenstein's writings, it was widely read and criticized by the Cambridge philosophical community during the first decades of the century (see section "Pragmatism and Truth as Usefulness"). A reference to it is also present in a conversation reported in PPO, 388–389.
7. Compare VRE (1902, 49, 103–104, 172, 229–230, 290) with Wittgenstein's MS 101, 11r, 18v, 31v; MS 102, 6v, 54v; MS 103, 2v, 6–8v, 13v. See also Monk (1991, 112).
8. See Goodman (2002, 42 ff.), Kober (2005, 234 ff.).
9. Putnam is also referring to Kierkegaard. See also Rhees (1984, 94). Cf. Kober (2005, 241).
10. See in particular Goodman (2002, 53 ff.) for a detailed analysis.
11. See, for instance, OC, §§360, 395, 397, 409, 422, 427; cf. Boncompagni (2013) and (2016, ch. 4).
12. Russell (1910, chs. 4 and 5), Moore (1922, ch. 3); cf. Goodman (2002, 12).
13. Cf. Ramsey (1991a, 15 n. 12, 22).
14. With thanks to Joachim Schulte for his advice on the translation. For a more complete analysis of this remark, see Boncompagni (2017).
15. The same can be said of Wittgenstein's attitude toward pragmatism in a 1932 lecture; see LWL, 75.
16. In particular in his concept of "linguistic commitment": see Boncompagni (2018).
17. Besides OC, §422, see AWL, 142; MS 114, 158; RPP I, §266.
18. Cf. Schulte (1999).
19. In this case, I do not agree with Goodman, when he claims that "Wittgenstein does not show *anywhere* a positive attitude towards pragmatism" (2002, 17). On Wittgenstein and pragmatism in general, see Boncompagni (2016).
20. Hence, this happens a couple of weeks before what is suggested by Goodman (2002, 60, 190 n. 1), who follows Hilmy (1987, 278 n. 319): both refer to a remark written on February 26 (MS 110, 118). Yet, Wittgenstein might have read PP (1890) even before February 1931; indeed, Wittgenstein's friend Ramsey had surely read PP (1890) by 1929 (see Ramsey 1991b, 76), and the two often read and discussed the same books at the same time.
21. Originally in TS 213, 33v; see also BBB, 78–79. See ter Hark (1990, 161).
22. See for instance AWL, 50, 79, 114, and WWCL, 107.
23. See also PPF §§43–44 and PI, §334.
24. On the if-feeling, feelings of tendency, and related themes, see PI, §§245, 251, 253, 591 ff., 609–610, 640; RPP I, §§174, 180, 242–243, 331, 334. Cf. also Goodman (2002, 119 ff.), Hilmy (1987, 123 ff.), ter Hark (1990, 161 ff. and 242 ff), ter Hark (2011, 500 ff.).

25. Cf. Goodman (2002, 89 ff.).
26. See also MS 124, 256–257; MS 129, 83–84; TS 241, 32; TS 242, 22; PI, §308. On the "unbridgeable gulf," see James (PP 1890, 138, 178).
27. Cf. Hallett (1977, 453). For a wide-raging examination of Wittgenstein's objection to James, but also to Russell and Ogden and Richards on meaning, see Hilmy (1987, ch. 4).
28. See PP (1890, 57 ff.) and cf. PPF, §260 ff and RPP I, §§202–206, 242, 247, 344, RPP II, §§571–572.
29. See also Z, §109.
30. This is Hallett's (1977, 399) interpretation. However, it must be observed that *here* James is not calling into question the relation between thinking and speaking. Moreover, as Goodman (2002, 125) underlines, James also points out that sometimes it is only after pronouncing a sentence that we realize what we were thinking (see PP 1890, 270), thus anticipating Wittgenstein's point.
31. See also §§ 335, 338; RPP I, §173 and RPP II, §575; Z §§1–2 and LEP, 44, 126, 245.
32. See Z, §§109–111, RPP I, §554 and RPP II, §§214, 220; originally in MS 136, 58b, with the name "Barnard" instead of "Ballard."
33. PI, §§243–315; see Stern (2011).
34. Cf. PPF, §7, LW I, §841–842. An early mention of James in connection with a "solipsistic language" is in AWL, 25. Yet, in James's defense, one might highlight that in another context, that of moral philosophy, James has been described as anticipating (once more!) Wittgenstein, and precisely with respect to the impossibility of a private language. Cf. Putnam (1995).
35. Cf. Steiner (2012, 275), Goodman (2002, 77).
36. Originally in MS 137, 29a. Cf. also MS 137, 66a and MS 138, 24b.
37. Originally in MS 169, 47v; Cf. also LW I, §246, 913. Notice that James too used these expressions: see for instance PU (1909, 109, 113) and ERE (1912, 47, 52).
38. See also MS 129, 107 and WWCL, 273.
39. See Boncompagni (2012).
40. Other phenomena I have not dealt with owing to a lack of space are: the feeling connected to a familiar and a foreign language; the "atmosphere" and the "fringe" of words; the sense of sameness; the inadequacy of our vocabulary in describing thoughts or feelings; the experiment of gazing at or repeating a word; the self and the "ownership" of objects and of sensations; memory. Goodman (2002) and, for PI, Hallett (1977) offer the most comprehensive accounts.
41. See the passage from MS 165 cited in the introduction; see also PI §571, PPF, §371; PGL, 45, 126, 323–324. Cf. Schulte (1999, 316), Hilmy (1987, 196), Hutchinson and Read (2013, 163), Goodman (2002, 64 ff.), and ter Hark (1990, 243–244). On Wittgenstein and scientism, see Beale and Kidd (2017).
42. See also AWL, 56; VW, 55. Cf. Schulte (1993, 121).
43. The "Lectures on Volition" (WWCL, 254–278), tentatively dated Michaelmas Term 1940, represent an interesting middle point, with Wittgenstein using and often criticizing James's PP but also affirming that "[i]n James' view there is something healthy" (257).
44. Schulte (1993, 133–134); ter Hark (1990, 215 ff.).
45. See also 277–278.
46. See PPF, sect. viii. Cf. ter Hark (1990, 209).
47. See also PI, §628 and, on feelings and kinaesthetic sensations, PI, §§621, 625.
48. See ter Hark (1990, 256–257).

49. Wittgenstein credits James for this image in MS 115 II, 217 (a partial correction and translation of the Brown Book into German).
50. See Goodman (2002, 114).
51. Cf. PBC, 401; Schulte (1993, 3, 76).
52. Cf. ter Hark (1990, 173).
53. Cf. BBB, 150 ff.
54. Plenty of references to James and many remarks on aspect-seeing can be found in RPP, PPF, PGL, and LW. Not only the reading of James, of course, but also the reading of Köhler, is responsible for this.
55. See also PGL 104, 139, 334, LW I, §556.
56. I am indebted to Joachim Schulte for his advice on the translation.
57. Cf. Marchetti (2015, 26, 252–257).
58. Cormier (2001) works on this idea, derived from Cora Diamond's reading of Wittgenstein (see in particular Diamond 1991), with an eye on James's conception of truth.
59. Cf. Goodman (2002, 64 ff.), Hutchinson and Read (2013, 163).
60. See also PGL, 145, 266.
61. See BT, sect. 44 and 55.
62. See Schulte (1999, 303–304).
63. I am indebted to Alex Klein and Russell Goodman for invaluable comments on an early draft of this chapter, which helped me improve it in a significant way.

Bibliography

Beale, J., and I. J. Kidd, eds. 2017. *Wittgenstein and Scientism*. London: Routledge.

Biesenach, H. 2014. *Anspielungen und Zitate im Werk Ludwig Wittgensteins*. Sofia, Bulgaria: St. Ohridski University Press.

Boncompagni, A. 2012. "Streams and River-beds. James' Stream of Thought in Wittgenstein's Manuscripts 165 and 129." *European Journal of Pragmatism and American Philosophy* 4(2): 36–53.

Boncompagni, A. 2013. "The 'Pragmatic Maxim' in Wittgenstein's *On Certainty*." In *Mind, Language and Action. Papers of the 36th International Wittgenstein Symposium (pre-proceedings)*, edited by D. Moyal-Sharrock, V. Munz, and A. Coliva. Kirchberg am Wechsel: Austrian Wittgenstein Society.

Boncompagni, A. 2016. *Wittgenstein and Pragmatism.* On Certainty *in the Light of Peirce and James*. London: Palgrave Macmillan.

Boncompagni, A. 2017. "Wittgenstein and Pragmatism: A Neglected Remark in Manuscript 107." In *Pragmatism and the European Traditions: Encounters with Analytic Philosophy and Phenomenology before the Great Divide*, edited by M. Baghramian and S. Marchetti. London: Routledge.

Boncompagni, A. 2018. "Wittgenstein on Meaning, Use and Linguistic Commitment." In *Wittgenstein in the 1930s: Between the* Tractatus *and the* Investigations, edited by D. G. Stern. Cambridge: Cambridge University Press.

Citron, G., ed., 2015. "Wittgenstein's Philosophical Conversations with Rush Rhees (1939–50): From the Notes of Rush Rhees." *Mind* 124(493): 1–71.

Cormier, H. 2001. *The Truth Is What Works. William James, Pragmatism and the Seed of Death*. Lanham, Maryland: Rowman & Littlefield.

Diamond, C. 1991. "Realism and the Realistic Spirit". In *The Realistic Spirit*. Cambridge, MA: MIT Press.
Drury. M. 1996. "1967 Dublin Lecture on Wittgenstein." In *The Danger of Words and Writings on Wittgenstein*. Bristol: Thoemmes Press.
Gale, R. 1999. *The Divided Self of William James*. Cambridge: Cambridge University Press.
Goodman, R. 2002. *Wittgenstein and William James*. Cambridge: Cambridge University Press.
Haack, R. 1982. "Wittgenstein's Pragmatism." *American Philosophical Quarterly* 19(2): 163–171.
Hacker, P. M. S. 1990. *Wittgenstein. Meaning and Mind (An Analytical Commentary on the PI, vol. 3)*. Oxford: Blackwell.
Hallett, G. 1977. *A Companion to Wittgenstein's* Philosophical Investigation. Ithaca, NY: Cornell University Press.
ter Hark, M. 1990. *Beyond the Inner and the Outer. Wittgenstein's Philosophy of Psychology*. Dordrecht: Kluwer.
ter Hark, M. 2011. "Wittgenstein on the Experience of Meaning and Secondary Use." In *The Oxford Handbook of Wittgenstein*, edited by O. Kuusela and M. McGinn. Oxford: Oxford University Press.
Hilmy, S. 1987. *The Later Wittgenstein. The Emergence of a New Philosophical Method*. Oxford: Blackwell.
Hutchinson, P., and R. Read 2013. "*Practicing* Pragmatist-Wittgensteinianism." In *The Cambridge Companion to Pragmatism*, edited by A. Malachowski. Cambridge: Cambridge University Press.
Kober, M. 2005. "'In the Beginning was the Deed': Wittgenstein on Knowledge and Religion." In *Readings of Wittgenstein's* On Certainty, edited by D. Moyal Sharrock and W. H. Brenner. London: Palgrave Macmillan.
Marchetti, S. 2015. *Ethics and Philosophical Critique in William James*. London: Palgrave Macmillan.
McGuinness, B. 1988. *Wittgenstein. A Life. Young Ludwig (1889–1921)*. London: Duckworth.
McGuinness, B., ed. 2012. *Wittgenstein in Cambridge. Letters and Documents 1911–1951*. Oxford: Wiley-Blackwell.
Monk, R. 1991. *Wittgenstein. The Duty of Genius*. London: Vintage.
Moore, G. E. 1922. "William James' Pragmatism," in *Philosophical Studies*. London: Routledge and Kegan Paul.
Moore, G. E. 1952. "An Autobiography." In *The Philosophy of G.E. Moore*, edited by P. A. Schilpp. New York: Tudor Publishing Company.
Nubiola, J. 2000. "Ludwig Wittgenstein and William James." *Streams of William James* 2(3): 2–4.
Pihlström, S. 2005. *Pragmatic Moral Realism*. Amsterdam: Rodopi.
Putnam, H. 1991. "Wittgenstein on Religious Belief." In *On Community*, edited by Leroy S. Rouner. Notre Dame, IN: University of Notre Dame Press.
Putnam, H. 1995. "The Permanence of William James." In *Pragmatism: An Open Question*. Oxford: Blackwell.
Ramsey, F. P. 1991a. *On Truth*. Edited by N. Rescher, U. Majer. Dordrecht: Kluwer.
Ramsey, F. P. 1991b. *Notes on Philosophy, Probability and Mathematics*. Edited by M. C. Galavotti. Neaples: Bibliopolis.
Rhees, R., ed. 1984. *Recollections of Wittgenstein*. Oxford: Oxford University Press.
Russell, B. 1910. *Philosophical Essays*. London: Longmans, Green & Co.
Russell, B. 1921. *The Analysis of Mind*. London: George Allen & Unwin.
Schulte, J. 1993. *Experience and Expression. Wittgenstein's Philosophy of Psychology*. Oxford: Oxford University Press.

Schulte, J. 1999. "Wittgenstein—auch ein Pragmatist?". In R. Raatzsch, ed., *Philosophieren über Philosophie.* Leipzig: Leipziger Universitätsverlag.

Steiner, P. 2012. "Une question du point de vu. James, Husserl, Wittgenstein et le sophisme du psychologue." *Revue Internationale de Philosophie* 1(259): 251–281.

Stern, D. 2011. "Private Language." In *The Oxford Handbook of Wittgenstein*, edited by O. Kuusela and M. McGinn. Oxford: Oxford University Press.

Wittgenstein, L. 1933. *Tractatus Logico-Philosophicus.* London: Routledge and Kegan Paul. [TLP]

Wittgenstein, L. 1967. *Lectures and Conversations on Aesthetics, Psychology and Religious Belief.* Edited by C. Barrett. Berkley: University of California Press. [LA]

Wittgenstein, L. 1969a. *The Blue and Brown Books.* Oxford: Blackwell. [BBB]

Wittgenstein, L. 1969b. *On Certainty.* Oxford: Blackwell. [OC]

Wittgenstein, L. 1979. *Notebooks 1914–1916.* Oxford: Blackwell. [NB]

Wittgenstein, L. 1980a. *Wittgenstein's Lectures Cambridge 1930–1932.* Edited by D. Lee. Oxford: Blackwell. [LWL]

Wittgenstein, L. 1980b. *Remarks on the Philosophy of Psychology.* 2 vols. Oxford: Blackwell. [RPP]

Wittgenstein, L. 1981. *Zettel.* Oxford: Basil Blackwell. [Z]

Wittgenstein, L. 1982. *Wittgenstein's Lectures Cambridge 1932–1935.* Edited by A. Ambrose. Oxford: Blackwell. [AWL]

Wittgenstein, L. 1988. *Wittgenstein's Lectures on Philosophical Psychology 1946–47.* Edited by P. T. Geach. Hemel Hempstead: Harvester Weathsheaf. [PGL]

Wittgenstein, L. 1990–1992. *Last Writings on the Philosophy of Psychology.* 2 vols. Oxford: Blackwell. [LW]

Wittgenstein, L. 1993. "A Lecture on Ethics." In *Ludwig Wittgenstein. Philosophical Occasions 1912–1951.* Edited by J. Klagge and A. Nordmann. Indianapolis, IN: Hackett. [LE]

Wittgenstein, L. 1996. *Familienbriefe.* Edited by B. McGuinness, M. C. Ascher, and O. Pfersmann. Vienna: Hölder-Pichler-Tempsky. [CF]

Wittgenstein, L. 2000. *Nachlass: The Bergen Electronic Edition.* Oxford: Oxford University Press. [BEE]

Wittgenstein, L. 2003. *Public and Private Occasions.* Edited by J. C. Klagge and A. Nordmann. Lanham: Rowman & Littlefield. [PPO]

Wittgenstein, L. 2009. *Philosophical Investigations.* Edited by P. M. S. Hacker and J. Schulte. Oxford: Wiley-Blackwell. [Part I: PI; Part II: PPF]

Wittgenstein, L. 2013. *The Big Typescript TS 213.* Edited by C. G. Luckhardt and M. A. E. Aue. Oxford: Wiley-Blackwell. [BT]

Wittgenstein, L. 2016. *Wittgenstein: Lectures, Cambridge 1930–1933. From the Notes of G.E. Moore.* Edited by D. G. Stern, B. Rogers, and G. Citron. Cambridge: Cambridge University Press. [M]

Wittgenstein, L. 2017. *Wittgenstein's Whewell's Court Lectures, Cambridge 1938–1941.* Edited by V. A. Munz and B. Ritter. Oxford: Wiley-Blackwell. [WWCL]

Wittgenstein, L., and F. Waismann 2003. *The Voices of Wittgenstein. The Vienna Circle.* Edited by G. Baker. London: Routledge. [VW]

CHAPTER 29

JAMES AND PHENOMENOLOGY

STEVEN LEVINE

Introduction

For a period of forty years, from the forties to the late seventies, *The Principles of Psychology* was intensively engaged by a series of philosophers in the phenomenological tradition. These philosophers were following a hint left to them by Edmund Husserl, who said that the *Principles* yielded him "some flashes." He went on: "I saw how a daring and original man did not let himself be held down by tradition and attempted to put down what he saw and describe it. Probably this influence was not without significance for me" (quoted in Spiegelberg 1981, 102). While the *Principles* includes an explanatory project that phenomenology eschews, its acute descriptions of consciousness make it prima facie an attractive resource for those who think that philosophy is concerned above all with the description of conscious lived experience. In light of this, philosophers such as Schütz, Gurwitsch, Linschoten, Wilshire, Edie, Wild, and Cobb-Stevens took up various themes in the *Principles*, leaving us with a quite rich interpretive tradition.[1] What I want to do in this chapter is assess the central claims of this tradition and see whether James's text supports them.

The Reversal Thesis

The phenomenological reading makes two central claims: (1) that James in the *Principles* articulates a proto-phenomenological theory of intentionality, and (2) that because of this, James came to think that psychology is not an autonomous science independent of philosophy. Here I discus the second claim and come back to the first in the next section.[2]

The phenomenological reading's second claim is radical considering the fact that it is James's stated intention in the *Principles* to treat psychology as a natural science, which in his view requires sticking to a "strictly positivistic point of view" (PP 1890, 6), one that eschews metaphysics. To stick to a strictly positivistic point of view is to keep one's explanations of phenomena within the boundary of the assumptions of the special science one is working in, and to not examine the validity of these assumptions in a more basic discourse. What are the assumptions of psychology as a special science?

> Every natural science assumes certain data uncritically, and declines to challenge the elements between which its own "laws" obtain, and from which its own deductions are carried out. Psychology, the science of finite individual minds, assumes as its data (1) *thoughts and feelings*, and (2) *a physical world* in time and space with which they coexist and which (3) *they know*. Of course these data themselves are discussable; but the discussion of them (as of other elements) is called metaphysics and fall outside the province of this book. This book, assuming that thoughts and feelings exist and are vehicles of knowledge, thereupon contends that psychology when she has ascertained the empirical correlation of the various sorts of thought and feeling with definite conditions of the brain, can go no farther—can go no farther, that is, as a natural science. If she goes farther she becomes metaphysical.[3] (PP 1890, 6)

James recognized that psychology was not yet a science but "only the hope of a science" (PBC 1892, 401). But for this hope to be made good we must act in light of the hope, acting as if psychology were a science. As James says, "I wished, by treating Psychology *like* a natural science, to help her become one" (EPs 1892, 270). And the main way that James did this was providing this science with "a useful basis for united action" (EPs 1892, 275), a basis found in the assumptions enumerated in the block quote. To continually invest itself in metaphysical controversies about how thought can know the physical world, or about the ultimate nature of our given thoughts—for example, whether they are the product of an underlying entity like the Soul or the product of an association of elementary ideas—is to divert psychology from its true task, from describing the various kinds of states of consciousness and then explaining them by correlating them with brain states.[4] Although James recognizes that we have little grasp on how brain states actually condition mental states, he proposes that we take as a working hypothesis "the uniform correlation of brain-states with mental-states" (PBC 1982, 13). Indeed, he proposes that we take the laws that govern this correlation to be "the ultimate laws for our science" (PP 1890, 6).

The phenomenological reading claims that James's psychology is not independent of metaphysics because the dualism that subtends it as an autonomous discipline—that is, between thought and world, subject and object—continually breaks down in the *Principles*. One sense in which dualism breaks down in the *Principles* is that at certain points James treats thought and its object as secondary modifications of a stream of consciousness in which no such dualism exists, foreshadowing his later view of pure experience.[5] The phenomenological reading highlights another reason for the breakdown: namely, the fact that in the *Principles* James articulates, almost despite himself, a theory of *intentionality*. The *Principles* contains an account of thought in which thought refers to, is intrinsically and not extrinsically "self-transcendent" to, an object akin to what phenomenologists call the intentional object.[6] As Wilshire puts it, "the very concept of a mental state involves the concept of its object; without this presupposition neither term in the relationship is intelligible. This is the doctrine of intentionality" (Wilshire 1968, 17). We shall come back to the meaning of this cryptic claim below.

The important point for now is this: if it is true that James articulates the intentionality of thought in the *Principles*, then the relation between philosophy and psychology cannot be what James officially claims it to be. Why? As we saw earlier, psychology has two steps, the description of states of consciousness and their explanation through their correlation with brain states. But as James himself notes in the last chapter of the *Briefer Course*, "[b]efore we can know just what sort of goings-on occur when thought corresponds to a change in the brain, we must know the *subjects* of the goings-on" (PBC 1982, 397). In other words, before we can identify correlations between mental and brain states, we first need to descriptively identify the types of mental states to be so correlated. But if thought is intentional in the way that James—according to the phenomenological reading—says it is, then to know which type of mental state is being correlated with a brain state, one must have already identified *its* cognitive object, since a thought, to be the thought it is, *involves* its object. If this is the case, then

> the specification of the cognitive relationship would have to be achieved *before* the attempt to determine the casual relationship could even begin.... Not only would it be impossible for James to leave the relationship of thought and thought's object unspecified, or regarded as external, while he pursues through empirical investigations causal laws correlating thought and brain, as he wishes to do, but he would have to regard the cognitive relationship as internal before he embarks on a causal pursuit. This would throw the natural scientific program itself from a logically prior to a logically posterior position in investigations of psychology. (Wilshire 1968, 16)

We could call this thesis, in which a natural-scientific psychology goes from a prior position to a posterior one vis-à-vis philosophy, the "reversal thesis."

This thesis admits of a weaker and a stronger reading. The weaker reading says that James's *thought* is committed to the thesis, not that *he* endorsed it. Here one distinguishes between what a thinker's thought commits him or her to from what the thinker took him or herself to be committed to. The stronger reading says that James's thought not only commits him to the reversal thesis, but that *he* endorses it. Wilshire argues for the stronger thesis by pointing to things that James himself says in the last chapter of the *Briefer Course*; for example, that in psychology the "waters of metaphysical criticism leak at every joint" (PBC 1892, 400). Based on such evidence, Wilshire says, with no qualification, that James was "forced to conclude that such a metaphysics must be logically prior to his natural scientific psychology, and that his psychology cannot stand by itself as an autonomous endeavor. The reversal is complete and its significance momentous" (Wilshire 1969, 27).

But I think that Wilshire cannot be right, for the simple reason that in two pieces written after the *Briefer Course*—"A Plea for Psychology as a 'Natural Science'" and in the preface to the Italian translation of the *Principles*—James continues to insist that psychology must continue to make the pragmatic presuppositions that determine it as a special science. While after the *Principles* James *himself* moved to metaphysical criticism, leaving psychology as a natural science mostly behind, this does not mean that he no longer endorsed the division of labor between psychology and philosophy. I think it is clear that he did. But this still leaves us with the weaker thesis, which is the one I will examine in the rest of the chapter.[7] In what follows, we shall evaluate its cogency by evaluating whether James articulated a proto-phenomenological conception of intentionality in the *Principles*, one in which thought and its object are internally and necessarily related.

The Psychologist's Fallacy and the Objectivist Misunderstanding of the Mind

To see whether James has a proto-phenomenological account of intentionality, we need to get clear about what thought involves. To do so, James argues, we must make a preliminary distinction among: (1) thought understood as a conscious mental state, (2) the object of thought as it is experienced from within the thought, and (3) the object of thought as posited by someone, the psychologist, who is situated outside of the thought and its object. To not make these distinctions is to open oneself to making what James calls the "psychologist's fallacy."

Overall, this fallacy involves the psychologist confusing "his own standpoint with that of the mental fact about which he is making his report" (PP 1890, 195). But there are two varieties of the fallacy. The first involves the psychologist substituting their third-personal description of a mental state, which includes all that they know about the state, for the first-person experience that is had by the subject of the state. Based on this, the psychologist assumes that "the mental state studied must be conscious of itself as the psychologist is conscious of it" (PP 1890, 195). This mistake, however, is based on another mistake, which gives us the second variety of the fallacy. Here is how James describes it:

> The psychologist . . . stands outside the mental state he speaks of. Both itself and its object are objects for him. Now when it is a *cognitive* state (percept, thought, concept, etc.), he ordinarily has no other way of naming it than as the thought, perception, etc., *of that object*. He himself, meanwhile, knowing the self-same object in *his* way, gets easily led to suppose that the thought, which is *of* it, knows it in the same way in which he knows it. (PP 1890, 195)

So the psychologist is apt to substitute their thought of the object for the thought of the object undertaken by the subject they are studying because they confuse thought with objects generally. And they do so because the language they use to describe subjective mental life is a language of "outer things" (PP 1890, 300). "Naming our thought by its own objects, we almost all of us assume that as the objects are, so the thought must be" (PP 1890, 194). In making this assumption, the psychologist comes to think:

1. As objects (in their reality) stay the same, so do thoughts;
2. As objects (in their reality) are composed of discrete parts, so are thoughts;
3. As objects (in their reality) are discontinuous with other objects, thoughts are discontinuous with other thoughts; and
4. As objects (in their reality) only have contingent and external relations to other objects, thoughts only have external and contingent relations to objects.

One of James's primary goals in chapter IX of the *Principles* is, according to the phenomenological reading, to break the grip of these objectivist misunderstandings of the mind. The difficulty is that they inform introspection itself. So more accurate introspection cannot by itself loosen their grip. To access thought's true nature, introspection must be supplemented by a "series of indirect considerations" (PP 1890, 226): for example, the fact that we feel the same things differently when in different emotions and moods; the fact that the eye is constantly modulating its intake of sensory information; the fact that for a sensation to recur it would have to occur in an unmodified brain, which is a physiological impossibility; etc.[8] When we take note of these indirect considerations, most of which are not first-personal, and have them inform our introspections, we are better able grasp the subjective features of our mental life. So while James does not, like Husserl, provide a method like the reduction and *epoché*[9] to access first-personal experience, he does, through the critique of the psychologist's fallacy and these indirect considerations, provide us with tools to clear away presuppositions that prevent us from grasping the subjective nature of mental life. If we use these tools properly, we will be able to see that:

a) Thought is in constant change;
b) Each thought is a unitary and singular pulse of consciousness that does not have parts, even if its object is complex and has parts;
c) Each thought is sensibly continuous with other thoughts;
d) Each thought refers to some object, what James calls thought's object, in an internal and necessary way.[10]

Let us go through these more carefully.

Thought and Some of Its Characteristics

For James, thought is given first-personally as constantly in change. "Now we are seeing, now hearing; now reasoning, now willing; now recollecting, now expecting; now loving, now hating" (PP 1890, 224–225). No one of these conscious states once past can recur in identical form. "Every thought we have of a given fact is, strictly speaking, unique, and only bears a resemblance of kind with our other thoughts of the same fact" (PP 1890, 227).

The idea that thought is in constant change and can never recur is resisted both by the psychologist and by "common experience" (i.e., common sense; PP 1890, 225). The psychologist recognizes that thought *appears* to change continually. But they think that that cannot be the case, due to their tacitly modeling thought on objects as they are in their reality. So they have to explain this appearance away. They do so by saying that our changing thoughts are the "resultant effect of variations in the *combination* of certain simple elements of consciousness that always remain the same. These mental atoms or molecules are what Locke called 'simple ideas'" (PP 1890, 225).

This conclusion is corroborated by common experience. For is it not obvious that when we experience the same patch of grass in the same light, we experience the same idea of green on both occasions? Is it not obvious that "thought of the object's recurrent identity is" nothing but "the identity of its recurrent thought" (PP 1890, 194)? James's answer is no:

> What is got twice is the same OBJECT. We hear the same note over and over again; we see the same quality of green, or smell the same objective perfume, or experience the same species of pain. The realities, concrete and abstract, physical and ideal, whose permanent existence we believe in, seem to be constantly coming up again before our thought, and lead us in our carelessness, to suppose that our "ideas" of them are the same ideas. (PP 1890, 225)

So here is why common experience confuses thought and object. Common experience has the "habit of not attending to sensations as subjective facts, but of simply using them as stepping-stones to pass over to the recognition of the realities whose presence they reveal" (PP 1890, 225). But if we could stop passing over the subjective facts, if we could attend to them, we would be able to see that it is not the successive states or thoughts that are the same green or are the same smell, but the *object* of those states, and that our thoughts of these objects are constantly changing.

Modeling thought on objects as they exist in the psychologist's reality has a second baleful effect, this one involving a view of the composition of thought:

> [W]e almost all of us assume that as objects are, so the thought must be.... [T]he perceptions of multiplicity, of coexistence, of succession, are severally conceived

to be brought about only through a multiplicity, a coexistence, a succession of perceptions. The continuous flow of the mental stream is sacrificed, and in its place an atomism ... is preached, for the existence of which no good introspective grounds can be brought forward. (PP 1890, 194–195)

In other words, in modeling thoughts on objects, one comes to assume that a complex object involving coexistent, multiple, or successive parts, can only be cognized by a thought which is itself comprised of such parts (be they simple atomic impressions or ideas). James's contrary view is this: "*There is no manifold of coexisting ideas; the notion of such a thing is a chimera. Whatever things are thought in relation are thought from the outset in a unity, in a single pulse of subjectivity, a single psychosis, feeling, or state of mind*" (PP 1890, 268). How does James establish this?

James challenges the atomist picture by asking whether such a view can make sense of the unity of consciousness necessary to experience a complex object as a single thing. In other words, he argues that it is hard on atomist grounds to understand how a multiplicity, coexistence, or succession of ideas could add up to a single thought of a multiplicity, coexistence, or succession. The atomist claims that a complex of ideas can add up to a thought of something complex because a "series of states is the awareness of itself" in the sense that "if the states be posited severally, their collective consciousness is *eo ipso* given" (PP 1890, 164n). In other words, the atomist claims that if you have a number of discrete states given severally (as a multiplicity, a coexistence, or a succession) that those severally given states add up to an awareness of all the states together. But if each item "is shut up in its own skin, windowless, ignorant of what the other feelings are and mean" (PP 1890, 162)—that is, if they are truly "discrete" and "separate" from one another as the atomist thinks—then it is unclear how this registering of the severally given states as a unity is possible. James nicely illustrates the problem for successive thoughts with this example:[11]

> Take a sentence of a dozen words, and take twelve men and tell to each one word. Then stand the men in a row or jam them in a bunch, and let each think of his word as intently as he will; nowhere will there be a consciousness of the whole sentence.[12] (PP 1890, 162)

To understand James's alternative account of the unity of consciousness, consider the thought "the pack of cards is on the table." James says:

> [T]he thought has time-parts. . . . Now I say of these time-parts that we cannot take any one of them so short that it will not after some fashion or other be a thought of the whole object "the pack of cards is on the table." They melt into each other like dissolving views, and no two of them feel the object just alike, but each feels the total object in a unitary undivided way. This is what I mean by denying that in the thought any parts can be found corresponding to the object's parts. Time-parts are not such parts. (PP 1890, 269)

To have a unified thought of this complex object, we don't have a thought that contains, as distinct atomic parts, the idea of the cards, the idea of the table, the idea of their relation, and so on. Rather, we have a single unified thought, "the pack of cards is on the table," that is of the complex yet unified object the-pack-of-cards-is-on-the-table.

But how can we say that a thought of a complex object is a single thought if the thought of it has different time-parts moving through the stream of consciousness? The answer begins by pointing out that time-parts are sensibly continuous with one another; "they melt into each other." Because they are sensibly continuous, the nature of each time-part involves the other time-parts, those just past and those just to come. Because of this, even if each part "feels" the object in a slightly different way as consciousness moves through time, they feel the object "in a unitary undivided way."

But even if this is so, why think that the time-part "the pack of cards" and the time-part "is on the table" comprise a single thought rather than two thoughts that are themselves sensibly continuous? We can establish their identity, James thinks, only by seeing that each sensibly continuous time-part is of the same "total" object, that is, is self-transcendent to the same object. To establish the unity of the time-parts of a single thought, a single pulse of consciousness, we must therefore have in view the self-identical object to which they refer. As such, the unity of consciousness necessary to think a complex object as a unity is accounted for not by the laws of association, as the empiricist thinks, nor by the fact that there is a self-identical subject who unified the disparate parts of the complex thought, as Kant thinks, but by the fact that the sensibly continuous time-parts of a single thought intend the same object:

> [The] sense of identity of the knowing subject is held by some philosophers to be the only vehicle by which the world hangs together. It seems hardly necessary to say that a sense of identity of the known object would perform exactly the same unifying function, even if the sense of subjective identity were lost. And without the intention to think the same outer things over and over again, and the sense that we were doing so, our sense of our own personal sameness would carry us but a little way toward making a universe of our experience. (PP 1890, 434–435)

The third mistake that is made by modeling thoughts on objects is that it leads us to overlook the sensible continuity not just of the time-parts of a single thought but of the stream of multiple thoughts as they unfold through time. To illustrate, take James's example of a sudden contrast in the successive parts of the stream, for example, a thunderclap. While one might think that this rends or interrupts the continuity of consciousness, one only thinks this because, once again, one is confusing "thoughts themselves, taken as subjective facts, and the things of which they are aware" (PP 1890, 233). While a thunderclap rends nature and introduces into it a chain of "discrete and discontinuous" (PP 1890, 233) spatio-temporal events, the coming and going of these events is given continuously, with no breaks. These events "no more break the flow of the thought that thinks them than they break the time and space in which they lie.... The transition between the thought of one object and the thought of another is no more a break in the thought than a joint in a bamboo is a break in the wood" (PP 1890, 233–234). So in confusing thought and object we are prone to

> overlooking, even when the things are contrasted with each other most violently ... the large amount of affinity that may still remain between the thoughts by whose means they are cognized. Into the awareness of thunder itself the awareness of the previous silence creeps and continues; for what we hear when the thunder crashes is not thunder *pure*, but thunder-breaking-upon-silence-and-contrasting-with-it. Our feeling of the same objective thunder, coming in this way, is quite different from what it would be were the thunder a continuation of previous thunder. The thunder itself we believe to abolish and exclude the silence; but the *feeling* of the thunder is also a feeling of the silence as just gone. (PP 1890, 234)

Hearing the thunder involves the feeling of the silence just gone because the silence is retained and intermixes with the hearing of the thunder, making the thunder-feeling distinct from what it would be in a different context. So although the feeling of thunder is a single pulse of consciousness, a pulse that has no atomic parts, the nature of this pulse partly depends on the relations it has to other thoughts in the stream.

But it is not only the thought of the thunder that is sensibly continuous with thought of the silence. There is also continuity in the *object thought about*. The *thunder that is heard* is continuous with the *silence that was heard*. As James puts it, "all our concrete states of mind are representations of objects with some amount of complexity. Part of the complexity is the echo of objects just past, and, in a less degree, perhaps, the foretaste of those just to arrive" (PP 1890, 572). Here the *object of thought*, the thunder, involves, as part of its sense, objects just past and the objects to come. To be aware of a temporally successive object like "thunder-breaking-on-silence," one must not only have subjective thoughts that are sensibly continuous, one must also perceive a complex object whose parts are sensibly continuous.

The phenomenological reading claims that this object, which James calls "thought's object," is manifestly not the same as the thunder as it exists for the psychologist who stands outside of the thought (PP 1890, 183–184). The thunder that exists in the psychologist's reality is a physical event that may be discrete and discontinuous with the silence just past, and may have parts that can be literally decomposed. When we incorrectly model thought on objects, it is discrete objects like this that we model it on. But there is another concept of object in James: *thought's object*. Here the object is not "thunder" but nothing short of "thunder-breaking-on-silence," all in hyphens. The phenomenological reading claims that James takes thought's object to be internally related to the thought of it. I examine this claim in the next section.

Thought and Its Object

For phenomenology, every intentional experience has two essentially correlated sides: the act of intending or meaning an object (*noesis*) and the object intended or meant (*noema*).[13] Although the object meant is not an immanent part of the experience but is merely meant by it, nonetheless the experience would not be the experience it is if it did not mean this object in just the way that it does. This is what Wilshire means by the cryptic idea that the doctrine of intentionality is based on the idea that "the concept of a mental state involves the concept of its object." The phenomenological reading claims that the *Principles* has a similar picture: the acts by which we intend the Same are acts of meaning, not merely psychological acts, and the self-identical object of these acts is not merely a physical object in space and time but an intentional object that is internally and necessarily correlated with such acts. Is this claim plausible?

In chapter XII of the *Principles*, James outlines what he calls the principle of constancy in the mind's meanings. This principle states that the "'*same matters can be thought of in successive portions of the mental stream, and some of these portions can know that they mean the same matters which the other portions meant.*' One might put it otherwise by saying that '*the mind can always intend, and know when it intends, to think of the Same*'" (PP 1890, 434). The "*sense of sameness*" articulated by this principle "is the very keel and backbone of our thinking" and is for James "the most important of all the features of our mental structure" (PP 1890, 434).[14] The "function by which a state of mind means to think the same whereof it thought on another occasion" (PP 1890, 442n) James calls a "conception." A conception "properly denotes neither the mental state nor what the mental state signifies, but the relation between the two, namely, the *function* of the mental state in signifying just that particular thing" (PP 1890, 436). So James distinguishes conceptions from the states of consciousness that are potentially their vehicles and from the mind-independent physical objects to which they might refer.

On the one hand, a conception cannot be identified with the multitude of conscious states that are potentially its vehicle. "[T]he thoughts by which we know that we mean the same thing are apt to be very different indeed from each other. We think the thing now in one context, now in another; now in a definite image, now in a symbol" (PP 1890, 454). One state of mind means the same thing as another state of mind not because they are the same mental state but because they involve the same conception. While states of mind are in constant change, conceptions, once formed, never change:

> Each conception . . . eternally remains what it is, and never can become another. The mind may change its states, and its meanings, at different times; may drop one conception and take up another; but the dropped conception can in no intelligible sense be said to *change into* its successor. The paper, a moment ago white, I may now see to have been scorched black. But my conception "white" does not change into my conception "black." On the contrary, it stays alongside of the objective blackness, as a different meaning in my mind, and by doing so lets me judge the blackness as the paper's

change. Unless it stayed, I should simply say "blackness" and know no more. Thus, amid the flux of opinions and of physical things, the world of conceptions, or things intended to be thought about, stand stiff and immutable, like Plato's Realm of Ideas. (PP 1890, 437)

So the flowing multitude of our changing thoughts can mean the same because they are vehicles for unchanging conceptions. And they must be unchanging, for otherwise we would not be able to distinguish whether the paper's change from white to black was merely a change in our conception of the paper, or a change in the paper itself. Sounding like Gottlob Frege and Husserl in their criticism of psychologism, James is here arguing that objective knowledge requires positing conceptions that do not change through time.[15]

On the other hand, conceptions are not to be identified with the physical objects that mental states signify, objects in the psychologist's reality. According to James, this is because conception and object can vary independently of one another. "Even now, the world may be a place in which the same thing never did and never will come twice. The thing we mean to point at may change from top to bottom and we be ignorant of the fact. But in our meaning itself we are not deceived; our intention is to think of the same" (PP 1890, 435). In other words, even if the world of physical objects changes from top to bottom, our thought's meaning the same does not change. This is because what is meant as the same has identity conditions that do not depend on the empirical world at all. "To learn whether black and white differ, I need not consult the world of experience at all; the mere ideas suffice. *What I mean* by black differs from *what I mean* by white, whether such colors exist *extra mentem meam* nor not. If they ever do so exist, they *will* differ" (PP 1890, 1239). It is clear that conceptions and actual physical objects cannot be identified.

But a conception does signify a relation to an object. How should we characterize this object? To answer this, we must examine James's distinction between the "object of thought" and the "topic of thought," which as Gurwitsch points out, is similar to Husserl's distinction between the object-as-it-is-intended and the object-which-is-intended:[16]

In popular parlance the word object is commonly taken without reference to the act of knowledge, and treated as synonymous with individual subject of existence. Thus if anyone ask what is the mind's object when you say "Columbus discovered America in 1492," most people will reply "Columbus," or "America." . . . They will name a substantive kernel or nucleus of the consciousness, and say that thought is "about" that—as indeed it is—and they will call that your thought's object. Really that is usually only the grammatical object, or more likely the grammatical subject, of your sentence. . . . [O]r you may call it the "topic" of your thought, or the "subject of your discourse." But the *Object* of your thought is really its entire content or deliverance, nothing more nor less. . . . It is nothing short of the entire sentence, "Columbus-discovered-America-in-1492" . . . with hyphens between all its words. (PP 1890, 265–266)

Thought's object is "neither more nor less than all that the thought thinks, exactly as the thought thinks it" (PP 1890, 266). But this includes not only what is thought about, but also the manner in which it is thought about, including the halo of obscure relations in which it is bathed. In phenomenological language, thought's object is the *object-as-it-is-intended*. Clearly this cannot be determined without reference to the thought that intends it. But neither can the thought be determined without reference to the object thought about. This is because, as we saw earlier with the pack of cards example, the sensible continuity of the time-parts of the thought cannot specify, by itself, whether such parts comprise a single thought of something or two sensibly continuous thoughts of it. It is also required that these time-parts be of the same "total object," which is the object-as-it-is intended by that thought. In light of this, we can understand what it means to say that the reference of thought to the object of thought is internal and necessary: the identity conditions of the thought depend on the object meant or intended by the thought.

The topic of thought is, we could say, the referent of thought. In phenomenological language, it is the *object-which-is-intended*. But we can view the topic of thought in two ways. First, we can view it from the psychologist's point of view. From this point of view, the topic is the *empirical referent* of the thought, which exists in what for the psychologist is *objective reality*.[17] This object is externally and contingently related to the thought that is of it. This is the object of which James speaks in papers such as "The Function of Cognition." There he gives an account in which thought's relation to its empirical referent is nothing magical, a matter of thought "jumping" or "transcending" the divide between mind and world and hitting upon the right object. Rather, reference is determined by "the procession of mental associates and motor consequences that follow on the thought, and that would lead harmoniously, if followed out, into some ideal or real context, or even into the immediate presence, of the [object]" (MT 1909, 34). Reference to an empirical object depends not on meanings that the thinker of the thought ascertains from within their experience, but on whether the associates of the thought in fact lead to the object "*through a context which the world supplies*" (EPh 1895, 74).

But the topic of thought can also be viewed from within the stream of thought. From this point of view, the topic is a *higher-order object of thought*. James says of this object that it is in one way "less than the thought's object . . . in another way it may be more" (PP 1890, 266). It is less than thought's object because, while the topic understood in this way denotes the object thought about, it does not specify what is thought about it. The objects of thought that pertain to specific thoughts do specify this. The topic is more than the object of thought, however, because within the stream we "as a rule . . . are fully aware that we have thought before of the thing we think of now. The continuity and permanency of the topic is of the essence of our intellection" (PP 1890, 454). In other words, the topic of thought is needed to make sense of the fact that from within the stream of thought different thoughts, for instance "Columbus discovered America in 1492" and "he was a daring genius," can nonetheless intend the same thing. Insofar as we can distinguish between the constantly changing thoughts that we have of something and the something that is thought of by those thoughts, we can say that the topic, when understood as a higher-order-object, transcends any given thought of it and therefore has what phenomenologists call *immanent objectivity*. In this way, the topic of thought is more than thought's object.

Selectivity, Conception, and the Mind

If we remember, the phenomenological reading is comprised of two basic theses: (1) that James in the *Principles* articulates a proto-phenomenological theory of intentionality, and (2) that because of this, James came to endorse the reversal thesis, that is, the thesis that philosophy's account of the mind as intentional is prior to empirical psychology's account of the mental. I think the phenomenological reading is right that there is a proto-phenomenological theory of intentionality in the *Principles*. But I don't think that this proto-theory can be understood independently of James's naturalistic account of the selectivity of the mind. I also don't think that it entails the reversal thesis. In this section and the next, I will justify these two claims.

The basic problem is that the phenomenological reading has too narrow a view of the *Principles* and its goals, and this blinds it to important features of James's account of conception. How is the phenomenological reading of James too narrow? The phenomenological reading posits that there is one program for psychology as a natural science in the *Principles*, the correlational program, when in fact there are two. This other program involves understanding conscious mental life functionally as intervening "between impressions made from without upon the body, and reactions of the body upon the outer world" (PP 1890, 19–20). While the correlational program aims at objective knowledge, its knowledge is restricted to what goes on in a subject, with its mental and brain states. The functionalist program, in contrast, stresses "that minds inhabit environments which act on them and on which they in turn react. . . . [I]n short, it takes mind in the midst of all its concrete relations" (PP 1890, 19). According to this program, therefore, mental life is essentially teleological, concerned with a creature's fundamental interest in achieving its ends so as to cope with a changing environment. Indeed, it is the "pursuance of future ends and the choice of means for their attainment" that is for James "the mark and criterion of the presence of mentality in a phenomenon" (PP 1890, 21).

John Dewey, for one, takes this to be the central program of the *Principles*, which gives his reading a quite different cast than the phenomenological reading. He agrees with the phenomenological reading that there are two strains in the *Principles*, one in which there is "a realm of consciousness set off by itself" (Dewey 1930/1981, 11) and one in which its official dualism breaks down. But whereas for the phenomenological reading the breakdown of the *Principles*' official dualism leads to the vitiation of its naturalist project altogether, for Dewey this breakdown is precisely what makes the *Principles*' naturalism possible. But instead of its naturalism being of the correlational type, it is a "hylomorphic" naturalism, "having its roots in a return to the earlier biological conception of the psyche, but a return possessed of a new force and value due to the immense progress made by biology since the time of Aristotle" (Dewey 1930/1981, 11). For Dewey, the importance of the *Principles* is that it begins the project of situating and embodying the mental in the bodily and the environmental, and it makes a start at the project through its account of sensorimotor and intellectual habits; the naturalistic account of attention; the non-dualist account of the self; the account of concepts as emergent from patterns of attention determined by a creature's biological and culturally developed interests; the account of reasoning and essence as essentially teleological; the account of instincts and emotion, in which "our mental life is" seen as "knit up with our corporal frame" (PP 1890, 1082); the account of the reflex arc in which the mental is for the sake of action; and the account of the will as a product of attention, itself undergirded by habits.

In light of this program, a characteristic of consciousness that we have not yet discussed comes to the fore: its selectivity, its being interested in, and attending to, one part of its object to the exclusion of others. According to James's naturalistic anthropology, creatures must selectively attend to objects because they find themselves coping with an environment that delivers far more information than they can utilize to prepare their behavioral responses. Because of this, they must, to have intelligible experience, accentuate certain of the salient qualities and relations found in the "much-at-once-ness," and ignore others.

There are multiple levels at which selection operates, for James. At the most basic level, a creature's sense organs are selective mechanisms that, for physiological reasons, reliably respond to some sensory groupings and not others. The experiencing subject has no say here. Then, through attention and discrimination, a creature orders the sensory field that makes it past this initial sorting. Which features of the sensory field a creature attends to and discriminates, and which features they ignore, is determined by their basic interests, both practical and aesthetic.

In creatures of higher complexity, this ordering of the sensory field is undertaken not just by attention but also by the use of conception, "teleological instruments" that help us to practically handle the much-at-once-ness. For James, conceptions result "from our attention singling out some one part of the mass of matter-for-thought which the world presents, and holding fast to it, without confusion. . . . [T]he conceptual function requires . . . that the thought should not only say 'I mean this,' but also say 'I don't mean that'" (PP 1890, 436–437). To use a Hegelian turn of phrase, conceptions are patterns of identity and difference that attention and discrimination carve out of the sensible stream to which we hold fast through time, and which we connect to similar patterns that are not now present. What patterns we carve will depend on our standing interests and purposes. The "*whole function of conceiving, of fixing, and holding fast to meanings, has no significance apart from the fact that the conceiver is a creature with partial purposes and private ends*" (PP 1890, 456). The whole point of meaning the Same, we could say, is to advance our interests and ends. Conceptions are powerful instruments to do that because they greatly expand our ability to foresee tendencies and to discern unity in complexity: "[B]y picking out . . . the items which concern us, and connecting them with others far away, which we say 'belong' with them, we are able to make out definite threads of sequence and tendency; to foresee particular liabilities and get ready for them; and to enjoy simplicity and harmony instead of what was chaos" (WB 1897, 90). So while James's account of the content of conceptions is quite Platonic, his account of their purpose is thoroughly pragmatic.

Faced with these two sides of conception, one might try to fashion a unified theory that does equal justice to the fact that it phenomenologically appears to us that we mean the Same and that its so appearing plays a functional role in a creature's goal-directed activity. The phenomenological reading does not take this course, instead claiming that the functionalist program depends on the phenomenological one.[18] Here is its argument for this conclusion.

Thought's object, if we remember, is not the physical object, but is the object "exactly as the thought thinks it, however complicated the matter and however symbolic the manner of the thinking may be" (PP 1890, 266). This is a fringed object, one whose mostly "dim" static and dynamic relations are given as "part of the object cognized." These relations are not just spatial and temporal but also, it must now be pointed out, dispositional and causal. So an object of thought is given not only as having spatial and temporal properties and relations but also as having certain powers to affect other things. These powers are given as part of the *object meant*, the object as it is intended. But as we would expect, corresponding to these given relational powers are subjective senses and feelings of meaning that intend them. "*The sense of our meaning is an entirely peculiar element of the thought*. It is one of those evanescent and 'transitive' facts of the mind which introspection cannot turn round on, and isolate and hold up for examination. . . . [I]t pertains to the 'fringe' of the subjective state, and is a 'feeling of tendency' " (PP 1890, 446). In being a feeling of tendency that pertains to the fringe of our subjective states, we can say that the sense of meaning is articulated by anticipations or expectations about how the total meant objects will behave, expectations that inform our future action and perception.

The point is that the phenomenological reading tries to account for the pragmatic relation between agent and object by claiming that whether our interests are satisfied or thwarted is best seen not as an empirical question but as a conceptual question about the relation of harmony or discord between our sense of meaning and the object meant. If there is a lack of harmony, we must alter our conception of an object by creating a new compound conception—one utilizing old conceptions that have not changed and new conceptions (see PP 1890, 442n). Here, the phenomenological reading claims, we are still immanent to the realm of meaning, to the realm of thought and its internal and necessary relation to its object.

I agree with the phenomenological reading that any account of *satisfaction* in James must involve his theory of meaning. The concept of satisfaction, which is the basis of James's theory of truth, is far more complicated than it is usually taken to be.[19] But what the phenomenological reading does not account for sufficiently is the fact that we cannot detach the question of whether there is harmony or discord between our sense of meaning and the object meant from our *real relations*[20] to objective reality.

Already in the *Principles*, James elaborated the doctrine, discussed earlier when describing the empirical referent of thought, in which for a state of mind "to take cognizance of a reality, intend it, or be 'about' it, is to lead to a remoter state of mind which either acts upon the reality or resembles it" (PP 1890, 445). To use James's example, just as a gun demonstrates what it is pointed at through a real relation to what it hits, that is, by breaking its target, a state of consciousness also demonstrates what objective reality it is pointed at through a real relation, through "the power of interfering with the course of . . . reality" (MT 1909, 22).[21] James takes it, because of his endorsement of the reflex-arc theory, that all "feeling is for the sake of action" and "all feeling results in action" (MT 1909, 23). So for a mental state q to be about y is for the actions that result from q to have practical consequences with respect to y—either practical consequences that flow from our acting directly "upon it through the bodily organs" (PP 1890, 213), or by our acting indirectly on certain intermediaries that would lead to the direct handling of y.[22]

According to this pragmatist or functionalist strain of James's thought, the expectations that comprise the sense of one's meaning are developed through an on-going learning process involving reality, rather than—as it is for Husserl—through the intuition of pre-existing meanings or essences. The phenomenological reading is right that James has a strong Platonist strain in his account of conceptions. Once a pattern of identity and difference is carved out of the sensible stream, we have a permanent conception that cannot be changed.[23] But a balanced reading of the *Principles* must also try to do justice to the fact that the internal relation between thought and its object articulated by a conception is bound up with how we act on, and are acted on, by reality in our goal-directed behavior. It must account for the fact that our intending or meaning the Same plays a functional role in our ongoing coping with a recalcitrant reality. Such a reading would see that James rejects the Kantian idea, which informs phenomenology, that there is a hard line between our intentional and real relations to things, and that his account of meaning is meant to be naturalistic in some important respect. I am not in a position to develop this reading here. I just want to point out that the phenomenological reading rejects the need to develop such a reading, and that this makes its account of James significantly one-sided.[24]

The Reversal Thesis Again

We are now, at long last, in a position to evaluate the reversal thesis. Again, the reversal thesis says this. The official program of the *Principles* is to correlate mental state and brain state. But we have found, through the discovery of intentionality, that to specify the content of a thought requires specifying what it is of—its intentional object—and this can only be done by philosophy (i.e., phenomenology) and not by psychology. So the naturalistic program of the *Principles* depends on a prior philosophical program.

But this thesis depends for its intelligibility on an either/or: either one accepts James's official dualism between subject and object, which underwrites his correlational program, or one accepts that the relation between thought and its object is an ideal and internal relation, which undermines dualism and so the autonomy of this naturalistic program. But if, as the second naturalistic project posits, intentional relations to objects must be understood within the context of a creature's ongoing attempt to cope with reality, then we can say that for James meaning finds its ground not in pure constitutional acts of the mind but in our embodied dealings with the world. Precisely how James's naturalistic story about meaning might work in detail is an open question. And precisely how that naturalistic story could be reconciled with James's account of intentionality remains open as well. But the very fact that these two questions remain open demonstrates something important: that it does not follow from James's articulation of a proto-phenomenological theory of intentionality that his project of developing a naturalistic psychology must collapse.

Notes

1. For the principle works of this tradition, see Schütz (1941/1966), Gurwitsch (1943/1966, 1947/1966), Linschoten (1968), Wilshire (1968), Wild (1969), Cobb-Stevens (1974), and Edie (1987).
2. In this chapter I just focus on these two central claims. Schütz and Gurwitsch made the first in the forties, while Wilshire put forward the second in the late sixties. It should be noted that phenomenological readers have also considered in detail James's account of the self, his theory of time consciousness, his theory of belief and reality, his theory of language, as well as his accounts of attention, will, and action. For James's account of the self, see Wilshire (1968, ch. 6), Wild (1969, ch. 4), Edie (1973), Cobb-Stevens (1974, ch. 4); for his account of time consciousness, see Cobb-Stevens (1974, ch. 3, 1998); for his account of belief and reality, see Wild (1969, ch. 6), Kersten (1969), Schütz (1945/1964), Cobb-Stevens (1974, ch. 6), Edie (1987, chs. 1 and 4); for his account of language, see Linschoten (1968, ch. 4) and Embree (1979); and for his account of attention, will, and action, see Wild (1969, chs. 5, 10, and 11), Cobb-Stevens (1974, ch. 7), Edie (1987, chs. 2 and 4).
3. In the *Principles* James uses both "thought" and "feeling" to stand for states of consciousness. In this chapter I use "thought" as the generic term for states of consciousness, including sensations. I only use his alternate term "feeling" when context demands it.
4. "The definition of psychology may be best given ... as the *description and explanation of states of consciousness as such*. By states of consciousness are meant such things as sensations, desires, emotions, cognitions, reasonings, decisions, volitions, and the like. Their 'explanation' must of course include the study of their causes, conditions, and immediate consequences, as far as these can be ascertained" (PBC 1892, 9).
5. See his account of the "spiritual self" in chapter X, and his account of our "original sensations" in chapter XVII, where James clearly presages his account of "pure experience" given later as part of his radical empiricism. For this point, see Dewey (1940) and Myers (1986, 61).
6. James also has theory in which thought's "self-transcendent function," i.e., its intentional reference to an object, is seen as falling "outside and not inside its being" (MT 1909, 20). I discuss this theory in "Selectivity, Conception, and the Mind."
7. Sometimes Wilshire puts forward a more modest thesis, namely, that the *Principles* is a text "at odds with itself" (Wilshire 1968, 211). On this view, the *Principles* makes a

phenomenological breakthrough, though the text does not consistently carry it out, leading to a deep tension between the natural scientific program, with its methodological dualism between thought and object, and the phenomenological tendency, which undermines that very dualism.

8. Wilshire dismisses James's forays into physiology and experimental psychology, saying that the results are "disappointing, if not embarrassing" (Wilshire 1968, 13). But Wilshire reads the import of these forays incorrectly, even when seen from the phenomenological point of view. Wilshire focuses only on the narrow issue of whether precise correlations between mental states and brain states are being arrived at. But the better way to see James's physiological discussions from the phenomenological point of view is as forms of evidence that help the psychologist better describe mental life as given first-personally. Of course, there are other, non-phenomenological, ways of reading James's relation to experimental psychology in the *Principles*. See Klein (2009).

9. Husserl thinks that for phenomenology to access its object, i.e., the world as it is manifest to consciousness, requires that we set aside, or put out of action, all of the presuppositions and convictions about conscious experience that we have accrued from the sciences and our cultural/historical inheritance. But we must be even more radical, Husserl thinks, because the greatest distortion in our account of consciousness arises from the temptation to understand consciousness in terms of the existing world that is given through it. To avoid this temptation, we need to put the "natural attitude" out of action by putting the world into "brackets." In enacting the *epoché*, we continue to be concerned with *the world*, but now as it is meant or intended, and so as the correlate of consciousness. For a comparison of the critique of the psychologist's fallacy with Husserl's *epoché* and reduction, see Giorgi (1981).

10. This list should not be confused with the five features of consciousness James takes to be basic, and that he discusses at PP (1890, 220). His list identifies some features of consciousness that I do not discuss here, and not all the features I discuss are on his list.

11. James has similar arguments for non-successive thoughts. See PP (1890, 163).

12. James recognizes that Kant and his followers also had "little trouble in showing that such a bundle of separate ideas would never form one thought at all," which led them to think "an Ego must be added to the bundle to give it unity, and bring the various ideas into relation with each other" (PP 1890, 267). But if one denies in the first place the idea that complex thoughts are composed of atomic impressions and ideas, as James does, then there is no reason to posit the Kantian "elaborate internal machine shop" (PP 1890, 344) to bring order to the manifold.

13. For these concepts, see Husserl (1913/1982, pt. 3, ch. 3).

14. This principle, it should be noted, applies not just to conceptual acts of consciousness but also to intuitive acts (sensory, perceptual, and orectic).

15. I think we can now begin to appreciate Husserl's claim that James helped free him from psychologism: "How little James's genius from observation in the field of the descriptive psychology of presentational experience entails psychologism, can be seen from the present work. For the advance in descriptive analysis that I owe to this distinguished thinker have only facilitated my release from the psychologistic standpoint" (Husserl 1913/2001, 1:324n).

16. See Gurwitsch's classic paper "On the Object of Thought" (Gurwitsch 1947/1966). For the original distinction, see Husserl (1913/2001, 2:113).

17. In an unpublished chapter of the *Principles*, "Object of Cognition and Judgments of Reality," James distinguishes between objects and reality. While the term *object* is "equivalent to the mental content, or deliverance or matter of consciousness," the term *reality*

signifies the realm of objects that have "status or existence outside of the particular feelings in which they appear" (MEN 1883, 265). Errors and illusions have objects, but they are not of reality.
18. See Wilshire (1968, 7–9, ch. 3) and Cobb-Stevens (1974, ch. 7).
19. See Cobb-Stevens (1974, ch. 8), where he compares James's account of truth as satisfaction with Husserl's account of truth as ideal adequation between meaning-intention and meaning-fulfillment.
20. My use of the concept of "real relation" is influence by Vincent Descombes, although he stresses the concept in the context of a discussion of Peirce's triadic semiotics. See Descombes (2014).
21. See Jackman (1998) and O'Shea (this volume) for good treatments of James's functionalist account of intentionality.
22. It is often conceded by phenomenological readers that James, soon after the *Principles*, replaced the phenomenological theory of intentionality with this functionalist theory of intentionality. See Wilshire (1968, 203–205). This they see as a misstep. My point here is simply that the functionalist theory was already operative in James's work at the time of the *Principles* and we have to account for that.
23. Although at certain points in the *Principles* James offers a decidedly non-Platonist theory of at least empirical conceptions: "In logic a concept is unalterable; but what are popularly called our 'conceptions of things' alter by being used. The aim of science is to attain conceptions so adequate and exact that we shall never need to change them. There is an everlasting struggle in every mind between the tendency to keep unchanged, and the tendency to renovate, its ideas. Our education is a ceaseless compromise between the conservative and the progressive faction" (PP 1890, 753).
24. I think C. I. Lewis is the philosopher who most clearly tried to integrate both sides of James's thought; unsuccessfully, I might add. Sometimes phenomenological readers of James realize that Maurice Merleau-Ponty is a better template for understanding James than is Husserl. I think this is a valuable insight, for Merleau-Ponty wishes to articulate a non-psychologistic theory of meaning or sense that nonetheless emerges out of our goal-directed embodied dealings with the world. See Merleau-Ponty (1945/2012).

References

Cobb-Stevens, Richard. 1974. *James and Husserl: The Foundations of Meaning*. The Hague: Martinus Nijhoff.
Cobb-Stevens, Richard. 1998. "James and Husserl: Time-Consciousness and the Intentionality of Presence and Absence." In *Self-Awareness, Temporality, and Alterity*, edited by Dan Zahavi, 41–57. Dordrecht: Kluwer.
Descombes, Vincent. 2014. *The Institutions of Meaning: A Defense of Anthropological Holism*. Translated by Stephen Adam Schwartz. Cambridge: Harvard University Press.
Dewey, John. 1930/1981. "From Absolutism to Experimentalism." In *The Philosophy of John Dewey*, edited by John J. McDermott, 1–12. Chicago: University of Chicago Press.
Dewey, John. 1940. "The Vanishing Subject in the Psychology of James." *The Journal of Philosophy, Psychology and Scientific Methods* 37 (22): 589–599.
Edie, James. 1973. "The Genesis of a Phenomenological Theory of the Experience of Personal Identity: William James on Consciousness and the Self." *Man and World* 6: 322–340.

Edie, James M. 1987. *William James and Phenomenology*. Bloomington: Indiana University Press.
Embree, Lester. 1979. "The Phenomenology of Speech in the Early William James." *Journal for the British Society for Phenomenology* 10: 101–109.
Giorgi, Amedeo. 1981. "On the Relationship among the Psychologist's Fallacy, Psychologism, and the Phenomenological Reduction." *Journal of Phenomenological Psychology* 12: 75–86.
Gurwitsch, Aron. 1943/1966. "William James's Theory of the 'Transitive Part' of the Stream of Consciousness." In *Studies in Phenomenology and Psychology*, 301–331. Evanston: Northwestern University Press.
Gurwitsch, Aron. 1947/1966. "On the Object of Thought." In *Studies in Phenomenology and Psychology*, 141–147. Evanston: Northwestern University Press.
Husserl, Edmund. 1913/1982. *Ideas Pertaining to a Pure Phenomenology and to a Phenomenological Philosophy, First Book*. Translated by F. Kersten. Dordrecht: Kluwer.
Husserl, Edmund. 1913/2001. *Logical Investigations*. Translated by J. N. Findlay. 2nd ed. 2 vols. New York: Routledge.
Jackman, Henry. 1998. "James' Pragmatic Account of Intentionality and Truth." *Transactions of the C. S Peirce Society* 34: 155–181.
Kersten, F. 1969. "Fanz Brantano and William James." *Journal of the History of Philosophy* 7: 177–191.
Klein, Alexander. 2009. "On Hume on Space: Green's Attack, James's Empirical Response." *Journal of the History of Philosophy* 47 (3): 415–449.
Linschoten, Johannes. 1968. *On the Way toward a Phenomenological Psychology: The Psychology of William James*. Pittsburgh: Duquesne University Press.
Merleau-Ponty, Maurice. 1945/2012. *The Phenomenology of Perception*. Translated by Donald Landes. New York: Routledge.
Myers, Gerald E. 1986. *William James: His Life and Thought*. New Haven: Yale University Press.
Schütz, Alfred. 1941/1966. "William James's Concept of the Stream of Thought Phenomenologically Interpreted." In *Collected Papers*, 3, 1–14. The Hague: M. Nijhoff.
Schütz, Alfred. 1945/1964. "On Multiple Realities." In *Collected Papers*, 1, 207–259. The Hague: M. Nijhoff.
Spiegelberg, Herbert. 1981. *The Phenomenological Movement: A Historical Introduction*. Dordrecht: Kluwer.
Wild, John Daniel. 1969. *The Radical Empiricism of William James*. Garden City, NY: Doubleday.
Wilshire, Bruce. 1968. *William James and Phenomenology: A Study of "the Principles of Psychology."* Bloomington: Indiana University Press.
Wilshire, Bruce. 1969. "Protophenomenology in the Psychology of William James." *Transactions of the Charles S. Peirce Society* 5 (1): 25–43.

Index

Abbot, Francis Ellingwood, 112–13
absolutism, 167, 391–98, 403–5, 430–31, 434–43, 469–70, 473–74. *See also* absolute *under* mind
abstraction, 55, 71–73, 123–24, 253–54, 275–76, 378–79, 439, 444, 458–60, 490–91
acquaintance, 67–69, 207–8, 272–75, 279–82, 294–97, 301–2, 361–62, 367, 416–17. *See also under* knowledge
action, 433, 444, 476
    attention and, 21–22, 27, 36–37, 93
    belief and, 225–29, 473–74, 499, 532, 537–38, 542
    brain and, 185
    cognition and, 187–89, 275–76
    consciousness and, 95, 185, 251–52, 478, 584–85
    democratic, 249
    emotion and, 52–53, 56–58
    ethics and, 199–211, 444–45, 496–99
    experience and, 347–48
    habit and, 525–26
    interest and, 87–88, 185
    reference and, 336–37
    reflex, 86–87, 92
    social, 253–54
    spontaneous, 92–93, 119–20
    truth and, 553
    will and, 36–37, 473–74
    See also will
Adams, Robert Merrihew, 222
adaptation. *See* evolution
Addams, Jane, 512
aesthetic appreciation, 113–14, 123–24

affect, affectivity, 45, 49, 53–54, 58, 475. *See also* emotions
Agassiz, Louis, 109–12, 141–42, 178
alienation, 440, 442, 444
Alston, William P., 222
American Academy of Arts and Sciences, 109
American Association for the Advancement of Science, 1
American Institute of Homeopathy, 139–40
American Medical Association, 139
American Philosophical Association, 1
American Psychological Association, 1, 12 n1
analogy, 320, 337, 342, 398, 405
Analysis of Mind, The (Russell), 542–43
Analysis of the Phenomena of the Human Mind (Mill), 66–67
analyst, logical, 531
anarchy, 252–55, 349
anatomy, 110–11, 134–35, 146–47, 178–82, 193, 362. *See also* physiology
Andrew, John, 258
Année Philosophique (journal), 469
anthropology, 167, 185, 188
anticipation, 23–25
Aristotelianism, 5, 439, 455, 497–98, 514–15
Arnold, Matthew, 240
asceticism, 209–10, 227
association, associationism, 25–26, 62–68, 78 n5, 183, 275–76, 376–77, 411–13, 419–20, 427 n17, 491–93
atavism, 161–62, 164–65, 168
atomism, 25, 31, 67–70, 77, 79 n12, 363–64, 413–15, 427 n19, 495, 517–18, 533, 575–76. *See also under* consciousness; experience; psychology

attention, 2, 19–23, 67–68, 72–73, 115–120, 127–28, 149, 183–85, 210, 556
    action and, 21–22, 27, 36–37, 93
    belief and, 19, 37–38
    body and, 23, 30, 34–35
    conception and, 74–76
    consciousness and, 28–33, 36–37, 116, 120–22
    experience and, 21, 375
    ideational preparation, 23–26, 29
    intellectual, 28–29
    interest and, 33–35, 561–62, 583–84
    ontological implications of, 35–37
    organic adjustment, 23, 29, 34
    perception and, 74–76, 479–80
    reactive spontaneity, 26–29, 34–35, 38–39
    sensation and, 583
    time and, 28–29
    as value-laden, 35
    voluntary, 36–37
    will and, 34–37, 561–62
authoritarianism, 502
automatic processes, 31
automatic writing, 158, 160
automatism, 85–88, 98–99, 101 n8, 121–22, 163–64, 362–63
autonomy, 246, 253
"Axioms and Postulates" (Schiller), 533

bacteriology, 137
Bain, Alexander, 8, 62–67, 78nn1–3, 119–20
Banks, Erik C., 283–84, 285 n8
Barrett, Lisa, 49
Barrett, William F., 158
Bastian, Adolf, 161–62
Beaunis, Henri-Étienne, 159–60
Bechtel, Edwin DeTurck, 393–94
behavior, 27
    belief and, 219
    prudent, 89–100, 102 n19, 102 n25
    purposive, 86–90
    reference and, 336–37
behaviorism, 23, 43, 542–43
belief, 2–3, 68–69, 168–69, 188–89, 210, 554
    action and, 225–29, 473–74, 499, 532, 537–38, 542
    attention and, 19, 37–38
    behavior and, 219
    emotion and, 44–45, 53–58

    ethics and, 496–501
    experience and, 412, 496, 516, 520–21, 532–33
    habit and, 525–26
    knowledge and, 349–50, 500–501
    moral, 220
    over-belief, 368
    as personal, 223–24
    probability and, 537–38
    religious, 148–49, 216–29, 229 n4, 232–33, 338–40, 352–54, 532, 535–36, 544–46, 552
    right to, 232–33
    science and, 162
    subjectivity and, 372
    trust and, 220
    truth and, 217–18, 221–22, 309–10, 314–17, 320–22, 333–34, 346, 349–52, 371–72, 494–98, 524–25, 531–41
    usefulness of, 535–41
    will to, 37–38, 217–18, 228–29, 352–53, 362–63, 372, 476–77, 483–84, 492–93, 540–41
    See also truth; will
Bentham, Jeremy, 236
Bergson, Henri, 8, 172 n17, 381–87, 444, 476–77
Berkeley, George, 61–62, 65–66, 271, 348, 360–61, 365, 376, 411–12
Berlin Academy of Sciences, 1
Berlin, Isaiah, 239
Bigelow, Jacob, 136–37
Binet, Alfred, 158
Bismarck, Otto von, 160–61
Blood, Benjamin, 148, 469–70
Blue and Brown Books, The (Wittgenstein), 561
Bode, Boyd Henry, 370, 377–79, 385, 387
body:
    attention and, 23, 30, 34
    black box of, 135–37
    consciousness and, 85–87
    emotions and, 34, 41–58
    in medicine, 135–41, 148
    mind and, 138–39, 147–48, 159, 359–66
    perception of, 34
    subjectivity and, 55–56
    unconscious processes of, 66–67
Bolzano, Bernard, 390
Bottazzi, Filippo, 169–70
Bourne, Ansel, 160, 172 n7
Bowditch, Henry, 142, 144–45
Bowen, Francis, 109

Bradley, Francis H., 166–67, 430–31, 435–37, 533
Braid, James, 160
brain, 44, 67, 80 n17, 347, 426 n6
    action and, 185
    consciousness and, 86–88, 95–100, 362–63, 572, 585
    default mode network, 22
    mind and, 363–66
    physiology and, 86–87, 362
    reactions and, 347–48
    sensation and, 69–70, 362
    See also cerebellum
Braithwaite, Richard, 542
Brentano, Franz, 269, 278
British Academy, 1
British Association for the Advancement of Science, 157
Brown-Séquard, Édouard, 142–43
Brown, Thomas, 62–63
Brücke, Ernst, 136
Buddhism, 456
Burali-Forti paradox, 403

Caird, Edward, 520–21
Cannon, Walter, 42–44, 48
Cantor, Georg, 390, 396–97, 399
Cantor's paradox, 403
capitalism, 252–53
care, 199–200, 209–11
Carlson, Thomas, 471, 485 n12
Carnap, Rudolf, 341
Carpenter, Joseph Estlin, 163
Carpenter, William B., 116, 162–63, 168
cases. *See* categories, categorization
Cassirer, Ernst, 472
categories, categorization, 290–92, 304, 350–51, 472–75, 481–83
    centrality and, 292
    chaining, 292, 294–95, 303–4
    no common properties, 292
    pluralism and, 337–38
Cattell, James McKeen, 155–57, 163, 168–69, 172 n20
causality, causation, 4, 44–57, 67, 85–86, 91–92, 95–99, 125, 139–41, 146–47, 193, 278, 362–66, 419–20
Cavell, Stanley, 203–4
cerebellum, 86, 93. *See also* brain

chance, 187–88, 398, 400–401, 440–41. *See also* novelty
Chapman, John Jay, 149
Charcot, Jean-Martin, 160
charity, 227
Chautauqua Lake Institution, 446
chemistry, 110, 134, 137–38, 141, 143, 178;
    mental, 64–65, 78 n8
choice, 89–91, 121–22, 473–75
Christian Science Church, 139, 151
Civil War, 208–9, 257–58
clairvoyance, 160. *See also* psychical phenomena
clarity, 20–22
classification. *See* categories, categorization
Clifford, William Kingdom, 2, 216–22, 328, 497–500, 546
Cobb-Stevens, Richard, 12, 570
cognition, 43–44, 491–92
    action and, 187–89, 275–76
    as active, 543
    animal, 284 n2, 285 n3
    attention and, 28–29
    conceptual dimensions of, 269–84, 284 n2, 285 n3, 285 n9, 290–97, 312–14, 382–83
    direct, 271–72, 279–84
    emotion and, 41–44, 554–55
    evaluation and, 186–87
    evolution and, 186–87
    experience and, 67–68
    interest and, 276–77
    language and, 275–79, 290–93, 556–57
    perceptual dimensions of, 269–84, 284 n2, 293–97, 312–14
    pluralism and, 277
    privateness of, 556–57
    reality and, 337
    relation and, 279–82
    as social, 295–300
collaboration, 190, 242, 248–49, 258–59
Colombetti, Giovanna, 58
combination, 64–65, 183, 376
common sense, 41–42, 101 n16, 127, 250, 283, 293–96, 311–16, 322–23, 334–36, 373–74, 575
communitarianism, 246
community, 258, 261–62, 498
    ethical, 248–50, 497–500

comparison, 94, 124, 259–60
complexity, 43, 48–51, 245, 253–54, 292, 376–77, 413–14, 427 n19, 428 n21, 436–37, 574–78
Comte, Auguste, 119, 360
concepts, conception, 25–26, 67–69, 269–84, 284 n2, 285 n3, 285 n5, 285 n9, 290–97, 301–2, 305 n4, 312–14, 433, 437–39, 442–44, 515, 579–85
    attention and, 74–76
    categories and, 481–82
    perception and, 74–76, 80 n22, 81 n25
    rationality of, 432–33
    See also percepts, perception
conceptualism, 382–83, 386
conflict, 250, 258–60
    order and, 260
    resolution, 232–33
    value and, 240–41
confusion, 20–21, 53–54, 75, 96, 100, 312, 423
consciousness, 80 n19, 100 nn1–2, 102 n21, 194 n3, 491–92
    action and, 95, 185, 251–52, 478, 584–85
    altered states of, 158, 167
    atomism and, 575–76
    attention and, 28–33, 36–37, 116, 120–22
    automaton theory of, 85–88, 98–99, 121–22, 362–63
    as autonomous and relational, 251–52
    awareness and, 30–31
    belief and, 37
    body and, 85–87
    brain and, 86–88, 95–100, 362–63, 572, 585
    categories and, 482–83
    compounding of, 379–80
    conception and, 579–85
    as conversing, 512
    determinism and, 91–92
    emotion and, 54–56
    environment and, 557–58, 582–85
    evaluation and, 87–90, 93–96, 99–100, 102 n24, 103 n27
    evolutionary theories of, 57, 84–88, 96–100, 102 n24, 120–25, 184–85, 365–66
    experience and, 189–90, 275–77, 282–83, 312–14, 365–67, 373–74, 379–84, 413–17, 511–13, 573–75
    experiments in, 86–93
    higher forms of, 228–29
    holistic view of, 467–68
    intentionality and, 571–72
    interest and, 115–16, 120–22, 184–86
    introspection and, 574
    meaning and, 556–57, 579–81, 584–86
    mind and, 67–68
    of objects, 573–78, 580–81, 584–86, 587 n9
    perception and, 481–82
    of reality, 365–66
    redintegration and, 115–16
    selectivity and, 583
    self and, 32, 366–67, 415
    sensation and, 182, 184, 273, 360–62, 365, 383
    stream of, 2, 30, 67–69, 182–84, 415–17, 426 n10, 482–84, 549, 556–58, 561–62, 571–72, 575, 577, 581
    subjectivity and, 270–72, 274–75, 282–83, 574–75
    time and, 577–78
    truth and, 374–75, 531
    unity of, 182–85, 576–78
    will and, 36, 383–84
consensus, 261–62, 310
consequentialism, 202–3, 237–38
conservatism, 255, 500
constructionism, 53
contestation, 188, 259–60
context, 37, 279–82, 297–99, 415–17, 516–17, 557–58. *See also* environment
contingency, 234, 249–50, 257, 262, 292, 440–41, 444–46, 574, 581
continuity, 367, 375, 377, 381–84, 391–92, 401–2, 417–18, 425, 479–80, 482–84, 577–78
contractarianism, 235
conversion, 55–56, 226–27
cooperation, 242, 247, 260, 262 n3, 298–99, 497–98
Cope, Edward Drinker, 122
correspondence, 113, 117–18, 121–22, 124, 277–78, 319, 333–38, 350, 363, 428 n21, 476, 495, 505 n38, 539–40, 584. *See also* truth
corroboration, 298–300, 309, 316–17
Costello, Harry, 541–42
Couturat, Louis, 399
Critical Philosophy of Immanuel Kant, The (Caird), 520–21

Critique Philosophique, La (journal), 114–15, 467–69, 473–77, 481–84
Croce, Paul, 157
Crookes, William, 158, 162
culture, 44–45, 51–53, 57–58, 520, 538. *See also under* emotions
Curie, Marie and Pierre, 158, 169–70

Damasio, Antonio, 44, 49–50
Darwin, Charles, 8, 46, 50–51, 54–57, 84–85, 96, 109–13, 122–23, 161–62, 178–79, 208–9, 347–48, 351–52, 368 n3, 477, 511–12. *See also* evolution
Dedekind, Richard, 390, 395–97, 401–2, 406 n6
deflationism, 494–95
Deigh, John, 44–45
"De la philosophie du XIXe siècle en France" (Renouvier), 114
Delboeuf, Joseph, 476–77
deliberation, 246, 249, 255, 258–59
democracy, 229, 234–35, 340–41, 442–43, 502–3, 538
  radical, 245–62
  social, 252–53
De Morgan, Augustus, 514–15
deontologism, 202–3. *See also* ethics
depression, 56, 113–14, 143, 452
description, 2, 56, 67, 208, 223–24, 273, 293, 493, 545, 564, 572–74
  knowledge by, 294, 301–2
desire, 35, 126, 217–18, 226–27, 243 n5, 413
  morality and, 235, 237
  obligation and, 247–49
Dessoir, Max, 158
determinism, 35, 61–62, 91–92, 101 n8, 467–70, 473–75, 481
  indeterminism, 343 n10, 362–63, 405, 445, 474–75
Dewey, John, 4–8, 12 n1, 126–27, 261, 328–32, 339–42, 351, 354 n4, 432–33, 490–91, 511–26, 531, 541–43, 582–83
dialectics, 436–39, 511–12, 516–17
dialetheism, 324
dialogue, 5–8
digital corpus, 5–7, 13 n7, 14 n8
dignity, 188–89
discrimination, 21, 67–74, 184, 583

distraction, 20–22, 27
diversity, 187–88, 242–43, 246, 252–54, 418, 421–22
"Divinity School Address, The" (Emerson), 459
Doctrine of Chances (Peirce), 499
dogmatism, 520–21
doubt, 166–67, 207–8, 218, 371–72, 432–33, 492–93. *See also* belief
dreams, 31, 159, 167, 274, 293–94, 532
Drury, Maurice, 543–44, 550
dualism, 57–58, 138–39, 147, 271, 276, 359–61, 366, 415–17, 423, 496–97, 571–72, 582–86
du Bois-Reymond, Emil, 136–38, 152 n2, 182
Du Bois, W. E. B., 255
Duns Scotus, John, 490
duration, 381–84. *See also* time
Dworkin, Ronald, 234–35, 259, 291–92

Eddy, Mary Baker, 139
Edie, James M., 570
education, 125, 162, 254–57, 341, 502–3
egalitarianism, 234, 236, 243 n3
egoism, 246, 252
  ethical, 236
Ekman, Paul, 49
eliminativism, 22, 45–46
Eliot, Charles William, 117–18, 143–45, 178
Elkin, Stephen, 259
Ellsworth, Phoebe, 44–45, 49
Emerson, Ralph Waldo, 8, 451–53, 455
Emmanuel Movement, 150
emotions, 2, 31, 61–62, 364, 491–93
  action and, 52–53, 56–58
  "autonomic specificity" hypothesis of, 44
  basic, 44–45, 49–50, 53
  belief and, 44–45, 53–58
  body and, 34, 41–58
  cognitive emotion theory, 43–44
  culture and, 44–45, 51–53, 57–58
  evolutionary theories of, 44, 51–55
  existential, 54–56
  experience and, 559–60
  instincts and, 50–53
  interest and, 34
  James-Lange theory of, 45–50, 559–60
  neuroscience and, 44, 49–50

emotions (*cont.*)
  non-human animals, 42–44
  reality and, 54–56
  spiritual, 227
  subtle, 48–53
  unconscious, 31–32
empathy, 250–51, 258
empiricism, 61, 64–66, 79 n9, 112–15, 119–20, 123–24, 137–38, 142–43, 182, 187, 193, 199–200, 205, 413, 431, 454, 471, 474–75, 483–84, 500
  free will and, 473–74
  holism and, 436
  immediate, 515–18
  logical, 341–42
  in medicine, 137–43, 146–48
  pluralistic, 391–94, 399–401, 404–5
  psychology and, 492–93
  rationalism and, 518
  realism and, 283
  tolerance and, 232–33
  See also Radical Empiricism
enactivism, 23, 58
Encyclopedia Logic (Hegel), 438–39, 442
Encyclopedia of Unified Science, 341, 344 n17
enhancement, 20–22, 26
Enquiry Concerning Human Understanding, An (Hume), 413
environment, 68–69, 77
  consciousness and, 582–83, 585
  ethics and, 126–27
  knowledge and, 124
  mind and, 117–25, 183–85
epiphenomenalism, 84–90, 98–100, 101nn8–9, 129 n10
epistemology, 19, 37, 56–57, 195 n15, 245, 481, 513–15, 519
  ethics and, 499–502
  realism and, 276–77
  of social toleration, 235, 241–43, 243 n6
  See also knowledge; pluralism; truth
equality, 254–55
Esquisse d'une classification (Renouvier), 476
Essais de critique générale (Renouvier), 468–70, 481
Essais sur les données immédiates de la conscience (Bergson), 476–77

ethics, 126–28, 184–85, 199–200, 202–11, 212 n10, 467–68, 481, 490–91, 563
  action and, 199–211
  applied, 205, 496–99
  belief and, 2, 220–22, 496–501
  casuistic, 247–48
  community and, 497–500
  descriptive, 204–5, 212 n10
  egoism and, 236
  "ethical republic," 247–49, 251–52, 257–58, 260–62
  experimentation and, 250, 258
  habit and, 199–200, 209–10
  hortatory, 204–11
  human personality and, 226–27
  knowledge and, 499–502
  logic and, 497–98
  meta-ethics, 205
  metaphysics and, 501–2
  normative, 205, 496–500
  objectivity and, 499–500
  perception and, 501–2
  pragmatist, 247
  as primary, 496–97
  psychology and, 248, 250–51
  reflection and, 201–2
  relativism and, 497–98
  religious experience and, 225–27
  social obligation and, 247–49
  systematic, 205–6
  as tragic, 247–48
eugenics, 161–62
evaluation, 84, 87–90, 93–96, 99–100, 102 n24, 103 n27, 186–87, 259–60
Evidence as to Man's Place in Nature (Huxley), 110–11
evidentialism, 216–18, 222
evolution, 44, 46, 50–57, 84–85, 96–100, 102 n24, 109–15, 118–28, 161–62, 178–79, 184–87, 208–9, 347–48, 351–52, 365–66, 368 n3, 382–83, 471, 477, 483–84, 493, 511–12
Évolution créatrice (Bergson), 382–84
Examination of Sir William Hamilton's Philosophy (Mill), 66–67
expectation, 24
experience, 3–4, 123–24, 404, 411–12
  action and, 347–48

atomistic, 495
attention and, 117, 119–20, 375
belief and, 412, 496, 516, 520–21, 532–33
chance and, 400–401
chaos of, 312–14
concepts and, 437–39, 442–44
consciousness and, 182–84, 275–77, 312–14, 365–67, 373–74, 379–84, 413–17, 511–13, 573–75
as dynamic, 516
emotion and, 559–60
evolution and, 127–28
first-person, 45, 47–49, 54–58, 84, 573–75
habit and, 525–26
immediacy of, 517, 522–23
individual, 165–66, 216, 223–24, 245
infinity and, 404
knowledge and, 348–49, 364–67, 374–75, 379, 382, 385–86, 415–17, 495, 514–15, 543
language and, 191
as lived through, 381–87
in medicine, 148–52
mind and, 365–66
moral, 205, 241
mystical, 227–28
novelty and, 398
of objects, 375–77, 385–86, 411–12, 415–25
ordinary, 424–25
perception and, 72
in philosophy, 146
pluralism and, 515–16
rationality and, 517–26
of reality, 186–88, 276–83, 383–87, 434–38
of relation, 373–78, 386–87, 411–25, 472, 514–17
religious, 223–28, 230 n6, 543–46, 552
self and, 366–67, 415
sensation and, 135–36, 560
of situation, 516–18, 522, 524
of space, 419–20, 423–24
subjectivity and, 312, 322, 375–78, 411–12, 415–17
systematizing, 313–16, 319, 322–23, 326 n26
of time, 24–25, 69–70, 397–98, 418–20, 450–51
unity and, 436–38, 440–42
of universals, 515–16, 522–26

of whole, 379–80
See also pure experience
experimentation, 42–46, 67, 84–93, 99–100, 126–27, 145–46, 210, 216–17, 246, 258, 431, 500, 587 n8
ethical, 250
physiological, 135–36
psychological, 158, 160, 168–69, 172 n7, 178

fallibilism, 372, 431, 494, 497–98, 500–502
Faraday, Michael, 162
Fechner, Gustav Theodor, 161, 167, 182
feeling, 270–75, 293–94, 554
cognition and, 554–55
feeling about, 280
meaning and, 555
of relation, 277–78
will and, 560–61
See also emotions
Fichte, Johann Gottlieb, 160, 167, 473
Fick, A., 363–64
finitism, 472, 478–79
First Essays (Renouvier), 472
First Principles (Spencer), 113–14, 119
Fiske, John, 112–13, 119
"Fixation of Belief, The" (Peirce), 520, 522
Flournoy, Théodore, 159–60, 482
focalization, 20–21
Foucault, Michel, 203–4
freedom, 233–34, 239, 245–46, 248–54, 257–58, 470–73
Frege, Gottlob, 331–32, 493, 579–80
French Revolution, 160, 535–36
Friesen, Wallace, 49
Frijda, Nico, 52–53
Frost, Robert, 343
Fullerton, George Stuart, 172 n15, 193
functionalism, 248, 281, 368 n3, 511, 582–85, 588 n22
Chicago, 512–26

Gale, Richard, 557
Galileo (Galileo Galilei), 155–56
Galston, William, 259–60
gaze, 23
germ theory, 137
Gibson, James, 77

Girel, Mathias, 118, 392
Goltz, Friedrich Leopold, 89–90, 99–100
Goodman, Russell, 543–44, 550–51
Gould, Stephen Jay, 98
Gray, Asa, 109
Gray, John, 259
Green, T. H., 430–31
Grier, Michelle, 393–94
Griffiths, Paul, 43–44
Gurney, Edmund, 158–60, 164–66
Gurwitsch, Aron, 570, 580–81

Haack, Susan, 498
habit, 2, 31, 65–66, 185, 226–27, 492–93
   action and, 525–26
   belief and, 525–26
   ethics and, 199–200, 209–10
   experience and, 525–26
Haeckel, Ernst, 161, 328
Hahnemann, Samuel, 144
Hall, G. Stanley, 145–46, 164–65, 168–69
hallucinations, 159–60, 163–65
Handbuch der physiologischen Optik
   (Helmholtz), 66–67, 182
Harris, W. T., 430–31
Harvard University, 1, 101 n9, 109–10, 117–18,
   134, 142–45, 178–81, 221–22, 349, 478–
   79, 541–42
hedonism, 236
Hegel, G. W. F., 8, 160, 167, 270–73, 279–81,
   332–33, 430–46, 468–70, 482, 511–
   13, 516–17
Heidegger, Martin, 45, 54–55
Heidenhain, Rudolf, 160
Helmholtz, Hermann von, 61–67, 78 n5, 79 n9,
   79 n12, 116, 129 n12, 136, 182, 374–75, 480
Hempel, Carl Gustav, 341–42
Herbart, Johann Friedrich, 64–65, 78 n5
Heretics Society, 544
Hering, Ewald, 63
Hilmy, S. Stephen, 556
history, 204, 208, 246, 249–51, 257–58, 301–2,
   321–22, 349, 442–43, 446, 512, 516–17
Hodgson, Richard, 155, 158, 168–69
Hodgson, Shadworth Hollway, 85, 115–18, 348,
   469–70, 479–82
Holcombe, William, 139–40

holism, 62, 67–70, 77, 148, 151, 183, 436–
   39, 467–68
Holmes, Oliver Wendell, Jr., 113–14, 178–79
Holmes, Oliver Wendell, Sr., 136–37, 144–45
Holt, Henry, 124–25, 181–82
homeopathy, 138–41, 143–44, 149–51
Honig, Bonnie, 259
hormones, 44
"How to Make Our Ideas Clear"
   (Peirce), 524–25
humanism, 54, 188, 346–47, 430, 461–62,
   535, 541–42
Humboldt, Wilhelm, 234–35
Hume, David, 8, 171 n4, 348, 375, 411–
   14, 474–75
   Copy Principle, 428 n21
humility, 241–43, 251, 501–2
Husserl, Edmund, 570, 579–81, 587 n9
Huxley, Thomas Henry, 86, 110–11, 146–47,
   156–57, 162, 171 n4, 185, 328
hydropathy. *See* water cures *under* medicine
hypnotism, 144, 158–64, 172 n7

idealism, 166–67, 170, 188, 193, 335, 394–405,
   430–31, 434–43, 467–68, 483–84, 493, 511,
   531, 533. *See also* absolutism
ideas, 25–29, 32. *See also* concepts
Idée de la personnalité humaine dans la
   psychologie moderne (Jeanmaire), 476
identity, 75–76, 194 n11, 366, 413, 416–20
imagination, 24, 26–27, 68, 80 n22, 418–22,
   425, 428 n21
imperialism, 252–53
inclusion, 242–43, 249, 255, 257, 460
"In Defense of Humanism" (Schiller), 535
individualism, 185–86, 189–90, 216, 223–24, 229,
   233, 245–46, 252–53, 297–300, 430, 501–2
inequality, 234, 255
inference, 31–32, 66, 73–74, 78 n5, 87–88, 182,
   239, 271–75, 280–82, 284 n2, 285 n9, 365,
   428 n22, 491–93
De l'infini mathématique (Couturat), 399
infinity, 390–91, 399, 472–75, 478–82
   new, 395–98
   totality and, 391–96, 399–405, 479–80
inquiry, 432–33, 490–91, 496–98, 500–501,
   516–18, 521–24

instincts, 31, 50–53, 364, 383
instrumentalism, 300, 315–16, 405
intellect, intellectualism, 208–9, 217–18, 334–35, 433–38, 442–43, 460, 521, 533
intensity, 22
intentionality, 43, 54–57, 269, 271–73, 277–78, 285 n6, 285 n8, 289–304, 370–73, 377–78, 386, 556–57, 570–72, 579–82, 585–86, 588 n22
   error and, 370–72, 374, 386–87, 388 n1
   truth and, 303–4, 305 n6
interactionism, 84–85, 88–89, 92, 98, 100, 101 n8
interdependence, 246
interest, 115–120, 124–28, 562–63
   attention and, 33–35, 561–62, 582–84
   cognition and, 276–77
   consciousness and, 87–88, 120–22, 184–86
   emotions and, 34
   as evaluative, 35
   perception and, 186
   universal, 259
   See also attention
International Congress of Psychology, 159–61
intimacy, 434–35, 440–44
Introduction à la métaphysique (Bergson), 380–82
introspection, 46–49, 61–62, 67, 93, 413, 425, 491–93, 554, 556, 574
intuition, 182, 383–85, 491–92

Jackman, Henry, 317
Jackson, A. C., 543–44
James, Henry, Jr., 453
James, Henry, Sr., 451–52
James, William:
   alternative medicine and, 139, 143–44, 150–52, 172 n7
   anti-dualism, 57–58
   criticism of Herbert Spencer, 116–25
   depression, 113–14, 143–44, 178–79, 452
   dialogism of, 5–8
   examinations, 144–45
   Gifford Lectures, 3, 223, 329–30, 532, 534
   Hibbert Lectures, 4, 346, 431–32, 533
   interest in psychical phenomena, 155–61, 163–71, 172 n7, 172 n20
   James-Lange theory, 45–50, 559–60
   Lowell lectures, 84–85, 163, 180–81, 347
   medical study, 134–35, 141–43, 178–79
   Memorial Hall, 294–99, 303–4, 335–37, 349
   Mind-Stuff Theory, 31, 67, 363–64
   as moral philosopher, 199–206, 208–11
   phenomenological holism, 77
   protest against American suppression of Philippine insurgency after Spanish-American war, 253–54
   Reactive Spontaneity Theory, 26–29, 34–35, 38–39
   relationship with Charles Sanders Peirce, 13 n3
   on religion, 166–67
   reputation, 1–5, 12 n1, 13 n7
   review of Thomas Huxley, 146–47
   scientific education, 109–10
   teaching appointment at Harvard, 1–2, 61, 78 n1, 117, 122–23, 134, 179–80
   Thayer Expedition to Brazil, 111–12, 141–42, 178
James, William, works by:
   "Are We Automata?" 84–88, 91–92, 98–99, 121–22, 181
   "Brain and the Mind, The," 84–85
   "Brute and Human Intellect," 118–19, 181
   "Dilemma of Determinism, The," 201, 398, 433
   "Does 'Consciousness' Exist?" 181, 190, 364, 366, 415–17, 511–12
   "Energies of Men, The," 181, 202–3
   Essays in Psychical Research, 156–57
   Essays in Radical Empiricism, 4, 177, 189, 202–3, 282–83, 293–94, 300, 359, 363, 386–87, 415–17, 426nn10–11, 478, 512–16, 549–50
   "Existence of Julius Cæsar, The," 352
   "Experience of Activity, The," 181
   "Feeling of Effort, The," 95, 476–77
   "Great Men and their Environment," 202–3
   "Humanism and Truth," 315, 350–51
   "Introduction to The Literary Remains of the Late Henry James," 201
   "Is Life Worth Living?" 221–22, 328
   "Knowing of Things Together, The," 194 n8, 281–83, 416–17
   Manuscript Lectures, 399–401

James, William, works by: (*cont.*)
- *Meaning of Truth, The*, 177, 187, 201, 269–70, 294, 321–22, 335–36, 349, 352, 450–51, 537–38, 553
- "Moral Equivalent of War, The," 233–34, 256–57
- "Moral Philosopher and the Moral Life, The," 103 n27, 126–27, 201–3, 206–8, 225–26, 235–36, 247–50, 474, 533
- ms. 4437 ("Infinity"), 399–401, 404
- "On a Certain Blindness in Human Beings," 201, 235–41, 250–51
- "On Some Hegelisms," 431–32, 435–36
- "On Some Omissions of Introspective Psychology," 477, 482–83
- "On the Function of Cognition," 181, 186–87, 269–75, 279–81, 293–94, 300, 348–49, 370–72, 374–75, 581
- "Original Datum of Space-Consciousness, The," 78 n6
- "Philosophical Conceptions and Practical Results," 2, 328–29, 471–72
- "Physical Basis of Emotion, The," 42
- "Plea for Psychology as a 'Natural Science,' A" 573
- *Pluralistic Universe, A*, 4, 148, 177, 187–91, 212 n13, 284, 286 n14, 346, 380, 384–85, 398, 404, 431–36, 440, 444, 498, 533
- *Pragmatism*, 3–4, 127–28, 177, 187, 201, 227–28, 229 n4, 232, 243, 249–50, 269–70, 277, 289, 309–11, 314–15, 319–21, 325 n17, 326 n26, 330–37, 340–41, 349–53, 450–55, 460–62, 532–35, 539, 549–50, 553
- "Pragmatist Account of Truth and Its Misunderstanders, The," 319
- *Principles of Psychology, The*, 1–2, 19–39, 41–42, 46–54, 57, 61–73, 77, 79 n15, 80 n19, 80 n21, 89, 92, 94, 123–25, 147–51, 158, 163–64, 167, 177, 180–87, 192–93, 201–3, 209–10, 216–17, 250–51, 269–72, 281–82, 289, 293–94, 300, 337, 347, 359–62, 365, 376, 414–17, 426nn10–11, 452–53, 469, 480–83, 491–93, 511–13, 534, 543–44, 549–50, 570–74, 579, 582–85, 588 n22
- *Psychology: The Briefer Course*, 30, 41–42, 46, 67–68, 72–73, 79 n15, 80 n19, 376, 549–50, 572–73
- "Psychological Theory of Extension, The," 78 n6
- "Quelques considérations sur la method subjective," 181, 467, 475–76
- "Reflex Action and Theism," 328, 433, 476
- "Relation between Knower and Known, The," 349
- "Remarks on Spencer's Definition of Mind as Correspondence," 118, 181, 201
- "Sentiment of Rationality, The," 140, 145, 221–22, 229 n4, 313–14, 328, 331–34, 351, 432–33
- *Some Problems of Philosophy*, 4, 177, 186, 270, 278–79, 385–86, 390–94, 401–5, 468–69
- "Spatial Quale, The," 67, 80 n21, 480–81
- "Stream of Thought, The," 182–83
- *Talks to Teachers on Psychology and to Students on Some of Life's Ideals*, 188–89, 202–3, 210
- "Thing and Its Relation, The," 347
- "Tigers in India, The," 349
- "Two English Critics," 349, 537–39
- *Varieties of Religious Experience, The*, 3, 13 n6, 44–45, 53–56, 158, 163, 167, 172 n16, 177, 180–81, 201–3, 216, 223–29, 229 n4, 329–34, 338, 353, 363, 368, 452–53, 460, 462, 532, 534, 543–45, 549–51
- "What Is an Emotion," 41–42, 50–51, 477
- "What Makes a Life Significant," 201, 443
- "What Pragmatism Means," 524–25
- "What Psychical Research Has Accomplished," 169
- "What the Will Effects," 477
- "Will to Believe, The," 149–50, 201–3, 216–22, 227–29, 229 n4, 232–33, 328, 497–98, 532, 534, 536, 545
- *Will to Believe and Other Essays in Popular Philosophy, The*, 2–3, 38, 44–45, 53–54, 168–69, 188–89, 431–32, 475–77, 483–84, 533
- *Works of William James, The*, 194 n2
- "A World of Pure Experience," 190, 277–78, 364, 411–12, 451, 514–15

Janet, Pierre, 158–60
Jarvis, E. A., 396
Jastrow, Joseph, 164–65, 168–69

Jeanmaire, Charles, 476
Journal of Philosophy, 377–78
Journal of Speculative Philosophy, 491–92
judgment, 43, 69, 123–24, 205–6
justice, 233–34, 245, 257

Kallen, Horace Meyer, 192, 346–47, 352, 469
Kant, Immanuel, 61–66, 70–71, 76, 79 n10, 81 n27, 117, 182, 247, 270–73, 279–81, 284 n2, 393–94, 404, 444, 467, 471–75, 481–84, 492–93, 501–2, 520–21, 577–78, 585
Keynes, John Maynard, 542
kinetoscope, 381–82
Klein, Alexander Mugar, 33, 177, 492–93
Klev, Ansten, 395–96
knowledge, knowing, 289–304
　absolute, 187
　by acquaintance, 294, 301–2, 361–62, 416–17
　belief and, 349–50, 500–501
　concepts and, 280–82, 294–97, 301–2
　environment and, 124, 127–28
　ethics and, 500–502
　experience and, 348–49, 364–67, 374–75, 379, 382, 385–86, 415–17, 495, 514–15, 543
　immediate, 279–82, 284 n2, 293–94
　interest and, 127–28
　knowledge about, 69, 272–75, 277–80, 294–302, 349, 361–62
　known-as, 348
　misrepresentation and, 302–4
　moral, 241–43, 243 n6, 250
　objective, 579–81
　of past, 301–2
　perception and, 294–97, 300–302, 543
　probabilistic, 187
　progress of, 250
　of reality, 289–90, 293–96
　representative, 349
　sensation and, 374–75
　shared, 385–87
　skepticism and, 500–501
　as social, 255–56, 271–72
　subjectivity and, 372
　truth and, 302–4, 371–72, 533
　of unobservables, 300–301
　virtual, 296–97, 301–2, 377
　See also belief; truth

Köhler, Wolfgang, 77, 561
Kulturkampf ("struggle for culture"), 160–61

Ladd, George Trumbull, 193
Lamarck, Jean-Baptiste, 96, 118–19, 129 n22, 130 n23, 477
Lamberth, David, 323
Lange, Carl, 42–43, 45–49
language:
　cognition and, 275–79, 556–57
　concepts and, 274–79, 290–93
　experience and, 191
　meaning and, 341
　moral, 205
　private, 556–57
　as social, 295–300, 303–4
　truth and, 337–38
Lavoisier, Antoine, 522
Le Bon, Gustave, 162
"Lecture on Ethics, A" (Wittgenstein), 544, 551–52
Lectures and Conversations on Aesthetics, Psychology, and Religion (Wittgenstein), 545
Lectures on the Elements of Comparative Anatomy (Huxley), 110–11, 146–47
Lenzen, Victor, 542
Lequier, Jules, 471–73
Lewes, G. H., 86–87, 99–100
Lewontin, Richard C., 98
liberalism, 234–35, 240, 246–47, 249, 259–61, 430
Linschoten, Johannes, 570
Locke, John, 25, 61–62, 183, 270–71, 375, 517–18, 575
Lodge, Oliver, 158
logic, 2–3, 123–24, 190–92, 194 n11, 195 nn12–13, 217–18, 286 n14, 521–23
　ethics and, 497–501
　of infinity, 391–96, 404–5
　natural, 493
　psychology and, 491–93
　of relations, 514–15
Logic: The Theory of Inquiry (Dewey), 512, 517–18
Lombroso, Cesare, 161–62
Lotze, Hermann, 64, 167, 435–37, 523

Lovejoy, Arthur Oncken, 352
Ludwig, Karl, 136

Mach, Ernst, 281–83
machine learning algorithm, 5–7, 13 n7, 14 n8
March Revolution of 1848, 160–61
Massachusetts Fifty-fourth Regiment, 257–58
materialism, 135–36, 145–49, 152 n2, 160–61, 166, 170–71, 185, 188, 193, 365, 431, 434–35, 458–59
mathematics, 2–3, 390–92
   of infinity, 395–405
   metaphysics and, 396–403, 405
McDermott, Robert, 156–57
McDougall, William, 49
McGuinness, Brian, 551
McTaggart, J. M. E., 533
Mead, G. H., 511–12
meaning, 3–4, 187, 221–22, 229, 331–32, 335–38, 490–91, 525–26, 554
   consciousness and, 556–57, 579–81, 584–86
   feeling and, 555
   linguistic, 341
   operation, 293–94, 300–304, 305 n12, 305 n14
medicine, 134–35, 163–64
   body's black box, 135–37
   degenerationism in, 163, 167
   holistic, 138–39, 151
   materialism and, 148–49
   medical hypnotism, 160, 162
   mind-cure, 139, 151
   scientific, 135–52
   sectarian, 137–52
   water cures, 139, 143–44
mediums, 155–63, 167–69
memory, 80 n22, 160, 184, 362, 383–85
   attention and, 21–22, 26–27
   episodic, 27
   perceptual, 27
   working, 27
Merleau-Ponty, Maurice, 45, 55
mesmerism, 160, 162
Metaphysical Club, 145, 178–79
metaphysics, 4, 68–69, 167, 192–93, 332–33, 359–68, 368 n3, 481
   ethics and, 501–2

   of infinity, 395–404
   intentionality and, 370–73
   mathematization of, 396–405
   moral, 205
   philosophy and, 390–92, 395–97, 404–6
   of pragmatism, 461, 501–2
   psychology and, 426 n11, 571–73
   of radical empiricism, 276, 281–82
Methods of Ethics, The (Sidgwick), 205–6
Methods of Study in Natural History (Agassiz), 110
Meynert, Theodor, 182, 362, 364
microscopes, 136–37
military, 256–57
Mill, James, 62–67, 411–12
Mill, John Stuart, 62–67, 119–20, 212 n8, 234–35, 240, 243, 411–12
Miller, Dickinson S., 370
mind, 378–79, 476
   absolute, 10–11, 370–71, 374–75, 379, 386–87, 437–41
   active, 115–25, 183–85, 194 n3
   atomism of, 363–64
   attention and, 19–24, 30–33
   body and, 138–39, 147–48, 159, 359–66
   brain and, 363–66
   divisions in, 159
   economy of, 361
   elementarism, 376–77
   environment and, 117–25, 183–85
   experience and, 183, 365–66
   external view of, 491–92
   internal view of, 383, 491–93
   mind-stuff theory, 363–64
   passive, 115–16, 123–24
   perception and, 117–18
   philosophy of, 19
   physiology and, 33
   psychical phenomena and, 158, 163–64
   psychology of, 493–94
   spontaneity of, 19, 183–84
   unconscious mental states, 24–25, 30–33
Mind (journal), 41–42, 50–51, 84–85, 165, 269–70, 371–72, 431–32, 481–82, 533–35
Mind! A Unique Review of Ancient and Modern Philosophy (Schiller), 533
Minot, Charles S., 164

miracles, 160–62
modernity, 156, 203–4
monism, 237–38, 431–46, 456, 460–62, 468–70, 482
  neutral, 283, 285 n8, 286 n12, 360, 542–43
"Montaigne, or the Skeptic" (Emerson), 455, 458–59
Moore, G. E., 205–6, 531–36, 539–41, 549–50, 553
morality, 188–89, 474
  absolutism and, 442
  action and, 444–45
  epistemology and, 241–43, 243 n6, 250–51
  experience and, 241
  moral equivalent of war, 256–57
  obligation and, 235–39, 245, 296–98, 502
  pluralism and, 188, 235–43, 260
  psychology and, 259–60
  rationalism and, 496–97
  as social and collaborative, 233, 242–43, 248–57, 260–62
  uncertainty and, 238–39, 258–62
  See also ethics
Morselli, Enrico, 166, 169–70
movement, 45–46, 62–64, 73, 78 n2, 78 n7, 80 n20, 81 n26, 392–93
Müller, Johannes, 135–36
Münsterberg, Hugo, 155–56, 169–70
My Philosphical Development (Russell), 543
Myers, Frederic W. H., 157–60, 163–66, 171 n4, 172 n16
Myers, Gerald, 32, 41–42, 147
mysticism, 460, 552

Nagel, Thomas, 240
National Academy of Science, 1, 172 n20
nationalism, 511
national service corps, 256–57
nativism, 61–64, 77, 78 n3, 79 n9
naturalism, 58, 109–10, 124–25, 156–57, 160, 166, 170, 182, 221–25, 347, 477, 482–84, 493, 498–501, 582–86
  scientific, 157–58, 164, 170–71
Naturphilosophie, 160
nervous system, 44, 69–70, 135–36, 347–48
neurasthenia, 143
Neurath, Otto, 342

neurology, 178, 185
neurophenomenology, 58
neuroscience, 44, 49–50, 185
Newcomb, Simon, 164–65
Newey, Glen, 259
New Monadology (Renouvier), 474
Nietzsche, Friedrich, 203–5
nihilism, 221–22, 230 n5
nominalism, 455–59, 490, 495, 498, 502–3, 517–18
"Nominalist and Realist" (Emerson), 455–57
norms, normativity, 493, 496–501, 520–22
Norton, Grace, 119–20
novelty, 193, 209–10, 261–62, 383, 390, 398, 401, 405, 473–74, 478
Nozick, Robert, 366
Nussbaum, Martha, 234–35

objectivism, objectivity, 276, 282–83, 366, 375–77, 385–86, 411–12, 415–25, 499–500, 521–22, 573–81, 585–86
obligation:
  moral, 235–39, 496–98, 502
  social, 245–51, 256
observation, 216–17, 413
occult. *See* psychical phenomena; spiritualism
On Certainty (Wittgenstein), 553
On the Origin of Species (Darwin), 109–11
ontology, 19, 35–38
  relativism and, 516–17
optics, 182
order, 208–9, 245, 252–54, 258–60
organization, 77
Osler, William, 138
Ostwald, Wilhelm, 330–32
Oxford University, 346–47, 404, 431–32, 533

Palladino, Eusapia, 169–70
Palmer, George Herbert, 431–32
parallelism, 147, 150–51
Parfit, Derek, 366
Pearson, Karl, 351
Peirce, Charles Sanders, 2–5, 8, 13 n3, 112–13, 145–48, 178, 186–87, 190, 193, 195nn12–13, 328–32, 343 n4, 432–33, 469–70, 482, 490–503, 512–15, 520–25, 531, 533, 539–42

percepts, perception, 67–68, 116, 269–84, 284 n2, 294–97, 377–78, 515, 531
   aspect-seeing, 562–63
   atomism of, 413–15, 427 n19
   attention and, 19, 21–26, 29, 74–76, 479–80
   of body, 34
   Conceivability Principle, 413–14
   concepts and conception, 25–26, 74–76, 80 n22, 81 n25
   consciousness and, 481–82
   constancy of, 73–74
   distraction and, 27
   emotions and, 41–42
   error and, 371, 387
   ethics and, 501–2
   experience and, 72, 411–12
   imagination and, 421–22
   individual, 186, 189–91
   interest and, 186
   knowledge and, 284 n2, 293–95, 300–302, 361–62, 543
   mind and, 117–18
   objectivity and, 375–77
   operation and, 293–94
   preperception, 24–25, 562
   reactive spontaneity, 26
   of reality, 280–84, 293–95, 311–15, 413, 420–22
   of relation, 417–25, 427 n17, 427 n19, 480
   self and, 417–18
   sensation and, 25–26, 68–75, 77, 79 n10, 80 n22, 81 n24, 182, 361–62, 428 n22
   Separability Principle, 413–14
   spatial, 2, 61–66, 70–77, 80 n20, 81 n23, 81 n25, 182, 313, 382–83, 479–80
   of time, 2, 24–25, 62–64, 479–80
   truth of, 313–16
   unconscious, 67
   unobservables, 300–301
   as value-laden, 35
   visual, 129 n12
Perry, Ralph Barton, 192, 212 n4, 542
personality, 53, 55, 185, 226–27, 451
perspectivism, 186, 190–91
Pflüger, Eduard, 86–87, 89–90, 99–100
phenomenalism, 371–75, 472–75, 478, 481–82

phenomenology, 2, 8, 32, 36, 58, 205, 275–76, 278, 283, 293–94, 359, 570–71
   of emotions, 44–45, 54–56
   holistic, 77
   intentionality and, 570–72, 579–82, 585–86, 588 n22
   and psychology, 77, 554, 558–59, 570–72, 582–86, 586 n7, 588 n22
   of sensation, 69
Phillips, Denis, 319
Philosophical Essays (Russell), 539
philosophy:
   American, 469
   analytic, 8, 205, 278, 328–29, 341–42, 343 n1
   Anglophone, 8, 19
   attention and, 19–21
   belief and, 2
   European, 4–5
   evolution and, 125–26
   experience and, 146
   individualism and, 246
   materialism and, 135–36, 152 n2
   mathematics and, 405
   metaphysics and, 390–92, 395–97, 404–6
   as method, 563
   of mind, 19, 100 n1, 102 n21, 467–68
   moral, 199–11, 237–38, 241–43, 243 n6, 474
   perspectivism, 186
   political, 232–35, 245–46, 252–62
   pragmatism and, 501–2
   psychology and, 19, 61–62, 177–93, 194 n10, 195 n15, 347–48, 405, 413–14, 467–68, 561, 570–73, 582
   realism and, 182, 185
   relevance of, 328–33, 339–43
   of religion, 3, 166–67, 216, 227–28
   of science, 330–31, 341–42, 390–91, 394, 404–6, 558–59, 582
   self and, 207–11
   temperament of, 475
   thought and, 2–3
   voice in, 5–8
phrenology, 363–64
physics, 137–38
physiology, 477–78, 587 n8
   of brain, 347, 362
   comparative, 179–80

of consciousness, 86–93, 99–100
experimental, 84–87, 90–93, 99–100, 135–36, 178
mechanistic, 91–92
optics and, 182
of perception, 62–64
psychology and, 1–2, 13 n2, 145–47, 159–60, 347–48, 483–84, 492–93
of sensation, 69–70, 182
Pihlström, Sami, 471, 563
Pillon, François, 114–15, 469, 471–72, 483–84
Piper, Leonora, 155–56, 158, 163–65, 168–69
Platonism, 166, 438–39, 495–96, 514–15, 583, 585, 588 n23
pleasure, 236–38
pluralism, 22, 37–38, 54, 58, 148, 187–93, 216, 229, 235–43, 243 n6, 245–46, 251–52, 260, 431, 434–35, 440–46, 450–51, 468–69, 472, 474–75, 502
  categorization and, 337–38
  cognition and, 277, 285 n5
  empiricism and, 391–92, 399–401, 405
  experience and, 515–16
  infinity and, 391–92, 399–401, 404–5
  realism and, 277
  reality and, 533
  religion and, 461–62
  social toleration and, 238–43
  truth and, 309–10, 318, 322–24, 326 n26, 337–39, 346–47, 351–54, 533
positivism, 112–14, 147, 166, 331–32, 360, 497–98, 571
  logical, 341–42
"Postulate of Immediate Empiricism, The" (Dewey), 515–17
practicality, 444–46
pragmatism, 2–5, 13nn3–4, 57–58, 127–28, 166–70, 183–93, 199–200, 203–5, 208–11, 212 n8, 227–28, 328–33, 340–43, 368, 450–53, 467–68, 471, 483–84, 492–93, 511–13, 531
  belief and, 338–40, 349, 352–54
  consciousness and, 54–55
  ethics and, 247, 250–51, 499–501
  individualism and, 501–2
  inquiry and, 432–33
  medicine and, 148
  metaphysics and, 461, 501–2

as method, 490–91, 494, 498, 500–502, 524–25, 536, 564
nominalism and, 490–91, 498, 502–3
ontology of, 35–38
philosophy and, 501–2
as political philosophy, 245–47, 252–62
positivism and, 331–32
psychology and, 501–2
rationalism and, 524–26
realism and, 276, 490–91, 498, 502–3
religion and, 3, 338–40, 352–54, 460–61
as social philosophy, 232–35
as temperament, 453–55, 457, 462, 463 n4
tolerance and, 251
truth and, 319, 321–24, 325 n17, 333–38, 346–51, 494–96, 524–25, 533, 541–44, 553–54
"Pragmatism" (Russell), 537–38, 542
predictive coding, 21
Principia Ethica (Moore), 205–6
Principles of Mathematics (Russell), 399, 402
Principles of Nature (Renouvier), 482
Principles of Psychology (Spencer), 66–67
Prinz, Jesse, 44, 49–50
probability, 495, 537–38
Proceedings of the American Society for Psychical Research, 158, 164–65
Proceedings of the Aristotelian Society, 539
progress, 161–62, 191–92, 206–8, 262, 497–98
progressivism, 234–35, 242–43, 254–55
prudence, 89–93, 95–100, 102 n19, 102 n25
psychical phenomena, 144, 148, 155–71, 171 n4
psychoanalysis, 150
psychology, 477–78, 490–93, 573–75
  abnormal, 158, 163, 180–81, 467–68
  atomism and, 67–70
  basic emotions theory, 49–50, 53
  of belief, 168–69
  brain and, 426 n6
  consciousness and, 54–55, 66, 84, 102 n21, 182–83
  crowd, 162
  degenerationism in, 163, 167
  ecological, 23
  empiricism and, 413–15, 492–93
  environment and, 77
  ethics and, 248, 250–51

psychology (cont.)
    evolution and, 46, 56–57, 84, 124–25, 368 n3
    experimental, 13 n2, 84, 158, 160, 168–69, 172 n7, 178, 492–93, 587 n8
    German, 19
    Gestalt, 77
    introspection and, 46–48, 556
    mental vivisection, 160
    metaphysics and, 192–93, 359–63, 368 n3, 426 n11, 571–73
    of mind, 379–79, 493–94
    morality and, 188–89, 205, 259–60
    phenomenology and, 56, 77, 554, 558–59, 570–72, 582–86, 586 n7, 588 n2
    philosophy and, 61–62, 177–93, 194 n10, 195 n15, 347–48, 405, 413–14, 467–68, 561, 570–73, 582
    physiology and, 1–2, 13 n2, 117–18, 145–47, 159–60, 347–48, 483–84, 492–93
    pragmatism and, 501–2
    professionalization of, 12 n1, 159–63, 168–69
    rationality and, 363–64
    realism and, 276
    of religion, 2–3, 216
    as science, 68–69, 79 n11, 145–46, 570–71, 573, 582
    sensation and, 66–67
    spiritualism and, 159–71
    stability and, 226–27
pure experience, 4, 182–85, 189–90, 281–84, 285 n8, 286 n12, 311–14, 324, 359–67, 368 n3, 415–17, 423–25, 426 n10, 571–72
purposiveness, 86–87, 89–90, 367–68
Putnam, Hilary, 495–500, 502–3, 552
Putnam, James Jackson, 92, 117–18, 150

"Qualitative Thought" (Dewey), 517–18
Quine, W. V. O., 324 n11, 516–17

race, racial theory, 161–62
    inequality and, 255
Radical Empiricism, 38, 127–28, 148, 166–67, 183, 189–90, 193, 194 n7, 276–78, 281–82, 305 n15, 347–48, 354 n2, 361–68, 370, 375–79, 385–86, 404, 411–15, 434–35, 450–51, 467–68, 474, 495, 501, 511, 513–18, 521, 526
Ramsey, Frank, 495, 542, 553

Ratcliffe, Matthew, 45, 54–55
rationalism, 187, 199–200, 205, 347, 363–64, 378–79, 431–36, 440–46, 454, 456, 477, 501–2, 513–18, 521–24
    criticism and, 520–22
    democracy and, 260–61
    ethics and, 499–500
    morality and, 496–97
    objectivity and, 521–22
    pragmatism and, 524–26
    radical, 518–26
Rawls, John, 234–35, 259
reaction, 26, 116–17
realism, 182, 185, 259–62, 271, 276–77, 334–36, 385, 455–59, 490–91, 498, 500–503, 514–15, 518, 524–25, 533
    conceptual, 439
    direct, 283–84
    empiricism and, 283
    indirect, 311–12
    metaphysical, 495
    natural, 501
    physical, 283
reality, 37–38, 54–56, 68–69, 127–28, 404
    absolute and, 440–41
    cognition of, 279–84, 337
    consciousness of, 365–66
    as experienced, 187–91, 276–77, 279–84, 314–15, 383–87, 413, 434–38
    feeling and, 270–75
    knowledge of, 289–90, 293–96
    objectivity of, 276, 282–83, 366, 385–86
    pluralism and, 533
    truth and, 277–79, 289–90, 311–17, 349–50
reason, reasoning, 67–78, 246, 250–51, 491–92
    moral, 205–6
    religious belief and, 228
    unconscious steps in, 31–32
recognition, 260, 297–98
redintegration, 115–16
reductionism, 45–46, 54, 366, 493
reference, 335–36, 349–51
    action and, 336–37
reflection, 91, 201–2, 204–5, 211
    historical, 246, 250
reflexes, 26, 86–87, 92, 184–85, 347–48, 362–63, 478

relationism, 272–73, 279–83
relativism, 251, 277, 317, 497–98, 502, 517
  ontological, 516–17
religion, 148–49
  belief and, 216–29, 229 n4, 232–33, 338–40, 352–54, 532, 535–36, 544–46, 552
  Catholicism and, 160–61
  conflict and, 240
  experience and, 3, 223–28, 230 n6, 543–46, 552
  morality and, 225–27
  naturalism and, 221–22
  as personal, 223–24
  philosophy of, 216, 227–28
  pluralism and, 461–62
  politics and, 224
  pragmatism and, 3, 460–61
  psychology of, 2, 216
  Reformation and, 160–61
  social role of, 227–28
  spiritual emotions, 227
  spiritualism and, 164–67
  tolerance and, 232–33
  truth and, 353–54
  See also belief; truth
Renouvier, Charles, 8, 48, 114–15, 118–19, 370–77, 385, 392–94, 400–404, 452, 467–84
representation, 23–26, 29, 64–65, 271–75, 476, 479
  conceptual, 280–81
  misrepresentation, 302–4, 371–74, 386–87
Representative Men (Emerson), 458
republic, ethical, 247–52, 257–58, 260, 262
resemblance, 417–19, 425
responsibility, 188, 245
Revue Philosophique, 476–77
Ribot, Théodule, 159–60
Richardson, Robert, 141–42
Richet, Charles, 166, 169–70
Robertson, G. Croom, 431–32
Robinson, Jenefer, 44, 49–50, 52–53
Rorty, Richard, 203–4, 319–20, 342, 490–91
Rousseau, Jean-Jacques, 535–36
Royal College of Science for Ireland, 158
Royce, Josiah, 8, 155–56, 165–67, 193, 348–49, 370–73, 377, 379, 384–87, 388 n1, 391, 395–405, 430–31, 435–37, 440–41, 469–70, 482, 541–42

Russell, Bertrand, 12 n1, 281–83, 294, 331–32, 346–49, 352–53, 399, 402–4, 531–43, 550–53

Saint-Simon, Henri de, 114
Santayana, George, 517–18, 534
Sartre, Jean-Paul, 56
satisfaction, 584
Schachter, Stanley, 42–43
Schelling, Ferdinand Canning Scott, 160, 167, 172 n17, 346–47, 351–52, 443, 490, 501–2, 531, 533–35, 541–42
Schlick, Moritz, 341
Schopenhauer, Arthur, 65, 160
Schütz, Alfred, 570
Science (magazine), 155, 164, 172 n20
Science of Logic (Hegel), 438–39
Second Essays (Renouvier), 472, 477
secularization, 161–62, 164–65
self, 426 n10
  as activity, 511–12
  consciousness and, 32, 67–68, 366–67, 415
  emotions and, 45, 56
  experience and, 366–67, 415
  hidden, 159
  identity and, 417–20
  introspection and, 554, 556
  multiple, 159
  perception and, 417–18
  in philosophy, 207–11
  self-cultivation, 199–201, 206–11
  time and, 418
  transcendent, 270–71, 279–80, 293–96, 571–72, 577–78, 586 n6
  wider self, 228–29
"Self-Reliance" (Emerson), 462
Sellars, Wilfrid, 271–73, 279–81, 284 n2
sensation, 67–68, 116, 182, 359–60, 433, 476, 491–93
  attention and, 23–30, 583
  bare, 74–75
  consciousness and, 184, 273, 360–62, 365, 383
  continuity of, 577–78
  experience and, 560
  immediate, 275–76
  knowledge and, 273–75, 361–62, 374–75

sensation (*cont.*)
    localized, 559–60
    nerve energies and, 135–36
    neural processes of, 69–70, 79 n12
    objectivity of, 360–62
    perception and, 25–26, 68–75, 77, 79 n10, 80 n22, 81 n24, 182, 361–62, 428 n22
    pure, 25
    selectivity and, 583
    space and, 182, 70–76, 78 n6, 360–61, 365
    time and, 577–78
    unconscious, 67
Senses and the Intellect, The (Bain), 66–67, 78 n1
sentimentalism, 496–500
sentinel hypothesis, 22
Shaler, Nathaniel Southgate, 144
Shaw, Robert Gould, 257–58
Shklar, Judith, 259
Sidgwick, Eleanor, 158–59
Sidgwick, Henry, 158–61, 166, 172 n17, 205–6
Singer, Jerome, 42–43
situational analysis, 8
skepticism, 147, 222, 305 n4, 454–59, 462, 463 n6, 499–501, 520–21
Skrupskelis, Ignas, 156–57
Smith, Alys, 534
Society for Psychical Research, 157–61, 164–65, 167–69, 172 n15, 172 n17
solidarity, 257–58
solipsism, 251–52, 378, 387
Solomon, Robert, 43
somnambulism, 31, 167
space:
    experience and, 419–20, 423–24
    infinity and, 478–81
    perception of, 61–66, 70–74, 77, 78 n6, 80 n20, 81 n23, 81 n25, 182, 313, 382–83, 427 n19, 479–80
    sensation of, 360–61, 365
    as subject in itself, 392–93
    time and, 382–83
    unitary, 76, 81 n25, 81 n27
    vision and, 77, 80 n20
Spencer, Herbert, 8, 66–69, 112–127, 183–85, 476, 480, 493
Spinoza, Baruch, 443

spiritualism, 144, 148–49, 158–71, 171 n4, 172 n15, 193
spontaneity, 26, 123–24, 183–84
stability, 226–27
Stanford Named Entity Recognizer (NER), 5–7, 13 n7, 14 n8
stimulation, 26
Stout, Jeffrey, 222
Strang, L. G., 151
Strauss, David Friedrich, 160–61
stream of thought (consciousness), 2, 30, 67–69, 182–84, 415–17, 426 n10, 482–84, 549, 556–58, 561–62, 571–72, 575, 577, 581
Studies in Humanism (Schiller), 534–35
Studies in Logical Theory (Dewey), 513, 516–17
Stumpf, Carl, 63–64, 373
subjectivism, 237–238, 493
subjectivity, 48–49, 52, 55–58
    belief and, 372
    consciousness and, 270–75, 574–75
    experience and, 312, 322, 375–78, 411–12, 415–18
    knowledge and, 372
    in medicine, 137–38
    rationality and, 432–33
    sensation and, 360–62
suicide, 56, 113–14, 221–22
Sully, James, 159–60
supernatural, 156–57, 160–61, 171 n4
survival hypothesis, 167
"Syllabus: Types of Philosophic Thought" (Dewey), 520
System of Synthetic Philosophy (Spencer), 113

Tarski, Alfred, 335
Taylor, James, 151
telepathy, 155–60, 165–66
theism, 431, 434–35
Thomson, J. J., 158
thought-transference, 160
time:
    attention and, 28–29, 116–17
    consciousness and, 577–78
    experience and, 397–98, 418–20
    infinity and, 478–81
    perception of, 24–25, 63–64, 427 n19, 479–80
    self and, 418

sensation of, 577–78
space and, 382–83
"specious present," 2, 24–25, 378, 381–82, 418, 427 n16
as subject in itself, 392–94
Time and Space (Hodgson), 115–18, 479–80
Titchener, Edward B., 155–56, 163, 168–69
Tocqueville, Alexis de, 253–54
tolerance, 229, 232–35, 238–43, 246, 251, 502
Tolstoy, Leo, 56
Tomkins, Silvan, 49
Tractatus Logico-Philosophicus (Wittgenstein), 531, 544, 551–52
trance states, 31, 155–56, 159–60, 163–64, 167
transcendentalism, 169, 201, 207–8, 222–28, 293–96, 338–40, 367–68, 439, 443, 481–82, 493–97, 518, 521
Treatise of Human Nature, A (Hume), 413, 420
trust, 220
truth, 3–4, 38, 187, 190–91, 277–79, 289–90, 309–17, 319–22, 333–34, 349–50, 490–92, 494–95, 498, 524–25
  absolute, 317–23
  action and, 553
  belief and, 217–22, 228, 309–10, 314–17, 320–22, 333–34, 346, 349–52, 371–72, 494–98, 524–25, 531–41
  buried secrets and, 321–22, 325 n22
  categories and, 350–51
  community and, 498
  consciousness and, 374–75, 531
  copy theory of, 314–17, 325 n12
  correspondence theory of, 334–38, 350, 539–40
  experience and, 450–51
  inquiry and, 498
  intentionality and, 303–4, 305 n6
  knowledge and, 289–90, 302–4, 371–72, 533
  language and, 337–38
  necessary, 210
  pluralism and, 318, 322–24, 326 n26, 337–39, 346–47, 351–54, 533
  probability and, 537–38
  reference and, 349–51
  relation and, 348, 374–77
  relative, 317–21, 325 n17, 326 n26, 502
  religious, 353–54

representation and, 374–75
satisfaction and, 584
usefulness and, 495–96, 539–44, 553–54
value and, 533
verifiability and, 296–97, 310, 320–21, 374–75, 386–87, 495–98, 539–41
tuned receptor cells, 77
tychism, 400–401
Tylor, E. B., 161–62
Tyndall, John, 162
tyranny, 239–40, 260–61

uncertainty, 238–39, 258–62
unconscious, 24–25, 30–33, 66–67, 73–74, 77, 79 n13, 116, 182, 491
unity, 249–51, 258, 576–78
universals, 514–15, 522, 524–26
University of California at Berkeley, 2
utilitarianism, 235–38, 248
utopia, 248–49, 252–53, 257, 259–60

vagus nerve, 44
value, 94–95, 103 n27
  conflict and, 240–41
  pluralist, 235–43, 246
  transcendent, 221–22, 227–28, 367–68
  truth and, 533
  in utilitarianism, 236–38
variation, 122–24, 187–88. *See also* evolution
Variation of Animals and Plants Under Domestication (Darwin), 112
verificationism, 331–32
violence, 255–57
Virchow, Rudolf, 161
vision, 31–32, 77, 80 n20, 129 n12. *See also* sensation
vitality, 138–41
volition, 36, 119–20, 160, 363, 413, 560–61. *See also* will
Volkmann, A. W., 63
voluntarism, 251–52

Wahl, Jean, 474
Waldron, Jeremy, 259
Wallace, Alfred Russel, 158–62
war, 233–34, 258
  moral equivalent of, 256–57

Ward, Thomas Wren, 113–14
Washington, Booker T., 255
Weinberger, Joel, 31
Weltanschauung, 186, 189–90, 315, 411–12, 518, 564
Whewell, William, 137–38, 157
Wild, John Daniel, 570
Wilkinson, James John Garth, 143–44
will, 2, 185, 383–85, 472–73
   action and, 36–37
   attention and, 19–22, 36–38, 561–62
   belief and, 37–38, 217–18, 228–29, 362–63, 372, 476–77, 483–84, 540–41
   consciousness and, 383–84
   feeling and, 560–61
   free, 34–35, 347, 354 n3, 362–63, 372, 467–68, 473–75, 478, 481–84
   phenomenology of, 36
   pure, 26

"William James's Conception of Truth" (Russell), 535–39
Williams, Bernard, 259
Williams, D. C., 192, 210
Wilshire, Bruce, 570–73, 579, 586 n7, 587 n8
Winkler, Kenneth, 370–71
Witmer, Lightner, 169
Wittgenstein, Ludwig, 8, 191, 203–5, 491–92, 531, 543–46, 549–64
Wolterstorff, Nicholas, 222
Wordsworth, William, 25
World and the Individual, The (Royce), 391, 395
Wright, Chauncey, 109, 112–13, 119–20, 178
Wundt, Wilhelm, 13 n2, 30–31, 64–67, 78 n5, 79 n12, 115–17, 147, 159–61, 168, 182–84, 511
Wyman, Jeffries, 110–11, 178

Zeno's paradox, 402–4